THE TRANSFORMATION OF ECONOMIC LAW

This book is written in honour of Hans-W. Micklitz for his 70th birthday and the closure of his 12-year term as the Chair for Economic Law at the European University Institute (EUI). Hans-W. Micklitz has gained international recognition for dedicating his extensive and fruitful career to diverse areas of law: European Economic Law, European Private Law, National and European Consumer Law, Legal Theory, theories of Private Law and Social Justice. This book is a product of the collaborative endeavour of its contributors, all of whom have a special connection with Hans-W. Micklitz as his doctoral supervisees or research assistants. The collection is to be read as the influence of Hans's dialogues in the early stage of the academic careers of 31 young legal scholars. The edited volume is divided into three sections devoted to subjects that have received Hans's attention during his time at the EUI: EU Consumer Law (part I); European Private Law and Access Justice (part II); the CJEU between the individual citizen and the Member States (part III).

The Transformation of Economic Law

Essays in Honour of Hans-W. Micklitz

Edited by
Lucila de Almeida
Marta Cantero Gamito
Mateja Durovic
and
Kai P. Purnhagen

With the assistance of Evgenia Ralli

•HART•
OXFORD • LONDON • NEW YORK • NEW DELHI • SYDNEY

HART PUBLISHING

Bloomsbury Publishing Plc

Kemp House, Chawley Park, Cumnor Hill, Oxford, OX2 9PH, UK

1385 Broadway, New York, NY 10018, USA

HART PUBLISHING, the Hart/Stag logo, BLOOMSBURY and the Diana logo are trademarks of Bloomsbury Publishing Plc

First published in Great Britain 2019

A catalogue record for this book is available from the British Library.

Library of Congress Cataloging-in-Publication data

Names: Micklitz, Hans-W., honouree. | Cantero Gamito, Marta, editor.

Title: The transformation of economic law : essays in honour of Hans-W. Micklitz / Edited by Marta Cantero Gamito, Lucila de Almeida, Mateja Durovic and Kai P. Purnhagen ; With the assistance of Evgenia Ralli.

Description: Chicago : Hart Publishing, 2019. | Includes bibliographical references and index.

Identifiers: LCCN 2019021099 (print) | LCCN 2019021911 (ebook) | ISBN 9781509932597 (EPub) | ISBN 9781509932580 (hardback)

Subjects: LCSH: Commercial law—European Union countries. | Consumer protection—Law and legislation—European Union countries. | Civil law—European Union countries.

Classification: LCC KJE6569 (ebook) | LCC KJE6569 .T74 2019 (print) | DDC 346.407—dc23

LC record available at https://lccn.loc.gov/2019021099

ISBN: HB: 978-1-50993-258-0
ePDF: 978-1-50993-260-3
ePub: 978-1-50993-259-7

Typeset by Compuscript Ltd, Shannon

FOREWORD 1

HOMAGE TO HANS-W. MICKLITZ

Academic life has many pleasurable and rewarding dimensions. An academic career usually spans several decades or more. Over the course of time, one encounters many people. I have listened to hundreds of lectures, presentations, seminars, over the course of 30 years as an academic. I have met many extremely interesting and gifted academics. Like everyone, I would imagine, there are only a handful of people who deeply impact one's own life and work. For me, Hans-W. Micklitz is one of those special people.

When I was interviewed for the Chair in Legal Philosophy and Legal Theory in 2008, I had never been to the European University Institute. Of course, I knew of the existence of the Institute but I had no connection with anyone before I took up my Chair in 2009. When I arrived in Florence in August of 2009, I had no idea what adventures would lie ahead for me. Over the course of the next eight years, I would experience an intellectually rewarding experience like none I have ever had. Hans-W. Micklitz is central to this narrative.

Every year the Institute takes in a new class of researchers. In 2009, the new class of law researchers was hosted by the law department to a one-day event where the researchers and professors would discuss their work and get to know one another. I did not know anyone and, as I rode the bus from Fiesole to a cloister outside Siena, I wondered what my new colleagues would be like. I spent the day listening to the researchers explain their doctoral projects and to my colleagues discussing their work. When Hans spoke about his work I knew I wanted to get to know him better.

The work day in Siena ended with a splendid dinner for the researchers and the professors. As luck would have it, I was seated next to Hans. In the space of less than ten minutes, we established our mutual admiration for a wide variety of philosophers and political theorists. We learned that we both enjoyed economic law and many of the same works of literature. When the meal ended, Hans offered to drive me back to Florence. During the drive, I recall we mainly discussed Marx's critique of Hegel on law and Kojeve's role in the reception of Hegel. I went home that night firm in my belief that the next eight years would be like none I had ever experienced before.

Hans and I met regularly during my initial years in Florence. He brought my level of competence in European law – especially economic law – far higher than I would ever achieve on my own. I read everything he suggested to me and

I learned an immense amount from him. I recall vividly the day Hans received word of his ERC grant. It was announced at Academic Council (the monthly meeting of all EUI professors) and Hans received thunderous applause. As a result of this grant, Hans was able to add a tremendous amount to the intellectual life of the law department. Speakers, conferences, PhD students and a host of ancillary activities all made for an intellectual feast. It was thrilling.

The law department had a regular practice of having professors present their work. While it was common for people to present completed articles, I always tried to present an idea or an argument and see what I got by way of feedback. I once presented an outline for a review of a book on constitutionalism. My outline was so threadbare that one of my colleagues criticised me for not presenting 'a paper'. Hans was the commentator for my presentation. In the course of half an hour, Hans tied my presentation to several previous works of mine on globalisation and trade law as well as several of my EUI seminars on topics as diverse as Hardt and Negri's *Empire* and transnational legal theory. Hans made connections in my own work that I had never seen before. I was astonished and grateful.

Of course, Hans and I taught seminars together. Two of these stand out for me. One of the many great things about the Institute is the chance to learn languages. When I came to the Institute, I spoke serviceable German but no language other than English. When my Italian developed, I suggested to Hans that we teach a seminar together on Italian Legal Philosophy. Of course, the seminar was to be in Italian. Hans' Italian was far better than mine but I thought we could pull it off.

Each week, I would send Hans a list of questions we could ask the participants and a key word vocabulary list. These helped me far more than they did Hans: he didn't need any crutches. Apart from succeeding with the language, Hans always had the most insightful things to say about the texts. Machiavelli, Bobbio and others were the subject of wide-ranging discussions about the nature of law, the role of politics in law and the particular way Italian legal philosophers conceptualise issues in legal theory. Teaching that seminar with Hans was an intellectual delight.

For my last seminar at the Institute, Hans and I decided to invite five leading scholars of transnational law to come and discuss their work with our group. For one week, Hans and I would discuss the seminar material with the researchers and the next we would have the guest speaker come in and defend their positions. By this time, Hans and I were like a well-oiled machine. Our dialogue with the speakers was peppered with interventions by the researchers who were simply extraordinary in their abilities.

For the last session – which represented my last hours teaching as a professor at the EUI – our guest was my dear friend Alexander Somek. To my mind, Somek is the best legal theorist in Europe. That said, we disagree on many things (especially how to read Wittgenstein). But the two hours with Hans and Sascha were the best two hours of my academic life. I may never have another time like it.

The ERC grant enabled Hans to conduct a grand intellectual experiment, one that resulted in the publication of his book, *The Politics of Justice in European*

Private Law. The book is a stunning intellectual achievement. The synthesis of theory, deep knowledge of EU law, and a subtle rendering of economic theory are simply without equal anywhere in the literature. This is a book that will be read widely and will have a major impact on the field.

In the Preface to the book, Hans kindly mentions the fact that I often told him 'You must write your book'. Hans always had many commitments. He devoted himself to the law department, his supervisees, and his American friend. The present volume is a testament to Hans by the many supervisees whose lives he has touched. He is as selfless as he is brilliant. I have learned so much from him. I shall be forever grateful to the forces that brought us together for what was, for me, the experience of a lifetime.

Dennis Patterson
Professor of Law and Philosophy
Rutgers University
25 January 2019

FOREWORD 2

VORWORT

Ich möchte meinen Freund und Kollegen Hans W Micklitz nicht über den grünen Klee loben, sowas gehört sich einfach nicht. Darüber hinaus wäre ihm eine Hommage auch sehr peinlich, weil man ihr geradezu wehrlos ausgesetzt ist, was er gar nicht gut leiden kann.

‚Wehrlos' mag nun ein wenig martialisch klingen – gleichwohl haben wir es in der Wissenschaft immer auch mit dem Kampf um die Wahrheit zu tun.

In unseren Forschungen, also jenen, an denen ich dann und wann beteiligt war, hat er sich nie – und das ist gravierend, auf Theorien und Sekundärdaten verlassen. Er hat sich auch nie in reiner Theorie verloren. Im Gegenteil, soweit ich das miterlebt habe, waren die Ergebnisse anderer Studien oder rechtsphilosophische Grundlagen immer wieder Startpunkte zu neuen Überlegungen und eben auch Forschungen. Wir können also sagen, Plato, Aristoteles, Cato und Caesar saßen genauso am Tisch wie Macchiavelli, Montesquieu und Napoleon.

In Begleitung und Kommentierung der Entwicklung der EWG- und EU-Rechtsgeschichte in den Bereichen des Wirtschafts- und Verbraucherrechts, mehr noch, wie der kürzlich erschienene tiefe Einstieg in *The Politics of Justice in European Private Law* zeigt, ist ihm nicht Bange, sich an die Wurzeln des europäischen und jeweils nationalen Selbstverständnisses vorzuarbeiten, um sie besser verstehen und explizieren zu können. Sobald wir von Wurzeln (radix) sprechen, drängt sich der Verdacht auf, Micklitz sei ein Radikaler.

Ja, genauso ist es auch. Hans ist ein Radikaler, wiewohl er diese Attribuierung in Bescheidenheit wohl ablehnen würde. Ein Radikaler der Wahrheitsfindung.

Als wir vor vielen, vielen Jahren erstmals zusammengearbeitet haben, ergab sich die Forschungsfrage zwischen ‚law in the books' und wirklichen Prozeduren, also zwischen ‚Soll-Zuständen' und ‚Ist-Zuständen' zu unterscheiden.

Also zwischen Normativität und Praxis und eben auch gesellschaftlicher Lebenspraxis, die sich so erstaunlich anders gebärdet, als vorgedacht. Diese sich sanft einschleichende Erkenntnis führte zu weiteren und weiteren Studien.

Das hört sich ziemlich harmlos an, offenbart aber einen Wissenschafts – und Forschergeist, der sich mal eben an die Realität heranwagt, statt dünne Bretter zu bohren.

Da reden wir dann von ‚Krise', die für Hans Micklitz in meiner soziologischen Betrachtung umstandslos zum allgegenwärtigen ‚normalen' Forschungsimpetus wird, aber wir reden auch über Struktur, dem feinen Gewebe der gesellschaftlichen Wirklichkeit.

Ich habe erst kürzlich in einem Telephonat erfahren, dass Hans Micklitz seine Annahmen der frühen 90er Jahren heute naiv vorkommen und muss ihm tröstend entgegenhalten, die Annahmen mögen ja vor 30 Jahren naiv gewesen sein, die empirischen Erhebungen und Ergebnisse dieser Zeit aber selbstredend nicht. Die stehen da protokolliert und sind heute noch in Buchform lesbar.

Ist das nicht kurios und wundervoll – die Ergebnisse des Forschenden überholen den Forscher?

Und das ist der Pivot!

Micklitz geht immer wieder das Wagnis ein, sich selbst der Naivität, oder um es konziliant zu formulieren, sich den eigenen Hypothesen und Prämissen in Enttäuschung zu stellen, ja er fordert diesen Konflikt mit unfertigem Wissen und der Realität geradezu heraus.

Er muss also über eine enorme Enttäuschungsbereitschaft verfügen. Das scheint mir der Kern seiner wissenschaftlichen Tätigkeit überhaupt zu sein.

Im dienenden Hintergrund stehen immer die Befunde Poppers (‚lasst Theorien sterben, aber nicht Menschen'), Thomas Kuhns ‚Paradigmenwechsel' in den Naturwissenschaften (ja, selbst dort) und schließlich auch die Ideologiekritik, die Kant, Hegel und Marx systematisch folgt.

Nehmen wir ganz kurz das ERPL-Projekt in den Blick, zu dessen Mitarbeitern Micklitz eine ganze Reihe von begabten und neugierigen PhD-Aspiranten anstiftete.

In meiner Erinnerung waren es mehr als 50 direkt gesprochene und per Audio offene Interviews mit beteiligten Richtern, Gerichtsprotokollen, die stenographisch festgehalten wurden, Beamten, Ärzten und Patienten, Experten des Konsumentenschutzes, selbstbewußten NGO-Aktivisten in Sachen Umwelt, Pressekonferenzen, wissenschaftliche Konferenzen mit Vertretern nationaler Kommunikationsgesellschaften, die oft, audiophon protokolliert über Tage dauerten, über alle sprachlichen Grenzen hinweg.

Wenn man so will, ein Wust von Primärdaten aus der wirklichen Welt. Grob geschätzt waren dies über viele 100 Stunden direkter Wirklichkeitssuche und darüber hinaus, Daten, die erhoben und analysiert werden sollten, von jungen Wissenschaftlern, die gerade deswegen auch begütigt werden sollten, in der Via Palazzine. Vor allem von der bewunderungswürdigen Alexandra, seiner Frau, die couragiert bei Essen und Trinken, Musik, Piano, Gesang und Darstellung dafür sorgte, im Leben zu bleiben.

Ganz im Ernst – das muss alles analysiert werden.

Und wer macht so etwas? Wer arrangiert diesen ‚pädagogischen Eros'. Diese Frage ist schnell beantwortet – Hans Micklitz, der viel gerühmte Experte, knüpft Zusammenhänge wie ein Weber, spinnt Fäden und aus dieser Textur heraus stachelt er seine Studenten und Kollegen auf, an der ‚Sache' zu bleiben, in Inspiration und Emsigkeit. Das mag nicht jedem gefallen. Ich selbst hatte oft den Eindruck,

Hans errichte so ganz im Geheimen eine Gelehrtenrepublik, die aber nicht in Selbstzufriedenheit ‚self-sufficiency' stillsteht, sondern fordert, ja auch provokativ fordert.

Eine Antwort, die mich überzeugt, ist das vorliegende Buch, es gibt Wissenschaftler jüngerer Generation, die diesen Faden aufnehmen.

Kleinmütigkeit darf man also dem ‚Anstifter' von Empirie nicht vorwerfen, im Gegenteil – das Visier ist immer aufgeklappt, jeder Befund wird geprüft und in endlosen Gesprächen gewichtet und höchstwahrscheinlich (so vermute ich) als Theorem den Überlegungen des Europäischen Rechtsexperiments hinzugefügt.

Das ist das Eine.

Das Andere aber ist, dass aus dieser genuin wissenschaftlichen Disposition, die sich nichts vormachen lassen will, die sich nicht mit Fragen der Demokratisierung von Forschung, nicht mit allfälligen Ideologemen des allgemeinen Betriebs gemein machen will, ein Eros – eine sinnliche Forschungslust resultiert – der so manchen (nicht alle) Aspiranten beflügelt, nun wirklich aus dem schicklichen Leben auszubrechen und zur ‚Sache' zu kommen:

Ich muß meinem Freund und Kollegen dieserhalb Tribut zollen. Ihm gelang und gelingt es immer wieder nachfolgende Generationen diese Akkuratesse und Delikatesse der Wahrheitssuche nahezubringen, sie zu stimulieren, nicht nachzugeben, die Bürde der Wahrheit oder Wahrheitsähnlichkeit auf sich zu nehmen.

Und unversehens sind wir in der alten ‚Humboldtschen' Universität des frühen 19. Jahrhunderts, Modell für viele andere aufstrebende Gesellschaften, in der alle Empirie- und Theoriestreitigkeiten produktiv ausgetragen wurden.

Ist also Hans W Micklitz ein Nostalgiker?

Nie im Leben.

Wissenschaft ist die Institution, beständig Kritik zu üben, Wissenschaft ist ein destruktives Geschäft in atemloser Fröhlichkeit – das allein ist ihre Aufgabe.

Niemals Glaube, niemals Überzeugung, nur Überprüfung des Ist-Zustandes in aller Welt.

Wie wir sehen, folgen andere und neue Generationen diesem Gedanken.

Und ich bin froh darum.

Thomas Roethe
Part-time Professor in the Law Department,
European University Institute

CONTENTS

1

Introduction

LUCILA DE ALMEIDA, MARTA CANTERO GAMITO,
MATEJA DUROVIC, KAI P. PURNHAGEN

This book is written in honour of Hans-W. Micklitz, an outstanding legal scholar and personality, who has gained international recognition for dedicating his extensive and fruitful career to diverse areas of law: European economic law, European private law, national and European consumer law and legal theory, theories of private law and social justice. This book is the product of the collaborative endeavours of its contributors, all of whom have a special connection with Hans-W. Micklitz as his doctoral supervisees or research assistants. In Summer 2019, the term of Hans-W. Micklitz as a holder of the Chair for Economic Law at the Law Department of the EUI – who is humble enough to insist on being addressed only as Hans – comes to an end. From 2007 to 2019, dozens of PhD and LLM supervisees, Max Weber and other post-doctoral fellows and research assistants have shared the wonderful experience of working and collaborating with Hans. In Summer 2019, Hans is also celebrating his 70th birthday.

During many decades of his impressive career, Hans has contributed to transforming the landscape the many areas of law listed above. Born in 1949, Hans studied law and sociology at Mainz, Lausanne/Geneva, Giessen and Hamburg. Prior to his appointment at the EUI, Hans was the Head of the Institute of European and Consumer Law (VIEW) in Bamberg. He worked as a consultant on diverse projects of the OECD, UNEP Geneva Switzerland/Nairobi Kenya and Consumers International (CI) Den Haag Netherlands/Penang Malaysia. Hans was a visiting scholar at the University of Michigan, Ann Arbor and Jean Monnet Fellow at the European University Institute, Florence. He was also a visiting professor at Somerville College at the University of Oxford and was a co-founder of the Centre of Excellence in Foundations of European Law and Politics at the University of Helsinki. The crowning of Hans' research excellence was that during his time at the EUI, he became the recipient of the extremely prestigious ERC Grant 2011–2016 on *European Regulatory Private Law: the Transformation of European Private Law from Autonomy to Functionalism in Competition and Regulation (ERPL).* Hans is currently a Finland Distinguished Professor (FiDiPro), a funding programme of the Academy of Finland, for the period 2015–2020. He also keeps ongoing consultancies for ministries in Austria, Germany, the UK, the European Commission, OECD, UNEP, GIZ and several non-governmental organisations. We are confident that Hans' scholarhip will not come to an end with his departure from the EUI, and that many new books, book chapters, articles, commentaries and theses will be written, edited and supervised under Hans' guidance.

This edited volume is a small gesture of appreciation to Hans from his EUI-related 'academic children'. Rather than representing a collection of chapters written by his academic peers, colleagues and friends (bearing in mind their number, such a project would certainly be unfeasible), this book has gathered the work of Hans' students. The collection of chapters is to be read as the influence of Hans' dialogues in the early stage of the academic career of 31 young legal scholars. The majority of the contributors are Hans' supervisees, but there are also post-doctoral researchers and research assistants who have had the chance to engage with his work in books and in person while at the EUI. Hans' scholarship has deeply influenced his supervisees and researchers to perceive the role and the rule of private and economic law in various social contexts, jurisdictions, and legal theories. The variety of legal issues covered in this book – from broad conceptualisation of consumer law and regulation to the role of national courts and the Court of Justice of the European Union – merely mirror Hans' relentless curiosity and academic excellence.

Besides being a leading legal scholar, Hans is a wonderful, wise and compassionate human being, always very kind, warm, supportive, ready to help and encourage his students and colleagues. This book celebrates Hans' career thus far, and explores the topical areas of law substantially shaped by his academic work. The 20 chapters of this edited volume are divided into three sections. Each section is devoted to a subject that has received Hans' attention while at the EUI:

I. EU consumer law;
II. European private law and access justice;
III. the CJEU between the individual citizen and the Member States.

The editors of this book owe Evgenia Ralli, one of the youngest of Hans' PhD students, a debt of gratitude for her incredible help with this book. Evgenia really went above and beyond to help us setting up this entire project, so all her efforts need to be highly appreciated, for without her, the publication of this book would not have been possible. The editors would also like to thank Hans' very appreciated friends and colleagues Dennis Patterson and Thomas Roethe for their forewords. We would also like to express our appreciation to Claudia de Concini, Hans' administrative assistant at the EUI for all her help with the organisation of the conference in Hans' honour at the EUI.

Working with Hans means that it is not only his office door that is always open – he also warm-heartedly opens the doors of his home. Alongside him stands Alexa, such a wonderful person, and a generous hostess who kindly welcomes us in Florence as very dear guests. Getting to know Alexa is also one of the privileges of working with Hans. Her thoughtful support extends beyond Hans, to his supervisees. Throughout and after our stays at the EUI, Alexa has remained a very important figure of our lives in Florence. We owe her much gratitude for being our 'accomplice' in making this possible. Danke, Alexa!

Finally, the editors wish to thank Hart Publishing, and Sinead Moloney in particular, for publishing this book and for the support shown to us from the very beginning. This unconditional support allows us, Hans' academic children, to pay our tribute and show our gratitude to the significant contribution that Hans-W. Micklitz has made to legal scholarship.

Part I. EU Consumer Law

EU consumer law is one of the cores of European private law. It is the subject that motivated Hans' legal scholarship throughout his academic career and the source of his inspiration to uphold claims about the foundations of the European justice.

Hanna Schebesta and *Kai P. Purnhagen* examine, in Chapter 2, the ambiguous concept of average consumer as established under Directive 2005/29/EC on unfair commercial practices. In particular, they examine how the CJEU has assessed the average consumer. In order to comprehend how the CJEU has understood the concept of average consumer, the authors apply a mixed-method approach combining doctrinal and empirical analysis. Doctrinal analysis determines where the 'average consumer' is used in EU law and how the respective legislative and juridical acts relate to each other. Subsequently, an empirical (qualitative software-supported) analysis determines how these legislative and juridical acts operationalise the 'average consumer' benchmark. Whereas a large bulk of jurisprudence concerns the average consumer test in primary law or has been applied to interpret secondary legislation which does not make explicit reference to the consumer benchmark, the analysis in this chapter is limited to those cases where a clear link between the wording of secondary law and the Court's jurisprudence can be established. This leaves aside the cases where the CJEU interpreted secondary legislation in light of primary law or primary law directly.

Mateja Durovic examines contract law remedies for the breach of the rules on unfair commercial practices. The main purpose of Chapter 3 is to assess recent developments in this area of law after the CJEU decision in *Bankia*. In *Bankia*, the CJEU provided some clarifications regarding the consequences of traders' engagement in unfair commercial practices and what national courts are expected (or rather not expected) to do according to the text of the Unfair Commercial Practices Directives (UCPD). The Court said that, contrary to the example of fairness of contract terms established by Directive 93/13/EEC on unfair contract terms, the national courts are not obliged to assess *ex officio*, ie by its own motion, whether a particular contract or any of its term has been concluded under the impact of unfair commercial practices. In such a manner, the CJEU has actually lowered the scope of protection offered by the UCPD and failed to provide a more effective protection to an individual consumer who has been affected by an unfair commercial practice. Eventually, this chapter demonstrates that in its decision in *Bankia*, the CJEU failed to explicitly confirm a closer connection between the rules on unfair commercial practices and contract law, and expand the application of *ex officio* obligation of the national courts of the Member States to verify fairness of the contract terms to the assessment whether a contract has been concluded as a result of unfair commercial practice.

Peter Rott examines a consumer perspective on algorithms. Chapter 4 takes the subjective consumer perspective rather than the perspective of objective compliance with the law. It looks at automated decision-making through algorithms, that tend to give no reasons, as perceived arbitrariness on the part of business operators. Where decisions are made directly by an algorithm or are prepared by an algorithm and then implemented by a natural person that does not have the intention and/or the ability to review the 'recommendation' of the algorithm, this type of procedure must, first of all, be made explicit to consumers so that they can avoid it by turning to a different trader. Where this is impossible because the trader in question has a dominant position on the market or the same algorithm is used by the vast majority of traders, safeguards that are typical for decisions of public authorities must be in place. Then, constitutional principles such as human dignity, the right to equal treatment and the rule of law require the trader to give comprehensible reasons for the decision; and the reason cannot solely be the result of a calculation exercise.

Irina Domurath examines the legal framework for consumer profiling under the new EU General Data Protection Regulation (GDPR). The problems discussed in Chapter 5 deals with privacy – including consent, anonymisation and data minimisation as well as discrimination. Manifold gaps in the legal framework with regard to data protection hinder individuals from understanding, tracing, or contesting the use of their data and profiles. Irina claims that because of the normative power of algorithmic governance generally and consumer profiles in particular, a system of 'technological totalitarianism' has developed, which escapes individual and traditional regulatory control. Recognising the vast research possibilities in this field, this chapter shows that many tools and principles already exist in the GDPR that could help to overcome those challenges, if they are strengthened with regard to unambiguity and enforcement and streamlined into all cross-cutting fields of law, including private law. Political debate needs to make explicit the societal effects and discuss the desirability of technological governance, if individuals and regulators are not to be subjected to unfettered algorithmic control of private companies.

Agnieszka Jabłonowska and *Przemysław Pałka* consider the interplay between the EU consumer law and artificial intelligence. Chapter 6 begins by addressing three topical issues in law and artificial intelligence (AI) scholarship: the definition of 'artificial intelligence', the problem of the 'black box' and liability for the actions of AI. Moreover, it addresses certain misconceptions present is legal discourses, and proposes conceptual distinctions to remedy them. The argument of the chapter subsequently moves forward to three issues specific to consumer law: the asymmetry between businesses and consumers; the emergence of AI applications in consumer markets; and some of the potential challenges which they raise, particularly those to consumers' autonomy. Deeper intellectual engagement with the challenges posed to the doctrine and the practice of consumer law by the development of AI is necessary before one can move to recommendations on how the law should be changed. The chapter concludes with a plea to develop AI-based applications empowering the consumers and the civil society.

Part II. European Private Law and Access Justice

Hans-W. Micklitz's legal scholarship has been rounded off with the development of his distinct vision on European private law. He understood that the guiding principles informing national private law, namely autonomy and freedom of contract, differed from those underpinning the EU legal order – European private law was not the harmonisation of domestic legal private law regimes. Moving away from the mainstream legal scholarship focused on the construction of a civil code for Europe, Hans became persuaded by the idea of understanding the positive and normative features of a private law that was genuinely EUropean.

Guido Comparato and Rónán Condon compare, in Chapter 7, the transformations taking place in European private law in recent years to the transformations first described a century ago in French legal scholarship, when confronted with the interpretation of the French Code Civil in a deeply changed social context. That scholarship, epitomised by personalities like Léon Duguit, challenged the dominant legal formalism. The authors argue that Duguit's legal functionalism remains a useful lens through which to examine contemporary transformations of private law and the state in an EU context. The contribution thus highlights the characteristics of those transformations separated by a century of legal evolution, attempting to trace them in the specific area of European private law.

Unlike the rules contained in nineteenth century codes, and that informed domestic private law regimes, Hans found that EU rules on private law had a regulatory purpose. These rules, moreover, were not to be found as a separated or dedicated branch of EU law, but were scattered along different internal market rules, at the intersections between public and private law. He was determined to identify and systematise these rules, and to test whether they had the necessary elements to constitute a legal regime of their own. This endeavour earned him an ERC Grant (2011–2016) to develop his ERPL Project at the EUI.

One of the main hypotheses on which ERPL was built was 'self-sufficiency'. *Marta Cantero Gamito and Federico Della Negra* sketch the postulates of this hypothesis in Chapter 8. Using the examples of telecommunications and investment services regulation, they find that the hypothesis of self-sufficiency is actually reflected in the law-making and enforcement of these two key sectors of the internal market. Both sectors are informed by a sector-specific rationality that permeates the contract rules contained in the sector-specific legal regimes. A sector-specific rationality emerges as a result of the configuration of the sector to attain regulatory outcomes, ie competition or consumer protection. This results in a transformed private legal order, created and enforced at the European level via old and new modes of governance.

In Chapter 9, *Lucila de Almeida and Fabrizio Esposito* engage with the distinct concept of access justice as proposed by Hans in his latest book, *The Politics of Justice in European Private Law*. The book is a thorough reflection on the relevant findings of his five-year ERPL project. By comparing the mature account and the critiques to the earlier account of 'access justice', the authors aim to shed lights on the most important features of Hans' theory of justice. The chapter first introduces the three conditions that materialise the notion of access justice – its distinctive normative ground represented by the ideas of fair access, the access to justice, and the societal justice. Second, the three conditions of the mature account of access justice are illustrated in the context of the EU energy law throughout the 30 years of positive integration. Third, the authors consider early critiques to access justice and reflect upon how the mature account of access justice addresses them. They conclude that the mature account of access justice has been largely successful in addressing these critiques.

The aspirations of the EU legal order to function independently from domestic legal regimes cover other areas beyond Services of General Economic Interest (SGEIs), for example, taxation and insolvency law. In this light, while the EU legal basis for the regulation of SGEIs is generally not contested, EU initiatives in other areas may involve a more complex justification. In this line, *Katerina Pantazatou* illustrates in Chapter 10 how a combination of recent developments has crafted a detailed justification for EU action in direct taxation. She shows how the financial and economic crisis, in conjunction with the globalisation and the digitalisation of the economy, has shifted the focus of EU taxation from the taxpayer to the Member States; from the elimination of double taxation to the prevention of tax avoidance. These advancements aim at promoting a fair and efficient tax system for the Digital Single Market, and may lead to the phasing out of intra-EU tax competition.

Annika Wolf and Heikki Marjosola in Chapter 11 provide an account of the evolution of EU insolvency law with a view to demonstrating that, in its attempts to harmonise insolvency law across Member States, the EU might adopt more drastic regulatory approaches (eg passing a Regulation) if Member States render incapable the putting in place of a coherent level playing field for insolvency proceedings across the EU.

Among the different regulatory approaches for the regulation of ERPL, the European Commission does not completely abandon the idea of crafting a unified EU contract law. This is the claim of *Antonio Marcacci* in Chapter 12. In his view, the European Commission is paving the way for establishing a 'brand new contract standard' for digital financial cross-border transactions. To conclude, new modes of governance are also identified in the EU regulation of food chains and financial markets.

In Chapter 13, *María Paz de la Cuesta de los Mozos and Elena Sedano Varo* examine experimentalism in these two sectors. They demonstrate that borrowing experimentalism as a governance and regulatory choice in the EU approach to food chains and financial markets is a manifestation of the broader ERPL phenomenon.

Shortly after the ERPL project was rolled out, Hans realised that the characteristics of this phenomenon were spilling over the internal market. The transformations operated in private law were also visible in the non-EU world. Therefore, after five years developing the positive and normative postulates of European Regulatory Private Law within the EU, he embarked in a journey to find ERPL in the legal practice that takes place beyond the confines of the EU marketplace. Hans is currently investigating this dimension in the context of his ongoing project on The External Dimension of European Private Law (EDEPL), funded by the Academy of Finland. Two chapters in this volume show that there is certainly a tendency towards the external impact of European private law.

Barbara Warwas and Zdeněk Nový focus in Chapter 14 on how arbitration has contributed to the development of ERPL not only in its internal but also in its external dimension. Providing a thorough analysis of the implications of the CJEU judgment in *Achmea* (C-284/18) and paying attention to EU rules on out-of-court procedures, they contend that a perceived embryonic EU proceduralisation of arbitration results in the harmonisation of dispute settlement in international economic law.

Rozeta Karova focuses in Chapter 15 on the development of the Energy Community and its importance in the second decade of its existence. The Energy Community, covering the territories from Lisbon to Tbilisi, is an example of how the EU internal energy market could be extended to third countries. Through a historical tour of the organisation, she illustrates that the Energy Community serves as a template for exporting EU values, principles and rules beyond the EU's borders. Even though the Energy Community became a central piece in the EU's external energy policy and a reference point for regional cooperation in energy, the full potential of the Energy Community Treaty has not yet been explored. Finally, the Energy Community serves as a framework for energy relationships with the EU neighbours.

Part III. The CJEU between the Individual Citizen and the Member States

Time and again the CJEU comes under fire. Sometimes this is from the Member States, claiming loss of sovereignty; at other times it is from the trade unions and public interest groups, who fear the downgrading of 'the Social'. Hans, instead, has argued the exact opposite, at least concerning the remedies in the social and the citizens' rights order. For Hans, only more judicial activism can overcome the lacunae which results from a rights-remedy-procedure mechanism that is too much designed to enforce economic freedoms. The CJEU's judgments have, therefore, been the starting point of many of Hans' works.

Bosko Tripkovic and Jan Zglinski demonstrate in Chapter 16 that there are certain structural and theoretically significant similarities between constitutional and private law pluralism in EU law. Using the notions of contestation and accommodation, the authors develop a comprehensive analytic framework, which accounts for the multiplicity of interactions between European and Member State legal, political, and evaluative structures, and integrates public and private law pluralisms into one coherent narrative. In contrast to the received wisdom that judicial institutions are at the forefront of contestation, the authors demonstrate that courts in fact facilitate the silent process of quotidian accommodation that occurs behind the scenes of grandiose legal and political conflicts.

Barend van Leeuwen claims that psychoanalytical concepts shed light on why preliminary references are made and on how the CJEU deals with them. In Chapter 17 the author examines a number of preliminary references to the CJEU from a psychoanalytical perspective to argue that psychoanalysis helps us to understand the interaction between national courts and the CJEU. Barend presents his argument in four steps. First, judges possess a legal 'mind', which is shaped by their national culture, national law and national legal training, in which EU law has to be accommodated. Second, the preliminary reference procedure establishes a therapeutic relationship between national courts and the CJEU. Third, psychoanalytical dynamics can be identified in this therapeutic relationship. Fourth, an analysis of these dynamics gives a better insight into the relationship and interaction between national courts and the CJEU in the preliminary reference procedure.

In Chapter 18 *Marija Bartl and Keiva Marie Carr* ask what lessons, if any, can be drawn from the decision in *Whitman and Others*, the most recent pronouncement on Brexit, if looked at through the prism of Kennedy's 'Three Globalisations of Legal Thought'. Setting out in turn the core characteristics of Classical Legal Thought, The Social, and Neo-Formalism, the authors proceed to critically examine the judgment, asking what light it sheds on the relation between law and politics in the EU. Kennedy's 'Three Globalisations of Legal Thought' in this regard provides useful analytics with which to explore the different legal consciousnesses that appear to co-exist in the judgment. Ultimately, the authors claim, *Wightman and Others* draws predominantly on the 'Social' legal thought, giving priority to the political expression and collective democratic rights of EU citizens.

Betül Kas explores, in Chapter 19, the transformation of the legal field by drawing on the socio-legal reconstruction of the *Janecek* case. *Janecek* concerns the private enforcement of EU environmental law before the national courts in the situation where the national authorities failed to comply with their planning obligations for clean urban air. Taking the 'law in action' the chapter draws on the perspective of the legal realist to reveal that no clear boundaries can be outlined between rights derived from the EU legal order and their enforcement by national institutions, remedies and procedures. Substance and procedure mutually influence each other.

Marco Rizzi and Lécia Vicente apply a comparative matrix methodology to distinguish the notions of defectiveness and, more prominently, causation as developed by the Supreme Court of the United States (SCOTUS) and the CJEU in vaccine liability cases. Chapter 20 discusses the legal frameworks governing the liability of vaccine manufacturers in the US and the EU to analyse then how the two courts have elaborated the nature and scope of the causal link. While the CJEU, continuing a controversial line of French jurisprudence on this matter, has adopted a form of dialectical reasoning in its interpretation of the Product Liability Directive, the SCOTUS stands firmly by a deductive way of causal inquiry, and follows a purely textual or plain meaning approach to the black letter law of relevant provisions.

In Chapter 21, *Annett Wunder* explores the use of the word 'solidarity' in the judgments of the CJEU. Solidarity has become a notion used frequently in the literature and the decisions of the Court. It appears on its own, but sometimes it is linked with other terms like European solidarity, national solidarity, financial solidarity, and furthermore, sometimes it is used as a synonym for equality or identity. The chapter argues that this knowledge may help us to better understand its usage in case law. The first part of this chapter defines solidarity; the second section looks at the use of the term 'solidarity' in the judgments of the CJEU; and the final part summarises the findings.

PART I

EU Consumer Law

2

An Average Consumer Concept of Bits and Pieces

Empirical Evidence on the Court of Justice of the European Union's Concept of the Average Consumer in the UCPD

HANNA SCHEBESTA* AND KAI P. PURNHAGEN**

If one were to ask an academic what Hans Micklitz is most famous for, most people would probably mention his works on consumer law. Indeed, no serious work on consumer law in the EU can nowadays do without a reference to Hans' work. This is not to say that most lawyers support or endorse his position. Quite the contrary, in Germany he is still mostly cited as a 'Mindermeinung' (*minority opinion*). A different picture emerges if one broadens the scope to the European and international level. Here, he is likewise recognised as a major scholar on the topic (among other topics), however, most people follow and endorse his work. To us, this does not come as a surprise. Most of his concepts, including those introduced into German national law, originate in the European or international legal sphere or stem from interdisciplinary analysis. Very uncommon to German civil law scholarship, Hans, as a true European, took these European, international and interdisciplinary approaches as a starting point and tried to make them fit into established legal systems.

A large part of Hans' works concerned the interpretation of the normative benchmark of the 'average consumer' at the EU level.[1] There is no doubt that

* Assistant Professor of Law, Wageningen University. Small descriptive parts of this chapter were already published in the chapter J-U Franck and K Purnhagen, 'Homo Economicus, Behavioural Sciences, and Economic Regulation: On the Concept of Man in Internal Market Regulation and its Normative Basis' in K Mathis (ed), *Law and Economics in Europe – Foundations and Applications* (Dordrecht, Springer, 2014) 329 ff. We thank Niels van der Linden for excellent research assistance.

** Associate Professor of Law, Wageningen University and Distinguished International Visitor, Rotterdam Institute of Law and Economics.

[1] See for example H-W Micklitz, 'Unfair Commercial Practices and Misleading Advertising' in N Reich et al (eds), *European Consumer Law* (Cambridge, Intersentia, 2014) 98.

many authors have so far worked on this topic.[2] However, with diversity of authors comes diversity in scholarship and background. Hence, the interpretation of the 'average consumer' has been subject to many views, approaches and analyses. Consumer protection lawyers, for example, criticise the concept for not reflecting a realistic notion of a consumer.[3] Such a view may be explained by a preconception of consumer law in EU law equalling consumer protection legislation in national laws. In such a view, anyone acting in a private capacity should be protected as a consumer also at EU level. Others emphasise that consumer protection is only needed in certain situations.[4] As a consequence others criticise the average consumer benchmark for not adequately reflecting such situational consumer protection.[5] Law and economics scholars in particular have paralleled the 'average consumer' benchmark to the economic concept of homo economicus.[6] This categorisation has been used by others as a point of departure for criticising the concept of the average consumer for not taking into account sufficiently the latest developments of behavioural sciences.[7] Among all these contributions, Hans' work stands out as one of the few who have tied their work on the average consumer benchmark rigorously close to the internal market rationale as developed by the Court of Justice of the European Union (CJEU).[8]

Hans Micklitz is one of the few who have pointed out that the average consumer benchmark is first and foremost a tool to manage the different levels of EU internal market order and accommodate the systematically different demands of consumers in the Member States.[9] While this finding has been true for many years, more recent developments in both, secondary legislation

[2] See lately especially G Howells and G Straetmans, 'The Interpretive Function of the CJEU and the Interrelationship of EU and National Levels of Consumer Protection' (2017) 9(2) *Perspectives on Federalism* E180.

[3] R Incardona and C Poncibò, 'The Average Consumer, the Unfair Commercial Practices Directive, and the Cognitive Revolution' (2007) 30 *Journal of Consumer Policy* 21.

[4] G Wagner, 'Mandatory Contract Law: Functions and principles in light of the proposal for a Directive on Consumer Rights' (2010) 3(1) *Erasmus Law Review* 47, 68.

[5] J Stuyck, 'Consumer Concepts in EU Secondary Law' in F Klinck and K Riesenhuber (eds), *Verbraucherleitbilder* (de Gruyter, 2015) 115 ff.

[6] JU Franck and KP Purnhagen, 'Homo Economicus, Behavioural Sciences, and Economic Regulation: On the Concept of Man in Internal Market Regulation and its Normative Basis' in K Mathis (ed), *Law and Economics in Europe – Foundations and Applications* (Dordrecht, Springer, 2014) 329 ff.

[7] G Howells, 'EU Consumer Protection Through Information – The Lessons Behavioural Economics Offers' in PC Müller-Graff et al (eds), *Europäisches Recht zwischen Bewährung und Wandel: Festschrift für Dieter H Scheuing* (Baden Baden, Nomos, 2014) 546 ff; J Trzaskowski, 'Behavioural Economics, Neuroscience, and the Unfair Commercial Practices Directive' (2011) 34(3) *Journal of Consumer Policy* 377 ff; V Mak, 'Standards of Protection: in Search of the "Average Consumer" of EU law in the Proposal for the Consumer Rights Directive' (2010) 18 *European Review of Private Law* 15, 27–29.

[8] Micklitz (above n 1) 98. See, for a strong endorsement of the claim to connect the average consumer test to the internal market rationale, S Weatherill, 'The Evolution of European Consumer Law: from well informed consumer to confident consumer' in H-W Micklitz (ed), *Rechtseinheit oder Rechtsvielfalt in Europa* (Baden Baden, Nomos, 1996) 423.

[9] Micklitz (above n 1) 98.

and the Court's jurisprudence seem to paint a different picture, where the average consumer benchmark is being interpreted as one which takes into account increasingly, among other features, more structural vulnerability levels of consumers at the EU level.[10] Taking Hans' approach seriously and contrasting it to recent developments of the average consumer benchmark, the question arises of whether both secondary legislation and the Court have taken a fundamental turn in the conceptualisation of EU consumer law in general and the average consumer benchmark in particular. Therefore, there might be a necessity to assess the relationship of the benchmark, the Court's jurisprudence and the resulting effects for European integration.[11] This asks for a more thorough investigation about the links of the average consumer concept in secondary legislation and the Court's case law.[12] In particular, this chapter will address the following research questions concerning the case law of the average consumer test in the Directive 2005/29/ EC on unfair commercial practices (UCPD):[13]

- How is the average consumer test conceptualised?
- How to determine the average consumer/how to fill in the test?
- Who is the average consumer (characterisation)?
- Who decides who the average consumer is (institutional dimension?)
- Is the 'average consumer' in the UCPD case law the same 'average consumer' as elsewhere?

In order to answer these questions, we are using a mixed-method approach, combining doctrinal and empirical analysis.[14] Doctrinal analysis will determine where the 'average consumer' is used in EU law and how the respective legislative and juridical acts relate to each other. Subsequently, an empirical (qualitative software-supported) analysis[15] will determine how these legislative and juridical

[10] H Schebesta and KP Purnhagen, 'The Behaviour of the Average Consumer: A Little Less Normativity and a Little More Reality in the Court's Case Law? Reflections on Teekanne' (2016) 41 *European Law Review* 589 ff; WH Edinger, 'Promoting Educated Consumer Choices. Has EU Food Information Legislation Finally Matured?' (2016) 39(1) *Journal of Consumer Policy* 9; Howells and Straetmans (above n 2).

[11] A first attempt has already been provided by Howells and Straetmans (above n 2).

[12] When referring to the Court, we refer to both the European Court of Justice and the Court of Justice of the European Union.

[13] Directive 2005/29/EC of the European Parliament and of the Council of 11 May 2005 concerning unfair business-to-consumer commercial practices in the internal market and amending Council Directive 84/450/EEC, Directives 97/7/EC, 98/27/EC and 2002/65/EC of the European Parliament and of the Council and Regulation (EC) No 2006/2004 of the European Parliament and of the Council ('Unfair Commercial Practices Directive').

[14] See, for this method at a generic level, T Hutchinson, 'The Doctrinal Method: Incorporating Interdisciplinary Methods in Reforming the Law' (2015) *Erasmus Law Review*, available at www.elevenjournals.com/tijdschrift/ELR/2015/3/ELR-D-15-003_006.pdf.

[15] The qualitative software supported analysis was conducted using MAXQDA in order to code the cases. For an elaboration of this method, see also H Schebesta, 'Content Analysis Software in Legal Research: A Proof of Concept Using ATLAS.ti' (2018) *Tilburg Law Review* 23.

acts operationalise the 'average consumer' benchmark. While in the research operation we have applied both methods in isolation, the findings presented here are the combined result from the application of both methods.

The structure of the chapter is as follows: first we will illustrate the relationship of the average consumer benchmark in secondary legislation to the Court's case law. We will show that out of all secondary legislation which explicitly uses the 'average consumer' in its wording, jurisprudence has only dealt with the UCPD. While we acknowledge that a large bulk of jurisprudence concerns the average consumer test in primary law, or has been applied to interpret secondary legislation which does not make explicit reference to the consumer benchmark, we limit our analysis to those cases where a clear link between the wording of secondary law and the Court's jurisprudence can be established. This will leave aside the cases where the CJEU interpreted secondary legislation in light of primary law or primary law directly. Consequently, we will investigate only the cases where the Court has operationalised the 'average consumer' benchmark of the UCPD. Lastly, we will summarise and analyse our findings.

I. The Relationship of the Average Consumer in Secondary Legislation to the Court's Jurisprudence

The average consumer is a trending topic, both in legal scholarship and in the Court's case law.[16] A total of 156 cases list the 'average consumer' in the operative part of the judgments, testifying to the importance of the concept in the CJEU's jurisprudence.

The Court developed the average consumer concept as an expression of the proportionality principle, to interpret the free movement of goods as enshrined today in Article 34 TFEU, and therefore as a standard of EU law confining domestic law that establishes obstacles to free trade. Subsequently, the Court applied this concept as a yardstick to construe which practices may be considered 'deceptive' under secondary law that harmonised domestic protective standards in order to ensure free trade in the internal market.[17] It made its way into secondary legislation first with the adoption of the UCPD in 2005, then subsequently into other provisions such as Regulation (EC) No 1924/2006 on Nutritional and Health Claims (NHCR)[18] and Regulation (EU) No 1169/2011 on Food Information to Consumers (FIR).[19] In line with the approach established in *Clinique*, the Court

[16] See, inter alia, Howells and Straetmans (above n 2).

[17] Case C-315/92, *Verband Sozialer Wettbewerb eV v Clinique Laboratoires SNC et Estée Lauder Cosmetics GmbH*, ECLI:EU:C:1994:34, [1994] ERC I-317, at [16].

[18] Regulation (EC) No 1924/2006 of the European Parliament and of the Council of 20 December 2006 on nutrition and health claims made on foods.

[19] Regulation (EU) No 1169/2011 of the European Parliament and of the Council of 25 October 2011 on the provision of food information to consumers, amending Regulations (EC) No 1924/2006

habitually referred to the average consumer concept in cases concerning secondary legislation which did not mention the average consumer benchmark explicitly, such as Directive 93/13/EEC on unfair contract terms[20] or Directive 2000/13/EC on the labelling, presentation and advertising of foodstuffs.[21] In fact, even today, the secondary instruments containing rules using the 'average consumer' concept remain limited to the already mentioned FIR, UCPD, and NHCR.

Both the FIR and the NHCR use the average consumer only in an isolated provision. Under the FIR, the nutrition declaration may be given 'by other forms of expression and/or presented using graphical forms or symbols in addition to words or numbers provided that the following requirements are met', namely if 'they are supported by scientifically valid evidence of understanding of such forms of expression or presentation by the average consumer' (Article 35(1)(d) FIR). The NHCR contains a general principle that 'the use of nutrition and health claims shall only be permitted if the average consumer can be expected to understand the beneficial effects as expressed in the claim' (Article 5(2) NHCR).

The UCPD therefore emerges as the only instrument that uses the concept of the 'average consumer' on a systemic level. Famously, it defines a practice as unfair if 'it materially distorts or is likely to materially distort the economic behaviour with regard to the product of the average consumer whom it reaches or to whom it is addressed, or of the average member of the group when a commercial practice is directed to a particular group of consumers'. A misleading practice under Article 6(1) is one that 'deceives or is likely to deceive the average consumer, even if the information is factually correct' and under Article 6(2) one that causes or is likely to cause 'the average consumer to take a transactional decision that he would not have taken otherwise'.

Similarly, the definition of misleading omissions strongly relies on the average consumer: 'it omits material information that the average consumer needs, according to the context, to take an informed transactional decision and thereby causes or is likely to cause the average consumer to take a transactional decision that he would not have taken otherwise' and it causes or is likely to cause 'the average consumer to take a transactional decision that he would not have taken otherwise'. An aggressive practice is found where 'it significantly impairs or is likely to significantly impair the average consumer's freedom of choice or

and (EC) No 1925/2006 of the European Parliament and of the Council, and repealing Commission Directive 87/250/EEC, Council Directive 90/496/EEC, Commission Directive 1999/10/EC, Directive 2000/13/EC of the European Parliament and of the Council, Commission Directives 2002/67/EC and 2008/5/EC and Commission Regulation (EC) No 608/2004.

[20] Council Directive 93/13/EEC of 5 April 1993 on unfair terms in consumer contracts, OJ L95, 21 April 1993, 29–34.

[21] Directive 2000/13/EC of the European Parliament and of the Council of 20 March 2000 on the approximation of the laws of the Member States relating to the labelling, presentation and advertising of foodstuffs.

conduct'. Therefore, the general concept of unfairness, the definition of misleading actions and misleading omissions and aggressive actions, and the necessary effect on the transactional decision of a consumer are tied to the concept of the average consumer.

As we have examined in greater detail elsewhere,[22] practices and requirements relating to information can be framed in two ways: (i) as 'objective' information requirements; and (ii) as 'subjective' requirements that relate to the understanding and processing of information by the consumer. Under the information-based approach, 'although the average consumer is mentioned, the Court takes a flight into a perceived objectivity found in examining the *quality of the information*, for instance whether information was accurate, complete, and sufficient'.[23]

Both the FIR and the NHCR prohibit a specific misleading aspect of information. The NHCR mandates that the average consumer must understand the *beneficial effects* expressed in a claim. The FIR mandates that the *form and presentation* of nutrition declarations must be understood by the average consumer. Interestingly, the FIR requires 'scientifically valid evidence' to support the understanding by the average consumer.

While the FIR in its Article 7 (in particular read together with Article 8 GFL) also determines whether information is misleading, both the NHCR and the FIR are legal frameworks that are primarily dedicated to the formulation of positive objective information requirements, such as the size of the font on packaging, standard information to be included, and so forth. The UCPD, by contrast, relies on the average consumer in order to determine whether information already used in the market is misleading.

While the NHCR (2006) and the UCPD (2005) are from the 'first legislative wave' of the average consumer, the FIR (2011), as the most recent instrument, makes reference to scientific studies, eg behavioural studies. This appears to accommodate the more modern version of the behaviourally-informed understanding of the average consumer that has since around 2005.[24]

Apart from the UCPD, the other legal instruments that explicitly deploy the average consumer have no case law on it. For this reason, and the systematic way in which the average consumer concept pervades the UCPD, we conducted a systematic research into the case law in order to provide a better understanding of how the Court has used and interpreted the average consumer concept where it is tied to a legal secondary framework.

[22] H Schebesta and KP Purnhagen, 'Is the "behavioural turn" in consumer law taken by Dutch courts?' (2017) *Tijdschrift voor Consumentenrecht en handelspraktijken* 272.

[23] Schebesta and Purnhagen (above n 22).

[24] G Howells, 'The Potential and Limits of Consumer Empowerment by Information' (2005) 32 *Journal of Law and Society* 349.

II. Overview of the Case Law on the UCPD Operationalising the 'Average Consumer'

There are currently 28 cases by the Court that include the search term 'average consumer' on the UCPD. This is explained by the fact that almost any UCPD case will cite a full UCPD article in the legal context that contains the keywords 'average consumer'.

Of these, 15 cases concerned strict rule interpretation, for instance a cluster of cases seeking interpretation on the exclusive nature of the grounds mentioned in Annex I; or interpretations relating to specific practices (pyramid scheme in *Nationale Lotterij*[25]); the relationship between different provisions (for instance between professional diligence and Article 6 in *CHS Tour Service*[26]); or the legality of national enforcement measures (in *Köck*[27]).

We identified 10 cases with a clear application of the average consumer concept (*Dyson*,[28] *Canal Digital*,[29] *Carrefour*,[30] *Perenicova*,[31] *Purely Creative*,[32] *Ving Sverige*,[33] *Wind Tre*,[34] *UPC*,[35] *Trento Sviluppo*,[36] *Sony*[37]). In two additional cases, the Court exclusively framed a question as a pure information case (*Verband Sozialer Wettbewerb*[38]), and in *Mediaprint*[39] the court speaks about the general public instead of the average consumer. The following section outlines the facts of the relevant cases, the provision relating to which and how reference was made to the average consumer.

Carrefour launched a television advertising campaign 'garantie prix le plus bas Carrefour' (Carrefour lowest price guarantee) that compared the price of brand products in its own shops with those of competitors by including favourable prices of its own larger outlets (hypermarches) compared to regular supermarkets for the competitors. The average consumer benchmark was therefore mostly undertaken under the advertising rules, ie Article 4(a) and (c) of Directive 2006/114/EC

[25] Case C-667/15, *Loterie Nationale – Nationale Loterij NV van publiek recht v Paul Adriaensen, Werner De Kesel, The Right Frequency VZW*, ECLI:EU:C:2016:958.

[26] Case C-435/11, *CHS Tour Services GmbH v Team4 Travel GmbH*, ECLI:EU:C:2013:574.

[27] Case C-206/11, *Georg Köck v Schutzverband gegen unlauteren Wettbewerb*, ECLI:EU:C:2013:14.

[28] Case C-632/16, *Dyson Ltd and Dyson BV v BSH Home Appliances NV*, ECLI:EU:C:2018:599.

[29] Case C-611/14, *Canal Digital Danmark A/S*, ECLI:EU:C:2016:800.

[30] Case C-562/15, *Carrefour Hypermarchés SAS v ITM Alimentaire International SASU*, ECLI:EU:C:2017:95.

[31] Case C-453/10, *Pereničová and Perenič v SOS financ spol sro*, ECLI:EU:C:2012:144.

[32] Case C-428/11, *Purely Creative Ltd v Office of Fair Trading*, ECLI:EU:C:2012:651.

[33] Case C-122/10, *Konsumentombudsmannen v Ving Sverige AB*, ECLI:EU:C:2011:299.

[34] Case C-54/17, *Autorità Garante della Concorrenza e del Mercato v Wind Tre SpA*, ECLI:EU:C:2018:710.

[35] Case C-388/13, *Nemzeti Fogyasztóvédelmi Hatóság v UPC Magyarország Kft*, ECLI:EU:C:2015:225.

[36] Case C-281/12, *Trento Sviluppo srl v Autorità Garante della Concorrenza e del Mercato*, ECLI:EU:C:2013:859.

[37] Case C-310/15, *Vincent Deroo-Blanquart v Sony Europe Ltd*, ECLI:EU:C:2016:633.

[38] Case C-146/16, *Verband Sozialer Wettbewerb eV v DHL Paket GmbH*, ECLI:EU:C:2017:243.

[39] Case C-540/08, *Mediaprint Zeitungs- und Zeitschriftenverlag GmbH & Co KG v 'Österreich'-Zeitungsverlag GmbH*, ECLI:EU:C:2010:660.

on misleading and comparative advertising,[40] only read in conjunction with Article 7(1)–(3) of the UCPD.

In *Canal Digital*, a subscription price was mentioned in internet and television advertisements, while an additional charge was mentioned less prominently or only upon additional clicks on a banner. The Court interpreted Articles 6 and 7 UCPD, and the notion of transactional decision, holding that it was for the national court to decide whether the communications were misleading. It provided guidance on what to take into consideration in the assessment of whether the average consumer was misled, for instance the fact that there is significant asymmetry of information that may easily give rise to confusion and consumer understanding. The Court further held that price is principally a factor affecting the transactional decision of the average consumer.

In *Wind Tre*, the company marketed SIM cards with pre-loaded and pre-activated services that were charged to the user if they were not expressly deactivated, without that user having been informed about the existence of these fee-based services. Ultimately the practice was found to be a 'per se' violation, as inertia selling prohibited by Annex I, point 29. The Court's argumentation did, however, venture into the average consumer concept in relation to Article 8 UCPD (aggressive commercial practices).

In *Dyson*, the CJEU established that the lack of reference to a vacuum cleaner's energy efficiency testing conditions is not capable of constituting a misleading omission under Article 7 of Directive 2005/29. What constitutes, or does not constitute, material information to the average consumer was judged exclusively on the basis of a systematic interpretation and took as a reference point the information required under EU law relating to the uniform energy label. The average consumer reaction was then extrapolated and applied in the context of the Energy Directive.

In *Ving Sverige* a travel agency's commercial was found to be a misleading omission, as there was insufficient or no information on the main characteristics of the trip, such as the price. In its treatment of the violation of Article 7, the Court speaks of consumer only, and does not specifically deploy the concept of 'average consumer'.

Purely Creative and Others concerned a number of practices relating to prize winning promotions. While some practices qualified as blacklisted practices, the information on the substance of the prize was examined by the Court under the 'average consumer' requirements in Article 5(2)(b) UCPD. It did so by identifying pieces of information that would be necessary, rather than judging the typical consumer reaction.

In *Perenicova* the Court held that a credit agreement showing an APR lower than the real rate constituted false information as to the total cost of the credit and hence the price referred to in Article 6(1)(d) of Directive 2005/29. The average consumer reaction, to be determined by the national court, would be necessary to judge whether such would influence the transactional decision of a consumer.

[40] Directive 2006/114/EC of the European Parliament and of the Council of 12 December 2006 concerning misleading and comparative advertising (codified version).

The *Sony* case concerned a commercial practice consisting of the sale of a computer equipped with pre-installed software without any option for the consumer to purchase the same model of computer not equipped with pre-installed software. The Court tested under Article 5(2) and 5(4)(a), using the 'average consumer' as a benchmark twice, for ascertaining the misleadingness, and for the transactional decision.

In *Trento Sviluppo*, a supermarket chain advertised a price reduction in leaflets for a laptop, which was not actually available to the consumer. The Court interpreted Article 2 and held that the 'transactional decision' of an average consumer would have to be interpreted widely.

In the *UPC* case, the erroneous information provided by a cable television service to its customer was regarded as misleading practice under Article 6(1) UCPD even where only one consumer was concerned.

We examined those cases in greater detail in order to study how the concept is used in the UCPD jurisprudence by the Court. Overall, a double layered average consumer emerges in the case law: first, on unfairness strictly of the practice (read: 'deceptiveness'), then second on the influence on the transactional decision. On content, the most important articles to be interpreted are naturally Article 7(1)–(3) of the UCPD and Article 6(1) of the UCPD. Interestingly, much depends whether these cases are framed as objective information questions or consumer reactions. The 'transactional decision' taken by the consumer risks becoming the Achilles' heel of the UCPD. While it was contended for a long period that this criterion does not provide an additional threshold, it increasingly seems to be the case that it does. Overall, the 'average consumer', despite guidance of the Court, falls fair and square into the realm of the national court.

III. Summary of the Court's Use of the Average Consumer Test in the UCPD

On the basis of a systematic qualitative analysis of the identified cases, the following picture emerges of the 'average consumer' concept in the CJEU's UCPD jurisprudence in terms of the meta-conception of the test itself, the characterisation of the average consumer, and the institutional dimension responsible for assessing the concept.

A. What is the Average Consumer Test?

The average consumer is conceptualised as the point of reference[41] or 'benchmark to be used'.[42] Specifically, for the UCPD, the Court held that 'the constituent

[41] *CHS Tour Services GmbH v Team4 Travel GmbH* (above n 26) para 43.
[42] *Canal Digital Danmark A/S* (above n 29) para 39.

features of a misleading commercial practice, as set out in that provision, are in essence expressed with reference to the consumer as the person to whom unfair commercial practices are applied'.[43] In other words, the average consumer is the reference point for determining any misleading commercial practice.

B. Who is the Average Consumer (Characterisation)?

Recital 18 UCPD specifies that the 'average consumer' test is not a 'statistical test' and that, 'to determine the typical reaction of that consumer in a given case, the national courts and authorities have to exercise their own faculty of judgment' a statement that is often taken over in the cases.[44] The benchmark to be used is that of the average consumer, 'who is reasonably well-informed and reasonably observant and circumspect, taking into account social, cultural and linguistic factors'. This definition is taken over in the overwhelming number of cases (*Wind Tre*, *Sony*, *Dyson*, *UPC*, *Canal Digital*, *Ving Sverige*, *CHS Tour Service*). This does not come as a surprise, as the definition had been developed initially in case law. Probably because recital 18 had been nothing else than a codification of case law, the 'typical reaction' of recital 18 did not receive specific attention in case law. However, the most recent cases refer to recital 18 as a source for the characterisation of the average consumer.[45] What these sweeping formulations mean can be inferred on the basis of the applications of the average consumer concept in cases. In the jurisprudence, the following variables or characteristics were used by the Court in order to interpret the average consumer: cases refer to consumer perception in the abstract[46] or deploy consumer awareness as a feature.[47] Other features used are the technical capacity of consumers[48] and the existence of an information asymmetry.[49]

Empirically there is a difference between 'the consumer in a specific context' and the 'average consumer'. There is tension between 'the average consumer' (general) and 'the average consumer, according to the context' (circumstance-specific). This is apparent, for instance, in the case of *Wind Tre*, in which the CJEU raised doubts whether the average consumer is sufficiently aware and technically informed about the pre-loaded and pre-activated mobile services for prepaid

[43] *CHS Tour Services GmbH v Team4 Travel GmbH* (above n 26) para 43; *Canal Digital Danmark A/S* (above n 29); *Ving Sverige* (above n 33) paras 22–23.

[44] *Canal Digital Danmark A/S* (above n 29) para 39; *Wind Tre* (above n 34), and *Purely Creative* (above n 32).

[45] *Purely Creative* (above n 32); *Canal Digital Danmark A/S* (above n 29); *Wind Tre* (above n 34).

[46] *Ving Sverige* (above n 33); *Carrefour* (above n 30); *Canal Digital Danmark A/S* (above n 29); *Dyson* (above n 28).

[47] *Sony* (above n 37); *Wind Tre* (above n 34).

[48] *Wind Tre* (above n 34).

[49] *Canal Digital*: 'offers for TV channels are characterised by a wide variety of proposals and combinations that are generally highly structured, both in terms of cost and content, resulting in a significant asymmetry of information that is likely to confuse consumers' (above n 29) para 41.

SIM cards. It then states that it is for the national court to establish the 'typical reaction of the average consumer in circumstances such as those at issue in the main proceedings' (*Wind Tre*, para 52).

Overall, there is no clear pattern on how the CJEU gives meaning to the average consumer, despite the fact that a solidifying body of case law on this concept has emerged. As a juridical concept, the CJEU seems to be struggling with providing meaning to its measurement and content and is still in the process of giving it sharper contours.

One exception exists. With respect to the transactional decision, the Court seems to accept a per se mechanism regarding price. Price 'is, in principle, a determining factor in the mind of the average consumer, when he has to make a transactional decision' (*Canal Digital*, para 46). Price therefore enjoys an a priori presumption of influencing the average consumer's behaviour with respect to the transactional decision.

An important issue that emerges clearly is the tension between subjective average-consumer-based framing of the argumentation and objective information requirements-based framing. What is the relationship between objective information requirements and the subjective consumer perception of information?

Some cases, while paying lip-service to the 'average consumer', in reality determine whether the information quality is sufficient. For instance, in *Wind Tre*, the Court held: 'It follows that for a service to be solicited the consumer must have made a free choice. That supposes, in particular, that the information provided by the trader to the consumer is clear and adequate' (para 45). Further, no reference to the consumer's perception or capacity to handle information is made in *Verband Sozialer Wettbewerb*, although this case concerned an interpretation of Article 7 UCPD:

> It is for the referring court to examine, on a case-by-case basis, first, whether the limitations of space in the advertisement warrant information on the supplier being provided only upon access to the online sales platform and, secondly, whether, so far as the online sales platform is concerned, the information required by Article 7(4)(b) of that directive is communicated simply and quickly.

In terms of information quality, there is an important difference between an omission under Article 7(1) UCPD and Article 7(3) UCPD and deception under Article 6 UCPD. Misleading omissions take into consideration in particular the limitations of the communications medium (time and space) and additional measures taken to make information available to consumers by other means. Such constraints cannot be taken into account under Article 6 UCPD (authoritatively argued in *Canal Digital*). Overall, as we have argued earlier,[50] it is possible to frame identical disputes through the concept of information quality, or through the capacity of consumers handling that information.

[50] Schebesta and Purnhagen (above n 22).

C. Who Decides Who the Average Consumer is (Institutional Dimension)?

Repeating the concept of the average consumer developed by the Court on fundamental freedoms, recital 18 UCPD specifies that, 'in a given case, the national courts and authorities have to exercise their own faculty of judgment'.[51] It is clearly the national court that has the mandate to apply and fill the average consumer with meaning. This general and theoretical rule is often repeated and it is firmly enshrined in the decentralised system of application of EU law that the actual application of the average consumer test to the facts is for the national courts to execute. This principle is strongly reflected in the case law on the average consumer.[52] More specifically, the Court emphasised that it is for the national court to ascertain the average consumer's reaction to a certain practice.[53]

While it is hence for the national courts to apply the average consumer, the degree of guidance from the Court varies between 'next to nothing' and providing detailed guidance that more or less solves the case's particulars: in *Carrefour* the Court stated that 'it is highly likely that the advertising would … be misleading'.[54] In *Canal Digital* the Court, by contrast, provided guiding principles and variables to be taken into consideration. In *Wind Tre*, there was a quasi-determination, only necessitating the national court to verify the facts:

> In the present case, it appears that the services at issue in the main proceedings were pre-loaded and pre-activated on the SIM cards without the consumer having been sufficiently informed of this beforehand, and that, in addition, the consumer was not informed of the costs connected with using those services; this, however, is for the referring court to verify. When the consumer has been neither informed of the cost of the services in question, nor even of the fact that they were pre-loaded and pre-activated on the SIM card that he bought, it cannot be considered that he freely chose the provision of those services.[55]

In terms of how strongly, and how, the Court guides the national courts, a mixed picture emerges. Sometimes the Court proceeds with straight postulates such as that the price influences consumers' transactional decisions, while at other times the facts are discussed in greater detail (eg *Carrefour*), whereas in other cases, the answer appears genuinely subject to the national court's determination (*Sony*). However, even where the Court exercises detailed guidance, any behavioural approach must necessarily be a mandate for the national courts.[56]

[51] *Canal Digital Danmark A/S* (above n 29) para 39.
[52] *Carrefour* (above n 30) para 31.
[53] Eg *Perenicova* (above n 31).
[54] *Carrefour* (above n 30) para 38.
[55] *Wind Tre* (above n 34) para 48.
[56] Schebesta and Purnhagen (above n 22).

IV. Analysis

The empirical analysis has revealed the muddy nature of the Court's treatment of the average consumer benchmark. There are few general lines which we can dissect from the empirical analysis.

The average consumer of the UCPD has matured to a self-referential 'average consumer' interpretation isolated from case law rendered in other areas. The UCPD case law interpretations of the average consumer notion are mostly self-referential, in the sense that they constitute a largely isolated bubble of cases, and do not frequently cite iconic average consumer case law rendered in other areas. This raises the question whether the 'average consumer' of the UCPD is not a specific kind of consumer, and test. Indeed, cases outside of the UCPD on secondary legislation which do not carry any – or only an embryonic – reference to the average consumer benchmark use the average consumer as it was developed in the interpretation of primary law. In the UCPD, most case law concerning the average consumer is codified, so that the UCPD itself contains the 'textual material' to define an average consumer test without reference to primary law. This is witnessed, inter alia, by the fact that most UCPD case law refers to the average consumer definition in the recitals, and not to the one originally developed in *Gut Springenheide*.[57]

Apart from these formal features, another explanation of the self-referential nature of the UCPD consumer lies in the specificity of the factual situations governed by the UCPD, as explained in the following.

The 'average consumer' concept performs a distinct function in UCPD adjudication. The purpose of the average consumer in the UCPD is twofold: first, it is the yardstick by which to *characterise a commercial practice*; second, it is used in reference to *whether a transactional decision was affected*. Regarding the first, the Court uses the average consumer to characterise a practice as misleading or not; in the words of the Court: 'the constituent features of a misleading commercial practice, as set out in that provision, are in essence expressed with reference to the consumer as the person to whom unfair commercial practices are applied'.[58] In the UCPD, practices are constructed as a unilateral act, and the 'average consumer' is a constitutive feature to characterise such practices as misleading or not. On this basis, it makes sense to reflect on the unilateral nature of practices versus bilateral contractual relations, as they appear in the case law on the Directive 93/13/EEC on unfair contract terms.

It is a different question to ask whether a practice is misleading towards the average consumer (generally) and therefore aims at the characterisation

[57] Case C-210/96, *Gut Springenheide GmbH and Rudolf Tusky v Oberkreisdirektor des Kreises Steinfurt – Amt für Lebensmittelüberwachung*, ECLI:EU:C:1998:369, para 31.

[58] *CHS Tour Services* (above n 41) para 43; *Canal Digital Danmark A/S* (above n 29); *Ving Sverige* (above n 33) paras 22–23.

of the practice (situation 1), or whether the question is that in a specific case constellation, given the specific circumstances, an average – in the sense of *typical* – consumer would have been misled (as suggested by the wording of recital 18, situation 2). The varying approaches on this in the case law research demonstrated that these different functions of the juridical concept are not clearly recognised in the Court's argumentation.

Empirically, the institutional mandate to fill the average consumer in situation 2 cases with meaning is placed on the national courts. The case law showed that the Court regularly places a strong mandate on the national courts in filling the meaning of the average consumer in situation 2, in every case at the very least paying lip-service to this delimitation. Tridimas[59] has created a typology of CJEU judgments that acknowledges the diverging degrees to which the judgments actually provide stronger or weaker guidance to the national courts. The surveyed case law indicated a sometimes stronger sometimes, and sometimes absent willingness of the Court to enter into an interpretation of the 'average consumer'.

One explanation for the EU approach in the case law of the Court is clearly institutional by nature. Most consumer law cases are preliminary reference procedures. In these, the national referring court is confronted with the factual situation that it sketches for the CJEU. The CJEU's mandate is exclusively to interpret EU law, and – strictly speaking – does not proceed to apply the law to the facts. The CJEU is not the final instance of a case and thereby not the element in the overall legal process that will apply the interpretation of the law on the facts of the case. These institutional constraints of the legal process place inherent limitations on the interpretation the Court can give to the average consumer. The fact that the mandate of interpretation is placed clearly on the national court is in line with recital 18, but it is not something stipulated in the articles of the UCPD themselves.

If the 'average consumer' serves as a constitutive feature of a misleading practice (situation 1), a stronger mandate for the CJEU to interpret the concept can be warranted. Whether the 'average consumer' case law is used in order to characterise a practice as unfair has important institutional implications. Where the 'average consumer' is a constitutive indicator about which practices are prohibited, the interpretation thereof becomes one of EU law interpretation. Only a specific average consumer understanding, in the specific context, would then refer to the factual circumstances which are situated in the realm of the national court. On this basis, we argue that the CJEU could pay stronger attention to the function that the 'average consumer' concept serves in situation 1 cases respectively, and where it is used to characterise a practice as unfair, to provide stronger guidance to national courts.

Where in UCPD litigation the average consumer is used in order to interpret (unilateral) commercial practices, there is a stronger interest in an EU-wide

[59] T Tridimas, 'Constitutional Review of Member State Action: The Virtues and Vices of an Incomplete Jurisdiction' (2011) 9(3)–(4) *International Journal of Constitutional Law* 737.

understanding, and this interpretation ultimately serves the characterisation of what is a misleading practice – it therefore makes sense to interpret such in the abstract, rather than rendering specific circumstantial interpretations of specific cases. Such an understanding could be used to justify a stronger interpretation by the CJEU in defining the contours of the 'average consumer' concept. This argument finds support in the UCPD itself. The black list in the Annex I to the UCPD circumscribes specific practices which the EU characterises as unfair (situation 1 cases). Hence, when determining the fairness of practices outside of the black list, it is safe to assume that the Court can employ similarly a more specific approach by providing more flesh on the bones of the average consumer concept.

Concluding, the Court provides very little guidance as to the interpretation and application of the average consumer benchmark. However, what we can learn from the little we have is that, at least for the UCPD, a fundamental turn is not yet fully developed, but there are careful steps in jurisprudence and the law itself to develop a more EU-wide version of the average consumer. As this is still largely a work in progress of EU institutions, works on the topic such as that conducted by Hans continue to be hugely relevant. The topic is and will be here to stay, and will increase in importance the more the body of EU law on the consumer grows in substance.

3

Private Law Consequences of Unfair Commercial Practices

MATEJA DUROVIC*

I. Introduction

The EU Directive 2005/29/EC on unfair commercial practices (UCPD)[1] is a piece of European consumer protection legislation which provides the widest and most powerful protection to the consumers.[2] The major goal of the UCPD is to provide unified European rules aimed at prohibiting of all unfair commercial practice from businesses which may potentially affect, directly or indirectly, the economic interests of one or more consumers.[3] On the ground of the text of this Directive, the Court of Justice of the European Union (CJEU or the Court) has in recent years developed a significant case law, providing the interpretation of numerous of its provisions and contributing to the Europeanisation of private laws in the Member States of the European Union.[4]

The purpose of this chapter is to critically examine one of the Court's latest decisions on the UCPD, the one in *Bankia*.[5] Moreover, this chapter strongly supports the idea proposed by the European Commission in the New Deal for Consumers on introduction of individual remedies in all Member States for all consumers who have been affected by unfair commercial practice.

In *Bankia*, the CJEU provided some clarifications regarding the consequences of a trader's engagement in unfair commercial practices and what the national court

* Lecturer in Contract and Commercial Law at King's College London.

[1] Directive 2005/29/EC of the European Parliament and of the Council of 11 May 2005 concerning unfair business-to-consumer commercial practices in the internal market and amending Council Directive 84/450/EEC, Directives 97/7/EC, 98/27/EC and 2002/65/EC of the European Parliament and of the Council and Regulation (EC) No 2006/2004 of the European Parliament and of the Council [2005] OJ L149/22.

[2] See HW Micklitz, 'The General Clause on Unfair Practices' in G Howells et al, *European Fair Trading Law. The Unfair Commercial Practices Directive* (Ashgate, 2006).

[3] Art 1 UCPD; Case C-388/13, *Nemzeti Fogyasztóvédelmi Hatóság v UPC Magyarország kft*, ECLI:EU:C:2015:225, para 32.

[4] M Durovic, *European Law on Unfair Commercial Practices and Contract Law* (Hart, 2016) 17 ff.

[5] Case C-109/17, *Bankia SA v Juan Carlos Mari Merino and Others*, ECLI:EU:C:2018:735.

are expected or, rather, not expected to do, according to the text of the UCPD. The Court said that, contrary to the example of fairness of contract terms established by Directive 93/13/EEC on unfair contract terms (UCTD),[6] the national courts are not obliged to assess *ex officio*, ie by the own motion, whether a particular contract or any of its term has been concluded under the impact of unfair commercial practices. In such a manner, the CJEU has actually lowered the scope of protection offered by the UCPD and failed to provide a more effective protection to an individual consumer who has been affected by an unfair commercial practice.

Such an approach is closely connected with a historically rather problematic and ambiguous relation between the rules on unfair commercial practices and contract law. One of the most unclear and least regulated parts of the UCPD has been related to the consequences of the trader's involvement in unfair commercial practices and the remedies that have to be available to the individual consumer in such situations.[7] The UCPD has introduced a formal independence between the European rules on unfair commercial practices and contract law.[8] However, despite the declaration of strict separation between these two areas of law, in reality the UCPD has had a major impact on contract law.[9] In its decision in *Bankia*, the CJEU failed to explicitly confirm a tighter connection between the rules on unfair commercial practices and contract law and expand the application of *ex officio* obligation of the national courts of the Member States to verify fairness of the contract terms to the assessment of whether a contract has been concluded as a result of unfair commercial practice.

II. The Development of the *Ex Officio* Obligation of Assessment of Fairness of Contract Terms

In its very fruitful case law on the rules of the UCTD, the CJEU has established and confirmed the obligation of the national courts to verify the fairness of all of the terms of consumer contracts.[10] This is the outcome of the Court's extensive interpretation of the rules of the UCTD and, in particular, those rules establishing the mechanism for how the fairness verification of contract term is to be performed by the national courts and what should be the legal consequences of stipulation of unfair contract term in consumer contracts.[11]

[6] Council Directive 93/13/EEC of 5 April 1993 on unfair terms in consumer contracts [1993] OJ L095/29.

[7] H-W Micklitz, 'Unfair Commercial Practices and European Private law' in C Twigg-Flesner (ed), *The Cambridge Companion to European Union Private Law* (Cambridge University Press, 2010) 231–32.

[8] Art 3(2) UCPD.

[9] M Durovic, 'The impact of Directive 2005/29/EC on unfair commercial practices on contract law' (2015) 23(5) *European Review of Private Law* 715, 748.

[10] See G Howells and G Straetmans, 'The Interpretive Function of the CJEU and the Interrelationship of EU and National Levels of Consumer Protection' (2017) 9(2) *Perspectives on Federalism* E180.

[11] Arts 3, 4, 6 and 7 UCTD.

As a result of the CJEU interpretation of the UCTD, today the Member State courts are required to check the fairness of contract terms even if the consumer, as a contractual party, has not raised the issue of the fairness of the contract terms. Eventually, if a contract term turns out to be unfair, the national courts are obliged to draw all the legal consequences established by the national law for unfairness of contract terms, eg that such a term is void.

The Court did not immediately establish this system of protection through the interpretation of the provisions of the UCTD, but this was a rather gradual development. The CJEU approach ended up being much more powerful than anyone could have expected at the moment when the rather sparse text of this Directive was adopted, with ambiguous and few rules on consequences of unfair contract terms.[12] In *Oceano*, as the first case that substantially examined the provisions of the Directive, the Court approached the consumer as a weaker party in a contractual relationship with trader 'as regards both his bargaining power and his level of knowledge'.[13] Furthermore, the consumer was indicated as an economically weak party with insufficient financial resources to initiate litigation before the court. While free legal aid programs may prove as a solution to this problem, what still remains problematic is the fact that the consumer is not aware of his rights.[14]

The lack of awareness surrounding his rights was the justification of the Court for the explanation of why the national courts do not need the motion of consumers in order to assess whether a contract term is unfair or not, but that they may assess it of its own motion. By this approach, the traditional law approach of *ignorantia legis non excusat*[15] was precluded on the basis that the consumer is a much weaker party.

Such an approach was confirmed in *Cofidis*, where the Court pointed out that national courts should assess – without the motion of consumers – whether a term is unfair because the consumer is 'unaware of his rights or because he is deterred from enforcing them on account of the costs which judicial proceedings would involve'.[16] In *Cofidis*, the Court reaffirmed the competence of the national courts to ascertain the illegality of an unfair term even in cases when the consumers do not themselves raise the issue of fairness within the time limit defined by national law. Furthermore, the Court pointed towards effective protection as the primary purpose of Directive 93/13/EEC.[17] In *Cofidis* the risk was presented that

[12] T Wilhemsson, 'Unfair Contract Terms' in G Howells et al, *Rethinking EU Consumer Law* (London, Routledge, 2017).

[13] Joined Cases C-240/98 to C-244/98, *Océano Grupo Editorial SA v Rocio Murciano Quintero ea*, ECLI:EU:C:2000:346, para 25; Case C-168/05, *Elisa María Mostaza Claro v Centro Móvil Milenium SL*, ECLI:EU:C:2006:675, para 25; Case C-40/08, *Asturcom Telecomunicaciones SL v Cristina Rodriguez Nogueira*, ECLI:EU:C:2009:615, para 29.

[14] *Océano Grupo Editorial SA v Rocio Murciano Quintero ea* (above n 13) para 26.

[15] Ignorance of the law is no excuse.

[16] Case C-473/00, *Cofidis SA v Jean Louis Fredout*, ECLI:EU:C:2002:705, para 34.

[17] ibid, 35.

the consumer might not use its right due to his ignorance, or due to the costs of the procedure.

In *Mostazza Claro*, the Court established the obligation of the national courts to assess whether a contractual term that is the subject of a dispute falls within the scope of Directive 93/13/EEC. This was justified by reason of the public interest that the regime set by this Directive is designed to protect.[18] The CJEU emphasised in its decision that the purpose of the UCTD is to strengthen consumer protection 'and, in particular, to raising the standard of living and the quality of life in its territory'.[19]

Moreover, the Court imposed the obligation upon the national courts to raise the motion of unfairness even in cases when the consumer is represented by a professional lawyer before the court in a particular case, ie a qualified person who possesses a high level of legal knowledge.[20] The special regime of protection by unfair contract terms imposes that 'the national court being required to assess of its own motion whether a contractual term is unfair, compensating in this way for the imbalance which exists between the consumer and the seller or supplier'.[21]

The fact that assessment of fairness of a contract term represents a duty, and not the mere power of the national courts, was confirmed in *Pannon*.[22] Furthermore, in this judgment the Court allowed the consumer to choose whether they wanted this option or not, as the Advocate General Trstenjak stressed in her Opinion in *VB*: '[t]he advantage of that approach is that it refrains from imposing protection on the consumer, but is based rather on the idea of protecting consumers by providing them with information'.[23]

In *Asturcom Telecomunicaciones*, the Court invoked the principle of public policy already present in national contract laws, pointing out that the obligation imposed by the UCTD that a consumer must not be bound by an unfair contract term must be regarded 'as a provision of equal standing to national rules which rank, within the domestic legal system, as rules of public policy'.[24] As a consequence, the national court is under the obligation to assess whether the contract is concluded contrary to the principle of public policy.[25] Moreover, national courts are obliged to ensure the establishment of all consequences under the national law, so that the consumer does not become bound by unfair contract terms.[26]

[18] *Elisa María Mostaza Claro v Centro Móvil Milenium SL* (above n 13) para 38.
[19] ibid, para 37.
[20] Joined Cases C-222/05 to C-225/05, *van der Weerd and Others* [2007] ECR I-4233, para 107.
[21] *Elisa María Mostaza Claro v Centro Móvil Milenium SL* (above n 13).
[22] Case C-243/08, *Pannon GSM Zrt v Erzsébet Sustikné Győrfi*, ECLI:EU:C:2009:350.
[23] Case C-137/08, *VB Pénzügyi Lízing Zrt v Ferenc Schneider*, ECLI:EU:C:2010:659, para 106.
[24] *Asturcom Telecomunicaciones SL v Cristina Rodriguez Nogueira* (above n 13) para 52.
[25] ibid, para 54.
[26] ibid, para 59.

The subsequent case law of the CJEU confirmed that public interest requirements impose the obligation on the national court to assess the fairness of a contract term in the circumstances of the case and to ensure that consumers are not bound by these clauses.[27] In order to ensure that consumers are fully liberated from all the consequences of the stipulated unfair contract terms, national courts have the right to declare the entire contract void.[28]

Eventually, the Court has confirmed this approach in its ruling in *Aziz*. In this decision, the CJEU has also explained further the meaning of the general fairness test, ie how the elements of the general fairness test are to be understood and applied by the national courts of Member States. In line with the decision of the Court, a contract term will be unfair if, first, the consumer would be in a more favourable situation of the term had not been included in the agreement, and, second, if the trader could have expected that the consumer would not have agreed to the contract term if it had been negotiable. These two conditions must be fulfilled cumulatively.[29] In its subsequent case law, the CJEU has confirmed that approach.[30]

The examination of the case law of the Court on the UCTD has demonstrated that, for the reasons of protection of the highest public interest, the CJEU provided a radically extensive, purposive and creative interpretation of the provisions of the UCTD.[31] Eventually, such an approach resulted in substantial interference, and effects on the national civil procedure laws of Member States.[32] A gradual evolution may be observed, from giving to the national courts a simple possibility of verifying the fairness of contract terms, to its mandatory requirement. This evolution seems to have achieved its peak in the Court's judgment in *Invitel*.[33] In this case, the Court pointed out that decision of the national court in which a contract term was found unfair has *erga omnes* effects on all consumer contracts that contain it, including the contracts of those consumers who did not initiate or join the process before the national courts on the assessment of fairness of a contract term.[34] All in all, such an interpretation of the CJEU has eventually turned a rather short and ambiguous UCTD into an extremely powerful instrument of consumer protection throughout the EU.

[27] *VB Pénzügyi Lízing Zrt v Ferenc Schneider* (above n 25); Order in Case C-76/10, *Pohotovosť sro v Iveta Korčkovská*, ECLI:EU:C:2010:685; Case C-472/10, *Nemzeti Fogyasztóvédelmi Hatóság v Invitel Távközlési Zrt*, ECLI:EU:C:2012:242.

[28] Case C-453/10, *Jana Pereničová and Vladislav Perenič v SOS financ spol sro*, ECLI:EU:C:2012:144, paras 35–36.

[29] ibid, para 67.

[30] Case C-92/11, *Banco Español de Crédito, SA v Joaquín Calderón Camino*, ECLI:EU:C:2012:349; Case C-488/11, *RWE Vertrieb AG v Verbraucherzentrale Nordrhein-Westfalen eV*, ECLI:EU:C:2013:180.

[31] H Schebesta, 'Does the National Court Know European Law? A Note on Ex Officio Application after Asturcom' (2010) 18(4) *European Review of Private Law* 847.

[32] See DU Galetta, *Procedural Autonomy of EU Member States: Paradise Lost?* (Springer, 2011).

[33] *Nemzeti Fogyasztóvédelmi Hatóság v Invitel Távközlési Zrt* (above n 27).

[34] ibid, para 44.

III. Indirect Effects of Unfair Commercial Practices on a Contract

In cases of unfair commercial practices, the actors are the same as in cases of unfair contract terms, with the equal presence of inequality of power: on the one side, there is a trader as a more powerful party, and, on the other side, there is a consumer as a weaker party. The judgment in *Perenicova* was the first case in which the Court had a chance to assess the relationship between the UCPD and contract law, ie the rules on unfair contract terms. The Court's decision is very important, because it explained for the first time the impact of unfair commercial practice on the fairness of a contract term, which is a legal issue that had not previously been clear.[35]

In its judgment, the CJEU stated that provision of untrue information about the annual percentage rate is to be considered as a form of misleading action, in accordance with Article 6 of the UCPD in relation to price provision. However, the unfairness of such a practice does not directly lead to the unfairness of a contract term concluded as a consequence of such a practice, but it represents one criteria that the national courts should take into consideration while assessing the fairness of a contract term as provided by the UCTD.[36] The explanation of the Court was primarily based on the fact that Article 3(2) of the UCPD indicates that the provisions of the Directive are without prejudice to contract law. Therefore, the fact that a contract was concluded as a consequence of unfair commercial practice cannot have any kind of direct effect on the validity of a contract.

Ultimately, there are two main consequences of the judgment: first, a stipulation of an unfair contract term shall be considered a form of unfair commercial practice, ie a form of misleading action; second, the breach of the rules on unfair commercial practices does not have any *direct* effect on the validity of a contract potentially affected by the unfair commercial practices. However, this breach represents one of the factors which may be taken in the consideration by the national courts of Member States when assessing the fairness of a consumer contract and its terms. The crucially important question has been what the impact of this decision on the national legal systems is, because the Member States have different approaches to the effects of breaches of the rules on unfair commercial practices on contract law.

The differences regarding contract law consequences among Member States have been regarded as one of the most problematic issues in the application of the UCPD.[37] In some Member States, the breach of unfair commercial practices has

[35] S Orlando, 'The Use of Unfair Contractual Terms as an Unfair Commercial Practice' (2011) 7 *European Review of Contract Law* 25.

[36] Case C-453/10, *Jana Perenicová and Vladislav Perenic v SOS financ spol sro*, ECLI:EU:C:2012:144, para 43.

[37] S Whittaker, 'Relationship with European and National Contract Laws' in S Weatherill and U Bernitz (eds), *The Regulation of Unfair Commercial Practices under EC Directive 2005/29: New Rules and New Techniques* (Hart, 2007) 151–54.

direct effects on the validity of the contract, causing a contract concluded under the unfair practice to become null and void. On the other hand, in other Member States, the breach of the UCPD as transposed in the national legal system has no direct effect on the life of a contract.

As a consequence of the confirmed strict maximum harmonisation character of the Directive, this decision of the Court opened up a question as to whether the national legal systems of Member States are allowed to keep their approaches towards the contract law consequences of unfair commercial practices, or whether they have to modify them in accordance with the judgment in *Perenicova*. The relevance of this issue can best be seen in the fact that the European Commission, in its submission to the Court, considered that national laws which provide direct contract law consequences of the rules on unfair commercial practices are to be considered as contrary to EU law.[38] The national contract law fortresses of Member States remained undisturbed, at least by *Perenicova* judgment.

Furthermore, following the case law of the Court on the UCTD and its emphasis on the public interest element, it can easily argued that the UCPD is also designed to protect the highest public interest. Namely, the main purpose of the UCPD is to protect the economic interest of the consumer by prohibiting all kinds of commercial practices by traders that may impair it.[39] To this end, this prohibition leads to the accomplishment of two extremely important goals of the EU: the achievement of a high level of consumer protection, and the strengthening of the internal market.[40] The UCPD accomplishes these two goals by providing the most complete legal mechanism for protection of consumers' free and informed choice, which enables the consumer to make his transactional decision while being fully aware of all the necessary information, and without any illegal influence by the trader.

Still, it seems that the CJEU in its decision in *Perenicova*, through allowing the national courts to take into consideration the breach of the rules on unfair commercial practices as one of the factors to be considered, left the door open to the national courts to apply their national rules and annul contracts if that is something defined by the national rules of Member States. The introduction of an obligation for the national courts of Member States to assess *ex officio* the fairness of a commercial practice and apply all relevant contract law consequences on a contract concluded under its impact, would not be contrary to the judgment of the CJEU in *Perenicova*. However, the opportunity to do so, and to adopt the same approach for the UCPD as for the UCTD, was missed, thanks to the CJEU's decision in *Bankia*.

[38] Opinion of Advocate General in Case C-453/10, *Jana Pereničová and Vladislav Perenič v SOS financ spol sro*, ECLI:EU:C:2012:144, para 41.

[39] Art 5(1) UCPD.

[40] Art 1 UCPD.

IV. The CJEU's Refusal of the Application of *Ex Officio* Doctrine

The UCPD's rules on enforcement and applicable remedies in case of breach of its provisions are very scarce. The focus of the Directive seems to be on the collective dimension of enforcement, and individual enforcement has been left aside.[41] The UCPD only requires that Member States need to ensure that there exist adequate and effective means to combat unfair commercial practices. Moreover, the sanctions for breach of unfair commercial practices are expected to be proportionate, dissuasive and efficient.[42] Therefore, one of the main tasks is how to secure the fulfilment of these requirements and the provision of an adequate protection to the consumers affected by the unfair commercial practices. It should be noted that the Commission's Consumer Market Study published in 2017 demonstrated that some 27% of consumers who were victims of unfair commercial practices did not take any action.[43]

A high level of consumer protection is guaranteed and highlighted by the EU Charter of Fundamental Rights, which represents an integral part of the Treaty.[44] In line with this fundamental principle of EU law, and following the extensive development of case law of the CJEU on the UCTD, which secured a high level of protection to consumers affected by the unfair contract terms, it seems reasonable to argue that for the equivalent purpose – a high level of consumer protection – the CJEU should pursue the same approach while interpreting the UCPD. In other words, the Court should impose an obligation on the national courts of Member States, when assessing a consumer contract, to check whether there was an unfair commercial practice. What the national courts should in particular verify is whether the fact that there is a presence of unfair commercial practice has some contract law consequences under the national contract laws of the Member State.

If the answer to this question turns out to be affirmative, in line with its case law on the UCTD, the national courts should be required to draw the appropriate consequences under the national law of the Member State.[45] What seems obvious is that the protection of consumers' economic interests by the UCPD needs to be recognised as being of highest public interest, and thus the *ex officio* doctrine should apply. Only such an approach can ensure that an individual consumer

[41] H-W Micklitz, 'Legal Redress' in G Howells et al, *European Fair Trading Law. The Unfair Commercial Practices Directive* (Ashgate, 2006) 220.

[42] Art 12 UCPD.

[43] See Consumer Market Study to support the Fitness Check of EU consumer and marketing law 2017, available at publications.europa.eu/en/publication-detail/-/publication/a8d7ca32-772c-11e7-b2f2-01aa75ed71a1/language-en/format-PDF.

[44] Art 38 Charter of Fundamental Rights of the European Union.

[45] *Telecomunicaciones SL v Cristina Rodriguez Nogueira* (above n 13) para 59; Case C-342/13, *Katalin Sebestyén v Zsolt Csaba Kővári, OTP Bank, OTP Faktoring Követeléskezelő Zrt and Raiffeisen Bank Zrt*, ECLI:EU:C:2014:1857, para 35.

is exempted from all negative contractual consequences of unfair commercial practice and thus appropriately protected.

The establishment of the *ex officio* doctrine for the unfair commercial practices' verification is in line with the decision of the CJEU in *Perenicova*. The mere fact that a trader was engaged in an unfair commercial practice would not automatically lead to the annulment of a contract concluded as the outcome of such practice, direct nullity of its term or any other contract law consequences. However, the national courts of Member States would have to check whether the facts connected to a particular unfair commercial practice have, under national contract law, any effect on the validity of concluded contract.

In that sense, the decision of the CJEU in *Perenicova* might have represented for the UCPD what *Oceano* has been for the UCTD: a cornerstone for the development of better protection for an individual consumer who has been affected by the breach of consumer law. However, the CJEU decided to take a different approach.

In its decision in *Bankia*, the CJEU found that it is not necessary for the national courts of Member States during mortgage enforcement proceedings to be able to review whether the enforceable instrument breaches the UCPD. This is because, as the Court pointed out, the provisions of the UCPD do not place such an obligation on the courts. When explaining its judgment, the Court referred to the different approaches taken in the UCPD and the UCTD. In particular, the Court pointed out to its decision regarding the UCTD in *Aziz*, due to the similarity of the subject matter of that case with the facts in *Bankia*. This is because both *Aziz* and *Bankia* dealt with mortgage enforcement proceedings. Moreover, the CJEU identified that there are differences between pursuing of the goals of the UCTD and the UCPD: although they are both designed to ensure the achievement of a high level of consumer protection, they do so by using different means.[46]

In that sense, the UCTD clearly secures that unfair contract terms are not to be binding on the consumer, whereas the UCPD has introduced a total prohibition of unfair commercial practices. The UCTD seeks to address the inequality of power between the parties which is created by the unfair term, while the UCPD only seeks to put an end to unfair practices, without an impact on the validity of the contract. In addition, the CJEU has underlined that, as clearly stated in its text, the UCPD is without prejudice to, in particular, individual actions brought by those who have been harmed by an unfair commercial practice.[47] The UCPD is, as well, without prejudice to EU and national rules on contract law, including the rules on the validity, formation or effect of a contract.[48]

The Court pointed out that a contractual term cannot be declared invalid even if it was agreed on between the parties to the contract on the basis of an unfair commercial practice.[49] Moreover, in *Bankia*, the CJEU confirmed that a finding

[46] *Bankia SA v Juan Carlos Mari Merino and Others* (above n 5) para 36.
[47] Recital 9 UCPD.
[48] Art 3(2) UCPD.
[49] *Bankia SA v Juan Carlos Mari Merino and Others* (above n 5) para 43.

that a commercial practice is unfair has no direct effect on whether the contract is valid, is in line with the UCPD.[50] Finally, the Court emphasised that, contrary to the situation in *Aziz*, where compensatory protection was found to not meet the requirements of the UCTD, in the case of unfair commercial practices, compensatory protection can be sufficient.[51] Still, the Court clarified that it is possible for the unfairness of practices to be considered during mortgage enforcement proceedings in the context of a review of unfair terms. Therefore, all of these are factors that, according to the CJEU, should justify the differences in the Court's approaches to these two European legal instruments which are both developed to secure fairness in business-to-consumer relations.

Still, despite this explanation, bearing in mind the CJEU's very clear approach to interpretation of the European rules on unfair contract terms as established by the UCTD, it is difficult to understand why the CJEU refused to follow the same approach in the case of the provisions of the UCPD. Despite the argumentation used by the Court, the reality is that both legal instruments are aimed at providing uniform legal standards for fairness in business-to-consumer relations and at contributing to the development of a common market by abolishing the differences which exist among the approaches of the national laws of EU Member States both towards fairness of commercial practices and fairness of contract terms.

V. European Consumer Policy Perspective and the Fitness Check

The need for clarification of the relationship between the rules on unfair commercial practices and contract law has been something that has attracted the attention of policy makers, especially the European Commission. What has become obvious is that, despite a clear separation between the rules of the UCPD and the contract law,[52] it has been possible to observe that the UCPD has had some effects on contract law.[53] That issue was one of the subjects of the European Commission's Fitness Check of consumer and marketing law. The results of the Fitness Check were published in May 2017 and these may be considered as a cornerstone for the massive planned project on reform of the entire corpus of European consumer law.[54]

[50] ibid, para 50.
[51] ibid, para 52.
[52] Art 3(2) UCPD.
[53] M Durovic, 'The impact of Directive 2005/29/EC on unfair commercial practices on contract law' (2015) 23(5) *European Review of Private Law* 715.
[54] European Commission, 'Study for the Fitness Check of EU consumer and marketing law', SWD(2017) 209 final, available at publications.europa.eu/en/publication-detail/-/publication/c70681c5-772f-11e7-b2f2-01aa75ed71a1/language-en/format-PDF/source-search.

In the Fitness Check project, the European Commission assessed the existing legislative instruments of which European consumer law consists. Accordingly, the Commission also examined the current status of the implementation of the UCPD in the national legal systems of the Member States. What has been emphasised as a particularly important practical problem is the question of regulation of contract law remedies for breach of the rules on unfair commercial practices. In particular, the main question is what kind of contract law remedies the consumer should have in cases where their contract stipulation has been affected by a commercial practice which then turns out to be unfair. Consequently, in order to provide a solution to this issue, the European Commission identified some possible policy options for the future.[55]

The Fitness Check demonstrates that, as a general observation, in all Member States, consumers may rely on different general contract law remedies in cases where the traders breached the rules on unfair commercial practices. There is no unified approach.[56] However, in the regulation of the link between the breach of the rules on unfair commercial practices and general contract law rules themselves, the contract law approaches among the Member States differ. This is because only a few Member States have established a direct link between the two areas of law. Moreover, even in cases when it has been established, the link between the rules on unfair commercial practices and contract law consequences thereof is defined in a heterogenous manner. In addition to the general contract law remedies, a number of Member States have adopted specific contract law remedies available to the consumers where they are victims of the unfair commercial practices.

In the study which preceded publication of the Report, the European Commission came up with three possible policy options related to the reform of the UCPD.[57] The first policy option was that no action should take place at European level, but the *status quo* should be preserved. The second policy option was the introduction of a link between breach of the rules on unfair commercial practices and the national contract law remedies as provided by the national laws of the Member States. The third option was the most radical one. It suggested the adoption of a common European contract law remedy for the breach of the rules on unfair commercial practices.[58]

The ideal solution would certainly be the development of a common European contract law remedy for the consumer who has been harmed by an unfair commercial practice. The main purpose of that remedy would be to put the consumer in the position they would be in had the unfair commercial practice not occurred. For example, that the contract concluded under the impact of an unfair commercial practice is not binding on the consumer, ie a similar solution to that in

[55] ibid.
[56] See Durovic (above n 4) ch V.
[57] 'Study for the Fitness Check of EU consumer and marketing law' (above n 54) 269–71.
[58] ibid, 270.

the UCTD.[59] The national legislation report regarding the potential development of direct contract law consequences of unfair commercial practices indicated that such a policy option is considered to be highly controversial, and stakeholders are divided in their opinion in this respect.[60]

Generally speaking, it appears that consumer organisations and entities in charge of consumer protection, such as consumer organisations and enforcement authorities, are in favour of the adoption of common European contract law remedies for the breach of unfair commercial practices. Contrary to this, businesses seem to be strongly against such an idea.[61] The Fitness Check Report pointed out that remedies against unfair practices were regulated differently at the national level and rarely applied 'despite the high reported incidence of UCPD infringements'. There was little case law showing 'a clear link between the remedies derived from the general contract law doctrines and the unfair commercial practices as established in the UCPD'.[62]

The Commission therefore concluded that the introduction of an EU-wide right to individual remedies would 'contribute to the circular economy' and serve 'as an additional deterrent against misleading claims about environmental and durability features of goods and services'.[63] According to the Report, this would be in line with the majority of stakeholders, which call for 'more effective and consistent enforcement of EU consumer law'.[64] However, there are a number of challenges for this policy option.[65] Having re-considered each of the three options, the European Commission has come up with a policy reform suggestion in its New Deal for Consumers.

VI. New Deal for Consumers and Private Law Remedies in Case of Unfair Commercial Practices

Following the publication of the Fitness Check Report, the European Commission published a new policy document, 'New Deal for Consumers' in April 2018.[66] The New Deal for Consumers proposes a number of changes to the UCPD.[67]

[59] Art 6(1) UCTD.

[60] 'Study for the Fitness Check of EU consumer and marketing law' (above n 54) 266.

[61] ibid, 269.

[62] ibid, 93.

[63] ibid, 77, 86.

[64] Fitness Check Report, 27. The results of the online public consultation indicated a vast majority support for the introduction of specific remedies among consumer organisations (95%), consumer respondents (75%), and public authorities (75%). Businesses and business associations were divided, with 45% of businesses and 10% of business associations in favour: see Fitness Check Report, 93.

[65] ibid, 270.

[66] European Commission, *Communication from the Commission to the European Parliament, the Council and the European Economic and Social Committee – A New Deal for Consumers*, COM(2018) 183 final.

[67] C Twigg-Flesner, 'Bad Hand? The "New Deal" for EU Consumers' (14 May 2018), final version published at (2018) 15 *European Union Private Law Review (GPR)* 166, 169.

In this consumer policy document the European Commission tries to address the issue of the ineffective individual remedies that consumers can rely on when being affected by unfair commercial practices, focusing here primarily on the availability of contract law remedies. This is because, while aiming at a total prohibition of unfair commercial practices, EU law has not provided a harmonised set of rules regarding individual remedies for consumers. The general problem with the lack of adequate, uniform and efficient enforcement of the rules at the European level was well demonstrated in the *Apple* case, an example of one of the biggest pan-European consumer law cases.[68]

Some EU Member States have adopted contract law remedies such as the right to terminate the contract and receive a refund, or have widened the application of traditional contract law concepts of misrepresentation and duress.[69] This issue has become very relevant after the global *Dieselgate* scandal, where European consumers were only able to seek remedies from the car dealer and not from the car producer, which was in fact responsible for the marketing of cars with misleading environmental claims, thus also breaching the rules of the UCPD.[70] This has been a problem that should be addressed at a more general and uniform level.[71]

Accordingly, the New Deal for Consumers aims to ensure that individual consumers in all Member States have the right to claim individual remedies when they are affected by any form of traders' unfair commercial practices. Therefore, the New Deal proposes the adoption of a new article of the UCPD, which would require that Member States have to provide both for contractual and non-contractual remedies to individual consumers who have been harmed by an unfair commercial practice.[72]

This amended part of the UCPD would not follow the maximum harmonisation approach, but would just set up minimum standards. As a minimum, the contractual remedies should include a consumer's right to terminate the contract.[73] In addition, each Member State should provide non-contractual remedies that would encompass the right to compensation for damages that an individual consumer has suffered as a consequence of an unfair commercial practice, irrespective of whether a contract has been concluded.[74] The Member States would be free to offer any other private law remedies to an individual consumer.

[68] M Durovic, 'The Apple Case: The Commencement of Pan-European Battle against Unfair Commercial Practices' (2013) 9(3) *European Review of Contract Law* 253, 265.

[69] For example, in the UK, amendments made to the Consumer Protection from Unfair Trading Regulations 2008 by the Consumer Protection (Amendment) Regulations 2014. However, these remedies are only available where there have been misleading actions and aggressive practices, and not for misleading omissions.

[70] 'Study for the Fitness Check of EU consumer and marketing law' (above n 54) part 3.

[71] See Volume 6 (2017), Issues 1 and 2 of the *Journal of European Consumer and Market Law* addressing the *Dieselgate* scandal in EU Member States.

[72] Proposed Art 11a UCPD.

[73] Proposed Art 11a(2) UCPD.

[74] Proposed Art 11a(3) UCPD.

VII. Conclusions

In its decision in *Bankia*, the CJEU has missed yet another opportunity to strengthen the relationship between the rules on unfair commercial practices on the one side, and the rules on contract law on the other side and to secure an adequate level of protection to an individual consumer harmed by unfair commercial practice. The previous chance was missed in *Perenicova* case. The hope after the judgment in *Perenicova* was that it would represent for the UCPD that which the decision in *Oceano* meant for the future expansion of the scope of the UCTD.

In other words, the judgment in *Perenicova* could represent a first step towards the introduction of a general obligation on the national courts to assess *ex officio* the contract law consequences on an individual consumer of an unfair commercial practice. In *Oceano,* the CJEU pointed out that this is the right of the national court of Member States: a mere possibility. However, through the subsequent case law, that mere possibility, an option, has been transformed into an active duty imposed on national courts, which has an *erga omnes* effects. It has been an extremely powerful transformation, indeed, of the scope of the UCTD.

In the UCPD, the securing of adequate contract law remedies to an individual consumer harmed by unfair commercial practice, and the confirmation of an explicit causal link between contract law and the law on unfair commercial practices is the only way forward and the only manner in which to provide a high level of protection to all consumers. However, what needs to be secured is that an individual consumer succeeds in practice to profit from that remedy. That is a goal which can be only achieved if there is an *ex officio* obligation on national courts to assess whether a consumer contract has been affected by an unfair commercial practice.

However, in its decision in *Bankia*, the CJEU has not used the possibility presented to it to widen the scope of application and increase the level of protection offered by the UCPD. That would have been a positive development, because it would have provided an individual consumer harmed by an unfair commercial practice with an excellent mechanism of protection. It can be seen as a missed opportunity for the Court, but is something that could potentially be remedied by the European legislator. Accordingly, the introduction of *ex officio* doctrine is something that should and could be done as a part of the legal reform inspired by the New Deal for Consumers programme.

4

A Consumer Perspective on Algorithms

PETER ROTT*

I. Introduction

I have known Hans Micklitz for more than 20 years. Over the years, or decades, Hans and I not only became friends but also kept finding new topics that we were both interested in, although we have sometimes looked at them in different ways. These topics included, among others, services of general interest, the liability of certification bodies (triggered by the breast implants scandal) and the collective enforcement of consumer rights. For this contribution, I chose a more recent field of interest of ours: algorithms, and how they, or rather their use, change the playing field between traders and consumers. As always, I take a consumer perspective on them, and I limit my observations to the algorithms' immediate effects on consumers.

In academic writing, we find much discussion about the way in which algorithms can improve decision-making of businesses (trying to exploit their customers' willingness to pay) as well as of consumers (trying to get the best deal); but also about the risk that algorithms might contain prohibited elements, such as discrimination. Hans Micklitz and colleagues from the Advisory Council for Consumer Affairs (*Sachverständigenrat für Verbraucherfragen*; SVRV) at the German Federal Ministry of Justice and for Consumer Protection have addressed this issue in an expert opinion of December 2016,[1] and they have proposed, among other things, that algorithms should be regulated by law, and that they should be transparent and open to objective assessment of their compliance with legal requirements. Control should be put in the hands of an expert committee.[2]

This chapter goes a step further by taking the subjective consumer perspective rather than the perspective of objective compliance with the law. It looks at automated decision-making through algorithms, that tend to give no reasons,

* Professor of Civil Law, European Private Law and Consumer Law at the University of Kassel, Germany.

[1] SVRV, *Verbraucherrecht 2.0 – Verbraucher in der digitalen Welt* (Berlin, SVRV, 2016); SVRV, *Digitale Souveränität* (Berlin, SVRV, 2017) 22.

[2] ibid, 67, 69 ff.

as perceived arbitrariness on the part of business operators, and suggests that it may be necessary to apply safeguards that are typically found in public law (against arbitrary decisions of public authorities) to the use of algorithms by private operators.

II. Algorithms and Their Use

Algorithms are nothing but mathematic formulas. Using algorithms in a legal context means to translate facts (that should be economically and/or legally relevant) into figures that support decision-making. As Hans Micklitz and his co-researchers at the EUI have aptly observed, the problem is not the algorithms as such but their use, and how that use changes the relations between actors, that is of interest.[3] In this chapter, I focus on the influence of the use of algorithms on the relationship between traders and consumers.

Algorithms can be used in many contexts and at different stages of the contact with consumers, and before contact is made. At an early stage, they can be used to explore consumer preferences, for example, relating to products, shopping environments (whether in real life or digital) or shopping times. Knowledge, or rather perceptions, of such preferences may then shape offers to the general public, for example by varying prices during the day based on consumer habits or needs, but also personalised marketing approaches, personalised offers or the rejection of an offer based on what the trader, or the automated system he uses, knows or believes he knows about the individual consumer.

Personalised advertisements are something that everybody has experienced who has ever bought on the Amazon platform. Nowadays, this is by no means limited to personalised messages. In contrast, most advertising that, for example, online news providers show us is personalised in the sense that it takes up our recent searches on internet, or more generally the websites we have visited.[4] The same applies to the advertising that we see on Smart TVs.[5] Even easier is the placement of personalised advertising in social media, where consumers readily disclose personal data to the public.[6]

Personalised offers may take this one step further in not only addressing our perceived needs or desires but also in exploiting our perceived willingness to pay, thus, to charge an individual price that the trader believes we will be ready to accept ('personalised pricing').

[3] See A Jabłonowska et al, 'Consumer law and artificial intelligence – Challenges to the EU consumer law and policy stemming from the business' use of artificial intelligence' *EUI Working Paper Series*, LAW 2018/11 (Florence, EUI, 2018) 4.

[4] See T Weichert, 'Scoring in Zeiten von Big Data' (2014) *Zeitschrift für Rechtspolitik* 168 ff.

[5] See S Bauer, 'Personalisierte Werbung auf Social Community-Websites – Datenschutzrechtliche Zulässigkeit der Verwendung von Bestandsdaten und Nutzungsprofilen' (2008) *MultiMedia und Recht* 435.

[6] See, for example, F Lichtnecker, 'Die Werbung in sozialen Netzwerken und mögliche hierbei auftretende Probleme' (2013) *Gewerblicher Rechtsschutz und Urheberrecht* 135.

Finally, the use of algorithms may lead the trader to reject certain customers for valid reasons or on grounds that he is not allowed to consider by law, in particular by anti-discrimination legislation. A special instance of the latter two categories is the provision or otherwise of credit, which may be rejected or granted on different conditions on the basis of a credit score.

III. Effects on Consumers

The different ideal types of uses of algorithms produce different effects on consumers, although these effects partially overlap. What I do not consider here, as I focus on effects, is the collection and the processing of data as such and their lawfulness under data protection law, as a trader may never use the data that he collected.

It is sometimes argued that the use of big data and algorithms can be beneficial for consumers as they receive advertisements and offers that are better targeted to their needs. Where this is actually the case, no consumer problem exists. Thus, this effect can be neglected for the purposes of this chapter. Clearly, however, this is not always the case.[7]

For the subsequent considerations, I use the categories of molestation, exploitation and discrimination. All these categories were present before the age of digitalisation, but their intensity may have increased.

A. Molestation

Molestation occurs frequently when the consumer receives advertisements or offers, primarily by email or SMS, and more recently when watching television or reading online newspapers with ads constantly popping up. This is, by the way, not exclusive to commercial actors: immediately after having searched online for literature on plastic waste in the ocean, I was shown a media campaign by the German Federal Ministry for the Environment, Nature Conservation and Nuclear Safety concerning plastic waste.

Some of these advertisements are more invasive than others. This is of course not new, but personalised advertising feels more invasive, as it shows that someone knows more about us than we have meant to tell them; or that someone has perceptions of us that we dislike.[8] And very often, the advertisement relates to traders, or products of traders, whose websites we have not visited before but who must have obtained our data from other sources.

[7] For a recent example, see the story of the journalist G Brockell who was still swamped with advertisements for baby products after a stillbirth; see NN, 'Trauernde Mutter schreibt bewegende Anklage gegen Tech-Konzerne' *Spiegel online* (12 December 2018), available at www.spiegel.de/netzwelt/web/gillian-brockell-journalistin-aergert-sich-nach-totgeburt-ueber-online-anzeigen-a-1243282.html.

[8] For example, following a research on unfair practice of online dating portals, I have received plenty of advertisements from online dating portals, and more explicit content.

B. Exploitation

Big data and the use of algorithms are also employed to improve the exploitation of the consumer's willingness to pay. Quite obviously, traders aim to find a price that is as high as possible but that the consumer will still pay. They will thereby be guided by experience, and experience will tell them that the willingness to pay varies on the timescale and between consumers. They may therefore engage in dynamic pricing, or even in personalised pricing. Dynamic pricing means the variation of prices during the year, the month or the day, depending on varying supply, varying demand or varying competition by other traders. This has always happened, for example in the form of winter sales, in peak times or in relation to foodstuff that is about to expire.[9] Petrol stations, whose prices have always been fairly dynamic,[10] were the first actors to vary prices during the course of the day. Big data and algorithms allow traders to refine and automatise the process and to react most speedily to changing demand and competition.[11] Internet sellers have begun to engage in dynamic pricing, and even supermarkets consider the introduction of electronic price tags on which prices could be varied electronically (but appear to have shied away from this until now, see below).[12] Price variations can in fact be enormous.[13] Studies have revealed that prices have varied by 240% within a couple of hours.[14]

One consequence of highly dynamic pricing is that consumers lose their idea of the 'real' price, the so-called 'reference price' (if they ever had one).[15] Consequently, the Consumer Centre of Northrhine-Westphalia has demanded that traders should be required to generally indicate the price development of the last 72 hours, which would reveal a policy of dynamic pricing.[16]

In terms of the exploitation of the consumers' willingness to pay, dynamic pricing is still rough as it extends to all consumers shopping at a given time of the day and can therefore only react to average preferences. For more specific targeting, traders must

[9] See, for example, H Zander-Hayat et al, 'Personalisierte Preise – Eine verbraucherpolitische Einordnung' (2016) *Verbraucher und Recht* 403, 404.

[10] See D Tietjen and BF Flöter, 'Dynamische und personalisierte Preise: Welche lauterkeitsrechtlichen Schranken gelten für Unternehmen?' (2017) *Praxis im Immaterialgüter- und Wettbewerbsrecht* 546.

[11] See G Wenglorz, 'Dynamischer Preis: Ein Fall für die Preisangabenverordnung?' in W Büscher et al (eds), *Marktkommunikation zwischen Geistigem Eigentum und Verbraucherschutz – Festschrift für Karl-Heinz Fezer zum 70. Geburtstag* (Munich, CH Beck, 2016) 957, 958. For petrol stations, see the Danish company a2i systems, at www.a2isystems.com; on which see S Schlechner, 'Why Do Gas Station Prices Constantly Change? Blame the Algorithm' *Wall Street Journal* (8 May 2017).

[12] See Tietjen and Flöter (above n 10) 546.

[13] For empirical evidence, see Marktwächter Digitale Welt, *Dynamische Preisdifferenzierung im deutschen Online-Handel* (2018) 13 ff. See also J Remmel, 'Die verbraucherpolitische Perspektive: aktuelle Entwicklungen im Online-Handel' (2016) *Wirtschaftsdienst* 875.

[14] See F Hofmann, 'Der maßgeschneiderte Preis' (2016) *Wettbewerb in Recht und Praxis* 1074, 1075.

[15] See also P Kenning and M Pohst, 'Die verbraucherwissenschaftliche Perspektive: von der Customer Confusion zur Price Confusion?' (2016) *Wirtschaftsdienst* 871, 873; Remmel (above n 13) 875 ff.

[16] See Verbraucherzentrale Nordrhein-Westfalen, *Verbraucherproblemen wirksam begegnen – Weichen richtig stellen* (2017), available at www.verbraucherzentrale.nrw/sites/default/files/migration_files/media247515A.pdf, 4.

therefore employ 'personalised pricing', that is, determine, from the available personal data of the consumer, the personal willingness to pay of that particular consumer. In the past, determinants of that personal willingness to pay have been seen in the use of particular devices (such as an iPhone) but even more in the personal purchasing and/or searching history of the particular consumer; this can mean, first, that consumers are offered different products or services, or that they are ranked in different ways, depending on the perceived, or calculated, preferences of the individual consumers ('price steering'),[17] and second, that consumers may be offered the same goods or services at different prices. Consumers may also be approached in different ways, for example, using different language.[18] While some authors have suggested that this could have a redistributive effect in that poorer consumers are charged less than wealthy consumers,[19] this may be doubted as it is not the aim of personalised pricing to act as Robin Hood but to increase the overall profit.

Otherwise, studies have revealed that the majority of consumers disapprove of dynamic pricing (beyond what is understandable and a well-established practice) as well as of personalised pricing, because they perceive it as unfair. This applies even to consumers who benefit from personalised pricing;[20] and it is the reason why traders usually (claim to) have abandoned such practices after they have been made public.[21]

C. Discrimination

If differentiation between individual consumers is based on specific data relating to, for example, sex or religion, differentiation may turn into discrimination in the terms of anti-discrimination laws, which may lead to the unjustified denial of access to goods or services or to less favourable conditions of access, and the related economic and psychological consequences.

D. Arbitrariness

Finally, and perhaps most importantly, algorithms are ever more used in the preparation of decision-making or for decision-making itself, without offering

[17] On an early example of hotel rankings shown by Orbitz, see A Hannak et al, *Measuring Price Discrimination and Steering on E-commerce Web Sites* (2014) 1, available at conferences.sigcomm.org/imc/2014/papers/p305.pdf.

[18] For examples, see P Rott, 'Der "Durchschnittsverbraucher" – ein Auslaufmodell angesichts personalisierten Marketings?' (2015) *Verbraucher und Recht* 163 with further references.

[19] See EI Obergfell, 'Personalisierte Preise im Lebensmittelhandel – Vertragsfreiheit oder Kundenbetrug?' (2017) *Zeitschrift für Lebensmittelrecht* 290, 294; Tietjen and Flöter (above n 10) 548; S Genth, 'Dynamische Preise: ein Gewinn für Handel und Verbraucher' (2016) *Wirtschaftsdienst* 863.

[20] See, for example, W Reinartz et al, *Preisdifferenzierung und –dispersion im Handel* (IFH Förderer, 2017) 10 ff; M Schwaiger and G Hufnagel, *Handel und elektronische Bezahlsysteme* (ABIDA, 2018) 13 ff.

[21] See again the example of Orbitz by Hannak et al (above n 17) 1.

the consumer the chance to talk to someone and find out about the reasons for the decision, and maybe to convince the person in charge that the decision was based on incorrect facts or on an incorrect interpretation of facts. Therefore, the consumer will know neither what facts the decision was based on nor why those facts made the algorithm come to that particular conclusion.[22] And even if there is a chance to ask why, for example, credit was not granted or why the conclusion of a supply contract was rejected, the (human) answer may simply refer to a score that was calculated by way of an algorithm,[23] and that answer will surely be correct, since the human being in charge will often not have knowledge about the relevant criteria and their relevance for the achieved score either. It is this perceived arbitrariness that makes people feel helpless and subjected to the unknown logics of a machine.

IV. Counter-Strategies?

A. Avoidance

The most obvious counter-strategy is not to use the internet, the viability of which is a question of lifestyle. For most people, this is not the way forward, as it means disconnecting from a major and ever-increasing source of information and social life likewise, not least because the analogue life is diminishing at almost the same pace. Equally unhelpful is the strategy not to consent to the use of cookies and the like when surfing the internet, which means that one cannot use most search engines and visit most websites.

Pop-up blockers and ad blockers are another common tool to block advertising. Globally, around 11% of consumers use ad blockers.[24] Ad blockers do not offer absolute protection against advertising, but clearly reduce the volume by only letting advertisements pass that the ad blocker provider classifies as acceptable, although ad blocker providers also allow traders to buy into the white list of acceptable advertising.[25] Ad blockers are not prohibited, as they serve the legitimate interest of consumers not to be molested by advertising.[26] Obviously, however, internet service providers who want to refinance their services through

[22] See also P Scholz, 'DSVGO Art. 22 Automatisierte Entscheidungen im Einzelfall einschließlich Profiling' in S Simitis et al (eds), *Datenschutzrecht* (Baden-Baden, Nomos, 2018) para 10.

[23] See, for example, the case decided by LG Berlin, 1 November 2011, 6 O 479/10 (2012) *Zeitschrift für Datenschutz* 74.

[24] See Pagefair, *2017 Adblock Report* (2017), available at pagefair.com/blog/2017/adblockreport.

[25] Which the *Bundesgerichtshof* found to be permissible, see BGH, 19 April 2018, I ZR 154/16 (2018) *MultiMedia und Recht* 817.

[26] See BGH, 24 June 2004, I ZR 26/02 (2004) *MultiMedia und Recht* 662; T Hoeren, 'Anmerkung' (2018) *MultiMedia und Recht* 821.

advertisements dislike ad blockers, and they have developed counter-strategies by way of blocking access for consumers that use ad blockers.[27]

At least, one may wish to avoid traders that engage in (rapid) dynamic pricing or in personalised pricing. This strategy, however, presupposes that it is possible to identify such traders, either through their information about their related business policy, or through information by third parties. These are not usually available, as traders try to hide such exploitation strategies from the consumer (so-called *fencing*),[28] rightly fearing the consumer's unhappiness with exploitation. At the same time, the simple fact that prices differ does not necessarily point at personalised pricing but can also be related to different circumstances, such as tax liability, delivery costs and the like. Thus, personalised pricing and related exploitation are not easy to detect even for consumers who try.[29]

B. Confusion and Manipulation

Clever consumers may adopt strategies to counter the negative effects of algorithms. For example, it has been shown that advertising algorithms get confused if several persons of different age and with different interests use the same computer. One could therefore intentionally sabotage the use of (correct) algorithms with nonsense searches on the internet or fake accounts.[30] This could mitigate molestation through personalised advertisement as well as personalised pricing, although more sophisticated algorithms should be able to find out and distinguish the different users. It means, however, that the consumer will have to invest time and effort to counter something that happens automatically at the other end. The inequality of terms is obvious.

Manipulation might also be a strategy to avoid unfavourable credit scores. This would, of course, presuppose that consumers know in which way they could influence that score, thus, which criteria are used and how they are weighed – which is exactly what those calculating the scores, such as credit rating agencies, keep secret. In fact, authors have pointed at the risk that consumers might use such knowledge for the purpose of manipulating their score.[31]

[27] See also Hoeren (above n 26) 821.

[28] See M Zhang and P Bell, 'Price Fencing in the Practice of Revenue Management: An Overview and Taxonomy' (2012) 11(2) *Journal of Revenue and Pricing Management* 146.

[29] See Hannak et al (above n 17) 3 ff; M Schleusener, 'Dynamisch und personalisiert: Wie entwickelt sich die Preissetzung im Online-Handel?' (2016) *Wirtschaftsdienst* 868, 870.

[30] See the methods applied by Hannak et al (above n 17). See also P Beuth, 'Dumme Maschinen sollten uns recht sein' *Spiegel online* (12 December 2018), available at www.spiegel.de/netzwelt/web/werbung-fuer-babybedarf-nach-totgeburt-dumme-maschinen-sollten-uns-recht-sein-a-1243348.html.

[31] See F Wäßle, 'BGH stärkt die Rechte der Auskunfteien erneut' (2014) *Betriebs-Berater* 846; J Taeger, 'Scoring in Deutschland nach der EU-Datenschutzgrundverordnung' (2016) *Zeitschrift für Rechtspolitik* 72, 73.

C. Price Comparison

One obvious strategy to find the best prices on the internet, thereby ideally avoiding the high tide of price increases, is price comparison. This is a strategy that the vast majority of consumers have already applied[32] and a strategy that is clearly favoured by the EU legislator that has introduced the Member States' duty to make available price comparison websites in a number of areas of law, including the Payment Accounts Directive 2014/92/EU.[33]

The problem is of course that price comparison tools must be able to cope with the dynamics of price development, or they will be inaccurate.[34] In a judgment of 2010, the German *Bundesgerichtshof* held that it is misleading if price increases are only reflected hours later on the price comparison website.[35] In this context, one should mention that with increasing automation, the price may change during the purchasing procedure; this is happening already now, for example on flight booking platforms such as Expedia, and it is also not unlikely to happen where the consumer has to make his way to the cheapest petrol station or even to the supermarket cashier.[36]

Moreover, price comparison sites would normally only reflect the price situation at a given time but do not indicate that the prices change, although there are examples of price comparison sites now that indicate the development of the average price of a given product on the timeline.[37]

Finally, how price comparison sites should cope with personalised pricing is fairly unclear. Here, the relevant strategy would seem to be to use different appliances in parallel for the search after the same product or service.

Such search strategies, however, have serious limitations, even if one leaves aside the fact that price comparison tools may not be reliable themselves but may omit relevant traders (that are not willing to pay commission).[38] First of all, comparing prices not only at a given moment but also on the timeline means

[32] In 2012, the European Commission emphasised the use of price comparison websites by consumers, see the European Commission Staff Working Document *Bringing e-commerce benefits to consumers*, SEC(2011) 1640 final, 4 and 19 ff.

[33] See Art 7 Directive 2014/92/EC [2014] OJ L 257/214.

[34] See also Recital (23) Payment Accounts Directive 2014/92/EC.

[35] See BGH, 11 March 2010, I ZR 123/08 (2010) *Gewerblicher Rechtsschutz und Urheberrecht* 936.

[36] See also Tietjen and Flöter (above n 10) 547.

[37] For example, idealo.de. See www.idealo.de/magazin/2017/03/08/neu-auf-idealo-de-bessere-suchfilter-uebersichtliche-preisentwicklung-und-feedback-button.

[38] See only the report of the German Federal Cartel Office (*Bundeskartellamt*), Konsultationspapier zur Sektoruntersuchung Vergleichsportale (December 2018), available at www.bundeskartellamt.de/SharedDocs/Meldung/DE/Meldungen%20News%20Karussell/2018/12_12_2018_SU_Vergleichsportale_Konsultation.html. See also BGH, 27 April 2017, I ZR 55/16, (2017) *Gewerblicher Rechtsschutz und Urheberrecht* 1265, where the court held the lack of information on the fact that the price comparison only included traders who paid commission was a misleading omission in the terms of unfair commercial practices law.

to allow a certain period of time for the search during which the dynamics of pricing can be explored. This is only possible where the consumer does not want to satisfy an urgent need. Second, comparing prices on the timeline results in the multiplication of time for the search, and therefore of the search costs, to an extent that makes price comparisons impossible or limits them to the search for more expensive goods or services. The situation is reminiscent of the studies concerning the time that one would have to invest to read all the standard terms of all the contracts that one concludes, and all the labels of products that one buys.

D. Consequences

No strategy is really promising. What remains is the sentiment of being subjected to arbitrary decision of others, or even worse, of machines.[39] This is also what consumers feel when their credit application is rejected because they are classified in a certain risk category without being told why their personal data leads to that categorisation.

V. Algorithms and the Law

Having identified a number of problems related to molestation, lack of price transparency and exploitation, the natural next step is the search for solutions that the law provides. In fact, some of the issues have been approached by the EU or by national legislators, although sometimes in an insufficient manner; others can only be addressed through the use of general concepts.

Algorithms need data input, which is why they have primarily been discussed in the context of data protection. The more useful the algorithm is meant to be, the more data it needs to be fed. The first step would therefore be to question why traders have so much data about us that they can use for algorithms that they deem helpful. There is good reason to believe that the current approach of data protection law, including the General Data Protection Regulation (EU) 2016/679 (GDPR), is insufficient to protect consumers against the uncontrolled use and processing of their personal data, as it relies on (somewhat fictitious) consent that one has to give if one does not wish to be disconnected. This, however, is not the topic of this chapter. Thus, for the following remarks, I shall assume that the relevant data that are fed into algorithms have been lawfully collected.

[39] See also Reinartz et al (above n 20) 14; TJ Tillmann and V Vogt, 'Personalisierte Preise im Big-Data-Zeitalter' (2018) *Verbraucher und Recht* 447, 448.

A. Molestation

i. Unfair Commercial Practices Law

Molestation of consumers has traditionally been addressed by unfair commercial practices law. Unfair commercial practices law has been used, more or less successfully, to fight unsolicited visits at the consumer's home, mail advertisement, cold calling, unsolicited faxes and email spam. Not least, some of these techniques have been dealt with by the Distance Selling Directives 97/7/EC[40] and 2002/65/EC[41] and can now be regarded as aggressive practices in the terms of Article 7 of the Unfair Commercial Practices Directive 2005/29/EC.[42]

Typical internet advertising by way of interstitials and pop-up windows is generally thought not to be an aggressive practice, because traders who offer content free of charge need it to refinance their activities. German courts have only held this to be an unfair commercial practice where it exceeds certain limits. For example, the LG Berlin held for a website with free of charge browser games that an interstitial that can be clicked away after five seconds is still acceptable. In contrast, the court saw a violation of unfair commercial practices law in an interstitial that could not be clicked away for 20 seconds.[43] Pop-up windows were held to be an aggressive practice in a case where each time when the consumer tried to close the window, other windows popped up and the consumer could only escape by closing the browser.[44] Since those decisions have been laid down, however, advertising practices on the internet have moved on, and there would seem to be reason to believe that some of the new practices are well beyond the acceptable level, for example, the frequent unwanted movies that absorb our monthly data budget of mobile phone contracts, or those advertisement windows where the exit button is hidden, through a nearly invisible extension of the window, at some unexpected spot on the screen. And even if the individual advertisement may not reach the level of unfairness yet, that may well be the cumulative effect of numerous advertisements on an internet page.[45]

This case law has, at first glance, nothing to do with the personalisation of unwanted advertising. In my opinion, however, that personalisation adds an extra level of molestation[46] that may tip the balance towards an aggressive practice.

[40] [1997] OJ L144/19.

[41] [2002] OJ L271/16.

[42] [2005] OJ L149/22.

[43] LG Berlin, 14 September 2010, 103 O 43/10 (2010) *Gewerblicher Rechtsschutz und Urheberrecht – Rechtsprechungs-Report* 333.

[44] LG Düsseldorf, 26 March 2003, 2a O 186/02 (2003) *MultiMedia und Recht* 486.

[45] The (potential) floodgate effect, and therefore the cumulative effects of practices, has been held to be decisive for the unfairness of, for example, cold calling and unsolicited emails. See BGH, 19 June 1970, I ZR 115/68 (1970) *Neue Juristische Wochenschrift* 1738, 1739 (cold calling); BGH, 11 March 2004, I ZR 81/01 (2004) *Neue Juristische Wochenschrift* 1655, 1657 (unsolicited emails).

[46] See above, section III.A.

ii. Data Protection Law

Below the level of aggressive practices, data protection law could help in that it puts limits to the collection and processing of personal data; this is, however, outside the scope of this chapter.

B. Exploitation

At first glance, exploitation by way of dynamic pricing or personalised pricing seems to be in line with the fundamental principle of freedom of contract. Everybody is free to contract, or not to contract, with other persons to the conditions that the parties choose to apply for their contract. In relation to price increases and decreases, the *Bundesgerichtshof* held in 2003 that the trader is free in his decision on the price. He can increase or decrease his publicly announced prices at any time, as he finds suitable, as long as this is not in breach of price laws and as long as the circumstances do not suggest an unfair commercial practice, the latter being possible where the price increases and decreases are used to disguise the 'real price' and make a rocket price appear reasonable.[47] In a decision of 1958, the *Bundesgerichtshof* had held that freedom of contract included the right to charge different customers different prices, unless special aggravating circumstances are in place.[48]

At the same time, price transparency is a core element of consumer law, including EU consumer law. This does not only find expression in the Price Indication Directive 98/7/EC[49] but also in numerous price-related information obligations of other EU consumer laws, such as Article 6(1)(e) of the Consumer Rights Directive 2011/83/EU,[50] or the annual percentage rate of Article 5(1)(g) and 19 of the Consumer Credit Directive 2008/48/EC,[51] and of Article 13(1)(g) and 17 of the Mortgage Credit Directive 2014/17/EU.[52] All this legislation, however, relates price transparency to the individual contract rather than relating the individual offer to offers that are made to other consumers, or at other times. Thus, although it shows the value of price transparency, it does not apply to the problem at hand.[53]

The legal solution can be found in unfair commercial practices law, and in particular in the prohibition of a misleading omission. According to Article 7(1) of the Unfair Commercial Practices Directive (UCPD), a commercial practice shall be regarded as misleading if, in its factual context, taking account of all its features

[47] See BGH, 13 March 2003, I ZR 212/00 (2003) *Neue Juristische Wochenschrift* 2096.
[48] See BGH, 18 April 1958, I ZR 158/56 (1958) *Gewerblicher Rechtsschutz und Urheberrecht* 487.
[49] [1998] OJ L101/17.
[50] [2011] OJ L304/64.
[51] [2008] OJ L133/66.
[52] [2014] OJ L60/34.
[53] See Tillmann and Vogt (above n 39) 452 ff.

and circumstances and the limitations of the communication medium, it omits material information that the average consumer needs, according to the context, to take an informed transactional decision and thereby causes or is likely to cause the average consumer to take a transactional decision that he would not have taken otherwise. Whether or not information is material depends on the consumer's knowledge and expectations, which are formed by his or her socio-cultural background.[54] Here, the traditional equal price policy of traders is relevant. Consumers are used to being charged equal prices, and they react with disaffirmation when they are confronted with dynamic pricing the reason for which they cannot trace, and even more when they are confronted with personalised pricing. Thus, the issue of being subjected to such strategies or otherwise will be relevant for their decision to interact with the trader in question. It is therefore material information in the terms of Article 7(1) of the UCPD that causes or is likely to cause the average consumer to take a transactional decision that he would not have taken otherwise. Traders have to inform consumers about their use of dynamic pricing and personalised pricing strategies.[55]

This would most likely have a clear negative impact on their business, as consumers may fear paying more than the average, or simply consider that particular trader to act unfairly; this, however, does not mean that the trader should have the right to disguise those practices, but on the contrary, that fairness dictates transparency.

One remaining problem in this context is that the UCPD does not require Member States to provide for individual remedies for breach. While some Member States have introduced, for example, a cancellation right, Germany is one Member State that has not conferred individual rights on consumers. Thus, a contract that is concluded through the use of an unfair commercial practice is still valid and binding on the consumer. This problem may, however, be solved with the proposed amendment to the UCPD as part of the so-called 'New Deal for Consumers'.[56]

C. Discrimination

Discrimination in relation to the supply of goods and services is dealt with by Directive 2000/43/EC implementing the principle of equal treatment between persons irrespective of racial or ethnic origin[57] and by Directive 2004/113/EC

[54] See also T Wilhelmsson, 'Misleading practices' in G Howells et al (eds), *European Fair Trading Law* (Aldeshot, Ashgate, 2006) 123, 152.

[55] See also Zander-Hayat et al (above n 9) 407 ff; Obergfell (above n 19) 298; Tillmann and Vogt (above n 39) 452 ff.

[56] See Art 1(4) of the proposal for a Directive on better enforcement and modernisation of EU consumer protection rules, COM(2018) 185 final, which envisages the insertion of a new Art 11a on redress into Directive 2005/29/EC.

[57] [2000] OJ L180/22, in particular Art 3(1)(h).

implementing the principle of equal treatment between men and women in the access to and supply of goods and services.[58] National legislators may have extended the prohibition to discriminate to other reasons. For example, the German legislator has extended the principle of equal treatment to religion, disability, age and sexual identity.[59] Obviously, this also applies where discrimination is hidden in an algorithm,[60] although the GDPR has not taken up this issue.[61]

Potential remedies under EU anti-discrimination law are an injunction and damages.[62] Moreover, the use of discriminating personalised prices may constitute an unfair commercial practice.[63]

According to German case law, however, anti-discrimination law does not apply to the relationship between a credit rating agency and a consumer, as the credit rating agency does not supply goods or services to the consumer but is only a third party with influence on the actual supply or service relationship with a trader.[64]

Another problem will lie in the detection and proof of discrimination.[65] Generally speaking, the burden of proof is with the claimant, although EU law provides for the reversal of the burden of proof in situations where the potential discrimination victim provides facts from which it may be presumed that there has been direct or indirect discrimination.[66] The reversal of the burden of proof, however, only relates to the causation between the special characteristics of the potential victim (for example, religion) and the different treatment. The consumer must still prove the different treatment as such, and he or she has no claim related to information from the trader on how he treated other consumers,[67] or what the score would be if, for example, the female claimant was male.[68]

One notable exception from anti-discrimination law is unequal treatment when it comes to credit, according to the German government. Credit is not regarded to be available to the public irrespective of the person concerned in the terms of Article 3(1) of Directive 2004/113/EC and is therefore considered to be outside the scope of application of that Directive.[69]

[58] [2004] OJ L373/37.

[59] See § 19 para 1 *Allgemeines Gleichbehandlungsgesetz* (General Act on Equal Treatment; AGG).

[60] See Genth (above n 19) 866; SVRV, *Verbrauchergerechtes Socring* (Berlin: SVRV, 2018) 135 ff.

[61] Only recital (71) of the GDPR mentions the risk of discriminatory profiling, see Scholz (above n 22) para 14.

[62] Whether or not the victim can also claim the conclusion of the desired contract is discussed controversially. See G Thüsing, 'AGG § 21 Ansprüche' in C Schubert (ed), *Münchener Kommentar zum Bürgerlichen Gesetzbuch*, vol 1, 8th edn (Munich, CH Beck, 2018) para 17 ff, with further references.

[63] For Germany, see Tietjen and Flöter (above n 10) 548.

[64] See OLG Munich, 12 March 2014, 15 U 2395/13, (2014) *Zeitschrift für Datenschutz* 570, 572.

[65] See also SVRV, *Verbraucherrecht 2.0* (above n 1) 70.

[66] See Art 8(1) of Directive 2000/43/EC and Art 9(1) of Directive 2004/113/EC.

[67] For details, see Thüsing, 'AGG § 22 Beweislast' in Schubert (above n 62) para 6 ff.

[68] See OLG Munich (above n 64) 573.

[69] See the explanations of the German government on the draft legislation to implement EU anti-discrimination law (2006) *Bundestags-Drucksache* 16/1780, 42. For a different view concerning small credit, see G Thüsing, 'AGG § 19 Zivilrechtliches Benachteiligungsverbot' in Schubert (above n 62) para 25.

D. Arbitrariness of Automated Decisions and Credit Scores

i. Automated Decisions

Automated decisions are, first of all, mentioned in Article 22 GDPR,[70] which is the successor provision to Article 15 of the replaced Data Protection Directive 95/46/EC.[71] Under Article 22 GDPR, the data subject shall have the right not to be subject to a decision based solely on automated processing, including profiling, which produces legal effects concerning him or her or similarly significantly affects him or her. The basic aim of this provision is related to human dignity and fundamental rights: the exercise of fundamental freedoms by human beings should not be subjected to the decision of an algorithm; a decision with legal effects should always be made by a natural person.[72]

The application of Article 22 GDPR on credit scoring is a matter of some debate. Taking into consideration the purpose of this provision, it should be clear that not only the automated rejection of a credit application comes under Article 22 GDPR but that the same applies where an employee rejects that application because of the score. Only a new decision, which takes other factors into account, constitutes a relevant human intervention.[73] These principles apply to internal scores (calculated by the bank) as well as to external scores (calculated by a credit rating agency), as the creditor usually will not collect all the pieces of information and process themselves into a credit score but rely on the credit score that a credit rating agency has calculated on the basis of the information it has available.[74] Whether or not the rejection of the conclusion of a (credit) contract produces a 'legal effect' in terms of Article 22(1) GDPR is a matter of controversy.[75] At least, it 'similarly significantly affects' the consumer.[76]

The majority opinion, however, seems to be that credit scoring normally comes under the exception of Article 22(2) no 1 GDPR, according to which the prohibition of Article 22(1) GDPR does not apply if the decision is necessary for entering into, or performance of, a contract between the data subject and a data controller. For credit scoring, the necessity of assessing the consumer's creditworthiness stems from consumer credit law.[77] According to Article 8 of the Consumer Credit

[70] Regulation (EU) 2016/679 on the protection of natural persons with regard to the processing of personal data and on the free movement of such data, [2016] OJ L 119/1.

[71] [1995] OJ L281/31.

[72] See Scholz (above n 22) para 3.

[73] See Scholz (above n 22) para 29; M Helfrich, 'DSVGO Automatisierte Entscheidungen im Einzelfall einschließlich Profiling' in G Sydow (ed), *Europäische Datenschutzgrundverordnung*, 2nd edn (Baden-Baden, Nomos, 2018) para 43 ff.

[74] See Scholz (above n 22) para 29; against Taeger (above n 31) 74 ff; M Martini, 'DS-GVO Art. 22 Automatisierte Entscheidungen im Einzelfall einschließlich Profiling' in BP Paal and DA Pauly, *DS-GVO – BDSG*, 2nd edn (Munich, CH Beck, 2018) para 24.

[75] For legal effect: Helfrich (above n 73) para 48; against Scholz (above n 22) para 34.

[76] See Scholz (above n 22) para 35. See also recital (71) para 1 GDPR.

[77] See Scholz (above n 22) para 43.

Directive 2008/48/EC as well as Article 18 of the Mortgage Credit Directive, the creditor must assess the consumer's creditworthiness before making the decision on the conclusion of a credit contract. To this end, he shall consult the relevant databases containing information about the credit history of the consumer; which in the German context is, in particular, the Schufa.[78] And even in relation to other contracts, in particular long-term contracts where the consumer's creditworthiness is of relevance, authors accept automated decision-making under the exception of Article 22(2) no 1 GDPR, although no legal requirement for a creditworthiness assessment exists.[79]

ii. Credit Scoring

a. Objective Requirements

Binding scoring standards do not exist, and certain scoring practices have been blatantly insufficient in the past.[80] Therefore, the German legislator introduced, in 2009, the requirement that the data used to calculate the probability value must be demonstrably essential for calculating the probability of the action on the basis of a scientifically recognised mathematic-statistical procedure.[81] Notably, this provision did not primarily aim at the protection of consumers, or data subjects, but at the protection of businesses who should be enabled to make sound business decisions.[82]

The GDPR embraces a similar but much weaker notion;[83] according to recital (71) paragraph 2 GDPR, in order to ensure fair and transparent processing in respect of the data subject, taking into account the specific circumstances and context in which the personal data are processed, the controller should use appropriate mathematical or statistical procedures for the profiling; which is not binding.

The special rule on scoring has been maintained after the entry into force of the GDPR, although some regard this as a breach of the GDPR.[84] It is now enshrined in § 31 *Bundesdatenschutzgesetz* (Federal Data Protection Act; BDSG).

[78] On which see, for example, M Beckhusen, 'Das Scoring-Verfahren der SCHUFA im Wirkungsbereich des Datenschutzrechts' (2005) *Zeitschrift für Bank- und Kapitalmarktrecht* 335.

[79] See Scholz (above n 22) para 43, with further references.

[80] For an example, see OLG Frankfurt, 7 April 2015, 24 U 82/14, (2015) *Neue Juristische Online-Zeitschrift* 1913. See also I Domurath and I Neubeck, *Verbraucher-Scoring aus Sicht des Datenschutzrechts* (Berlin, SVRV, 2018) 23 ff.

[81] § 28b no 1 BDSG of 2009. For detailed discussion, see R Metz, 'Scoring: Licht im Tunnel' (2009) *Verbraucher und Recht* 403; R Metz, 'Scoring: New Legislation in Germany' (2012) 35 *Journal of Consumer Policy* 297.

[82] See Domurath and Neubeck (above n 80) 7.

[83] See also SVRV, *Verbraucherrecht 2.0* (above n 1) 62 ff.

[84] See E Ehmann, 'Anhang 2 zu Artikel 6 Datenverarbeitung bei Verbraucherkrediten, Scoring und Bonitätsauskünften' in Simitis, Hornung and Spiecker (above n 22) para 17 ff.

b. Information

According to § 34 BDSG of 2009, the consumer had the right to be informed about the type of data that was used for the calculation of the score and the coming into being and the relevance of the score in the individual case and in plain and intelligible language.[85] In the aftermath, there was some debate about what exactly this entailed. Whereas it was clear that the consumer had to be informed about the data that was included in the calculation of the score, one consumer claimed that § 34 BDSG also related to information about the way that the pieces of information were weighed and what comparison groups were used. The latter was rejected by Schufa, relying on the protection of its business secrets – a decision that the *Bundesgerichtshof* confirmed in 2014.[86] In other words, the consumer does not have the right to know what the algorithm does with his or her data, and the court has not verified either whether a scientifically recognised mathematic-statistical procedure has been applied.[87] A constitutional complaint against that court decision is still pending in the Federal Constitutional Court.[88]

§ 34 BDSG of 2009 has been repealed, as Articles 13–15 GDPR address the issue. Article 13 GDPR addresses personal data that are collected from the data subject. According to Article 13(2)(f) GDPR, the data controller shall, at the time when personal data are obtained, provide the data subject with information concerning the existence of automated decision-making, including profiling, referred to in Article 22(1) and (4) and, at least in those cases, meaningful information about the logic involved, as well as the significance and the envisaged consequences of such processing for the data subject. The same applies, according to Article 14(2)(g) GDPR, to personal data that has not been obtained from the data subject. Finally, under Article 15(1)(h) GDPR, the data subject shall have the right to obtain from the controller confirmation as to whether or not personal data concerning him or her are being processed, and, where that is the case, access to the personal data and information on the existence of automated decision-making, including profiling, referred to in Article 22(1) and (4) and, at least in those cases, meaningful information about the logic involved, as well as the significance and the envisaged consequences of such processing for the data subject.

Unsurprisingly, a debate has started on what 'the logic involved' entails. Authors that had been unhappy with the above-mentioned decision of the *Bundesgerichtshof* maintain that the logic involved includes the weighing of the factors that are used for the calculation of a score.[89] Even the disclosure of the score formula is thought to be necessary in exceptional cases, if this is the only way by which the person

[85] § 34 para 2 BDSG of 2009.
[86] See BGH, 28 January 2014, VI ZR 156/13, (2014) *Neue Juristische Wochenschrift* 1235.
[87] See Weichert (above n 4) 169.
[88] File number 1 BvR 756/14.
[89] See A Dix, 'DSGVO Art. 13 Informationspflicht bei Erhebung von personenbezogenen Daten bei der betroffenen Person' in Simitis et al (above n 22) para 16.

concerned can avoid and rectify an incorrect calculation.[90] In contrast, those authors who had already defended the judgment of the *Bundesgerichtshof* consider the requirements of Article 13(2)(f) GDPR to be even weaker than those of the former § 34 BDSG.[91]

VI. Control of Algorithms

A. Control by an Independent Public Authority?

The solution that the *Sachverständigenrat für Verbraucherfragen* proposed is that algorithms should be controlled by an independent public authority.[92] This is regarded as striking a balance between the consumer's interest in not being subjected to random, arbitrary or even discriminatory calculation models, and the trader's interest in the protection of his business secrets.

In fact, that model has formed part of German data protection law for a while in the case of credit scoring. It was introduced in 2009: the data protection authorities were put in charge of controlling whether the probability value was essential for calculating the probability of the action on the basis of a scientifically recognised mathematic-statistical procedure.[93] Opinions on its success are mixed. While some authors refer to the expertise of German data protection authorities,[94] critiques emphasise their lack of resources.[95]

That lack of resources will surely not become a smaller issue with the increasing use of algorithms in all areas of life and business. For that reason, it does not seem to be an option for the future. More than that, any sort of control is bound to fail in relation to self-learning algorithms, as they may very soon differ from what has been approved by the competent authority.

B. Control by Private Certification Bodies?

The standard solution, in particular of EU law, to avoid the limitations of resources of public authorities is certification by private certification bodies that are, more or less, supervised by public authorities. Indeed, we also find this model for data

[90] See Dix (above n 89) para 16; A Roßnagel et al, 'Was bleibt vom Europäischen Datenschutzrecht? – Überlegungen zum Ratsentwurf der DS-GVO' (2015) *Zeitschrift für Datenschutz* 455, 458; against BP Paal and M Hennemann, 'DS-GVO Art. 13 Informationspflicht bei Erhebung von personenbezogenen Daten bei der betroffenen Person' in Paal and Pauly (above n 74) para 31.

[91] See Taeger (above n 31) 75.

[92] See above, I.

[93] § 38 BDSG of 2009; see also J Taeger, 'Anmerkung' (2014) *MultiMedia und Recht* 492, 493.

[94] See Taeger (above n 93) 493; SVRV, *Verbraucherrecht 2.0* (above n 1) 61.

[95] See Weichert (above n 4) 170.

protection law in Article 42(1) GDPR.[96] That a certification system for algorithms would be preferable to public law control may be doubted.[97] It may be sufficient to refer to the devastating experience with the certification of medical devices and the breast implants scandal around the French producer Poly Implant Prothèse[98] and to the positive credit ratings that Lehman Brothers received from Standard & Poor's just before its bankruptcy.[99] Lastly, certification would encounter the same problems as public law approval when it comes to self-learning algorithms.

C. Control by Courts?

Ex-post control by courts may be able to consider the individual case; it would, however, presuppose that cases reach the courts in the first place. One may suspect that consumers whose credit applications are rejected and who are denied the conclusion of a supply contract will not have the financial resources to access the court system in the first place. Moreover, court procedures are simply too slow to cope with the ever-changing challenges of the digital world.[100] Thus, although control by courts should definitely be possible, it will not be able to remedy the problem at large.

VII. A Duty to Explain Decisions?

All the above solutions, the effectiveness of which must be doubted anyway, will most likely not reduce the consumer's sentiment of being subjected to the arbitrariness of traders, or to the algorithms they use; and the meaning of the new data protection rules granting a right to be informed about the logic involved in an automated decision is unclear.[101] It therefore seems apt to look for other remedies against the arbitrariness of decision-making.

Until now, arbitrariness has primarily been an issue of public law, including constitutional law; this has often been related to the right of human dignity, the rule of law or the right to equal treatment. One emanation of this is the obligation of public authorities to give reasons for all their decisions. In numerous decisions,

[96] For detailed discussion, see G Hornung and S Bauer, 'Privacy through Certification? – The New Certification Scheme of the General Data Protection Regulation' in P Rott (ed), *Certification – Trust, Accountability, Liability* (Cham, Springer, 2019) 109.

[97] See also Domurath and Neubeck (above n 80) 13.

[98] On which see P Rott, 'Certification of Medical Devices – Lessons from the PIP Scandal' in Rott (above n 96) 189.

[99] On which see A Halfmeier, 'Liability of Rating Agencies under German and European Law' in Rott (above n 96) 231.

[100] See also SVRV, *Verbraucherrecht 2.0* (above n 1) 70.

[101] See above, section V.D.ii.b.

the German Federal Constitutional Court pointed at the constitutional principle that the citizen who is affected by the decision of a public authority has the right to be given reasons for the decision, as only then is he able to defend his rights.[102]

The right not to be subjected to arbitrariness and the right to be given reasons for decisions includes the individual possibility to understand and to control the reasons given. Control by (even independent) third actors is insufficient, as it would mean that the individual is compelled to trust in their assessment, without having the opportunity to control and challenge that assessment. In a recent case concerning the determination of areas in which rent control (*Mietpreisbremse*) applies, the government of the State of Hesse had argued that the explanation for the relevant secondary legislation (which the law required) had been present, although it had not been published together with the legislation. The Regional Court of Frankfurt rejected this argument and held that, with an unpublished explanation, the landlord concerned could not know whether an explanation existed at all, and if so, whether that explanation satisfied the relevant requirements.[103]

Comprehensibility means that the addressee is able to understand the reasons. Therefore, reasons must be given in a language that the layperson can understand, rather than merely in legal terminology.[104] Even more, a simple figure – a score – would be insufficient explanation for a decision.

Can this kind of argument be transferred into private law relationships between traders and consumers, taking into consideration the principle of freedom of contract? There have been developments that suggest such an approach, primarily because the lines between the spheres of public law and private law are increasingly blurred, and private actors have gained immense factual power.

This is, for example, reflected in the case law of the Court of Justice related to the fundamental freedoms of the TFEU. In the case of *Fra.bo*,[105] the German *Deutsche Vereinigung des Gas- und Wasserfaches eV* (DVGW) had denied certification of copper fittings produced and distributed by the Italian producer Fra.bo, thereby effectively denying Fra.bo access to the German market. Although DVGW is a private organisation, the Court of Justice treated this as an obstacle to the free movement of goods.[106]

In Germany, the debate on the application of fundamental rights in private law relationships has been revived through a recent decision of the Federal

[102] See, for example, BVerfG, 16 January 1957, 1 BvR 253/56, (1957) 6 *Entscheidungen des Bundesverfassungsgerichts* 32, 44.
[103] See LG Frankfurt, 27 March 2018, 2-11 S 183/17 (2018) *BeckRS* 4544.
[104] See P Tiedemann, 'VwVfG § 39 Begründung des Verwaltungsakts' in J Bader and M Ronellenfitsch (eds), *BeckOK VwVfG*, 41st edn (Munich, CH Beck, 2018) para 4.
[105] Case C-171/11, *Fra.bo SpA v Deutsche Vereinigung des Gas- und Wasserfaches eV (DVGW) – Technisch-Wissenschaftlicher Verein*, ECLI:EU:C:2012:453.
[106] For details, see H-W Micklitz and R van Gestel, 'European Integration through Standardization: How Judicial Review is Breaking Down the Club House of Private Standardization Bodies' (2013) 50 *Common Market Law Review* 145.

Constitutional Court, which has in the aftermath been taken up by civil courts in relation to powerful players in the digital world.[107] The Federal Constitutional Court had to decide on the lawfulness of a ban of a football fan from all games of the *Bundesliga*. While the Federal Constitutional Court held that the fundamental right to equality did not amount to a general obligation of private actors to treat all private persons equally, this is different where a private actor offers goods or services to the public at large and makes far-reaching decisions on the participation of others in social life. In this situation, the private actor must not exclude others arbitrarily from access to his goods or services. Instead, he must provide objective reasons that justify his decisions. According to the Federal Constitutional Court, this is connected with procedural requirements. In the instant case, these included a hearing of the football fan concerned. Moreover, the private actor must give reasons that allow the person concerned to enforce his rights.[108]

Such influence on access to the market can also be attributed to relevant players on the internet. They have not only attracted the attention of cartel authorities[109] but have also been addressed due to their relevance for social life. In the aftermath of the above-mentioned decision of the Federal Constitutional Court, civil courts prohibited Facebook from deleting posts arbitrarily that the courts held to be covered by the right to free speech of Article 5 of the Basic Law (*Grundgesetz*), and to ban user accounts containing such posts.[110]

The logic of the above-discussed court decisions would also apply to Schufa. Schufa rules the German credit rating market with a market share of 80–100% in certain sectors such as banking.[111] It is their scores that are used by all kinds of suppliers and service providers in their decision to conclude a contract or otherwise and to determine the conditions of such a contract. Thus, the Schufa score is absolutely crucial for the consumer's access to the market.[112] This suggests that it must not be arbitrary and that, on demand, Schufa must give (real) reasons for the score, which is more than mere information about the data that went into the score.

[107] See only BP Paal and M Hennemann, 'Meinungsvielfalt im Internet' (2017) *Zeitschrift für Rechtspolitik* 76; S Müller-Riemenschneider and L Specht, 'Anmerkung' (2018) *MultiMedia und Recht* 547; A Peukert, 'Gewährleistung der Meinungs- und Informationsfreiheit in sozialen Netzwerken' (2018) *MultiMedia und Recht* 572, 575. In wise anticipation see K-H Ladeur, 'Ausschluss von Teilnehmern an Diskussionsforen im Internet – Absicherung von Kommunikationsfreiheit durch "netzwerk-gerechtes" Privatrecht' (2001) *MultiMedia und Recht* 787.

[108] See Bundesverfassungsgericht (Federal Constitutional Court; BVerfG), 11 April 2018, 1 BvR 3080/09 (2018) *Neue Juristische Wochenschrift* 1667.

[109] See, for example, Bundeskartellamt, *Facebook-Verfahren – FAQ* (2018), www.bundeskartellamt.de/SharedDocs/Publikation/DE/Diskussions_Hintergrundpapier/Hintergrundpapier_Facebook.html; id, *Einleitung eines Missbrauchsverfahrens gegen Amazon* (2018), www.bundeskartellamt.de/SharedDocs/Meldung/DE/Pressemitteilungen/2018/29_11_2018_Verfahrenseinleitung_Amazon.html.

[110] See LG Frankfurt, 14 May 2018, 2-03 O 182/18 (2018) *MultiMedia und Recht* 545; LG Berlin, 9 September 2018, 27 O 355/18. For critique, see M Beurskens, '"Hate-Speech" zwischen Löschungsrecht und Veröffentlichungspflicht' (2018) *Neue Juristische Wochenschrift* 3418, 3419.

[111] See wikipedia, *Schufa* (2018), de.wikipedia.org/wiki/Schufa.

[112] See also Weichert (above n 4) 169.

And if Schufa should not be able to explain the score because it has developed through self-learning, then it must not be used.

In conclusion, what is needed to avoid arbitrariness is procedural safeguards, including an obligation to give reasons for decisions.

VIII. Conclusions

Promising self-help strategies of consumers against molestation, exploitation, discrimination and arbitrariness that are caused or aggravated by the use of algorithms are not available. Therefore, these effects must be addressed by the law.

Molestation by way of personalised advertising can, in principle, be countered by means of unfair commercial practices law, although courts would seem to have to be less generous in accepting aggressive advertising as the price to be paid for the use of offers on the internet free of charge.

Dynamic pricing and personalised pricing run counter to the deeply-rooted general expectation that prices shown on internet or on price tags are reasonably stable and only changed for a reason, and that they are generally applicable prices. Information on dynamic pricing and personalised pricing is therefore 'material' in the terms of Article 7(1) of the UCPD. Thus, the use of dynamic pricing and personalised pricing is only permitted if the trader makes this transparent. This means, of course, that consumers may turn away from traders that apply such practices if they dislike them.

Discrimination is obviously prohibited. To make that prohibition more effective, the burden of proof not to engage in discriminatory practices should be more clearly on the trader, and it should be accompanied by a strengthened right to information for the consumer.

What remains is the problem of being subjected to decisions that an algorithm makes directly or that are prepared by an algorithms and then implemented by a human being who does not have the intention and/or the ability to review the 'recommendation' of the algorithm. This type of procedure must, first of all, be laid open to consumers so that they can avoid it by turning to a different trader. Where this is impossible, because the trader in question has a dominant position on the market or the same algorithm is used by the vast majority of traders, those dominant private actors or the originators of relevant scores are to be treated like public authorities. Then, human dignity, the right to equal treatment and the rule of law require the trader to give comprehensible reasons for the decision, and the reason cannot solely be the result of a calculation exercise.

5

Technological Totalitarianism: Data, Consumer Profiling, and the Law

IRINA DOMURATH*

When writing a PhD on European consumer law, it is impossible to escape the influential Bremen School as represented not only by Hans Micklitz's thought but also by the late Norbert Reich – Hans' supervisor – and Peter Rott – Hans' supervisee and my doctorate supervisor. Ever since I first came to the EUI as a visiting researcher in 2013, I have worked closely with Hans. And after completing my PhD, I continued working with him in his capacity as a member of the Advisory Council for Consumer Affairs at the Ministry of Justice and for Consumer Protection in Germany. During this time, we explored some of the newest of Hans' manifold interests: the legal problems involved in the data economy and technology. This contribution is largely based on that cooperation,[1] in gratitude for the many engaging and beautiful stays at the EUI and the always fruitful and challenging discussions.

I. Markets, Data, Profiling

In *The Empire of Things*,[2] Trentmann backtraces how the consumer society developed, first slowly, but then increasingly gaining momentum spurred by industrialisation and mass production. By now, we live in a time of ubiquitous markets. Almost everything is becoming a tradable good or service, a commodity. The modern consumer society is reaching far beyond the traditional commodities.

* Post-doctoral researcher at University of Amsterdam, Department of Private Law, Centre for the Study of European Private Law.

[1] As such, this contribution is based on previous research work, see I Domurath and I Neubeck, 'Verbraucher-Scoring aus Sicht des Datenschutzrechts' (2018) *Veröffentlichungen des Sachverständigenrats für Verbraucherfragen*. The previous co-author has given consent to expanding the original piece for this contribution. All responsibility lies with the author.

[2] F Trentmann, *The Empire of Things – How We Became a World of Consumers, from the Fiteenth Century to the Twenty-First* (New York, Harper Collins, 2016).

Once considered pivotal for the construction of societies, energy, water, and telecommunication sectors are being re-conceptualised as private markets, in which consumers are supposed to shop around for suitable goods and services as if they were comparable to a pair of trousers or a washing machine. The marketisation of education and housing sectors is following suit. The transformation of health care looms large.

The latest object of commodification is data.[3] Data has become an economic product. In times of global recession, the data economy is booming. But it is not only the data economy based on data collected through polls and active relinquishment. It is the data generated passively through internet use, mobile phones, fitness bracelets and the like. Information such as heartbeats and steps taken during the day become included in big data sets that are traded as a commodity on global markets. What is next? In a lead article at the beginning of 2018 on brain-computer interfaces, *The Economist* welcomed the turning of 'firing of neurons' into a to-be-harnessed resource.[4]

Big data is also increasingly used for profiling purposes. Profiling is a term from information science that refers to the construction and application of user profiles through computerised data analysis, increasingly involving the processing of large quantities of aggregated data. During the profiling process, data is analysed and evaluated with the help of algorithms or heuristics, and the constructed profiles are applied as a basis for a decision-making, for example in public policy or marketing. Profiling relies on data mining technologies and algorithms.[5]

Profiling not only enables public authorities to use statistical patterns and correlations for criminal enforcement, but is also well established in the private sector.[6] Financial institutions use profiling technologies habitually for fraud prevention and creditworthiness assessment, in order to minimise the risk involved in giving credit to customers.[7] Nowadays, profiling has become a standard in modern business operations. Private companies offer 'targeted services' to consumers in accordance with their preference and shopping profiles, using profiling to predict the behaviour of different types of customers, and model

[3] A Schwartz, 'Legal Implications of Imperfect Information in Consumer Markets' (2004) 151(1) *Journal of Institutional and Theoretical Economics* 31, 38.

[4] 'Using Thought to Control Machines', *The Economist* (6 January 2018).

[5] B Anrig et al, 'The Role of Algorithms in Profiling' in M Hildebrandt and S Gutwirth (eds), *Profiling the European Citizen – Cross-Disciplinary Perspectives* (Dordrecht, Springer Netherlands, 2018).

[6] For an overview of the use of artificial intelligence in different sectors, see A Jablonowska et al, *Consumer law and artificial intelligence – Challenges to the EU consumer law and policy stemming from the business' use of artificial intelligence – Final report of the ARTSY project*, EUI Working Paper LAW 2018/11 (Florence, European University Institute, 2018).

[7] F Ferretti, 'A European perspective on consumer loans and the role of credit registries: the need to reconcile data protection, risk management, efficiency, over-indebtedness, and a better prudential supervision of the financial system' (2010) 33(1) *Journal of Consumer Policy* 1; F Ferretti, '*The Law and Consumer Credit Information in the European Community – The* Regulation *of Credit Information Systems* (London, Routledge Cavendish, 2008); A Rona-Tas, 'The role of credit bureaus in globalised economies: why they matter less than we think and how they can matter more' in H-W Micklitz and I Domurath (eds), *Consumer Debt and Social Exclusion in Europe* (Farnham, Ashgate Publishing, 2015).

marketing strategies accordingly.[8] A high 'customer lifetime value', referring to the profit made for a company by one customer over her lifetime – leads to preferential treatments, better offers, better customer service.[9] Also on labour markets, profiling technologies are increasingly used by employers monitoring their employees' online behaviour or ranking skills.[10] And, finally, insurance companies increasingly offer rates and services based on individuals' behaviour and characteristics.[11]

In this contribution, I analyse the role of data protection law in this development. The main, and in the international context probably most elaborate, legislation dealing with data protection is the EU General Data Protection Regulation (GDPR). In Section II, I will outline the main issues in profiling. While some of the problems are not new, for example the correctness of the data used for profiling, others emerge only or are amplified through the use of big data and modern data-processing technologies. Similarly, many issues discussed belong to the field of general data protection, for example the consent of the data subject in the data collection and use, whereas other problems are specific to profiling processes, such as the problem of discriminatory decision-making. This shows that profiling cuts across the whole field of data protection law but also other types of regulation. The problems discussed here concerning privacy – including consent, anonymisation and data minimisation, discrimination and automation, purposes of data collection, and transparency and truthfulness of data – are by no means meant to be an exhaustive analysis of the topic. Given the constraints of space, any overview of data protection and profiling can only be illustrative.[12]

Section III then analyses the tools of the GDPR to respond to those issues. We will see that the GDPR does not address all these issues effectively. Manifold gaps in the legal framework with regard to data protection hinder individuals from understanding, backtracing, or contesting the use of their data. Coupled with the normative power of algorithmic governance, a system of 'technological totalitarianism'[13] has developed, which poses challenges to traditional regulation. Even though much of the analysis could be extended and researched in more detail, this contribution shows already that many tools and principles exist in the GDPR that can help to overcome those challenges, but they need to be strengthened with

[8] M Kamp et al, 'Profiling of Customers and Consumers – Customer Loyalty Programmes and Scorign Practices' in Hildebrandt and Gutwirth, *Profiling the European Citizen* (above n 5).

[9] See www.sueddeutsche.de/wirtschaft/konsum-die-vermessung-des-kunden-1.4264260 (last accessed 23 March 2019).

[10] N Leopold and M Meints, 'Profiling in Employment Situations (Fraud)' in Hildebrandt and Gutwirth (above n 5).

[11] See for example www.theglobeandmail.com/globe-drive/adventure/trends/why-ontario-drivers-pay-the-highest-car-insurance-rates-in-the-country/article19522860/ and www.nytimes.com/2012/03/19/health/policy/women-still-pay-more-for-health-insurance-data-shows.html (both last accessed 23 March 2019).

[12] For example, I do not analyse the right to be forgotten or the right to data portability. Liability issues and problems of enforcement are also omitted.

[13] Term borrowed from F Schirrmacher (ed), *Technologischer Totalitarismus* (Berlin, Suhrkamp, 2015).

regard to unambiguity and enforcement. The final part of Section III summarises findings and open questions. Section IV contains a further discussion of the legal and societal problems involved in profiling and sketches possible ideas to make the data protection framework more appropriate for dealing with challenges posed by big-data profiling technologies. The contribution ends with a few remarks on the challenges of regulation through technology at the intersection with data protection.

II. Profiling in the GDPR

A. Definitions and Goals: Data Law as Consumer Law

In Article 4(4) GDPR profiling is defined as:

> any form of automated processing of personal data consisting of the use of personal data to evaluate certain personal aspects relating to a natural person, in particular to analyse or predict aspects concerning that natural person's performance at work, economic situation, health, personal preferences, interests, reliability, behaviour, location or movements.

Hand in hand with much EU legislation, for example in consumer law, the GDPR attempts a balancing act between protective and enabling goals. For example, Recital 6 acknowledged that rapid technological change has 'transformed both the economy and social life, and should further facilitate the free flow of personal data …, while ensuring a high level of the protection of personal data'. As the justification for EU action often lies in the disparities between Member States' legal orders and the resulting impediments for the internal market, the GDPR also aims at ensuring a 'consistent' (not necessarily 'high') level of protection for data, while preventing 'divergences hampering the free movement of personal data within the internal market', see Recital 13. In line with other developments in EU law, most notably services of general economic interest, where citizens' rights against the state are substituted with consumer rights against private companies,[14] also in the GDPR citizen rights become consumer rights. Building up a data economy is a pronounced goal of the EU[15] and citizens as consumers are allotted the role of fostering the economy by engaging in market transactions and fulfilling their desires and needs on those markets.

In this vein, data consumers are given a broad range of rights in the GDPR. They can, for example, access their personal information with the data controller

[14] H-W Micklitz, 'Universal Services: Nucleus for a Social European Private Law' in M Cremona (ed), *Market Integration and Public Services in the European Union* (Oxford, Oxford University Press, 2011).

[15] See ec.europa.eu/digital-single-market/en/policies/building-european-data-economy (last accessed 23 March 2019).

(Article 15 GDPR), have the right to rectify false information (Article 16 GDPR), restrict processing of their personal data in certain circumstances (Article 18 GDPR), and transfer their data from one controller to the other (Article 20 GDPR). While these rights might, in principle, strike a balance between protective and enabling goals, this contribution shows that the problems involved in profiling are not solved by granting those individual rights. Individuals face substantial obstacles in enforcing their rights.[16] Similarly to the limitations of the idea of consumer empowerment through information in general consumer law,[17] 'do-it-yourself' data protection[18] runs into conceptual and practical problems and is, therefore, not an effective tool of data protection. Regulatory oversight is needed in addition to individual rights to make data protection law effective.

B. Legal Problems in Data Use for Profiling

Profiling and scoring raise many political, societal, legal, and ethical problems. Legally, the automatic or semi-automatic generation and application of profiling technologies raises issues relating to the purpose of data collection, privacy, discrimination, and transparency.[19]

First of all, profiling raises privacy concerns. This is because profiling technologies enable far-reaching monitoring of an individual's behaviour and preferences and can reveal personal or private information about individuals that they might not even be aware of themselves. The most prominent example of such practices is the well-known case of the department store Target, in which the US-based retail department store identified the pregnancy of a teenager with the help of customer tracking technology and revealed it to her family by sending coupons for baby products to her house.[20]

[16] For the problems involved in individual enforcement of data protection law, see R Podszun et al, 'Die Durchsetzung des Datenschutzes durch Verbraucherrecht, Lauterkeitsrecht und Kartellrecht' (2016) *Neue Juristische Wochenschrift* 2987; G Spindler et al, *Rechtsdurchsetzung im Verbraucherdatenschutz: Bestandsaufnahme und Handlungsempfehlungen* (Berlin, Friedrich-Ebert-Stiftung, 2016); I Domurath and L Kosyra, 'Verbraucherdatenschutz im Internet der Dinge' in *Veröffentlichungen des Sachverständigenrates für Verbraucherfragen* (Berlin, Advisory Council for Consumer Affairs, 2016).

[17] GG Howells, 'The Potential and Limits of Consumer Empowerment by Information' (2005) 32(3) *Journal of Law and Society* 349; T Wilhelmsson, 'The Abuse of the "Confident Consumer" as a Justification for EC Consumer Law' (2004) 27(3) *Journal of Consumer Policy* 317.

[18] T Matzner et al, 'Do-It-Yourself Data Protection – Empowerment or Burden?' in S Gutwirth et al (eds), *Data Protection on the Move – Current Developments in ICT and Privacy/Data Protection* (Dordrecht, 2016).

[19] L Lessig, *Code* (New York, Basic Books, 2006); DJ Solove, *The Digital Person – Technology and Provacy in the Information Age* (New York, New York University Press, 2004). While liability and accountability also reflect important legal problems in profiling, they are outside of the scope of this contribution.

[20] See www.businessinsider.com/the-incredible-story-of-how-target-exposed-a-teen-girls-pregnancy-2012-2 (last accessed 11 December 2018).

Second, profiling technologies are by their very nature discriminatory. While this problem is not new to profiling practices, the use of big data allows unparalleled kinds of social sorting and segmentation. The automation of discriminatory decision-making processes adds a new structural layer to the problem. In accordance with their 'digital reputation',[21] profiled individuals can pay higher prices and they may run increased risks of exclusion from access to goods and services because catering to their needs is less profitable.

Third, big data analyses and predictions are based on vast amounts of data that are often collected for no particular purpose. In fact, all kinds of data are gathered, stored, processed, evaluated, and analysed for all kinds of different purposes. It is the promise of big data analyses that they are able to uncover correlations and patterns from an aggregate pool of data. This questions the very nature of data policies of companies, in which the purposes of data collection are set out.

Connected to this problem is, fourth, that that the process of profiling is mostly invisible. Most of the time, individuals are not aware that they are being profiled. This problem is amplified through purpose-changes of the data use.[22] Even if the profiled individual knew, profiling practices and the profiles themselves are often legally protected by intellectual property or trade secrets. One prominent case of a woman in Germany challenging the scoring formula of the Schufa, the biggest German credit-scoring bureau, illustrates this problem. The German Supreme Court had decided that the formula forms part of the Schufa's protected business interest.[23] This secrecy disturbs the procedural (and substantive) equality of arms and access to due process: if a person does not have access to the information that forms the basis for certain advantages or disadvantages, she cannot contest the way she is being treated.[24] This makes it is virtually impossible to control the correctness of the data, contest the sorting into a certain profile, or to object to the profile process.

III. Responses of the GDPR

How does the GDPR respond to those problems involved in profiling? While some of the problems are dealt with in specific provisions, for example Article 22 GDPR or Article 6 GDPR, there are also general principles of data protection law that also apply to profiling practices, Article 5 GDPR. The Article 5 principles play

[21] F Pasquale, *Black Box Society – The Secret Algorithms that Control Money and Information* (Cambridge, Mass, Harvard University Press, 2015) 19.

[22] M Leese, 'The new profiling: algorithms, black boxes, and the failure of anti-discriminatory safeguards in the European Union' (2014) 45(5) *Security Dialogue* 494, 504.

[23] BGH, 28.01.2014 – VI ZR 156/13. The case currently lies with the German Constitutional Court.

[24] Leese (above n 22) 504.

an important role in the interpretation and application of the GDPR rules[25] and should not be understood as mere self-commitments of the industry,[26] but as basic obligations.[27] Violations of the Article 5 GDPR principles belong to the especially sanctioned ones, Article 83 V GDPR.

A. Privacy Concerns

This section shows that the most prominent legal concern involved in profiling – privacy – is only inadequately addressed in the GDPR, even though privacy protection is a major legal concern of the GDPR. Article 5(1) lit f) GDPR requires that data is:

> processed in a manner that ensures appropriate security of the personal data, including protection against unauthorised or unlawful processing and against accidental loss, destruction or damage, using appropriate technical or organisational measures ('integrity and confidentiality').

In this section, we will, first, analyse the legal bases for data collection and processing generally: the consent of the profiled individuals and the necessity for the performance of a contract. Second, we will look into the requirements of using anonymised or pseudonymised data. Both anonymisation and pseudonymisation could be suitable tools to address privacy concerns in data collection and processing. Third, one of the general principles of data protection is analysed: data minimisation. We will see that none of these regulatory tools is able to address privacy concerns involved in profiling in a sufficient way.

i. Legal Basis

Article 5(1) lit a) GDPR prescribes that data should be processed lawfully, fairly, and in a transparent way. Data processing without a legal basis is prohibited. This means that the controller must ensure the lawfulness of the data collection and analysis process, including the information of the data subject, and the existence of automated decision-making in terms of Article 22 GDPR, the involved logic, as well as the significance and envisaged consequences of such processing.[28]

[25] JP Albrecht and F Jotzo, *Das neue Datenschutzrecht der EU* (Baden-Baden, Nomos Verlagsgesellschaft, 2017) margin note 1 to Art 5 GDPR.

[26] S Pötters, 'Artikel 5 DSGVO' in P Gola (ed), *Datenschutz-Grundverordnung: DS-GVO. VO (EU) 2016/679* (München, CH Beck Verlag, 2017) margin note 4 to Art 5 GDPR; EM Frenzel, 'Artikel 5 DSGVO' in BP Paal and DA Pauly (eds), *Datenschutz-Grundverordnung Bundesdatenschutzgesetz: GD-GVO BDSG* (München, CH Beck, 2018) margin note 2 to Art 5 GDPR.

[27] P Reimer, 'Artikel 5 DGSVO' in G Sydow (ed), *Europäische Datenschutzgrundverordnung* (Baden-Baden, Nomos Verlagsgesellschaft, 2017) margin note 2 to Art 5 GDPR.

[28] Article 29 Data Protection Working Party, *Guidelines on Automated individual decision-making and Profiling for the purposes of Regulation 2016/679* (Brussels, 2017) 10.

Article 6(1) lit a) and b) GDPR establishes that the consent of the data subject and the necessity for contract performance are possible legal bases for data processing. It states:

> Processing shall be lawful only if and to the extent that at least one of the following applies:
>
> a) the data subject has given consent to the processing of his or her personal data for one or more specific purposes;
>
> b) processing is necessary for the performance of a contract to which the data subject is party or in order to take steps at the request of the data subject prior to entering into a contract;

a. Consent

Consent of the individual forms part of EU primary law, Article 8(2) Charter of Fundamental Rights, and enables the data subject to dispose of personal data at his own discretion. As such, consent is an expression of self-determination. The importance of consent in the GDPR framework cannot be understated. The lack of consent (or another legal basis) leads to the unlawfulness of the data collection and processing. In this sense, consent is a 'formal' tool of protection, as it is not concerned with any material unlawfulness or unfairness.

The requirement of consent as a means of personal data protection is based on the assumption that the 'consumer' can act reasonably circumspectly and can adapt his actions in a rational manner and in accordance with his preferences. The main issue to be addressed through the requirement of consent is a structural information asymmetry between data processor and data subject. The disclosure of information is supposed to remedy this information asymmetry – an approach well known and critically discussed in the field of consumer protection generally.[29] In data protection law, consent requires that it must be clear beforehand what personal data is being collected for which purpose.[30] It implies, for example, that a data broker cannot sell consumer profiles to financial companies, which then define consumers into categories for offering different financial products – including payday or high-cost loans – without consumer permission or knowledge of the underlying data.[31] Article 13 GDPR prescribes the kind of information that has to be submitted to the data subject.

[29] See for example WC Whitford 'The Functions of Disclosure Regulation in Consumer Transactions' (1973) *Wisconsin Law Review* 400; Schwartz (above n 3) 31; Howells (above n 17); SI Becher, 'Asymmetric Information in Consumer Contracts: The Challenge That Is Yet to Be Met' (2008) 45(4) *American Business Law Journal* 723; O Ben-Shahar and CE Schneider, 'The Failure of Mandated Disclosure' (2011) 159 *University of Pennsylvania Law Review* 647.

[30] S Schulz, 'Artikel 7 DSGVO' in Gola (above n 26) margin note 31 to Art 7 GDPR.

[31] Article 29 WP, *Guidelines on Automated individual decision-making* (above n 28) 10.

The requirements for valid consent follow from Articles 4 Nr 11 and 7 II, IV GDPR. Consent is defined in Article 4(XI) GDPR as

> any freely given, specific, informed and unambiguous indication of the data subject's wishes by which he or she, by a statement or by a clear affirmative action, signifies agreement to the processing of personal data relating to him or her.

As Article 4(XI) GDPR makes clear, consent must be freely given, specific, informed and unambiguous. In practice, all those terms are highly problematic.

First and foremost, the way in which the individual is to be informed is problematic. Many data protection policies are too long, so that they are hardly ever read. A study showed that one internet user would need to invest around 244 hours a year to read once the data policies of all visited webpages.[32] The increasing use of mobile devices makes it even harder to grapple with long privacy policies.[33] In addition, privacy policies of companies often do not comply with the requirements to be 'specific' and 'unambiguous'. They are often unspecific, surely in order to enable usage of data that is as broad as possible. The contexts of the data collection and possible receivers of data are frequently enumerated only as examples and not exhaustively. In those cases, policy statements do not make clear which data precisely is being processed, saved, or forwarded to third parties.[34] Such practices make privacy statements vague and unclear, and, hence, not sufficient to inform the data subject. As a consequence, the legal power of consent of the data subject is undermined because the very basis for that consent, information, is not ensured.

The second problematic requirement of a valid consent as the basis for data collection and processing is the requirement for the consent to be given 'freely'. Here, the real choice of consumers is questionable because of feared detriment, power imbalances, lack of necessity of the data collection, and bundling practices. Finally, the so-called privacy paradox hinders an approach that could give real-life effective consent. We will turn to these issues in more detail now.

According to the Article 29 Data Protection Working Party (Article 29 WP), the element of free will implies real choice and control for the individual concerned. It means that consent will be invalid if the person concerned is unable to refuse or withdraw consent without detriment.[35] Such detriment exists if it involves any costs for the data subject, for example the downgrading of the performance of the service.[36] Voluntariness of the consent implies that it must be possible to give consent to different concrete and partial data processes. Only then can choice truly be effected.

[32] AM McDonald and LF Cranor, 'The Cost of Reading Privacy Policies' (2008) 3(4) *Journal of Law and Policy for the Information Society* 543, 563.

[33] On the different reasons for the ineffectiveness of current information means, see N Helberger, *Forms matter' – Informing consumers effectively*, Study commissioned by BEUC X 2013/89 (Brussels, BEUC, 2013).

[34] See for example concerning data policies in the internet of things: Domurath and Kosyra (above n 16).

[35] Article 29 Data Protection Working Party, *Guidelines on Consent under Regulation 2016/679* (Brussels, 2017) 6.

[36] ibid, 11.

The burden of proof should lie with the data processor. This reversal of the burden of proof would take into account imbalances of power. Even though the GDPR is aware in Recital 43 of imbalances in power mainly in relation to public authorities, the Article 29 WP points out for consideration that situations of coercion, deception, intimidation, or negative consequences can also occur in employment situations or in other relations between private parties.[37] Thus, in order to assess the voluntariness of consent, it must be analysed carefully, whether there is a clear power imbalance between the data subject and the data processor. It is unlikely that an employee will contest the data processing of an employer. Similarly, individuals do not contest the data processing of a business professional, if she wants or needs to access certain goods or services offered by that professional, be it a washing machine or a health insurance policy. It is questionable whether the voluntariness of consent is actually assessed. This would require substantive inquiry into each and every specific case, usually by a court, entailing enforcement problems.[38]

The requirement of real choice must be viewed in conjunction with the necessity requirement of Article 7 IV GDPR and Recitals 42 and 43. Article 7 IV GDPR makes clear that in order to evaluate the voluntariness of consent, it must be examined whether the data is necessary for the execution of the underlying contract. The requirement of 'necessity' needs to be interpreted strictly, in that there must be a direct and objective link between the data processing and the purpose of the contract execution.[39] The Article 29 Data Protection Working Party explains that, for example, a mobile app for photo editing does not need geo-localisation or online behavioural advertising in order to provide a functioning core service. If users cannot use the app without consenting to these purposes, consent cannot be considered as having been freely given. Thus, the data collector and processor cannot rely on consent but needs to find another valid legal basis. Whether this test would be fulfilled in practice is, albeit in need of further research, doubtful.

Moreover, Article 7 IV GDPR prohibits situations in which consent to the data process is 'bundled' with the acceptance of the general terms and conditions, or the provision of a contract is tied to a request for consent to process personal data that is not necessary for the performance of the contract or services. In such cases, it is presumed that consent is not given freely.[40] The bundling prohibition becomes important for profiling when, for example, the granting of a credit is premised on the consent in the data processing for the creditworthiness assessment. While the assessment of repayment capacity might be 'necessary' for granting the credit, there is usually no need for data processing, if, in the case of an online retailer,

[37] ibid, 8.
[38] Podszun et al (above n 16); Spindler et al (above n 16); Domurath and Kosyra (above n 16).
[39] Article 29 WP, *Guidelines on Consent* (above n 35) 9.
[40] ibid.

a customer pays in advance. In that case, the tying of consent in data processing to the execution of the contract would be prohibited.[41]

The prohibition of bundling is to ensure that contract and consent are not blurred and that data processing cannot become directly or indirectly the counter-performance of a contract. At the same time, the ever-spreading practice of offering 'cost-free' products and services in return for data collection and processing run counter to this goal.[42] Many apps and internet-based applications are based on so-called 'free-of-charge' licence agreements. Some have argued from an economic incentives standpoint that the prohibition of bundling should not be applied to these licence agreements. They contend that the bundling prohibition is not violated if more protective, albeit fee-based, options are available to the user, who can choose between fee-based and free-of-charge products and services. Otherwise, the prohibition of bundling could lead to a decrease of 'free-of-charge' offers.[43] However, this argument overlooks that the bundling prohibition also serves to protect less financially able users from giving up their data because of financial pressure. If left unfettered, the data economy could develop in a way that individuals with less financial resources tend to give their consent to data processing in order to gain access to goods and services 'free of charge', whereas other individuals could afford to pay themselves out of data collection by paying for a less data-intrusive option.

Finally, the so-called privacy paradox renders consent ineffective. It describes the discrepancy between the value given by individuals to their privacy in general and the supposed decrease in value given to privacy by individuals when they give up their data in return for a cheaper product in particular. In such cases, the free will of the person concerned might be impaired, because the opposite decision – ie not giving up data – can involve substantial cost. Furthermore, actual privacy preferences are difficult to implement for individuals due to constantly changing technologies and data protection policies of webpages.[44]

These problems show that consent as the most prominent legal basis for data collection and processing needs to be seen critically. They cast serious doubt on the ability of the requirement of consent to enable true choice for individuals.[45]

[41] A Koreng and M Lachenmann, *Formularhandbuch Datenschutzrecht* (München, CH Beck, 2018) 960 ff.

[42] See for example bigdatascoring.com/; also www.faz.net/aktuell/feuilleton/silicon-demokratie/kolumne-silicon-demokratie-bonitaet-uebers-handy-12060602.html (last accessed 23 March 2019).

[43] Schulz (above n 30) margin note 27 to Art 7 GDPR.

[44] G Hull, 'Successful Failure: What Foucault Can Teach Us About Privacy Self-Management in a World of Facebook and Big Data' (2015) 17(2) *Ethics and Information Technology* 89; also W Hoffmann-Riem, 'Verhaltenssteuerung durch Algorithmen' (2017) 142(1) *Archiv des öffentlichen Rechts* 1, 21.

[45] The same holds true for the right of individuals to revoke consent. For a proposal for a solution, also with regard to the right to be forgotten, see E Politou et al, 'Forgetting personal data and revoking consent under the GDPR: Challenges and proposed solutions' (2018) 1 *Journal of Cybersecurity* 4.

b. Necessity

The consent of the data subject is not necessary under Article 6(1) lit b), when the data processing is 'necessary for the performance of a contract to which the data subject is party or in order to take steps at the request of the data subject prior to entering into a contract'. The scope of the provision is different from the one on consent, where 'necessity' is used in order to identify allowed or prohibited tying practices: if the data is unnecessary for the execution of the contract, the data processor needs to get the specific consent of the concerned data subject under lit a – otherwise the consent will not be given 'freely'; in contrast, if the data is necessary for contractual performance under lit b, the consent can be tied to the terms and conditions and will satisfy the requirement of voluntariness.

Also in this provision, the scope of 'necessity' is highly unclear and disputed. On the one hand, data that are the essential basis for calculations and decision-making regarding a concrete transaction are 'necessary', for example in the case of insurers who can decide whether to offer an insurance contract to their customers depending on the latters' risk profile.[46] Similarly, although an online retailer can process customers' credit card information for payment purposes and address data for delivery, it cannot condition the completion of a purchase agreement on building a profile of their customers' tastes and lifestyle choices based on the latters' visits to the retailer's website. Since the requirement of 'necessity' must be interpreted narrowly,[47] Article 6(1) lit b) GDPR is treated similarly to a legal exception – the general rule being the consent of the concerned data subject. It is, however, questionable whether this narrow interpretation is observed in practice and whether there is anybody who can actually control and verify 'necessity'. Research has already pointed to lack of potent enforcement agencies in the field of data protection.[48]

ii. Anonymisation and Pseudonymisation

Besides the condition of a legal basis, there are more substantial provisions in the GDPR that can be used to address privacy concerns of profiled individuals. A prominent means to secure the privacy of the data subject is to use only anonymous or pseudonymised data. The GDPR defines anonymous data in Recital 26 as 'information which does not relate to an identified or identifiable natural person or to personal data rendered anonymous in such a manner that the data subject is not or no longer identifiable'. The Article 29 WP states that effective anonymisation must prevent all parties from singling out an individual in a dataset, from linking records, and from inferring any information in a dataset; this implies that

[46] J Kühling and B Buchner, *Datenschutz-Grundverordnung, Bundesdatenschutzgesetz: DS-GVO/BDSG* (München, CH Beck, 2018) margin note 46 to Art 7 GDPR.

[47] Article 29 WP, *Guidelines on Consent* (above n 35) 13.

[48] Spindler et al (above n 16); Domurath and Kosyra (above n 16).

it is not enough to remove identifying elements, but that additional measures to prevent identification have to be taken.[49] De-identification must be irreversible.[50] Pseudonymised data, in turn, is data that can be attributed to an individual through the use of additional information, and thus makes it possible to identify an individual, Recital 26 GDPR. Article 4 V GDPR defines pseudonymisation as the processing of personal data so that the data cannot be attributed to an individual without the use of additional information, provided that such information is kept separately and is subject to technical and organisational measures to ensure non-attribution to the individual data subject.

The GDPR does not prescribe anonymisation or pseudonymisation of personal data. As for anonymisation, we can only note that the GDPR does not apply to the processing of anonymous data (Recital 26 GDPR). The underlying assumption is that the anonymous data is not 'personal' data, because the individual is not identifiable. It remains a technical question to what extent anonymisation processes and technologies are actually able to create truly anonymous datasets. Concerning pseudonymisation, Recital 28 GDPR introduces pseudonymisation as a specific means of data protection and Recital 29 GDPR encourages pseudonymisation by the same controller, who should keep additional information for attributing the personal data to an individual separately.

It is unclear whether anonymisation and pseudonymisation are incompatible with the very nature of profiling. Research indicates that profiling should be possible without identifying the person concerned in the sense of data protection law.[51] At the same time, individualisation of the data might be an inherent step in assigning a profile to an individual. Thus, even though the GDPR aims at encouraging the use of anonymised or pseudonymised data, this might not be feasible in profiling. Be that as it may, this shows that data controllers might be required to justify at least the individualisation in their profiling processes.

iii. Data Minimisation

Another tool to address privacy concerns over the collection and use of data is the data minimisation principle. It is a cornerstone of data protection law. Article 5 I lit c) GDPR states that personal data shall be:

> adequate, relevant and limited to what is necessary in relation to the purposes for which they are processed ('data minimisation').

The precise meaning of the terms 'adequate', 'relevant', and 'necessary' is, however, unclear. Definitions and policy instructions are missing. It is unclear whether

[49] Article 29 Data Protection Working Party, *Opinion 05/2014 on Anonymisation Techniques* (Brussels, 2009) 14.

[50] ibid, 7.

[51] W Schreurs et al, 'Cogitas, Ergo Sum. The Role of Data Protection Law and Non-discrimination Law in group Profiling in the Private Sector' in Hildebrandt and Gutwirth (above n 5).

the data minimisation principle is a manifestation of a general proportionality principle or not.[52] The Article 29 WP contends that the data minimisation principle implies that, for example within the frame of automated decision-making processes according to Article 22 GDPR, the responsible data processor must justify their need to collect personal data or at least consider using aggregated, anonymised or (if sufficiently safe) pseudonymised data.[53]

Even though it is clear that the data processor is accountable for observing the data minimisation principle, Article 5 II GDPR, it is much less obvious how the profiling company can prove the use of minimised data or its proportionality. Is a mere statistical correlation between the data and the pursued purpose enough? It might be sufficient to prove that the profiling could not have been done in the same way with less or different data and that the benefits of the scoring are not disproportionate to the interference with the right of the data subject. Who is supposed to control adherence to the principle? All this is unclear. In the end, the data minimisation principle is too vague to correct deficiencies immanent in profiling and big data analyses.

B. Discrimination and Automation

In profiling, discrimination looms large. Most of the discrimination is inherent in the decision to give access to goods and services. For example, creditworthiness assessments usually discriminate against poorer individuals vis-à-vis people with more financial resources: the former might be barred from access to credit. Car insurers have in the past discriminated against men, because, statistically, they are more involved in accidents: this involves higher contributions.[54] Health insurers charge higher contributions for women, despite laws to the contrary, because they tend to put more costs on the health sector.[55] It is to be noted that these problems have not come into existence only since big-data profiling technologies have become ubiquitous. However, the use of such technologies can amplify and reinforce discriminatory structures and infuse them with a perceived objectivity.[56] Automation carries the danger of unwarranted discrimination.[57]

[52] P Schantz, 'Artikel 5 DSGVO' in HA Wolff and S Brink (eds), *BeckOK Datenschutzrecht* (München, CH Beck, 2017); against: Frenzel (above n 26) margin note 35 ff.

[53] Article 29 WP, *Guidelines on Consent* (above n 35) 11.

[54] See the Globe and Mail article, above n 11.

[55] For the US: B Alemayehu and KE Warner, 'The Lifetime Distribution of Health Care Costs' (2004) 39(3) *Health Services Research* 627; see also the *New York Times* article, above n 11.

[56] For example cultural stereotyping in the financial sector extends to and can also be amplified by algorithmic profiling, see I Ramsay, 'Consumer Credit Law, Distributive Justice and the Welfare State' (1995) 15 *Oxford Journal of Legal Studies* 177, 194.

[57] K De Vries, 'Identity, profiling algorithms and a world of ambient intelligence' (2010) 12(1) *Ethics and Information Technology* 71, 83.

The GDPR is rather silent on this topic. While it acknowledges in Recitals 75 and 85 GDPR that personal data breaches can lead to discrimination, it does not prohibit such discrimination. The GDPR tools here are the 'classical' ones: legal basis for data collection and use, information of the data subject. It is then for the individual to take up the fight with the data processor. The problems involved in data protection law enforcement through individuals have been noted above. As seen in the case of a woman in Germany who – unsuccessfully – tried to get information on the scoring formula of the biggest German credit bureau,[58] individual complaints might not be a suitable approach, as long as that formula is considered a legally protected trade secret.

The GDPR only indirectly influences discriminatory practices. Inasmuch as profiling overlaps with automated decisions, the GDPR acknowledges the amplification effect of automation on discrimination. Article 22 GDPR gives profiled individuals the right to not be subject to solely automated decision-making processes. Notwithstanding the wording of Article 22 GDPR in terms of 'right', the Article 29 WP contends that Article 22 GDPR establishes a general prohibition of solely automated decisions. It implies the necessity of human involvement in terms of a review by someone who has the authority and competence to change the decision.[59]

Be that as it may, the 'prohibition' of solely automated decision-making in Article 22 GDPR is deceptive for several reasons. First of all, even if somebody with sufficient competence reviewed the automated decision, humans tend to trust in the results of algorithmic categorisation. Machines are considered to not make mistakes, so they can bureaucratically institutionalise discrimination.[60] In reality, the delineation between automated and human decisions is not that clear cut: a process in which a human decides whether to agree the loan based on a profile produced by a purely automated process might not be so different from an automated credit-granting decision based solely on an algorithm, especially if the human only follows the result of the automated process. In the end, the humans who are supposed to control the algorithmic decisions could lose true agency.[61] Second, the exceptions contained in Article 22 GDPR cover a wide range of actual business practices, which, as a consequence, fall outside of the scope of the prohibition. For example, Article 22 II lit a) GDPR allows solely automated decision-making, if it is 'necessary' for entering into or performing obligations under a contract. Here, we come back to the problems involved in assessing the necessity of data collection and use (see above III.A.i.b).

Third, there is also a more general problem involved in automated discrimination. There is a 'deep-seated' epistemological conflict between anti-discrimination

[58] BGH (see above n 23).
[59] Article 29 WP, *Guidelines on Automated individual decision-making* (above n 28) 9.
[60] De Vries (above n 57) 83.
[61] Leese (above n 22) 505.

rules that rely on the establishment of causality on the one hand and data-driven analytics that build ever-changing hypotheses on the basis of correlations in databases that increasingly operate with self-learning algorithms on the other.[62] This reflects a fundamental problem in the use of technology and reliance on correlations for profiling.[63] It also relates to the correctness of the profile and the question whether an individual has the right to be profiled in a 'correct' and truthful way (see below, Section III.D).

C. Purpose

With regard to the problems of the purpose of big data analyses, the GDPR sets out requirements for data controllers. Article 5(1) lit b) GDPR stipulates that data must be

> collected for specified, explicit and legitimate purposes and not further processed in a manner that is incompatible with those purposes; further processing for archiving purposes in the public interest, scientific or historical research purposes or statistical purposes shall, in accordance with Article 89(1), not be considered to be incompatible with the initial purposes ('purpose limitation').

The goal of the purpose limitation principle is to achieve transparency and traceability of data processing.[64] It is often called the essential constructive principle[65] or the pivotal basis of data protection law.[66] It is necessary to limit careless data collection and processing and trading. The purpose limitation principle works together with the principle of storage limitation, which ensures that data is not kept for longer than the purpose of the data processing requires. Article 5(1) lit e) GDPR states that data should be 'kept in a form which permits identification of data subjects for no longer than is necessary for the purposes for which the personal data are processed'.

The basis of the purpose limitation principle is the assumption that the goals of data collection and processing are clear *a posteriori*.[67] This implies that the profiling company needs to make sure that the original cause of data collection is compatible with the purpose of the scoring process. In addition, it requires that the

[62] ibid, 501, 503, 505. In security issues, the discriminatory problem is enhanced because 'normality' is no longer defined by social or legal norms, but in terms of a statistical normal distribution of characteristics.

[63] For further discussion, see Domurath and Neubeck (above n 1) 22 ff.

[64] Frenzel (above n 26) margin note 27 to Art 5 GDPR.

[65] Schantz (above n 52) margin note 13 to Art 5 GDPR.

[66] Frenzel (above n 26) margin note 23 to Art 5 GDPR; Schantz (above n 52) margin note 12 to Art 5 GDPR.

[67] Leese (above n 22) 504; see also BJ Koops, 'The (In)flexibility of Techno-Regulation and the Case of Purpose-binding' (2011) 5(2) *Legisprudence* 171, 181.

purpose specification in data policies be clearly formulated[68] from the viewpoint of the objective recipient of the declaration, so that it is unequivocally understandable what the data is going to be used for.[69]

The very assumption that the goals of data collection and use are clear *a posteriori* renders the purpose limitation unable to address big data processing of data for scoring purposes. Big-data analyses are based on an indiscriminate use of data; their value derives from the aggregation of vast amounts of data, irrespective of whether they are necessary or useful for a specific underlying contract. Much of the data used for profiling collected by the private sector is only initially for private business purposes. There is a so-called function creep inherent in data collection process, as technological systems push for functions expansion.[70] Algorithmic profiling based on big data analyses makes it virtually impossible to determine beforehand what personal data is used, for which purposes, and who uses it.[71] Potentially, every bit of data can become valuable in the future, especially for subsequent security monitoring.[72] An obvious case in point is the disclosure of user data of a cell phone user from usage records to security agencies in case of a crime or security threat.

Reflecting the ambiguity in purpose specification in times of big data, the interpretation of the purpose limitation principle allows for very broad formulations.[73] For example, it does not bind the data controller to the initial purpose of data collection; it just needs to be assessed whether the new type of data processing is compatible with the initial purpose.[74] This broadness is related to the absence of specific legal requirement and a lack of clarity concerning the level of abstraction for the specification of the purpose. For example, it is unclear whether the purpose needs to refer to the type of business of the profiling company (eg consumer credit scoring) or the type of contract for which the data is being collected and processed (eg consumer credit agreement).[75] This is also connected to problems of consent (see above, Section III.A.i.a.).

[68] G Ziegenhorn and K von Heckel, 'Datenverarbeitung durch Private nach der europäischen Datenschutzreform' (2016) 22 *Neue Zeitschrift für Verwaltungsrecht* 1585, 1589; CF Culik and N Döpke, 'Zweckbindungsgrundsatz gegen unkontrollierten Einsatz von Big Data-Anwendungen' (2017) 5 *Zeitschrift für Datenschutz* 226, 227.

[69] T Helbing, 'Big Data und der datenschutzrechtliche Grundsatz der Zweckbindung' (2015) 4 *Kommunikation & Recht* 146.

[70] Koops (above n 67) 181.

[71] For example, in the US, and probably not just there, a credit card company took into account whether a prospective customer attended marriage counselling, as there was statistical evidence that divorce can spill over into financial distress: Pasquale (above n 21) 31.

[72] Leese (above n 22) 504.

[73] Culik and Döpke (above n 68) 227; N Härting, 'Zweckbindung und Zweckänderung im Datenschutzrecht' (2015) 68 *Neue Juristische Wochenschrift* 3284, 3286; different: P Schantz, 'Die Datenschutz-Grundverordnung – Beginn einer neuen Zeitrechnung im Datenschutzrecht' (2016) 26 *Neue Juristische Wochenschrift* 1181, 1843.

[74] M Albers, 'Artikel 6 DSGVO' in Wolff and Brink (above n 52) margin note 68 ff to Art 6 GDPR.

[75] U Dammann, 'Erfolge und Defizite der Datenschutzgrundverordnung' (2016) 7 *Zeitschrift für Datenschutz* 307, 312.

It becomes clear that the purpose limitation principle does not generally question big data processes.[76] Accelerated by a technological function creep, broadly formulated privacy policies render purpose limitation virtually ineffective.

D. Transparency and Truthfulness

The last legal problem to be addressed in this contribution is the transparency and correctness of data used for profiling. In addition to Article 5(1) lit a) GDPR, which prescribes that data should be processed lawfully, fairly, and in a transparent way, Article 5(1) lit d) states that the data should be 'accurate and, where necessary, kept up to date'. Furthermore, 'every reasonable step must be taken to ensure that personal data that are inaccurate, having regard to the purposes for which they are processed, are erased or rectified without delay ("accuracy")'. Transparency and correctness of the data are inherently connected. Without transparency, data subjects cannot assess the accuracy of the data used for their profiles. Secrecy and opacity are to be avoided; otherwise the right under Article 16 GDPR to rectify wrong data grasps at nothing.

Despite these and other provisions in the GDPR, transparency is not guaranteed in practice. The main issue is, again, enforcement. Pasquale gets to the heart of the problem:

> Knowledge is power. To scrutinize others while avoiding scrutiny oneself is one of the most important forms of power. Firms seek out intimate details of potential customers' and employees' lives, but give regulators as little information as they possibly can about their own statistics and procedures. Internet companies collect more and more data on their users but fight regulations that would let those same users exercise some control over the resulting digital dossiers … It matters because authority is increasingly expressed algorithmically … The values and prerogatives that the encoded rules enact are hidden within black boxes.[77]

Pasquale shows that there is a discrepancy between the practices of companies (and other entities that use algorithms for any kind of decision-making) and the ability of regulators to exercise any kind of legality control over those practices. The right of individuals to trace the use of their personal data, as for example in Article 15 GDPR, runs into a deadlock when opposed to legally protected trade secrets of the company that is profiling them. Transparency is increasingly lost in a 'black box'[78] of algorithms that determine opaque decision-making structures. In order to avoid obvious negative effects of secrecy and opacity, from the viewpoint of data protection law, regulatory oversight is therefore crucial.

[76] Culik and Döpke (above n 68) 230.
[77] Pasquale (above n 21) 3–4.
[78] Pasquale (above n 21).

And another point must be made here. Big data analyses are not concerned with the correctness of individual data at all. Profiling can take place efficiently without correct data. Being based on statistical inferences, big data analyses rely on the logic that what is incalculable on an individual level is calculable on a collective level.[79] Through the aggregation of information of many individuals, the likes and dislikes of one individual are predicted, presuming that people who have shared preferences in the past will also share them in the future.[80] While those statistical inferences can work in some cases, tensions can arise because any profile inherently relates to a 'community', which the individual is considered to be part of because of certain shared characteristics. Those probabilistic groupings are simply not concerned with truthfulness. This shows that individuals do not have the right to be profiled 'correctly'. This is not only problematic from the viewpoint of data protection and the right of individuals to self-determination, which the GDPR aims at fostering, but also from the viewpoint of the effectiveness of profiling.

E. Findings and Open Questions

The examination of these problems involved in profiling practices shows that, currently, the GDPR is not able to address the data protection challenges involved in profiling. The protective gaps permeate the whole legal framework regarding privacy issues, discrimination, purpose, and transparency problems.

First and foremost, with regard to privacy concerns, the main legal basis for data collection and use, consent, is fraught with legal and actual problems. For example, its mere basis – the provision of information – is bound to be ineffective, as information is hardly read or readable. Page-long privacy statements are often not comprehensible to individuals, and difficult to read, especially as people increasingly switch to mobile devices. Privacy statements used by companies are often opaque and intransparent. Second, in the data economy, in which data collection and processing is ubiquitous, consent is rarely voluntary. In practice, access to goods and services – especially when offered free of charge – depends enormously on the consent of individuals to data collection, so that consent effectively becomes the counter performance of a contract. This shows that the bundling prohibition is toothless. Moreover, the privacy paradox and difficulties to implement changing privacy preferences add to the inability of consent to fulfil its function to enable true choice for individuals.

Another problem concerns the effectiveness of the data protection principles. The data minimisation principle, which could in theory put boundaries to big data-based profiling, is interpreted so broadly that it does not effect the minimisation of data collection and use. The same holds true for the purpose

[79] De Vries (above n 57) 80.
[80] De Vries (above n 57) 77.

limitation principle. It is interpreted in a way that enables profilers and other data collectors and processors to formulate their privacy policies in a very broad way. Another problem is that it runs counter to the very essence of big data analyses, which are based on the sifting of indiscriminate, vast amounts of data, the use of which cannot be determined a priori. Also, the attempt of the GDPR to achieve more transparency of data collection and use is bound to fail. In practice, the algorithms that companies use for data analyses and profiling are part of their trade secrets.

This is connected to another blind spot of the data protection principles: the lack of possibility to detect infringements and sanction them according to Article 84 V GDPR. This means that even though the privacy policies of companies will mostly not comply with those principles,[81] infringements will probably remain largely undetected and unsanctioned.

Finally, it becomes clear that many provisions of the GDPR concerning profiling cannot improve data protection rules, if the regulatory framework is not to make profiling as a business practice impossible. It is clear that the data minimisation principle would, if interpreted and enforced strictly, disable probably most big data analyses. This would run counter to strong business interest in the data economy generally, and of providers of profiling and targeted services specifically. Furthermore, as discrimination is inherent in profiling, the GDPR cannot prohibit discrimination based on individual characteristics that are reflected in their data. Cultural stereotyping permeates automated decision-making structures. The GDPR addresses this problem only indirectly through the prohibition of solely automated decision-making. However, the provision of Article 22 GDPR might have no practical consequences, because the actual substantial involvement of a human reviewer is bound to be highly influenced by the automated decision. Here, we feel the consequences of not extending the non-discrimination principle in EU law fully to the field of consumer law.[82]

The gaps in the legal framework and in the effectiveness of the approach put into focus the problems of liability and accountability. These topics are outside of the scope of this chapter. In further research, important questions need to be answered. Where profiling causes harm in terms of privacy or discrimination, it is unclear who is to be held accountable: the software programmer, the profiling service provider, or even the profiled user? This issue of liability is especially complex in a data economy where algorithms are, first, not programmed by individual programmers, but by big teams of programmers, and second, increasingly self-writing based on machine-learning technologies. Further research in this regard is indispensible. Similarly, existing research into the regulatory capture of twenty-first century technology is in urgent need of being expanded. The role of algorithms in regulation, their effectiveness and limitations as well as the risks

[81] See for the internet of things and purpose limitation, Domurath and Kosyra (above n 16).
[82] Jablonowska et al (above n 6) 17.

involved in their use, must be carefully studied, not only from legal, but also economic, sociological, and psychological perspectives. Societal discourse needs to be open and aware of all benefits and risks.

IV. Further Discussion

Our examination has shown that profiling poses a number of challenges. Society needs to think over the ubiquitousness of profiling and the normative power of algorithmic governance. Legally, profiling intersects with regulation, private law and human rights dimensions.

A. Technological Totalitarianism and the Granular Society

A system of downright governance through technology has developed. Nowadays, algorithms determine access to goods and services, both for consumption and basic needs. Whereas some decades ago, credit-scoring formulas determined access to consumer credit only, nowadays credit scores are powerful doors to a range of activities that are vital for participation in society, from obtaining a house to live in[83] to access to employment or affordable insurance.[84] Algorithms determine the kind of access a person has to goods, housing, health care, insurance and much more. Brownsword predicts that within the next 42 years, 'technological management' will co-exist with legal, moral and social norms as a regulatory instrument.[85] Pasquale argues that, at least on financial markets, the use of algorithms has become so ubiquitous that regulation has already been replaced by automation.[86]

This system of algorithmic power can be called totalitarian. Totalitarianism derives from several elements: the ubiquitousness of algorithmic decision-making; the inability of regulators to effectively control the development of algorithmic governance; the inability of individuals to understand, backtrace, and contest the use of their personal data; and the shaping of social norms through normative effects of profiling. This contribution has addressed the first three elements, including remarks on the inability of regulators to effectively control ubiquitous algorithmic decision-making; the respective gaps in the GDPR have been identified. The other element, the shaping of social norms, merits a few remarks.

[83] Concerning the powers of financial institutions (and their credit scores) to determine access to housing, see I Domurath, *Consumer Vulnerability and Welfare in Mortgage Contracts* (Oxford, Hart, 2017) 170.

[84] Pasquale (above n 21) 23.

[85] R Brownsword, 'Law, Innovation and Technology in the year 2061: from law to technological management' (2015) 7(1) *Law, Innovations and Technology* 1.

[86] Pasquale (above n 21) 105. See also Jablonowska et al (above n 6) 9 ff, for use of artificial intelligence.

The inability of individuals to influence in any way the collection and use of their data and the shaping of social norms are connected to the normative power of technological regulation (regulation through technology). First of all, we have seen that the rights of individuals to exercise influence over the use of their data is, in practice, very limited. Solove uses the metaphor of Kafka's *The Trial* to refer to the helplessness, frustration, and vulnerability of individuals vis-à-vis large (bureaucratic) organisations that have control of a dossier with vast amounts of information over their personal lives.[87] Second, even if individuals could understand and backtrace the collection and use of their personal data, technical rules are basically self-enforcing, so that they pre-empt resistance as a primary driver for legal change.[88] Third, as profiles determine access to goods and services, they can influence individual behaviour, as individuals can attempt to change their profiles and their interactions with others in order to gain access to goods and services. In a Foucaultian view, discipline proceeds by forcing the individual to conform to a model of desired characteristics and behaviour.[89] While this might be an inherently human behaviour that also exists in other social contexts (eg at school, where pupils can study harder in order to improve their grades), we must take into account the ubiquitousness of profiling and, thus, the crucial power of profiles in determining access to goods and services. With spreading profiling practices, hardly any realm of social interaction will escape relentless observation and judgement. This means that technological rules become the rules of society. This can have negative impacts on the experience and use of personal freedom.

As space for personal freedom narrows, individual identity dissolves. According to Deleuze, contemporary profiling disassembles individuals into 'dividuals',[90] meaning that the individual is no longer the smallest unit in society, as they are broken down into different data points. Individuals are absorbed into a more or less random community, and deconstructed into different roles. Being part of a community of shared certain criteria in one field (eg pregnant women under 25) does not mean that all individuals assembled under this community actually have anything in common besides those criteria (eg being vegetarian). The same holds true for other groups the individual is classed into. Different and overlapping categorisations not only lead to an 'unacceptable amount of blunt probabilistic heuristics and discriminatory categorizations', but can also impede individuals from relating their identity to them.[91] This also leads to a segmentation of the market according to different consumer-identities and lifestyles, a practice, albeit widely used for several decades, that has reached a new level

[87] Solove (above n 19) 9.

[88] For an overview of the literature that also takes account of the diverging (minority) view that techno-regulation can be more flexible than traditional regulation, see Koops (above n 67) 176 ff.

[89] Leese (above n 22) 500.

[90] G Deleuze, 'Postscript on the Societies of Control' (1992) 59 *October* 3.

[91] De Vries (above n 57) 81.

of sophistication with targeted advertising and recommendation algorithms.[92] Even though segmentation enables targeting and, thus, may be efficient from the competitive-strategic point of view of companies, it can also be destructive of the social fabric of societies.[93] We can even go as far as claiming that this granularity of modern society dissolves our social reality, threatening justice and democracy as the very pillars of our societies.[94]

These thoughts question whether the current regulatory framework is at all able or even designed to catch the technological characteristics of profiling in particular, and the data economy in general. Technology-driven innovation seems to advance with a large disregard for protective standards for data. In the end, a value discussion needs to take place making clear what the end goal of data protection laws should be: the fostering of a data economy, including profiling, in which personal data flows freely; or the protection of the privacy of individuals with all the limitations to the data economy entailed. Similarly, academic and societal debates need to determine which forms of discrimination – which is, after all, inherent in automated profiling processes – are warranted and which are not.[95]

B. An Intersection of Laws

It is vital to acknowledge that regulators and society at large have and must exercise some legal control over technological developments. Profiling technologies in particular challenge all aspects of the law: regulation of markets, data protection, and contract law. Data protection can play a vital role in connecting regulation and private law.

The regulatory challenges of technological change are increasingly discussed in the literature. A whole new corpus of academic commentary on the intersection of data protection and competition and consumer law has emerged.[96] The regulatory challenges are also well outlined in the final report of Hans Micklitz's last collaborative research project on the use of artificial intelligence in business (*ARTSY*):[97] discussions on the normative framework especially concerning discrimination, targeted services and other issues involved in profiling; questions of technological feasibility of those normative goals; the respective design of governance structure;

[92] ibid, 77.

[93] OH Gandy, 'Engaging rational discrimination: exploring reasons for placing regulatory constraints on decision support systems' (2008) 12(1) *Ethics and Information Technology* 29.

[94] C Kucklick, *Die granulare Gesellschaft* (Berlin: Ullstein Buchverlag GmbH, 2016).

[95] Also De Vries (above n 57) 83.

[96] F Costa-Cabral and O Lynskey, 'Family ties: the intersection between data protection and competition in EU Law' (2017) 54(1) *Common Market Law Review* 11; N Helberger et al, 'The Perfect Match? A Closer Look at the Relationship between EU Consumer Law and Data Protection Law' (2017) 54(5) *Common Market Law Review* 1427; W Kerber, 'Digital markets, data, and privacy: competition law, consumer law and data protection' (2016) 11 *Journal of Intellectual Property Law & Practice* 856.

[97] Jablonowska et al (above n 6) 57–70.

and the broader implications for society. Hans and his collaborations suggest that a bottom-up approach is useful to grapple with technological challenges of artificial intelligence in different fields of regulation.[98]

However, the challenges are not only of a regulatory nature. Private law (no matter whether understood in a 'pure' or more 'regulatory' sense) especially needs to be rethought. In times of ubiquitous markets and commodification, private law naturally plays a pivotal role in ordering society. Contracts between private parties are important institutions in facilitating market exchanges and can be the framework for social ordering and imposing social obligations.[99] As profiling affects market exchanges, it also affects contractual relations. Profiles nowadays fulfil a gatekeeper function for access to an increasing number of different goods and services, some of them for consumption, but some of them for the satisfaction of basic needs. This development indicates the need to transform the goals, purposes, and rules of private law.

In many ways, private law is already transforming.[100] Especially in consumer (contract) law, the changes through technology and data are already visible.[101] Data protection and contract law cut across different regulatory sectors and are, thus, pivotal in the articulation and protection of privacy interests in all market segments. But more needs to be done. The questions raised in the *ARTSY* project are only a starting point.

From a normative point of view, the goal of fostering a data economy with fluid transfer of data must take into account the legal problems in data use for profiling. Data protection law should not be reduced to data law[102] that disregards protective

[98] P Palka et al, *Before Machines Consume the Consumers – High-Level Tagewaways from the ARTSY Project*, EUI Working Paper LAW 2018/12 (Florence: European University Institute, 2018) 2.

[99] In credit relations, this role of contracts is already acknowledged because they not only structure contingent expectations of the contract parties concerning their transaction, but also because credit is inherently connected to distributive justice and welfare. See J Beckert and W Streeck, 'Economic Sociology and Political Economy A Programmatic Perspective' (2008) MPlfG Working Paper 08/4, 22; J Beckert, 'Capitalism as a System of Contingent Expectations – Toward a Sociological Microfoundation of Political Economy' (2012) *MPlfG Discussion Paper* 12/4; Ramsay (above n 56); I Domurath, 'Mortgage Debt and the Social Function of Contract' (2016) 22(6) *European Law Journal* 758.

[100] For example H-W Micklitz, 'The Transformation of Private Law Through Competition' (2016) 22(5) *European Law Journal* 627; H-W Micklitz, 'Constitutional transformation of private law pillars through the CJEU' in H Collins (ed), *European Contract Law and the Charter of Fundamental Rights* (Antwerp, Intersentia, 2017).

[101] For example: M Fries, 'PayPal Law und Legal Tech – Was macht die Digitalisierung mit dem Privatrecht?' (2016) *Neue Juristische Wochenschrift* 2860; MBM Loos, 'Standard terms for the use of the Apple App Store and the Google Play Store' (2016) 5(1) *Journal of European Consumer and Market Law* 10; C Busch et al, 'Discussion Draft of a Directive on Online Intermediary Platforms' (2016) 5(4) *Journal of European Consumer and Market Law* 164; C Busch et al, 'The Rise of the Platform Economy: A New Challenge for EU Consumer Law?' (2016) 5 *Journal of European Consumer and Market Law* 2.

[102] Similarly to the expulsion of the concept of protection from consumer law: H-W Micklitz, 'The Expulsion of the Concept of Protection from the Consumer Law and the Return of Social Elements in the Civil Law: A Bittersweet Polemic' (2012) 35(3) *Journal of Consumer Policy* 283; reiterated for the regulation of and through technology in Jablonowska et al (above n 6) 9 ff.

elements in favour of facilitating economic exchange. Moreover, since profiles can determine the access to goods and services, and, thus, the access to contractual relations about the provisions of those goods and services, contract law must take into account the connection between consent to privacy policies and consent to enter into contractual agreements. Legal debates in this regard must go beyond the discussions on payment through data or data ownership.[103] The limits that the connection of contracts with profiles pose in terms of freedom of choice, freedom of contract, and, more profoundly, freedom of self-expression, need to be recognised as much as problems of discrimination.

Brownsword contends that a precautionary approach should be adopted vis-à-vis the development and use of 'smart machines' for the sake of human dignity.[104] Orientation at the fundamental right to human dignity implies empowering individuals to make their own choices as well as constraining certain practices. Precaution means that regulation must hold the risks involved in technological governance at an acceptable level. This contribution has shown that there are many gaps in the legal framework that could be filled with a precautionary approach. For example, anonymisation could be adopted as the basis for legality. If the data processor wants to use individual personal data, proof of strict causality could be required for 'necessity'. Most of the current profiling practices would have to significantly adapt to such regulation. Strong oversight and enforcement mechanisms are urgently needed.

But it is not only the right to human dignity that should play out in a new all-encompassing legal approach to market regulation, data protection, and contract law. The right to human dignity, the right to liberty, the right to respect for family life and home, and the right to the protection of personal data, freedom of thought and expression, equality and non-discrimination are not just mere aspirational standards; they are human and fundamental rights that form part of the primary law of the EU.

[103] Much research is being done in this regard, see for example BJ Evans, 'Much Ado About Data Ownership' (2011) 25(1) *Harvard Journal of Law & Technology* 69; G Hornung and T Goeble, '"Data Ownership" im vernetzten Automobil' (2015) 31(4) *Computer und Recht* 263.

[104] R Brownsword, 'From Erewhon to AlphaGo: for the sake of human dignity, should we destroy the machines?' (2017) 9(1) *Law, Innovation and Technology* 117; Brownsword (above n 85); R Brownsword and M Goodwin, *Law and the Technologies of the Twenty-First Century: Text and Materials* (Cambridge, Cambridge University Press, 2012).

6

EU Consumer Law and Artificial Intelligence

AGNIESZKA JABŁONOWSKA* AND PRZEMYSŁAW PAŁKA**

The chapter considers the interplay between the EU consumer law and artificial intelligence. It begins by addressing three topical issues in law and AI scholarship: the definition of 'artificial intelligence', the problem of 'black box' and liability for the actions of AI. It addresses certain misconceptions present in legal discourses, and proposes conceptual distinctions to remedy them. The argument then moves to three issues specific to consumer law: the asymmetry between businesses and consumers, the emergence of AI applications in consumer markets, and some of the potential challenges which they raise, particularly those to consumers' autonomy. Deeper intellectual engagement with the challenges posed to the doctrine and the practice of consumer law by the development of AI is necessary before one can move to recommendations on how the law should be changed. The chapter concludes with a plea to develop AI-based applications that empower consumers and civil society.

I. Introduction

Artificial intelligence is about to go mainstream in European legal scholarship. The unquestionable success of this technology across different sectors of the economy – from energy, to retail, to healthcare – has led to a proliferation of scholarly contributions and political strategies during the last couple of years. The next EU Commission is expected to make AI one of its strategic priorities, akin to Junker's Digital Single Market. The audience interested in AI will therefore gradually broaden, from scholars interested in technology, to scholars working in particular legal fields, where AI will become one of many phenomena to be taken

* PhD researcher at the University of Lodz. Supported by the Foundation for Polish Science (FNP).
** Private Law Fellow at Yale Law School's Center for Private Law, Resident Fellow at Information Society Project.

into account, as was the case with the internet. The societal changes caused by AI are significant, and so research concentrating on identification of promises and challenges, as well as possible ways to respond to them, is important and should be applauded. At the same time, the tone and content of some of these contributions suggest that AI is just hype. Hence, many predictions made about its course, as well as concerns raised, should be treated with critical reservation. In this chapter, we want to draw from the lessons we have learned during our work in the last couple of years, and anticipate some questions and issues we believe will be discussed over the coming years by European lawyers, especially those interested in consumer law and policy.

In particular, we build upon the results of the ARTSY Project[1] led by Hans Micklitz for the last two years, in which we had the pleasure to participate. Its ambition was to map the ways in which the AI is being used in the private sector, and identify the challenges for EU consumer law and policy. The final results are presented in the form of a comprehensive report[2] and high-level takeaways,[3] and the reader is invited to consult those documents. We do not want to replicate the Project's conclusions here. Rather, we build upon them and offer reflections about three substantive matters we consider scholarly interesting and societally important: the asymmetry between businesses and consumers; the emergence of AI applications in consumer markets; and some of the potential challenges which they raise. These reflections are the most consumer-oriented part of the chapter, presented in Sections IV–VI.

Hans Micklitz's contribution to the scholarly community is not limited to the impressive substantive results of his studies. Equally important is his way of thinking: the urge to be critical, and to go against the current; to be sceptical of hype and herd behaviour; to think outside of the box, and break down the established labels; to take time to observe and reflect, before rushing to conclusions. Along these lines, we begin the chapter by tackling three 'topical' issues in the field of AI and law: the problem of its definition, the problem of the 'black box' and the problem of liability for AI's actions. To do so, we open in a provocative manner, and want to argue that none of them actually is a problem. Rather, we tend to see them as problems because of conceptual confusions. We clarify the concepts, propose several distinctions to help structure the debates, and suggest alternative ways of tackling these questions.

[1] ARTSY Project (ARTificial intelligence SYstems and consumer law & policy) was conducted over the course of 2017 and 2018 at the European University Institute in Florence, with Hans Micklitz being the Principal Investigator. It was funded by the Berkman Klein Center for Internet and Society as a part of the Ethics and Governance of Artificial Intelligence Fund. See artsy.eui.eu/.

[2] A Jabłonowska et al, 'Consumer Law and Artificial Intelligence: Challenges to the EU Consumer Law and Policy Stemming from the Business' Use of Artificial Intelligence. Final report of the ARTSY project' (2018) EUI Working Paper LAW 2018/11, available at cadmus.eui.eu/handle/1814/57484.

[3] P Pałka et al, 'Before Machines Consume the Consumers: High-Level Takeaways from the ARTSY Project' (2018) EUI Working Paper LAW 2018/12, available at cadmus.eui.eu//handle/1814/57485.

Finally, we want to give due respect to Hans Micklitz's deep commitment to society, and the belief that, as scholars, we owe a debt to the people around us. In his work, Hans beautifully connects the ability to slow down and theorise, with the conviction that at the end of the day, what we do should serve a societal purpose; that action research is something not only compatible, but also deeply intellectually connected, with the theory. To do so, we briefly reflect upon the ways in which AI can be used to empower consumers and civil society, what the legal and political preconditions are for this to happen, and what we should do next.

II. Definition of Artificial Intelligence. Or, What Is This 'AI'?

It seems to be a good practice in the field of AI and law to begin a paper by stating that there is no commonly agreed upon definition of AI. This statement is correct, but hardly helpful. In the end, an author and the readers should share an understanding of what is it that they are talking about. The lack of *the* definition does not remove the author's obligation to clarify what is the object of the inquiry. Given that one can expect the number of legal papers concerned with AI to grow, it is worthwhile to begin our considerations by addressing the questions: why is there no agreed upon definition of AI?; and what are the alternative ways to begin a paper, which actually confer some added knowledge?

Let us begin by stating that a lack of a definition is not a problem it itself. There are quite a few fundamental concepts: 'human being', 'politics', 'economy', or – yes – 'law', which lack a commonly agreed upon definition. But this does not stop us from studying them, or having some real world impact upon them. What matters, however, are the reasons why scholars would like to have a definition. What are the functions a definition is supposed to serve? There are two. First, the role of a definition is to delineate the object of inquiry. What is it that we are talking about? When we say 'artificial intelligence', do we mean 'self-driving cars', 'a discipline in engineering', 'Google translate'? This is something we need to agree upon, to avoid talking past one another. Second, once the object of inquiry is clarified, a role of a definition is to tell us something about it. What are the features/characteristics of the phenomenon under consideration? This is something we should do, to avoid talking about our (possibly mistaken) idea about the reality, instead of the reality itself. So the reflex to define – in order to delineate and increase understanding – should be applauded. However, these functions do not have to be served by an Aristotelian definition *per genus et differentiam*. There are other ways. A lack of such a definition does not remove an obligation to clarify. It is helpful, however, to inquire into why is there no commonly agreed upon definition of AI. There are two reasons.

First, the same term is currently being used to refer to very different phenomena. And this is not a bad way to start. We should not begin research by being underinclusive, for the sake of a neat definition. The buzzword 'artificial intelligence' captures a series of intuitions, fears and hopes in people's minds. Scholars who try to generalise sometimes have very different things in mind. Some will be concerned with robots becoming conscious, like those in *I, Robot* or *Westworld* (which are not coming about anytime soon) and talk about 'robot rights' or 'personality for AI'. Some others will think of high-frequency trading agents, taking decisions 'autonomously' (which have been with us for a decade now) and ponder the need to update financial market regulation. There are scholars concerned with credit-scoring by algorithms (which are real, but technologically simple, and for now do not rely on AI), and there are those interested in moral considerations made salient by self-driving cars.[4] All of these phenomena have something in common with artificial intelligence. At the same time, they are very different from one another. Some exist already, some do not. Some pose threats to health and life, some to other legally protected values. Just as we do not define a 'human intelligence' for the sake of regulating human behaviour, there is no reason to believe that we will need *the* definition of AI, either for scholarship, or for regulation.

Second, perspective matters. An engineer sitting in a lab and trying to build a computer that will pass the Turing test[5] has something else in mind than a policymaker trying to understand what are the problems with companies using AI to deliver targeted advertising to consumers. Consider three definitions, first two commonly invoked after Russell and Norvig's classic textbook,[6] and the third used by us in the ARTSY project:

(1) 'The art of creating machines that perform functions that require intelligence when performed by people';[7]
(2) 'The study of computations that make it possible to perceive, reason and act';[8]
(3) 'A socio-technological practice where an entity, private or public, uses machine learning tools to generate new knowledge out of large amounts of data, and/or act upon that knowledge, in order to automate and optimize certain process, as well as undertake new, previously impossible, tasks'.[9]

The first two define an academic discipline, or a goal of a scholarly endeavour. The object of inquiry is what engineers do in their labs. The *genus* being 'the art' or

[4] G Contissa et al, 'The Ethical Knob: Ethically-Customisable Automated Vehicles and the Law' (2017) 25 *Artificial Intelligence and Law* 365.

[5] A test for an 'intelligent machine' has been proposed by Alan Turing, who argued that we could deem one to be so, if a human talking to it (by textual means) was unable to tell whether the entity on the other side is a human or a machine.

[6] SJ Russell and P Norvig, *Artificial Intelligence: A Modern Approach*, 3rd edn (Pearson Education, 2016).

[7] R Kurzweil, *The Age of Intelligent Machines* (Cambridge, Mass, MIT Press, 1990).

[8] PH Winston, *Artificial Intelligence*, 3rd edn (Addison-Wesley, 1992).

[9] Pałka et al (above n 3).

'the study' clearly indicates that.[10] By comparing definitions (1) and (2), one can see what the disagreement is in the engineering community. The first camp is interested in creating machines that will act like humans and deliver outputs which look human, even if they are achieved through very different means. The second is concerned with processes, and tries to replicate a human way of thinking inside a machine. Both of them, in addition, have a universal ambition.

The third definition is different in two ways. First, its *genus* is 'practice'. It is not concerned with what engineers try to achieve, but what is actually happening on the market right now.[11] Second, it does not have a universal ambition. It defines the term for the purposes of studying the practice from the point of view of consumer law. It clearly delineates what is meant, at the same time being open to the idea that for the purposes of studying self-driving cars, autonomous weapons or a field of investment, 'AI' will be defined differently. Differently, because a different set of phenomena will be under consideration, and because that set might have different unifying features.

The reader will have noticed the risk of defining AI *ignotum per ignotius* in the third definition. Its understanding presupposes the knowledge of what machine learning is. Why is this so, and what is it?

For the purposes of pondering effects of technology on law, and considering potential regulation, one should concentrate on what is possible/existent, or what will be so in the foreseeable future. Machine learning is just one type of artificial intelligence,[12] but the only type that currently works and is used in the practice.[13] That is why it makes sense for legal scholars to be clear about the types of technologies they refer to when invoking the term 'AI'. What is machine learning, then?

Machine learning turns upside down the traditional approach to computer science.[14] Traditionally, a programmer would write a series of instructions for the machine, which the latter would subsequently execute. For certain tasks – like creating spreadsheets – this works well enough. But for others – like machine translation or image recognition – traditional programming came short of rendering satisfactory results. In machine learning, a developer will give a computer a big data set – a series of inputs and outputs one could say – and let the machine, relying on a learning algorithm, to figure out the way to get there. For example, to teach a computer to recognise traffic signs, an image recognition learning algorithm will receive one billion photos of such signs, and one billion photos without them.

[10] If one wanted to define 'law' in a similar manner, one could speak of 'the art of commenting on legal material in a way that finds order, provides guidance, and expresses critical take on the subject': the study of something.

[11] If one wanted to define 'law' in a similar manner, one could speak of 'the ways in which legal actors, like judges or attorneys behave, and the reasons they provide for doing so': the actual practice.

[12] E Alpaydin, *Machine Learning. The New AI* (MIT Press, 2016).

[13] N Cristianini, 'The Road to Artificial Intelligence: A Case of Data over Theory' (2016) *The New Scientist*, available at www.newscientist.com/article/mg23230971-200-the-irresistible-rise-of-artificial-intelligence/.

[14] Alpaydin (above n 12).

The output will be a trained algorithm, a new piece of code capable of conducting a certain task. These algorithms, later, can be incorporated in a piece of software (an app, a website, a desktop computer program) that a user can employ.

This approach has now successfully been deployed in numerous ways: machine translation, image recognition, spam detection, health diagnosis, fraud detection etc. And this is the 'artificial intelligence' that 'is everywhere' nowadays. Which points to the final question: how should one then begin a paper about law and AI?

First, it seems to be a good idea to specify what exactly one has in mind: current practice or a possible future? If the former, to clarify what exactly are the techniques used in a given sphere, by whom, and for what purpose. If the latter, to rely on technical research making clear whether we are talking about foreseeable applications (like new types of natural language processing), or far removed speculations (like conscious machines). For example, 'this paper is about the machine learning tools advertisers use to better understand consumer reaction to ads, and in consequence develop more effective ones'. The beauty of this approach is that it gets real. The difficulty is that it requires empirical research, often interdisciplinary in nature, which is much more effort-intensive than armchair philosophy. But it is the way to go.

Second, one has to remember that AI is not a one thing, it does not have one definition, does not pose the same types of problems everywhere, and so will have to be tackled case-by-case. The times when one could speak of 'regulation of AI' and come across with a meaningful contribution, are over. What exactly do you want to think of, when you speak of 'artificial intelligence'?

III. Black Box

A commonly repeated wisdom is that programs relying on artificial intelligence, or even better – on 'algorithms' – are 'black boxes'. We do not know what is going on inside, how they perform their tasks. Some people express fear that we will never know. Others set up for the task of 'opening' black boxes and advocate for 'the FDA for algorithms' or 'more research on explainability'. However, just like 'AI', 'black box' is a buzzword used frequently to denote different things. In this section, we want to introduce two distinctions: between legally- and technically-induced black boxes; and between private and public use of algorithms. And we argue that even though there are many challenges surrounding different algorithmic technologies, the 'black box problem' is a much smaller problem (at least from regulatory perspective) than people tend to assume.

To begin, let us address yet another concept that often gets used rather frivolously: 'algorithm'. An algorithm, from the technical standpoint, is a sequence of unambiguous instructions to be followed by an agent. This agent can be a human, or a computer (an artificial agent). Consider an example. Imagine your friend is hosting a party, but there is too much stuff to do, so you volunteer to help. She asks you to offer drinks to the guests. You're stressed, and do not know how to go about it, so your friend gives you the following instruction:

1. Look at the guests, and when you see one not holding a drink, approach and ask whether he or she wants one;
2. IF NOT, exclude this guest from the pool for 20 minutes and go back to step 1.
3. IF YES, ask what drink would they like.
4. IF we have that drink, serve it, wish them a lot of fun, and go back to step 1; IF we do not have that drink, proceed to step 5
5. List the drinks which we have. IF the guest chooses one, serve it, wish them a lot of fun, and go back to step 1; IF the guest does not want one anymore, execute step 2.

The instruction above is an algorithm. Now, the agent executing it is you – a human – but it could just as well be a robot. All this is to say than an algorithm and an agent (often an artificial agent) executing it are not the same types of entity.

A 'black box' is an agent whose instructions we do not know. There are two reasons why do not know it (not mutually exclusive): because the agent, or its employer/owner (i) does not want to tell us what the instruction is (and claims to have a legal title not to tell us); or (ii) does not himself understand what the instruction is. Those, respectively, are legal and technical black boxes.

Legal black boxes emerge when a company which develops or uses a tool invokes a trade secret, or another legal reason, not to share the instruction (the algorithm) that the tool follows. This, often, can be quite simple algorithms. In fact, many algorithms labelled 'black boxes' do not rely on artificial intelligence. Consider two examples that captured significant public attention in the past: the German SCHUFA case, and the COMPAS risk-assessment tool used in the American criminal justice system, ie the 'proprietary' nature defence – 'I came up with this algorithm, it took me time and effort, and I will not share, because others will replicate it'. In many cases, such a defence makes sense. In other cases, there will be public policy reasons for not disclosing the instructions. Algorithms used by agents at the airports that choose whom to control, or by tax authorities choosing whom to inspect, probably should remain secret, in order not to be 'gamed' by the bad guys. However, in all these cases it is technically possible to understand the algorithm by humans. And there are many ways in which, in order to make sure that there is no discrimination, or other undesirable consequences, they could be controlled by experts, without full disclosure to the public. One can imagine administrative agencies overseeing financial markets, or consumer relations, being given a competence to inspect them, while at the same time being legally obliged not to disclose. Especially for algorithms that are privately developed, but used as a part of the exercise of public power (by the criminal justice system, tax authorities, in visa lotteries etc) there should be someone competent (legally and technically) to audit them. To achieve this, however, no rocket science is needed; only changes in law and organisation.

Technical black boxes are those that emerge as a result of a learning algorithm finding patterns in vast collections of data. And indeed, in software relying on AI, certain steps are 'mysterious' to a human, in the sense that we do not really know how the machine gets from point A to point B. Many examples have caught the media's attention. The, by now famous, AlphaGO has learned how to beat human masters in the Go game, first by studying thousands of games of amateurs and professionals,[15] and then got even better simply by playing against itself.[16] Human experts do not know *how* the machine is 'thinking', while at the same time it outperforms every human on the planet. DeepMind, AlphaGo developers, captured the general public shock on their website, writing:

> During the games, AlphaGo played a handful of highly inventive winning moves, several of which – including move 37 in game two – were so surprising they overturned hundreds of years of received wisdom, and have since been examined extensively by players of all levels. In the course of winning, AlphaGo somehow taught the world completely new knowledge about perhaps the most studied and contemplated game in history.[17]

The game example is, well, a toy example but the similar technical black boxes occur in systems with high societal and practical relevance. Medical applications detecting cancer, or deciding whether to use chemotherapy; self-driving cars learning how to drive and how to behave in different situations; machine translation (potentially soon to be used in courts and administrative proceedings) all have this 'mystery' part in them, where we do not know how exactly they perform their tasks. Is it a problem for regulation? If so, it is much smaller than we tend to assume, because there is really a lot that we do know. We know why the machine is trying to get to point B from point A, and in what circumstances it has learned to do so, and who was in charge of these circumstances.

Imagine that a small child, who cannot read or write, points to a jar labelled 'Cookies' and asks what the sign says. You answer, and the child spends a while looking at it. On a different day, the child takes a piece of paper, scribbles something, and tells you 'this says Cookies'. Indeed, that is what the output looks like. You're happy and proud, congratulate the child, and ask it to write 'cook'. 'I have no idea how to write that' is the answer. You ask the child to show you the letter 'c'. 'What's a letter?' you hear in reply. The child does not know the letters, it cannot 'write' in the sense of the word as you understand it. Nevertheless, the child has learned to create a sign indicating 'Cookies'. You do not know *how* it learned to do so – definitely not in the 'standard' way. What the child paid attention to, and how it managed to remember the 'cookies' shape is a mystery to you. A black box. At the same time, you know what data the child was exposed to. The sign 'Cookies', paired

[15] D Silver et al, 'Mastering the Game of Go with Deep Neural Networks and Tree Search' (2016) 529 *Nature* 484.

[16] D Silver et al, 'Mastering the Game of Go without Human Knowledge' (2017) 550 *Nature* 354.

[17] See deepmind.com/research/alphago/.

with the meaning of the sign that you provided. And you know what the task was: to learn how to write 'Cookies'.

The same is often the case with most machine learning systems. Their programmers/operators might not know precisely how the machine has figured out how to perform the task at hand, but they know quite well what (types of) data it had access to, or what the task was that it was supposed to learn to perform. Hence, it is a significant overstatement to say that 'no-one understands' what the machine is doing. Of course, in many applications, it would come in useful to know a little bit better how exactly the machine has learned what to do. From the perspective of the computer science, this is a widely acknowledged challenge, and a promising venue of research. However, from the regulatory point of view, this is often a third order problem. What matters for regulation is: what tasks the developers want the machines to execute; in what ways have they trained them; and, where there is a risk of a known undesirable output (discrimination, for example), what precautions have been undertaken at the implementation stage (the algorithm is not the same thing as the agent; the agents might have additional layers of instructions, not necessarily relying on AI). To use yet another distinction and popular buzzword, what we are dealing with is first and foremost organisational opacity, not a technical one.[18] Instead of focusing on 'explainability' of a 'black box', we should focus on the processes of development and deployment, and the vast majority of answers can be found there.

With so many different types of black boxes, again the 'problem' is legion, and will need to be tackled case by case, often using very different legal and technical means. If one wishes to write about the black box in a particular societal practice, a good way to start is to ask: what type of a black box are we dealing with here? And what exactly is the problem caused by it?

IV. Liability

The third issue often invoked at the early stages of discussions about legal status and regulation of artificial intelligence is the issue of liability. A familiar story would begin by warning us that machines are getting 'smarter and smarter', 'autonomous', 'reprogram themselves', and so as a result no one knows what exactly they will do. In such a world, the narrative continues, who is/should be liable? The owner? The seller? The programmer? The question is difficult and complex, it would seem, and so this paradigmatic shift, 'the responsibility gap', needs to be addressed soon by researchers and policy. Or so we are told.

As we hope is clear by now, many of these assumptions are quite stretched. Granted, tools using artificial intelligence are more sophisticated than traditional

[18] See H Chulu, 'Let us end algorithmic discrimination' (2018) *Medium*, available at medium.com/techfestival-2018/let-us-end-algorithmic-discrimination-98421b1334a3.

software, and their actions are harder to predict, but we are very far from a world in which machines are 'autonomous' in the sense that they start doing things by themselves. How they achieve their goals might be difficult to explain, but it is still very much humans who give them the goals, and are capable of foreseeing negative consequences. In this sense, an action of an AI-powered system is never an accident. It is always a result of a quite informed decision, taken by a human, to deploy the tool in a given context, with clearly specified objectives in mind. Hence, we want to argue, the liability gap is a much smaller problem than many tend to assume. Nevertheless, the question is there to be answered. To do so, we want to introduce two distinctions: between moral and legal liability; and between compensatory and preventive functions of legal liability.

As a matter of moral philosophy, the question of who is *actually* culpable if a machine relying on AI does something wrong is interesting and – arguably – challenging. However, it is a separate question from the legal one. As a matter of law, a situation in which we ascribe civil liability to an entity who had no fault is neither new nor challenging. Liability for the actions of children or animals is one example. Strict liability for 'dangerous' products is another. Is the producer of Coca Cola cans morally liable for the fact that one in billion explode? Not really. Is he legally liable? Yes, fully. In yet another domain, traffic law provides a good example. Quite often the person who was actually at fault – driving without slowing down on the main road – will not be found guilty by the law, as long as he or she had a right of way. Traffic law is a good starting point, because it shows how we manage to fully separate the moral question from the legal one, and at the same time ensure that the law's compensatory function is realised. A system of strict liability, with a recursive claim, paired with mandatory insurance at various stages, shows that the question 'who pays?' can be both answered unambiguously, and fully separated from the question of who is 'actually' morally liable.

However, ensuring that people harmed are duly compensated is not the only function of legal liability. Arguably, as a society, we want to live in a world in which someone who is harmed receives compensation; but we would prefer to live in a world in which that someone does not get harmed in the first place. Hence, liability also serves a preventive function. People do not want to be liable and have to pay; and so they act more carefully, or do not commit certain acts in the first place. With machines, however, this will not necessarily be the case. Machines need to be programmed/trained to act in a certain way or not. And creating an incentive to design them in such a way does not have to come in a form of rules on liability. Many other options are on the table. Mandatory or optional certification, certain good practices (like impact assessments) in the design process, transparency and accountability mechanisms etc are just some examples of other means of achieving the goal of machines not breaking the law.

What is very important is the realisation that an exact choice of means will be different in different cases, both for technical and for normative reasons. Sometimes the creation of standards will be possible and helpful, sometimes not. Sometimes keeping a 'human in the loop' is possible, sometimes very difficult.

And sometimes (when life and health are at risk) we might want to have these costly processes legally required, while in other cases we might think that the cost is too high to bear.

The question of liability is therefore a problem of complexity of situations, not complexity of technology. When encountering this question, it is useful to remember that: (1) moral and legal responsibility are not necessarily connected to one another; (2) ensuring that there will be someone to pay is not equal to ensuring that law's preventive function is realised; and (3) liability rules (and other preventive measures) can and will differ case by case, depending on technical and normative divergences.

To sum up the argument until now: the three issues discussed above, namely the definition of artificial intelligence, the problem of the 'black box', and the questions regarding the liability for harms caused by the systems relying on AI, are common to all legal and policy considerations surrounding the themes of AI governance and regulation. They are relevant to European consumer law, but equally useful for those looking at AI from other normative angles. All three are topical issues, but pose different actual problems than usually assumed, stemming usually from conceptual confusions. In the next four sections, we look at issues specifically pertaining to European consumer law and policy.

V. Asymmetry

Among public policy reasons for establishing a consumer protection framework, the disparity of power between consumers and traders appears to be a central theme. Special consideration for consumer interests is generally explained by their weaker position with respect to levels of knowledge, resources, experience and the bargaining power.[19] This imbalance is seen as a source of potential concern about efficiency, distributive justice and individual rights. In discussions among scholars and policymakers the junction between these three (and perhaps more) perspectives often remains debatable.[20] Ultimately, compound justifications appear to be most common and the emphasis placed on particular elements depends not only on the regulatory theory to which one subscribes, but also on the more general background (political, institutional) of the whole regulatory enterprise. This is well illustrated by the case of the EU – a context which Hans Micklitz has explored in great detail. His analyses of the nexus between consumer law and internal market

[19] See eg cases C-137/08, *Pénzügyi Lízing*, ECLI:EU:C:2010:659, para 46 and C-105/17, *Kamenova*, ECLI:EU:C:2018:808, para 34.

[20] Cf S Grundmann et al (eds), *Party Autonomy and the Role of Information in the Internal Market* (de Gruyter, 2001); F Rischkowsky and T Döring, 'Consumer Policy in a Market Economy. Considerations from the Perspective of the Economics of Information, the New Institutional Economics as well as Behavioural Economics' (2008) 31 *Journal of Consumer Policy* 285; I Benöhr, *EU Consumer Law and Human Rights* (Oxford, Oxford University Press, 2013).

policy, including his powerful conception of 'access justice',[21] have shed light on the specific dynamics in European law and policy-making. At the same time, he has constantly remained on the lookout for the other, more socially-oriented face of consumer policy at both national and European level.[22] As the ongoing socio-technological developments, including those related to AI, will continually push us to reflect on the consumer protection instruments we have in place, the need to specify and agree on their underlying rationales will become even more pressing.

Much attention will probably remain, and rightly so, on the information asymmetry. It is a prominent aspect of the consumer's weaker position and fits well both with economic reasoning and with autonomy theory.[23] In simplified terms: without sufficient transparency of prices, quality and terms, consumers cannot make informed and therefore efficient choices, which in turn reduces suppliers' incentives to compete on these parameters.[24] Consumers are perceived as rational actors capable of processing the relevant information and taking decisions that match their preferences and increase their utility. Such an approach was eagerly taken up by the EU legislator, who has often prioritised the tools that serve 'consumer empowerment', such as disclosure duties.[25]

As signalled before, however, the idea that consumers can improve the functioning of the market through their transactional decisions is not the only perspective that shapes European law and policy-making. Legislation and case law on unfair terms in consumer contracts shows that consumers might be in need of more substantive protection when they are faced with contracts of adhesion.[26] The concept of 'vulnerable consumers' has also gradually emerged from the growing body of EU law, highlighting the fact that consumers who are not 'reasonably well-informed and reasonably observant and circumspect'[27] do not necessarily have themselves to blame and may require a more targeted protection.[28] Later insights from behavioural economics have added further nuance to this picture, by pointing, among others, to certain systematic biases which affect consumer

[21] H-W Micklitz, 'Social Justice and Access Justice in Private Law' (2011) EUI Working Paper LAW 2011/02, available at cadmus.eui.eu/handle/1814/15706.

[22] H-W Micklitz, 'The Expulsion of the Concept of Protection from the Consumer Law and the Return of Social Elements in the Civil Law: A Bittersweet Polemic' (2012) 35 *Journal of Consumer Policy* 283.

[23] Rischkowsky and Döring (above n 20); O Ben-Shahar and CE Schneider, *More Than You Wanted To Know: The Failure of Mandated Disclosure* (Princeton University Press, 2014).

[24] I Ramsay, *Consumer Law and Policy: Text and Materials on Regulating Consumer Markets*, 3rd edn (Oxford, Hart, 2012).

[25] H-W Micklitz, 'The Consumer: Marketised, Fragmentised, Constitutionalised' in D Leczykiewicz and S Weatherill (eds), *The Images of the Consumer in EU Law: Legislation, Free Movement and Competition Law* (Oxford, Hart, 2016).

[26] C Willett and M Morgan-Taylor, 'Recognising the Limits of Transparency in EU Consumer Law' in J Devenney and M Kenny (eds), *European Consumer Protection: Theory and Practice* (Cambridge, Cambridge University Press, 2012).

[27] See eg Case C-210/96, *Gut Springenheide*, ECLI:EU:C:1998:369, para 31.

[28] N Reich, 'Vulnerable Consumers in EU Law' in Leczykiewicz and Weatherill (above n 25).

choice on a much wider scale.[29] The question which can now be asked is whether the changing technological landscape, and especially the developments in AI, are making this type of consideration more or less pronounced.

As should already be clear from sections II and IV, there will not be a single answer, considering that AI is not a single 'thing'. But first, it is helpful to take a step back and look at the process of digitalisation more generally and consumers' place in it. There are two contrasting viewpoints.[30] On the one hand, with an instantaneous access to the internet and a variety of digital tools, contemporary consumers appear to be much better placed to find and compare information and exchange experience. Through this they can become more capable of assuming the role that neoclassical economists and, to a certain extent, the EU legislator have imagined for them.[31] On the other hand, due to the growing quantity of information, consumers often cannot meaningfully process and evaluate it on their own.[32] Both perspectives are true, even if they partially remain in tension. It is precisely this information paradox that has driven the development of a new generation of online intermediaries, such as search engines and social media, which allow consumers to navigate the information universe.

Although the solution came with a new unknown – as to how personalisation actually takes place and what it can lead to, this uncertainty has not weakened the demand for filtering tools and the pace of the technological progress. AI, or more precisely machine learning, is arguably the single most significant development in this process so far. It takes knowledge generation to the next level and makes it possible to create an entirely new value out of the information overload. The results seem ambiguous. Consumers gain access to potentially more relevant information about parts of the socio-economic landscape as well as to innovative products, such as personal digital assistants, which bring a new dimension to everyday convenience. At the same time, their continuous use of data-driven services and products (the line becomes blurred) contributes to the growing knowledge – and power – of their counterparts. What exactly the underlying trade-offs are often remains less clear, arguably as a result of both consumers' cognitive limitations and different 'black box' problems (Section III). This potentially adds to the already extensive insights traders have about the markets[33]

[29] B Schüller, 'The Definition of Consumers in EU Consumer Law' in Devenney and Kenny (above n 26); A-L Sibony and G Helleringer, 'EU Consumer Protection and Behavioural Sciences: Revolution or Reform?' in A Alemanno and A-L Sibony (eds), *Nudge and the Law: A European Perspective* (Oxford, Hart, 2015).

[30] JK Winn, 'Is Consumer Protection an Anachronism in the Information Economy?' in JK Winn (ed), *Consumer Protection in the Age of the 'Information Economy'* (Routledge, 2006).

[31] For a critical view see: C Coteanu, *Cyber Consumer Law and Unfair Trading Practices* (Routledge, 2005).

[32] More generally on the so-called information overload, see G Howells, 'The Potential and Limits of Consumer Empowerment by Information' (2005) 32 *Journal of Law and Society* 349; Willett and Morgan-Taylor (above n 26); Ben-Shahar and Schneider (above n 23).

[33] M Weber, *Max Weber on Law in Economy and Society* (Harvard University Press, 1954).

and consumers – including their biases and misperceptions.[34] With AI, the possibilities of leveraging these factors to suppliers' advantage can increase even more.

From this we can conclude that AI surely has a *potential* for increasing the asymmetry between consumers and traders. An important question is how far this change is actually taking place and whether it is part of an evolution, or rather a disruption. How much broader is the knowledge which can now be inferred about consumers by looking at behaviours of countless other individuals? How does it translate into the existing regulatory rationales, eg does it affect consumers' ability to 'act rationally'? Recognising that knowledge *about* consumers is now a crucial element of the traders' informational advantage rightly brings the associations with data protection law to mind. It would be a mistake, however, to focus one's attention solely on this domain. Rather, a combined reflection about data protection, consumer law, further neighbouring domains such as anti-discrimination law, and their underlying paradigms should be encouraged.[35]

VI. AI Applications, Public Regulation and Private Commitment

There seems to be a broad consensus that the corporate use of machine learning is, in itself, neither good nor evil. What rather needs to be assessed are specific applications of AI in consumer markets. To analyse the latter – both individually and as a broader socio-technological practice – a great amount of (largely empirical) work is yet to be done. Still, considering the current stage of knowledge, and especially the asymmetrical dynamics mentioned above, it is not surprising that remarkable deployments of AI in the private sector are causing mixed reactions.[36]

It might be for these reasons that some of the leading companies engaged in the AI game have tried to position themselves as more than just profit-driven corporations. Both Facebook and Google pride themselves on their researchers' publications in leading scientific journals, along with their generous support of academic and social projects.[37] What is more, the industry leaders are increasingly

[34] JD Hanson and DA Kysar, 'Taking Behavioralism Seriously: The Problem of Market Manipulation' (1999) 74 *New York University Law Review* 630.

[35] W Kerber, 'Digital Markets, Data, and Privacy: Competition Law, Consumer Law and Data Protection' (2016) 11 *Journal of Intellectual Property Law & Practice* 856; N Helberger et al, 'The Perfect Match? A Closer Look at the Relationship between EU Consumer Law and Data Protection Law' (2017) 54 *Common Market Law Review* 1427; P Hacker, 'Teaching Fairness to Artificial Intelligence: Existing and Novel Strategies against Algorithmic Discrimination under EU Law' (2018) 55 *Common Market Law Review* 1143.

[36] See eg BEUC, 'Automated Decision Making and Artificial Intelligence – A Consumer Perspective' (2018) BEUC Position Paper, available at www.beuc.eu/publications/beuc-x-2018-058_automated_decision_making_and_artificial_intelligence.pdf.

[37] See eg research.fb.com/category/facebook-ai-research/; www.blog.google/outreach-initiatives/google-org/ai-social-good/.

interested in more than direct consumer interactions. One can observe a growing market not just for data, but also for machine learning tools to be used by programmers.[38] This adds a further dimension to the discussions about the appropriate governance model for AI development and deployment.[39]

At this point legal scholars would welcome a categorisation of some kind. What types of AI applications can we possibly expect to see in the market practice? When thinking about consumer markets, one can be tempted to distinguish between AI-based services designed for the use by consumers and those applied by businesses in marketing and customer relations. This is helpful to some extent. The former group would cover, for example, automated translation tools, recommender systems and personal assistants, while personalisation of commercial practices and contractual conditions or chatbots used in customer service would fall into the latter.[40] One needs to remember, however, that in reality the boundaries are more difficult to draw. This falls in line with the broader developments in the digital markets – monetisation strategies can be diversified and indirect, different commercial relationships might be interconnected and the distinction between products and services often becomes blurred (with much of the exchange taking place on a long-term 'as is' basis). A given AI-based solution thus does not become more or less problematic due to the category in which it fits, but rather as a result of its overall context.

There might nevertheless be some guidelines of a more general nature that we would like AI developers to consider at the programming stage. This view seems to be substantiated by recent developments in the industry itself. ISO and IEEE have been active in developing standards for different aspects and use cases of AI applications.[41] As far as individual companies are concerned, most illustrative are probably the 'AI principles', which Google recently committed itself to follow in the hope to 'lead by example'.[42] The motives for this move have already been questioned – and perhaps rightly so.[43] Equally intriguing are the narratives which accompany such bottom-up efforts – ones that typically pertain to ethical, not legal, considerations. In fact, however, the connection between many of these initiatives and consumer law or the neighbouring domains, especially data protection and anti-discrimination law (Hans Micklitz would not approve of an overly sharp distinction), is readily apparent. In a field so complex and dynamic, getting

[38] See eg facebook.ai/developers/tools; cloud.google.com/automl/; aws.amazon.com/machine-learning/.

[39] Consider the idea of the European AI-on-demand platform as a possible response, see: European Commission, 'Horizon 2020 Work Programme 2018–2020 Part 5.i Information and Communication Technologies', 55, available at ec.europa.eu/research/participants/data/ref/h2020/wp/2018-2020/main/h2020-wp1820-leit-ict_en.pdf.

[40] Jabłonowska et al (above n 2).

[41] See www.iso.org/committee/6794475.html; https://standards.ieee.org/news/2017/ieee_global_initiative.html.

[42] See www.blog.google/technology/ai/ai-principles/.

[43] In particular, the move is being linked to a controversial military contract concluded by the company with the US Department of Defense.

right the relationship between public and private, and between the law, economy and ethics becomes particularly important.

What, then, are the main recurring themes in the ethical and legal discussions about AI within the industry? Certainly, a lot attention is devoted to discriminatory outcomes and their distributional effects.[44] Considering that AI applications rely, at least partially, on human inputs (sourcing data, training algorithms), they are also susceptible to human imperfections. In contrast to single human errors and biases, however, once deployed, AI applications can carry large-scale implications and their shortcomings are not always easy to detect.[45] Since being prejudiced against the underprivileged and minorities is one of the last things major AI stakeholders would like to be associated with, preventing unfair bias seems to be an area of joint efforts. In its proudly unveiled principles, Google undertakes to avoid 'unjust impacts on people, particularly those related to sensitive characteristics such as race, ethnicity, gender, nationality, income, sexual orientation, ability, and political or religious belief'. Of course, this is not something we should be taking for granted, or considering to be a problem solved. After all, until not long ago Facebook did not see anything wrong in allowing advertisers to target ads by race and ethnicity,[46] and the measures Google takes or intends to take to fulfil its declaration remain largely unclear.

Still, the growing number of the studies exploring technological measures for addressing the problem of unfair bias in machine learning gives grounds to hope that similar commitments can be more than just empty words.[47] Such a broad, multi-stakeholder interest in this area is certainly a welcome development. At the same time, as has been pointed out in the literature, hitherto attempts at formalising fairness seem to rely on a limited perception of equality, understood as non-discrimination on the basis of a particular sensitive characteristics, such as gender or ethnicity.[48] This may be due to the current legal landscape, whose focus similarly remains on historically disadvantaged groups. From that perspective, certain characteristics mentioned by Google (eg income) appear to even go beyond the catalogues enshrined in law. An important question is, once again, when and how such legal-ethical conditions are being specified and implemented and who decides if they have been fulfilled. Finally, it is necessary to reflect on the more general limits of the sensitive characteristics (or protected classes) approach,

[44] T Zarsky, 'Understanding Discrimination in the Scored Society' (2014) 89 *Washington Law Review* 137; S Barocas and AD Selbst, 'Big Data's Disparate Impact' (2016) 104 *California Law Review* 671; PT Kim, 'Auditing Algorithms for Discrimination' (2017) 166 *University of Pennsylvania Law Review Online* 189; Hacker (above n 35).

[45] C O'Neill, *Weapons of Math Destruction: How Big Data Increases Inequality and Threatens Democracy* (Allen Lane, 2016).

[46] See www.propublica.org/article/facebook-promises-to-bar-advertisers-from-targeting-ads-by-race-or-ethnicity-again.

[47] See P Gajane and M Pechenizkiy, 'On Formalizing Fairness in Prediction with Machine Learning' (2017), available at arxiv.org/abs/1710.03184.

[48] R Binns, 'Fairness in Machine Learning: Lessons from Political Philosophy' (2018) 81 *Proceedings of Machine Learning Research* 149.

as laid down in applicable legal frameworks. Arguably, AI systems can significantly transform the underlying populations over time as well as generate new societal segments, composed of multiple parameters, on a continuous basis.[49] This adds a new dimension to the existing line of research which investigates the problems of stigmatisation and exclusion in a broader societal context.[50] We also cannot forget that legislative and judicial responses to the instances of discrimination tend to divide public opinion. From a governance perspective this implies that the questions raised by AI often cannot be 'dealt with' on a one-off basis. Addressing its impacts will rather be a long-term process, requiring the engagement of multiple stakeholders and civil society.

VII. The Autonomy of Humans and the Autonomy of Machines

We have already expressed our scepticism about the gravity of the legal problems caused by machines acquiring 'autonomous' qualities. This does not mean that autonomy is entirely irrelevant in the context of AI. In fact, the contrary is true. However, as is argued here, the focus should remain on the autonomy of humans.

This, at least theoretically, should bring us, lawyers, onto familiar ground. When thinking about autonomy in the legal context, 'private autonomy' – a traditional concept of private law and the main embodiment of the freedom of contract – is likely to be the first association to come to mind. Much of the scholarship over recent decades has been concerned with the conceptualisation of both terms and their evolution.[51] The classical theory underscored the freedom of formally equal contract partners in shaping their relationships; as long as they *appear* to have agreed on a given transaction, the state should not intervene. Conceivable exceptions on the grounds of fairness have been those related to procedure, not substance and revolved around the so-called 'vitiating factors'.[52] With industrialisation and the consumer society the discussion began to focus on the need for *overriding* private autonomy, in order to protect the party which is factually and

[49] LT Liu et al, 'Delayed Impact of Fair Machine Learning' (2018) 80 *Proceedings of the 35th International Conference on Machine Learning* 3150; A Vedder and L Naudts, 'Accountability for the Use of Algorithms in a Big Data Environment' (2017) 31 *International Review of Law, Computers & Technology* 206.

[50] Eg intersectionality, see L McCall, 'The Complexity of Intersectionality' (2005) 30 *Signs: Journal of Women in Culture and Society* 1771.

[51] PS Atiyah, *The Rise and Fall of Freedom of Contract* (Oxford, Clarendon Press, 1979); H-W Micklitz, 'On the Intellectual History of Freedom of Contract and Regulation' (2015) 4 *Penn State Journal of Law and International Affairs* 1.

[52] P Cartwright, *Consumer Protection and the Criminal Law: Law, Theory, and Policy in the UK* (Cambridge University Press, 2001); E Mik, 'The Erosion of Autonomy in Online Consumer Transactions' (2016) 8 *Law, Innovation and Technology* 1.

structurally weaker.[53] However, as Hans Micklitz has shown in his work, there are also other ways of looking at autonomy.[54] This becomes particularly apparent when EU law is considered – one in which these traditional theoretical underpinnings do not play a pivotal role and can be approached without prejudice. The concept of the 'regulated autonomy' tries to capture this multidimensional nature of autonomy in the European legal context.[55] Through this lens, European private law can be viewed as at the same time 'establishing market freedoms, therefore increasing private autonomy' and 'set[ting] boundaries to this newly created autonomy'.[56] In doing so, the EU creates its own model of freedom of contract, characterised by the coexistence of these enabling and restricting (framing) dimensions.[57]

The challenges posed by AI clearly call for a deeper reflection on the nature of autonomy and conditions under which it might be desirable for lawmakers to step in. This is true not only for contract law, but also, among others, for unfair commercial practices law. Indeed, concerns have already been voiced about the use of algorithmic agents, including AI powered, by the traders to exert powerful influence on consumer behaviours. We, too, consider this to be among the major threats of the traders' growing technological sophistication vis-à-vis consumers.

Crucially, the knowledge businesses may acquire through AI must be viewed in a broader context: with increasing digitalisation on a more general level it is currently possible to adjust not only the form and content of commercial messages to particular consumers, but also the place and time.[58] Some recent studies began to explore the possibility of conceptualising such personalised practices under Directive 2005/29/EC on unfair business-to-consumer commercial practices in the internal market (UCPD).[59] With further advances in facial recognition, the

[53] S Weatherill, 'Justifying Limits to Party Autonomy in the Internal Market – EC Legislation in the Field of Consumer Protection' in Grundmann et al (above n 20).

[54] For an equally relevant take on the regulatory dimension of autonomy in private law, see S Grundmann, 'On the Unity of Private Law. From a Formal to a Substance-Based Concept of Private Law' (2010) 18 *European Review of Private Law* 1055.

[55] G Comparato and H-W Micklitz, 'Regulated Autonomy Between Market Freedoms and Fundamental Rights in the Case Law of the CJEU' in U Bernitz et al (eds), *General Principles of EU Law and European Private Law* (Wolters Kluwer, 2013).

[56] H-W Micklitz and D Patterson, 'From the Nation State to the Market: The Evolution of EU Private Law' (2012) EUI Working Paper LAW 2012/15, available at cadmus.eui.eu//handle/1814/22415.

[57] ibid.

[58] R Calo, 'Digital Market Manipulation' (2013) 82 *The George Washington Law Review* 995; Mik (above n 52).

[59] Directive 2005/29/EC of the European Parliament and of the Council of 11 May 2005 concerning unfair business-to-consumer commercial practices in the internal market and amending Council Directive 84/450/EEC, Directives 97/7/EC, 98/27/EC and 2002/65/EC of the European Parliament and of the Council and Regulation (EC) No 2006/2004 of the European Parliament and of the Council ('Unfair Commercial Practices Directive') [2005] OJ L149/22. See N Helberger, 'Profiling and Targeting Consumers in the Internet of Things – A New Challenge for Consumer Law' in R Schulze and D Staudenmayer (eds), *Digital Revolution: Challenges for Contract Law in Practice* (Nomos/Hart Publishing, 2015); Mik (above n 52); M Sax et al, 'Health as a Means Towards Profitable Ends: mHealth Apps, User Autonomy, and Unfair Commercial Practices' (2018) 41 *Journal of Consumer Policy* 1.

importance of these questions will increase even more. A somewhat different line of research inquires about the impact of the delegated decision-making on autonomy and dignity.[60] This may seem like a different debate; yet, because of some of the elements of market transformation mentioned above, the line may be thinner than it looks at first sight. Just think about personal digital assistants and the vanishing divide between information and advertising.[61]

Against this background it seems pertinent to reflect on the parameters which one should take into account when deciding about the balance between the law's enabling and restricting dimensions. As mentioned above, the EU seems to be primarily concerned with market integration. It recognises the need for increased 'consumer trust' in the market in general, and in the internal market in particular, and fosters this trust through a variety of tools.[62]

Trust also seems to be at the forefront of emerging European policy on AI, as epitomised by the recently adopted Ethics Guidelines for Trustworthy Artificial Intelligence. To what extent such a paradigm is indeed justified, and to what extent it is fulfilled, is a more complex matter, which we have touched upon in Section V. In any case, when traders' AI practices are opaque and potentially manipulative, consumers' trust in the market seems to rest on a weak foundation.

Let us have a brief look at the instruments which lawmakers can use to expand or restrict the autonomy of different market actors. Earlier reference to the UCPD brings substantive rules on misleading and aggressive commercial practices to mind. Depending on the Member State, these can be enforced mainly through actions for an injunction brought by consumer organisations or through administrative decisions taken by consumer protection agencies.[63] So far Member States' procedural autonomy in this field has remained rather broad, and the European Court of Justice has not triggered the process of proceduralisation comparable to the one known from its case law on Directive 93/13/EEC on unfair terms in consumer contracts.[64] Notably, the recent 'New Deal for Consumers' package, adopted by the European Commission, puts emphasis on a more harmonised enforcement.[65] The proposed amendments to the UCPD refer to 'contractual and non-contractual remedies', which should be available to consumers harmed by

[60] R Brownsword, 'From Erewhon to AlphaGo: For the Sake of Human Dignity, Should we Destroy the Machines?' (2017) 9 *Law, Innovation and Technology* 117.

[61] ME Stucke and A Ezrachi, 'How Digital Assistants Can Harm Our Economy, Privacy, and Democracy' (2017) 32 *Berkeley Technology Law Journal* 1239; L Adam and H-W Micklitz, 'Information, Beratung und Vermittlung in der digitalen Welt' (2016) SVRV Working Paper No 6, available at www.svr-verbraucherfragen.de/dokumente/information-beratung-und-vermittlung-in-der-digitalen-welt/.

[62] Weatherill (above n 53).

[63] H-W Micklitz and G Saumier (eds), *Enforcement and Effectiveness of Consumer Law* (Springer, 2018).

[64] Council Directive 93/13/EEC of 5 April 1993 on unfair terms in consumer contracts [1993] OJ L95/29; see eg cases C-388/13, *UPC Magyarország*, ECLI:EU:C:2015:225, paras 57–59 and C-109/17, *Bankia*, ECLI:EU:C:2018:735. See also M Namysłowska and A Jabłonowska, 'Member States Interests and the EU Law on Unfair B2C and B2B Practices' in M Varju (ed), *Between Compliance and Particularism. Member State Interests and European Union Law* (Springer, 2019).

[65] COM(2018) 183 final.

unfair commercial practices, as well as penalties, which should be added to the menu of sanctions available to the competent public authorities (administrative or judicial).[66] One can discuss at length whether the proposed approach is right or wrong, needed or not. The bottom line remains that all of these measures are inherently reactive. Assuming that commercial practices relying on AI could be qualified as infringements of the UCPD, such infringements would first need to be identified, which considering the personalised and elusive nature of commercial practices in the digital age may not be so easy to do, at least not with the current tools. For consumers, the ability to unilaterally terminate the contract could be a way of reversing the consequences of decisions taken while being subject to an undue influence. Similarly, however, if this remedy is work, it cannot be difficult to seek. Perhaps some inspiration could be found in the interface between public and private enforcement of competition law, although yet again, this is a complex matter, which cannot be addressed here in due detail.

There is, however, more to this debate than the right mix of remedies under UCPD. We have already emphasised the need for an integrated reflection into different domains. The previous section mentioned some aspects of anti-discrimination law, suggesting this is to be a field where the cooperation between public and private stakeholders is especially promising. With respect to the topic addressed here – the impact on consumers' transactional decisions – the convergence of public and private interest is less pronounced, which possibly draws us towards more traditional tools of consumer protection, such as the ones discussed above. However, as we have seen, these are not without problems of their own. More importantly perhaps, they seem to address the crux of the problem, the impact on consumers' autonomy, only in a very indirect way – by providing for a fairly broadly phrased prohibition and ex post sanctioning in the hope of achieving a dissuasive effect. At the same time, in discussions about consumers and digitalisation, more and more attention appears to be directed to the ex ante perspective – what businesses can (or can be required to) do, also in a technological sense, to ensure that consumer autonomy is preserved. To be sure, this is not a dimension consumer law has not been preoccupied with so far: quite the contrary – various pre-contractual information requirements bear witness to its importance.[67] However, in more recent years, other tools, especially those of data protection law, are clearly gaining prominence. Specific requirements associated with consent, transparency and control over the use of data, or privacy by design and by default are some of the most emphasised themes.[68] With all the public

[66] COM(2018) 185 final, Art 1.

[67] See eg the discussions surrounding the adoption of Directive 2011/83/EU of the European Parliament and of the Council of 25 October 2011 on consumer rights, amending Council Directive 93/13/EEC and Directive 1999/44/EC of the European Parliament and of the Council and repealing Council Directive 85/577/EEC and Directive 97/7/EC of the European Parliament and of the Council [2011] OJ L304/64.

[68] See especially guidelines and opinions of Article 29 Working Party and the European Data Protection Supervisor.

attention devoted to the General Data Protection Regulation (GDPR)[69] they have been extensively explored and publicised. The impact on market practice is also visible. Now is the time to look at all these tools and their practical operation in still more detail and connect the respective debates.

VIII. Instead of Conclusions: Empowerment

All the discussion up to this point has been concerned with AI-powered and big data-fuelled tools, developed and used by big business and/or state exercising its policing power in criminal justice or tax collection. This is because, as of late 2018, actual usage of AI is almost exclusively the domain of corporations and the state. The reason is simple: creation of new AI applications is resource-intensive, requires substantial funding, and relies on the existence/creation of enormous data sets, readily available to online giants and law enforcement agencies. However, it does not have to be that way.

In the spring of 2016, one of us was eating an ice cream and enjoying the sun in the gardens of Villa Schifanoia in Florence, when Hans Micklitz – passing by – stopped and said:

> You know what? I think we should build a software that will read online terms of service and highlight unfair contractual clauses. These contracts are way too long for anyone to read; and consumer law is a mess. Everyone would be way better off if computers could do that'. The initial response was a list of reasons why this cannot work: we are not programmers, natural language is complex, law cannot be formalised … but Hans just raised his hand, stopped the outpour of scepticism, and said: 'instead of telling me why this cannot be done, make a list of conditions for making it possible. Let's try'.

Half a year later, a prototype of that software was finished,[70] and a year later an article with the theory of consumer empowerment using technology was published.[71] That piece of software did not rely yet on artificial intelligence; but the project did not stop there. In the summer of 2017 a new project – Claudette – was launched, with the ambition of automating the analysis of online terms of service[72] and privacy policies[73] using machine learning: all this within the paradigm of

[69] Regulation (EU) 2016/679 of the European Parliament and of the Council of 27 April 2016 on the protection of natural persons with regard to the processing of personal data and on the free movement of such data, and repealing Directive 95/46/EC (General Data Protection Regulation) [2016] OJ L119/1.

[70] The reader can download it at uterms.software/download/.

[71] H-W Micklitz et al, 'The Empire Strikes Back: Digital Control of Unfair Terms of Online Services' (2017) 40 *Journal of Consumer Policy* 367.

[72] M Lippi et al, 'CLAUDETTE: an Automated Detector of Potentially Unfair Clauses in Online Terms of Service' (2018), available at arxiv.org/abs/1805.01217.

[73] G Contissa et al, 'Claudette Meets GDPR: Automating the Evaluation of Privacy Policies Using Artificial Intelligence' (2018), available at papers.ssrn.com/sol3/papers.cfm?abstract_id=3208596.

empowering individuals and civil society using technology. This is Hans Micklitz in action. He is both a thinker, and a doer.

Within this spirit, we want to conclude the chapter with this message: artificial intelligence can and should be used to empower the individuals and the civil society. Clearly, the challenges it raises are real, and should be tackled by law and/or policy. However, legal and political response to the developments of artificial intelligence should not limit itself to addressing these challenges only. Law should also, if not even more, concentrate on enabling the creations of AI-powered systems to help empower the people. What would that mean?

In the domain of consumer law, individuals and civil society organisations enjoy numerous rights and competences. Countless information obligations give consumers a right to access information about the products and services they use. Unfair contractual terms rules give consumers and their organisations standing to challenge certain clauses in boilerplate contracts that create an imbalance of rights and duties to the detriment to consumers. GDPR contains numerous information duties for the data controllers, and so consumers (data subject) have a right to know who uses what data about them and for what purpose. Unfair commercial practices legislation enables us to challenge misleading and/or aggressive ads and offers. We have a lot of rights. But who has the time and the power to make use of them? Put provocatively, the problem of consumers and NGOs is not the lack of the powers, but rather too few resources and factual abilities to make use of them.

That is where AI can be of help. Reading of contracts and privacy policies can be automated. Analysis of what apps actually do can be automated. Communication with businesses and consumer protection bodies can be automated. We could imagine a world in which consumers are equipped with apps that read the agreements they accept for them, detect unfair clauses, and notify the companies and the enforcers. We could live in a world where ads are assessed for unfairness. We could live in a world where the exercise of many rights – for example, the right to object to data processing – is automatic. A large part of the work initiated by Hans Micklitz within this strand concentrated on outlining the theoretical preconditions for these developments, and presenting proof of the concept. On the technical side, we are not far from that world. The problem again is resources. What is needed, as of today, is an interdisciplinary collaboration of engineers and lawyers, and the financial means for engaging in costly development processes.

To paraphrase President Kennedy, who – as Hans Micklitz often reminds us – was one of the major figures in the development of the consumer law: ask not only what consumer law can do with artificial intelligence, ask what artificial intelligence can do for consumer law.

PART II

European Private Law and Access Justice in its Internal and External Dimensions

7

The General Transformations of Private Law Since Léon Duguit

Autonomy, Responsibility and Sovereignty in European Private Law

GUIDO COMPARATO* AND RÓNÁN CONDON**

This contribution compares the transformations taking place in European private law in recent years to the transformations first described a century ago in French legal scholarship confronted with the interpretation of the French Code Civil in a deeply changed social context. That scholarship, epitomised by personalities like Léon Duguit, challenged the dominant legal formalism, with its emphasis on the subjective right, insisting instead that private law and the state perform social functions. Duguit's legal functionalism remains a useful lens through which to examine contemporary transformations of private law and the state in an EU context. In fact, contemporary law is characterised by new economic, technological, and societal processes which produce an increased level of complexity linked to new 'transformations' of private law. This contribution thus highlights the characteristics of those transformations separated by a century of legal evolution attempting to trace them in the specific area of European private law. A considerable difference between 'then' and 'now' is that those processes of transformation that Duguit noted now take place beyond a territorially-defined state in the context of market-building in a supranational arena. This leads to a greater, and unimagined, blurring – if not bypassing – of the public-private divide. Duguit's 'legal theory without sovereignty' well describes these developments, but is now under pressure from renewed idealisms.

* Lecturer in Law at Birkbeck College, University of London.
** Assistant Professor in Law at Dublin City University.

I. Introduction

It is a common theme of legal scholarship that the law, both private and public, is in a continuous process of transformation.[1] Focusing on legal evolution in the European context, in particular, it was suggested a decade ago that private law is experiencing a transformation from autonomy to functionalism in competition and regulation.[2] The imprints of that development can be found in several arenas, as will be highlighted in the following pages of this chapter. Claims that contemporary law and society is undergoing deep and structural change are, of course, commonplace. What is more difficult is to make sense of these changes within a convincing analytical framework. When examining contemporary changes, one can look back to look forward. Looking back, then, the French legal scholar Léon Duguit sketched a plausible account of changes of private law and the state since the French *Code Civil*'s (hereinafter Code Civil) inauguration. He attempted to apply the lens of social science to law in an effort to explain the evolution of private law and the state in *belle époque* France and beyond. Our question is what can we still learn from Duguit's social and functional approach to law in the EU context? And, indeed, what if anything has changed? Before this can be done, however, it will be necessary to retrace Duguit's criticism of the *Code Civil* and its purported metaphysics.

II. Context: The *Code Civil* at 100

By the early 1900s, the *Code Civil* had entered its second century. Napoleon's enduring triumph was a product of Enlightenment rationalism and natural law. A bailiwick against the worst excesses of the *ancien régime*, it carved out a sphere of non-domination for the sovereign individual. If the *ancien régime* had revivified *imperium* in public law, the *Code* now revived the Roman concept of *dominium* in a recrudescent private sphere.[3] Thus, the sovereign individual whose political rights had been declared luminously in the *Declaration de droit de l'homme et du citoyen* (the Declaration of the Rights of Man and the Citizen) only a few years earlier found, in the *Code*, his civil rights from property, family, to contract and tort expatiated in some 2,881 articles. These rights were conceived at base as absolute, subjective rights. That is, rights that exclude the state from the private

[1] The word 'transformation' is deliberately chosen. For discussion of analogous notions such as 'legal change' and 'evolution', see A Watson, 'Comparative Law and Legal Change' (1978) 37(2) *The Cambridge Law Journal* 313; S Worthington et al (eds), *Revolution and Evolution in Private Law* (Oxford, Hart, 2018).

[2] H-W Micklitz, 'The Visible Hand of European Regulatory Private Law – The Transformation of European Private Law from Autonomy to Functionalism in Competition and Regulation' (2009) 28(1) *Yearbook of European Law* 3.

[3] L Duguit, *Les transformations générales du droit privé depuis le Code Napoléon* (Paris, Librairie Félix Alcan, 1912) 120.

sphere of market and family. Thus, in the words of the *Code Civil* property rights may be exercised '*de la manière la plus absolue*'[4] and contracts are acts of the will, private legislation that cannot be easily altered once freely entered: '*les conventions légalement formées tiennent lieu de loi à ceux qui les ont faites* …'[5] Not only was the state ringfenced, but the authority of the old corporations or guilds was sapped. By excluding the state and corporation from large fields of social activity, the great productive energy of society is unleashed as probably the most notable moment in that long historical process which was later characterised as a move from status to contract.[6]

But if the subjective right is a *sine qua non* for the emergence of a private law society, by the early-1900s the mood music had changed.[7] A century of industrialisation bequeathed mass labour movements, mass accidents, mass politics, vertically integrated firms, and the gradual centralisation of power in an increasingly bureaucratised state. By the early 1900s, the time was right to reassess legal and social change since the *Code*. Against this background, in a series of lectures given at the University of Buenos Aires in Argentina in 1911, Léon Duguit discussed the 'general transformations of private law' which took place since the *Code Napoléon*.[8] In his lectures, Duguit's primary contribution is methodological. He develops a coherent legal sociology, which he applies to private law. His starting-point is that in classical legal scholarship the individual, and indeed the state, is given a '*volonté*' – whether individual will or the '*volonté commune*'.[9] By founding public and private law on subjective right, it places individual and state apart from society. But neither conception, Duguit argues, is in step with '*la realité*'. Duguit's commonest refrain is that the state and the individual are a priori and metaphysical concepts projected on to law and society. He wishes instead to develop a scientific theory shorn of preconceptions, using legal cases and legislation as social facts to illustrate his counterpoint: that out of the individualism of Enlightenment Europe a social law is emerging.

By focusing on cases and legislation – constructing his theory bottom-up – the *a priorism* and metaphysics of natural law is replaced by an *a posteriori* and social scientific method.[10] With Comte and the *philosophes* he disparages, he views

[4] Code Civil, Art 554. 'Ownership is the right to enjoy and dispose of things in the most absolute manner, provided they are not used in a way prohibited by statutes or regulations'.

[5] Code Civil (above n 4) Art 1134. Agreements lawfully entered into take the place of the law for those who have made them'. Many Code Civil articles are devoted to the circumstances in which consent is vitiated, namely, duress, fraud and mistake.

[6] H Sumner Maine, *Ancient Law: Its Connection with the Early History of Society, and Its Relation to Modern Ideas* (London, John Murray, 1861).

[7] F Böhm, 'Rule of Law in a Market Economy' in A Peacock and H Willgerodt (eds), *Germany's Social Market Economy: Origin and Evolution* (London, Palgrave McMillan, 1989) 46.

[8] Duguit (above n 3).

[9] L Duguit, *L'État, Le Droit Objectif et la Loi Positive* (Paris, Thorin et Fils, 1901).

[10] It is hard to deny the heavy influence of Durkheim on this point, see E Durkheim, 'Rules for the Observation of Social Facts' in (WD Halls trans) *The Rules of the Sociological Method* (New York, Free Press, 1982) 60.

society as progressing in phases; with Durkheim, he views law through the lens of social solidarity.[11] The *Code Civil* is an epochal moment, to be sure, but to grasp contemporary law and society one should not elevate it to a totem. Social facts (*les faits*) vary with the effluxion of time. In Duguit's words, '*dans la réalité des choses, il y a une transformation continuelle et perpétuelle des idées et des institutions*',[12] and while the text of the *Code Civil* may not have changed, its meaning and scope varies under the pressure of these ineluctable societal forces.[13] The *Code Civil*, then, with all its symbolic value, represented for Duguit an important moment of comparison, a yardstick to measure how legal reality (*la realité*) had changed since 1804, not only in France but in all 'civilised' countries. Leaving aside references to the degrees of 'civilisation', particularly widespread at that time, Duguit projects far from a paean to the *Code Civil*, describes a newer and more recent transformation which marks a possible rupture with the traditional description of the whole global legal history of that time. Now, it is true that Duguit is not alone in theorising on the emergence of social law. He is part of a realist school of *avant garde* scholars.[14] What is distinctive in *les transformations du droit privé* is how Duguit systematically retraces the emergence of social law through property, contract and tort, tying this transformation to the idea of social interdependence or solidarity.

The greater societal complexity of early twentieth century society is given expression in new laws and re-interpretations, which limit the absolute rights of the *Code Civil* with respect to the social function. This has led, first, to a new social law mediating group, as distinct from individual interests, which reflects how society has developed since the *Code*. Each group has a social function to fulfil because greater factual interdependence necessitates new bonds of solidarity. What Duguit recognises, in essence, is a move from individualism to solidarity or 'socialism'.[15] Duguit issues an explicit and important disclaimer that the term does not coincide with socialism as a political doctrine. Second, Duguit, as primarily a public law scholar, links the changes affecting private law notions of contract, tort, and property to more general modifications affecting the state itself. Two years later he would go on to publish a new book, discussing this time the 'transformations of public law'.[16] In this sense, and following a 'social' approach to legal studies which had already taken root in Germany,[17] Duguit was able not only to

[11] ibid; Durkheim censured Comte's stadialism. While Duguit shared the idea of social progress with Comte, he did not think that contemporary society is an end-state.

[12] 'In social reality, there is a continual, ongoing transformation of ideas and of institutions'.

[13] Duguit (above n 8) 4–5.

[14] See O von Gierke, *Die soziale Aufgabe des Privatrechts* (Berlin, Springer, 1889).

[15] The difference with Durkheim, of course, is that Durkheim claimed that law functions as an agent of solidarity. However, how it achieves this depends on the structure of social relations more broadly. Duguit instead argues for evolution. For a comparison of Durkheim and Duguit, see R Cotterrell, *Emile Durkheim. Law in a Moral Domain* (Edinburgh University Press, 1999) 39.

[16] L Duguit, *Les transformations du droit public* (Paris, Armand Colin, 1913).

[17] See O von Gierke, *Die soziale Aufgabe des Privatrechts* (Berlin, Springer, 1889).

identify an evolution in the law but rather to link the profound social and political transformations of his time to the evolution of private law as well, even behind the seeming timelessness of the *Code Civil.*

That critical link between state and private law transformations, which Duguit first recognised, remains extremely prescient today, in particular taking into account tendencies towards functionalisation on the one hand and the phenomena of globalisation, supranationalism, and transnational network governance on the other hand, which rather appear to be weakening the link between state and law. But appearances may be deceiving because, as will be shown, transformation does not imply displacement. For these reasons, the rest of this chapter will attempt to re-read Duguit's transformations and relate them to the more recent transformations taking place in our current European society, 100 years after that move was first described. Before focusing squarely on contemporary European private law, in homage to Duguit's method, we will retrace twentieth-century law as our yardstick – like Duguit, looking back to look forward.

III. The Birth of the Social: Private Law and *La Fonction Sociale*

Léon Duguit was a professor in Public law at the University of Bordeaux in the same period in which Émile Durkheim lectured on social sciences at the same university and laid the foundations of sociology as an autonomous science. Leaving aside some differences between their approaches,[18] it is perhaps unsurprising that the two professors shared some common beliefs concerning the relationship between law and society. More precisely, Durkheim in social science and Duguit in legal science contested the universality of the law – and in particular of the *Code Civil* – rather suggesting that the law depended on society and evolved with it. Most importantly, Durkheim and Duguit share a common supposition that social facts such as the law must be explained in terms of their contribution to social integration. This requires setting aside a priori natural law concepts. A second shared supposition is that the more complex the society, the more *private* law is the means through which social solidarity is achieved. By examining the transformation of private law as *datum*, then, a window is opened onto the contemporary form social solidarity or interdependence takes.

The way concepts such as property, contract, tort, state and so on have evolved in legal practice then enables the social scientist to draw broader conclusions about societal integration. In *belle époque* France, where the universal ideals of Enlightenment and an authoritative view of sovereignty had already been merged within the framework of the *Code Civil*, the legal repercussions of the sociological

[18] See Cotterrell (above n 14) 39.

approach were likely to be received with suspicion or even hostility among traditional lawyers. Unperturbed, Duguit in *Transformations du droit privé*, declared that the *Déclaration des droits de l'homme et du citoyen* of 1789 and the *Code Napoléon* the main principles on which those texts were based, national sovereignty and the natural right of the individual, were in fact 'already dead'.[19] Duguit arrived at his conclusion by examining social facts, namely the evolution of case law and legislation from the *Code* onwards.

Thus, in his sixth lecture on propriety he documented a long list of limitations to the right of property, otherwise traditionally construed as 'absolute', which were continuously posed by the state whenever a public interest in intervening on private ownership emerged.[20] One of his main examples is *la loi du 28 juillet 1885*, and also *la loi du 15 juin 1905*. These laws allowed the state to install telephone technical infrastructure on private land without indemnity unless damage is caused. Such laws reflect how the formerly absolute right to property is increasingly qualified by the need to reconcile individual and group interests in society. Critical infrastructure in the social interest cannot be compromised by antiquated notions of property as exclusive right. The idea of a 'social function' of property would later become a common theme in legal scholarship, particularly in the aftermath of World War II, up to the point that the term was recognised even in constitutional charters, notably the Italian Constitution of 1946, as well as, following a particular development which will be discussed in the following pages, in the EU.

While the idea of 'social function' has been most discussed with regard to property, the same principle also applies to other areas of private law, including contract and torts. With regard to contracts, and more broadly *l'acte juridique*, the autonomy of the individual is recognised and safeguarded by the law only insofar as the 'goal' pursued by the individual is deemed worthy of protection by the legal system. It is not even sufficient that the goal is lawful; what is now required is that the pursued goal is one of '*solidarité sociale*', a goal having '*une valeur sociale*'.[21] Duguit's analysis goes further, in fact, by focusing on the empirical reality of the market of that time, in which technology and automation were creating new forms of contracting. Thus, he describes phenomena like the 'contracts of adhesion' and 'collective contracts', with the latter manifest both in '*concession de service public*' and 'collective labour contract'.[22] In those cases, Duguit claims that it is hard to apply the traditional category of 'contract' as based on private autonomy without subterfuge. Instead, Duguit refers to these contract forms as '*convention-loi*', a hybrid between

[19] L Duguit, *Law in the Modern State* (New York, BW Huebsch, 1919) XLI.

[20] MC Mirow, 'The Social-Obligation Norm of Property: Duguit, Hayem, and Others' (2010) 22 *Florida Journal of International Law* 191 suggests that much of Duguit's approach and analysis of the idea of property's social function was based on the approach developed by Henri Hayem in his 1910 doctoral thesis at the University of Dijon, *Essai sur le droit de propriété et ses limites* (Paris, Rousseau, 1910).

[21] Duguit (above n 3) 96.

[22] ibid, 127.

agreement and legislation. Similar developments had already troubled Durkheim, who noted that '*tout n'est pas contractuel dans le contrat*',[23] mentioning immediately afterwards – this time in possibly more conservative terms – that the only arrangements to be called contracts are those which have been freely agreed upon by the parties. A few years later, the private law scholar Emmanuel Lévy[24] would go one step further by noticing that in fact '*tous les contrats ont quelque chose de collectif*'.[25]

It is in describing these new forms of 'contracts' (*les faits*), as termed by traditional scholarship, that Duguit was able to draw a parallel between the evolution of the state and of private law: '*de même que disparaît l'autonomie de l'individu, de même disparaît la souveraineté de l'État*'.[26] The concession of public service contract illuminates the fact that the very role of the state was changing. By examining legal practice, as opposed to scholarly exegesis on the subjective right, it became clear that the state had transformed from the night watchman of the nineteenth century. The old-school liberalism, with its abstract notion of *imperium*, appeared inaccurate. Newer regulatory objectives demanded a more interventionist state, which was better described in functional than sovereigntist terms.[27] New elements such as most notably technological advancements and new social expectations engendered by them ('[t]he time is not far distant when every house will demand electric light',[28] says Duguit), created a new need for the state to be actively involved in the provision of those services. In this respect, the main ideas of Duguit are expressed in his writings dealing more specifically with the transformations of *public* law, later translated in English by Frida and Harold Laski.[29]

The radical idea of Duguit is that a conceptualisation of the state should do away with the notion of sovereignty. That concept appeared misplaced for a plurality of social and legal reasons. On the one hand, the pretence of making sovereignty reside in the nation appeared doubtful looking at the geopolitical reality; on the other hand, sovereignty is based on a notion of *imperium*, which does not appear to reflect the way in which the state concretely operated in society. In fact, the state will have, as it was beginning to do from the end of the

[23] É Durkheim, *De la division du travail social. Étude sur l'organisation des sociétés supérieures* (Paris, Félix Alcan, 1893) 230.

[24] On Lévy's sociology of law, see C Didry, 'Emmanuel Lévy et le contrat, la sociologie dans le droit des obligations' (2004) 56–57(1) *Droit et société* 151.

[25] E Lévy, *La vision socialiste du droit* (Paris, Marcel Giard, 1926) 99.

[26] Duguit (above n 3) 136. 'At the same time that individual autonomy disappears, so too does state sovereignty'.

[27] Elsewhere Duguit rails against the metaphysics of state sovereignty, which for Duguit personifies the state and obscures the social fact that state power is a relationship of domination in which sovereigntist rhetoric obfuscates the relationship of submission to superior force, see Duguit (above n 9) 9–10. 'Qu'on appelle Etat un groupement humain, fixé sur un territoire déterminé, ou les plus forts imposent leur volonté aux plus faibles, nous les voulons bien. Qu'on appelle souveraineté politique ce pouvoir des plus forts sur les plus faibles: nous y donnons les mains. Aller au-delà, c'est entrer dans l'hypothèse'. He continues, the state is 'une affirmation métaphysique, point de réalité': at 26.

[28] Duguit (above n 18) 47.

[29] ibid.

nineteenth century and more obviously at the start of the twentieth, to provide individuals with basic services like postal services, public light, transport, instruction. In this context, the state mostly has to 'organise' society rather than simply 'defending' it: 'the ruling class to-day must not only abstain from certain things, but must perform other things'.[30] To do that, the state might also require new forms of interaction with contracts. The idea of 'public service' should thus be the new basis of modern public law.[31]

If the transformation of contract and property is linked very closely to the changing role or function of state, tort law takes on a greatly enhanced position vis-à-vis these more established bodies of law. It will be recalled that while the *Code Civil* devotes 853 articles directly to property and contract, tort law (delict) is given short treatment in four articles:[32] Articles 1382–86. The core idea of classical tort law is that it is only those harms caused by another's subjective fault that give rise to non-contractual liability.[33] This is set out succinctly in Article 1382: '*Tout fait quelconque de l'homme, qui cause à autrui un dommage, oblige celui par la faute duquel il est arrivé à le réparer*'.[34] As Duguit argues, this concept of delict is consistent with the general commitments in the *Code Civil*: it is concerned with subjective fault or, in other words, the acting individual in the world who, deliberately or through his imprudence, harms another individual. Unless the harms that befall an individual can be imputed to the acts of another, then the loss lies where it falls as a consequence of *fortuna* or a lack of self-help.[35] However, tort law is not immune from the transformation of state and society. What social function, then, does tort law fulfil? For Duguit, the key conceptual move is from individual, subjective '*imputabilité*' to managing objective, social '*risque*'.[36] Classical, interpersonal law has not entirely disappeared, of course, but it has been supplemented by principles that aim to allocate the costs of accidents between individuals and groups.[37]

The most telling manifestation of this shift is from individual fault to strict liability for incidental accidents of industrialisation.[38] Duguit takes the *loi du*

[30] ibid, 29.

[31] ibid, 44.

[32] Directly, because other articles deal with intangible property.

[33] Subjective here means as a result of personal acts; it does not imply that the standard of care is based on the tortfeasor's state of mind.

[34] Any act whatever of man, which causes damage to another, obliges the one by whose fault it occurred, to compensate it.

[35] See F Ewald, *L'Etat Providence* (Paris, Grasset, 1986).

[36] Duguit (above n 3) 139.

[37] Very perceptive on this point: Albert A Ehrenzweig, 'Negligence without Fault' (1966) 54 *California Law Review* 1422, focusing on transformations within tort law, as distinct from supplemental legislation.

[38] This transformation rests on viewing accidents as incidental and statistically regular occurrences that can be controlled, rather than the unfortunate hand of providence. Duguit's sociological predecessor is Comte; in statistics, Quetelet – see Ewald (above n 33), and (S Utz trans) 'The Return of Descartes Malicious Daemon: An Outline of the Philosophy of Precaution' in T Baker and J Simon (eds), *Embracing Risk: The Changing Culture of Insurance and Responsibility* (Chicago, Univerisity of Chicago Press, 2002) 273.

9 avril 1898 (workplace accidents) as illustrating a deeper point. This law, very similar to those implemented throughout the industrialised West, effectively indemnified workers for workplace accidents by obliging employers to compensate them without proof of fault. The deeper point is that the drift of modern law is towards making those who introduce a risk liable for the accidents that are caused when these risks materialise in harm.[39] While society as a whole benefits from group activity, the members of these groups benefit more directly from their activities: '*Si celui-ci en a le bénéfice immédiate, il est juste qu'il supporte le risque que fait courir aux individus et aux autres groupes la mise en œuvre de cette activité*'.[40] Today, we refer to this as strict enterprise liability. Duguit's primary focus was on the idea that the groups that cause accidents are also those that benefit from these activities and his concept is of social justice for risk creation by groups. Consistent with his critique of *imperium*, the state in this view is also a group and liability should be placed at its door as much as that of enterprises. Neither 'metaphysical' concepts of *dominium* or *imperium* should obscure the fact that group activities generate social risks, which following his idea of interdependence should be assumed by the risk creator.[41]

His group-based theory is cogent if one focuses on the defendants of a tort action as placeholders for manufacturers, employers, the state, all of which now have social *duties* to fulfil. Duguit's contribution is remarkably prescient because, together with contemporaries such as Saleilles and Josserand, he notes that tort law in the twentieth century became a form of social or regulatory law.[42] While it is true that enterprise strict liability never fully or unambiguously displaced individual fault, it created a second track of 'organisational liability'. Duguit's blindspot, as we noted, is that if tort law is about dividing managing risks, between those groups who create risk and those who suffer their consequences, he underestimates that responsibility for causation (social justice) is not necessarily the only or, indeed, the most effective way to divide risk. In other words, the 'socialisation du droit' does not flow only towards strict liability.[43] This 'blindspot' is a consequence of his method, which attempts to explain all law as attempts to achieve social integration. His second prescient observation is that state sovereignty is an *a priori* and metaphysical concept and it should not exclude the development of tort law principles where its activities result in harm to individuals. These observations helped concretise a distinct state liability law in France and beyond. Once again, like his researches on property and contract, Duguit envisions an emerging organisational form of liability founded on social solidarity, which does not

[39] The doctrine of vicarious liability, or in French law *faute d'autrui*, is another clear example of this trend. For a comparative analysis, see P Giliker, *Vicarious Liability in Tort: A Comparative Perspective* (Cambridge, Cambridge University Press, 2010).

[40] Duguit (above n 3) 140. 'It is just that those who benefit directly from group [activity] should shoulder the risk that may harm other individuals and groups'.

[41] ibid, 139.

[42] D Green, 'Tort Law Public Law in Disguise' (1960) 38(1) *Texas Law Review* 251.

[43] Duguit (above n 3) 139.

distinguish between state or private actors. All are submitted to the need of rules for social interdependence.

Thus, by tracing changes to property, contract and tort (*les faits*) Duguit is able to note the changing role and function of state and society. Both the emergence of public services as the new goal of the state and the social function in the area of private law are both manifestations of the same basic truth: law is a manifestation of social solidarity and it is based on social interdependence[44] rather than individualism. For that reason, the system encapsulated in the *Code Civil*, regardless of its persistent black-letter rules, is no longer a reflection of the reality of the law, as it stands, or its underlying ethic of social justice.

IV. The Turn of the Twenty-first Century: Law and Society Above and Beyond the State

The twentieth century belonged to the social, but does the twenty-first? Duncan Kennedy suggests that, after the second globalisation of legal thought consisting of the success of 'the social', the law has more recently steered away from that phase, introducing a new era, or a third globalisation of legal thought, whose contours appear less clearly defined as the one of the preceding phases.[45] If that is true and the 'social' is disappearing – most manifest in the alleged crisis of the welfare state, which represented the clearest recognition of the rationality of the social[46] – is the analysis of Duguit still of any use in conceptualising a very different historical period characterised by a redefinition of legal thought and the eclipse of the state by functional transnational networks? How many of the ideas of interdependence and social function still play a role in particular in the current European law scenario?

One should start from the fundamental contribution of Duguit regarding the recognition of the link between private law and the State – as the law depends on society and the state represents the organised form of society. If Duguit noted that 'we have witnessed in the last half of the nineteenth century an immense economic change',[47] equally important changes took place in the twentieth, again of a technological, economic and in consequence societal nature. This has led to the emergence of newer goals which are pursued by public institutions. On closer inspection, this trend does not contradict Duguit's intuition. The French professor

[44] ibid, 26.

[45] D Kennedy, 'Three Globalizations of Law and Legal Thought: 1850–2000' in DM Trubek (ed), *The New Law and Economic Development. A Critical Appraisal* (Cambridge, Cambridge University Press, 2006) 19.

[46] M Camdessus, 'Worldwide Crisis in the Welfare State: What next in the context of Globalization?' Address by the Managing Director of the International Monetary Fund at a seminar organised by Observatoire Chrétien des Réalités Economiques Paris, France, 15 October 1998.

[47] Duguit (above n 18) XLII.

recognised that it was impossible to ultimately create a list of legitimate ends for the state to pursue: that would depend on the political and social needs of a particular moment, so it would be perfectly acceptable that, over time, a new society would develop newer ends. Claiming the contrary would negate the whole idea of legal transformation and absolutise certain public law principles, running against the whole starting point of the social dependence of the law, and, indeed, running against Duguit's scientific method. Private law, in that view, will always be open to the pursuit of further public policy objectives, as its internal rationality – now, just as in Duguit's time – cannot be described as entirely self-contained and fully autonomous.

It is clear that the debate between autonomists and instrumentalists is still very much alive, and while it is generally conceded that private autonomy does not exist in a vacuum, some public policy objectives might be deemed to be legitimate as functionalisations of private autonomy while others might not.[48] Without delving into those debates, it can only be mentioned here that, as new state policies develop, these interventions might be coloured by various ideological considerations, depending on the direction in which the state will want to steer individual behaviour. Thus, the use of terms like 'the social', 'socialisation', or even 'socialism' should not mislead us, as Duguit himself had warned us: the state might pursue objectives which are not 'socialist' at all in political terms but still based on the idea that one should pursue a 'social function'. A clear example of this possibility appeared a few years after Duguit: fascism admitted the functionalisation of individual conduct up to the suppression of freedom for overarching public reasons. In light of this, the preoccupation of Duguit of highlighting that 'socialism' did not refer to the political notion becomes particularly relevant, as the social does not coincide with the welfarist.

The second aspect in which the thought of Duguit is both actual and outdated resides in the role of the state in the economy. Describing the current tendencies of his time, Duguit predicted a growing involvement of the state in the regulation of private affairs. In his view, the state would become more and more involved in the provision of public services. In that regard, more recent trends showed that in fact the state has, up to a certain extent, withdrawn from the direct provision of those services. In the third wave described by Kennedy, the state has started relying more strongly on the market itself as the means through which social goals may be achieved. Services such as transport, education, energy, to name just a few, have in more recent years been outsourced to the market by privatisation and liberalisation. This has happened against the background of rising new economic ideals highlighting the importance of free markets as well as processes of transnationalisation

[48] The extent to which private law is closed in its own rationality or can pursue some further objectives is still debated, see the 'middle ground position' advocated by H Dagan, 'The Limited Autonomy of Private Law' and the comment to it by G Teubner, 'State Policies in Private Law? A Comment on Hanoch Dagan', both in (2008) 56(3) *The American Journal of Comparative Law* at 809 and 835 respectively.

of the economy, which seem to suggest an overall shift from 'government' to 'governance'.[49] Various attempts have been made in the literature to reconceptualise the role of private law in this changed 'after-Welfare State' context, in which the fading of the state let the question arise as to who should in practice functionalise private law.[50] Even if this development would appear to prove Duguit's prediction wrong, on a closer look this does not appear to be the case.

In the first place, the current trends of transnationalisation and globalisation confirm the loss of centrality of the notion of sovereignty as intended to be a prerogative of the nation and thus of the revolutionary nation-state. The current global scenario proves the increasing problems with a conception of statehood which makes the law coincide with the imposition of a state embodying a sovereign nation. Two tendencies appear relevant in that respect: supranationalism, as the development of institutions like the EU which produce an increasing amount of law and regulation impacting private relations; and transnationalism, as the norms produced by non-state actors beyond traditional systems of national law-making. Both developments pose a threat to an exclusively national conception of sovereignty as the one referred to by classical conceptions of public law, which indeed reveals itself to be ill-placed to make sense of the rules produced in those venues, sometimes hardly definable as 'law' despite their occasionally considerable prescriptive significance. While this breaks the link between state and private law, it does not break the more fundamental one between law and society, even if poses a challenge to it.

Alternative conceptualisations have been proposed, overcoming the public/private distinction and suggesting 'polycontexturality' as the relevant approach.[51] At all events, this does not contradict the transformation described a century ago, as the starting point of those analyses was in fact not the state per se, but rather society. For Durkheim, in fact, the political society is 'the complex group of which the state is the highest organ',[52] which does not mean that the state is the only form of social organisation capable of exerting power or possibly functionalising individual behaviours.[53] It is furthermore worth noting that these developments have not led to the extinction or an obsolescence of the concept of the state. Rather than disappearing, economists and political scientists alike rather point to a redefinition of its role. In that sense, Stiglitz has spoken of how globalisation impacted on the economic role of the state,[54] while a new strain of research has emphasised the importance of state support in the development of even the most innovative

[49] JN Rosenau and E-O Czempiel (eds), *Governance Without Government: Order and Change in World Politics* (Cambridge, Cambridge University Press, 1992).

[50] See P Zumbansen, 'Law After the Welfare State: Formalism, Functionalism and the Ironic Turn of Reflexive Law' (2008) 56 *American Journal of Comparative Law* 769.

[51] G Teubner, 'After Privatisation? The Many Autonomies of Private Law' (1998) 51 *Current Legal Problems* 393.

[52] É Durkheim, *Professional Ethics and Civic Morals* (London, Routledge, 1957) 48.

[53] Cotterrell (above n 14) 154.

[54] J Stiglitz, 'Globalization and the economic role of the state' (2003) 12 *Industrial and Corporate Change* 3.

technological industries.[55] In short, neither the state nor private law has disappeared; they have instead transformed.

In the second place, those developments had impacted directly on the 'social function' of private law. The retreat of the state from the provision of public services has coincided with an increase in the supervision and regulation of the private actors who provide those services in the market – regardless of their organisation in the form of a nation-state or not. The societal expectation in the provision of services has not disappeared and might, on the contrary, have rather increased, but those demands might have to be satisfied by non-state actors. The development went much beyond what Duguit introduced: in his view, the main functionalisation took place in the realm of property law, while the most relevant developments in the area of contract consisted of contracts of adhesion and collective contracts. We now clearly witness a functionalisation of private autonomy as well, while analogous developments take place in tort law. A few examples drawn from the European supranational experience will clarify this point.

V. Functionalisation of Contract Law

Private law has historically been employed as a nation-building and a market-building tool. The unification of law through the recognition of some basic principles allowed for the construction of nationally unified markets and later industrialisation, while it also served the symbolic need of unity necessary to the creation of the state.[56] Relatively more recently, attempts have been made to create private law codes at a supranational level.[57] While the Euronationalist attempt to propose the symbolic value of private law unification at the European level has proved to be an unfortunate attempt which has produced more resistance and hostility than acceptance, the function of market-building has been definitely more successful. The recognition of the four fundamental freedoms at the level of the Treaties had the immediate effect of extending party autonomy across European national borders, allowing private individuals and companies to more easily engage in contractual relations with other subjects in other European countries.[58] Just as this result was initially reached through market freedoms, later the process of creeping constitutionalisation of EU law created new umbrella principles allegedly encompassing freedom of contract. Article 16 of the Charter of

[55] M Mazzucato, *The Enterpreneurial State. Debunking Public vs Private Sector Myths* (Anthem Press, 2013).

[56] G Comparato, *Nationalism and Private Law in Europe* (Oxford, Hart, 2014).

[57] Communication from the Commission to the European Parliament and the Council, 'A more coherent European Contract Law. An action plan' COM(2003) 68 final.

[58] P-C Müller-Graff, 'Basic Freedoms – Extending Party Autonomy across Borders' in S Grundmann et al (eds), *Party Autonomy and the Role of Information in the Internal Market* (Berlin, Walter de Gruyter, 2001) 133.

Fundamental Rights of the EU in particular acknowledges a 'freedom to conduct a business' which was soon tested by scholarship and the CJEU as the possible constitutional anchorage for the protection of freedom of contract. This was made explicitly clear in 2013 in the *Sky Österreich* case, when the CJEU stated that the freedom 'covers the freedom to exercise an economic or commercial activity, the freedom of contract and free competition'.[59] All this would point in the direction of an increased reliance on freedom of contract and thus a return to the autonomy of the will of the individuals, back to a liberal individualistic conception of freedom of contract removed from the 'social' discourses of the 1900s. That is undoubtedly an aspect of the process of constitutionalisation of private autonomy, which has already led to criticism in the literature with specific regard to its repercussions in the area of labour law and must not be underestimated.[60]

At the same time, nonetheless, the process of constitutionalisation leads to further consequences. The first aspect, obviously, is the need to balance constitutional rights, so that freedom of contract will have to be interpreted also in light of other principles, possibly of a welfarist nature such as most notably the case of the right of housing.[61] More fundamentally, that balancing exercise is the demonstration that constitutionalisation means that freedom of contract will also have to be construed in light of the other goals pursued in the EU. This aspect becomes clear looking at the evolution of the concept in the case law of the CJEU. If *Sky Österreich* expressed the principle in the clearest terms in 2013, in fact the constitutionalisation, or rather marketisation, of autonomy, goes back to an older time. The case of *Nold* in 1974 is revealing. The case originated from the complaint of a German coal dealer that a decision of the European institutions restricting its economic freedom was infringing on freedoms safeguarded by the German Constitution, including personal freedom (Article 2) and right to private property (Article 14).

Leaving partially aside the important constitutional dimension of the dispute and focusing on its private law aspect, the complaint was thus apparently based on an individualist notion of the protection of freedom of contract according to which this should embed the power of an individual to do whatever it pleases. A form of 'negative' freedom to put it in Berlin's famous terms.[62] And yet, the European Court of Justice rejected that interpretation, on the contrary pushing towards a 'positive' notion of freedom of contract which recognises its functionality to overall social ends and values. The Court stated that:

> if rights of ownership are protected by the constitutional laws of all the Member States and if similar guarantees are given in respect of their right freely to choose and practice

[59] *Sky Österreich GmbH v Österreichischer Rundfunk*, Case C-283/11, para 42.

[60] G Davies, 'Freedom of Contract and the Horizontal Effect of Free Movement Law' in D Leczykiewicz and S Weatherill (eds), *The Involvement of EU Law in Private Law Relationships* (Oxford, Hart, 2012) 53.

[61] Case C-145/11, *Mohamed Aziz v Caixa d'Estalvis de Catalunya, Tarragona i Manresa (Catalunyacaixa)*; Case C-34/13, *Kušionová v SMART Capital as.*

[62] I Berlin, 'Two Concepts of Liberty' in I Berlin, *Four Essays on Liberty* (Oxford, Oxford University Press, 1969) 118.

> their trade or profession, the rights thereby guaranteed, far from constituting unfettered prerogatives, must be viewed in the light of the social function of the property and activities protected thereunder.[63]

Thus, as early as the 1970s, as economic freedoms are recognised they are also subjected to the limitations imposed, again, by the 'social function' of property. Even so, the social function is rooted less in notions of social justice and more in a market-building project.

The same reasoning, now covered by references to the freedom to conduct a business, has been employed to advance a variety of relevant aims of the EU. These have ranged from more traditionally 'welfarist' goals such as the protection of the worker,[64] to more recent attempts to regulate the developing information society.[65] In all these instances, the Court of Justice has not taken an a priori stance either in support of or against freedom of contract but has rather expanded or restricted it considering its particular social function. In fact, the Court has constantly referred to its new classic formula:

> freedoms are not absolute rights, however, but must be considered in relation to their social function. Consequently, restrictions may be imposed on their exercise provided that the restrictions correspond to objectives of general interest and do not constitute in relation to the aim pursued a disproportionate and intolerable interference, impairing the very substance of the rights guaranteed.[66]

It is in light of these considerations that it has been suggested in legal scholarship that private autonomy in the EU, while recognised on the one hand, it is necessarily 'framed'[67] or paradoxically 'regulated' on the other hand.[68]

The notion of social function of property thus lies at the core of the later development of the European case law functionalising even private autonomy. It would nonetheless be incorrect to infer the whole evolution of a concept from just the case law. Quite to the contrary, Duguit showed that the main functionalisation was coming from an increase of special statutes outside the code, and at the present day the most evident instrumentalisation of private autonomy is operated again by regulation – often including also the activities of independent regulatory agencies – to which the approach of the CJEU has offered legal justification

[63] Case C-4/73, *J Nold, Kohlen- und Baustoffgroßhandlung v Commission of the European Communities*, para 4.

[64] Joined Cases C-184/02 and C-223/02, *Kingdom of Spain and Republic of Finland v European Parliament and Council of the European Union.*

[65] Case C-275/06, *Productores de Música de España (Promusicae) v Telefónica de España SAU*, 2008 I-00271; Case C-70/10, *Scarlet Extended SA v Société belge des auteurs, compositeurs et éditeurs SCRL (SABAM)*; Case C-360/10, *Belgische Vereniging van Auteurs, Componisten en Uitgevers CVBA (SABAM) v Netlog NV*.

[66] *Spain and Finland v European Parliament and Council* (above n 64) para 52.

[67] N Reich, *General Principles of EU Civil Law* (Cambridge, Intersentia, 2014).

[68] G Comparato and H-W Micklitz, 'Regulated Autonomy between Market Freedoms and Fundamental Rights in the Case Law of the CJEU' in U Bernitz et al (eds), *General Principles of EU Law and European Private Law* (Alphen aan den Rijn, Kluwer Law International, 2013) 121.

through the above-mentioned decisions. Again, the areas which have been interested by phenomena of liberalisation and (only seeming) deregulation offer the clearest examples of that trend. The various directives issued by the EU in the area of private law also present the same aspect when it comes to the autonomy of the individuals: they are in the first place expanding it to the extent that they are meant to build an internal market, but they often do that by posing a series of conditions to the way in which that freedom has to be exercised.

Instruments through which private behaviour can be 'steered' include the imposition of information duties – one of the favourite approaches in large part of EU consumer law – a system of incentives and disincentives, as well as various rules of conduct with more or less bite. Fields which present highest risks coupled with higher social and economic relevance, such as notably in the case of the financial sector, present that aspect particularly clearly. Certainly, there is not only one strategy through which that objective is achieved. Therefore, in the case of consumer credit and mortgage law, we have witnessed a progressive shift from an approach based on the information paradigm to forms of regulation without clearly defined sanctions for non-compliance to, more recently, more defined sanctions. Similarly, the approach of the Markets in Financial Instruments Directive (MiFID, now MiFID II, and Markets in Financial Instruments Regulation or MiFIR) meant to impose 'know-your-customer' and 'know-your-product' obligations create a new level of control on the activities that can be performed by private individuals when these involve a considerable level of (systemic) risk.

The question here is not whether those approaches should be welcomed or not, or if they are sufficiently effective; what is more relevant to point out is that regulation (effective or not, controversial or not) is more incisively affecting private autonomy, further confusing the already blurred line between public and private law.

VI. Functionalisation of Tort Law

In EU liability law, what Duguit refers to as the '*conception traditionnelle*' is inapt. This traditional conception of private law (the individual) as *dominium*, and public law (the state) of *imperium* in public law[69] is gradually being displaced by a law of societal responsibility for third-party harms. This is distinct from 'the social', which was concerned with group-(social) justice in tort law. Instead, the EU (particularly the CJEU) is constructing a liability regime – in bits and pieces – that attempts to make society itself responsible for societal risks.[70]

[69] Duguit (above n 3) 120.

[70] Risks that do not simply materialise in the harm to concrete individual, but which following Beck, have society-wide consequences if they eventuate in harm. See U Beck, *Risikogesellschaft. Auf dem Weg in eine andere Moderne* (Frankfurt am Main, Suhrkamp Verlag, 1986).

This is achieved by expanding the addressees of liability in EU law. Private actors are given public or societal responsibilities (market making and regulation), while public actors are treated as if they were private actors (no sovereignty, liability without fault). These changes are most obvious in the case law surrounding the New Approach to Technical Standards, but functionalisation of roles (market building and regulation) is a wider phenomenon.

The two tracks of liability traditionally have been the Product Liability Directive (85/374/EEC) and state liability.[71] The Product Liability Directive is a break-even point, which is on the precipice between the social and the post-social thinking of the internal market project. Duguit would surely have recognised the underlying philosophy of this recital: 'liability without fault on the part of the producer is the sole means of adequately solving the problem, peculiar to our age of increasing technicality, of a fair apportionment of the risks inherent in modern technological production'. However, the justification for harmonising liability – the building of an internal market – would have been anathema to him because it is no longer rooted in social justice, but instead instrumentalises the individual to build markets. When these two concerns conflicted, it was the market that won out in cases such as *Commission v France*,[72] *Gonsales Sanchez*[73] and *Skov*.[74] On the other side, state liability is a residual remedy that is activated almost exclusively in cases where the state fails to implement EU law, but it has been enlarged in recent years into misapplication of EU law cases.

The interesting theme in state liability cases is that the state is not recognised as sovereign – instead, it is treated like an administrative agency which exercises discretion according to a test of sufficiently serious breach of EU law. These two branches of law are coalescing now in regulated markets for goods where state liability and private liability commingle – and are *supplemented* by a third and fourth route to liability, namely the responsibility of private actors for public functions and the possibility of individual responsibility in EU law.[75] The idea that rights have a social function remains; however, how social solidarity is achieved appears to require addressees of liability to fulfil, simultaneously, several functions – building a market and regulating the risks attendant to the market. In what follows, we will examine the slow emergence of what we refer to as the

[71] Council Directive 85/374/EEC, of 25 July 1985 on the Approximation of the Laws, Regulations and Administrative Provisions of the Member States Concerning Liability for Defective Products [1985] OJ L210 29, 30 (Product Liability Directive).

[72] Case C-52/00, *Commission v France* [2002] ECR I-3827.

[73] Case C-183/00, *Gonzalez Sanchez v Medicinia Asturiana SA* [2002] ECR I-3901.

[74] Case C-402/03, *Skov Æg v Bilka Lavprisvarehus A/S* and *Bilka Lavprisvarehus A/S v Jette Mikkelsen and Michael Due Nielsen* [2006] ECR I-00199.

[75] Case C-470/03, *AGM-COSMET Srl v Suomen valtio, Tarmo Lehtinen* [2007] ECR I-2749, see para 98: 'Union law does not preclude an individual other than a Member State from being held liable, in addition to the Member State itself, for damage caused to individuals by measures which the individual has taken in breach of Union law'.

third route to liability, namely the liability of private actors for failure to fulfil (traditionally) public functions.[76]

The New Approach to Technical Standards is an important testing ground for these claims. The New Approach at a most basic level provides market access in the absence of legislation on product standards. Instead, following the logic of *Cassis de Dijon*, mutual recognition of standards takes its place, which allows for proportionate measures in the name of health and safety.[77] The formulation of standards is largely assigned to private standardisation bodies, and compliance and monitoring is assigned to mostly private notification bodies in accordance with a notification procedure.[78] The relevant producer may then select a notification body from a list, which certifies product compliance at the pre-market stage and has some post-market compliance duties. The producer, in essence, contracts for compliance and monitoring with the notification body. Post-market, state regulatory bodies, also have duties to ensure compliance with standards.[79] The notification bodies are, in theory, supervised also by the public authority. The New Approach clearly solves a problem of decisional supranationalism by co-opting private actors into a regulatory framework that mixes private regulation and public supervision, bypassing the need for EU-level legislation, which would be cumbersome and inefficient. But who's liable if the system breaks down? Can Duguit help us?

One of Duguit's methods was to look to case law to develop theory. In his methodology, this is a posteriori as distinct from a priori. When we examine the case law we find an emerging law on the liability of secondary tortfeasors emerging 'in bits and pieces'. The most recent, relevant case is *Schmitt*.[80] In that case, the relevant question obtained to the liability of a notification body under the (old) Medical Devices Directive (Directive 93/42/EEC).[81] That Directive sets out several pre- and post-market surveillance requirements.[82] It will be recalled that Poly Implant Prothèse (PIP) went bankrupt after it emerged that their managing director had been fraudulently filling silicone implants with low-grade silicone, leading to accusations that it harmed women. The company, PIP, because it was insolvent, could not be pursued in national law or per the Product Liability Directive (organisational liability), so the claimants brought class action claims in a

[76] This theme is not only present in New Approach case law, but underpins cases such as *Viking* and *Laval*, as Azoulai noted several years ago: L Azoulai, 'The Court of Justice and the social market economy: The emergence of an ideal and the conditions for its realization' (2008) 45(5) *Common Market Law Review* 1335.

[77] H Schepel, *The Constitution of Private Governance: Product Standards in the Regulation of Integrating Markets* (Oxford, Hart, 2005) ch 2.

[78] For a more detailed, and nuanced, account see MP Egan, *Constructing a European Market: Standards, Regulation and Governance* (Oxford, Oxford University Press, 2001) ch 6.

[79] Public bodies may withdraw a product, but only in accordance with a strict procedure that requires notification of the EU Commission.

[80] Case C-219/15, *Elisabeth Schmitt v TÜV Rheinland LGA Products GmbH*, ECLI:EU:C:2017:128.

[81] Recently replaced by Regulation 2017/745.

[82] Annex II, sections 3.3, 5.3 and 5.4.

number of jurisdictions including France and Germany against *TÜV*, the notification body (secondary tortfeasor).

The relevant legal questions were whether, first, the Medical Devices Directive contemplates the liability of notification bodies and, second, whether this gives rise to individual causes of action or 'subjective' rights based on the Directive. The CJEU held that Directive 93/42/EEC did contemplate liability pursuant to the consumer protection dimension of the Directive. The Court noted that there was a general obligation to discharge surveillance powers with due care and diligence or else the obligations under the directive would be 'dead letter'.[83] However, following *Paul*,[84] it did not give rise to a subjective right based on EU law.[85] The Court, further, seems to equate recovery against the notification body and recovery against the state.[86] Thus, from the point of view of consumer protection, a rather unsatisfactory picture emerges: the CJEU held that while notification bodies and the state may be addressees of liability, based on an interpretation of the Directive, EU law creates an obligation, but national law must provide the corresponding right or cause of action.[87] Nonetheless, the import of such a judgment should not be underestimated – alongside the organisational liability introduced by the Product Liability Directive is an emerging governance or network liability of secondary tortfeasors which does not distinguish formally between private and public actors. In other words, all parties in the regulatory process – whether formally designated public or private have duties under EU law which, *ex hypothesi*, give rise to liability when they are breached. These may be breached on several legal bases – whether based on product liability law ('producer' liability), *qua* individual (*AGM.COS.MET*), *qua* state or *qua* 'private' certifiers fulfilling regulatory functions. This emerging law is taking small steps, to be sure, but it is important to bear in mind the underlying concept. That is, EU law imposes duties on parties not only to open markets, but to regulate them for risks.

What the CJEU focuses on is their *function* in an overall, transnational governance architecture of ex ante and ex post regulation. Duguit would surely have recognised this for what it is: yet another step in the erosion of the public-private

[83] See paras 44–46.

[84] Case C-222/02, *Peter Paul and Others v Bundesrepublik Deutschland* [2002] ECR I-9425.

[85] A number of scholars have noted, rightly I submit, that applying the *Schutznorm* reasoning in *Paul* outside of financial services is inappropriate: M Tison, 'Do not Attack the Watchdog! Banking Supervisor's Liability after Peter Paul' Financial Law Institute Working Paper Series 2005 02.26; N Reich, 'Product Liability and Beyond: An Exercise in "Gap-Filling"' (2016) 24 *European Review of Private Law* 619, 635.

[86] This is more transparent in AG Sharpton's Opinion, para 33 in discussing the limits of liability noting that the Product Liability Directive is not the only avenue for legal recourse in EU law: 'Plainly, however, that directive does not limit the obligations as to product safety to the manufacturer alone. … [it also] imposes a number of duties on Member States'. She further states that notified bodies must also be within the scope of application of the liability rule.

[87] See N Reich, 'Rights without Duties? Reflections of the State Liability Law in the Multilevel Governance System of the Community: Is There a Need for a more Coherent Approach in European Private Law' *EUI Working Paper Law 2009/10.*

divide, and, from a tort law perspective, the socialisation of risks. Micklitz might argue that this reflects a concept of societal responsibility, as distinct from social justice, where private actors incur liability for failing to fulfil public functions and public actors are submitted to the discipline of private law remedies on an equal footing with private actors.[88] More broadly, it is yet more evidence of the de-centring of the state in society and the challenges it poses in terms of developing liability rules for heterarchical regulatory networks.

VII. The Return of Sovereignty?

Duguit's analysis is grounded in a critique of the traditional notion of sovereignty. It is the attenuation of that principle which leads to the above-mentioned developments both in public and in private law, as *de même que disparaît l'autonomie de l'individu, de même disparaît la souveraineté de l'État*.[89] If these tendencies characterise the so-called second globalisation of legal thought, as described by Kennedy, the same trend of attenuation of sovereignty became more explicit in the third phase of that globalisation, characterised this time by a move towards neoliberalism and transnationalism. In that context, state sovereignty is confronted with new international, supranational, and transnational actors, challenging the state as the sole forum of law-making.

These additional layers of regulatory complexity aggravated the crisis of sovereignty – at least of external sovereignty – which even appeared too compromised with the disasters produced by aggressive forms of nationalism in the twentieth century, so that a 'mutual limitation of sovereignty' appeared as an effective way to ensure peace in Europe.[90] While the global reach of the economic system continues to underline the increased interdependence of countries and private actors at the transnational level, facilitated and intensified by the development of technology,[91] at the theoretical level system theory suggests the irreversibility of increased complexity, becoming the reference point for the conceptualisation of transnational law.

But this state of affairs is currently facing resistance. On the one hand, realist economists and sociologists continue sagaciously emphasising that, even in the transnational context, the state is in fact still the most relevant actor,[92] and that

[88] H-W Micklitz, *The Politics of Justice in European Private Law. Social Justice, Access Justice, Societal Justice* (Cambridge, Cambridge University Press, 2018).

[89] Duguit (above n 3) 136.

[90] J Habermas and J Derrida, 'February 15, or What Binds Europeans Together: A Plea for a Common Foreign Policy, Beginning in the Core of Europe' (2003) 10 *Constellations* 291.

[91] On the role of technology, J Stiglitz, 'Globalization and the economic role of the state' (2003) 12 *Industrial and Corporate Change* 3, 3.

[92] R Gilpin, *Global Political Economy. Understanding the International Economic Order* (Princeton, Princeton University Press, 2001) 15.

despite the attempts of liberalising the movement of factors of productions – one of the aspects which is suggested as being at the basis of transnationalisation – states in fact still keep a strong and sometimes dramatic control over the circulation of some of those,[93] so that transnational theorists might underestimate how states continue to pursue overt and covert mercantilist policies. On the other hand, international and supranational institutions are contested, as they are continuously challenged by the changing preferences of sovereign states. The EU, with its reliance on a 'pooled sovereignty'[94] and its extensive liberalisation of factors of productions, is in fact also crossed by sovereigntist tendencies, either of a nationalist identitarian or a national democratic inspiration, which question its existence or its current supranational structure, regarded as oppressive either of national identities and therefore as a threat to the 'nation state', or of social conflicts and therefore as a threat to the 'welfare state'.[95] In this intricate political scenario, in which the interconnections of external and internal sovereignty become more visible,[96] is Duguit's view of private law, which takes as its starting point a critique of sovereignty, still relevant?

Even leaving aside the most evident instances represented by the defeat of the idea of a common European sales law, repercussions for private law are immediate: the question is whether a sovereign state which is pursuing a protectionist policy accepts forms of instrumentalisation of private autonomy meant to build an internationally competitive market? Will a domestic court award damages based on the economic considerations of a transnational standardisation body instead of its own criteria of justice possibly rooted in specific social notions of the good? Is national democracy even compatible at all with international economic integration, to the extent that the latter limits the room for manoeuvre of the former?

As Hans Micklitz has pointed out, in any case, there does not appear to be a 'safe way back' to the nineteenth or the twentieth century.[97] Neither do the current sovereigntist tendencies – if there is anything inherently new about the message, considering the uninterrupted relevance of the state in world politics – necessarily point to the imminent reversal of the so-far described transformations of private law. Duguit's critique of sovereignty was not primarily inspired by ideological preferences – even despite the particular historical period in which

[93] A Borón, *Empire and Imperialism. A Critical Reading of Michael Hardt and Antonio Negri* (London, Zed, 2005) 42.

[94] RO Keohane, 'Ironies of Sovereignty: The European Union and the United States' in JHH Weiler et al (eds), *Integration in an Expanding European Union. Reassessing the Fundamentals* (Oxford, Blackwell, 2003) 312. The idea is most recently discussed by B Fekete, 'The Limits of Sovereignty Pooling: Lessons from Europe' in M Belov (ed), *Global Constitutionalism and Its Challenges to Westphalian Constitutional Law* (Oxford, Hart, 2018) 133.

[95] A Somma, *Sovranismi. Stato, popolo e conflitto sociale* (Rome, Derive Approdi, 2018).

[96] C Eckes, 'The reflexive relationship between internal and external sovereignty' (2015) 18(1) *Irish Journal of European Law* 33–47.

[97] H-W Micklitz, 'The Legal Subject, Social Class and Identity-based Rights' in L Azoulai et al (eds), *Constructing the Person in EU Law. Rights, Roles, Identities* (Oxford, Hart, 2016) 290.

he wrote – but instead on pragmatic considerations relating to organic solidarity: looking at *la réalité* of his time, which had less to do with the position of France in the international context and more with the development of industrialisation and the simple desire of the citizens to have electricity provided in their houses. By those lights, the renewed appeal of nineteenth-century sovereignty cannot coincide with the restatement of nineteenth-century law. Society has become too complex – this is Duguit's message – for simple, ideological solutions to societal problems.

There is surely a lesson to be learned for scholars faced with contemporary upheavals brought about by intensified transnationalism in law and economy. For Duguit, and for contemporary scholarship, grounding legal analysis on a pragmatic look at the reality of social facts, with a (post)modern sensitivity to the '*réalité*' that many of those facts are not given but constructed, resounds as a valuable suggestion for resisting the symbolic appeal of renewed, but atavistic, political idealisms. New ways to re-embed the social in a transnational setting are required. In this respect, private law has an important but unrealised role to fulfil.

8

Some Reflections on the Self-Sufficiency of European Regulatory Private Law

MARTA CANTERO GAMITO* AND FEDERICO DELLA NEGRA**

I. Introduction

The European Regulatory Private Law (ERPL) project, and hence ERPL as a concept, was built around four pillars (hybridisation, self-sufficiency, convergence, and conflict and resistance).[1] Within the ERPL project, we have discussed 'self-sufficiency' at length.[2] In this chapter, we merely give some brushstrokes of our research as part of the project and provide our own reflections on self-sufficiency, the concept that has accompanied us throughout our PhD journey. We present self-sufficiency in two specific sectors of internal market regulation: electronic communications (more commonly known as telecommunications) and investment services.

This chapter, which is a result of joint research conducted by the authors, proceeds as follows. Part II introduces the idea of the self-sufficiency of ERPL. Then we go on to examine self-sufficiency in our respective sectors, telecoms and investment services. Accordingly, part III has been drafted by Marta and part IV has been drafted by Federico. Some reflections on self-sufficiency are provided at the end of the chapter by way of conclusion.

* Assistant professor of law at CUNEF (Madrid) and Associate professor of IT law at the University of Tartu.

** Federico Della Negra obtained his PhD in Law at the EUI and is a legal counsel at the European Central Bank. The views expressed in this article are purely personal, and they are in no way intended to represent those of the ECB.

[1] See H-W Micklitz, 'A Self-Sufficient European Private Law – A Viable Concept?' in H-W Micklitz and Y Svetiev (eds), *A Self-Sufficient European Private Law – A Viable Concept?* (2012) *EUI Working Papers Law* 2012/31.

[2] We fondly remember the well-spent afternoons in Sala Europa, Capella, and even Hans' office, in Villa Schifanoia.

II. The Self-Sufficiency of ERPL

Self-sufficiency in ERPL is understood as an all-inclusive discourse that encompasses and embraces an entire legal sector since its birth (law-making) up to its enforcement under a sector-specific logic.[3]

Our role within the project was to test the self-sufficiency hypothesis in our respective sectors. Self-sufficiency, thus, became the perspective from which to examine ERPL. It ought to be also understood as a form of interaction between ERPL and national private law.

Self-sufficiency has a descriptive and a normative meaning.[4] First, it describes the emergence of a broad set of rules that have remained largely separate from traditional private law and, instead, are to be found within sector-specific regulation. This sectoral approach resulted in the creation of regulatory silos, which are difficult to reconcile with the 'almost mythological image of systematics and coherence of traditional national private law'.[5] Second, it claims that it is wrong to keep this large regulatory framework separate from the traditional national private laws.[6] This normative claim is important, in that it underlines the need to ensure, even when EU law does not expressly harmonise national private laws, a minimum level of effectiveness of EU law and effective judicial protection for EU citizens.

Apart from operating under the logic and rationale(s) of the sector concerned, a self-sufficient ERPL manages its way to operate with minimal interaction with national actors.[7] The thesis of a self-sufficient ERPL proposes that the principles and rules adopted by the EU in specific sectors of the internal market are autonomous from the national private law rules applicable in these markets.[8]

Hans developed the concept of self-sufficiency in the context of a potential 'transformation of private law from autonomy to functionalism in competition and regulation'.[9] In essence, while the national private law enshrined in the nineteenth century codifications is largely based on the principle of private autonomy, ERPL is based on the need to achieve market integration. This goal affects (the purpose of) national private law, re-orientating it towards the achievement of the internal market. Moreover, in contrast to the private law principles contained in those civil codes, there is also room for social policy elements within ERPL. ERPL is based on the idea of 'access justice'.[10]

[3] H-W Micklitz and D Patterson, 'From the Nation State to the Market: The Evolution of EU Private Law' (2012) *EUI Working Papers LAW* No 2012/15, at 14.

[4] JM Smits, 'Self Sufficiency of European (Regulatory) Private Law: A Discussion Paper' in Micklitz and Svetiev (above n 1) 83, 86.

[5] H-W Micklitz et al, 'The Regulatory Character of European Private Law' in C Twigg-Flesner (ed), *Research Handbook on EU Consumer and Contract Law* (Cheltenham, Edward Edgar, 2016) 44.

[6] Smits (above n 4) 83, 86.

[7] Y Svetiev, 'Dimensions of Self-Sufficiency' (2013) *EUI Working Papers LAW* No 2013/05.

[8] Micklitz (above n 1) 6.

[9] Micklitz and Svetiev (above n 1) 6.

[10] H-W Micklitz, 'Social Justice and Access Justice in Private Law' (2011) *EUI Working Paper LAW* No 2011/02.

Access justice is the EU model of justice that enables market access for citizens and consumers, especially those most vulnerable, where national private law is not capable of providing such access. However, while access justice is a concept different from the different Member States' models of social justice, domestic private law regimes can complement it.[11] This recent development in Hans' access justice thesis is crucial for the understanding of self-sufficiency.

Self-sufficiency is not a binary concept. This means that the self-sufficiency of ERPL does not work towards total independence but towards providing minimum requirements of market access (safety net), capable of functioning independently from national private law but not necessarily without it. Such a baseline is pervading (intrusion) and challenging the domestic understanding(s) of justice (substitution) in such a way that national private legal orders will eventually come together. In order words, ERPL sets the foundations for the harmonisation of European private law.

Testing self-sufficiency was indeed a challenging exercise. However, this does not mean that it was not an enjoyable trip. Methodologically, disclosing evidence of self-sufficiency was something that could not have been done without empirical research – we needed to understand what was going on inside each sector. Within the ERPL project, and with the invaluable help and support of one of Hans' dearest colleagues, Thomas Roethe, we were determined to find out the 'stable practice'[12] to be found inside each silo. The following sections summarise those findings.

III. Self-Sufficiency in EU Electronic Communications

Private law has suffered a transformation in many ways. One of them comes from the liberalisation of formerly publicly provided utilities. Electronic communications have been regulated at EU level in a comprehensive way, including the regulation of private law relations that take place among participants of telecommunications markets. Overarching principles for the telecoms sector such as universal service and non-discriminated access greatly define the context of contractual relations arising from transactions within the sector. In this manner, the examination of ERPL in the EU telecoms sector reveals that contract law elements in the EU regulatory framework for electronic communications contribute to achieving regulatory goals, ie they perform a regulatory task. This regulatory function redefines the confines and purposes of traditional private law.

In the telecoms sector, the interaction between private law and its new regulatory task is articulated through the institutional and procedural structure devised for electronic communications in Europe. The regulation and practice of the sector

[11] H-W Micklitz, *The Politics of Justice in European Private Law* (Cambridge, Cambridge University Press, 2018).

[12] Smits (above n 4) 86.

follow a sector-specific logic. For example, the resolution of disputes and generation and application of substantive rules usually follows sector-related patterns. Here, not only the substance of the rules, but also their sector-specific regulatory governance, are devised to deliver regulatory and policy outcomes. This requires considering sector-specific contract rules from their making to their enforcement or, in Hans' words, 'from cradle to grave'. Accordingly, this part of the chapter illustrates the impact over the three layers that underpin the postulates of self-sufficiency: making, substance and enforcement.

A. Law-Making

From the perspective of law-making, the starting hypothesis is that telecommunications regulation involves its own sector-specific decision-making and implementation procedures, largely intended to give effect to the substantive provisions to achieve regulatory outcomes. It is in the making of telecommunications regulation that its contractual provisions are instrumentalised in order to serve the desired regulatory functions.

Liberalisation entailed a shift from national regulation to supranational law-making in formerly public services. The opening of the market (Article 106 TFEU) and consumer protection (Article 169 TFEU) provided the legal basis for the first generation of EU telecommunications rules. But priorities have evolved over time, and while the promotion of competition and consumer protection were still main priorities, the second (2002) and third (2009) packages of EU telecommunications rules were more focused on the regulatory harmonisation of the internal market for telecoms based on Article 114 TFEU.

Similarly to energy and financial regulation, the level of technical complexity of the telecoms regulatory framework involved the establishment of National Regulatory Authorities (NRAs) to oversee the regulatory process at national level. NRAs were established as a way of securing liberalisation via the establishment of an overly sophisticated institutional design. Additional supervisory mechanisms at EU level were put in place, including the creation of a network for cooperation in regulatory affairs. This network has reached its most advanced stage so far with the establishment of the Body of European Regulators for Electronic Communications (BEREC) in 2009. BEREC is the outcome of the path dependency of a set of practices that were followed in previous years, which first emerged as informal cooperation with the creation of the Independent Regulators Group (IRG) and that was later institutionalised under a formal organisation fostered by the European Commission, the European Regulators Group. BEREC was originally meant to be a European agency. Instead, its current structure is the result of political fragmentation. However, the reality is that BEREC, as a forum of regulators, in combination with other sector-specific supervisory mechanisms, delivers a high level of regulatory convergence, with the advantage of bypassing complex political commitments such as those associated with the establishment of a fully-fledged European Agency and the problematic task of endowing it with competencies.[13]

The empirical research conducted revealed that the dominant task to achieve sector-specific regulatory goals influences the interplay between NRAs and the EU and that hierarchy, and hence centralisation, is the only option for the EU legislator to achieve sector-specific outcomes.

B. Substantive Law

The underlying hypothesis when it comes to substantive law is that the described regulatory approach pervades and even shapes substantive rules. Contract law rules contained within telecommunications regulation appear to pursue a broader set of functions as opposed to the traditional functions of private law.

The internal market has been the driving force behind the private law found in regulated sectors, and contracts have become an instrument of higher policy (and regulatory) objectives. Contract law becomes competitive contract law.[14] Consequently, sector-related rights and remedies for private parties must be read in light of regulatory goals. Private law here seems to be used for economic regulation under a public interest rationale, eg universal access and end-to-end connectivity.

Market access is the key. For instance, under telecommunications regulation, there is an obligation to grant access and interconnection to the network infrastructure to alternative operators and to ensure access to all consumers who request it. This has influenced contracts in two ways. On the one hand, a competitive internal market approach has developed contractual elements oriented to the empowerment of the consumer. On the other hand, a universal service approach has strived for the protection of the most vulnerable consumers.

The self-sufficiency idea is then based on the assumption that sector-specific elements of contract law differ from traditional private law because certain mandates, such as obligations to contract to preserve universal access, are not found anywhere within traditional private law rules or civil codes. The different national private legal regimes and general contract law seem to be insufficient to fulfil the regulatory role of contracts in the telecoms sector. Additionally, following the principle of national procedural autonomy, EU law is not supposed to provide for European remedies. However, the introduction of the possibility to switch for free provided as part of the Universal Services Directive would serve as a basis

[13] By way of example, the conferring of powers to the European Securities and Markets Authority (ESMA), which gave rise to Case C-270/12, *UK v European Parliament and Council* (ESMA case), ECLI:EU:C:2014:18. See also Case C-217/04, *UK v European Parliament and Council* (ENISA case), ECLI:EU:C:2006:279.

[14] H-W Micklitz, 'The Concept of Competitive Contract Law' (2005) 23 *Penn State International Law Review* 549, 555.

for new remedies (intrusion), and ultimately replacing (substitution) national civil remedies, eg switching operators at zero cost as a sector-related remedy.

A competitive internal market approach yields new elements for private law. A clear example is the right to switch service providers. On the other hand, a universal service approach is far removed from traditional private law, where the freedom of contract is the ultimate rationale and imposes obligations to contract as a safety net for vulnerable consumers. Accordingly, in regulated markets, contract law provisions are isolated from consumer law and although they further certain redistributive goals, contract law provisions in regulated markets are a *lex specialis*. Indeed, private and civil law regimes remain applicable to telecommunications contracts even by traditional judicial schemes of enforcement. Yet, different approaches yield different outcomes, because they are built according to different rationales. It is also evident that new (specialised) bodies have emerged for the enforcement of the sector-related provisions, especially for the resolution of business-to-business (B2B) and business-to-consumer (B2C) disputes arising in connection to the provision of telecommunications services.

Contractual relationships ought to be interpreted according to public law considerations. As a result, the existence of a sector-specific rationality creates tensions between the public and the private domain (public vis à vis private principles). The lines between public and private law get blurred.

C. Enforcement

The successful application of substantive rules depends on the effectiveness of its enforcement system. In the telecoms sector, as in consumer-related disputes in general, only a few disputes reach the courts. This is due to the fact that, at least in telecommunications, the adjudication of private law disputes is moving away from courts to extra-judicial enforcement, giving a significant role to Alternative Dispute Resolution (ADR) and even administrative enforcement in the form of regulatory adjudication. The vast majority of telecoms-related disputes are resolved via extrajudicial mechanisms in both market levels, wholesale (B2B) and retail (B2C). In fact, the establishment of out-of-court procedures was a requirement of the EU legal framework for telecoms. This requirement seems to be used as one of the many other political strategies to advance internal market-building processes.[15] It remains to be seen, however, if it really enhances consumers' confidence and consumer protection in the market.

The enforcement of telecommunications rules largely relies on sector-specific dispute settlement in an attempt to more effectively give effect to the substantive

[15] ADR is one of the levers to boost and strengthen the internal market; see COM (2011) 206 final, pp 9–10.

law provisions contained therein. In other words, sector-specific mechanisms for the resolution of telecoms-related disputes are also regulatory oriented. Be that as it may, the examination of the use of out-of-court mechanisms for the resolution of telecoms-related problems could serve as an illustration of a process of 'de-judicialisation';[16] the enforcement of EU law is moving towards softer solutions coming from public and private bodies other than courts.

The goal-enforcing role of regulation, traditionally assigned to public bodies, is now shared with enforcement by private parties. The civil judiciary appears to be relatively ill-suited to deliver regulatory outcomes and therefore it adopts a residual role in the enforcement of telecoms-related contracts. In view of this, the regulatory role of the judiciary in the telecoms sector, while remaining an option, is superseded by the more prominent role given to out-of-court dispute settlement schemes. It is also observed that some sector-specific schemes for dispute settlement are based on trust and non-legal categories as an externality of the reflexivity of the sector. Beyond private civil law enforcement, sector-specific schemes for dispute resolution seem more effective.[17]

To conclude, this brief exposition of the transformations operated in the making, substance and enforcement of contract rules in telecoms from the perspective of self-sufficiency sketches the wider transformation(s) of private law. The rationality of the sector permeates the entire legal discourse (public and private) while providing a justification for the incorporation of regulatory elements into private law and vice versa. Consequently, it is contended that the sharp distinction between private law and public regulation is no longer relevant.

IV. Self-Sufficiency in Investment Services

In the investment services sector too, an evolving EU regulatory framework, which has become more and more specific, prescriptive and intrusive for private autonomy, co-exists with national private laws, which apply horizontally to all private relations. More importantly, in the absence of EU rules on remedies and procedures, these rules are provided for by national private law. The problem that arises in investment services regulation is whether and to what extent general private law concepts (eg good faith, duty of care, causation) should be used to 'enforce' sectoral EU requirements.

Investment services regulation is a privileged point of view from which to assess the concept of self-sufficiency in EU law. Investment services have been

[16] H-W Micklitz, 'The Visible Hand of European Private Law – The Transformation of European Private Law from Autonomy to Functionalism in Competition and Regulation' (2009) 28 *Yearbook of European Law* 3.

[17] M Cantero-Gamito, 'Dispute Resolution in Telecommunications: A Commitment to Out-of-Court' (2017) 25 *European Review of Private Law* 387.

subject to an increasing number of regulatory requirements in order to achieve the internal market and to protect investors. The global financial crisis triggered a new wave of harmonisation.[18] However, in spite of the large detriment suffered by retail investors due to misconduct in the wake of the global financial crisis, the EU did not introduce an express private law remedy for breaches of these requirements.

Against this backdrop, the following pages seek to understand whether and to what extent it is possible to identify a self-sufficient, or autonomous regulatory regime for investment services in the EU, exploring the law-making, substantive law and enforcement dimensions. The main focus of this research is the MiFID II,[19] which was adopted on 14 April 2014 and entered into force on 3 January 2018, repealing the MiFID I.[20]

A. Law-Making

Law-making in investment services regulation is based on the four-layer regulatory approach set out in 2001 by the so-called Lamfalussy Report.[21] According to this regulatory approach, the ordinary legislative procedures of Article 294 TFEU should be used only to set out regulatory principles (level 1) and the Commission should then adopt detailed rules by means of delegated or implementing acts under Articles 290 and 291 of the TFEU (level 2). Specialised administrative bodies should be in charge of providing non-legislative guidance to market participants via soft-law acts (level 3) and the Commission should ensure through appropriate enforcement actions Member States' compliance with binding EU law (level 4).

Before the global financial crisis, the Committees of national regulators (or Lamfalussy Committees) provided non-binding guidance to the Commission for adoption of Level 2 acts and soft law for Level 3 acts. In particular, the Committees of European Securities Regulators (CESR) enhanced convergence in national supervisory practices, mainly through guidelines and Q&As,[22]

[18] See in particular M Andenas, 'Harmonising and regulating financial markets' in M Andenas and C Baasch Andersen (eds), *Theory and Practice of Harmonisation* (Cheltenham, Edward Elgar, 2012) 1.

[19] Directive 2014/65/EU of the European Parliament and of the Council of 15 May 2014 on markets in financial instruments and amending Directive 2002/92/EC and Directive 2011/61/EU (MiFID II) [2014] OJ L173/349.

[20] Directive 2004/39/EC of the European Parliament and of the Council of 21 April 2004 on markets in financial instruments amending Council Directives 85/611/EEC and 93/6/EEC and Directive 2000/12/EC of the European Parliament and *of the Council and repealing Council Directive 93/22/EEC* (MiFID I) [2004] OJ L145/1.

[21] Final Report of the Committee of Wise Men on the Regulation of European Securities Markets 2001 (Lamfalussy Report).

[22] See P Schammo, *EU Prospectus Law. New Perspectives on Regulatory Competition in Securities Markets* (Cambridge, Cambridge University Press, 2011) 21.

but proved to be ill-suited to ensure adequate cooperation and information exchange between NCAs and to take effective actions to ensure a consistent application of EU law.[23]

To overcome these deficiencies, the co-legislators established, on the basis of Article 114 TFEU, the European Supervisory Authorities (ESAs) – European Securities and Markets Authority (ESMA), European Banking Authority (EBA), European Insurance and Occupational Pensions Authority (EIOPA) – with the main objective 'to protect the public interest by contributing to the short, medium and long-term stability and effectiveness of the financial system, for the Union economy, its citizens and businesses'.[24] The ESAs, together with the ESAs Joint Committee, the national competent authorities (NCAs) and the European Systemic Risk Board (ESRB) form the European System of Financial Supervision (ESFS).

The ESAs not only provide technical advice to the Commission for the adoption of delegated acts, but they may also adopt, upon legislative delegation, draft regulatory and implementing technical standards which have to be endorsed and enacted by the Commission, in the form of delegated or implementing acts, under Articles 290 and 291 of TFEU, to acquire binding legal effects. In order to respect the limitations set out by the *Meroni* judgment,[25] and substantially reaffirmed in the 'short-selling judgment',[26] the ESMA Regulation specifies that these standards shall be technical and shall not imply strategic decisions or policy choices.[27]

In relation to MiFID II ESMA gave its technical advice to the Commission for adoption of Level 2 legislation.[28] The technical advice covered a large part of the conduct of business rules, including product governance obligations and product intervention powers. In fact, the EU legislators favoured the instrument of delegated acts to implement conduct of business rules and confined draft regulatory technical standards to certain technical aspects of the best execution rule.[29] This may suggest that the development of Level 2 conduct of business rules was perceived as a potentially controversial matter, involving policy choices.

[23] See J De Larosière, *Report* (Brussels, 25 February 2009) para 162.

[24] Art 5(1) of Regulation (EU) No 1095/2010 of the European Parliament and of the Council of 24 November 2010 establishing a European Supervisory Authority (European Securities and Markets Authority), amending Decision No 716/2009/EC and repealing Commission Decision 2009/77/EC (ESMA Regulation) [2010] OJ L 331/84.

[25] Case C-9/56, *Meroni v High Authority*, ECLI:EU:C:1958:7.

[26] *UK v European Parliament and Council* (above n 13).

[27] Art 10(1) and 15(1) ESMA Regulation. For the difference between regulatory and technical standards see in more detail T Tridimas, 'Financial Supervision and Agency Power: Reflections on ESMA' in N Shuibhne and LW Gormley, *From Single Market to Economic Union: Essays in Memory of John A Usher* (Oxford, Oxford University Press, 2012) 70.

[28] ESMA, Final Report. ESMA's Technical Advice to the Commission on MiFID II and MiFIR. 19 December 2014. ESMA/2014/1569.

[29] Art 27(10) MiFID II.

B. Substantive Law

With regard to the substantive law aspects of investment services regulation, self-sufficiency could be measured with regard to the type and scope of harmonisation.[30] When harmonising national laws in a particular field of its competence, the EU may decide to grant the Member States the right to impose stricter requirements where necessary to achieve a specific objective (minimum harmonisation), or to prohibit the Member States from doing so, typically to ensure a level playing field (maximum harmonisation). In addition to this, the EU may harmonise only regulatory requirements or also the remedies and procedures for breaches of these requirements. Finally, harmonisation may be carried out via directly applicable acts (Regulations) or acts that require transposition into national law (Directives).

The first form of investment services regulation in the EU is the Investment Services Directive (ISD).[31] This Directive introduced the single passport and minimum authorisation requirements as well as several conduct of business principles to ensure that firms behave fairly and honestly with their clients. Member States were left free to introduce more stringent conduct of business requirements.

In 2004 the MiFID I[32] replaced the ISD, and set out specific conduct of business rules, further detailed by the 2006 Commission MiFID I Directive,[33] to protect clients against misconduct. MiFID I harmonised also the powers of competent authorities, required the Member States to lay down effective, proportionate and dissuasive administrative measures or sanctions or administrative sanctions for breaches of the Directive and encouraged the Member States to set up extra-judicial mechanisms for out-of-court resolution of consumer disputes.[34]

In 2014 MiFID II, replaced MiFID I, tightened MiFID I conduct of business rules, and introduced new product governance obligations. This type of requirement, combined with the new product intervention powers granted by MiFIR[35] to national and EU authorities, aims to prevent detriment caused by mis-selling at the point of sale of financial instruments and therefore reflects a more intrusive and paternalistic approach to retail client regulation.[36] MiFID II also strengthens

[30] See in more detail, F Della Negra, 'The regulatory design and goals of civil liability in EU securities regulation after the global financial crisis: trends and perspectives' in M Andenas and OO Cherednichenko, *Civil Liability after the Crisis* (forthcoming).

[31] Council Directive 93/22/EEC of 10 May 1993 on investment services in the securities field [1993] OJ L141/27.

[32] Recital No 71 MiFID I.

[33] Commission Directive 2006/73/EC of 10 August 2006 implementing Directive 2004/39/EC of the European Parliament and of the Council as regards organisational requirements and operating conditions for investment firms and defined terms for the purposes of that Directive (Commission MiFID I Directive) [2006] OJ L241/26.

[34] Arts 50, 51 and 53 MiFID I.

[35] Regulation (EU) No 600/2014 of the European Parliament and of the Council of 15 May 2014 on markets in financial instruments and amending Regulation (EU) No 648/2012 (MiFIR) [2014] OJ L173/84.

[36] M Andenas and HY Chiu, *The Foundations and Future of Financial Regulation* (London, Routledge 2014) 139.

supervisory powers and administrative enforcement (Article 70) requires the Member States to establish mechanisms to compensate clients for losses suffered as a result of breaches of the Directive (Article 69) and to set up extra-judicial mechanisms for out-of-court resolution of consumer disputes (Article 75). An important novelty of MiFID II is that its Level 2 has been adopted in the form of a Regulation, which is a directly applicable act and could, therefore, be invoked by investors against the firm in a civil proceeding (horizontal direct effect).

Over three generations of Directives, the intensity of harmonisation has changed. MiFID I removed the host state power to implement and supervise the conduct of business rules and introduced, in principle, a maximum harmonisation standard for these rules.[37] MiFID II confirms the MiFID I's choice in favour of maximum harmonisation, thus limiting the possibilities for Member States to introduce more stringent requirements to protect investors.[38] The scope of harmonisation, with regard to private law aspects, has only marginally changed. MiFID II, like its predecessor, did not introduce rules to harmonise the private law remedies for breaches of conduct of business rules. Harmonisation of civil liability standards has been perceived as legally and politically problematic, given the divergent standards of liability in place in Member States.[39]

C. Supervision and Enforcement

With regard to supervisory and public enforcement powers, self-sufficiency could be measured taking into account the competences of the EU and national competent authorities.

Within the ESFS, the NCAs continue to carry out day-to-day supervision over investment services providers and the ESAs have a defined number of tasks and powers,[40] including product intervention powers and direct supervision of Credit Rating Agencies (CRAs) and Trade Repositories (TRs).[41] Therefore, the ESAs'

[37] Art 4(1) MiFID I. See in favour of the maximum harmonisation, PO Mülbert, 'The Eclipse of Contract Law in the Investment Firm-Client-Relationship' in G Ferrarini and E Wymeersch, Investor Protection in Europe: Corporate Law Making, The MiFID and Beyond (Oxford, Oxford University Press, 2006) 299. Contra OO Cherednychenko, 'Full Harmonisation of Retail Financial Services Contract Law in Europe: A Success or a Failure?' in S Grundmann and YM Atamer (eds), *Financial Services, Financial Crisis and General European Contract Law* (Kluwer Law International, 2011) 243.

[38] Art 24(12) MiFID II.

[39] T Tridimas, 'EU Financial Regulation: Federalization, Crisis Management and Law Reform' in P Craig and G De Burca (eds), *The Evolution of EU Law*, 2nd edn (Oxford, Oxford University Press, 2011) 794.

[40] See Arts 17, 18 and 19 of ESAs founding regulations; product intervention and direct supervisory powers vis-à-vis Credit Rating Agencies and Trade Repositories.

[41] Currently, ESMA supervises eight registered TRs, 26 registered CRAs and four certified CRAs (ESMA's supervision of credit rating agencies, trade repositories and monitoring of third country central counterparties 2017 Annual Report and 2018 Work Programme, 8 February 2018 ESMA80-199-153) p 6.

competencies do not replace the ones of the NCAs, but add to the NCAs' competencies in order to ensure a higher level of supervisory convergence and the protection of the financial stability of the EU in specific circumstances. It is therefore not possible to identify a self-sufficient or autonomous EU regime for financial supervision and public enforcement.

This, of course, does not mean that the acts of the ESAs are irrelevant for the private law relationships between financial market participants. Supervisory acts not only have vertical effects against (or in favour of the) supervised entities; they also produce horizontal effects, ie they may affect the private law relations between the supervised entity and its clients.[42]

i. Private Enforcement

In the context of private enforcement, self-sufficiency takes up a particular meaning. It should not be understood in an institutional but in a more substantive law sense, namely to indicate the type of standards used by national courts and adjudicators to resolve disputes. Such standards may diverge from the strict application of substantive law, involving the consideration for EU law standards, ie via the mechanism of consistent interpretation, or application of EU general principles.

ii. Judicial Enforcement

Conduct of business rules may be enforced via judicial or extra-judicial proceedings. Differently from other experiences in Europe[43] and abroad[44] MiFID II, like its predecessor, did not grant investors a private law remedy for breaches of its conduct of business rules, nor did it define the civil law consequences stemming from their violation. As a result, given that these aspects fall outside its harmonisation's scope, Member States remain free to govern them but subject to the principles of equivalence and effectiveness.[45]

However, as the CJEU held in *Genil v Bankinter*[46] and in *Banif Plus Bank Zrt v Márton Lantos*,[47] Member States shall determine the contractual consequences of non-compliance with those obligations in accordance with the principles of equivalence and effectiveness. These two principles should be interpreted with

[42] See also F Della Negra, 'The Effects of the ESMA's Powers on Domestic Contract Law' in M Andenas and G Deipenbrock (eds), *Regulating and Supervising European Financial Markets: More Risks than Achievements* (Berlin/Heidelberg, Springer, 2016) 139.

[43] See in the UK the Financial Services and Markets Act, s 138D, in Ireland the Central Bank (Supervision and Enforcement) Act 2013 (No 26/2013), s 44, and in Portugal Art 304a of Código dos Valores Mobiliários (Decreto-Lei n. 486/99) Diário da República no 265/1999, Série I-A de 1999-11-13.

[44] See in Singapore the Financial Advisers Act (Chapter 110, 2007 Revised Edition) 1B, s 25.

[45] Case C-604/11, *Genil 48 GL v Bankinter*, para 57.

[46] Case C-604/11, *Genil v Bankinter*, ECLI:EU:C:2013:344, para 57.

[47] Case C-312/14, *Banif Plus Bank Zrt v Márton Lantos*, ECLI:EU:C:2015:794, para 79.

regard to MiFID I and II; the case law shows that the CJEU takes into account factual and practical dimensions of effectiveness related to the specific situation at stake.[48]

Research has shown that, notwithstanding of the absence of express private law remedies for breaches of conduct of business rules, national courts have granted to investors a remedy based on general contract or tort law.[49] This trend is most visible in continental Europe, where courts acknowledge, on the basis of different private law categories, the civil law effects of the conduct of business rules in advised and non-advised transactions, especially with unsophisticated retail clients. By contrast, British courts are more reluctant to grant civil law effects to regulatory duties.[50] Only in advised transactions, ie when the investment service is provided under an advisory contract, have the UK courts accepted that the general private law duty of care should be interpreted in light of the applicable conduct of business rules. In non-advised transactions, instead, courts have generally refused to interpret common law duties in light of regulatory duties. However, it should be noted that the different approaches of national courts in the UK and continental judicial may be influenced by the specific factual and institutional context.

In the UK disputes litigated in courts generally concern highly sophisticated investors, who are supposed to possess a high level of experience and expertise in financial service contracts. In continental Europe, judicial disputes relate to unsophisticated retail clients, who face information and bargaining power asymmetries vis-à-vis the firm.

In addition to this, in the UK the Financial Ombudsman Service (FOS) adjudicates most of the retail client disputes. The FOS makes use of regulatory standards when deciding the disputes and it is not bound by common law. In continental Europe, although the recourse to ADR bodies has significantly increased after the crisis, national courts continue to adjudicate a high number of retail client disputes.

iii. Out-of-Court Enforcement

MiFID II requires (MiFID I merely encouraged) Member States to set up procedures for the 'out-of-court settlement of consumer disputes concerning the provision of investment and ancillary services provided by investment firms' and to ensure that all investment firms adhere to one or more such bodies implementing such complaint and redress procedures.

[48] Case C-453/00, *Cofidis SA v Jean-Louis Fredout*, ECLI:EU:C:2002:705, para 37. See F Cafaggi and P Iamiceli, 'The Principles of Effectiveness, Proportionality and Dissuasiveness in the Enforcement of EU Consumer Law' (2017) 3 *European Review of Private Law* 575, 578.

[49] See F Della Negra, *MiFID II and Private Law. Enforcing EU Conduct of Business Rules* (Oxford, Hart, 2019) 166 and D Busch and C Van Dam, 'A Bank's Duty of Care: Perspectives from European and Comparative Law' in D Busch and C Van Dam (eds), *A Bank's Duty of Care* (Oxford, Hart, 2017) 373.

[50] Della Negra (above n 49) 168.

MiFID II does not require ADR bodies to apply legal principles and rules to resolve a dispute. The ADR bodies may use different legal basis to resolve the dispute (eg legal provisions, considerations of equity, codes of conduct), provided that the types of rules used are made publicly available, and the persons in charge of the procedure need to have (only) a general understanding of the law.[51] However, it has been shown that ADR bodies set up within supervisory authorities do apply regulatory standards to resolve disputes.[52] This type of adjudication does not simply produce 'a settlement for the parties', but determines how regulatory duties and supervisory expectations should be interpreted in the concrete case and in this sense they truly complement the investors' protection mandate of supervisory authorities.[53]

ADR bodies tend to apply regulatory standards when adjudicating retail disputes and this has the positive effect of fostering the effectiveness of EU conduct of business rules via ADR procedures.[54]

In conclusion, the main contribution that the concept of self-sufficiency brings to EU investment services regulation is to underline the need for an effective application of EU law and for effective protection of individual rights. However, as OO Cherednichenko put it, the self-sufficiency of EU investment services regulation 'is a matter of degree rather than an absolute'.[55] Whereas law-making and substantive law could be regarded as self-sufficient from national law, supervision and enforcement still crucially rely on national laws and institutions.

V. Conclusions

The examination of ERPL from the perspective of self-sufficiency reveals an emerging legal practice that allows us to perceive contract law within a regulated sector as a set of rules that necessarily function linked to their institutional and procedural environment with the aim of producing regulatory outcomes. This legal practice consists of an amalgam of dualities where different actors (national/supranational), rules (public/private, binding/non-binding) and market-levels (wholesale/retail) share common sector-specific rationality. By establishing a common sector-specific discourse along each of the 'silos', we conclude that the these sectors are self-sufficient, generally functioning in a self-standing and coherent manner. Such an approach involves the transformation of the private law contained in sector-specific regulation.

[51] Art 7(1)(i) and Art 6(1)(b) ADR Directive.

[52] See in particular Della Negra (above n 49) 124.

[53] See H-W Micklitz, 'The Transformation of Enforcement in European Private Law: Preliminary Considerations' (2015) 4 *European Review of Private Law* 502 and Cantero-Gamito (above n 17).

[54] See Della Negra (above n 49).

[55] OO Cherednychenko, 'Financial Consumer Protection in the EU: Towards a Self-Sufficient European Contract Law for Consumer Financial Services?' (2014) 10(4) *ERCL* 495.

In EU telecoms and investment services regulation we find at least three different transformations for private law:

(i) a shift in the regulatory paradigm: from the contract law rules contained in national civil codes or common law to sector-related rules governing private relationships;
(ii) a move from freedom of contract to regulated autonomy: from autonomy to mandated (B2B) and universal (B2C) access to markets and justice as a result of the EU internal market-building project;
(iii) a more regulatory oriented adjudication and interpretation of contract-related rules and principles, which involves a profound transformation of traditional civil law remedies, often enforced by sector-specific actors.

The narrative that pervades these transformations discloses the potential of regulatory-infused contract law to function as a proxy for the harmonisation of private law in Europe and hence to substantially contribute to the integration of the internal market.

9

In Search of a Grand Theory of European Private Law: Social Justice, Access Justice, Societal Justice and Energy Markets

LUCILA DE ALMEIDA* AND FABRIZIO ESPOSITO**

I. Introduction

A theory is grand when it is bold enough to embody 'the sociological imagination'.[1] Among theorists committed to the epistemology of science, grand theorists that embody the sociological imagination are those who seek big visions in order to achieve lucid summations of what is going on in the world. It is the quality of all that is intellectually ambitious to tie micro-levels of reality to explain social reality. In times of specialisation in all social science, H-W Micklitz – the main character in this *liber studentium* – envisioned the development of a grand theory and stands alongside the grand theorists carefully chosen in his collection *Privatrechtstheorie*.[2] Since 2007, the European University Institute has been the location of Hans' intellectual journey to give meaning to Europe's justice, in contrast to the emerging critique of Europe's justice deficit in the aftermath of the Eurozone crisis.

Hans, as he instead asks to be called by his students, successfully led the European Regulatory Private Law (ERPL) project throughout five-years of his awarded ERC Advanced Grant. While the ERPL project enabled Hans to gather prominent and young scholars to research and develop large empirical data that upheld his theory, the ERPL provided to us – as young scholars – the opportunity

* Postdoctoral Researcher, University of Helsinki, and Research Associate at the Robert Schuman Centre for Advanced Studies, Florence School of Regulation Energy & Climate.

** Postdoctoral Research Fellow, Edmond J Safra Centre for Ethics, University of Tel Aviv.

[1] C Mills, *The Sociological Imagination*, 14th anniversary edn (Oxford, Oxford University Press, 1959).

[2] S Grundmann et al (eds), *Privatrechtstheorie: moderne Theoriebildung im globalen Raum zwischen Rechts- und Gesellschaftswissenschaften* (Tübingen, Mohr Siebeck, 2015).

and privilege to meet and contribute to such intellectual endeavours. Like other contributors to this edited volume, we had the honour to contribute to the ERPL project – Lucila as research associate and Fabrizio as a collaborator, an experience that we are now pleased to share with a broader audience.

This chapter engages with what is arguably the most ambitious outcome of the ERPL project, namely an account of the justice dimension of the EU, which challenges 'the seemingly dominating justice deficit discourse in EU legal scholarship' and finds that, overall, '[t]he story is one of success'.[3] This story is told in Hans's latest book, *The Politics of Justice in European Private Law: Social Justice, Access Justice, Societal Justice*,[4] which offers nothing less of a grand theory about the descriptive and normative foundations of the European private law throughout the integration project.

Hans firmly connects the European integration project to the transformations in the global economy; transformations that are so radical to deserve the title of 'third industrial revolution'.[5] Against this background, the EU is described as a catalyst for changes to the political, legal and economic orders in Europe. The main character of this story is the construction of the distinct concept of 'access justice', argued to be a more positive and more promising development of European integration than the 'pure market justice' identified by the European' sceptics.

Access justice is a distinct concept from the Member States' understanding of social justice, as well as from Hans' account of societal justice. The core of access justice is 'materializ[ing] the theoretical chance of EU citizens to participate in the market so as to make it a realistic opportunity'.[6] To make access a realistic opportunity, a complex, multi-level institutional system built on the co-responsibility of many different actors has been taking shape over the years. Access justice at the EU level is then connected to – and it is slowly evolving into, if you wish – a pan-European societal justice.

As we shall see, Hans's account of access justice in *The Politics of Justice in European Private Law* is greatly sophisticated. It is the result of relentless reviews and maturation over a decade. By borrowing Hans' words, 'ten years of thinking and writing were also ten years of discussions, of feedback and of rewriting';[7] the intellectual journey that began with the bold statements in 'The Visible Hand of European Regulatory Private Law',[8] to be later refined in *The Many Concepts of Social Justice in Private Law*.[9]

[3] H-W Micklitz, *The Politics of Justice in European Private Law: Social Justice, Access Justice, Societal Justice* (Cambridge, Cambridge University Press, 2018) 385.

[4] Micklitz (above n 3).

[5] J Rifkin, *The Third Industrial Revolution* (Basingstone, Palgrave Macmillan, 2011).

[6] Micklitz (above n 3) 2.

[7] Micklitz (above n 3) Preface XVI.

[8] H-W Micklitz, 'The Visible Hand of European Regulatory Private Law – The Transformation of European Private Law from Autonomy to Functionalism in Competition and Regulation' (2009) 28 *Yearbook of European Law* 3.

[9] H-W Micklitz (ed), *The Many Concepts of Social Justice in European Private Law* (Cheltenham, Edward Elgar, 2011).

The concept of access justice in European private law, as it stands, deserves deep reflection and extended discussion. In this chapter, however, we intend to do something less ambitious. We intend to start a conversation – something Hans finds very important in academia – on the descriptive, conceptual, and normative attractiveness of access justice. To achieve this end, this chapter is structured as follows. Section II articulates the mature account of access justice and relates it to social and societal justice. Section III put these three concepts of justice into the context of the energy markets, which Hans claimed play a prominent role in EU economic (or private) law.[10] Section IV introduces several critiques to earlier accounts of access justice. In Section V, this allows us to consider how the mature account of access justice addresses them. Section VI concludes.

II. The Mature Account of Access Justice

In this section, we introduce the mature account of access justice articulated in *The Politics of Justice in European Private Law*.[11] This task is greatly simplified by the rich and clear articulation of the concept of access justice Micklitz offers in the last chapter of the book.

> [Access justice] is bound to the completion of three requirements: first, breaking down barriers which limit participation and access; second, strengthening the position of workers and consumers to enforce their rights in a multi-governance legal order and, third, establishing an institutional design which can cope with the move from social protection laws to the laws on the labour and consumer market.[12]

Let us look at these three requirements more in detail. The first requirement entails that 'all market participants, including consumers, must have a fair and realistic chance of entering the market […] as well as of partaking in [its] benefits'.[13] Universal services obligations play an essential role in ensuring the openness of markets for vulnerable market participants. The law of the labour and consumer market society contributes to the access of both vulnerable and weak market participants. The system is built around the concepts of fair and discrimination-free access, imbalance of power, and, to a growing extent, good faith.

The second requirement has to do with the effectiveness of the rights of market participants, and therefore with the effectiveness of their enforcement. The focus is, therefore, on rights, remedies and procedures. Dispute settlement bodies play an important role in giving substance to the concept of a high level of consumer protection enshrined in the Treaty.[14] Notably, the role of collective entities and the

[10] Hans makes the bold conceptual move of equating private law with economic law: Micklitz (above n 3) 4.
[11] Micklitz (above n 3) 391.
[12] ibid.
[13] ibid.
[14] Micklitz (above n 3) 303.

right granted by the EU are more developed in consumer law in comparison to non-discrimination and labour law.[15]

The third and last component of access justice requires the participation of civil society at large 'in the making of the rules that underpin modern private law relations and their enforcement'.[16] Hans calls this third component of access justice 'societal' private law. The name shows the intimate connection between access and societal justice. Here 'private law plays an eminently societal role in the building of a legal order and a civil society beyond the nation-state'.[17] At this level, market citizens have new responsibilities. New forms of participation are open to market citizens and their associations; they can participate in 'the shaping of codes, guidelines, recommendations'.[18] Also, new forms of enforcement and monitoring are surfacing. Hans, however, notes that there is still much unexploited potential for participation – something that should be considered when lamenting the democratic deficit of the Union.

Against the claims that European integration is built upon pure market justice, Hans introduces a distinctive concept of justice – access justice – and distinguishes it from two other categories of social justice: the Member States' understanding of social justice; and societal justice. The separation between access, social, and societal justice is not sharp. 'Access justice should be understood as a thin version of social distributive justice. However, in its participatory form it turns into societal justice'.[19] The connection is well exemplified by telephone and internet disconnection: '[h]aving no access equates to social and societal exclusion'.[20] Hans is referring to very practical problems associated with being off-grid. Think of the importance of long-distance communication to establishing and maintaining personal, meaningful relations with friends and relatives; or of the increasing importance of smartphones for travelling (maps, booking, planning, etc). These are just two instances of the disruptive effect losing access to telecommunications has on our interconnected lifestyle.

Access justice 'does not aim to replace national patterns of justice. European societal justice reaches beyond access justice, beyond the market and into a European society'.[21] The national level remains entrusted with the task to provide social justice, which 'is bound to the idea of redistribution of wealth and loss shifting from the richer to the poorer part of the society'.[22] For Micklitz, social justice includes also the protection of the weaker parties in contractual relations.[23] It is primarily at the national level that the concept of social justice is specified and

[15] ibid, 336–37.
[16] ibid, 391.
[17] ibid, 358.
[18] ibid, 365.
[19] ibid, 2.
[20] ibid, 302.
[21] ibid, 390.
[22] ibid, 4.
[23] ibid, 5.

put into practice by the Member States 'according to their available resources and the willingness of [...] citizens to pay through higher taxes';[24] the EU task in this context is that of setting minimum standards.

The distinction between social and societal justice is terminologically elusive but conceptually sharp and significant. In contrast to social justice, the concept of 'European societal justice' has an expressive function; it expresses the idea that 'European justice is not limited to a kind of materialised access to the market'.[25] However, societal justice is still developing and 'relates to the people within the developing European society'.[26] With this, Micklitz wants to emphasise that in the governance structures of the developing European society, the citizens in their different social roles (consumer, employer, employee, etc) individually and in organised forms will be more and more co-responsible with the Union and the Member States for the governance of the European market society.

III. Access Justice in EU Energy Market

We began this chapter arguing that a theory is 'grand' when it is ambitious enough to link fragmented pieces of micro-reality in order to make sense out of our social world. Against pragmatism and EU scepticism, Hans, we noted, envisioned a grand theory of European's justice. He does so through navigating into the bits and pieces of what he calls a 'tripartite private order'.[27]

Beneath *The Politics of Justice*, the tripartite private order mirrors an analytical choice of structuring the European private law around three different categories – universal service obligations (USOs), the law of the consumer and labour market society, and the societal private law. The tripartite private order, therefore, is the result of a methodological and political choice of shedding light on private relationships where individuals are weakest parties and addressees of rights. These individuals are employees, consumers, and costumers of services essential to life like electricity, gas, water, and internet connection. In Hans' own words:

> [t]here is no legal person anymore in the third globalization, but where individual rights turn into identity-based rights, which can be only shaped along the line of groups to which the individuals belong.[28]

In this section, we do not intend to summarise the vast evidence that upholds Hans' theory of justice in private law. Instead, we choose to illuminate his distinct concept of access justice in one of the tripartite categories of law – USOs – and more specifically EU energy law. We do so because EU regulation of the energy

[24] ibid, 12.
[25] ibid, 391.
[26] ibid, 392.
[27] ibid, 283.
[28] ibid.

markets, alongside two other silos (telecommunication and financial services)[29] was the cornerstone of the ERPL project and, furthermore, was led by one of us.

To understand the reasons why energy law, and more specifically USOs applied to the energy markets, belong to a tripartite private order, one has to retrace the liberalisation, privatisation and re-regulation of public incumbents and its reflection on the law of regulated markets. Before it, USOs were conducted by vertically integrated operations benefiting from exclusive rights, and often public ownership. Operations were commonly defined as public acts, public contracts or, as in good French, *service public*.[30] Hand-in-hand technology, ideology and geopolitical changes[31] triggered the deregulation of former public operations. Exclusive rights were revoked, total or partial public ownership moved to hands of private shareholders, and enhancing competition became an inherent policy in all regulated markets. States outsourced USOs,[32] and with it, a process of privatisation of legal relationships was set in motion.

Among the various meanings of privatisation,[33] the most valuable to the theory of access justice is the privatisation of legal relationships between individuals and essential services' providers. The deregulation of former public operations turned the beneficiary of public services into customers and contractual parties in commercial or consumer contracts with service providers.[34] In jurisdictions with no specific rules, these contracts fell under general contract law. Non-payment for a service is a breach of contract and, hence, an indebted customer can be deprived of receiving a service and, at worse, be liable for the financial harm caused to the counterparty. Furthermore, general contract law does not uphold legal claims against providers who refuse to provide a service, eg the refusal to supply because of a client's overindebtedness.

As the privatisation of legal relationships placed the disputes between the recipients and providers of USOs to civil courts, dramatic cases of customers' disconnection from the electricity and gas grid for overindebtedness exposed the fragility of the liberalisation and privatisation of USOs. The cases prompted the need for political reaction, and Brussels answered the call by advancing a re-regulation of the energy markets at the EU level.

Following Hans' account of the genealogy of access justice, this re-regulation at the EU level marks the moment when access justice started taking shape in energy law. This brings us back to the late 1990s, when the first energy Directives were enacted. If access justice is bound to the completion of 'three requirements',

[29] See the contributions of M Gamito and F Della Negra in this volume.

[30] W Friedmann, *Law in a Changing Society* (abridged edition, London, Penguin Books, 1964).

[31] R Millward, *Private and Public Enterprise in Europe: Energy, Telecommunications and Transport, 1830–1990* (Cambridge, Cambridge University Press, 2005).

[32] J Freeman and M Minow (eds), *Government by Contract: Outsourcing and American Democracy* (Cambridge, Mass, Harvard University Press, 2009).

[33] The meaning of privatisation as described by G Teubner, 'After Privatization? The Many Autonomies of Private Law' (1998) 51 *Current Legal Problems* 393.

[34] Micklitz (above n 3) 289–90.

these three requirements have been the cornerstone of the EU regulation of the energy market since the early stage of the positive integration; they have maintained this role over the years and throughout subsequent reforms.

A. First Condition: Access Justice versus Market Access

The first requirement of access justice refers to breaking down barriers which limit participation and granting fair access to markets. The first article of the Directives in both the electricity and gas markets – 96/92/EC and 98/30/EC –[35] explicitly stated that the EU legislation laid down common rules relating to 'access to the market', to be understood also as market access. Despite the fragmented case law back then, the CJEU showed some signs of convergence around a principle of market access when interpreting the provisions on the free movement of goods and persons.[36] The EU legislation made it incontestable for the energy services. These first normative propositions relate explicitly to the notion of access to market entered and, once entered into the legal discourse, they reshaped the market reality.

The notion of market access and Hans' account of access justice have similarities but are not the same concept. None of them has a clear-cut definition though. In the Treaty of European Union, the market access rationale lies on the four freedoms[37] and the rules competition law. In particular, as regards the former, the link between non-discrimination principles and market access rationale grounds on a doctrinal construction of the CJEU's ruling that struck down national rules precluding foreign workers and undertakings to access markets. The EU legislation, instead, goes beyond the negative integration and advances the notion of access regulation or access regimes.[38] The latter encompasses a set of rules conferring to customers and new entrants the right to access energy markets against incumbents' discriminatory behaviour. It also imposes on the Member States the obligation of setting regulatory regimes to ensure equal treatment of all market participants. For example, the imposition of tariffs to access network systems is grounded on the rationale that all energy retailers hold the right to equal treatment to access the network. Tariff regime excludes the possibility of network operators negotiating access to transmission and distribution systems in a discriminatory way, which would later reflect on the energy bills of all final customers.[39]

[35] Directive 96/92/EC of the European Parliament and of the Council of 19 December 1996 concerning common rules for the internal market in electricity, Directive 98/30/EC of the European Parliament and of the Council of 22 June 1998 concerning common rules for the internal market in natural gas.

[36] C Barnard, 'Fitting the Remaining Pieces into the Goods and Persons Jigsaw?' (2001) 26 *ELRev* 35; C Barnard and S Deakin, 'Market Access and Regulatory Competition' in C Barnard and J Scott (eds), *The Law of the Single European Market: Unpacking the Premises* (Oxford, Hart, 2002).

[37] ibid.

[38] GR Faulhaber, 'Will Access Regulation Work?' (2008) 61 *Federal Communications Law Journal* 6.

[39] J-M Glachant, 'Regulating Networks in the New Economy' (2012) 3 *Review of Economics and Institutions* 1; J-M Glachant, 'Governance in Network Industries: Lessons Learnt from New Institutional Economics' (2014) 15 *Competition and Regulation in Network Industries* 157.

Commonly, market access in regulation is perceived from the incumbents' side – the right of an incumbent to access a public tender, a transmission system network, or a certain organised wholesale platform. From the consumption side, market access defines the right of customers to be connected to network systems – 'accessibility to all',[40] access to information,[41] and to the competitive market, the latter to be understood as the customers' right to choose one out of two service providers at least.[42]

Different from market access, Hans' account of access justice emphasises the fairness of private relationships. Furthermore, Hans rather focuses on USOs – the private relationship between incumbents and individuals as consumers. 'All market participants, including consumers, must have a fair and realistic chance of entering the market'.[43] Granting to individuals the access to competitive energy markets that, nevertheless, have all service providers charging unaffordable prices fulfils the conditions of market access on the one hand, but not of access justice on the other. Those individuals are deprived of accessing markets of essential services nonetheless.

The first requirement of access justice is noticeable in the provisions dealing with households' rights to reasonable prices, and in the protection of vulnerable consumers. While the first package of Directives was merely meant to ensure 'equality of access for EU [energy] companies to consumers',[44] the regulatory reform in the second energy package introduced social rules in the contractual relationship between energy providers and individuals. Ever since, EU legislation has ensured electricity services to households at 'reasonable, easily and clearly comparable and transparent prices',[45] and gas 'of a specified quality at reasonable price'.[46] The reasons behind the reasonable prices to consumers can be seen with particular clarity in the CJEU's judgment in *Federutility and Others*, when the Court decided for the legality of having 'reference prices' for gas provided that such interventions:

> Pursue a general economic interest consisting in maintaining the price of the supply of natural gas to final consumers at a reasonable level having regard to the reconciliation which the Member States must make, taking account of the situation in the natural gas sector, between the objective of liberalisation and that of the necessary protection of final consumers.[47]

[40] Directive 2009/72/EC of the European Parliament and of the Council of 13 July 2009 concerning common rules for the internal market in electricity and repealing Directive 2003/54/EC, Rec 60.

[41] For instance, the case law ruling on the right of Roma to access the meter information, Case C-83/14, *CHEZ Razpredelenie Bulgaria*, ECLI:EU:C:2015:480; and Case C-394/11, *Belov*, ECLI:EU:C:2013:48.

[42] Art 2(12) Directive 2009/72/EC. See also F Esposito and L Almeida, 'A Shocking Truth for Law and Economics: Consumer Welfare Explains the Internal Market for Electricity Better Than Total Welfare' in K Mathis and BH Huber (eds), *Energy Law and Economics* (Dordrecht, Springer, 2018).

[43] Micklitz (above n 3) 391.

[44] Art 3(2) Directive 96/92/EC; Art 3(2) Directive 98/30/EC.

[45] Art 3(3) Directive 2003/54/EC; Art 3(3) Directive 2009/72/EC.

[46] Annex A Directive 2003/55/EC; Annex A Directive 2009/73/EC.

[47] Case C-265/08, *Federutility and Others*, ECLI:EU:C:2010:205.

Federutility is a landmark case for reinforcing the obligation of the Member States to reconcile the objectives of the liberalisation with the necessary protection of final consumers. Therefore, the former could not undermine the latter.

In parallel to the consumers' right to reasonable prices, the second package also introduced the notion of vulnerable consumers, to which Hans pays great attention in *The Politics of Justice*.[48] Vulnerable consumers are the weakest among consumers. The second energy package introduced the notion of vulnerable consumers by imposing on Member States the obligation to provide 'appropriate measures to help them avoid disconnection'.[49] This then was an emphatic response of the EU legislator to the above-mentioned dramatic cases of disconnection for indebtedness. By referring to vulnerable consumers as a group of consumers running the risk of being disconnected from the grid, the second package of Directives implicitly linked the concept of vulnerable consumers to poverty. Later, the third enegy package amended the legal text and made uncontestable the tie between the concept of vulnerable consumers and poverty. The energy Directives establish that 'Member States shall define the concept of vulnerable consumers which may refer to energy poverty and, inter alia, to the prohibition of disconnection of [either electricity or gas] to such customers' in critical times.[50]

Almost ten years after the introduction of the notion of vulnerable consumers in EU energy law, the consumer's rights to protection while in vulnerable conditions has expanded to other contexts in the EU legislation.[51] This was the case since the EU Regulation on security of gas supply (SoS). The EU SoS Regulation grants to households the right to uninterruptable gas supply even in critical situations, such as the Russian-Ukraine gas supply crisis in January 2009, which brought widespread disruption to the gas supply for most Member States.[52]

Hans' account of access justice in the energy market stops in the enactment and aftermath developments of the third energy package. Notwithstanding the timeframe of *The Politic of Justice*, the materisalisation of access justice promises to be greatly expanded if the EU Parliament approves the fourth package. The most recent and ongoing regulatory reform, known as the clean energy package, was a mere political aspiration while Hans drafted *The Politics of Justice in European Private Law*. Today, while we finalise this chapter, the European Commission proposal reached the European Parliament and deserves a few words.

[48] Micklitz (above n 3) 310–14.

[49] Art 3(5) Directive 2003/54/EC; Art 3(3) Directive 2003/55/EC.

[50] Art 3(7) Directive 2009/72/EC; Art 3(3) Directive 2009/73/EC.

[51] Regulation (EU) 2017/1938 of the European Parliament and of the Council of 25 October 2017 concerning measures to safeguard the security of gas supply and repealing Regulation (EU) No 994/2010, Art 6(1).

[52] L de Almeida, 'SoS Back-and-Forth? Minimum v. Exhaustive Harmonization of Entitled Protected Customers in Gas Supply Crises: Eni and Others' (2018) *Helsinki Legal Studies Research Paper No* 52.

The clean energy package, if approved as it stands, will considerably enlarge the application of access justice in the energy markets. The Commission proposal, which is referred to as a 'fair deal for consumers',[53] encompasses provisions granting consumers fair access to new and emerging markets in the energy sector. These are, for example, new ancillary services and business models that are entering into the energy market because of technological innovations. The electricity Directive proposal contains a new chapter entitled 'consumer empowerment and protection'. It encompasses provisions granting to households, inter alia, the right to install or upgrade their smart meters 'under a fair and reasonable condition',[54] the 'right to access energy community's networks [...] on fair and cost-reflective terms',[55] and the right to self-generate electricity and feed it into the grid subject to non-discriminatory network charges.[56] If approved, the clean energy package will deserve an entire chapter to put it into the context of the concept of access justice. The task is for the near future, hopefully.

B. Second Condition: Access (to) Justice

The second component of access justice, and the least controversial of the three, concerns the effectiveness of the rights of market participants – to be meant effectiveness of enforcement. The European Commission has correctly noted, 'rights which can be not enforced are worthless'.[57] In other words, EU law indeed creates rights for individuals, but those rights have no worth if neither EU nor national laws furnish remedies and procedures to their effectiveness. *The Politics of Justice in European Private Law*, therefore, grounds the second condition of access justice on the importance of ensuring enforcement tools from two-sided approaches: public and private enforcement.

The Treaty of European Union has always relied on national courts as the first guarantors of the effectiveness of EU law. Therefore, having national procedures that grant access to courts is *sine qua non* to grant all individuals and undertakings the possibility to challenge a violation of the Treaty by the Member States. The EU legislation on the energy markets, instead, started to impose on the Member States the obligation to set procedures and remedies to ensure the effectiveness of the EU regulatory regimes outside national courts. To ensure that, a combination of the public and private enforcement was set in motion.

[53] COM(2016) 864 final/2, Proposal for a Directive of the European Parliament and the Council on common rules for the internal market in electricity (23.2.2017) 1.

[54] COM(2016) 864 final/2, Art 21(1).

[55] COM(2016) 864 final/2, Art 16.

[56] COM(2016) 864 final/2, Art 15.

[57] SEC(2011) 173, Commission, Public Consultation towards a Coherent Approach to Collective Redress, 2.

From the side of private enforcement, the EU legislator has overcome the principle of national procedure autonomy and, furthermore, imposed on the Member States the obligation of setting out-of-court dispute settlement procedures. To understand this EU approach, we need to go back to the second energy packages.

The second energy Directives imposed on Member States the obligation to set 'transparent, simple, and inexpensive procedures for dealing with their complaints'.[58] Back then, these Directives determined the setting of procedures without referring to them as out-of-court dispute settlements. This then changed when the third energy package entered into force. This later amendment introduced the expression 'out-of-court dispute settlement procedures'. Since then, Member States should consider that customers have the right to access 'transparent, simple and inexpensive … out-of-court dispute settlement procedures'.[59] Furthermore, EU energy law was then later complemented by the approval of the Alternative Dispute Resolutions (ADR) Directive, which regulates, among other aspects, the governance of those dispute settlement bodies.[60]

The second condition of access justice sheds light on the access to justice in the modes of the EU. Whilst the EU has no competence to regulate national court procedures and grant fair and realistic access to courts for consumers, ADRs have been an alternative way to provide consumers with access to justice; a way of realistic dispute for the violation of USOs.

Besides private enforcement, public enforcement has also entered into Hans' account of access justice. The second energy package introduced to the Member States the obligation to set independent national regulatory authorities (NRAs)[61] and 'appropriate mechanism for the … control and transparency so as to avoid any abuse of dominant position, in particular to the detriment of consumers'.[62] Following the provisions of these Directives, some Member States opted to delegate to the NRAs the authority to impose penalties on the undertakings that fail in complying with their USOs. The Directives of the third energy package, in contrast, enlarged the list of 'duties and powers' of the NRAs and included the responsibility of 'helping to ensure, together with other relevant authorities, that the consumer protection measures … are effective and enforced'.[63] The NRA has been an important institution to ensure the effectiveness of consumers' rights by either imposing penalties on non-compliant undertakings or by bringing an action against them before the national courts.

[58] Annex A(f) Directive 2003/54/EC; Annex A(f) Directive 003/55/EC.

[59] ibid.

[60] Directive 2013/11/EU of the European Parliament and of the Council of 21 May 2013 on alternative dispute resolution for consumer disputes and amending Regulation (EC) No 2006/2004 and Directive 2009/22/EC (Directive on consumer ADR).

[61] Art 23(1) Directive 2003/54/EC; Art 25(1) Directive 2003/55/EC.

[62] Art 23(8) Directive 2003/54/EC; Art 25(7) Directive 2003/55/EC.

[63] Art 37(1)(n) Directive 2009/72/EC; Art 41(1)(o) Directive 2009/73/EC.

C. Third Condition: Societal Justice to Mitigate Democratic Deficit

The third and last component of access justice is societal justice, as it is termed by Hans. It captures the engagement of 'market citizens and their associations'[64] in the multi-level governance of European private law-making.

The notion of societal justice is more specific than the usual advocacy for stakeholders' engagement in the regulation of energy markets. Individuals as consumers, consumer associations, and civil societies, rather than legal entities, are at the core and the centre of Hans' account of societal justice. It alludes more to a contemporary way of overcoming the lamented democratic deficit of the Union.

Until very recently, EU governance of energy markets had no reference to the obligation of ensuring the participation of civil society in the law-making process. The situation changed with the recent approval of the EU Regulation on the Governance of the Energy Union and Climate Action in December 2018.[65] For the first time, EU legislation imposes on the Member States the obligation to establish a multilevel climate and energy dialogue including civil societies.

> Each Member State shall establish a multilevel climate and energy dialogue pursuant to national rules, in which local authorities, civil society organizations, business community, investors and others relevant stakeholders and the general public can engage and discuss the different scenarios for energy and climate policies, including for the long term, and review progress.[66]

Before the EU Regulation on the Governance of the Energy Union, public engagement in the law-making process rested on the notion of stakeholders. The issue with such provisions is the vagueness of the meaning of 'stakeholders'. Which stakeholders should be involved in the law-making to fulfil due process? Therefore, a law-making process that requires stakeholders' engagement might open a room to the voice of civil society, but the effective involvement of this distinct category of associations depends on their capacity to respond to public consultations.

The engagement of stakeholders is observed in the development process of network codes in the European Energy markets. Generally speaking, network codes are a significant and growing set of the EU implementing acts regulating the operation of transmission systems. The network codes development process involves a complex of procedures pre-comitology, where the main characters are

[64] Micklitz (above n 3) 365.

[65] Regulation (EU) 2018/1999 of the European Parliament and of the Council of 11 December 2018 on the Governance of the Energy Union and Climate Action, amending Regulations (EC) No 663/2009 and (EC) No 715/2009 of the European Parliament and of the Council, Directives 94/22/EC, 98/70/EC, 2009/31/EC, 2009/73/EC, 2010/31/EU, 2012/27/EU and 2013/30/EU of the European Parliament and of the Council, Council Directives 2009/119/EC and (EU) 2015/652 and repealing Regulation (EU) No 525/2013 of the European Parliament and of the Council (Text with EEA relevance).

[66] Art 11 Regulation (EU) 2018/1999.

the Agency for Cooperation of Energy Regulators (ACER) and the European Network of Transmission System Operators (ENTSOs).

It is not on our purpose to describe all the stages of the pre-comitology law-making process of network codes. Nonetheless we point out the four steps where the EU Regulation imposes on the ACER and the ENTSO-e the obligations of pursuing stakeholders' consultation: first, by the ACER before establishing the annual priority list, which sets out the areas for which network codes are to be developed;[67] second, by the ENTSO-e while drafting the framework guidelines setting out strategic goals for the network codes to be developed by the ACER;[68] third, by the ENTSO-e while developing network codes based on the framework guidelines;[69] and, finally, by the ACER again while conducting further consultations when reviewing the draft network code developed by ENTSO-e.[70]

Some of the complex technical issues taken into account in the network codes directly impact on the relationship between consumers and energy providers. For example, the methodology to calculate network tariffs and re-dispatch are regulated in the network codes and, nonetheless, are costs that are reflected in the electricity bills of all consumers. This is the reason why civil society and consumer associations might, and should, engage in the law-making process of network codes.

The EU Regulation setting the law-making of the network codes and the Regulation on the Governance of the Energy Union turn the engagement of civil society in the EU law-making to possible and obligatory respectively. Nevertheless, the distinct feature of societal justice also has a soft approach to European private law, sometimes called European private orders.

The engagement of civil society in the making of recommendations and guidelines matters for Hans' purpose of societal justice despite its lack of legal normativity. The voluntary engagement of civil society in the making of non-legal normative documents is rather common in the energy sector. The Commission has annually hosted the Citizen's Energy Forum as a platform to collect inputs from consumer associations and civil society at large. The Forum has kick-off initiatives for producing guidelines and recommendations in various subject matters; a prominent example for our purposes is the 'Vulnerable Consumers Working Group Guidance Document'[71] on the best practices to protect vulnerable consumers in Member States. Another relevant initiative was led by the Council of European Energy Regulators (CEER), the association of national regulatory

[67] Regulation (EC) No 714/2009 of the European Parliament and of the Council of 13 July 2009 on conditions for access to the network for cross-border exchanges in electricity and repealing Regulation (EC) No 1228/2003, Art 6(1).

[68] Art 6(3) Regulation 714/2009.

[69] Art 10(1) Regulation 714/2009.

[70] Art 6(7) Regulation 714/2009.

[71] Available at ec.europa.eu/energy/sites/ener/files/documents/20140106_vulnerable_consumer_report_0.pdf, last accessed 25 March 2019.

authorities in the energy market. CEER launched a public consolation on 'how to involve and engage consumer organisation in the [national] regulatory process' and published the evaluation of responses as reports for public consultation.

If one looks back over the 13 years of market integration in the energy sector, Hans is correct in noting that there is still much unexploited potential for civil society participation. The development in the last five years, though, shows the awakening of EU energy law to the importance of involving stakeholders and, later, civil society properly. It looks a promising new path towards societal justice in EU energy law.

IV. Early Critiques to the Early Account of Access Justice

We devoted the previous section to summarising the mature account of access justice, and we put it in the context of the energy market. In this section, we introduce several critiques moved to the earlier accounts of access justice. This review will allow us to emphasise, in the next section, the intellectual development of Hans' theory over the years, thereby substantiating the initial claim of this chapter about *The Politics of Justice in European Private Law*, namely that it offers a grand theory of law.

We divide the critiques into conceptual and normative critiques. Of course, this division is made primarily for expository purposes, and other taxonomies could be possible. The common denominator of the conceptual critiques is their focus on the conceptual structure of access justice, of which the vagueness, ambiguity, and indeterminacy are lamented. Vagueness would affect in particular the concept of 'market', while the concept of 'consumer' would be ambiguous. Indeterminacy derives instead from the interaction between different requirements of access justice. The normative critiques engage with the substantive and institutional dimension of the framework, as well as with its effectiveness. We expose these critiques in their order of presentation.

Hesselink and Dagan find the concept of the 'market' that we are given access to by access justice is in need of clarification. 'What if the market is in fact a jungle, without any guarantees of at least the minimal contractual justice, eg protection against unfair exploitation?' asks Hesselink.[72] Almost answering this (rhetorical) question, Dagan observes that '[e]qual access to an unjust market does not generate just results'.[73] In other words, both authors stress the fact that ensuring access to unfair or unjust markets is a meagre, if any at all, result in terms of justice.

[72] M Hesselink, 'Post-private Law?' in KP Purnhagen and P Rott, *Varieties of European Economic Law and Regulation*' (Dordrecht, Springer, 2014) 41; M Hesselink, 'Private Law, Regulation, and Justice' (2016) 22(5) *European Law Journal* 681, 690–91.

[73] H Dagan, 'Between Regulatory and Autonomy-Based Private Law' (2016) 22 *European Law Journal* 644, 656.

The second layer of conceptual critique lies on the notion of consumer. Hesselink[74] points out a tension in the concept of consumers benefiting from access justice. In fact, in 2012 Hans suggested that the 'responsible' consumer is granted access justice, and the 'vulnerable' consumer receives social justice.[75] This view marks a fracture with the earlier analysis, where access justice seems to be addressed to the whole population of consumers, responsible and vulnerable alike. Accordingly, the concept of consumer is ambiguous in relation to access justice. 'Consumer' sometimes refers to 'any consumer' and other times refers to the 'responsible consumer' only.

Hesselink also identifies a source of indeterminacy for access justice. The critique is connected closely to the just-mentioned ambiguity of the term consumer and is articulated in two steps. First, the potential of access justice to reach an overlapping consensus between 'utilitarians' and 'liberal egalitarians' is noted.[76] Then, Hesselink observes that the idea of an overlapping consensus does not avoid indeterminacy when the underlying rationales of utilitarian and liberal egalitarian political theories clash. Accordingly, when there is a trade-off between, on the one hand, 'opening up more markets to more people' and, on the other hand 'protecting particularly vulnerable consumers and […] combating discrimination', access justice does not offer a useful normative framework.[77]

Moving to the normative level, we start from two important substantive critiques. According to the first, weaker parties in general and consumers, in particular, are instrumentalised under EU law, so that they become tools to advance the integration of national legal systems. The instrumentalisation of parties conflicts with a concept that is central to private law relations, namely their interpersonal[78] or relational[79] character. Contractual parties have duties and owe something to each other; they have rights against and can demand something of each other. However, if the reason for enacting EU consumer law is merely ensuring some collective goal like the maximisation of total welfare or establishing the internal market, this relational dimension is lost. Notably, Hans shared this critique. In fact, he went as far as to suggest that in EU law *pacta sunt servanda* has been substituted by *pacta sunt in efficientiam*.[80]

[74] Hesselink, 'Post-private Law?' (above n 72) 40–41.

[75] H-W Micklitz, 'Do Consumers and Businesses Need a New Architecture of Consumer Law? A Thought-Provoking Impulse' (2012) *EUI Working Papers LAW 2012/23* 67–68, translation of *Brauchen Konsumenten und Unternehmen eine neue Architektur des Verbraucherrechts? Gutachten A zum 69. Deutschen Juristentag* (Munich, Verlag CH Beck, 2012).

[76] Hesselink, 'Private Law, Regulation, and Justice' (above n 72) 689–90.

[77] Hesselink, 'Private Law, Regulation, and Justice' (above n 72) 690.

[78] ibid.

[79] Dagan (above n 73) 645.

[80] Micklitz (above n 75) 34. In our research, we have explored a different connection between allocative efficiency and economic activities. Allocative efficiency can be conceived of as being about consumer welfare instead of total welfare. See Esposito and Almeida (above n 42); F Esposito, 'Law and Economics United in Diversity: Minimalism, Fairness, and Consumer Welfare in EU Antitrust and Consumer Law' (dissertation, Florence, European University Institute, 2018). This is an important step towards recovering the compatibility between the relational dimension of contract law and efficiency.

The second critique has to do with the type of substantive reasons that ought to matter in the normative evaluation of access justice. Interestingly, Dagan and Hesselink disagree on this point. This critique is in between the substantive and institutional levels. In fact, Dagan defends the importance of the distinction between private and public law, which are respectively connected to two different concepts of justice, relational and distributive justice. For Dagan, without denying the importance of collective goals, what has to be attained with access justice are relations between free and equal persons respecting each other. Hesselink instead requires more. We should not settle for anything less than relations that consider market agents as 'full persons', whose dignity has to be respected, to the effect that not all the relevant concerns are relational.[81] Accordingly, Dagan invokes an institutional separation of competences to narrow the set of reasons that count in a normative account of the marketplace. Hesselink, instead, is not willing to accept such a separation.

Finally, Hesselink advances a different institutional critique, which is directed to the legitimacy of the EU legislative process. In his view, the strong technocratic element distinctive of sector-specific legislation 'is in direct collision with the very basic principle that the addressees of laws, including private laws, should be able to regard themselves also as their authors'.[82] What is at stake is nothing less than a legal system in which the addressees of the law are 'dominated by rule choices made by others'.[83]

V. How the Mature Account Addresses the Early Critiques

Access justice is embedded in a thick conceptual web, made of notions of justice and institutions, competencies and responsibilities. Sections II and III introduce the reader to Hans's mature account of access justice. Access justice is at the core of a refined theory of European justice that Hans forged by engaging with early critiques throughout the development of the ERPL project. While section IV has reported some of the critiques moved to access justice in the past, we devote this last section to assessing the extent to which the mature account of access justice addresses the critiques articulated in the previous section.

As seen, the critiques to the early account of access justice are conceptual and normative. The conceptual critiques deal with the concept of 'market' that is vague, of 'consumer' that is ambiguous, and with the indeterminacy of the framework when certain conflicts arise. The normative ones relate to the instrumentalisation

[81] Hesselink, 'Post-private Law?' (above n 72) 36 and 40; Hesselink, 'Private Law, Regulation, and Justice' (above n 72) 686 and 693.

[82] Hesselink, 'Private Law, Regulation, and Justice' (above n 72) 693.

[83] ibid, 693, fn 73.

of weaker parties, to the types of reasons that ought to matter in evaluating market behaviour, and to the legitimacy of an allegedly technocratic Union.

The mature account of access justice introduces notable improvements at the conceptual level that significantly reduce the bite of the conceptual critiques. First, there is little room left for concerns about the market we are granted access to being a jungle; the focus 'is not much access, per se, but access to the market under "fair conditions"'.[84] The ambiguity of the concept of consumer is now embraced; access means different things for different types of market participants. The confident market citizen needs only the guarantee of that minimum level of protection that will suffice to make cross-border economic activities appealing; the socially and/or economically vulnerable consumer needs more. And yet, a unifying element can be found:

> The same philosophy guides the mandatory EU rules on labour, nondiscrimination and consumer law. They are meant to bring the consumer and the worker into a legal position where she or he is equipped with the necessary set of rights to participate in the Internal Market.[85]

With regard to the indeterminacy following from the tension between granting more access and protecting the socially and economically vulnerable, we observe the following. Hans ascribes to the Union a strong commitment to social inclusion, implying that 'nobody gets lost'.[86] This commitment is not absolute, however. Its actual scope is determined with balancing acts structured around the rationality doctrine: '[t]hose who restrict the rights, expectations and needs of the vulnerable and the weak find themselves under a constant obligation to provide substantial reasons'.[87] In sum, Hans addresses this critique of indeterminacy by pointing to the existence of a meta-level of normative discourse.

Let us now move to the normative critiques. The first critique focuses on the instrumentalisation of weaker parties, whose interest would be in a tool for the pursuit of collective goals. The second has to do with the type of reasons that ought to matter in the justification of market arrangements. Lastly, the technocratisation of EU law-making would challenge the legitimacy of the Union.

Micklitz is (now) explicitly suspicious about the instrumentalisation critique. 'Both the Member States and the EU use, more or less, the same tools for achieving justice through public regulation [...]. Law is instrumentalised for social purposes' by both Member States and the Union.[88] This position follows straightforwardly from the basic assumptions underlying the story of the success of justice in European private law. In a globalised economy, the local markets of the Member States would be too small to ensure prosperity to local market participants.

[84] Micklitz (above n 3) 20.
[85] ibid, 22.
[86] ibid, 316.
[87] ibid, 345.
[88] ibid, 33.

Such a view does not imply – this is the crucial point – that the Union rejects the normative commitments animating national economic law.

The extent to which one finds this position persuasive also depends on the stance taken with regard to the second normative critique. In fact, the complex interaction between social, access, and societal justice in the market society is very much in line with the kind of holistic normativity demanded by Hesselink. Market citizens are not only self-responsible; they also hold moral and legal responsibilities towards others. Hans acknowledges the significance of Dagan's challenge explicitly, and agrees with him that 'social inclusion is an option not an obligation'.[89] Hans goes beyond conceding the point to Dagan, and adds that the tension between 'the autonomy-based foundation of access justice and [its] collective dimension' is released by the procedural and institutional components of access justice.[90]

Before elaborating further on this point, it is convenient to extend the discussion to the legitimacy critique. Hans declares that 'the relationship between the regulatory power of the EU and its legitimacy' falls outside the scope of his mature account of access justice.[91] This is indeed a huge and delicate debate, and we understand the decision to erect this kind of protective belt around the analysis. *The Politics of Justice in European Private Law* is definitely rich enough already for a single book! However, we fear that such a strategic move rests uncomfortably with the great emphasis placed on the importance of the co-responsibility of the market citizen and the significant role assigned to civil society in the procedural and institutional components of access justice.

As seen in Section I, the procedural and institutional components of access justice ascribe to all market participants – individually and collectively organised – a key role in the enforcement and in the shaping of the content of economic law. This key role is central to ensure the autonomy of market participants. This idea is indeed in line with Dagan's own view of the institutional setting required to ensure individual autonomy. Dagan, in fact, holds that much of the plurality of options needed to ensure our contractual autonomy can be expected to be created by 'bottom-up, demand-driven strategies'.[92] From this perspective, the European experiment, with its increasing societal participation in private law-making, is certainly going in the right direction. The same considerations have a direct bearing also on the legitimacy critique, at least in the version articulated by Hesselink. The more developed the participatory component of access justice, the harder it becomes to describe market participants as the addressees of the law are 'dominated by rule choices made by others'.[93]

[89] ibid, 26.
[90] ibid.
[91] ibid.
[92] H Dagan and M Heller, *The Choice Theory of Contracts* (Cambridge, Cambridge University Press, 2017) 114.
[93] Hesselink, 'Private Law, Regulation, and Justice' (above n 72) 693, fn 73.

VI. Conclusion

Hans W Micklitz is one of the most prolific and original European private lawyers of his generation. *The Politics of Justice in European Private Law* is arguably his most ambitious publication. It is a vibrant and insightful book that will inspire future research on European private law. The most ambitious outcome of the book is, therefore, the mature account of a distinct European justice – access justice. Access justice and its co-product, societal justice, are the result of many years of tireless research on, reflection about, and analysis of the transformation of European private law.

The Politics of Justice in European Private Law, as it stands, deserves deep reflection and extended discussion. In this essay, we did something less ambitious instead. We started a conversation – something Hans finds very important in academia – about the descriptive, conceptual, and normative attractiveness of access justice.

We envision this chapter as a starting point to the scholarship that will take up Hans' rich, insightful, and thought-provoking ideas. To this end, we have done three things. First, we have summarised the mature account of access justice, the central notion of Hans's intellectual achievement. We have introduced the reader to the three conditions that materialise the notion of access justice – its distinctive normative ground represented by the ideas of fair access, the access to justice, and the societal justice. Second, we have shown how the three conditions of the mature account of access justice have manifested themselves in EU energy law throughout the 30 years of positive integration. Third, we have considered early critiques to access justice and reflected upon how the mature account of access justice addresses them.

We look forward to the academic conversation on Europe's social justice, access justice, and societal justice and to see the role that Hans' ideas will play in it.

10

The Evolution of Direct Taxation in the EU: A Multi-Variable Equation

KATERINA PANTAZATOU*

I. Instead of an Introduction

A chapter on taxation in a book dealing with 'European economic law' needs no particular introduction. The start of my PhD at the European University Institute coincided more or less with the break out of the financial crisis. I intended to write a PhD in the – at the time – burgeoning field of the interrelationship between direct taxation and EU law. Hans Micklitz told me, when he was assigned as my thesis supervisor, that he is no tax lawyer and that we should, somehow, find some sort of compromise to examine taxation beyond its technicalities but read it in its context instead. This is why we decided to look into the reasons why it never developed into an EU competence, how the EU has managed to intervene in this allegedly hard core national policy area through the case law of the Court of Justice of the European Union (CJEU) but also to examine its future, especially in the context of the crisis, of the still (at the time) forthcoming banking union and the capital markets union. I am grateful to Hans Micklitz for being able at that time to see the broad picture and the interdependencies of taxation with other policy areas. There is no better way to proclaim his insightfulness to pursue that topic than showing how relevant it still is, 10 years later. I am grateful for all the things he taught me but above all for being such a wonderful person and guide in life.

This chapter discusses the evolution of direct tax law in the EU, post-crisis. I discern two main lines of influences. First, the financial crisis in itself and the interdependencies it has created for taxation through: (a) the increased need to produce more revenue for the national budgets; (b) the new economic governance framework; (c) the financial assistance mechanisms and the tax-related conditionalities attached to the financial assistance; (d) the 'saving' of the banking sector via state aid in the beginning of the crisis; (e) the development of the banking union;

* Associate Professor in tax law, University of Luxembourg.

(f) the growing need for the creation of an EU budget and the attribution of tax raising powers to the EU. Second, the change of focus observed both at a global level and an EU level, precipitated by the recent tax scandals and the financial crisis; combatting tax avoidance and ensuring that taxes are paid where profits arise or where value is created, through tax coordination became a priority. I examine each of these two lines in turn.

II. The Financial Crisis

The crisis that broke out in 2008 started as a financial and sovereign debt crisis, and it soon became a political crisis questioning the legitimacy of the Lisbon Treaty's institutional set-up and democratic accountability.[1] In the EU, the Euromemorandum Group had noted in the first years of the crisis that 'the effective crisis management at the EU level was substantially thwarted by the failure of the EU to coordinate, or even harmonize tax matters'.[2] At a global level, however, it is widely accepted that tax was not among the root causes of the 2008 global financial crisis, although it has been acknowledged that tax measures may have contributed in exacerbating non-tax incentives to greater leverage, greater risk taking and a lack of transparency.[3]

Faced with such unprecedented multiple crises, the EU was caught off-guard. In an effort to both patch things as swiftly as possible as well as to re-design the institutional and legal framework to avoid any future crises, the European economic Constitution has undergone changes that to some scholars seem like a total overhaul,[4] whereas others argue that it has been rather a different institutional practice that complemented the existing rules.[5]

The financial crisis should be regarded as a catalyst for taxation in the EU for several reasons. First, because the need for an increase in Member States' revenue became imperative. In particular in crisis times, attempts to solve budgetary problems (both at national or supranational levels) rely predominantly on increasing one's tax revenues, usually through direct or indirect taxation.[6] The budgets' shrinkage,

[1] Throughout this paper, I use the term 'crisis' in a sense encompassing the above terms.

[2] Euromemo Group, 'Confronting the crisis: Austerity or Solidarity' EuroMemorandum 2010/2011, available at www.euromemo.eu/euromemorandum/euromemorandum_2010_11/.

[3] G Lloyd, 'Moving Beyond the Crisis: Tax Policies for the Soundness of Financial Markets' in JS Alworth and G Arachi (eds), *Taxation and the Financial Crisis* (Oxford, Oxford University Press, 2012) 190.

[4] C Joerges, 'The European Economic Constitution and its Transformation through the Financial Crisis' in D Patterson and A Söderstn (eds), *Blackwell Companion to EU Law and International Law* (Wiley-Blackwell, 2016) 242–61.

[5] B De Witte, 'Euro Crisis Responses and the EU Legal Order: Increased Institutional Variation or Constitutional Mutation?' (2015) 11 *Constitutional Law Review* 434, 436.

[6] J Leaman, 'The Fiscal Lessons of the Global Crisis for the European Union: The Destructive Consequences of Tax Competition' in J Leaman and A Waris (eds), *Tax Justice and the Political Economy of Global Capitalism, 1945 to the Present* (New York, Berghahn, 2013) 87.

the increasing need to raise revenue through taxation and the public outrage at attempts to avoid taxation, shifted the Member States' focus to anti-avoidance measures.[7] Despite some descending voices coming from the traditional winners of tax competition in the EU, these anti-avoidance measures were initiated by the base erosion and profit shifting (BEPS) Package and soon materialised in secondary EU law. I will turn to these developments in the second part of this chapter.

Second, the crisis initiated a re-consideration of the fiscal/budgetary framework in force until then. It produced an allegedly more robust monitoring and sanctions-based system in order to ensure that Member States would comply with the debt and deficit ceilings set out already in the Stability and Growth Pact (SGP) of 1997. One of main characteristics of the post-crisis EU fiscal government is its institutionalisation – if not constitutionalisation – through a series of provisions in secondary law (Six Pack[8] and Two Pack),[9] soft law (the European Semester) and an intergovernmental agreement (the Fiscal Compact).[10] One does not have to go to great lengths to explain the interrelationship between tax and fiscal policies. Taxation and fiscal policies are not only related via a causal and consequential relationship (ie the money to be spent accrues, in essence, from the revenue collected through taxes), but they both incorporate basic tools that currently are arguably reserved to the Member States and prevent the completion of EU integration. The more the EU is involved in the budgetary policies of the Member States, the more inevitable it becomes that tax policies are also affected.

This alleged more consistent fiscal entrenchment and the continuous monitoring by the Commission of national budgets had an impact on Member States' national tax systems as well. In the economic governance limb, the prescribed consolidated budgetary policies come together with, besides expenditure restraints, specific direct tax policy requirements. Balanced budget provisions, like the ones included in the Six-Pack and the European Semester, require national governments to adopt budgets that raise enough revenue to cover expenditure.

[7] In particular, see below, especially the Anti-Tax Avoidance Directive and the growing number of Directives in the area of exchange of information between Member States and companies' reporting requirements; L Faulhaber, 'Sovereignty, Integration, and Tax Avoidance in the European Union: Striking the Proper Balance' (2010) 48 *Columbia Journal of Transnational Law* 177.

[8] Regulation 1175/2011 amending Regulation 1466/97 on the strengthening of the surveillance of budgetary positions and the surveillance and coordination of economic policies [2011] OJ L306/12; Regulation 1177/2011 amending Regulation 1467/97 on speeding up and clarifying the implementation of the excessive deficit procedure [2011] OJ L306/33; Regulation 1173/2011 on the effective enforcement of budgetary surveillance in the euro area [2011] OJ L306/1; Directive 2011/85/EU on requirements for budgetary frameworks of the Member States [2011] OJ L306/41; Regulation 1176/2011 on the prevention and correction of macroeconomic imbalances [2011] OJ L306/25; Regulation 1174/2011 on enforcement measures to correct macroeconomic imbalances in the euro area [2011] OJ L306/8.

[9] Regulation (EU) No 472/2013 on the strengthening of economic and budgetary surveillance of Member States in the euro area experiencing or threatened with serious difficulties with respect to their financial stability and Regulation (EU) No 473/2013 on common provisions for monitoring and assessing draft budgetary plans and ensuring the correction of excessive deficit of the Member States in the euro area.

[10] The Treaty on Stability, Coordination and Governance in the Economic and Monetary Union.

The changes in the national tax systems, in particular the biggest 'sufferers' from the crisis, need not necessarily consist only of an increase in tax rates but also of a review of 'tax expenditure' and the improvement of the efficiency of tax collection and administration.[11] In this regard, the encroachment of fiscal policies presumably might have a 'domino' effect to the very closely related field of direct taxation, since first, direct taxation constitutes an instrument of the implementation of fiscal policies. In addition, the (fiscal) Country Specific Recommendations (CSR) that are proposed to the Member States by the Council of Ministers, in the context of the European Semester, provide the fiscal targets and the means to achieve them through *general guidelines* over a period of 12–18 months. Very often, these recommendations include tax-specific changes and proposals.

Third, an initial reaction to the crisis was to control the Member States' attempts to rescue banks and to assess national support to private undertakings through the lens of the existing EU state aid rules. As no risk management mechanism existed at the time, the Commission applied looser criteria when assessing requests to grant aid in order to avoid a total failure of the banking sector. At a later stage, the focus shifted to legislation designed to strengthen financial supervision within the internal market.[12] The newly established banking union was built upon a better monitoring and resolution framework for financial institutions.[13] However, at the beginning of the crisis, the lack of an effective banking supervision framework forced many governments to rescue banks with public finances due to the wider effects a bank collapse would have on the state's economy.[14] Because of the domino effect, other Member States would be affected by a potential collapse of a systemic bank. 'Saving' the defaulting bank – either via state aid, or via (eventually) resorting to lending mechanisms such as the European Stability Mechanism (ESM), would certainly have tremendous repercussions for the Member State at issue. Indicatively, according to a 2012 Commission estimate, more than €4.5 trillion of taxpayer money were used to rescue banks in the EU in the period of the crisis until that point.[15] This certainly contributed to the prevailing feeling of injustice that many individual (and corporate) taxpayers witnessed as the 'too big to fail' theory did not apply to them.

[11] European Commission, 'Taxation Papers: Monitoring tax revenues and tax reforms in EU Member States 2010 – Tax policy after the crisis', *Working Paper 24/2010*, p 9.

[12] See for instance, Communication from the Commission, 'European Financial Supervision' COM(2009) 252 final; Regulation (EU) No 1092/2010 on European Union macro-prudential oversight of the financial system and establishing a European Systemic Risk Board.

[13] Regulation (EU) No 806/2014 establishing the Single Resolution Mechanism (SRM); Council Regulation (EU) No 1024/2013 establishes the Single Supervisory Mechanism as a system to supervise banks in the euro area and other participating EU countries and Regulation (EU) No 1022/2013 aligns the existing legislation on the establishment of the European Banking Authority (EBA) to the modified framework for banking supervision.

[14] D Chalmers (et al), 'The retransformation of Europe' in D Chalmers et al (eds), *The End of the Eurocrat's Dream – Adjusting to European Diversity* (Cambridge, Cambridge University Press, 2016) 2.

[15] European Commission 'A Roadmap towards a Banking Union', COM (2012) 510, p 3.

Fourth, and related to point three, is the development of the banking union, which was necessitated after the crisis broke out. Banking union's relation to taxation is twofold. The first point is preventing 'significant banks' from failing through increased monitoring and supervision. Post-crisis, and following the recommendations of the G20 and the Financial Stability Board (FSB),[16] the EU Member States agreed to construct banking union to limit the use of public funds in case of failure of one or more financial institutions, and to mitigate cross-border and bank-sovereign contagion effects. Banking union was envisaged to consist of three pillars, namely centralised bank supervision, resolution, and common deposit insurance, the last of these remaining to be implemented. Bank supervision under the auspices of the Single Supervisory Mechanism (SSM) and the ECB at its core directly supervise the most 'significant' banks in the Eurozone in order to provide for a level playing field for all banks, and ensure effective and credible enforcement of the EU prudential rules in order to avoid bank failures (preventive pillar).[17] Second, if the banks fail, banking union establishes the least costly of the taxpayers' resolution framework, in sharp contrast to the past state aid solution. Once a bank is declared as 'failing or likely to fail', then it is up to the competent resolution authorities – the Single Resolution Board (SRB) at the EU level and the national resolution authorities at a national level – to resolve the bank in question according to certain rules and criteria provided by the EU legislature.[18] This resolution mechanism, entitled Single Resolution Mechanism (SRM), aims to preserve the critical functions of failing banks and to minimise the cost for taxpayers. The SRB owns an EU fund, the Single Resolution Fund (SRF), which is to be used to cover all resolution-related expenses.[19]

Fifth, the Member States in dire financial condition were bailed out through different means of contested legality and legitimacy. Whether the financial assistance came via Memoranda of Understanding (MoU) as in the case of Greece, or through the European Financial Stability Facility (EFSF) or the ESM as in the cases of Ireland, Portugal and Spain, it always came attached to strict conditionality that very often imposed tax-specific changes to the national tax systems of the assisted states. Indicatively, the Council Decision of 10 May 2010 lays down a very specific list of measures to be undertaken by Greece, such as

> (a) a law introducing a 'progressive tax scale' for all sources of income and a horizontally unified treatment of income generated by labour and capital assets; (b) a law *repealing all exemptions and autonomous taxation provisions in the tax system*, including income from special allowances paid to civil servants.[20]

[16] Financial Stability Board, *Key attributes of effective resolution regimes for financial institutions* (October 2011).

[17] For more details see IG Asimakopoulos and K Pantazatou, 'Assessing the post-crisis European Economic Constitution: the fiscal perspective' in H Hofmann et al (eds), *The Metamorphosis of the European Economic Constitution* (Cheltenham, Edward Elgar, forthcoming).

[18] Art 32(1) BRRD; Art 18(1) SRMR.

[19] Arts 1 and 67–78 SRMR.

[20] See Art 2 Council Decision 2010/320/EU, 10 May 2010.

This is only one example of the increase of the interference and the indirect shaping of the national tax systems by the EU. Similarly, the commitments Cyprus undertook in the MoU framework include inter alia:

> On the revenue side, we increased excise taxes and VAT rates … At the onset of the program, we will implement measures amounting to 2.2 percent of GDP through the adoption of legislation and Council of Minister decisions, as needed (prior action). *On the revenue side, these measures will include: (i) increasing the corporate income tax rate from 10 to 12.5 percent; (ii) raising the bank levy rate from 0.11 to 0.15 percent; (iii) raising the withholding tax rate on interest received to 30 percent; and (iv) reforming the property tax;* and (v) other. These measures are expected to yield 2 percent of GDP' (emphasis added).[21]

As the Financial Facility Agreement (FFA) shows, Cyprus and its tax competitive scheme, together with the low corporate tax rates, have been in the lens of the 'strong' Euro Member States, notably Germany and France, for a long time now. The low tax rates Cyprus provided to attract capital and investment have been identified as a 'risk' the investors have to bear for their choices, according to Schäuble.[22] Despite, however, being legally a low tax jurisdiction, Cyprus's FFA and MoU demanded an increase of its corporate tax rates from 10% to 12.5% in order to qualify for the financial assistance by the ESM. Ireland could have fallen under the same requirement, especially as France and Germany were persistently calling on the Irish prime minister to increase its low corporate tax rates of 12.5% as a condition for any bail-out.[23] This requirement was, however, not included in the official bailout agreement, possibly by virtue of the British support of Ireland and the successful negotiations of Ireland with the Troika. The acceptance by the assisted Member States of tax-related conditionalities included in the rescue plans resulted in more tax integration and more fiscal federalisation of the EU.[24] The 'most powerful' or 'donor' Member States were allowed to interfere in the recipient states' tax systems and to impose on them not only principles of 'good budgetary governance' but also the principles of 'good tax competition', as the example of Cyprus illustrates.

Sixth, the voices advocating attributing the EU or the EMU a fiscal capacity have increased by reason of the crisis.[25] Creating an EMU budget or increasing the

[21] Paragraphs 22 and 24 of the Memorandum of Understanding between the 'Troika' and Cyprus, 29 April 2013.

[22] Q Peel, 'Germany senses unfairness over Cyprus plan', *Financial Times* (2 April 2013), www.ft.com/intl/cms/s/0/31a5505c-f8ed-11df-99ed-00144feab49a.html#axzz2ZVz9nZbf.

[23] See for instance P Davies, 'Lobbies say Ireland's 12.5% rate is secure', *Financial Times* (26 November 2010), www.ft.com/intl/cms/s/0/31a5505c-f8ed-11df-99ed-00144feab49a.html#axzz2ZVz9nZbf;Charlemagne, 'Tax Torment', *The Economist* (17 March 2011).

[24] L Hinnekens, 'Story and Fundamentals of Direct Taxation at Work in the EU' (2012) 5 *EC Tax Review* 7.

[25] See for instance H Van Rompuy (et al), 'Report: Towards a Genuine Economic and Monetary Union', 5 December 2012; J-C Juncker (et al), 'Completing Europe's Economic and Monetary Union', 22 June 2015; M Poiares Maduro, 'A new governance for the European Union and the Euro: Democracy and Justice' *EUI RSCAS Policy Paper 2012/11*.

EU budget would possibly (but not necessarily) imply giving the EU tax raising powers. A fully-fledged fiscal union would, consequently, necessitate the development of a stronger capacity at the European level, capable of managing economic interdependencies, and ultimately the development at the EU or euro area level of a fiscal body, such as a treasury office. For a fully-fledged fiscal union to be completed the EU budget should be financed through EU taxes.

Different degrees of fiscal integration have been advocated throughout the crisis, both with regard to their intensity as well as the participating states. The 'Van Rompuy report', for instance, recommended that the central level of the euro area should be equipped with powers for common decision-making on national budgets or else be given a fiscal capacity of its own.[26] Similar to the existing minimal EU budget, a fiscal capacity could be funded from contributions of Member States in relation to their economic output, or via a fixed share of national taxes (eg value-added tax), or a common European tax like the financial transaction tax (FTT), which, however, unlike the FTT would have to be collected in all Member States. Such an option would require Treaty amendments, providing, inter alia, the legal basis for 'a new taxation power at the EU level, or a power to raise revenue by indebting itself on the markets (presently barred by Articles 310 and 311 TFEU)'.[27]

While legal basis issues could be a problem for granting the EU a full fiscal capacity, the primary advantage of such a development would be the increase of the EU budget. The second big advantage is that the transfer of tax-raising powers to the EU, provided it is democratically legitimised, would 'democratise' also the EU's spending powers. Third, 'fiscal transfers' between Member States currently being prohibited under Articles 123 and 125 TFEU but still taking place via the ESM and the ECB's unconventional monetary policy measures,[28] would now be legitimised in the spirit of inter-state solidarity.

This final point deserves further attention. If fiscal transfers *stricto sensu* indeed take place in the context of the ESM and the ECB's unconventional measures, this becomes problematic for two reasons: first, because the EU, with the exception of cohesion policy, is not a redistributive state. Budgetary and fiscal powers, as the *BVerfG* reminded us in both the *Gauweiler*[29] and *Weiss* references,[30] belong to the constitutional core and identity of the Member States. If an EU body with such functions were to be established then it must be legitimised to do so, at least from

[26] Van Rompuy (et al), ibid.

[27] European Commission, A blueprint for a deep and genuine economic and monetary union – Launching a European Debate, (30 November 2012) COM(2012) 777 final/2, 33.

[28] I am referring here to the outright purchase programmes initiated by reason of the crisis by the ECB. These programmes took different forms throughout the ECB's unconventional mode; namely, the securities market programme (SMP), the – not so far implemented – outright monetary transactions programme (OMT), and quantitative easing (QE).

[29] Case C-62/14, 16 June 2015, *Gauweiler and Others v Deutscher Bundestag* (OMT case), ECLI:EU:C:2015:400.

[30] Case C-493/17, 11 December 2018, *Weiss and Others*, ECLI:EU:C:2018:1000.

a competences and a democratic accountability perspective.[31] Hence, eventual funding by other states' taxpayers would at least require an enhanced democratic legitimacy expressed, for instance, via an increased participation of the European Parliament (EP), which has not been the case so far.[32] The implication of such a transfer would be that the participant states jeopardise their budgetary autonomy, an argument that is, currently, valid for the financially assisted (from the ESM) states,[33] but which has been brought forward also by Germany in the context of the ECB's unconventional measures. The second criticism relates to the two related 'market-based prohibitions' in the Treaty, notably Articles 123 and 125 TFEU and to the moral hazard the existence of such a crisis resolution mechanism may cause. In other words, Member States' fiscal behaviour could be affected towards more fiscal profligacy.

The perennial question is, hence, whether these programmes can have negative repercussions for the Eurozone taxpayers, in case of one country's default. In other words, whether there is a risk when the ECB buys government bonds from 'weak' countries that it assumes a credit risk, which, in case of default of the country at issue, means the losses of the ECB would be borne by the Member States and, effectively, the taxpayers of the fiscally sound Eurozone countries. The question of who will bear the losses if things go wrong is fundamental. If one accepts that this possibility actually exists, then the budgetary powers of the Member States are in fact at stake because of the ECB's decisions. If we extend this argument, the ECB indirectly encroaches upon an area strictly reserved (until recently at least) to the Member States.[34]

These questions have been actively debated in literature with both sides finding support.[35] In legal literature, the different unconventional monetary policy measures of the ECB have been repeatedly found to entail hidden transfer mechanisms, the overstepping of the ECB into fiscal policy making and an overstretch of

[31] As the Court noted in *Pringle* about Art 136(3) TFEU and the ESM: 'The provision serves to safeguard the stability of the monetary union and specifically does not make it possible to introduce a comprehensive liability and transfer union, but instead gives selective authorisation, in a situation which is sufficiently clearly discernible [...]', para 178.

[32] As M Dawson and F De Witte argue: 'While it could have partly legitimized the Union's shift to greater re-distributive decision-making, the EP has played no role of significance in either the ESM or the Fiscal Compact': M Dawson and F De Witte, 'Constitutional Balance in the EU after the Euro-Crisis' (2013) 76 *Modern Law Review* 817, 832.

[33] C Calliess, 'The Governance Framework of the Eurozone and the Need for a Treaty Reform' in F Fabbrini et al, *What Form of Government for the European Union and the Eurozone?* (Oxford, Hart, 2016) 49.

[34] K Pantazatou and I G Asimakopoulos, 'Conventional and Unconventional Monetary Policy' in F Fabbrini and M Ventoruzzo (eds), *European Economic Law* (Cheltenham, Edward Elgar, forthcoming).

[35] See, for instance, H-W Sinn arguing against the QE: 'This is tantamount to illegal government financing through the money-printing press. If the ECB buys sovereign bonds, the governments will issue new bonds, in effect drawing their funding from the printing press. This is prohibited by Article 123 of the EU Treaty and would require clearing by the German Constitutional Court', available at www.cesifo-group.de/ifoHome/presse/Pressemitteilungen/Pressemitteilungen-Archiv/2015/Q1/press_20150122_ezb.html (accessed 25 March 2019).

the ECB's mandate to ensure price stability.[36] In economics, however, part of the criticism could be rebutted by the generally accepted view that central banks cannot 'go bust', as they hold the monopoly for issuing new currency.[37] Bond-buying programmes could become implicitly 'costly' for taxpayers to the extent that they involve increasing the money supply, as they can contribute to inflation.[38]

The other crisis resolution mechanism, the ESM asserts that: 'The ESM lends hundreds of billions of euros to programme countries. But *this does not cost taxpayers any money*, because the ESM raises the money it needs in financial markets'[39] (emphasis added). This statement seems to ignore the fact that if one state fails to repay the money, then, in accordance with Article 25 of the ESM Treaty, the losses shall be covered first by the reserve funds, whose guarantors are the participating states, demonstrating a first hybrid indirect form of redistributions. In addition to that, Recital 12 of the ESMT provides that in case debt sustainability is not restored '[I]n accordance with IMF practice, in exceptional cases an adequate and proportionate form *of private sector involvement* shall be considered [...]'.

An EU tax that would lead to the creation of a larger EU budget, a part of which would be possibly earmarked to resolve such crises, would certainly rectify many of the deficiencies of the current system. Despite the lack of political agreement and the legal basis obstacles, the most recent proposal to overcome the shortcomings of the Eurozone governance is the creation of a European Monetary Fund (EMF) that would allow for financial aid to countries hit by economic shocks. The EMF would replace the ESM and would have extensive competences, including acting as a lender of last resort in banking crises. The proposal was linked to the re-consideration of the introduction of a European minister of economy and finance for the Eurozone. According to the proposal, the European Council would be given the possibility to approve or reject bail-out programmes, the disposition of more instruments and more money to support crisis-afflicted states and banks and would be obliged to report regularly to the EP and national parliaments on its activities, with a view to achieving greater democratic control. If it materialised, it would present the ultimate, so far, 'fiscal transfers' mechanism as it would provide for grants and loans to countries in need, but it would still remain very far from being granted any tax-raising powers. However, Member States' reactions to the Commission's blueprint for the fund have been lukewarm.[40] The main fear has

[36] D Wilsher, 'Law and the Financial Crisis: Searching for Europe's New Gold Standard' (2014) 20 *European Law Journal* 241; K Tuori, 'Has Euro Area Monetary Policy Become Redistribution by Monetary Means? 'Unconventional' Monetary Policy as a Hidden Transfer Mechanism' (2016) 22 *European Law Journal* 838, 856; M Ioannidis, 'Europe's new transformations: How the EU economic constitution changed during the Eurozone crisis' (2016) 53 *Common Market Law Review* 1237, 1240 and 1252 ff.

[37] WH Buiter, 'Can central banks go broke?' (2008); D Bunea et al, 'Profit distribution and loss coverage rules for central banks' (2016) *ECB Paper Series* No 169.

[38] For an overview, see bruegel.org/2015/01/qe-and-central-bank-solvency/.

[39] See www.esm.europa.eu/about-us/how-we-work.

[40] J Brunsden and M Khan, 'Brussels calls for creation of European Monetary Fund', *Financial Times* (6 December 2017), available at www.ft.com/content/3dc16660-da8a-11e7-a039-c64b1c09b482.

been that the Fund would be controlled by EU institutions and would lack the necessary additional democratic guarantees that would come with such extensive fiscal powers. Its effectiveness has also been contested as, similar to the ESM, it has been criticised for creating moral hazard and an uneven burden – sharing that would certainly not function as a future crises' preventive mechanism.[41]

III. New Context, New Focus: Tax Planning, Aggressive Tax Planning, Tax Avoidance and Tax Evasion

A. The Past and the Shift

The focus of the scarce secondary legislation adopted in the area of direct taxation before the crisis has been the removal of tax-related obstacles in the internal market.[42] As the unanimity requirement, enshrined in the relevant approximation of (tax) laws provision, Article 115 TFEU, obstructed the adoption of extensive secondary legislation, this role fell on the CJEU, which has rightfully been presented as the motor of tax integration.[43] Furthermore, harmful tax practices would be tackled via soft law means, namely, the Code of Conduct for Business taxation. The Code targets 'potentially harmful' tax measures (PHTMs) on business – regulations and administrative practices as well as provisions that are 'unfairly' competitive by virtue of 'a significant effect on the location of business activity'.[44]

Other efforts to harmonise legislation concerning indirect taxation on financial transactions by introducing the FTT or to establish a single set of rules to calculate companies' taxable profits in the EU through the Common Consolidated Corporate Tax Base (CCCTB) were met with scepticism by many Member States and have not, so far, developed into binding legislation. The CCCTB proposal emerged in 2011 as a Commission initiative to enhance coordination among

[41] C Fuest, 'A three-step plan for a better European Monetary Fund', *EurActiv* (5 January 2018), available at www.euractiv.com/section/economic-governance/opinion/a-three-step-plan-for-a-better-european-monetary-fund/.

[42] Until 2008 the secondary legislation in force in direct taxation consisted of the following six Directives; Directive 2003/49/EC; Directive 2003/48/EC; Directive 90/434/EEC 1990; Directive 90/435/EEC; Directive 90/436/EEC, and Directive 77/799/EEC.

[43] M Graetz and AC Warren Jr, 'Dividend Taxation in Europe: When the ECJ makes tax policy' (2007) 44 *CMLR*; M Gammie, 'The role of the European Court of Justice in the Development of Direct Taxation in the European Union' (2003) *Bulletin, IBFD*; J Snell, 'Non discriminatory tax obstacles in Community Law' (2007) 56 *International & Comparative Law Quarterly* 355; S Kingston, 'The Boundaries of Sovereignty: The ECJ's Controversial Role: Applying Internal Market Law to Direct Tax Measures' (2006) 9 *Cambridge Yearbook of European Legal Studies*.

[44] European Commission, Communication: 'A Package to Tackle Harmful Tax Competition' (5 November 1997) COM (1997)564 final, Annex 1, C. The Code's coverage of 'business taxes' appears to be quite broad, although manifestly excluding indirect taxes and direct taxes on individuals.

Member States in order to eliminate tax obstacles and reduce market distortions. The adoption of the CCCTB would bring about winners and losers as a result of the reallocation of the corporate tax base among the Member States. While the Commission's impact assessment has shown that, in general, the smaller Member States would lose and the large Member States would win tax base, a rebutting survey by Ernst and Young argued otherwise.[45] Several states made use of their 'yellow card privileges' and opposed the first proposal, arguing that the proposal did not comply with the principle of subsidiarity.[46] Despite the first lukewarm reactions, the Commission proposed to re-launch a modified version of the CCCTB in October 2016, which remains to be adopted.

Whether successful or not, most of these approximation of laws attempts aimed to remove the remaining tax obstacles in the internal market, notably double taxation. Soon, however, it became apparent that the loss of tax revenue for individual Member States and the EU as a whole through tax evasion and tax avoidance practices constituted another major problem deserving its own set of solutions. In 2012, the European Commission reported that around €1 trillion is lost to tax evasion and avoidance every year in the EU.[47] The report does not specify whether this loss arises from illegal practices only, namely tax fraud and tax evasion, or whether the estimation includes also tax avoidance and aggressive tax planning.[48] A reason for this ambiguity could be the lack of a clear definition of the aforementioned terms. This was not only an EU problem. On 19 July 2013, the OECD published its action plan on BEPS. The underlying reasoning, at a global level, was that citizens and governments that were harmed by these practices perceived the minimisation of the tax burden of Multinational Enterprises (MNEs) as unfair. Indeed the fact that the world's biggest multinational conglomerates manage to earn trillions of dollars around the world, yet many seem to pay virtually no tax anywhere is framed as a justice issue because it shifts the burden of taxpaying to those who cannot similarly avail themselves of sophisticated tax planning strategies.[49] However, as the OECD points out, most of the schemes employed by the MNEs to avoid paying their share of taxes are not illegal. The fact that these practices are considered as legal, besides discouraging voluntary compliance by all taxpayers, also 'undermines the fairness and integrity of tax systems because businesses that operate across borders can use BEPS to gain a competitive advantage over enterprises that operate at a domestic level'.[50]

[45] Ernst & Young, 'Study on the Economic and Budgetary Impact of the Introduction of a Common Consolidated Corporate Tax Base in the EU' (January 2011).

[46] M Vascega and S van Thiel, 'The CCCTB Proposal: The Next Step towards Corporate Tax Harmonization in the European Union?' (2011) 51(9/10) *European Taxation* 374, 377.

[47] European Commission, 'Clamping Down on Tax Evasion and Avoidance: Commission Presents the Way Forward' 6 December 2012, available at europa.eu/rapid/press_release_IP-12-1325_en.htm.

[48] Tax evasion comprises predominantly cases of (illegal) non-disclosure of income, whereas tax avoidance consists of the shifting of profits to other low or no-tax jurisdictions.

[49] A Christians, 'Distinguishing Tax Avoidance and Evasion: Why and How' (2017) 3(2) *Journal of Tax Administration* 9.

[50] OECD, www.oecd.org/tax/beps/beps-about.htm.

This feeling of unfairness with regard to the payment of taxes due, in conjunction with the increased mobility of taxpayers facilitated by increasing globalisation and the digitalisation of the economy, brought again to the fore the need to take action against tax avoidance practices.[51] In order for tax systems to become more fair and just, the scope of what is considered impermissible had to grow or the cause and/or circumstances that create tax avoidance practices have to be tackled. Until recently, only tax fraud and tax evasion, ie the reporting of false information or the non-disclosure of income, were considered outright illegal. Tax avoidance, which can materialise through several different practices, and still remains to be defined clearly and consistently, belonged in some sort of grey zone that was neither legal nor outright illegal, but definitely possible. In agreement with this, Pierre Moscovici noted, in the aftermath of the Panama Papers, that

> [t]hese aggressive tax planning optimisation schemes, many of them appear to be completely legal. So we have to respond on the legal front by establishing a new legal framework. If this is legal, as many people claim, then we need to change the law.[52]

The core concept of tax avoidance is linked to the possibility to obtain a tax advantage 'by exploiting the friction between the form, which [the taxpayers] choose from those that do not trigger the liability to tax, and the substance, which is akin to events that would otherwise trigger the liability to tax'.[53] The EP has defined corporate tax avoidance as the use of

> loopholes and mismatches between different countries' tax systems and profits-and-losses shifting via *aggressive tax planning*, with a view to reducing companies' tax bill as a result of the diminution of their taxable revenues. It generally remains *within the boundaries of the law*, contrary to tax evasion and fraud which are both illegal[54] (emphasis added).

According to the Commission, aggressive tax planning consists of 'taking advantage of the technicalities of a tax system or of mismatches between two or more tax systems for the purpose of reducing tax liability'[55] including, inter alia, practices of rearrangement of international flows to avoid repatriation of taxes; reallocation of the tax base to a lower-tax country and the reduction of the tax base via

[51] In 1996, OECD countries launched their harmful tax practices initiative aimed at combatting international tax evasion by promoting transparency and exchange of information both within and outside the OECD. The 2000 OECD report, 'Towards Global Tax Co-operation', included a list of 35 jurisdictions that were found to meet the tax haven criteria set out in an earlier report issued in 1998.

[52] J Stone, 'Paradise Papers: Rich tax avoiders are "vampires", EU finance chief Pierre Moscovici says' *The Independent* (14 November 2017).

[53] P Pistone, 'The Meaning of Tax Avoidance and Aggressive Tax Planning in European Union Tax Law: Some Thoughts in Connection with the Reaction to Such Practices by the European Union' in AP Dourado (ed), *Tax Avoidance Revisited in the EU BEPS context* (IBFD, Amsterdam 2017).

[54] European Parliament, 'Understanding the OECD tax plan to address 'base erosion and profit shifting' – BEPS', Briefing, June 2017, p 2.

[55] European Commission (2012), Commission recommendation of 6 December 2012 on aggressive tax planning (2012/772/EU).

a double deduction or double non-taxation.[56] However, a common or shared definition of tax avoidance in tax systems is still lacking. Anti-avoidance measures reflect accurately the big differences between the Member States' tax policies and the inadequacy of the previous legal framework to tackle the arising asymmetries: what is 'tax avoidance' from one Member State's perspective is simply an exercise of the freedoms from another state's point of view.[57] If one adds to this the recently-coined term 'aggressive tax planning', the boundaries between the permissible and the impermissible become even more blurred.

In the absence of a common concept of tax avoidance in tax systems, one can rely on anti-abuse measures to counteract tax avoidance practices. After all, tax avoidance is fundamentally abuse of law, in that the tax practice or scheme at issue relies on the literal interpretation of the law, but circumvents its purpose.[58] Countries have their own General Anti-Avoidance Rule (GAAR) that set different criteria on what constitutes abuse and avoidance in the tax sphere. In 2016, the EU adopted the Anti Tax-Avoidance Directive (ATAD) and enacted, inter alia, a GAAR concerning the Member States of the EU, requiring that each Member State establish a domestic GAAR meeting certain baseline requirements.

Counteracting this feeling of injustice created by tax avoidance practices employed mostly by MNEs became a fundamental priority at a global level. Therefore, even earlier than 2013 and the BEPS initiative, the focus of global initiatives and EU secondary legislation has shifted to combatting tax avoidance. The underlying idea is to ensure that profits are taxed where they should, that is, either where the economic activity takes place or where value is created, and not in low or no-tax jurisdictions. What was, until very recently, a national matter, ie to counteract abusive tax practices through GAARs or Controlled Foreign Corporation (CFC) rules, or thin capitalisation rules or transfer pricing rules has now become the subject of a coordination approach through the BEPS initiative. The CJEU would often review the compatibility of those national tax measures vis-à-vis the fundamental freedoms, but in principle, this case law was the first and only to produce some first segments of a common approach on what constituted abuse and what did not.[59] However, since 2015, national tax systems have as a reference point, to say the least, the BEPS actions in order to become more tax avoidance-proof. I turn now to address the BEPS initiative, in order to proceed with analysing how this has affected the EU tax legal order.

[56] European Commission, 'Aggressive tax planning indicators – Final Report', Taxation Papers, *Working Paper No 71 – 2017*, p 23.

[57] T O'Shea, 'Some ECJ Guidance on Abusive Tax Practices in the European Union' (2008) 50 *Tax Notes International* 241.

[58] R Karimeri, 'A Critical Review of the Definition of Tax Avoidance in the Case Law of the European Court of Justice' (2011) 6/7(39) *Intertax* 296, 297.

[59] The landmark cases in the area of abuse in taxation are: Case C-255/02, judgment of 21 February 2006, *Halifax and Others*, ECLI:EU:C:2006:121 in the field of indirect taxation and Case C-196/04, judgment of 12 September 2006, *Cadbury Schweppes and Cadbury Schweppes Overseas*, ECLI:EU:C:2006:544 in the field of direct taxation.

B. Global Initiatives: Base Erosion and Profit Shifting

The BEPS Project is a joint OECD and G20 countries' project aiming to set up an international framework to combat tax avoidance by MNEs using base erosion and profit shifting tools, that is, tax avoidance strategies that exploit gaps and mismatches in tax rules to artificially shift profits to low or no-tax locations.[60] The project was initiated in 2013. The OECD has outlined BEPS as follows:

> BEPS relates chiefly to instances where the interaction of different tax rules leads to double non-taxation or less than single taxation. It also relates to arrangements that achieve no or low taxation by shifting profits away from the jurisdictions where the activities creating those profits take place. No or low taxation is not per se a cause of concern, but it becomes so when it is associated with practices that artificially segregate taxable income from the activities that generate it. In other words, what creates tax policy concerns is that, due to gaps in the interaction of different tax systems, and in some cases because of the application of bilateral tax treaties, income from cross-border activities may go untaxed anywhere, or be only unduly lowly taxed.[61]

In 2015, the OECD presented 15 Actions that range from the taxation of the digital economy (Action 1) to dispute resolution between countries (Action 14), all of which aim to 'equip governments with domestic and international instruments to address tax avoidance, ensuring that profits are taxed where economic activities generating the profits are performed and where value is created'.[62]

Currently, the Inclusive Framework on BEPS brings together over 124 countries and jurisdictions to collaborate on the implementation of the BEPS Package. While it has been acknowledged that the main source of these tax avoidance schemes is the interaction of existing different rules, rather than one rule per se (or the absence thereof), the BEPS package's goal is to tackle – in a coordinated manner – the *causes* and *circumstances* creating BEPS practices, rather than just suppressing the actual use of BEPS practices.[63]

C. EU Initiatives: Building on Anti-Tax Avoidance, Reporting and Exchange of Information

In 2013 when I defended my thesis I argued, inter alia, that the restraint of unanimity embedded in Article 115 TFEU, the legal basis for the adoption of any direct tax measures, would prevent the adoption of any secondary law in the near future. I was wrong.

[60] See www.oecd.org/tax/beps/.

[61] OECD, *Action Plan on Base Erosion and Profit Shifting* (OECD Publishing, 2013) 10.

[62] See www.oecd.org/tax/beps/beps-actions.htm.

[63] European Parliament, 'Understanding the OECD tax plan to address 'base erosion and profit shifting' – BEPS', Briefing, June 2017, 3.

The global initiatives to curtail tax avoidance practices could not leave the EU intact. All EU Member States, with the exception of Cyprus, are Members of the Inclusive Framework on BEPS that counts, as of January 2019, 127 members.[64] BEPS is built around three axes: the improvement of the coherence of tax rules across borders; the reinforcement of substance requirements; and the enhancement of transparency and certainty. The EU took quick steps in order to implement, to the extent possible, some of the BEPS Actions. In January 2016, the EU adopted the Anti-Tax Avoidance Package that aimed to ensure fairer, simpler and more effective corporate taxation in the EU through preventing aggressive tax planning and boosting tax transparency.[65] Same as in BEPS, in order to combat tax avoidance, the Package intends to promote the principle that companies are taxed wherever value is created in the EU.

i. *Tax Scandals and the Need for Tax Transparency*

A first reaction to the tax avoidance practices and the feeling of injustice they created was to build upon more tax transparency through the exchange of tax information among Member States. This led to the repeal and subsequent expansion of the 'mutual assistance Directive'[66] by Directive 2011/16/EU (DAC 1) that establishes a more elaborate, in comparison to the past, system of exchange of taxpayers' information. DAC 1 distinguishes between three types of exchange of information: exchange of information on request (referring to a specific case); spontaneous exchanges (no prior request by the recipient state, no systematic basis of exchange); and automatic exchanges (systematic exchange of predefined tax information on a regular basis). For the non-automatic exchange of tax information the exchanged data has to be *foreseeably relevant* to the administration and for the enforcement of domestic tax laws of the recipient Member State. The Directive prohibits fishing expeditions, in line with the commentary of Article 26 OECD Model Convention. The *mandatory* Automatic Exchange of Information (AEOI) in DAC 1 covers only specific tax data; namely, income from employment; directors' fees; life insurance products (not covered by other Union legal instruments on exchange of information and other similar measures); pensions; ownership of and income from immovable property.[67]

[64] See www.oecd.org/tax/beps/inclusive-framework-on-beps-composition.pdf.

[65] The EU Anti Tax Avoidance Package adopted by the European Commission on 28 January 2016 consisted of four documents: a proposal for an Anti Tax Avoidance Directive (ATAD); a Communication on an External Strategy for Effective Taxation; the amendment to the Directive on mutual assistance to apply automatic exchange of information to country-by-country reporting; and the recommendation on tax treaties adding the 'genuine economic activity' test to the Principal Purpose Test (PPT) rule.

[66] Council Directive 77/799/EEC was repealed by Directive 2011/16/EU (DAC 1) which has subsequently been amended several times.

[67] Art 8(1) Directive 2011/16/EU.

In the EU, the Common Reporting Standard (CRS)[68] was implemented through the EU Revised Directive (DAC 2) on Administrative Cooperation.[69] DAC 2 amended DAC 1 and it, inter alia, broadened the scope of the collection of data that is covered by AEOI. Under DAC 2, Member States are obliged to *automatically* exchange financial account information, abolishing effectively and finally bank secrecy within the EU.[70] DAC 2 implementation into national law was preceded by the infamous 'Swiss leaks' which revealed that HSBC PB had allegedly concealed over €5.7 billion in tax havens for its French clients alone. It was followed by the Lux Leaks scandal, revealed on 5 November 2014, when the ICIJ published hundreds of advance tax rulings on its website that concerned private tax agreements between multinational companies and the Luxembourgish authorities. A former employee of PWC discovered the documents in October 2010. Following these revelations, Luxembourg became a 'tax heaven by administrative practices'. All these revelations about the 'hidden wealth of nations'[71] that is channeled to tax havens by reason of laws protecting tax and bank secrecy could not be left unanswered. Public unrest was large as both MNEs and rich individuals could evade taxes by channelling their profits to very low or no-tax jurisdictions. This discontent was expressed in a multi-faceted way; not only in terms of more legislation, but also 'fast-track' legislation. 'Before Luxleaks, a text on taxation was negotiated for seven years,' said a top EU official. 'Now, it is seven months'.[72]

In the aftermath of LuxLeaks and the state aid investigations (at the time) of Advance Pricing Arrangements (APAs) and Tax Rulings,[73] DAC 1 was further amended by Directive (EU) 2015/2376 (DAC 3) on mandatory automatic exchange of information in the field of taxation. DAC 3 concerns the mandatory automatic exchange of tax information on advance cross-border rulings and APAs. The fear that because of this automatic exchange of information an increased number of taxpayers will become reluctant to file an APA application, in order to prevent their structures from being exposed, seems to be confirmed.[74]

[68] The CRS, developed in response to the G20 request and approved by the OECD Council on 15 July 2014, calls on jurisdictions to obtain information from their financial institutions and automatically exchange that information with other jurisdictions on an annual basis.

[69] Directive 2014/107/EU.

[70] Already under Art 18(2) of DAC 1 a Member State could not refuse to provide information just because 'this information is held by a bank, other financial institution, nominee or person acting in an agency or a fiduciary capacity or because it relates to ownership interests in a person'. Prior to that, see the Savings Income Directive that provided for mandatory and automatic exchange of savings account information between Member States.

[71] I am referring here to the famous book by G Zucman, *The Hidden Wealth of Nations* (University of Chicago Press, 2015) which addresses the question of how wealth is hidden in tax heavens and what can be done for this to be prevented.

[72] Q Aries, 'EU vows to act quickly on Panama Papers' *Politico* (4 July 2016).

[73] APAs and tax rulings mean essentially any agreement or communication addressed by a Member State to the person or group of persons at issue, with a view to, inter alia, interpreting the tax laws of that Member State and, usually, providing the tax to be paid by that person. For the cases, see n 93.

[74] See J Schaffner and S Balliet, 'Luxembourg and BEPS, EU State Aid Investigations and LuxLeaks: And What about Luxembourg?' (2016) July/August *International Transfer Pricing Journal* 279.

DAC 4 was adopted in May 2016.[75] It constituted one of the first elements of the January 2016 package of Commission proposals to strengthen the rules against corporate tax avoidance.[76] One and a half months after the publication of this package, in an all-time record, the Council reached a political agreement on the first part of the package, the mandatory exchange of country-by-country reporting to tax authorities. The directive builds on the 2015 OECD recommendations to address BEPS (Action 13).[77] DAC 4 provides for AEOI regarding country-by-country reports of a multinational company's group allocation of income, tax and business activities on a country by country basis. The rules only apply to MNEs with a minimum consolidated group turnover of €750 million. The relevant reporting entity will have to submit to the tax authorities of its residence Member State certain information (including turnover, pre-tax profit, income tax paid and accrued, number of employees, capital, tangible assets, and business activities) on an annual basis and for each tax jurisdiction where they do business. The residence Member State will then have to automatically exchange data with the other relevant Member States (ie where the MNEs are either resident or subject to tax through a permanent establishment). The idea behind DAC 4 is that tax avoidance risks related to transfer pricing are minimised and that the exchange of information will 'enable the tax authorities to react to harmful tax practices through changes in the legislation or adequate risk assessments and tax audits'.[78]

Furthermore, the Commission, being aware of the fact that tax authorities need greater access to information on the beneficial owners of intermediary entities in order to combat tax evasion, proposed another Directive to amend DAC 1 and the Fourth Anti-Money Laundering Directive (AMLD).[79] DAC 5[80] gives the possibility to tax authorities to access beneficial ownership and due diligence information as those are collected in the context of the anti-money laundering legal framework. In line with the Fourth AMLD and in order to minimise tax evasion Member States like the UK and France have already introduced beneficial ownership registries, making public or at least available to the relevant authorities beneficial ownership data.[81]

[75] Directive (EU) 2016/881.

[76] See ec.europa.eu/taxation_customs/business/company-tax/anti-tax-avoidance-package_en (accessed 25 March 2019).

[77] OECD/G 20 Base Erosion and Profit Shifting (BEPS) Project, Action 13: Guidance on the Implementation of Transfer Pricing Documentation and Country-by-Country Reporting.

[78] Directive (EU) 2016/881 of 25 May 2016 amending Directive 2011/16/EU as regards mandatory automatic exchange of information in the field of taxation, Preamble Recital 3.

[79] Directive (EU) 2015/849.

[80] Council Directive (EU) 2016/2258 amending Directive 2011/16/EU as regards access to anti-money-laundering information by tax authorities.

[81] In the UK, the 'People with Significant Control (PSC) beneficial ownership register' for companies is available to the public as opposed to the 'Trust Register' that will not be open to the public. In France, the 'French Trust register' is open only to specific designated authorities and professionals following the decision of the 'Conseil Constitutionnel', that ruled that public access to the trust register was unconstitutional on the ground that it created a disproportionate breach of privacy rights of individuals taking part in trust arrangements.

In the aftermath of Panama Papers, Pierre Moscovici told reporters that the use of offshore companies to hide what he called 'shocking amounts' of financial assets from tax authorities was 'unethical'.[82] He estimated that the tax shelters resulted in an annual loss of some €1 trillion in public finances.[83] The EU's answer to Panama Papers was DAC 6.[84] According to DAC 6, intermediaries, that is, for instance, accountants, advisers, lawyers and banks who sell reportable cross-border tax arrangements to their clients, should report information on the arrangement to the tax authorities of their home Member State. DAC 6 not only establishes mandatory disclosure rules for intermediaries on potentially aggressive tax-planning arrangements, but also provides for the automatic exchange on tax planning cross-border arrangements.[85]

ii. The Anti-Tax Avoidance Directive

The ATAD[86] has been characterised by many as the turning point in the history of EU tax legislation.[87] The ATAD establishes a *minimum framework* that Member States have to implement in order to cope with tax avoidance practices that, according to its title, 'directly affect the functioning of the internal market'. It is the first coordinated effort to interpret in specific the G20/OECD BEPS ideals, as it constitutes a 'regional' implementation of the BEPS holistic approach, which is much more consistent with the BEPS spirit, than the unilateral measures that have been taken by some EU Member States.[88]

This is the first time in the history of EU direct taxation, that a directive has had such a broad scope; the ATAD applies to all taxpayers that are subject to corporate tax in a Member State, including permanent establishments (PEs) of third country entities. As it aims to lay down rules against the erosion of tax bases in the internal market and the shifting of profits out of the internal market, it lays down rules of substantive law that go far beyond the reach of existing directives in the field of direct taxation both quantitatively and qualitatively.[89] It, hence, focuses on different practices that could facilitate tax avoidance and it, thus, establishes general rules

[82] Aries (above n 72).

[83] ibid.

[84] Council Directive (EU) 2018/822 amending Directive 2011/16/EU as regards mandatory automatic exchange of information in the field of taxation in relation to reportable cross-border arrangements.

[85] Art 8ab (13) provides that 'The competent authority of a Member State where the information was filed pursuant to paragraphs 1 to 12 of this Article shall, by means of an *automatic exchange*, communicate the information specified in paragraph 14 of this Article to the competent authorities of all other Member States'.

[86] Directive 2016/1164 Laying down Rules against Tax Avoidance Practices that Directly Affect the Functioning of the Internal Market [2016] OJ L193/1.

[87] See Pistone (above n 53) and D Gutman et al, 'The Impact of the ATAD on Domestic Systems: A Comparative Survey', *European Taxation* (January 2017) 2.

[88] AP Dourado, 'The EU Anti Tax Avoidance Package: Moving Ahead of BEPS?' (2016) 44(6/7) *Intertax* 440.

[89] Gutman et al (above n 87).

on limitations to the deductibility of interest, exit taxation, a general anti-abuse rule, controlled foreign company rules and rules to tackle hybrid mismatches. The general aim is not only to counter tax avoidance practices but also avoid creating other obstacles to the market, such as double taxation.[90]

The uniqueness of this unprecedented undertaking is, further, backed by the 'fast track' time-frame within which the ATAD was adopted, despite the unanimity obstacle enshrined in Article 115 TFEU. This was not only due to the need to fulfil the timeframe for BEPS implementation, but is in itself symptomatic of the level of urgency felt across EU Member States to respond to the challenges raised by the globalisation and the digitalisation of the economy.[91]

As expected, however, the ATAD not only represents a noble effort among Member States to cooperate in curtailing anti-tax avoidance practices, it also aims to establish a level playing field across Member States against tax avoidance practices. This means that lenient approaches to tax avoidance as a form of tax competition, adopted by certain Member States, will also have to be curtailed.[92] Indeed, as *Luxleaks* and other infamous recent state aid cases[93] reveal, several states have facilitated MNEs in avoiding paying their fair share of taxes where profits and value are generated. In an effort to attract investment and companies, traditional countries engaging in tax competition[94] had either introduced specific tax incentives towards that purpose, or had used their national legislation and tax treaty network towards this direction. As Kemmeren observes, these states were not really interested in cooperating with each other to align tax systems, as long as they thought that they had more to gain from tax competition than from tax coordination.[95] Getting the 'sworn opponents' to tax cooperation to agree on such a package speaks volumes about the public outrage that followed both the state aid cases and the tax scandals. The crisis and the huge budget deficits could only reinforce this argument.

IV. Conclusion

One cannot but observe that direct taxation has experienced a total overhaul in recent years in the EU. Nobody could have foreseen a few years ago that bank

[90] Recital 5, Council Directive (EU) 2016/1164.

[91] R de la Feria, 'Harmonizing Anti-Tax Avoidance Rules' (2017) 3 *EC Tax Review* 110.

[92] ibid.

[93] See, for instance, Case T-516/18, *Luxembourg (Engie) v Commission*; Case T-816/17, T-318/18, *Luxembourg (Amazon) v Commission*; Cases T-778/16, T-892/16, C-12/18, C-678/17, *Ireland (Apple) v Commission*; Cases T-760/15, T-636/16, T-877/16, *Netherlands (Starbucks) v Commission*; Cases T-759/15, T-755/15, *Luxembourg(FCA) v Commission.*

[94] Tax competition is very difficult to define. While several attempts have been made, notably by lawyers and economists, a commonly accepted definition is still lacking. The same applies to the two most distinctive categories of tax competition, namely 'good' tax competition and 'harmful' tax competition.

[95] E Kemmeren, 'Where is EU Law in the OECD BEPS Discussion?' (2014) 4 *EC Tax Review* 190.

secrecy would be practically abolished, that tax information would automatically be exchanged among Member States and that 'aggressive tax planning' schemes would be so much opposed. This has been caused by a series of – depending on one's stance – fortunate or unfortunate events. The financial crisis increased the states' need for revenue. The tax scandals, in conjunction with the imposed austerity measures, created to the 'average taxpayer' a feeling of injustice and unfairness. He bore the burden of contributing to the public finances whilst MNEs were saving billions through tax planning schemes. The latter were given more opportunities to engage in such practices through increasing globalisation and the digitalisation of the economy. This triangular relationship resulted in the production of a series of secondary legislation, built on tax transparency and anti-tax avoidance that for the first time in the history of the EU goes deep into the core of national tax systems. The main problem in the EU is no longer double taxation but instead non-taxation. This was the obvious and, to a certain extent, agreed upon result, precipitated by the fertile ground at global level and the BEPS project.

The second result of the crisis was much more subtle and, certainly, less collaborative. Both 'donor' and 'recipient' Member States have experienced an encroachment upon their budgetary and, by implication, tax sovereignty. The former via the crisis resolution mechanisms, namely, the ESM and the ECB's unconventional monetary policy tools, and the latter via the tax and budget-specific conditionalities attached to their financial assistance agreements.

All these direct and indirect implications of the crisis have resulted in the development of a level playing field in the internal market, where tax competition is no longer tolerated. If one adds to this the recent two proposals for Directives in the taxation of the digital economy in order to promote a fair and efficient tax system in the EU for the Digital Single Market,[96] we can safely assume that the crisis has functioned in several ways as the catalyst in changing the focus from 'no double taxation' to 'no zero taxation' and in producing the most important pieces of secondary legislation since the founding of the EU.

[96] Proposal for a Council Directive on the common system of a digital services tax on revenues resulting from the provision of certain digital services, COM(2018) 148 final and Proposal for a Council Directive laying down rules relating to the corporate taxation of a significant digital presence, COM (2018) 147 final.

11

The Evolution of European Insolvency Law from Regulatory Competition to Harmonisation

ANNIKA WOLF* AND HEIKKI MARJOSOLA**

Whether companies operate within a national or a European marketplace, a proportion of them will inevitably be unable to meet their financial obligations and will ultimately fail. The Europeanisation of national economies has increased the likelihood of cross-border insolvency proceedings in Europe. Achieving predictability, certainty and transparency in such multinational proceedings in Europe, and dealing with a debtor in default with the least possible delay and expense to the benefit of all stakeholders, are issues that have been addressed by the European institutions. The European legislator has issued two regulations: the European Insolvency Regulation (EIR, 2000) and a revision of it (EIR recast, 2015). In 2016, the European Commission published an ambitious proposal for a directive on preventive restructuring proceedings (Directive Proposal)[1] to further accelerate harmonisation in this area of law, which has much impact to achieve a common market.

This contribution discusses the evolution of EU insolvency law. Insolvency law will here be understood broadly as covering all kinds of insolvency rules ranging from early intervention measures (before serious financial distress has materialised), to timely restructuring (ensuring the preservation of viable business operations in the face of financial trouble), to the liquidation of assets, and to giving a second chance via debt discharge.[2] EU insolvency law is developing from what is still essentially a private international law model towards a

* Annika Wolf, Professor of Corporate Finance, Project Finance and Entrepreneurship, University of Applied Science Emden/Leer, Germany.
** Heikki Marjosola, Assistant Professor of Financial Law, University of Helsinki, Finland.

[1] European Commission proposal for a Directive of the European Parliament and of the Council on preventive restructuring frameworks, second chance and measures to increase the efficiency of restructuring, insolvency and discharge procedures (Directive Proposal), COM(2016) 723 final, 22.11.2016.

[2] ibid, explanatory memorandum, 2.

more harmonised approach. However, even if the Directive Proposal admittedly represents a significant change of course, it leaves certain key areas of private law untouched. The project, therefore, bears many of the hallmarks of what Hans Micklitz has termed European Regulatory Private Law. The current approach to EU insolvency law is one that accommodates the private law pluralism of national private legal orders but also builds on a distinct normative model making far fewer compromises when it comes to the ongoing process of Europeanisation.[3]

Following this introduction, Section I of the contribution reviews the evolution of EU insolvency law. Section II outlines the current economic state of the EU. This is particularly important in order to rationalise the nature of the proposed legislative intervention by the Directive Proposal. Section III focuses particularly on the Commission's strong commitment to ensuring that viable businesses in financial distress have access to coherent insolvency frameworks across all Member States and the possibility of restructuring at an early stage. The contribution concludes with an evaluation of whether the Directive will achieve its goals.

The paper's focus is appropriate to honour Hans Micklitz in recognition of his many contributions to scholarship in private law, and is an acknowledgement of his interests and pursuits. Beyond personal mentorship and encouragement, Hans Micklitz has provided us with insight and wisdom to contemplate the multifaceted nature of regulation in European law. Over his distinguished career, he has devoted much effort and applied his unique skills to teaching and scholarship in different areas of law. Hans Micklitz has inspired us as he has inspired cohorts of legal scholars and professionals. Our understanding of European law now is, and will always remain, inextricably tied to his important work.

I. The Evolution of EU Insolvency Law

The story of European integration is a story of gradual legal harmonisation of an increasing number of goods and services markets. Sixty years ago, the EEC Treaty[4] entered into force, extending the idea of one common market from the European Coal and Steel Community to all markets. Originally, Article 100 EEC Treaty was a compromise, implementing harmonisation only by directives and only by unanimity in the European Council. In order to further promote European integration, the 1985 Single Market programme[5] and the 1986 Single European Act (SEA)[6] created a further basis for harmonisation. With the new Article 100a, the

[3] H-W Micklitz, 'The Visible Hand of European Regulatory Private Law – The Transformation of European Private Law from Autonomy to Functionalism in Competition and Regulation' (2009) 28.1 *Yearbook of European Law* 3, 6.

[4] See eur-lex.europa.eu/legal-content/EN/TXT/?uri=LEGISSUM%3Axy0023.

[5] White Paper from the Commission to the European Council, 'Completing the Internal Market (Milan, 28–29 June 1985)' 14 June 1985, COM (85) 310.

[6] See www.europarl.europa.eu/factsheets/en/sheet/2/developments-up-to-the-single-european-act.

European Economic Community (EEC) introduced qualified majority voting in the European Council, greatly facilitating legal harmonisation. On the other hand, the Member States' approval of the SEA was made possible by certain important exceptions to some areas of national law and also by introducing a complex procedure that allowed individual Member States certain special rights. The SEA, and the 1992 Internal Market programme that followed it, endorsed minimum harmonisation and mutual recognition as a regulatory principle, thus allowing room for the dynamics of regulatory competition.[7]

Eventually, gradual deregulation prompted by regulatory competition made the case for full harmonisation by means of regulations. Being directly applicable, regulations prevent Member States from diluting the harmonising effects of a directive. In addition, the increasing density and detail of EU legislation limit the scope for national implementation laws and also raise doubts as to whether the implementation of a directive in national law does more harm than good.[8]

When it comes to insolvency law, it is by now well known that private international law in Europe has been unable to ensure equal treatment of creditors across national borders.[9] Efforts began in 1960 when the EEC first began to address the challenges of cross-border insolvency proceedings,[10] recognising that there was an 'obvious need to regulate the insolvencies of entities whose affairs transcend borders'.[11] The challenge to the ECC committee on international insolvency in drafting a Bankruptcy Convention was to establish a procedure that would harmonise the Member States' different laws and resolve the issues that arose when companies had assets in different Member States. These efforts needed to consider the two competing approaches in dealing with international insolvency issues: the territorialist approach; and the universalist approach. The universalist approach requires a single insolvency procedure that would be applicable in the EU, while under the territorialist approach each Member State would conduct its own insolvency proceedings with respect to assets located within its national jurisdiction and would disregard any parallel proceedings in another Member State.[12] An extreme universalist approach is the unitarian approach, where only one forum is responsible for overseeing the entire insolvency proceeding, to the exclusion of any other forum.[13]

[7] JM Sun, and J Pelkmans, 'Regulatory Competition in the Single Market' (1995) 33 *Journal of Common Market Studies* 67, 69.

[8] J Basedow, '60 Jahre Rechtsharmonisierung oder: vom unaufhaltsamen Drang zur Verordnung' (2018) *Europäische Zeitschrift für Wirtschaftrecht* 1, 2.

[9] IF Fletcher, 'International Insolvency: A Case for Study and Treatment' (1993) 27 *International Law* 429, 433.

[10] M Balz, 'The European Union Convention on Insolvency Proceedings' (1996) 70 *American Bankruptcy Law Journal* 485, 489.

[11] J Goldring, 'The new European insolvency regulation – a synopsis' (2002) 18(2) *Insolvency Law & Practice* 52.

[12] Fletcher (above n 9) 433.

[13] Balz (above n 10) 492.

After agreeing on the unitarian approach,[14] the EEC committee adopted a Draft EEC Bankruptcy Convention[15] in 1970 (Bankruptcy Convention 1970). However, there was no general acceptance because the new Member States made somewhat adverse comments, which led the EEC committee to amend the 1970 Bankruptcy Convention, significantly diluting its uniform law provisions. The new version was called the 1980 EEC Draft Bankruptcy Convention (1980 EEC Draft).[16] This remained unpopular in its original draft, even with revisions in 1982 and 1984, and never gained enough support from the Member States due to the enormous range of differences in countries' national laws and their distinctions between restructuring and insolvency proceedings.[17] In 1985, the EEC committee finally abandoned the 1985 EEC Draft. Negotiations were resumed in 1989 when the Council of Strasbourg began drafting the European Convention on Certain International Aspects of Bankruptcy (Istanbul Convention).[18]

The 1980s were a period of great change in insolvency law,[19] with many Member States amending their insolvency laws by introducing or expanding restructuring proceedings in addition to liquidation proceedings.[20] Those attempts were ironically resulting in less harmonisation among the Member States' national insolvency laws than the Istanbul Convention aimed towards[21] with adopting a flexible approach to the universalist theory whereby one main insolvency proceeding would be opened and administered in one Member State that was the 'centre of [the insolvent debtor's] main interests'.[22] It also supplemented the main proceedings with secondary proceedings in any other Member State in which the debtor had an 'establishment'.[23] The secondary proceedings would be administered under national law to resolve other legal issues.[24] The lack of definition of 'centre of main interests' and 'establishment' was criticised because the ambiguity of these terms was likely to lead to differing national interpretations, forum shopping and disputes over jurisdiction which could not be resolved by the Court of Justice of the European Union,[25] and, in fact, lead to more diversity instead of more harmony.[26]

[14] LA Burton, 'Toward an International Bankruptcy Policy in Europe: Four Decades in Search of a Treaty' (1999) 5(1) *Article 8 Annual Survey of International & Comparative Law* 205, 210.

[15] EC Doc IIII721BO (1990).

[16] C Tjur, 'An Analysis of the 1980 Draft EEC Bankruptcy Convention' (1982) 109 *International Business Law* 22, 24.

[17] Fletcher (above n 9) 437; Balz (above n 10) 492.

[18] European Convention on Certain International Aspects of Bankruptcy (Istanbul Convention), 5 June 1990, 30 ILM 165 (1991), also referred to as the Strasbourg Convention. See JL Westbrook, 'Theory and Pragmatism in Global Insolvencies: Choice of Law and Choice of Forum' (1991) 65 *American Bankruptcy Law Journal* 457, 487.

[19] Burton (above n 14) 213.

[20] Balz (above n 10) 499.

[21] ibid, 498.

[22] Istanbul Convention, Art 4(1). The Convention contains a rebuttable presumption that this is the country of incorporation.

[23] ibid, Art 17.

[24] ibid, Arts 19–22.

[25] Fletcher (above n 9) 439.

[26] Burton (above n 14) 215.

The EU Council of Ministers, as the principal law-making body of the EU, noted the absence of a European insolvency treaty as a 'shortcoming in the completion of the internal market'.[27] In 1989, it formed a working group to propose a new draft, published in 1995 as the European Union Convention on Insolvency Proceedings (EU Convention).[28] This again failed for various reasons,[29] among others the continuing lack of a comprehensive definition of the 'centre of main interest'.[30] Unlike the previous attempts, the EU Convention authorised the CJEU to interpret the Convention with binding effect on all signatories[31] and to give advisory opinions at the request of national courts.[32] Despite the promising outlook for a ratified insolvency convention, the attempt again failed.[33]

Consideration was given to adopting a multilateral treaty,[34] voluntary cooperation between nations or enacting individual national laws whereby countries guide their courts through cross-border insolvency proceedings.[35] International approaches included adhering to the Cross-Border Insolvency Concordat (Concordat),[36] which already contained provisions dealing with forum shopping and the location of the 'nerve centre',[37] or adopting the United Nations Commission on International Trade Law's Model Law on Cross-Border Insolvency,[38] which provides a uniform standard for recognising foreign insolvency proceedings and facilitating cooperation across borders[39] and also uses the terms 'centre of main interests' and 'establishment'.[40] The proceedings in question were again only insolvency proceedings with liquidation as an outcome.[41]

The adoption of the EIR[42] was a major step forward in the effective and efficient administration of cross-border insolvency proceedings within the EU.[43]

[27] Explanatory Report to the EU Convention on Insolvency Proceedings, 35 ILM 1223 (1996) p 2.
[28] European Union Convention on Insolvency Proceedings (EU Convention), 35 ILM 1223 (1996).
[29] For the reasons, see Burton (above n 14) 217.
[30] IF Fletcher, 'The European Union Convention on Insolvency Proceedings: An Overview and Comment with US Interest in Mind' (1997) *23 Brooklyn Journal of International Law* 25, 36.
[31] EU Convention, Arts 43–46.
[32] ibid, Art 65.
[33] Fourteen Member States signed. The UK refused to in retaliation for the total beef ban the EU had imposed (thanks to Mad Cow Disease) prior to the signature. See Burton (above n 14) 223 ff.
[34] Balz (above n 10) 529.
[35] Fletcher (above n 9) 441.
[36] Burton (above n 14) 226 ff.
[37] International Bar Association Section of Business Law, 'Committee on Cross-Border Insolvency Concordat (Concordat)' (15 September 1995) 9.
[38] United Nations Commission on International Trade Law's Model Law on Cross-Border Insolvency, 36 ILM 1386 (1997). In contrast to the Concordat, the provisions of the Model Law will become law in those nations that adopt it. See 'Guide to Enactment of the UNCITRAL Model Law on Cross-Border Insolvency', UN Commission on International Trade Law, 30th Sess, at 7, UN Doc AlCN.9/442 (1997).
[39] 'Guide to Enactment of the UNCITRAL Model Law' (above n 38) 8.
[40] ibid, Art 2(a), (f).
[41] ibid, Arts 9–13, 23–24.
[42] Council Regulation (EC) No 1346/2000 on insolvency proceedings (EIR), OJ L160, 30.6.2000, 0001–0013.
[43] ibid, Recital 2.

This came into force on 31 May 2002. The objective of the EIR was to ensure that cross-border insolvency proceedings operate efficiently and effectively for the proper functioning of the internal market,[44] introducing uniform conflict-of-law rules for these proceedings within the European Union[45] (except Denmark). The EIR did not harmonise the widely differing substantive laws among Member States, but instead set various provisions on jurisdiction, recognition and the applicable law. It, therefore, was primarily a private international law instrument in character.[46]

It designated the debtor's centre of main interests (COMI) as the Member State whose courts may open insolvency proceedings, and is an instrument to mediate between potentially competing courts in Member States in order to determine which country has jurisdiction over the insolvency of a particular debtor.[47]

The EIR was also intended to combat forum shopping within the EU because it 'is necessary for the proper functioning of the internal market to avoid incentives for the parties to transfer assets or judicial proceedings from one Member State to another, seeking to obtain a more favourable legal position (forum shopping)'.[48] The concepts of COMI and forum shopping were the subjects of various questions posted to the CJEU in the following years because the EIR did not provide much legal certainty and predictability with regard to the COMI. The CJEU established in *Eurofood*,[49] its first landmark case, that the COMI would be the registered office, which was recognisable by creditors and both objective and ascertainable to third parties. Other CJEU judgments further defined the COMI.[50]

With an unsustainable economic environment in most Member States after the financial crisis of 2007/2008, business insolvencies became a threat to the overall

[44] ibid, Recital 2.

[45] ibid, Recital 11.

[46] ibid, Recitals 8, 11.

[47] ibid, Recital 12.

[48] ibid, Recital 4.

[49] Case C-341/04, *Re Eurofood IFSC Ltd* [2006] Ch 508. See A Wolf, 'Success and Failure in Cross-Border Insolvency Proceedings of Multinational Corporations – Parmalat – A European and American Perspective', *2006 III Gold Medal Prize in International Insolvency Studies*, Master Thesis supervised by H-W Micklitz, available at www.iiiglobal.org/sites/default/files/annikawolf.pdf.

[50] In *Re Standard International Bank and Others* [2009] EWHC 1441 (Ch), *Kaupthing Capital Partners Master LP Inc* (31 March 2010, unreported) (Ch D), the CJEU referred COMI to the 'ordinary course of business'; in *ReCi4net.com Inc* [2005] BCC 277; *Re Damovo Group SA* (unreported, 25 April 2007) (Ch D); *Re Lennox Holdings plc* [2009] EWHC B11 (Ch); *Re Collins & Aikman Europe SA Collins and Others* [2006] EWHC 1343 (Ch); *Re Stanford International Bank Ltd* [2010] EWCA Civ 137, COMI was located at the place with 'head-office functions'; in Case C-396/09, *Interedil Srl (in liquidation) v Fallimento Interedil Srl and Another* the CJEU referred to 'administration of interests […] with a minimum level of organization [and] degree of stability'; in *Re Ci4net.com Inc* [2005] BCC 277, *Olympic Airlines SA Pension and Life Assurance Scheme v Olympic Airlines SA* [2012] EWHC 1413 (Ch) of an 'economic activity [that is] not transitory'. In addition, COMI should be 'determined on an entity-by-entity basis', see Case C-191/10, *Rastelli Davide e C Snc v Jean-Charles Hidoux*, COMI should be determined 'on the day of the insolvency application', see Case C-1/04, *Re Staubitz-Schreiber* and 'not the date of the hearing', see *Shierson v Vlieland-Boddy* [2005] EWCA Civ 974.

economic prosperity of the European internal market.[51] Flexible insolvency frameworks and corporate rescue have become much-discussed issues in the EU. Between 2009 and 2011, approximately a quarter of all the insolvencies in the EU (200,000 each year) had a cross-border element. The social costs of these insolvencies included 1.7 million jobs lost each year.[52] This underlines the importance of a coherent legal framework in this area of law.

The discussion has centred on certain forum-shopping issues where viable but financially distressed companies have sought to restructure their financial debts in English courts as going concerns instead of being administered in an insolvency proceeding under their own national laws and eventually liquidated. In particular, the English scheme of arrangement has proven to be a flexible tool to seek financial relief for non-English companies with a COMI in a different Member State[53] but with 'a sufficient connection'[54] to avail themselves of an opportunity to a financial restructuring in an English High Court. Many financially distressed but still solvent companies followed the call to London.[55]

The European Commission began reviewing the EIR in 2012, and in December 2012 published a proposal for amendment. The amendments were approved by the European Parliament in May 2015, with the 'EIR recast'[56] coming into force in June 2017. With a ten-year experience in dealing with definitions of the place of jurisdiction (COMI), recognition and enforcement issues, the EIR recast provided clarification on old questions.[57] It also introduced new provisions considering dealing with groups of companies.[58] The scope of the recast extends to restructuring proceedings which promote the rescue of economically viable but distressed businesses and which give a second chance to entrepreneurs,[59] thereby moving

[51] Commission Staff Working Document, 'Impact Assessment accompanying Commission Recommendation on a New Approach to Business Failure and Insolvency' (Impact Assessment), SWD(2014) 61 final, 12.3.2014, 2 and Communication from the Commission to the European Parliament, the Council and the European Economic and Social Committee 'A new European approach to business failure and insolvency' (Communication new European approach), COM(2012) 742 final, 2.

[52] ibid, Impact Assessment, 2.

[53] There were various attempts to shift COMI by German companies to have access to an English court, see A Wolf, 'Promoting an Effective Rescue Culture with Debt-Equity-Swaps? A Comparative Study of Restructuring Public Companies in Germany and England' (2015) *Nomos Verlag* 195 ff.

[54] The 'sufficient connection' was established by the High Court, see *Re Hellas Telecommunications (Luxembourg) II SCA* [2009] EWHC 3199 (Ch), *Re La Seda De Barcelona SA* [2010] EWHC 1364 (Ch).

[55] See *Trimast Holding Sarl v Tele Columbus GmbH* [2010] EWHC 1944 (Ch), *Re Rodenstock GmbH* [2011] EWHC 1104 (Ch), *PrimaCom Holding GmbH and Others v Credit Agricole and Others* [2011] EWHC 3746 (Ch), *Van Gansewinkle Groep BV* [2015] EWHC 2151 (Ch).

[56] Regulation (EU) 2015/848 of the European Parliament and the Council of 20 May 2015 on Insolvency Proceedings (EIR recast), OJ L141, 5.6.2015, 0019–0072.

[57] ibid, COMI is the place 'where the debtor conducts the administration of his interests on a regular basis and which is ascertainable by third parties' (Recital 28), 'presumed to be the registered office' (Recital 30) and which has 'not been moved within the 3-month period prior'. (Recital 31).

[58] ibid, Chapter V, Art 56ff.

[59] ibid, Recital 10. The EIR recast does not include the scheme of arrangement in Annex A because it is not an insolvency proceeding but a proceeding governed by company law: UK Companies Act 2006, Pt 26, ss 895–899.

towards a new approach to helping businesses overcome financial difficulties, all the while protecting the rights of creditors to recoup their money.

II. The Current Economic State in the EU: Some Context

The current European Commission has introduced various internal market policies in order to strengthen the EU's economy and to stimulate investment.[60] Insolvency and restructuring proceeding is a key instrument that has been singled out with a view to boosting investment. According to the Commission, 'well-functioning insolvency frameworks are crucial for the investment decisions since they define rights of creditors and borrowers in the event of financial difficulties'.[61]

In 2016,[62] there were 169,455 corporate insolvencies in Western Europe. Although this represented a 3.3% drop compared to 2015 (the third decline in a row),[63] the numbers of corporate insolvencies were still higher than before the crisis. Moreover, they do not reflect the great variation in numbers of insolvencies in individual countries. There were actually increases in corporate insolvencies compared to the previous year in Denmark (+65.6%),[64] Luxembourg (+12.6%), the UK (+12.2%),[65] Switzerland (+6.7%), Austria (+2.1%) and Norway (+1.8%).[66] On the positive side, 11 countries in Western Europe registered a decline in corporate insolvencies. These included Greece (−42.9%), Spain (−20.0%), the Netherlands (−16.5%), France (−8.4%),[67] Germany (−7.0%),[68] Finland and Sweden (both −6.4%), Belgium (−6.1%), Italy (−6.0%) and Portugal and Ireland (both −1.6%).[69]

[60] Communication from the European Commission on Action Plan on Building a Capital Markets Union, COM(2015) 468 final, 30.9.2015; Upgrading the Single Market: more opportunities for people and business, COM(2015) 550 final, 28.10.2015; Energy Union Package, COM(2015) 080 final, 25.2.2015; A Digital Single Market Strategy for Europe, COM(2015) 192 final, 6.5.2015; A Fair and Efficient Corporate Tax System in the European Union, COM(2015) 302 final, 17.6.2015; On steps towards Completing Economic and Monetary Union, COM(2015) 600 final, 21.10.2015.

[61] Communication from the European Commission on Annual Growth Survey 2016, COM(2015) 690 final, 26.11.2015, 8.

[62] The 2016 corporate insolvency data on European companies in this paragraph reflect the background to the decision by the Directive Proposal (above n 1) Section 2.2.4.

[63] Creditreform Wirtschaftsforschung, www.creditreform.at/presse/insolvenzstatistik-europa.ht, Unternehmensinsolvenzen in Europa, Jahr 2017/18, 1–2.

[64] ibid, 6. The main reason behind the surge in corporate insolvencies in Denmark was a delay in processing insolvency data from previous years.

[65] ibid, 4–5. Even though insolvencies were now below the 2008/2009 pre-crisis level, the numbers registered an increase because of fear of repercussions from Brexit.

[66] ibid, 2.

[67] ibid, 3. The first drop in insolvencies in five years.

[68] ibid, 4. Germany was one of the two countries in the sample which registered fewer insolvencies in 2016 compared to the pre-2008/2009 level.

[69] ibid, 2–3. The remarkable decline in southern countries such as Greece and Spain may also be due to businesses simply being closed down without necessarily declaring insolvency, as the severe consequences of the debt crisis were still being felt in these two countries.

In spite of these positive developments, the number of insolvencies remained higher than in 2011, the year before the European sovereign debt crisis.[70]

Insolvency law has become predominantly a single market issue. As the Commission states in the Proposed Directive, 'a higher degree of harmonisation in insolvency law is … essential for a well-functioning single market and for a true Capital Markets Union'.[71]

III. Commitment to More Harmonisation in EU Insolvency Law

In March 2014, the European Commission presented a recommendation on a new European approach to business failure and insolvency.[72] After the financial crisis, the unsustainable economic environment and business insolvencies became a detriment to the overall economic prosperity of the European internal market,[73] and forum shopping and corporate rescue were much-discussed issues. At that time, some Member States were in the process of reforming their insolvency frameworks, causing again more diversity than harmonisation.

The European Commission opted for a recommendation instead of a directive because it was concerned that a legislative measure could delay national reforms. It comes as no surprise that the Commission found national laws to differ significantly when dealing with companies in financial distress. The variations in the national restructuring frameworks could result in uncertainty and unpredictability about legal outcomes, resulting in unnecessary costs and limitations on the way to receiving fresh money to finance a restructuring. The non-binding recommendation aimed to provide a minimum standard[74] and 'greater coherence between the national insolvency frameworks in order to reduce divergences and inefficiencies [… and …] to also facilitate the restructuring of groups of companies irrespective of where the members of the group are located in the Union'.[75] The objective of the recommendation was to improve the conditions for preventive proceedings and to discourage the prevailing tendency towards insolvency proceedings and thus liquidation, by instead encouraging early restructuring.[76] Furthermore, the recommendation aimed to lower investment costs in Member States, increase recovery

[70] ibid, 7.

[71] Directive Proposal (above n 1) 2.

[72] Communication from the Commission to the European Parliament, the Council and the European Economic and Social Committee – A new European approach to business failure and insolvency, COM(2012) 742 final; Report from the Commission to the European Parliament, the Council and the European Economic and Social Committee on the application of Council Regulation (EC) No 1346/2000 of 29 May 2000 on insolvency proceedings, COM(2012) 743 final.

[73] Impact Assessment (above n 51) 2; Communication new European approach (above n 51) 2.

[74] ibid, No 3.

[75] ibid, Recital (11).

[76] ibid, Recital (1).

rates for creditors, and remove difficulties in restructuring groups of companies operating in different Member States.[77]

By adopting the series of common principles, the Commission hoped to ensure that viable businesses in financial difficulties would have access to national insolvency frameworks. These, in turn, would enable the companies to restructure at an early stage with the aim of preventing them from becoming insolvent, thereby maximising their overall worth for all the stakeholders. The recommendation asked the Member States, inter alia: to enable an early restructuring of distressed companies; to allow out-of-court restructuring for debtors; to allow businesses in difficult financial positions to request a period of stay of insolvency proceedings to develop a rescue plan; to help both debtors and creditors to follow a rescue plan to save viable companies; and lastly, to minimise the negative consequences of piling up debts by encouraging a discharge for a maximum period of three years so that entrepreneurs could have better chances of (re)launching their businesses.[78]

Although the Recommendation was not binding, Member States were encouraged – if not urged – to implement its core principles. Eighteen months later, the Recommendation was reviewed and assessed by the European Commission,[79] which concluded that the desired harmonised changes across all the EU Member States had not been achieved: compliance with the recommendation's objectives and provisions still varied significantly among Member States. The evaluation concluded that the Recommendation was not a successful approach to achieve more harmonisation across national insolvency frameworks and to facilitate the rescue of companies in financial distress.[80] Consequently – and unsurprisingly – the Commission started working on a directive.

The current proposal for the directive was issued in November 2016.[81] The Proposed Directive focuses on three key areas: (1) preventive restructuring frameworks; (2) second chance; and (3) efficiency of restructuring, insolvency and discharge procedures.[82] The proposal is the outcome of several insolvency initiatives by the European Commission to achieve a broad acceptance if approved: public consultations,[83] an expert group,[84] a conference on the convergence of

[77] ibid, No 2.

[78] European Commission press release (2014): 'Insolvency: Commission recommends new approach to rescue businesses and give honest entrepreneurs a second chance,' Brussels, 12 March 2014.

[79] Directorate-General Justice & Consumers of the European Commission, 30 September 2015, 1.

[80] ibid, 5, No 4.

[81] Directive Proposal (above n 1) Recital 47.

[82] ibid.

[83] For in-depth studies on the provisions and an overview of the legal framework, see INSOL Europe's 'Study on a new approach to business failure and insolvency – Comparative legal analysis of the Member States' relevant provisions and practices' (2012) Tender No JUST/2012/JCIV/CT/0194/A4. See also University of Leeds, 'Study on a new approach to business failure and insolvency – Comparative legal analysis of the Member States' relevant provisions and practices' (2014) Tender No JUST/2014/JCOO/PR/CIVI/0075.

[84] For more information about the Expert Group, its mandate and its members, and also the agendas and minutes of meetings, see ec.europa.eu/transparency/regexpert/index.cfm?do=groupDetail.groupDetail&groupID=3362.

insolvency frameworks within the European Union,[85] an impact assessment[86] and other key policy documents.[87]

The Directive Proposal's focus on preventive restructuring procedures has a clear rationale: the draft explicitly recognises that there exists a positive correlation between creditor recovery rates and the quality of Member States' restructuring and insolvency frameworks. In Member States where restructuring instead of liquidation is the most common insolvency proceeding, recovery rates are significantly higher, creditors recovering on average 83% of their claims in restructuring against an average of 57% in liquidation.[88]

While the EU itself respects different legal traditions and values,[89] this is a clear statement of favouring further harmonising of legal standards in restructuring and insolvency law within the Union. Overall, the new or amended legal rules should shift the focus away from liquidation towards early restructuring, developing a new approach to helping businesses overcome financial difficulties. In the best case, if the directive were to be adopted in its original text, it would have far-reaching implications for the national laws of some Member States while providing minimum standards to be met by all Member States. However, considering the results and comments during the consultation phase,[90] it is doubtful whether a more harmonised framework will actually be the result. Although the Directive Proposal requires Member States to implement the provisions in national law, the Member States are free to decide on the means of achieving the Directive's objectives, with some leeway as to the exact rules to be adopted in their national frameworks to ensure some minimum standards.

In terms of enforcement, the Directive would also offer a rare opportunity for most national legislatures in Europe to set up specialised insolvency courts and introduce special training for their judges,[91] thereby reaching deep into national sovereignty. Some Member States already have specialised courts, despite variations in the degree of participation by courts depending on the proceedings or thresholds.[92] Those Member States have judges that have a long experience of restructuring and insolvency proceedings. Some of them are not only legally but also commercially trained, and have experience working as professionals in this

[85] Conference organised under the auspices of the Slovak Presidency of the Council of the European Union, 12.7.2016, see ec.europa.eu/justice/newsroom/civil/events/160712_en.htm.

[86] Impact assessment, see ec.europa.eu/justice/civil/files/insolvency/impact_assessment_en.pdf.

[87] European Insolvency Initiatives, see ec.europa.eu/justice/civil/commercial/insolvency/index_en.htm.

[88] Directive Proposal (above n 1) Explanatory Memorandum, 3.

[89] E Jayme, 'Die kulturelle Dimension des Rechts – ihre Bedeutung für das Internationale Privatrecht und die Rechtsvergleichung' (2003) *Bd 67 RabelsZ* 211, 214.

[90] Among others: www.citizensinformationboard.ie/downloads/social_policy/submissions2017/EU_Commission_Proposed_Insolvency_Directive.pdf.

[91] Directive Proposal (above n 1) Art 24(2).

[92] For England and Wales, see the Insolvency Act 1986, s 117. France has launched 18 specialised insolvency courts for large cases, especially in the context of cross-border proceedings and insolvency cases involving groups of companies, following the enactment of the '*Macron law*', No 2015-990 of 6 August 2015.

area of law before being appointed to the bench.[93] This ensures effectiveness in the process with generally shorter duration of proceedings and fewer costs, while the judgments inherit legal certainty, predictability for creditors and debtors to give them legal certainty in and about the process.[94] This is also one of the reasons for them having become preferred jurisdictions (forum shopping) for restructurings.[95] Most Member States do not have specialised courts and judges, but instead have many regional courts.[96] The Directive Proposal emphasises courts with greater expertise, achieved by initial and further training required of insolvency judges to gain specific knowledge, thereby decreasing the perceived advantage some Member States' debtors attribute to other Member States' administrative and judiciary authorities.

In negotiating the proposal, the European Commission needed to convince the European Parliament and the Council about its objectives for minimum standards. With several pushbacks by the Member States and more than two years of discussions and consultations, the European Parliament published its committee report in August 2018[97] and confirmed to enter into inter-institutional negotiations in September 2018.[98] While there were several amendments proposed to the general wording of the Directive Proposal with regard to preventive proceedings, there were no comments on the judicial and administrative authorities. The Council finally published its compromise in October 2018.[99] The Council agreed to the main elements of the Directive Proposal for preventive proceedings, but requested more flexibility to amend the Member States' existing legal frameworks. While there was consensus to provide access to preventive restructuring proceedings for viable business in distress, there were concerns that the viability test would unnecessarily delay the opening of insolvency proceedings for unviable companies, hence leading to value destruction and higher costs. Therefore, the Council compromise allows for an optional viability test under certain conditions.[100] The compromise also gives Member States more flexibility to the involvement of judges, and where and whether training for these is mandatory.[101] With all European institutions' positions published and negotiations started, the Directive is expected to be published in early 2019.[102]

[93] Wolf (above n 53) 95, 96.

[94] P Wood, *The Law and Practice of International Finance* (Sweet & Maxwell 2008) 1–23.

[95] D Jasper, *Forum Shopping in England und Deutschland* (Duncker & Humblot 1990) 21, 26.

[96] In Germany, the last insolvency reform also included reforming the judiciary with a plan to have one insolvency court in each judicial district, which failed for political reasons, see Bundesministerium für Justiz (BMJ), RegE-EUSG, BT-Drucks 17/7511, (s (2)(2)(4) RegE-ESUG) and p 2.

[97] See www.europarl.europa.eu/sides/getDoc.do?type=REPORT&mode=XML&reference=A8-2018-0269&language=EN.

[98] See oeil.secure.europarl.europa.eu/oeil/popups/ficheprocedure.do?reference=2016/0359%28COD%29&l=en#tab-0.

[99] Council of the European Union, Interinstitutional File: 2016/0359(COD), data.consilium.europa.eu/doc/document/ST-12536-2018-INIT/en/pdf.

[100] ibid, p 3 and proposed amendments to Recital 12, 17a, 17b, Art 1a.

[101] ibid, proposed amendments to Art 24b, Art 26.

[102] Legislative materials until 12 December 2018 have been considered.

IV. Conclusion

The European Commission has put much effort into progressing with its approach to harmonise insolvency law across Member States. The EU approach has finally evolved to preventive restructuring proceedings in order to rescue companies in financial distress for going concerns instead of insolvency proceedings aimed at liquidation.

The actions by the European Commission, with the timely evaluation of the Recommendation's implementation and the Directive Proposal, underline the urgent need for greater coherence among Member States. Some of the Proposal's objectives are quite ambitious, not only considering the amendment of substantive law but also other areas in need of improvement, in particular, among others, the need for judicial and administrative authorities to have the necessary expertise and specialisation, and the need for more specialised courts. These objectives will be challenging for some Member States to adopt and to implement in national law. This process, however, will only begin once a directive has been passed and adopted. If the Directive does not lead to the desired outcome of a level playing field for all Member States, the next step will be a regulation, with EU law establishing itself as an independent legal order alongside national law or as supra-national law. It is important that the EU retains a holistic view of its own legal system because the elements must interlink, as is the case in national legal systems.

12

Digitally-Provided Financial Services under EU Law

Overcoming the Current Patchwork of Europeanised Private International Law and Sectorially-Harmonised National Private Laws

ANTONIO MARCACCI*

I. Introduction

At the end of the 1990s, the European Commission launched the then-considered forward-looking idea of a pan-European private law code merging national legal traditions – both civil and common – and, eventually, replacing them (horizontal approach). The project never became law, and today cross-border transactions are still governed by the Rome I (contracts) and Rome II (liability claims) Regulations, namely a Europeanised private international law, with the EU law-maker paying most of its attention to harmonise sectors of national private laws (vertical approach).

However, the world has changed in the last couple of decades, and technological development applied to business poses real challenges for the current legal architecture. FinTech is the best example: an umbrella term merging 'finance' and 'technology' where the provision of financial services is carried out via technological tools. Within this new context, the Commission seems to have partially retraced its steps and with the recent Green Paper on the Retail Financial Services[1]

* Antonio Marcacci, EUI PhD in Law, is a Senior Banking Compliance Professional. This Chapter stems from the following publication: Antonio Marcacci, 'Digitally-provided Financial Services under EU Law: Overcoming the Current Patchwork of Europeanized Private International Law and Sectorially-harmonized National Private Laws' (2017) 12 *Studi sull' integrazione europea* 3.

[1] European Commission, Green Paper of the European Commission on retail financial services: Better products, more choice, and greater opportunities for consumers and businesses, COM(2015)630 final.

(hereinafter the Green Paper) it looks determined to establish a legal level-playing-field for digital-based cross-border transactions in retail financial services. What the European Commission seems to have in mind is overcoming the current 'patchwork'[2] of Europeanised private international law and sectorially-EU harmonised national laws with a pan-EU network of mandatory contract rules for digital provision of financial services.

Very interestingly, the strategy the EU Commission seems to have in mind – accessing financial services from anywhere in Europe, better information to customers, improving redress and quality of enforcement through out-of-court procedures, easing cross-border provision of products – reproduces some basic features of the European Regulatory Private Law theory, such as competitive and contractual transparency, standardisation of contracts via information duties, elimination of market distortions, post-contractual cost-free or cost-reduced withdrawal and cancellation rights, and legal protection through an alternative dispute resolution mechanism (ADR). It thus seems possible to assume that the EU Commission's Green Paper is heralding the long-awaited great leap forward: the establishment of an autonomous legal framework for retail financial services; the embryo of a pan-EU contract law.

II. The Fintech Resolution: When Technology Creates a New (Cross-Border) Market and Makes the Law Look Older

The word FinTech stands for 'financial technology'; it is an umbrella term combining 'finance' and 'technology', and conveys the clear idea of financial services and products provided through technological tools, ie basically over the internet.[3] The financial industry sector providing FinTech-based services has been growing dramatically in recent years – from less than $1 billion in 2008 to $12 billion in 2014[4] – due to low-cost entry barriers and high-profit expectations.

[2] The idea of a shift from a patchwork to a network in legal terms was originally employed by Paul Geller: see P Geller, 'From Patchwork to Network: Strategies for International Intellectual Property in Flux' (1998) 9 *Duke Journal of Comparative & International Law* 69.

[3] *Investopedia* gives the following definition of FinTech: 'Fintech, a portmanteau of 'financial technology,' is used describe new tech that seeks to improve and automate the delivery and use of financial services. At its core, fintech is utilised to help companies, business owners and consumers better manage their financial operations, processes and lives by utilising specialised software and algorithms that are used on computers and, increasingly, smartphones. When fintech emerged in the 21st Century, the term was initially applied to technology employed at the back-end systems of established financial institutions. Since then, however, there has been a shift to more consumer-oriented services and therefore a more consumer-oriented definition. Fintech has expanded to include any technological innovation in – and automation of – the financial sector, including advances in financial literacy, advice and education, as well as streamlining of wealth management, lending and borrowing, retail banking, fundraising, money transfers/payments, investment management and more': *Investopedia* 'Fintech Definition' (2019, www.investopedia.com).

[4] 'Slings and arrows' *The Economist* (9 May 2015).

FinTech firms can provide a wide array of services to both consumers and undertakings through new business models and technologies, such as peer-to-peer lending (which directly meets loan demand and supply on crowd-funding platforms[5]), distributed ledgers (on which virtual currencies such as Bitcoin are based); mobile stock trading (securities trading executed on mobile devices[6]), online advice for savings investment (which combines human and technological factors), money transfer tools and digital wallet payments (such as Apple Pay[7]). Not all of them are new, out-of-the-blue services: the way they are provided is new though.

Digitalisation, as the evolution of current business models and services and the creation of new ones through digital technology,[8] is the new mantra. More and more European banking and financial institutions are very likely to leverage on FinTech to provide services previously offered only through traditional direct, frontal channels, with the intention of reaching more and more clients throughout the entire EU. In the short-to-mid term, a wise combination of innovation (internet-based) and tradition (face-to-face-based) is a direction banking and financial institutions are evidently willing to take. In the long term, physical location will increasingly be less important, and firms would be in a position to compete anywhere in the EU, with the result of opening up competition at European level.

However, this new business model would pose challenges for the current EU legal framework governing financial services, in particular the provision of services on a cross-border basis: the more fragmented and non-uniform the legal landscape in the EU, the harder for EU financial firms to take full advantage of an already-existing (and growing) internet-based single market grounded on new technologies.

The European Commission is aware of the limits of the current legal framework when it comes to governing digitally-based transactions and its approach goes well beyond the financial services sector. In 2015, the Commission even included the completion of the Digital Single Market in its ten political priorities and delineated a policy strategy based on fair competition and easy access for both undertakings and consumers.

[5] Crowd-funding is defined by the International Organization of Securities Commissions as 'an umbrella term describing the use of small amounts of money, obtained from a large number of individuals or organizations, to fund a project, a business or personal loan, and other needs through an online web-based platform'; E Kirby and S Worner, 'Crowd-funding: An infant industry growing fast' (2014) *Staff Working Paper of the IOSCO Research Department*, 4, available at www.iosco.org.

[6] Trades are executed through an application to be downloaded on a cell phone which lets users buy and sell individual stocks. See *Investopedia*, 'Mobile Trading' (2017, www.investopedia.com).

[7] Apple Pay is a mobile payment and digital wallet service provided by Apple Inc and powered by several iPhone devices, see www.apple.com.

[8] The European Commission has also launched the Digital Single Market strategy with the aim to bring 'down barriers to unlock online opportunities': European Commission, *Digital Single Market*.

Within this context, the Commission has recently issued a Green Paper on Retail Financial Services[9] with the goal to improve transparency and competition, and ease the cross-border supply of financial services, still very limited[10] when compared to the actual size of the European economy. The next section will present a case study which shows how difficult it is for a European investment firm to provide services on a cross-border basis without the grounding platform of a single EU contract law.

III. Cross-Border Provision of Financial Services Now

In 2001 the European Commission published its 'Communication on European Contract Law',[11] which was meant to open the door for a general debate – involving European institutions and stakeholders – about the establishment of a common pan-European Contract Law. The questioned raised by the Commission focused on the approach taken so far: a vertical, selective approach aimed at harmonising national-based specific contracts and specific marketing techniques, which was perceived as increasingly ineffective from a Single Market viewpoint.

The Commission felt the need for a 'farther-reaching … action in the area of contract law'.[12] The main concern was the assumption that the co-existence of several national contract laws within the EU could – either directly or indirectly – hinder the correct and efficient functioning of the internal market.[13] In particular, attention was focused on conflicts arising between mandatory rules of the laws of two different Member States in case of cross-border contracts,[14] and on the fact

[9] 'Financial services' is an umbrella term covering all retail finance-based services, namely insurance, loans and banking services, payments, savings and investment services. This chapter is focused only on investment services.

[10] European Commission (above n 1) 6.

[11] European Commission, Communication from the European Commission to the Council and the European Parliament on European contract law, COM(2001)398 final.

[12] ibid. Previous seminal academic studies had been published on the issue of a European Contract Law, as mentioned in the 2001 Commission Communication (ibid): A Hartkamp et al (eds), *Towards a European Civil Code* (The Hague, Kluwer Law International, 1998); O Lando and H Beale (eds), *Principles of European Contract Law Parts I and II* (The Hague, Wolters Kluwer, 2000); Academy of European Private Lawyers, *European Contract Code – Preliminary draft* (Pavia, Università di Pavia, 2001).

[13] As Karsten and Petri point out: 'The way European contract law has been established as a policy through two consultation procedures confirms its character as an internal market project'. See J Karsten and G Petri, 'Towards a handbook on European contract law and beyond: the Commission's 2004 Communication 'European Contract Law and the revision of the acquis: The way forward' (2005) 28 *Journal of Consumer Policy* 31, 34.

[14] In the words of the European Commission: 'Normally … different national regimes do not create any problems for cross-border transactions, as parties can decide which law will govern their contract. By choosing one national law, they accept all the mandatory rules of that law, as well as those non-mandatory rules which they do not replace by different terms. However, conflicts may arise between mandatory rules of the laws in one country with contradictory mandatory rules of another national law. These conflicts between different mandatory rules may have a negative impact upon cross-border transactions. Although not required by national laws, certain clauses in contracts may result from

that disparate national rules may bring about higher transaction costs,[15] which may result in a disincentive to conclude a transaction, or even to enter the market at all,[16] with detriments for both consumers[17] and businesses.

With the 2001 Communication, the Commission put forward four possible legislative outcomes: (i) no action; (ii) the promotion of the development of a common contract law principles set which would lead to more convergence of national laws, in particular through standardisation of contracts at European level (still national-based contracts but standardised by means of European rules); (iii) the improvement of the quality of the legislation already in place; and, finally, (iv) the adoption of a new comprehensive legislation at European level. The fourth option was the most appealing as it would have meant either a replacement of national laws, or a coexistence of a new European contract law alongside national laws; or a combination of the two, depending on the parties' choices.[18]

The 2001 Communication was followed by the Action Plan[19] of February 2003[20] and by its 2004 follow-up 'European Contract Law and the revision of the acquis: The way forward'[21] Communication.[22] Soon after, the European Commission asked the Study Group[23] and the Aquis Group[24] – both made up of distinguished scholars

common practice in a given member state, especially if such practice has been formalised in standard contracts. It may be hard to agree a contract containing terms and conditions different from those generally applied in a particular member state': European Commission (above n 11) 9.

[15] Literature on transaction costs is wide. A clear legal approach on this topic is given by P Schlag, 'The Problem of Transaction Costs' (1989) 62 *Southern California Law Review* 1661.

[16] European Commission (above n 11) 9.

[17] On the protection of the contract's weaker counterparty and the 2001 Communication, see S Weatherill (ed), 'The Protection of the Weak Party in a Harmonised European Contract Law' (2004) *Journal of Consumer Policy Special Issue*.

[18] European Commission (above n 11) 12–17.

[19] European Commission, Communication from the European Commission to the European Parliament and the Council – A more coherent European contract law – An action plan, COM(2003)68 final. In the words of Karsten and Petri, 'While the 2001 Communication on European contract law was a fanfare, opening a platform for an official debate on European contract law, the 2003 Action Plan channelled the discussion by setting the parameters for further consideration': see Karsten and Petri (above n 13) 33.

[20] The Action Plan set forth measures aimed at overcoming hurdles hampering the correct functioning of the internal market and the uniform application of the EU law. These measures were: (i) a more coherent *acquis* in based on common basic rules and terminology; (ii) the use of converging standard terms for trans-border contracts; (iii) further reflections on whether non-sector-specific measures may be needed: see European Commission, ibid, 11. See also J Karsten and AR Sinai, 'The Action Plan on European Contract Law: Perspectives for the Future of European Contract Law and EC Consumer Law' (2003) 26 *Journal of Consumer Policy* 159.

[21] European Commission, Communication from the Commission to the European Parliament and the Council – European Contract Law and the revision of the acquis: the way forward, COM/2004/0651 final.

[22] The 2004 Communication (ibid) set the agenda for the development of a European Contract Law. Karstan and Petri points out how the Commission was given a strong mandate to develop measures (i) and (ii) and to set the agenda for their implementation. See Karsten and Petri (above n 13) 34.

[23] The Study Group on a European Civil Code 'is a network of academics, from across the EU, conducting comparative law research in private law in the various legal jurisdictions of the Member States': see libguides.bodleian.ox.ac.uk/c.php?g=423166&p=2889490.

[24] The Acquis Group 'targets a systematic arrangement of existing Community law which will help to elucidate the common structures of the emerging Community private law': see www.acquis-group.jura.uni-osnabrueck.de.

from top European universities – to work on a 'Common Frame of Reference' (CFR),[25] whose draft[26] was submitted in 2009 and looked 'very much like a fully-fledged European civil code'.[27] A proposal for a Regulation on a Common European Sales Law[28] ensued, but it never became law. Thus, so far, there is no European Contract Law applicable to contracts concluded on a cross-border basis.

As Professor Micklitz rightly points out:

> what is missing at the EU level is, in continental language, a European civil code or, in common law language, a European law on contract and tort. (…) Therefore, trans-border conflicts within the EU have to be solved through private international law means.[29]

To cut a long story short, the EU law, on the one hand, harmonises national private laws *without* replacing them with a single EU private law, and, on the other hand, establishes a common EU standard for private international laws.

Traditionally speaking, private international law[30] provides for two main tools to overcome cross-border contractual issues: the first one is the determination of which law is applicable to a specific contract, while the second one is the adoption of uniform rules for the international provision of services and sale of goods.[31] In the first case, the parties of a contract coming from two different jurisdictions are asked to agree on which national law should apply to their contract. In this respect, the 1980 Rome Convention on the Law Applicable to Contractual Obligations[32] was the key instrument and it also determined which law was applicable when no choice was made. In the second case, the most important instrument is, instead, the 1980 United Nations Convention on contracts for the international sale of goods.[33]

However, when looking at the European level, one finds out that private international law has been 'Europeanised' through the adoption of Regulations,

[25] As reported by H-W Micklitz, 'The internal vs the external dimension of European private law – a conceptual design and a research agenda' (2015) *EUI Working Papers LAW 2015/35*, 1.

[26] C von Bar et al (eds), *Principles, Definitions and Model Rules of European Private Law, Draft Common Frame of Reference (DCFR)* (ec.europa.eu, 2009).

[27] Micklitz (above n 25) 1. About the reactions to the DCFR, see inter alia, O Lando, 'The structure and legal values of the common frame of reference (CFR)' (2007) 3(3) *European Review of Contract Law* 245; G Alpa et al (eds), *il Draft Common Frame of Reference del diritto privato europeo* (Padova, 2009); F Cafaggi and H-W Micklitz, *European Private Law after the Common France of Reference* (Cheltenham, 2010).

[28] Proposal for a Regulation of the European Parliament and of the Council on a Common European Sales Law, COM(2011) 635 fin.

[29] Micklitz (above n 25) 1–2.

[30] The Duke University's International Legal Research Tutorial defines private international law as the law governing 'the choice of law to apply when there are conflicts in the domestic law of different nations related to private transactions between those nations': law.duke.edu.

[31] European Commission (above n 11) 7.

[32] 1980 Rome Convention on the law applicable to contractual obligations (consolidated version) [1998] OJ C27, 26.1.1998, 34.

[33] The United Nations Convention on contracts for the international sale of goods (Vienna, 1980), www.uncitral.org.

in particular: (i) Rome I[34] on the determination of which national law is to be applied to contractual obligations in civil and commercial cross-border situations; and (ii) Brussels Regulation I-bis[35] on jurisdiction and the recognition and enforcement of judgments in civil and commercial matters. When it comes to consumer contract law and, in particular, to the cross-border provision of financial services to consumers, Article 6 of Rome I and Section 4 of Brussels I-bis are the key bricks of the legislation.

Section 4 of Brussels I-bis concerns the jurisdiction over consumer contracts, that is those contracts concluded by a consumer – defined as someone acting outside their trade or professional duties – and a professional – namely, someone who pursues commercial or professional activities which are directed into the Member State of the consumer's domicile, and the contract at hand falls within the scope of such activities (Article 17). Contracts concerning the provision of financial services are implicitly covered by this Section. Article 18, however, is particularly important since it defines the consumer's right to bring proceedings against the professional either in the courts of the Member State where the consumer is domiciled or in the courts of the Member State where the counterparty is domiciled. Unlike the professional – who can only sue the consumer before the courts of the latter's home state – the consumer is entitled to choose in which Member State their proceedings can be brought (protection of the so-called 'passive consumers', ie when the professional directs their business to the Member State of the consumer's domicile).

Article 6 of Rome I, instead, sets forth the principle that a contract concluded by a consumer and a professional – acting in the exercise of their trade or profession – is governed by the law of the country where the consumer has their habitual residence. Similarly to Article 17 of Brussels I-bis, paragraph 1 of Article 6 of Rome I protects the so-called 'passive consumer', as it is restricted to contracts related to a commercial or professional activity that is either carried out in the country where the consumer has their habitual residence or directed to that country.[36] Notably, paragraph II of Article 6 confirms the parties' freedom to choose the law applicable to their contract. However, such a choice may not deprive the consumer of the legal protection granted by their home country's provisions that cannot be contractually derogated and that, in the absence of choice, would be applicable on the basis of paragraph 1. Indeed, the protection of the passive consumer stands even where

[34] Regulation 593/2008 of the European Parliament and of the Council of 17 June 2008 on the law applicable to contractual obligations (Rome I).

[35] Council Regulation 1215/2012 of the European Parliament and of the Council of 12 December 2012 on jurisdiction and the recognition and enforcement of judgments in civil and commercial matters (recast).

[36] The so-called 'active consumers' are, indeed, excluded from such protection as para 4(a) reads as follows: 'Paragraphs 1 and 2 shall not apply to: a contract for the supply of services where the services are to be supplied to the consumer exclusively in a country other than that in which he has his habitual residence'.

the professional's country's law is chosen, due to the fact that the substantial gist of the legal safeguard afforded by the consumer's country cannot be overcome.[37]

Very importantly, paragraph II of Article 6 carves out specific features not falling under the Regulation's remit, such as: (i) rights and obligations which constitute a financial instrument; (ii) rights and obligations constituting the terms and conditions governing the issuance or offer to the public and public take-over bids of transferable securities; (iii) the subscription and redemption of units in collective investment undertakings in so far as these activities do not constitute provision of a financial service.[38] The first element concerns the content of a financial instrument itself whereas the second deals with the rules regulating the issuance (primary markets) and offer (secondary markets) of financial instruments: both aspects are strictly linked with the legal-economic environment of the issuer and a stretch of the Rome I Regulation up to this point would have probably meant a hardly justifiable intrusion into a very sensitive area of national private law.[39] The element dealing with the subscription and redemption of UCITS stocks by and large follows the same logic.[40] However, what matters the most for this chapter is the fact that Rome I clearly applies to the cross-border provision of financial services, as shown by the case study below.

Particular attention should be paid to the way in which Rome I tries to strike the right balance between the freedom to provide services and the preservation of

[37] On Europeanised private international law and consumer protection under EU Law relevant to this chapter, Gilles rightly points out how 'it is the combination of an inherent difference in bargaining strength between the parties to a consumer contract and the "dematerialised" nature of electronic commerce which justifies special consideration of the connecting factors to determine the choice of law of an electronic consumer contract': LE Gillies, 'Choice-of-law Rules for Electronic Consumer Contracts: Replacement of the Rome Convention by the Rome I Regulation' (2007) 3 *Journal of Private International Law* 96. See also G Finocchiaro, 'European Law and Consumer Protection in the Information Age' (2003) 12 *Information and Communications Technology Law* 111; B Ubertazzi, *Il regolamento Roma I sulla legge applicabile alle obbligazioni contrattuali* (Giuffré, Milan, 2008). On the early impact of the internet on private international law, see the following forward-looking article: R Schu, 'The Applicable Law to Consumer Contracts Made Over the Internet: Consumer Protection Through Private International Law?' (1997) 5 *International Journal of Law and Information Technology* 192.

[38] A very recent and shrewd analysis of this aspect is supplied by ME De Maestri, 'Il consumatore di servizi finanziari nelle norme di diritto internazionale privato dell'Unione europea' (2016) 2016 *Economia e Diritto del Terziario* 167. See also F Garcimartin Alferez, 'New Issues in the Rome I Regulation: The Special Provisions on Financial Market Contracts' (2008) 10 *Yearbook of Private International Law* 245.

[39] In the words of Garcimartin Alferez: 'In general terms, the application of Article 6 to some financial instruments or transactions, such as a public offer, could imply the interference of different laws depending on the habitual residence of the investor when he is acting outside his trade or profession. This could impede the uniformity of the legal regime applicable to those instruments or transactions, which is a key element for ensuring their economic function': F Garcimartin Alferez, 'The Rome I Regulation: Exceptions to the Rule on Consumer Contracts and Financial Instruments' (2009) 1 *Journal of Private International Law* 89.

[40] In the words of Garcimartin Alferez: 'all subscribers are governed by the same rules as regards issues such as the right to redeem, fees or the right to receive certain information. In general terms, all issues pertaining to the function, the structure, the management, operation and administration of the fund should be subject to a single law, regardless of the habitual residence of the subscribers': ibid, 93.

the consumer's home country's legal protection. Here a question might usefully be posed: would a national consumer protection measure – surviving through the Rome I's trade-off – pass the European Court of Justice's test on the freedom to provide services? The test the CJEU has crafted over time – in particular, since the *Webb* case[41] – provides for the four following points to be verified against the consumer's home country's restriction, which should: (i) be justified by the general public interest; (ii) be applicable on a non-discriminatory basis, namely it must apply to both national and foreign suppliers; (iii) not be disproportionate in accomplishing its policy aims; and (iv) ensure that its pursued purposes are not equally achieved by the supplier's State laws.[42]

On the whole, a plausible answer to the question raised above is: would it depend on the concrete national consumer protection measure envisaged by the consumer's home country legislation? Should the concrete consumer protection measure not unreasonably curb or impair the efficient and non-discriminatory provision of financial services on a cross-border basis, then it would survive as the result Rome I's trade-off. And the converse holds true.

Nonetheless, albeit an economic analysis of the law falls outside of the scope of this chapter, it can be conjectured that the mere application of the different consumer protection norms penetrating a contract governed by the law of another Member State is itself disincentivising due to the fact it raises extra costs on the part of the service supplier, costs related to regulatory compliance and prospective enforcement. If there were a single EU contract law applicable to consumer contracts concerning investment services, then the cross-border provision of such services would be falling into such an EU framework, and compliance and enforcement costs would likely be abated.

As a matter of fact, had the fourth option mentioned above become statutory reality, then the provision of financial services on a cross-border basis would already be governed by a truly single and common European Contract Law. As will be explained below, this might be the rekindled objective of the European Commission with its recent Green Paper on Financial Services.

When looking, instead, at the harmonisation of national private-law norms, what we find is a very complex phenomenon labelled 'European Regulatory Private Law'. This is used to describe (the emergence of) a self-sufficient European private law[43] which enshrines a twofold aim: easing private relationships (the 'private' side of the law), and realising public policy goals (the 'public' side of the law).[44] In order

[41] Judgment of the European Court of Justice of 17 December 1981, Case 279/80, *Webb*.

[42] R Smits, *The European Central Bank, Institutional Aspects* (The Hague, Kluwer, 1997) 245.

[43] H-W Micklitz et al (eds), 'European Regulatory Private Law – The Paradigms Tested' (2014) *EUI Working Paper LAW Series*, as mentioned by V Mak, 'The Consumer in European Regulatory Private Law' (2015) *Tilburg Private Law Working Paper Series*.

[44] ibid, 2.

to achieve its goals, the ERPL, then, uses tools traditionally viewed as in contrast with each other: rules of private law (such as mandatory contractual terms) and rules of public administrative law.[45] The contrast springs from the traditional roles played by private and public law, individual autonomy grounded on the freedom of contract versus regulation as a means of heteronomy.[46] Against this backdrop, the ERPL, even if it coexists with national private laws, has so far used harmonising public-law tools to penetrate into the private-law realm[47] of national legal traditions.

Importantly, the ERPL looks like a Janus-faced phenomenon, as it can have either an active role (the adoption of harmonising rules which directly replace old national norms not consistent with the EU public policy goals, ie the efficient functioning of the market) or a negative role (through the abolition of barriers to the integration of the internal market erected by national rules).[48] The more active the role, the harder the thrust of the ERPL, so that the adoption of a sector-related regulation introducing a brand-new, opt-in contract law standard for a specific field such as financial services would be a great leap forward for the ERPL, even greater than the shift from minimum to maximum harmonisation.

The policy goal that the EU law-maker has in mind – and this is particularly true for the banking and financial sector – is market efficiency, gauged in economic terms:[49] market stability,[50] and a concept of justice based on the opportunity to enter in and join the market. The private law produced by this law-maker is neither based on freedom of contract or *l'autonomie de la volontè*, nor on tort,

[45] H-W Micklitz, 'The Visible Hand of European Regulatory Private Law – The Transformation of European Private Law from Autonomy to Functionalism' (2009) 28 *Competition and Regulation. Yearbook of European Law* 3.

[46] G Comparato, 'Private Autonomy and Regulation in the Eu Case-Law' in Micklitz et al (above n 43).

[47] In the words of Professor Mak: 'inroads into party autonomy in private law can be explained, or even justified, in the light of the EU's internal market policy': Mak (above n 43) 4.

[48] ibid.

[49] The definition of 'economic efficiency' has been the subject of much debate for many decades and it is sufficient here to mention the two most important methods still used: the Pareto optimum and the Kaldor-Hicks criteria. The first term describes a situation where 'no one can be made better off without making someone else worse off'. In its strong form, the Pareto efficiency states that 'state A is preferred to state B when state A is ranked higher than state B for one person and all other persons rank A at least as high as B. If the utility (well-being) of each individual is higher in state A, then state A is preferred according to the weak form of Pareto efficiency'. The second method claims that 'state *a* is preferable to another state if, in the other state, it is not possible, hypothetically, to carry out lump-sum redistribution so that everyone could be made as well off as in state *a*.' Citations are from RO Zerbe Jr, *Economic Efficiency in Law and Economics* (Cheltenham, Edward Elgar, 2001), with the author citing RW Boadway and N Bruce, *Welfare Economics* (New York, Blackwell, 1984).

[50] European Commission, Communication from the Commission to the European Parliament, the Council, the European Economic and Social Committee and the Committee of the Regions, COM(2015)468 fin (Brussels, 2015).

unerlaubte Handlung or *responsabilitè d'autrui*.[51] Instead, this private law – which affects private law juridical relations even if it is not based on contracts – turns the market into a grounding principle and itself into a tool geared to grant the efficient functioning (and the very existence) of the market (the functional turn in European private law).[52] The result is a private law which is regulatory in the sense that it is used to 'constitute the Internal Market and it is competitive as the philosophy behind the regulatory measures relies heavily on market freedoms and competition'.[53]

The ERPL develops through certain key parameters[54] which highlight the functional role of the law towards the market as grounding principle. In particular, consumer protection through information disclosure is granted on the basis of the economic function played by the weaker party and is accompanied by contract standardisation, which not only eases information exchange (propaedeutic to market efficiency) but also reduces negotiation timing (enhancing competition among services providers): the purpose is not to grant autonomy to the parties, but, rather, improve market functioning (functional role of private law). The weaker party is invited to enter the market and benefit from it and what the law is supposed to do is grant fair access (access justice)[55] instead of focusing on more traditional forms of (social) justice (as national private laws usually do). Finally, effective legal redress strongly leverages on ADR mechanisms, which are less expensive and faster than traditional courts, and on public enforcement carried out by market supervisors, which use their enforcement powers as a tool to regulate market players' behaviour, overcoming the separation between substantive and procedural law typical of continental private legal orders.[56]

All this means that, to date, a contract concluded by two counterparties residing in two different Member States is governed by a 'Europeanised private international law'[57] while EU-harmonised national rules still apply. The case study below applies such a general stance to a concrete situation concerning the cross-border provision of investment services from one Member State (Germany) directly to another Member State (Italy). The outcome of this case study seems to prove that current legal framework is of little help for the intra-EU cross-border provision of investment services.

[51] Micklitz (above n 25) 1.
[52] Micklitz (above n 45).
[53] ibid, 6.
[54] ibid, 26.
[55] *Zugangsgerechtigkeit* in the words of Micklitz (above n 25).
[56] R Michaels and N Jansen, 'Private Law Beyond the State? Europeanization, Globalization, Privatization' (2006) 54 *American Journal of Comparative Law* 843, quoted by Micklitz (above n 25) 6.
[57] Micklitz (above n 25) 4.

IV. A Case Study: Intra-EU Cross-Border Provision of Investment Services

To understand how far the absence of a European Contract Law may affect specific areas of business, a short case study[58] on the cross-border provision of investment services within the EU will be described in this section. The case concerns a hypothetical German investment firm 'XYZ' licensed to provide investment services in Germany and willing to offer such services to Italian consumers without owning subsidiaries in Italy. The services offered could be, for instance, portfolio management,[59] reception and transmission of orders,[60] and investment advice,[61] and customers would be likely to fall into the MiFID macro-category of retail[62] clients.

The legal regime through which XYZ Firm may choose to operate is the distance marketing of financial services. This regime is governed by a simple directive (Directive 2002/65/EC[63]) which does not introduce a separate opt-in EU contractual framework to apply to distance contracts and, by combining minimum and maximum harmonisation provisions, leaves Member States the power to adopt other rules than those set forth by the Directive itself. The result is that firms are de facto required to adhere to different legal regimes,[64] even if these are harmonised in several areas such as information duties[65] and cooling-off periods.[66]

On the one hand, the investment service agreement between XYZ Firm and an Italian consumer entered into through a means of distance communication[67] (usually, over the internet) would be governed by German law. XYZ Firm would be performing investment services via phone, the internet or – if so requested by

[58] Please, note that the case herein described is an academic exercise and any resemblance to real events and/or real persons is unintended.

[59] '"Portfolio management" means managing portfolios in accordance with mandates given by clients on a discretionary client-by-client basis where such portfolios include one or more financial instruments', Art 4(8), Directive 2014/65/EU of the European Parliament and of the Council of 15 May 2014 on markets in financial instruments.

[60] When an 'intermediary, having received a purchase or sale order from the client, instead of carrying it out personally, sends it to another intermediary for execution', CONSOB, *What an investment service is*, www.consob.it.

[61] '"Investment advice" means the provision of personal recommendations to a client, either upon its request or at the initiative of the investment firm, in respect of one or more transactions relating to financial instruments', Art 4(4), Directive 2014/65.

[62] '"Retail client" means a client who is not a professional client': Art 4(11) Directive 2014/65. A '(p)rofessional client is a client who possesses the experience, knowledge and expertise to make its own investment decisions and properly assess the risks that it incurs': Annex II Directive 2014/65. To be considered professional, a client must comply with the criteria laid down in Annex II of MiFID II.

[63] Directive 2002/65/EC of the European Parliament and of the Council of 23 September 2002 concerning the distance marketing of consumer financial services.

[64] B Bartels et al, *European Banking and Financial Services Law*, 5th edn (Ghent, Larcier, 2012) 265.

[65] In particular, Arts 3, 4 and 5.

[66] The right of consumers to withdraw from a contract during a cooling-off period is regulated by Art 6.

[67] '"Means of distance communication" refers to any means which, without the simultaneous physical presence of the supplier and the consumer, may be used for the distance marketing of a service between those parties': Art 2(e) Directive 2002/65.

the customers – even via ordinary post, whereas orders from customers would be alternatively transmitted via phone, internet, or ordinary post. Each client would be assigned to a so-called 'investment adviser',[68] a Germany-based XYZ employee tasked with taking care of the customer relationship by, for instance, advising clients and handing over call minutes.

On the other hand, as stated above, Article 6(2) of Rome I Regulation governing intra-EU private international law clearly states that

> the parties may choose the law applicable to a contract (…) such a choice may not, however, have the result of depriving the consumer of the protection afforded to him by provisions that cannot be derogated from by agreement by virtue of the law which, in the absence of choice, would have been applicable.[69]

This means that the German-law-governed investment service agreement would have to contain consumer protection clauses as provided under Italian law, which makes the business model more expensive and, thus, far less appealing for XYZ Firm.

More importantly, under the distance marketing of financial services regime, investment adviser would not be allowed to provide investment services directly to customers upon direct meetings. Taking into account that investment of personal savings is a very sensitive area, a face-to-face relationship is very much needed[70] in order to achieve an efficient provision of services such as portfolio management and advice (let alone the new 'independent advice'[71] service recently introduced by MiFID II). On the basis of that, XYZ Firm may instead choose to base its investment advisers in Italy so as to let them meet their Italian customers on a regular basis. However, this would imply leveraging on the MiFID passport, namely either the exercise of cross-border investment activities (Article 34 of Directive 2014/65/EU[72]) through tied-agents[73] or the establishment of a branch (Article 35 of Directive 2014/65/EU[74]) which, again, uses tied-agents located in the host Member State, Italy, necessary to reach out to all of XYZ Italian clients and prospective clients.

In either case, XYZ Firm would have to, first and foremost, comply with the reporting requirements to be submitted to the German Federal Financial Supervisory Authority (BaFIN) – since the Home State control regime applies – as set forth by

[68] The term 'adviser' is used in the financial industry but other names can be simultaneously employed, such as 'family banker', 'personal banker', or 'private banker'.

[69] Regulation 593/2008.

[70] Communication from the Commission to the Council and the European Parliament – Review of the distance marketing of consumer financial services Directive (2002/65/EC), COM(2009)626 fin.

[71] Art 24(4) and 24(7) Directive 2014/65, MiFID II.

[72] Directive 2014/65/EU.

[73] According to MiFID II, '"tied agent" means a natural or legal person who, under the full and unconditional responsibility of only one investment firm on whose behalf it acts, promotes investment and/or ancillary services to clients or prospective clients, receives and transmits instructions or orders from the client in respect of investment services or financial instruments, places financial instruments or provides advice to clients or prospective clients in respect of those financial instruments or services' Art 4(1, 29), Directive 2014/65.

[74] Directive 2014/65.

Section 24a of the German Banking Act[75] on the establishment of a branch and provision of cross-border services in other EU Member States and implementing the MiFID passport in Germany. According to such reporting requirements, XYZ Firm is to notify the list of investment services it intends to provide to Italian customers.

In any case, XYZ Firm would have to comply with some specific Italian mandatory rules concerning aspects not covered by the European passporting mechanism, such as the written form of the agreement,[76] segregation of assets (the XYZ branch must ensure the its clients' funds are kept a part from its own funds),[77] and specific conduct of business obligations for the provision of investment services such as portfolio management.[78]

As a matter of practice, the only business model which would let XYZ Firm reach out to all of its Italian customers is to use Italian tied-agents, which implies offering investment services on a door-to-door basis[79] and the related duty to use only off-premises investment advisers authorised in Italy.[80] The XYZ Italian tied-agents would, then, have to be registered as '*consulenti finanziari abilitati all'offerta fuori sede*' (off-premises advisors) in a specific catalogue held by the *Organismo di vigilanza e tenuta dell'albo unico dei Consulenti Finanziari*,[81] supervised by the Italian Securities Market Authority, CONSOB. Finally, the service provision contract between with the XYZ tied-agents and their customers would be subject to Italian law and related conduct of business rules (harmonised under MiFID I and II – but, still, national rules).

Distance marketing of financial services? Establishment of a branch via the MiFID passport? Off-premises offer of investment services through tied-agents? This short case study shows that if the German XYZ Firm took the decision to provide investment services to Italian customers on a cross-border basis, then it would be required to comply with a dense patchwork of rules related to both the

[75] *Gesetz über das Kreditwesen*, vgl.§1Abs.1S.1, Abs.1a S.1, Abs.1b: an English translation is available at the BaFIN official website www.bafin.de.

[76] Art 23 ('*Contracts*') of the Italian Financial Law, Decreto legislativo 24 febbraio 1998, n 58. The remedy provided is the nullity of the entire contract which can be enforced only by the customer.

[77] Art 168 ('*Confusione di patrimoni*') of the Italian Financial Law. The violation of the segregation of assets duty is punished by imprisonment for between six months and three years and by an administrative fine ranging from €5,165 to €103,291.

[78] Art 24 ('*Gestione di portafogli*') of the Italian Financial Law. In more detail, this article provides that: (1) the customer may issue binding instructions concerning the transactions to be performed; (2) the customer may withdraw from the contract at any time, without prejudice to the right of withdrawal of the bank pursuant to Art 1727 of the Italian Civil Code; and (3) the power to exercise voting rights in relation to financial instruments under management may be conferred upon the bank by means of a proxy granted in writing and for each shareholder's meeting. The remedy provided is the nullity of the single transaction which can be enforced only by the customer.

[79] Also harmonised by EU law through Directive 2011/83/EU of the European Parliament and of the Council of 25 October 2011 on consumer rights. This Directive follows a full harmonisation approach but it does not establish a single European Market for off-premises contracts. The outcome is that firms and investment firms must comply with the host country's national legislation.

[80] Art 78 ('*Offerta fuori sede*') of the CONSOB's *Regolamento recante norme di attuazione del decreto legislativo 24 febbraio 1998, n. 58 in materia di intermediari*.

[81] The official website is www.albopf.it.

Italian and German legal systems, even when such rules are harmonised under European directives, like MiFID. If there were a fully-fledged, opt-in pan-EU contract law, then XYZ Firm could avoid complying with national rules and directly apply the EU rules to its cross-border contracts. Significantly, this is what the Commission seems to have in mind.

V. … And Then: The Commission's Green Paper on Retail Financial Services

At the end of 2015, the European Commission launched a new Green Paper on Retail Financial Services[82] with the aim of creating a 'true European market' for such services, which would bring more 'choice for consumers, allow successful providers to offer their services throughout the EU, and support new entrants and innovation'. Digitalisation and competition are intertwined leitmotifs: the first one represents the *sine qua non* condition for having cross-border purchases of financial services and it is meant to lead to the second one and (hopefully) to an increased general welfare.[83] In the words of the Commission: 'Digitalization should in principle foster cross-border activity, without requiring firms to establish themselves in other Member States'.[84]

The key concern of the European Executive is that, for the time being, too few retail financial service purchases take place across borders.[85] This would be due to the fact that the market is characterised by fragmentation and lack of competition, with limited cross-border activity, which would lead to the exploitation of rent positions on the part of some industry sectors at the detriment of consumers, to unjustifiable price and choice differentials for the same product from one Member State to another, and to a minimal switching possibility from one provider to another.

The goal is threefold, with two out of three aims having a purely economic dimension, while the third is more political:

(i) supply side: pushing companies based in one Member State to offer their services/products anywhere in the EU;
(ii) demand side: enabling consumers to buy services/products from a provider based in another Member State;
(iii) freedom of movement: achieve full 'portability' of financial services/products for citizens when they move from one Member State to another.

[82] European Commission (above n 1).
[83] In the words of the EU Commission: 'better products, more choice and greater opportunities for consumers and businesses': European Commission (above n 1) 12.
[84] European Commission (above n 1) 11.
[85] The Green Paper mentions several recent studies which show limited cross-border activity: the share of consumers purchasing banking products from another Member State was less than 3% for credit cards, current accounts and mortgages, only 5% for loans, and out 3% in terms of total gross written premiums in 2011 and 2012: European Commission (above n 1) 6.

The Green Paper covers all retail financial services – banking, investment/securities, and insurance – which are treated as services belonging to the very same market, and it examines: (i) the current state of the Single Market for retail financial services, taking into account that digitalisation has pushed integration on the provision of such services; and (ii) the actions needed to take down barriers that deter consumers and businesses from going cross-border.

The Commission recalls its recent efforts aimed at restoring market participants' trust, such as the empowerment of consumers so as to enable them to make informed investment decisions through increased disclosure and transparency requirements; or the boost to competition in the payment accounts market through an EU-wide right of access to basic payment accounts. Thus, the Commission reaffirms the importance of the 'disclosure of information paradigm'[86] and the idea of fairness/justice which equates the possibility to access the market.[87]

In more detail – and as far as investment services are concerned – the Commission sketches its strategy through the following prongs:

- standardised information disclosure so as to enable facilitated access to a wider range of products and cross-border comparison of different products which would lead to a more competitive market;
- opening up access to services from anywhere in the EU by overcoming geo-blocking restrictions;
- increasing consumers' trust and confidence by establishing efficient cross-border redress based on ADR mechanisms;
- allowing electronic signature and verification of identity in order to take full advantage of digital tools while fully taking into account anti-money laundering needs;
- making it easier for firms to comply with legal requirements applicable in other Member States;
- creating an autonomous EU regime for cross-border transactions or fostering a stronger harmonisation in order to create more legal certainty for both consumers and suppliers.

When responding to the Commission on the points raised by the Green Paper, ESMA has highlighted what I think are three key points: (i) oversight convergence among national supervisors; (ii) more harmonised enforcement procedures; and (iii) a prospective autonomous legal regime. The first point is particularly important due to the fact that MiFID strongly relies on public supervision and enforcement even when it comes to ensure investor protection: national supervisors are

[86] On the importance of disclosure as an investor protection tool under the EU law see N Moloney, *How to Protect Investors. Lessons from the EC and the UK* (Cambridge, Cambridge University Press, 2010) 288–344.

[87] On the concept of justice in the EU law: H-W Micklitz, 'Social Justice and Access Justice in Private Law' (2011) *EUI LAW Working Papers Series*.

granted the power to oversee the correct application of investor protection clauses enshrined in contracts concluded by services providers and their customers. The further convergence suggested by ESMA is aimed at bringing national, public administrative approaches on investor protection clauses closer.

The second point is private enforcement. However, given the lack of competence on the part of the EU on civil procedures, ESMA does not even hint at the solution adopted for a unitary patent protection system[88] but, instead, backs the Commission by affirming the importance of ADR mechanisms, low cost and easy to access for consumers. Finally, the third point is the endorsement of the rather cryptic proposal of an autonomous EU-wide regime which might be used as a 29th legal framework, replacing national applicable laws if so agreed by the counterparties.

As just pointed out, this is quite cryptic. The Commission has not revealed in the Green Paper what it has in mind, but it is not groundless to assume that the desired outcome of this Paper would be the adoption of a Regulation establishing a brand new, alternative contractual regime for cross-border businesses, applicable throughout the EU, which the counterparties would be free to choose over traditional regimes. What the Commission longs for is the completion of point (iv) of the 2001 Communication. Alternatively, it may try to push for further (full) harmonisation, but this would overcome the 'Europeanised private international law' issue which contributes to curbing the blossoming of the intra-EU cross-border market.

VI. … If So, On Which Basis? The Embryo of an Autonomous European (Regulatory) Contract Law

The European Commission seems to be working towards a separate contractual regime based on standardised information disclosure aimed at creating a level playing field able to grant access to both consumers and businesses and which leverages upon ADR schemes to boost legal certainty and increase consumers' trust and confidence. What the Commission seems to have in mind is a leap forward from the current regulatory approach on national private laws, towards the establishment of a standalone EU Contract Law.

What emerges from the Commission's Green Paper looks like the embryo of a proto-legal framework that very much resembles the main features of the ERLP. The market and its effective functioning – instead of the freedom of contract – is the leitmotif of the Commission, which aims at easing private relationships to realise

[88] The Agreement on a Unified Patent Court has established a pan-European, single patent legal regime for the settlement of patent disputes. The EU itself has implemented the Agreement by adopting an enhanced-cooperation based Regulation for the creation of a unitary patent protection system (Regulation 361/1).

a public policy goal, that is an efficient cross-border retail financial market. Retail investors are viewed as the weaker parties who need to be protected so that they feel comfortable to enter the cross-border digital market. Standardised information and effective legal redress through ADR mechanisms are employed to this end.

Cross-border competitive comparison of different retail financial products, overcoming of geo-blocking restrictions, and contractual transparency are functional tools leading to a more efficient market where products' details are easily comparable and information barriers are cut down in a way that contractual parties (both the stronger and the weaker) are in a position to understand – but, at least for the weaker party, not to modify – the reciprocal rights and duties.

On a more business-friendly side, the EU law-drafter looks prone to introduce a coherent legal scheme for electronic signature and verification of identity so as to let undertakings take full advantage of digital tools without overlooking anti-money laundering needs. Moreover, for those legal requirements falling outside the scope of such an opt-in European contract law for cross-border retail financial services, the Commission is committed to increasing harmonisation in order to reduce the compliance burden for undertakings.

VII. Conclusions

Digital technology is rapidly changing business and business practice, and the law is running the risk of not being able to keep pace with an evolving world. This chapter has tried to show how the current fragmented EU legal regime for the provision of cross-border investment services is not helping business to efficiently operate. The EU Commission has always pursued the aim of establishing an efficient single financial market, and the law has been widely instrumentalised to this goal – as the theory of the European Regulatory Private Law describes. However, unlike in the past, when the European Civil Code died in its cradle, this time the EU Commission seems to be keen to take the plunge and, by rekindling its old dream of a unified EU contract law, establish a brand new contract standard for financial cross-border transactions, thus replacing the classic harmonisation approach with a 'civil code-like' one. Such an EU contract standard would be a separate, opt-in, vertically-crafted contract for retail financial services, likely to become a bellwether for a general horizontally-crafted contract applicable to the entire market. It might be too early to anticipate how far the EU Commission will go, but the Green Paper clearly shows the path.

13

On Regulatory Experimentalism in European Private Law: The Legal Laboratory of Food and Finance

MARÍA PAZ DE LA CUESTA DE LOS MOZOS*
AND ELENA SEDANO VARO**

Experimentalism has made a jump from political science into legal scholarship. However, its reception in private law spheres has been contested. This chapter offers an overview of experimentalist thinking in EU private law. Then, it assesses the EU regulation of food chains and financial markets as test fields or laboratories of experimentalism. The assessment of the two laboratories follows the same structure: first, they describe how the conditions for experimentalist governance have taken shape in the respective sectors; second, they explore the experimentalist features revealed by the EU's newly-designed regulations. Finally, the chapter takes stock of these findings and concludes.

I. Introduction

The authors of this chapter came of age with the financial crisis in the headlines. The fall of Lehman Brothers and the economic debacle that ensued provided the background for our university years. It was some time later that the two of us met in Florence as PhD researchers. Under the supervision of Hans Micklitz, we both were trying to come to terms with the transformation that the crisis had operated on the legal categories that we had studied during our student years. In recent years we have become familiar with the regulatory dimension of private law in the EU as explored in Hans' work.[1] Private law is no longer the exclusive realm of

* PhD researcher at the Department of Law of the European University Institute (EUI).
** PhD researcher at the Department of Law of the European University Institute (EUI).

[1] H-W Micklitz, 'The Visible Hand of European Regulatory Private Law' (2009) 22 *Yearbook of European Law* 3.

freedom of contract, if ever it was. The private branch of EU law in consumer law and in the regulated sectors has been put at the service of EU regulatory goals and the construction of the internal market.[2] With Hans, we have not only learned to look at private law from a new perspective, we have learned, most of all, how to ask the right questions.

The purpose of this chapter is to explore the 'institutional' framework of regulatory private law in the EU. More specifically, we ask ourselves whether the design of EU private law-making can be said to respond to the features of experimentalism as described in political science.[3] This is to say, has norm-setting and norm-enforcement of private law rules in the EU responded to the four key elements of experimentalism: establishment of framework goals; autonomy of lower-level units in decision-making; definition of reporting duties; and peer-review and regular revision of the goals, metrics and procedures?[4]

In order to answer our question, this chapter builds on two case studies or laboratories: finance and food. The 2008 crisis hit both these sectors. Restructuring measures were urgently taken to avoid further chaos and to shield the sectors from the ensuing period of instability. While the two sectors seem far apart, they turned out to be closely interconnected. For example, due to the sensitivity of financial speculation in the food and agricultural sectors, the European Commission created in 2012 an Expert Group on Agricultural Commodity Derivatives and Spot Markets.[5] The Expert Group includes representatives from the Member States as well as associations of an assortment of agricultural sectors, and intends to inform the legislator on the evolution of food financial markets. Moreover, the MIFID II Directive has launched specific restrictive measures on the speculation with agricultural commodities. MIFID II includes a regime of position limits for agricultural commodities aimed at preventing market abuse. The new directive also greatly intensifies the reporting requirements of those positions, by setting an obligation of public disclosure once a week.[6]

The chapter is structured as follows. After this brief introduction, we examine the defining features of experimentalism and their relationship to private law (Section II). We then present the case studies: food (Section III) and

[2] OO Cherednychenko, 'Contract Governance in the EU: Conceptualising the Relationship between Investor Protection Regulation and Private Law' (2015) 21 *European Law Journal* 500, available at doi.org/10.1111/eulj.12130.

[3] On experimentalism see MC Dorf and CF Sabel, 'A Constitution of Democratic Experimentalism' (1998) 98 *Columbia Law Review* 267, available at doi.org/10.2307/1123411. See also CF Sabel and J Zeitlin, 'Experimentalism in the EU: Common Ground and Persistent Differences' (2012) 6 *Regulation & Governance* 410, available at doi.org/10.1111/j.1748-5991.2012.01157.x.

[4] CF Sabel and J Zeitlin, 'Learning from difference: The new architecture of experimentalist governance in the EU' (2008) 14 *European Law Journal* 271, 273–74.

[5] *Decision* of the Director General, DG *Agriculture* and Rural Development, October 2012, establishing an Expert Group on Agricultural Commodity Derivatives and Spot Markets. More information on the activities of the Expert Group can be accessed at ec.europa.eu/agriculture/cereals/commodity-expert-group_en.

[6] Arts 57 and 58 Directive 2014/65/EU.

finance (Section IV). Both case studies are organised in the same way. First, we explore whether the transforming conditions of the sector have conditioned the structural changes of law-making in the EU. Second, we explore the evolution of the respective regulation to the extent it displays emerging experimentalist features. Finally (Section V), we take stock of our findings and offer some concluding remarks on the nature of experimentalist private law in the EU.

II. Experimentalism in Private Law

The idea of experimentalism has been coined by political scientists in the study of mechanisms of public governance. From a European perspective, experimentalism has brought together the different features that the legal literature has attributed to law-making in the EU: its deliberative nature,[7] its informal mechanisms,[8] and its multi-level structure.[9] But unlike the previous theories, experimentalism does not concern itself with the characteristics of an institutional architecture set in stone. Because its focus is functional,[10] experimentalism is compatible with different institutional architectures as long as they permit decision-making processes to carry out four key functions. These four functions are: the collective establishment of framework goals by the EU institutions and Member States;[11] the autonomy of lower-level units in decision-making; the definition of reporting duties and peer-review and the regular revision of the goals, metrics and procedures on account of the implementation experience.[12] In this sense, experimentalism is a *recursive* method of decision-making that comprises 'a set of practices involving open participation by a variety of entities (public or private), lack of formal hierarchy within governance arrangements, and extensive deliberation throughout the process of decision making and implementation'.[13]

Experimentalism can be successfully implemented as long as certain conditions are met. For experimentalism to work, there needs to be a situation of strategic uncertainty (lack of agreement between policy-makers on the best strategy to regulate a given sector) and a 'multipolar or polyarchic' distribution

[7] C Joerges and J Neyer, 'Transforming Strategic Interaction into Deliberative Problem-Solving: European Comitology in the Foodstuffs Sector' (1997) 4 *European Journal of Public Policy* 609.

[8] T Christiansen and S Piattoni (eds), *Informal Governance in the European Union* (Manchester, Manchester University Press, 2000).

[9] R Dehousse, 'Regulation by Networks in the European Community: The Role of European Agencies' (1997) 4 *Journal of European Public Policy* 246.

[10] Sabel and Zeitlin (above n 4) 274.

[11] ibid, 274. See also Y Svetiev, 'The EU's Private Law in the Regulated Sectors: Competitive Market Handmaiden or Institutional Platform?' (2016) 22 *European Law Journal* 662.

[12] G de Búrca et al, 'New Modes of Pluralist Global Governance' (2013) 45 *NYU Journal of International Law and Politics* 723, 737–38.

[13] ibid, 738.

of power (where no single actor has the capacity to impose its own view).[14] At first sight, experimentalism seems to have sufficient bearings in the architecture of EU private law. The multiplicity of stakeholders in EU law-making and the need to coordinate the responses of Member States to the challenges of globalisation means that 'European regulatory private law is much more appropriate for experimentalism than traditional private law … [and] the limits of EU competences are compensated for by innovative competence creeping through experimentalism'.[15]

Through this prism, experimentalism has been identified with a problem-solving rationale particular to EU private law.[16] This rationale would be explained because, unlike the Member States, the EU does not have a legal and political tradition of its own that needs to be protected from the political disturbances of globalisation. Its hands are free to experiment with its own regulatory response. This distance from the ground level has often justified the suspicion of some over the lack of legitimacy of European institutions,[17] but it also 'allows for local tailored solutions, while providing mechanisms for peer review and monitoring of the design and effects of such solutions'.[18]

However, such an understanding of experimentalism is said to hide the political and redistributive elements of regulation.[19] If merely understood as a problem-solving approach, experimentalism runs the risk of reinforcing previously existing inequalities precisely because it lacks its own normative content. For this reason,[20] experimentalism would need to be 'modified' in the sense of ensuring the possibility of 'substantive deliberation' and of guaranteeing certain safeguards of protection in favour of weaker economic players (*ultimum remedium*).[21]

All in all, the attractiveness of experimentalism as a theory is that it offers an alternative explanation to regulatory competition and legal harmonisation as the EU approach to private law. Because it is a recursive and dynamic method of governance, it is compatible with diverse regulatory outcomes. Its detractors, however, see in experimentalism's lack of normative content a carte blanche for any pre-existing (im)balance of interests. Whatever the case, assessing the merits and pitfalls of experimentalism in EU private law needs to move past the idea that

[14] Sabel and Zeitlin (above n 4) 280.
[15] H-W Micklitz, 'The internal vs. the external dimension of European private law – a conceptual design and a research agenda' (2015) *EUI LAW Working Paper* 35/2015, 9.
[16] Svetiev (above n 11).
[17] Sabel and Zeitlin (above n 4) 271.
[18] Svetiev (above n 11) 662.
[19] M Bartl, 'Internal market rationality: In the way of re-imagining the future' (2018) 24 *European Law Journal* 99, 113.
[20] V Mak, 'Who Does What in European Private Law – and How Is It Done? An Experimentalist Perspective' (2017) Tilburg Law School Legal Studies Research Paper Series No 8/2017, 14.
[21] ibid, 12.

there is necessarily a hardline between procedure and substance.[22] Instead, the kind of questions that need to be asked are:

> whether the theory fits with lawmaking processes in the field, in terms of the participating lawmaking entities and the procedures of interaction and deliberation between them; and whether the goal [of achieving a 'high level of consumer protection'] is achieved through these strategies.[23]

III. The Food Laboratory

This section provides an overview of the restructuring of the food supply chain and the evolving approach of the European Commission to the regulation of UTPs in the food supply chain. The Commission's efforts date back to 2009, with the release of a first communication on a better functioning food supply chain.[24] They culminate in the recent proposal for a directive on business-to-business (B2B) unfair trading.[25] This overview assesses the experimentalist features of the European approach to sustainable practices in the food chain. It also reveals the limitations of the experimentalist approach to coordinate the definition of legal thresholds for protection, such as the definition of general clauses against UTPs, the definition economic dependence and even the possible definition of SMEs as weaker contractual parties.[26]

A. The Transforming Supply Chain or the Conditions for Experimentalist Governance

In 2008 the global food sector got into a spin.[27] A combination of factors resulted in a situation of market instability and food insecurity with profound effects on developing and developed economies. The financial crisis and the hikes in the price of agricultural commodities sank economic actors across the world in a

[22] See Micklitz (above n 15) 13.
[23] Mak (above n 20) 15.
[24] COM(2009) 591.
[25] COM/2018/0173 final.
[26] The definition of the personal scope of the Directive has been one of the main battlefields of the legislative procedure. While the Commission's initial proposal was limited to relations including SME suppliers, the final text has broadened its scope. Much to the dismay of the European retail sector, the new text covers mid-range companies at all levels of the food chain with a turnover of €350 million. Moreover, Member States are free to extend the rules beyond this threshold. For a review of the ongoing legislative procedure, see H Schebesta et al, 'Unfair Trading Practices in the Food Chain: Regulating Right?'(2019) *EJRR* (forthcoming), also available as a working paper at ssrn.com/abstract=3267118.
[27] See FAO Report, 'The State of Food Insecurity in the World 2008: High Food Prices and Food Insecurity – Threats and Opportunities' (2008).

situation of uncertainty and growing social unrest. Amid the havoc, the European food and agricultural policy, once a bulwark of European integration, entered a much-needed period of re-adjustment. The challenges that the European agro-food sector faced were numerous: growing food demand; new consumption trends; climate change; technological transformation and trade liberalisation.[28]

From the 1990s on, the rise of cross-compliance under public procurement rules[29] and the new WTO discipline on agriculture brought about the re-design of the Common Agricultural Policy (CAP) against a domestic background of budget constraints and market imbalances.[30] As the former CAP progressively retreated from direct intervention mechanisms in food markets,[31] the private law of contract gained a new role as a regulatory mechanism to canalise support towards agricultural SMEs and to balance bargaining power differences across food chains.[32] The structural crisis of agro-food supply chains and the technology-led transformation of the food sector opened leeway for a new European approach towards unfair trading practices (UTPs) in the food supply chain.

At first sight, the conditions for experimentalist governance were met. The goal behind the emerging approach was to promote the competitiveness of the European food sector in an environment of inherent uncertainty marked by structural imbalances, price volatility and the uneven allocation of decision-making powers across a variety of public and private actors with divergent interests.[33]

B. The Emergence of Experimentalist Features in B2B Fair Trading in the Food Chain

Ascertaining whether there is experimentalism in the regulation of trading practices in the food supply chain and of what type requires taking a closer look at the last ten years of regulatory innovations. This task requires an understanding of

[28] The global value chain literature has analysed in depth the elements driving the transformation of global agricultural markets. It also has brought attention to the different structural features of supply chains and their impact on governance models. See J Humphrey and O Memedovic, 'Global value chains in the agrifood sector' (2006) UNIDO Working Paper (2006); J Lee et al, 'Global value chains and agrifood standards: challenges and possibilities for smallholders in developing' (2012) 103(31) *Proceedings of the National Academy of Sciences* 12326.

[29] Kai P Purnhagen and P Feindt, 'A principles-based approach to the internal agricultural market' (2017) 5 *European Law Review*.

[30] Communication from the Commission to the European Parliament and the Council – Preparing for the 'Health Check' of the CAP reform COM (2007) 722.

[31] For an overview of various aspects of the recent CAP reforms, see G Anania et al, *The Political Economy of the 2014–2020 Common Agricultural Policy: An Imperfect Storm* (Centre for European Policy Studies, 2015).

[32] Illustrating this contractual turn, see the report commissioned by the French government on agricultural policy: JB Danel et al, 'Rapport sur la contractualisation dans le secteur agricole' (Conseil général de l'alimentation, de l'agriculture et des espaces ruraux, 2012).

[33] See European Commission, 'Report on the Competitiveness of the European Agro-Food Industry' (17 March 2009) 33 ff.

the role that the EU has played in the design of the procedures of interaction and deliberation among the entities participating in the governance design of the food supply chain.[34]

It could be argued that the European Commission has tried to open a space of deliberation to manage political tensions through the creation and promotion of multi-stakeholder fora representing (even if not necessarily in a balanced manner) a diversity of interests. From this perspective, the creation of this space is the expression of the Commission's preference for a *recursive review process*[35] over the enactment of new EU legislative instruments. As we shall see, the recursive process of monitoring and review has been carried out by the groups of experts set up by the Commission to watch over the correct functioning of the food supply chain.

In April 2008, the European Commission set up a High-Level Group (HLG) on the Competitiveness of the Agro-Food Industry.[36] The mission of this group was to identify the key challenges faced by a restructuring European agro-food industry and to put forward policy recommendations across several fields of action. The correct functioning of the food supply chain against the risk of bargaining power imbalances figured prominently among the concerns of the HLG.

The composition and functioning of the HLG arguably incorporated some experimentalist mechanisms in that it created a space for peer review. The HLG was made up of representatives of the European Commission, the Member States, and different sectors of the agro-food industry including consumers and civil society. Until 2010, the Group met on three occasions: June 2008, March 2009 and June 2009. All its publications were made public. The decisions of the group required a consensus. If there was no consensus, the documents reflected the dissenting opinions.[37]

This method of working would be reinforced in the coming years. In this regard, the final report of the HLG recommended that

> the European Commission in collaboration with the Members States and stakeholders should establish a European forum that will address the relationships among the players in the food chain, and in particular between producers/processors/distributors and will identify various parameters of importance for the good functioning of the food chain with the aim to adopt an EU wide code of conduct.[38]

The Commission ratified the recommendations of the HLG.[39] It broadened the scope and membership of the HLG with the establishment of the new High Level

[34] In answer to Mak (above n 20) 15.

[35] ibid, 14.

[36] By Decision of the European Commission, 28 April 2008 (2008/359/EC) [2008] OJ L120/15.

[37] See Annex 1 to the European Commission, Report on the Competitiveness of the European Agro-Food Industry, 17 March 2009.

[38] See recommendation no 15 in the European Commission, 'Report on the Competitiveness of the European Agro-Food Industry', 17 March 2009. Notably, the representatives of the retail industry did not support this recommendation.

[39] Communication from the Commission, 28 October 2009, 'A Better Functioning Food Supply Chain in Europe', COM (2009) 591 final.

Forum for a Better Functioning Food Supply Chain (HLF)[40] with the mission of implementing the recommendations of the HLG. With the establishment of the HLF, the Commission intensified some of the experimentalist features of the group. Specifically, the Commission proposed to collaborate with Member States to identify the issues posed by unequal bargaining power and to facilitate the exchange of best practices between regulatory agencies. Simultaneously, the Commission proposed to develop, together with relevant stakeholders, a set of EU-wide voluntary standard terms for the food supply chain. Finally, it also proposed to assess the effects of unfair trading practices in the internal market and the eventual need for further European action.[41]

Under the auspices of the HLF, representatives of the industry, Member States and civil society engaged in a multi-stakeholder dialogue on the causes, origins and strategies regarding trading practices in the food supply chain. This multi-stakeholder dialogue resulted in an interesting development in the form of a list of good practices for the food supply chain.[42] This list was to assume the role of the EU-wide voluntary standard terms promised by the Commission. Its role was to inform the contract terms and procurement policies of the signatories and it also informed the reform of trading legislations of some Member States.[43] In January 2013, the HLF endowed the Principles with a new governance structure to be known as the Supply Chain Initiative (SCI).[44] A governance group was created to monitor the evolution of the SCI and promote its implementation at the national level. It was composed of EU level associations representing the interests of the food and drink industry, food brands, retailers, SMEs and agricultural traders. The main feature of the SCI was to incorporate a voluntary registration system that offered the original seven signatories an alternative mechanism for the resolution of their disputes. However, the SCI lacked the support of key stakeholders like farmers and meat processors, who remained unconvinced of the independence and transparency of the dispute resolution system.

In parallel to the set-up of the SCI and following the rejection of the initiative by producers' associations, the European Commission launched a Green Paper Consultation on UTPs.[45] It gathered information from over 200 stakeholders – representing the industry, civil society and Member States – on the incidence, effects and possible remedies against the risk of UTPs in the chain. On the basis of

[40] Decision of the European Commission, 30 July 2010, [2010] OJ C210/4.

[41] ibid, 7.

[42] Vertical Relationships in the Food Supply Chain: Principles of Good Practice, see www.supplychaininitiative.eu/sites/default/files/b2b_principles_of_good_practice_in_the_food_supply_chain.pdf.

[43] For example, in Italy the list was incorporated into Art 62 of Decreto-Legge 24 gennaio 2012, n 1, amended by Legge 24 marzo 2012, n 27.

[44] See www.supplychaininitiative.eu/.

[45] European Commission, Green Paper on unfair trading practices in the business-to-business food and non-food supply chain in Europe, COM(2013) 37, 31 January 2013.

these findings, the Commission published a new communication in 2014.[46] In this Communication, the Commission rejected the proposal to take EU-wide action in the form of a harmonising instrument. Instead, it put forward three recommendations for action whereby the Commission expressed its support for reinforced private regulation initiatives like the SCI and its national sister platforms. It invited Member States to assess and relaunch their legislative framework against UTPs and underlined the need for effective enforcement, by reinforcing the investigation and sanction mechanisms of private and public regulatory frameworks.

Responding to this invitation, it has been up to Member States to revise their own regulatory frameworks against UTPs. Arguably, this process of national revision has allowed Member States to cater for tailored measures at the local level. Across different Member States, new regulatory responses have been developed at different intensities and speeds.[47] As a result, it is possible to find different degrees of complementarity between the public and the private sector in the enforcement design against UTPs. These divergences partly respond to the differences in the structure of the agricultural sector across member states and the differences in the degree of consolidation of agricultural activities across European regions. A majority of Member States have opted for a public regulatory model, where enforcement is carried out by a public agency endowed with investigation and sanctioning powers. Traditionally, this has been the case in France, where the bulk of enforcement against UTPs is carried out by the *Direction générale de la concurrence, de la consummation et de la repression des fraudes*, even though the recent development of the *Médiateur des relations commerciales agricoles* has approximated the French model to a mixed system. In other countries with a public regulatory model, enforcement against UTPs is carried out by the competition authority. This is the case in Germany, where the *Bundeskartellamt* has played a significant role in the fight against abuses of economic dependence. Additionally, countries that previously had no specific legislation addressed at UTPs have introduced new rules and granted enforcement powers to their competition authority or a newly-created agency. This has been the case in Poland, which in 2017 granted its competition authority new enforcement powers against UTPs. The UK, Spain and, since 2015, Slovenia, have opted for a mixed enforcement system. These models include a mechanism of mediation between businesses administered by a public agency or ombudsman, like the British Groceries Code Adjudicator or the Spanish AICA. Finally, other countries like Belgium and the Netherlands have opted for a purely private regulatory approach.[48]

[46] European Commission, Communication on Tackling unfair trading practices in the business-to-business food supply chain, COM(2014) 472 final.

[47] For a complete overview of UTP legislation across Europe, see the report prepared for the European Commission by A Renda et al, 'Study on the legal framework covering business-to-business unfair trading practices in the retail supply chain' (2014), available at publications.europa.eu/en/publication-detail/-/publication/c82dc8c6-ec15-11e5-8a81-01aa75ed71a1/language-en.

[48] For periodically updated comparative information on enforcement activities against UTPs across the EU, consult the webpage of the Spanish Agency: www.aica.gob.es/informes-9467910320160211.

In 2015, the Commission published a new report on UTPs in the food supply chain that reviewed the effectiveness of the different national frameworks against UTPs.[49] The Commission dismissed the need for further action at the EU level and committed to monitoring the evolution of the newly-designed private and public regulatory frameworks of the member states. To this effect, the mandate of the HLF was renovated to steer the dialogue among stakeholders and oversee the development of the SCI.[50]

In contrast to the experimentalist zeal of the Commission, the European Parliament,[51] the Council,[52] and the Economic and Social Committee called upon the Commission to propose a uniform regulatory framework on UTPs across the EU.[53] In April 2018,[54] the Commission published a proposal for a directive on UTPs, together with the results of the impact assessment.[55] However, the proposal retains an institutional focus, which at first sight seems compatible with an experimentalist approach. The main goal is to design effective enforcement mechanisms in view of the fragmented legal landscape and the limited enforcement capacity of voluntary initiatives.[56] In substantive terms, the original proposal does not provide a definition of UTP and its scope is limited to the relationship between SME-suppliers and retailers and to a limited number of trading practices already regulated by most Member States. The amendments of the European Parliament[57] and the interinstitutional agreement of 19 December 2018 have extended the scope of the proposal.[58] Even though all the details are yet to be known, the final text adds new prohibited UTPs unilaterally imposed to the original list. The list, unlike in the Unfair Commercial Practices Directive,[59] is not preceded by any general

[49] COM(2016) 32 final.

[50] Commission Decision of 1 June 2015 establishing the High Level Forum for a better functioning food supply chain (2015/C 179/03).

[51] Resolution of the European Parliament, 7 June 2016, on unfair trading practices in the food supply chain (2015/2065(INI)).

[52] Council Conclusions of 12 December 2016, 'Strengthening farmers' position in the food supply chain and tackling unfair trading practices'.

[53] COM(216) 32 final.

[54] European Commission, Proposal for a Directive on unfair trading practices in business-to-business relationships in the food supply chain, COM(2018)173.

[55] SWD(2018) 92 final.

[56] See Explanatory Memorandum to the text of the Proposal, COM(2018)173, 2–3.

[57] Draft European Parliament Legislative Resolution, on the proposal for a directive of the European Parliament and of the Council on unfair trading practices in business-to-business relationships in the food supply chain, available at oeil.secure.europarl.europa.eu/oeil/popups/ficheprocedure.do?reference=2018/0082(COD)&l=en.

[58] After six trilogues, an interinstitutional agreement has been reached in a seemingly rushed manner. This has a lot to do with the approaching European elections, which will be celebrated in the spring of 2019. After a failed attempt to reach an agreement at the beginning of December 2018, the Austrian presidency of the Council and the then upcoming Romanian presidency restarted negotiations before Christmas 2018. This last effort resulted in the interinstitutional agreement of 19 December 2018. The agreement needs to be approved by the Council and the Parliament, but it makes it more likely that if no changes are introduced, the Directive will be adopted before the end of the legislature.

[59] Directive 2005/29/EC, 11 May, concerning unfair business-to-consumer commercial practices in the internal market, [2005] OJ L149/22.

clause on 'fair trading'. Additionally, the final text purports to cover agricultural and food products and services in all of the food chain and to extend protection to all small and mid-range businesses 'with differentiated thresholds of protection'.[60] Throughout the different versions of the text, however, enforcement has remained a key element of the proposal.

That enforcement is a key issue in the approach to UTPs was already suggested by the so-called Brugge Study.[61] Perhaps for this reason, the bulk of the original proposal concerned the institutional dimension of the fight against UTPs.[62] The original proposal set a series of minimum requirements to be met by national enforcement authorities. These are considered indispensable to overcome the limitations to enforcement that stem from the so-called fear factor, that is, the fear of the weaker party to lodge a complaint against their commercial partner for fear of compromising the contract. In this sense, the proposal reinforces the role of administrative agencies after the fashion of some Member States, notably the British Code Adjudicator but also the Spanish AICA. According to the original text, Member States shall nominate a competent enforcement authority or designate as competent already existing authorities, such as consumer agencies or competition authorities. These public agencies shall be capable of initiating investigations on their own accord, gathering information, terminating the infringement, fining the offenders and publishing their names. Moreover, national enforcement authorities are called to integrate in a coordination mechanism or forum chaired by the European Commission. The purpose of this forum would be to facilitate the exchange of data and the exchange of best practices through annual meetings and reports and to assist each other in their enforcement activities.

The future adoption of the Directive does not entail necessarily the end of the experiment, especially because it allows Member States to maintain a great degree of autonomy in defining UTPs and types of businesses covered.[63] In this sense, the proposal reveals the possibility of integrating harmonisation within an experimentalist governance framework.[64] However, even an intermediate and experimental regulatory approach cannot escape the tensions between the diverging interests of suppliers and retailers in the food chain. These tensions have been illustrated by the Parliamentary discussions of the Commission's proposal and are reflected in the content of the somewhat rushed interinstitutional agreement. While the amendments of the European Parliament to introduce a definition of UTP and of

[60] See European Commission's Press Release, 19 December 2018, Agreement on unfair trading practices in the food supply chain will protect all EU farmers, available at europa.eu/rapid/press-release_IP-18-6790_en.htm. See also, Press Release of the Council of the EU, 19 December 2018, Fairer contractual relations in the agri-food chain agreed. Available at www.consilium.europa.eu/en/press/press-releases/2018/12/19/fairer-contractual-relations-in-the-agri-food-chain-agreed/.

[61] See Renda et al (above n 47) 18.

[62] Proposal for a Directive on UTPs (above n 54) Arts 4–7.

[63] ibid, Art. 3.

[64] See Mak (above n 20) 17, where she discusses the merging of harmonisation into the coordination mechanisms of legal pluralism.

abuses of economic dependence have been rejected, the final proposal extends the list of prohibited practices and the personal scope of the proposal to cover SMEs and mid-range businesses in the food chain. This extension is questionable from the perspective of agricultural policy, which is the legal basis of the proposal.[65] The (limited) available evidence on the incidence of the fear factor also casts doubts on the desirability of this extension, which would put enforcement in the hands of a European network of administrative agencies for all B2B relations in the food supply chain.

Still, the need for coordinated enforcement in the governance of the supply chain is recognised by the Parliament's text and by the final proposal. The final features of this coordination mechanism are not yet fully known. These concern the type of conflict rule to determine the competent authority, the intensity of cooperation,[66] its peer-review functions, their relationship with mediation mechanisms and the frequency of their meetings and their reporting activities.

Whether the Proposal completes the legislative procedure or not, the correct functioning of the food supply chain requires the coordination of multiple actors, public and private, who operate at the national, European and global level, and that apply different thresholds of 'unfairness'. Co-ordination points to procedure, which then again, puts us technically on the experimentalist side.[67]

IV. The Finance Laboratory

This section outlines the historical features of the restructuring of the EU approach to the regulation of finance, and describes how the institutional transformation of rule-making in the EU has sided with the transition from a system of refined self-regulation of financial transactions to a public standardisation of contracts. Second, the section characterises the powers of the European Supervisory Authorities (ESAs) in an attempt to illustrate how the architectural set up of the new European System of Financial Supervision provides fertile ground for experimentalism.[68] The ESAs are a forum of interaction of the EU institutions, Member States, stakeholders as well as associations of consumers whose ultimate goal is to establish a single rulebook applicable to all financial institutions in the EU.[69]

[65] See Schebesta et al (above n 26).

[66] Y Svetiev, 'Networked Competition Governance in the EU: Delegation, Decentralization or Experimentalist Architecture?' in C Sabel and J Zeitlin (eds), *Experimentalist Governance in the European Union* (Oxford, Oxford University Press, 2010).

[67] Micklitz (above n 15) 15–16.

[68] In favour of this thesis see M Cremona and H-W Micklitz (eds), *Private Law in the External Relations of the EU* (Oxford, Oxford University Press, 2016) 20.

[69] See Recital 5 Regulation (EU) No 1093/2010, [2010] OJ L331/12, Regulation (EU) No 1094/2010, [2010] OJ L331/48, Regulation (EU) No 1095/2010, [2010] OJ L331/84 establishing the ESAs.

A. The Financial Crisis as the Right Circumstance for Experimentalist Governance

With the partial repeal of the Glass-Steagall Act in 1998 and until the wake of the 2007 financial downturn, regulation in the financial markets worldwide dropped to a minimum as a consequence of the intellectual impulse of the so-called Washington Consensus. The efficient-market and rational-expectations hypothesis suggested that conditions for efficiency and equilibrium were valid even in environments evolving at the speed of light, such as financial markets.[70] But upon the breakdown of the global financial system in 2007, regulators came to terms with their inability to catch up with a beam of light. The fear that law was falling short to offset the contorted predatory behaviour of financial actors was confirmed by the collapse of the financial system following the bankruptcy Lehman Brothers. By the time Lehman failed, the market of mortgage backed securities had grown to an uncontrollable size, a size that was unwarranted by the role it served to the real economy.[71] The system imbalances were transmitted through the network of properties and there was no insurance, no type of collateral, that could withstand the shock.[72] The chain of contagion continued and in the two following months, the losses of the Standard & Poors index amounted to more than $10 trillion.

All in all, the laissez-faire policies introduced by the Gramm – Leach – Biley Financial Modernization Act of 1998 in the United States (the substitute for the Glass-Steagel Act) had led investment banks to a disastrous speculation fervour.[73] As a response to the crisis, global leaders agreed that the first line of defence against market instability was sound regulatory standards.[74] Since that precise moment, the global approach to financial regulation has evolved dramatically. Regulation has stepped in to address market failures such as information asymmetries or bounded rationality, and the disclosure-based paradigm has been substituted by heightened product governance. From the words of Alan Greenspan 'regulation of … transactions that are privately negotiated by professionals is unnecessary',[75] we have jumped to the pledge of the G20 in 2008 to 'strengthen our regulatory regimes, prudential oversight, and risk management, and ensure that all financial

[70] A Turner, *Economics After the Crisis: Objectives and Means* (Cambridge, Mass, MIT Press, 2013).

[71] FSA, 'The Turner Review : A Regulatory Response to the Global Banking Crisis' (March 2009) 49.

[72] In fact the insurance firm AIG collapse immediately after Lehman Brothers, in late 2008; the federal government bailed out AIG for $180 billion, and technically assumed control, because some believed its failure would endanger the financial integrity of other major firms that were its trading partners.

[73] RP Buckley and D Arner, *From Crisis to Crisis* (Kluwer Law International, 2011) 114–16.

[74] G20, 'Declaration: Summit on Financial Markets and the World Economy' November 2008. See also Leaders' Statement, The Pittsburg Summit (24–25 September 2009).

[75] Alan Greenspan was specifically referring to derivative transactions, FRB, 'Testimony, Greenspan – The Regulation of OTC Derivatives – 24 July 1998', available at www.federalreserve.gov/boarddocs/testimony/1998/19980724.htm, accessed 27 March 2019.

markets, products and participants are regulated or subject to oversight, as appropriate to their circumstances'.[76]

One could argue that the immediate regulatory reaction to the 2007 crisis was to set forth a myriad of 'traditional' standards, meaning that rules were hierarchically imposed. A good example is the regulatory framework for over-the-counter (OTC) derivatives, a sector in which, before the 2007 downturn, boilerplate contracts were mostly drafted by so-called norm-enterpreneurs[77] such as the International Swaps and Derivatives Association (ISDA) or the International Organization of Securities Commissions (IOSCO).[78] The transition from a system of refined self-regulation or transnational private law to an increasingly public regulatory space is well epitomised by the G20 Pittsburgh summit of 2009.[79] On that occasion, the G20 leaders introduced the paramount regulatory framework for OTC derivatives, including the obligation to clear OTC contracts to a particular intermediary (clearing houses or central counterparties). Although these international standards are not legally binding, their status changes when they become part of EU or national law.[80] In the EU, the principles for the regulation of OTC derivatives agreed upon by the G20 have been translated into the MIFID Regulation[81] and developed further by 17 regulatory technical standards (see below) drafted by European Service and Market Authority (ESMA).[82]

The argument we put forward in this section is that the regulatory intervention unleashed by the 2007 regulatory crisis has only been possible thanks to a multi-level collaboration among different actors coordinated by the ESAs under an experimentalist vest. The working methods amid the ESAs endorse participatory and deliberative rule-making that accommodate the knowledge of different players, thus granting adaptability to the legal order. Moreover, the division of rules in a set of legislative principles plus three different layers of rule-making (of different legal nature, as explained below) by expert administrative agencies conveys dynamism therein. This capacity to respond to rapidly evolving environment is crucial nowadays, when the ESAs are facing a new challenge just as disruptive technologies[83]

[76] Declaration of the Summit on Financial Markets and the World Economy, 15 November 2008, Washington DC, www.un.org/ga/president/63/commission/declarationG20.pdf.

[77] The term is coined by Calliess and Zumbansen when describing the state of the art in markets rule-making. G-P Calliess and P Zumbansen, *Rough Consensus and Running Code: A Theory of Transnational Private Law* (Oxford, Hart, 2010) 107.

[78] N Moloney, *EU Securities and Financial Markets Regulation*, 3rd edn (Oxford, Oxford University Press, 2014) 857.

[79] See H Marjosola, 'Regulate Thy Neighbour: Competition and Conflict in the Cross-Border Regulatory Space for OTC Derivatives', who gives an overview of the changes in the regulation before and after the crisis.

[80] See eg F Weiss and A Kammel (eds), *The Changing Landscape of Global Financial Governance and the Role of Soft Law*, XXII (Leiden, Brill – Nijhoff, 2015) VIII.

[81] Regulation (EU) No 600/2014 [2014] OJ L173.

[82] See the list of regulatory technical standards at ec.europa.eu/info/sites/info/files/mifir-level-2-measures-full_en.pdf.

[83] CM Christensen et al, 'What Is Disruptive Innovation?' (2015) *Harvard Business Review* 11.

accelerate the pace of financial innovation.[84] These two circumstances (the regulation of a sector that had previously leaned towards de-regulation and the arrival of technological breakthrough) determine a strategic uncertainty that paves the way to experimentalism.[85] Such an argument is unfolded in the next subsection.

B. The Emergence of Experimentalist Features in the European System of Financial Supervision

As early as 2001, the Lamfalussy Report recognised the importance of assembling a multi-layered governance structure that could address the deficiencies of a regulatory framework that was 'too slow, too rigid, complex and ill-adapted to the pace of global financial market change'.[86] For this reason, the 'wise men' published the Lamfalussy Report calling for an unprecedented institutional intervention in order to build up an integrated financial market in the EU. A second factor prompted by Financial Services Action Plan (a plan of 42 articles launched in 1999 for the harmonisation of the financial services markets in the EU) was the need to even out divergences and inconsistencies in the supervisory practices and sanctioning regime among Member States. In fact the discordant framework jeopardised competitive neutrality, a situation that could only be dealt with by a streamlined interface for regulatory cooperation.[87] Lamfalussy advanced a solution to these deficiencies in the form of a system that relied upon a network of three committees in which national authorities and local supervisors gathered together and exchanged information. There was one committee for the securities market (CESR), one for banking (CEBS) and one for insurance and occupational pensions (CEIOPS). The committees embodied the comitology principle, meaning that, in their function of assisting in the making of secondary law, they were chaired by the European Commission, which ensured the equitable and balanced representation of the Member States.[88]

Nevertheless, there was a major flaw that rendered the system of the so-called 'L3L' committees ill-suited to combat the structural problems of financial regulation. The committees lacked the powers necessary to harmonise the legal framework for financial services,[89] and among national supervisors coordination

[84] There are some who even speak of the a Fourth Industrial Revolution. See K Schwab, *The Fourth Industrial Revolution* (New York, Crown Publishing, 2017).

[85] Sabel and Zeitlin (above n 4) 280.

[86] Committee of Wise Men on the Regulation of European Securities Markets, Final Report (2001) 7, available at ec.europa.eu/finance/securities/docs/lamfalussy/wisemen/final-report-wise-men_en.pdf.

[87] ibid.

[88] See P Craig and G de Búrca, *EU Law: Text, Cases, and Materials* (Oxford, Oxford University Press, 2015) 115–17. On comitology, see also CF Bergström, *Comitology: Delegation of Powers in the European Union and the Committee System*, Oxford Studies in European Law (Oxford: Oxford University Press, 2005).

[89] J Zeitlin, 'EU Experimentalist Governance in Times of Crisis' (2016) 39(5) *West European Politics* 1078, available at doi.org/10.1080/01402382.2016.1181873.

was poor and cooperation too scarce.[90] Such structural problems were aggravated by the 2007 financial downturn, resulting in the collapse of the committees. As a matter of fact, the powers of the three committees were too weak to fight against the effects of a destabilising international macro-economic policy that had led to the building up of a flattening cheap leverage. These conditions triggered a Copernican revolution[91] under the auspices of the Larosière Group[92] and set in motion a far-reaching regulatory agenda to improve riskcyclical management and enhance convergence in supervisory practices. The Lamfalussy architecture was reinforced by the creation of the European System of Financial Supervision and the substitution of the 'L3L' committees by the ESAs. Mirroring the old committees, there is one ESA for each sector, so the ESMA, the European Insurance and Occupational Pensions Authority (EIOPA) and European Banking Authority (EBA).

The European System of Financial Supervision has created a multi-layered governance structure with two different levels (European/national) and two different pillars (micro-prudential/macro-prudential).[93] This chapter is concerned with micro-prudential supervision led by the ESAs. The ESAs coordinate the network of Competent Authorities (CAs) that are in charge of day-to-day supervision. Therefore, the ESAs have both rule-making and supervisory powers, in a recognition that supervision spills over into rules and vice-versa.[94] Rule-making tasks include: advising on the adoption of level 1 legislation; adopting binding technical standards that once endorsed by the European Commission become level 2 regulatory or implementing technical standards (from now RTS or ITS);[95] and finally passing a myriad of level 3 soft law measures of diverse levels of coerciveness[96] that qualify and complete the single rulebook.

At first sight, the extensive transfer of legislative prerogatives to the ESAs can seem like a shift towards operational centralisation.[97] This is particularly true for the banking sector, where the Banking Union completes the Europeanisation

[90] N Moloney, 'EU financial market regulation after the global financial crisis: "more Europe" or more risks?' (2010) *Common Market Law Review* 1319.

[91] See S Cappiello, 'RSCAS 2015/77 The Interplay between the EBA and the Banking Union,' 2015, referring to the powers that EBA has been endowed with.

[92] See The High Level Group on Financial Supervision in the EU, chaired by Jacques de Larosière, Report (2009), 6, available at ec.europa.eu/economy_finance/publications/pages/publication14527_en.pdf.

[93] For a clear picture of the division of tasks after the creation of the new supervisory actors, see Larosière report, ibid, 57.

[94] N Moloney, 'The European Securities and Markets Authority and Institutional Design for the EU Financial Market – a Tale of Two Competences: Part (2) Rules in Action' (2011) 12 *European Business Organization Law Review* 183, available at doi.org/10.1017/S1566752911200016.

[95] The scope of RTS and ITS is defined by the sectoral legislation. RTS and ITS are adopted in accordance with the procedure set in Arts 10–15 Regulation (EU) No 1093/2010, [2010] OJ L331/12, Regulation (EU) No 1094/2010, [2010] OJ L331/48, Regulation (EU) No 1095/2010, [2010] OJ L331/84 establishing the ESAs.

[96] Moloney (above n 78) 856.

[97] Eg RA Epstein and M Rhodes, 'The Political Dynamics behind Europe's New Banking Union' (2016) 39(3) *West European Politics* 415.

of supervision. However, this vision is segmented and disregards the actual twists and turns of the working method and decision-making processes inside the EBA. We explore below the working methods of the EBA when adopting binding technical standards (RTS or ITS), as well as guidelines and recommendations, and argue that they are more akin to experimentalism than to traditional centralisation. Special attention is devoted to the collaboration between the public and the private sectors in this regard.

Applicable to both hard and soft law adopted by the EBA are three reasons that contrast the idea of centralisation. First, the institutional composition of the EBA follows a federal logic, as its Board of Supervisors is composed of the heads of each national supervisor.[98] As a result, when exercising its regulatory prerogatives 'the EBA does not, and cannot, impose "its" view against the collective view of the national competent authorities. Rather, their (majority) view is its view'.[99] Second, content-wise, these norms (EBA level 2 and 3 rules) incorporate best practices stemming from national authorities since representatives of these later are comprised in operational committees, working groups and thematic hubs.[100] This exerts as a method of inter-institutional peer review and multipolar collaboration. Third, the working methods employed therein also benefit from cross-sectoral expertise as they widely include broad participation of stakeholders.

Against the idea of power concentration in the hands of the EBA is the space for deliberation left to consultations and dialogue held with interest groups. In the case of binding technical standards, there is a phase of compulsory consultations during their drafting.[101] The consultation is usually initiated by the publication of the dedicated paper with the draft technical standard and some questions addressed to the stakeholders that regard each of the norm's provisions. Financial institutions (as well as other commentators)[102] are requested to send their written comments within a period of three months. Respondents may request the EBA to treat their comments as confidential but any decision by the authority not to disclose the responses shall be reviewable by the EBA's Board of Appeal and the European Ombudsman.[103] In conclusion, the drafting of technical standards is open to a multi-stakeholder dialogue that makes up for a recursive method of decision-making.

[98] See Art 40 Regulation (EU) No 1093/2010, [2010] OJ L331/12.

[99] E Ferran, 'The Existential Search of the European Banking Authority' (2016) 17(3) *European Business Organization Law Review* 300, available at doi.org/10.1007/s40804-016-0048-9.

[100] ibid, 300–301.

[101] Arts 10(1) and 15(1) Regulation (EU) No 1093/2010, [2010] OJ L331/12.

[102] When conducting consultations, the EBA shall seek in particular the opinion of Banking Stakeholders Group. The EBA's Banking Stakeholder Group is composed of 30 members selected in balanced proportions to be an agent of credit and investment institutions operating in the Union, their employees, consumers and other users of financial services as well as top-ranking academics.

[103] See eg Consultation on Draft Regulatory Technical Standards on the methods of prudential consolidation under Art 18 of Regulation (EU) No 575/2013 (Capital Requirements Regulation – CRR).

The EBA also adopts extensive guidelines and recommendations that can be seen as taking away options and discretion from Member States.[104] This idea is reinforced by the fact that guidelines and recommendations are not always called upon by the primary legislation.[105] The EBA can also adopt guidelines under its own initiative by virtue of Article 16 of EBA's Regulation. Although these are formally non-binding instruments, they come with 'comply or explain' attached, which reinforces their legal value. 'Comply or explain' requires competent authorities to inform the EBA about their intention to comply/not comply with a new guideline or recommendation.

In our view, extensive soft regulation through guidelines and recommendations – despite what appearances may suggest – does not stand for a move towards centralisation precisely because of the deliberative approach, informal mechanisms and multi-level structure of the rule-making processes chosen by the EBA. The regulatory intervention unleashed by the 2007 regulatory crisis necessitates of a trial and error set-up that is only possible thanks to a multi-level collaboration: first, among the EU institutions and agencies;[106] second, with the national competent authorities – as the EBA embraces the comitology principle and endorses an array of interests from different national authorities; and finally with the private sector, the player detaining the technical knowledge that the public sector necessitates to complete the regulatory framework.

The dialogue between the EBA and the industry is particularly solid due to the mutable nature of financial assets and the dizzying innovations of financial engineering.[107] In recent years, new business models have broken into financial markets and disrupted the level playing field by introducing brand-new products and technologies that seek to automate the delivery of financial services. This bunch of business innovations is commonly known as financial technology (Fintech) and is giving many headaches to regulators. For example, one of the most prominent dilemmas posed by Fintech is the legal and accounting characterisation of cryptocurrencies. Because of their lack of backing by a trusted third party (traditionally money is backed by central banks), cryptocurrencies are extremely volatile, so it is difficult to capture their value. The regulatory responses have varied enormously, being even reckoned by some as a Ponzi scheme to lure and

[104] See S Grundmann, 'The Banking Union Translated into (Private Law) Duties: Infrastructure and Rulebook' (2015) 16(3) *European Business Organization Law Review* 366, doi:10.1007/s40804-015-0021-z.

[105] In particular in this case by the Capital Requirements Regulation, the Capital Requirements Directive or the Bank Recovery and Resolution Directive.

[106] The ESAs Regulations provide for a form of peer review: the so-called Joint Committee of European Supervisory Authorities. The Joint Committee is a permanent forum composed of representatives of each of the three ESAs and aimed at enhancing the cooperation between them. It meets at least twice a month and its main function is to ensure cross-sectorial consistency. There are some fields, usually particularly connected with the safeguard of financial stability, in which ESAs are required to cooperate more intimately and coordinate before adopting binding technical standards.

[107] K Pistor, 'A Legal Theory of Finance' (2013) 41(2) *Journal of Comparative Economics* 328, available at doi.org/10.1016/j.jce.2013.03.003.

defraud investors.[108] In fact the Chinese market already closed its doors in 2017 to cryptocurrency trading and subsequently tightened the prohibition by preventing local banks from operating in international exchanges of cryptocurrencies.[109]

The EBA has not yet given a regulatory solution to this issue, but to resolve the puzzle and ensure technological neutrality it is studying the possibility of setting up regulatory sandboxes.[110] The initiative to put in motion such an innovative test chamber for regulation comes up from an intensive lobbying activity by the Banking Stakeholders Group.[111] A regulatory sandbox is a safe legal space for experimentation in which companies can test innovative products, services or even business models.[112] Typically, a waiver is conceded by the supervisor so companies working under the umbrella of a regulatory sandbox receive legal advice to avoid incurring the legal consequences that they would otherwise incur by engaging in such activities.[113] In return for a reduced risk of being punished, innovators have to share information with the regulator and collaborate to design an optimal regulatory solution. This mechanism encompasses a two-way knowledge exchange: supervised entities share an amount of information that goes well beyond what they would share outside the sandbox, which in turn helps supervisors to design more appropriate rules.[114] All in all, regulatory sandboxes are of paramount importance to a recursive review process over the regulation of new financial practices.

V. Conclusions

In 2016 the European Regulatory Private Law (ERPL) project led by Hans came to an end.[115] Many of our colleagues, who have also contributed to this book, dedicated their PhDs to conducting empirical research that has proven how the

[108] 'Don't Be Surprised Floyd Mayweather and DJ Khaled Are Caught up in a Cryptocurrency Scam – They Are Basically Ponzi Schemes' *Independent* (23 October 2018), available at www.independent.co.uk/voices/floyd-mayweather-dj-khaled-cryptocurrency-scam-bitcoin-ico-ponzi-scheme-centra-tech-a8597416.html. See also the joint ESA's warning on virtual currencies, at www.esma.europa.eu/sites/default/files/library/esma50-164-1284_joint_esas_warning_on_virtual_currenciesl.pdf.

[109] It is to be noted, however, that the Chinese government is promoting a national blockchain project, thus imitating the strategy they already followed with Western social networks: that of emulating and confiscating the idea. See 'Experts Fear China Losing 90% Control Over Bitcoin Market, Forgetting Gov't Ban,' CCN, 10 July 2018, available at www.ccn.com/experts-fear-china-losing-90-control-over-bitcoin-market-forgetting-govt-ban/.

[110] EBA's Fintech Roadmap, March 2018.

[111] See 'Regulatory sandboxes, A proposal to EBA by the Banking Stakeholders Group' 20 July 2017, available at eba.europa.eu/documents/10180/807776/BSG+Paper+on+Regulatory+Sandboxes_20+July+2017.pdf.

[112] FCA, 'Regulatory Sandbox' (November 2015) 2.

[113] D Arner et al, 'Fintech and regtech in a nutshell and the future in a sandbox' (2017) 3(4) *Research Foundation Briefs*.

[114] DA Zetzsche et al, 'Regulating a Revolution: From Regulatory Sandboxes to Smart Regulation' (2017) 23 *Fordham Journal of Corporate and Financial Law* 31, 59–60.

[115] 'European Regulatory Private Law: the Transformation of European Private Law from Autonomy to Functionalism in Competition and Regulation' (ERPL).

traditional notion of private law is being continuously re-shuffled by new EU substantive laws, decision-making processes and enforcement mechanisms.[116] In line with the broader topology of the private law of the *acquis communautaire*, ERPL does not focus on establishing a level playing field for an autonomous civil society. Rather, as Micklitz remarks,[117] EU law regards its private branch as an instrument for pursuing collective objectives, and particularly specific goals of the internal market project.[118] Through the food and finance laboratories, this chapter has endeavoured to demonstrate that this regulatory rationale,[119] together with the need to accommodate rule-making in environments evolving at full speed, has brought about a new approach to regulation with an experimentalist design.

Experimentalism and close cooperation among different institutions and the private sector can be understood as the chosen method to accommodate a variety of interests. In the food sector, we have described how the European Commission opts for an open space of deliberation when regulating UTPs and how the workings of the HLG and HLF have incorporated extensive experimentalist features. By the same token, the shape of the single rulebook for financial products and services is conditioned by the working methods inside the EBA, which give room to lower-level units to contribute to the regulatory framework. Moreover, the European System of Financial Supervision yields a peer-review forum for different national supervisors and stakeholders. This recursive review over regulation is exacerbated in the case of regulatory sandboxes for sectors such as Fintech, where strategic uncertainty is all-pervasive.

Embracing an experimentalist approach, the EU legal order manages political tensions by opening up its ins and outs to a space of deliberation. The creation and promotion of multi-stakeholder forums is expected to guarantee the representation of a complex multiplicity of interests. It also endows the legislator with the power of monitoring the effects of different regulatory solutions before opting for a definite legal frame. The two case studies presented in this chapter have illustrated the safeguards in place to compensate for the perils of regulatory capture intrinsic to experimentalism.[120] The most important of these safeguards is the potential

[116] See F della Negra, *MiFID II and Private Law: Enforcing EU Conduct of Business Rules* (Oxford, Hart, 2018); M Cantero Gamito, 'The Private Law Dimension of the EU Regulatory Framework for Electronic Communications : Evidence of the Self-Sufficiency of European Regulatory Private Law' (EUI PhD Thesis, 2015); B van Leeuwen, *European Standardisation of Services and Its Impact on Private Law : Paradoxes of Convergence* (Oxford, Hart, 2017); L de Almeida, 'Integration through Self-Standing European Private Law : Insights from the Internal Point of View to Harmonization in Energy Market' (EUI PhD Thesis, 2017); B Kas, 'Hybrid Collective Remedies in the EU Social Legal Order' (EUI PhD Thesis, 2017).

[117] H-W Micklitz, 'The Visible Hand of European Regulatory Private Law' (2009) 22 *Yearbook of European Law* 3.

[118] See also OO Cherednychenko, 'Contract Governance in the EU: Conceptualising the Relationship between Investor Protection Regulation and Private Law' (2015) 21(4) *European Law Journal* 500, available at doi.org/10.1111/eulj.12130.

[119] See also Bartl (above n 19) 99–115.

[120] See Bartl (above n 19) 113.

openness of the rule-making process to every stakeholder who may want to assert their interests.

Notwithstanding, the experimental design of knowledge production may jeopardise epistemic pluralism. The 'problem-solving' strategy devises a technocratic road to political problems and conceals the (knowledge) access barriers that lay citizens may encounter. Even when they have a direct or indirect interest in a regulatory outcome, ordinary citizens lack the necessary expertise to give informed and persuasive arguments on food or financial regulation.[121] As a result, the preference for an experimentalist set up, even if optimal from a problem-solving perspective, can amplify existing inequalities and have detrimental distributive effects.

[121] For an illustrative example on the case of financial regulation see C Ford, *Innovation and the State: Finance, Regulation, and Justice* (Cambridge, Cambridge University Press, 2017) 39–41.

14

The Recent Developments in Arbitration and the European Regulatory Space

ZDENĚK NOVÝ* AND BARBARA WARWAS**

I. Introduction

We happily offer this paper to celebrate the 70th birthday of our dear professor, Hans Micklitz. It is an enormous honour and pleasure to contribute to this book.

In writing this chapter, we have tried to build on the ideas we learned from Professor Micklitz. First is a 'stand and stare' approach: to observe and look beyond ordinary things and labels, not to follow blankly conventional truths, and not to yield to a herd behaviour.[1]

At a more concrete level, it is noted that the Court of Justice of the European Union (CJEU), as well as Member States' courts, are not only interpreters of EU legal rules, but also political actors.[2]

The authors' academic work concerns predominantly arbitration, and therefore this chapter will be devoted to that area. We make our implicit assumption explicit that we consider arbitration as a valuable dispute resolution method. At the same time, we are aware of the fact that arbitration might not be viable for all types of disputes.

The chapter is divided into two main sections: the first predominantly deals will the *Achmea* judgment. As such, it concerns the role of investor-state arbitration under EU law. The second section examines the emerging role of arbitration, understood broadly, in shaping European regulatory private law.

* Section II was authored by Dr Zdeněk Nový, Assistant Professor at the Faculty of Law, Masaryk University, Brno, The Czech Republic. All views expressed are those of the author.

** Section III was authored by Dr Barbara Warwas, Professor (Lector) in Multilevel Regulation at The Hague University of Applied Sciences. All views expressed are those of the author.

[1] See H-W Micklitz et al, 'Methodology in the New Legal World' (2012/13) *EUI Working Papers*, www.cadmus.eui.eu/bitstream/handle/1814/22016/LAW_2012_13_VanGestelMicklitzMaduro.pdf?sequence=1&isAllowed=y 23. All websites referred to in this chapter were last accessed on 15 December 2018, unless indicated otherwise.

[2] See generally H-W Micklitz, *The Politics of Judicial Cooperation in the EU: Sunday Trading, Equal Treatment and Good Faith* (Cambridge, Cambridge University Press, 2005).

II. The Implications of the *Achmea* Judgment for International Arbitration in the European Union

Achmea, the Dutch company, merged with the company Eureko offering, inter alia, health insurance, in Slovakia.[3] Health insurance was provided through two Slovak companies, Union Insurance and Union Healthcare. After the change of the Slovak government in 2006, Eureko's investment in Slovakia, prompted by previous liberalisation of the health insurance market, was allegedly destroyed by a series of legislative measures of this state. Therefore, Achmea commenced an arbitration based on the bilateral investment treaty (BIT) between the Netherlands and Slovakia.[4] The arbitral tribunal sitting in Frankfurt am Main in Germany found that Slovakia had violated certain standards of treatment under BIT.[5]

Subsequently, Slovakia asked German courts for the annulment of such award. It argued that Article 8 BIT, enabling an investor to initiate arbitration against the state, is incompatible with Articles 18, 267 and 344 of the Treaty on the Functioning of the EU (TFEU).[6]

The case had to be resolved in the final instance by *Bundesgerichshof* (BGH).[7] BGH was not sure whether Article 344 TFEU, which says that Member States may not submit a dispute concerning interpretation and application of EU law to other judicial mechanism than to the CJEU, was applicable.[8] In the BGH's opinion the answer should have been in the negative, as the dispute at hand does not fall within the scope of Article 344 TFEU.[9]

BGH also wanted to know whether Article 267 TFEU precluded a dispute resolution clause in Article 8 BIT allowing an investor to commence arbitration against a Member State.[10] It found that arbitrators may not refer a preliminary ruling to the CJEU, and therefore uniform application of EU law could not be ensured.[11] Nonetheless, BGH noted that the uniformity of EU law may be guaranteed by the Member State's court reviewing the arbitral award.[12]

[3] Judgment of the Court (Grand Chamber) of 6 March 2018, Case C-284/16, *Slowakische Republic v Achmea BV*, ECLI:EU:C:2018:158.

[4] Agreement on Encouragement and Reciprocal Protection of Investments between the Kingdom of the Netherlands and the Czech and Slovak Federal Republic, www.investmentpolicyhub.unctad.org/Download/TreatyFile/2080

[5] Permanent Court of Arbitration Case No 2008–13, *Achmea BV (Claimant) v The Slovak Republic (Respondent)*, Final Award, UNCITRAL, 7 December 2012, para 352, www.italaw.com/sites/default/files/case-documents/italaw3206.pdf.

[6] Achmea judgment (above n 3) para 14.

[7] *BGH Beschluss vom 3 März 2016, no I ZB 2/15 in dem Verfarhen auf Aufhebung eines inländischen Schiedspruchs*, www.juris.bundesgerichtshof.de/cgibin/rechtsprechung/document.py?Gericht=bgh&Art=pm&Datum=2016&Sort=3&nr=74612&linked=bes&Blank=1&file=dokument.pdf.

[8] Achmea judgment (above n 3) paras 16–17.

[9] ibid, paras 15–16.

[10] ibid, para 18.

[11] ibid, para 19.

[12] ibid, para 20.

However, BGH doubted that the arbitral award in issue would be contrary to public policy, being one of very few reasons for its annulment under the German Code of Civil Procedure.[13]

Advocate General Wathelet submitted an extensive and thoughtful reasoning, accompanied by a number of references to cases and other authorities.[14] He found that there is no incompatibility between Article 8 BIT and EU law.[15] The Advocate General recognised that the arbitral tribunal at hand could be considered as a 'court or tribunal' in the sense of Article 267 TFEU.[16] Moreover, the dispute between Achmea and Slovakia did not come under Article 344 TFEU.[17] He also did not see any sign of discrimination that would trigger the application of Article 18 TFEU.[18]

Interestingly, and perhaps significantly, the CJEU did not refer to a single argument made by Advocate General Wathelet's Opinion. The CJEU just recalled in passing that it the Advocate General's opinion was not binding in any way.[19]

A. The CJEU's Reasoning

The CJEU first noted a fundamental principle of autonomy of EU law on international and national law. Such autonomy is justified due to the existence of special characteristics in EU law, such as primacy or direct effect.[20] Autonomy therefore requires that an international agreement between Member States shall not affect the allocation of powers under Treaties.[21] Thereafter, the CJEU recalled that there is a principle of sincere cooperation among states, as well as mutual trust as its corollary.[22] The specific 'nature' and autonomy of EU law may be maintained only by a 'judicial system' composed of the CJEU and Member States' courts that ensure 'consistency' and 'uniformity' of interpretation of EU law.[23] It is only for these courts to ensure a 'judicial protection of the rights of individuals' stemming from EU law.[24] The central element of judicial protection is the preliminary ruling procedure, which also guarantees the specific nature and observance of essential principles of EU law.[25]

[13] ibid.
[14] Opinion of AG Wathelet delivered on 19 September 2017 in Case C-284/16, *Slowakische Republic v Achmea BV*.
[15] ibid, para 273.
[16] ibid, paras 83–109.
[17] ibid, paras 138–53.
[18] ibid, paras 54–59.
[19] *Achmea* judgment (above n 3) para 27.
[20] ibid, para 33.
[21] ibid, para 32.
[22] ibid, para 34.
[23] ibid, para 35.
[24] ibid, para 36.
[25] ibid, para 37.

The CJEU examined Article 8 BIT. It found that its section (6) required that the arbitral tribunal is obliged to apply Dutch or Slovak law. Since EU law is part of both legal orders, it must apply before arbitrators as well.[26]

The CJEU then sought to analyse whether an arbitral tribunal established by virtue of Article 8 BIT pertains to the EU 'judicial system'.[27] The answer was in the negative, since the arbitral tribunal did not belong to the EU judicial system due to its 'exceptional nature', and therefore could not ask the CJEU for a preliminary ruling.[28] Such arbitral tribunal cannot be considered in particular as a court or tribunal of 'a Member State' and has no 'links with the judicial systems' of the Member State.[29]

The CJEU also found that the BIT requires the arbitral award be final, meaning that there is no appeal procedure.[30] The review of such award under German law as the *lex loci arbitri* is limited. In commercial arbitration, the CJEU says, consistency with EU law would be ensured in the course of the review of a commercial arbitral award.[31] This is not so with investment arbitration, for two reasons: first, investment arbitration, in contrast to commercial ones, does not 'originate in the freely expressed wishes of the parties', but from a treaty;[32] second, by concluding this treaty (BIT), the Member States 'remove from the jurisdiction of their own courts [*sic*], and hence from the system of judicial remedie[s]'.[33]

Article 8 BIT impedes the mutual trust among Member States, observance of the particular nature of the EU legal order, as well as the application of preliminary ruling procedure.[34] For all these reasons, Article 8 BIT is incompatible with the principle of sincere cooperation.[35] As a result, the CJEU found that:

> Articles 267 and 344 TFEU must be interpreted as precluding a provision in an international agreement concluded between Member States, such as Article 8 of the Agreement on encouragement and reciprocal protection of investments between the Kingdom of the Netherlands and the Czech and Slovak Federative Republic, under which an investor from one of those Member States may, in the event of a dispute concerning investments in the other Member State, bring proceedings against the latter Member State before an arbitral tribunal whose jurisdiction that Member State has undertaken to accept.[36]

[26] ibid, para 40.
[27] ibid, para 43.
[28] ibid, para 45.
[29] ibid, paras 49–50.
[30] ibid, paras 51, 53.
[31] ibid, para 54.
[32] ibid, para 55.
[33] ibid.
[34] ibid, para 58.
[35] ibid.
[36] ibid, the dispositive part.

B. Arbitration and EU Law: A Precursor to an Analysis of the *Achmea* Judgment

International arbitration and its actors seek to liberate themselves as far as possible from the limits provided by national laws and a formalism of court procedures.[37] Submitting to arbitration removes the existing or future disputes from the competence of Member States' courts. This implies that the case will be resolved outside the EU judiciary system, which consists solely of the CJEU and Member States' courts.

While Member States' courts must interpret and apply EU law in conformity with the CJEU case law, no such duty exists under EU law for arbitrators.[38] It is thus not certain whether correct interpretation and application of EU law would be ensured in international arbitration.

Arbitration borrows applicable rules to the substance of the dispute from national laws as well as non-state sources.[39] As the number of EU legal rules increases, there is more probability that these rules would apply also in international arbitration.

Investment arbitration then brings its 'own' substantive law, ie international law.[40] A number of vaguely drafted investment treaties,[41] often dating back to the pre-accession period, is thereby binding on Member States.[42] Both EU law and international investment law then regulate responsibility for Member States' breaches of their respective rules. The conflict between EU law and investment arbitration thus came to a head as soon as Member States were required to comply with contradictory obligations arising from the two systems.[43]

Investment arbitration adds a political dimension to a tension with EU arbitration law.[44] Investment arbitrators are said to favour investors, mostly

[37] See R David, *Arbitration in International Trade* (Deventer, Kluwer Law and Taxation, 1985) 10–11.

[38] See the Opinion of AG Saggio delivered on 25 February 1999 in Case C-126/97, *Eco Swiss v Benetton International*, para 52(1).

[39] See, for instance, N Blackaby and C Partesides with A Redfern and M Hunter, *Redfern and Hunter on International Arbitration Student Version*, 6th edn (Oxford, Oxford University Press, 2015) 190–216.

[40] N Blackaby, 'Investment Arbitration and Commercial Arbitration (or the Tale of the Dolphin and the Shark)' in L Mistelis and JDM Lew (eds), *Pervasive Problems in International Arbitration* (Alphen aan den Rijn, Kluwer Law International, 2006) 222.

[41] The vagueness of investment protection standards, as 'fair and equitable treatment', is intentional, and inherent perhaps. As it is impossible to foresee all possible breaches of investor rights, the treaty drafters preferred general standards to specific rules. For a deeper analysis see F Ortino, 'Refining the Content and Role of Investment "Rules" and "Standards": A New Approach to International Treaty Making' (2013) 28 *ICSID Review* 154–55.

[42] eg BIT at hand.

[43] Commission Decision (EU) 2015/1470 of 30 March 2015 on State aid SA.38517 (2014/C) (ex 2014/NN) implemented by Romania – Arbitral award Micula v Romania of 11 December 2013 (notified under document C (2015) 2112) (only the Romanian text is authentic) (text with EEA relevance) OJ L232, 4.9.2015, 43–70.

[44] See generally J Bonnitcha et al, *The Political Economy of the Investment Treaty Regime* (Oxford, Oxford University Press, 2017) 181–232.

multinational corporations.[45] They also pay no regard to public interest of the host state.[46] Arbitrators interpret bilateral investment treaties extensively whereby they fetter the regulatory space of host states.[47] There is inconsistency in decision-making of investment arbitral tribunals as well.[48]

It is submitted that the above critique of investment arbitration is too harsh and lacks support in theory and practice. Thus, before endorsing the idea of an inevitable demise of investment arbitration, certain arguments might be considered. First, investment arbitration has a preventive character.[49] Both the threat and reality of investment arbitration may streamline the conduct of Member States, so that they observe rule of law and seek to provide good administration of internal affairs.[50] Second, investment arbitration may be the only effective means of redress where an investment has been interfered with by a Member State.

The *Achmea* judgment sparked significant ado in the investment arbitration community.[51] An elite club of arbitrators and counsels seems to be afraid of a sharp decrease in the number of cases based on intra-EU BITs. On the other hand, *Achmea* has received a frenetic applause by the proponents of 'an ever closer Union'[52] who believe that Member States' courts, with the compulsory assistance of the CJEU, are the only decision-makers called upon to resolve all imaginable disputes.[53]

The following analysis is not going to settle who is 'right' or 'wrong' in the *Achmea* debate. Rather, it will demonstrate that the CJEU's reasoning has significant shortcomings and leaves many important questions unanswered, including how an investor may realistically enforce its rights against an EU host state.

[45] For the critical analysis of this argument see A de Mestral, 'Investor-State Arbitration between Developed Democratic Countries' in A de Mestral (ed), *Second Thoughts Investor-State Arbitration between Developed Democracies* (Waterloo, Centre for International Governance Innovation, 2017) 15.

[46] ibid, 19.

[47] ibid, 23–26.

[48] As to the need of consistency see eg G Kaufmann-Kohler, 'Is Consistency a Myth?', www.arbitration-icca.org/media/4/92392722703895/media012319141360720009500062.pdf

[49] See P Lalive, 'Some Threats to International Investment Arbitration' (1986) 1 *ICSID Review* 26–27.

[50] See W Sadowski, 'Protection of the Rule of Law in the European Union through investment treaty arbitration: is judicial monopolism the right response to illiberal tendencies in Europe?' (2018) 55 *CMLR* 1025; JE Alvarez, 'Is Investor-State Arbitration Public' (2016) 7 *JIDS* 541, 558.

[51] See eg P Pinsolle and I Michou Arbitration, '*Achmea v Slovakia* Judgment of the CJEU, is it really the end of intra-EU Investment Treaties?', www.quinnemanuel.com/media/1418711/the-achmea-judgement-ending-intra-eu-investment-treaties.pdf.

[52] Judgment of the Court (Full Court) in Case C-621/2018, *Wightman, Greer, Smith, Martin, Stihler, Maugham, and Cherry v Secretary of State for Exiting the European Union*, ECLI:EU:C:2018:999, para 4.

[53] B Hess, 'The Fate of Investment Dispute Resolution after the Achmea Decision of the European Court of Justice' Max Plank Institute Luxembourg for Procedural Law Research Paper Series No 2018 (3), www.mpi.lu/fileadmin/mpi/medien/events/2018/4/3/WPS3_2018_The_Fate_of_Investment_Dispute_Resolution_after_the_Achmea_Decision_of_the_European_Court_of_Justice.

i. Commercial versus Investment Arbitration

The CJEU in the *Achmea* judgment made a distinction between international commercial and investment arbitration, which has become crucial for many aspects of its analysis.

Commercial and investment arbitrations share certain features and diverge in others. However, one common feature is that no arbitration may arise without the consent of the parties.[54] What seems thus unconvincing is that the decisive difference between investment and commercial arbitration should rest, in the CJEU's view, on the idea that commercial arbitration is based on agreement between parties, whereas investment arbitration is based on a consent in an international treaty. This issue was of particular importance, as the CJEU had previously held with regard to commercial arbitration that a limited review of arbitral awards is justifiable, since it flows from the requirement of efficiency of enforcement of arbitral awards.[55]

In fact, it is a prevailing view that bilateral investment treaties normally contain a standing offer of the contracting states to the effect that an investor may commence investment arbitration if a legal dispute arises between the two. The acceptance of this standing offer of the state makes an agreement to arbitrate the matter before investment arbitrators.[56] Article 8 BIT therefore embodies only this offer to arbitrate, and does not 'in itself constitute a consent to arbitrate'.[57] As a result, commercial and investment arbitration differ only in the form of consent, not is its substance, ie agreement between the parties.

Furthermore, the two kinds of arbitration coalesce into one in the enforcement stage. In other words, in many instances, investment and commercial arbitration share the rules for annulment, recognition and enforcement of arbitral awards, eg the New York Convention[58] or procedural rules of *lex arbitri*.[59]

There is also another paradox hidden behind the CJEU's 'commercial/investment' divide. The CJEU has said in a few cases that an arbitral award contradicting

[54] See United Nations Conference on Trade and Development, *Dispute Settlement*, Consent to arbitration 1, www.unctad.org/en/Docs/edmmisc232add2_en.pdf.

[55] *Achmea* judgment (above n 3) para 54, with further reference to the CJEU case law. See also the judgment in Case C-126/97, *Eco Swiss China Time Ltd v Benneton International NV*, ECLI:EU:C:1999:269, para 35 (*Eco Swiss*).

[56] AK Bjorklund, 'Contract Without Privity: Sovereign Offer and Investor Acceptance' (2001) 2 *Chicago Journal of International Law* 183.

[57] Blackaby (above n 40) 219.

[58] Convention on the Recognition and Enforcement of Foreign Arbitral Awards (NY Convention). Interestingly, the CJEU said that Art 85 of the Treaty Establishing European Communities (now Art 105 TFEU) 'may' ('*kann*', '*peut-être*') be considered as a public-policy ground under the NY Convention. See *Eco Swiss* (above n 55) para 39.

[59] ICSID regime presents a mixed solution. Originally intended as a forum for resolution of disputes arising from contracts between investors and states, the ICSID has become dominated by cases stemming from breaches of international treaties. See AR Parra, *The History of ICSID*, 2nd edn (Oxford, Oxford University Press, 2017) 124–25.

EU public policy must be annulled.[60] If commercial and investment arbitrations are worlds apart, so the European public policy reasoning adopted in the case law relating to commercial arbitration should not apply to the review of investment arbitral awards by Member States' courts.

It remains unclear whether a Member State's court requested to annul an arbitral award arising out of an intra-EU BIT would feel obligated to do so as a matter of EU law, since the category of European public policy has thus far applied solely in the context of commercial arbitration.

Furthermore, commercial arbitration is no different to investment arbitration in that the arbitration agreement removes the jurisdiction of Member States' courts.[61] This is precisely why parties enter into an arbitration agreement: they do not wish to submit their dispute to a court.[62] Investment treaties then have given preference to arbitration exactly because national courts might not constitute a neutral forum for resolution of investment disputes.[63] It is immaterial, for this purpose, whether this 'removal' is due to an arbitration agreement in a contract or is finalised as an acceptance of the standing offer in an investment treaty. Commercial and investment arbitrations would thus be equally irreconcilable with EU law.

Why was the CJEU so much at pains to highlight the difference between the two kinds of arbitration, besides an attempt to justify non-following of its previous case law related to the limited review of awards? An answer might be that a holistic approach to arbitration, meaning the same treatment of commercial and investment arbitration, could reveal that EU has never had competence over arbitration as such.[64] Accordingly, there has been no comprehensive regulation of arbitration in EU law.[65]

Consequently, if there is no competence over arbitration in general, neither does it exist with regard to its sub-species, ie commercial and investment arbitration. There is especially no competence to regulate arbitrability of disputes. EU law generally does not limit parties' freedom to choose their dispute resolution mechanism. On the contrary, certain parts of EU law support individuals' autonomy to choose a dispute resolution mechanism.[66]

[60] Judgment of the Court (First Chamber) of 26 October 2006 *Elisa Maria Mostaza Claro v Centro Móvil Milenium SL*, ECLI:EU:C:2006:675; *Eco Swiss* (above n 55).

[61] *Achmea* judgment (above n 3) para 55.

[62] See David (above n 37) 10; see also WL Kidane, *The Culture of International Arbitration* (New York, Oxford University Press, 2017) 96.

[63] C Schreuer and R Dolzer, *Principles of International Investment Law*, 2nd edn (Oxford, Oxford University Press, 2012) 235–36.

[64] See N Reich, 'More Clarity after "Claro"? Arbitration clauses in Consumer Contracts as and ADR (alternative dispute resolution) mechanism for effective and speedy dispute resolution, or as "deni de justice"?' (2007) 1 *European Review of Contract Law* 52, 55.

[65] J Gaffney, 'Should the European Union Regulate Commercial Arbitration?' (2017) 33 *Arbitration International* 1.

[66] EU law support choice-of-court agreements as an expression of party autonomy to choose its forum. There is no reason why party autonomy should permit choice of courts to a different extent than arbitration does. See generally X Kramer and E Themeri, 'The Party Autonomy Paradigm: European and Global Developments on Choice of Forum' in V Lazić and S Stuij (eds), *Brussels Ibis Regulation. Short Studies in Private International Law* (The Hague, TMC Asser Press 2017) 27.

Additionally, CJEU analysis takes no account of the existence of investment contracts.[67] An investment contract is different to other, 'ordinary', contracts in two respects. First, one of the contracting parties is always a state. Second, the breach of an investment contract may under certain circumstances amount to violation of an investment treaty.[68] Would a dispute arising from an investment contract be a commercial arbitration or investment one according to the interpretation of the CJEU?

In summary, the CJEU reached a result opposite to that which it probably sought, by making a somehow artificial distinction between investment and commercial arbitration. The reason for different treatment of commercial and investment arbitration must lie elsewhere than in drawing a black-or-white picture of arbitration in the EU.

As will be demonstrated also below, the CJEU undermined its own argumentation on preliminary rulings by clinging to the commercial/investment arbitration divide.

ii. Investment Arbitrators Cannot Ask for a Preliminary Ruling

At the outset, it is paradoxical that Article 267 TFEU, which has never been addressed to arbitrators, should serve as a legal basis for why arbitrators cannot ask for a preliminary ruling. The problem thus lies in the narrow scope of Article 267 TFEU and not the arbitrator's lack of will to apply EU law.[69] It is tantamount to circular reasoning to say that arbitrators are not able to refer preliminary rulings and therefore they cannot protect EU values, since they are not addressed by Article 267 TFEU.

Moreover, it is common knowledge that commercial arbitral tribunals cannot submit a request for preliminary ruling to the CJEU.[70] Nevertheless, both 'commercial' and 'investment' arbitrators may seek such a ruling by asking national courts in the seat of arbitration to do so.[71] Thus, it is not impossible to ensure uniform and effective application of EU law in an intra-EU arbitration.

[67] As to investor-state contracts see eg A von Walter, 'State Contracts and the Relevance of Investment Contract Arbitration' in M Bungenberg et al (eds), *International Investment Law* (Baden Baden, CH Beck/Hart/Nomos 2015) ch 3 at 81.

[68] It is so when the BIT contains a so-called umbrella clause. See AG's Opinion in *Achmea* (above n 14) para 202.

[69] See G Carducci, 'A State's Capacity and the EU's Competence to Conclude a Treaty, Invalidate, Terminate and "preclude" in *Achmea* – a Treaty or BIT of Member States, a State's Consent to be Bound by a Treaty or to Arbitration, under the Law of Treaties and EU Law and the CJ's Decisions on EUSFTA and *Achmea*. Their Roles and Interactions in Treaty and Investment Arbitration' (2018) 33 *ICSID Review* 598.

[70] See CJEU judgment of 23 March 1982, Case 102/81, *Nordsee Deutsche Hochseefischerei GmbH v Reederei Mond Hochfischerei Nordstern AG & Co KG*, ECLI:EU:C:1982:107, paras 2–16, plus dispositive part; confirmed eg by *Eco Swiss* (above n 55) para 40.

[71] See eg § 1050 German Code of Civil Procedure; see also the English Arbitration Act 1996, s 45. See also GM Alvarez, 'The Achmea Case: More Question than Answers?' (2018) 15 *Revista Brasieleira de Arbitragem* 152.

From the perspective of a 'strategy', arbitrators' exclusion and separation from an EU judicial system could not improve the effectiveness and uniformity of application of EU law. Had investment arbitrators been made or recognised as part of the EU judicial system, the room for excuses as to why arbitrators took no account of EU law would have been reduced. Member States' courts would have then remained a safeguard against the wrong application of EU law. Such an approach was suggested by Advocate General Wathelet, in vain, alas.[72]

We have analysed above the distinction between commercial and investment arbitration made by the CJEU. In accordance with this approach, commercial arbitrators cannot refer preliminary rulings to the CJEU because their jurisdiction stems from an arbitration agreement as a contract. In consequence, investment arbitrators should be able to seek a preliminary ruling, as their jurisdiction stems from an international treaty as a part of the Member State's laws.[73] In short, if the latter's jurisdiction does not arise *ex contractu*, it may only do so *ex lege*. The argument referring to the 'exceptional'[74] nature of the investment arbitral tribunals, whatever 'exceptionality' means, cannot doubt this conclusion. Investment arbitrators therefore should be able to refer preliminary rulings to the CJEU as a matter of EU law.

iii. The Monopoly of the CJEU Over Interpretation and Application of EU law

The CJEU has a central role in the binding interpretation of EU law. Let us recall that the CJEU was not able to accept that the European Court of Human Rights (ECtHR) would have the final say about interpretation and application of EU law.[75] While it seems that the CJEU was perhaps bound to decide as it eventually did with regard to the European Convention on Human Rights (ECHR), the same conclusion does not ring true for investment arbitration. The CJEU will always have final say over the latter, because EU law is binding on Member States' courts reviewing arbitral awards, which are in turn obliged to refer preliminary rulings to the CJEU.

However, the CJEU is not the only court that has jurisdiction to interpret and apply EU law. For instance, a Swiss court may need to interpret EU law in order to resolve a dispute and the court has competence to do so. The same holds true for the ECtHR, which may need to interpret EU law from time to time.[76] Thus, there has never been full monopoly over interpretation and application EU law by either the CJEU or Member State courts.[77]

[72] See generally AG's Opinion (above n 14).
[73] See AG's Opinion (above n 14) para 96.
[74] *Achmea* judgment (above n 3) para 45.
[75] Opinion 2/13 of the Court (Full Court) of 18 December 2014.
[76] See eg ECtHR judgment (Grand Chamber), 23 May 2016, App No 17502/07, *Avotiņš v Latvia*.
[77] Carducci (above n 69) 599.

The CJEU found that the dispute resolution clause in Article 8 BIT would undermine its (non-full) monopoly over interpretation and application of EU law. Article 344 TFEU stipulates that 'Member States undertake not to submit a dispute concerning the interpretation or application of the Treaties to any method of settlement other than those provided for therein'.[78]

In the view of the CJEU, this provision means that Member States cannot submit to investment arbitration with an investor.[79] However, the *Achmea* judgment contains no explicit interpretation of Article 344 TFEU. *In claris non fit interpretatio* perhaps. Yet, the meaning of the provision does not appear manifestly clear.

It would have been particularly helpful had CJEU dealt with the scope *ratione personae* of Article 344 TFEU. From a textual analysis, in conjunction with Opinion 2/13, it seems that only disputes between Member States fall within the purview of the said provision.[80]

If this is so, there could not be an incompatibility between Article 344 TFEU and Article 8 BIT. An incompatibility might have arisen only between Article 344 TFEU and Article 10 BIT, as both regulate disputes between Member States.[81] The rule of effectiveness in interpretation of international treaties requires that neither article in BIT be considered without legal effect.[82] Articles 8 and 10 BIT do not cover the same disputes, as one of these provisions would be then redundant in the BIT.[83]

In addition, the scope *ratione materiae* of Article 344 TFEU encompasses disputes 'concerning the interpretation or application of the Treaties'.[84] Interpretation might show that there is no incompatibility between Article 344 TFEU and Article 8 BIT, since each regulates entirely different matters; in any case, they do not cover the 'same-subject matter'.[85]

Investment tribunals resolve disputes related to investment, not disputes relating to the interpretation and application of EU law. Yet, the disputes under

[78] See the text of Art 344 TFEU.

[79] *Achmea* judgment (above n 3) para 32.

[80] The CJEU indicates in the Opinion 2/13 that Art 344 TFEU overlaps with Art 33 ECHR. The latter provision deals only with inter-state application, not individual-against-state application under Art 34 ECHR. See CJEU Opinion 2/13 of 18 December 2013, para 209. That Art 344 TFEU concerns only state-to-state disputes has also been confirmed by investment tribunals. See *Blusun SA, Jean Pierre Lecorcier and Michael Stein (Claimants) v Republic of Italy (Respondent)*, ICSID case No ARB/14/3, para 289; see also Permanent Court of Arbitration Case No 2010–17, *European American Investment Bank AG (Austria) (Claimant) and the Slovak Republic (Respondent)*, Award of Jurisdiction, 22 October 2012 paras 254, 255.

[81] See the wording 'disputes between Contracting Parties' contained in Art 10(1) and (2) BIT.

[82] See R Gardiner, *Treaty Interpretation*, 2nd edn (Oxford, Oxford University Press, 2015) 180.

[83] This would in turn breach the principle of effectiveness, which is a firm part of international treaty law. See ibid, 179.

[84] See the text of Art 344 TFEU.

[85] *A contrario* Art 59(1) of the Vienna Convention on the Law of Treaties (Vienna, 23 May 1969, United Nations Treaty Series Vol 155 p 331).

Article 8 BIT, including the dispute between Achmea and Slovakia, are not disputes over the interpretation and application of the founding Treaties. They are disputes related to an alleged breach of an investment standard or standards under a BIT. The arbitral tribunal in the *Vatenfall* case recently confirmed this conclusion, stating that the *Achmea* judgment does not bar jurisdiction of an investment tribunal established by virtue of the Energy Charter Treaty.[86]

Finally, there may be disputes from an intra-EU BIT, which do not involve an EU law element at all.[87] In such a case, there is room for neither the application of EU law nor an intervention by the CJEU.

iv. *Investor Rights as a Missing Link*

What is at stake in investment arbitration is not just state obligations, but also the rights of investors. The latter are a missing link in the *Achmea* judgment.

Investment claims have been largely untested before Member States' courts. It remains unknown whether investors would be able to invoke their rights under an investment treaty before national courts.[88] It is also an open question whether national courts would give a direct legal effect to the provisions of an intra-EU BIT. In any case, an investor would not know whether the BIT has any legal effect in Member States' law unless it seeks to invoke it in the courts.[89]

Investment arbitration thus offers one of the few avenues, if not the only one, by which an investor may seek protection of its rights. In any case, no such redress exists for an investor in EU law.[90] Such a remedy could be available for breach of EU law by Member States, but not for breaches of standards of investment protection. Thus, the CJEU's 'judicial remedies' in Article 19(1) TFEU are merely hypothetical for investors seeking to enforce their investment claims. What is more, recent concerns regarding the protection of the rule of law by the judiciary in Poland

[86] *1. Vattenfall AB; 2.Vattenfall GmBH; 3.Vattenfall Europe Nuclear Energy GmBH; 4. Kernkraftwerk Krümmel GmBH & Co OhG; 5. Kernekraftwerk Brunsbüttel GmBH & Co oHG (Claimants) and Federal Republic of Germany (Respondent)*, ICSID Csse No ARB12/12, Decision on the *Achmea* Issue, 31 August 2018, www.italaw.com/sites/default/files/case-documents/italaw9916.pdf.

[87] For instance, *Anglia Auto Accessories Limited (Claimant) v Czech Republic (Respondent)*, SCC Final Award, Arbitration Case V 2014/181, 10 March 2017; *IP Busta & JP Busta (Claimants) v Czech Republic (Respondent)*, SCC Final Award, Case V 2015/14, 10 March 2017, www.mfcr.cz/cs/zahranicni-sektor/ochrana-financnich-zajmu/arbitraze/prehled-rozhodcich-nalezu.

[88] For a discussion on the nature of investor rights under investment treaties see BL Smit Duijzenkunst, 'Treaty Rights as Tradable Assets: Can Investor Waive Investment Treaty Protection?' (2010) 25 *ICSID Review* 409.

[89] What is more, it would be for national courts to decide whether they would give a direct legal effect to the provisions of an intra-EU BIT. An investor thus would not know whether the BIT has any legal effect in the Member State's law unless the investor seeks to invoke it in the courts. See also H Perezcano, 'Risks of a Selective Approach to Investor-State Arbitration' in A de Mestral (ed), *Second Thoughts: Investor-State Arbitration between Developed Democracies* (Waterloo, Centre for International Governance, 2017) 487–88.

[90] *Achmea* judgment (above n 3) para 17.

demonstrate how leaving the resolution of investment disputes solely to national courts may be a risky practice.[91]

Moreover, Achmea as an investor in the present dispute is a company with its registered office in a Member State, hence enjoying legal protection by EU law.[92] It is surprising that the CJEU did not consider the effects on its judgment on this EU company. The Court should have taken into account the EU law principles of legal certainty and protection of acquired rights, as well as effective judicial protection.[93] The CJEU interfered with all these principles, as it has effectively deprived the company of any forum in which to enforce its rights. The arbitral award in favour of Achmea does not appear to be enforced or subject to new litigation in national courts.

As a result, contrary to what is required by Article 47 of the Charter of the Fundamental Rights of the European Union (Charter), the investor does not enjoy effective judicial protection.[94] In addition, a final and enforceable arbitral award is a 'possession' under Article 1 of the ECHR,[95] and possibly also under Article 17 of the Charter.[96] Thus, it is feasible that Germany, by non-recognition of the award in favour of Achmea by virtue of the CJEU judgments, might breach the ECHR. It will be interesting to see whether German courts follow the ruling of the CJEU or the ECHR.

Finally, it is difficult to accept that a business risk should automatically entail as a consequence the impossibility of enforcement of an award. Moreover, if this is a part of business risk, it could be borne by companies like Achmea, but not small or middle-size investors. With regard to these categories of investors, the CJEU in its judgment in *Achmea* has thrown out the baby with bathwater.

All in all, it is not viable for investors to pursue their rights before Member States' courts, while a multilateral investment court is yet to come into existence, if it ever does.[97] Thus, to preclude investment arbitration based on intra-EU bilateral investment treaties denies access to justice for a significant number of investors.

[91] *Proposal for a Council Decision on the determination of a clear risk of a serious breach by the Republic of Poland of the rule of law* COM (2017) 835 final (20 December 2017). These concerns originate both in Poland and abroad. See generally Sadowski (above n 50) and M Hazelhorst, 'Mutual Trust under Pressure: Civil Justice Cooperation in the EU and the Rule of Law' (2018) 65 *Netherlands International Law Review* 103.

[92] EU companies should not be less protected than EU citizens as a matter of EU law. See generally art 49 TFEU.

[93] As to the first two principles see HG Schermens and DF Waelbroeck, *Judicial Protection in the European Union* (Kluwer Law International, 2001) 64–65, 70–71. For the principle of effective judicial protection see Art 47 Charter.

[94] Charter of Fundamental Rights and Freedoms of the European Union EJ C83/389 (30 March 2010).

[95] See Judgment, Appl no 13427/87, *Stran Greek Rafineries and Stratis Andreadis v Greece* and Judgment, Final, 4 October 2010, Appl no 12312/05, *King Stib and Majkić v Serbia.*

[96] The preamble of Charter refers to common constitutional traditions as well as the international obligations of Member States, namely the ECHR. It may thus be presumed that interpretation of the ECHR by the ECtHR ought to play a significant role in interpreting the Charter.

[97] However, there has been a considerable effort to establish a multilateral investment court by the Working Group III of United Nations Commission on International Trade Law, See the documents published by WG III, www.uncitral.org/uncitral/en/commission/working_groups/3Investor_State.html.

C. Further Consequences of the *Achmea* Judgment

The judgment brings one apparently 'technical' issue to the fore. The CJEU said that the provision of Article 8 BIT is 'precluded'. A 'preclusion' in this context makes little sense in legal terminology.[98] International treaties and their provisions cannot simply be 'precluded'. The CJEU thus does not say what legal implications BGH should derive from the *Achmea* judgment in the case before it. Should BGH try to subsume the 'preclusion' under one the reasons in the German Code of Civil Procedure for annulment of the arbitral award?[99] There is no clear answer to this question.

Nonetheless, the message hidden between the lines of the CJEU's dictum seems to be addressed primarily to the Netherlands and Slovakia, as well as other Member States. In other words, the CJEU has signalled that it might not oppose it if Member States brought their intra-EU BITs to an end.[100] Likewise, it may be a warning message to those Member States that have been reluctant to give up their BITs, one of them being the Netherlands. The latter announced its withdrawal from the BIT at hand about three months after the *Achmea* judgment.[101] In any case, since the CJEU rendered its judgment some investors have withdrawn their investment claims.[102] Thus, the judgment has had a far-reaching deterrent effect, beyond the parties to the original dispute.

The *Achmea* judgment also gives the Commission a legal support (*sic*) for developing its project on an EU permanent investment court.[103]

Moreover, in *Vattenfall*, *Masdar* and *UP*, investment arbitral tribunals refused in unison to decline their jurisdiction, despite the existence of the *Achmea* judgment.[104] However, these cases concern either the Energy Charter Treaty as a treaty binding on EU itself or ICSID arbitration, which has an autonomous system of annulment as well as recognition and enforcement of awards.[105] In short, these are arguably situations different to the one in *Achmea*.

[98] For instance, 'invalidity' would be perfectly understandable.

[99] Art 1059(2) German Code of Civil Procedure.

[100] See the Member States' reaction in Declaration of the Representatives of the Governments of the Member States, of 15 January 2019 on the Legal Consequences of the Judgment of the Court of Justice in Achmea and on Investment Protection in the European Union, www.ec.europa.eu/info/sites/info/files/business_economy_euro/banking_and_finance/documents/190117-bilateral-investment-treaties_en.pdf, accessed 27 March 2019.

[101] See PJ Kuijper, 'The-Netherlands Draws Consequences from-the Achmea Case What Consequence Will-the CJ draw?', www.acelg.blogactiv.eu/2018/05/07/the-netherlands-draws-consequences-from-the-achmea-case-what-consequence-will-the-CJ-draw-by-pieter-jan-kuijper.

[102] See eg 'Airbus withdraws arbitration demand over $3.7 billion helicopter deal', www.defensenews.com/industry/2018/05/22/airbus-withdraws-arbitration-demand-over-37-billion-helicopter-deal.

[103] See *A New System For Resolving Disputes Between Foreign Investors And States In A Fair And Efficient Way*, trade.ec.europa.eu/doclib/docs/2017/september/tradoc_156042.pdf.

[104] *Masdar Solar & Wind Cooperatief UA (Claimant) v Kingdom of Spain (Respondent)*, ICSID Case No ARB/14/1, Award, 16 May 2018, para 162; *UP (formerly Le Chèque Déjeuner) and CD Holding Internationale (Claimant) v Hungary (Respondent)*, ICSID Case No ARB/13/35, Award, 9 October 2018, 252–67, all the awards at www.italaw.com.

[105] The International Energy Charter, Consolidated Energy Charter Treaty, Part III, www.energycharter.org/fileadmin/DocumentsMedia/Legal/ECTC-en.pdf; Arts 53–55 Convention on the Settlement of Investment Disputes between States and Nationals of Other States, www.icsid.worldbank.org/en/documents/icsiddocs/icsid%20convention%20english.pdf.

Yet, Member States' courts might not share this view of arbitral tribunals. Relying on the *Achmea* judgment, Spain is vigorously defending against enforcement actions by an investor.[106]

To sum up, some Member States and the Commission may be satisfied with the *Achmea* judgment. However, this decision is bad news for investors deprived of the only way of protecting their legal claims. Worse, the CJEU does not indicate any viable alternative redress for investors.

III. Arbitration and the Advancement of European Regulatory Private Law

Against the background of the preceding discussion on the role of investor-state arbitration in the EU legal order, in this section of the chapter I examine the emerging role of arbitration in the development of the European Regulatory Private Law. The major hypothesis underlying this part of the chapter is that arbitration has contributed to the development of the new generation of European private law, namely European Regulatory Private Law. Furthermore, it is argued that both the substance and the procedural aspect of the European Regulatory Private Law have been recently transformed by arbitration actors and the changing face of arbitration practice. This has occurred with a support from the European Commission, and somewhat in the shadow of the tacit hostility of the CJEU to arbitration.

The starting point for such a discussion concerns the changing functions of arbitration in general and a shift from 'global' to 'regional' and back in arbitration practice. This shift is particularly visible in the context of the relationship between arbitration and EU law. Because arbitration and EU law have stopped being mutually exclusive systems, arbitration is playing an increasing role in generating internal European private law (and its 'regulatory' variant). This also determines the external dimension of European private law, where the European regulations of arbitration are being adopted in trans-border settings. This shift therefore has implications for a-national arbitration practice. As such, globalisation is no longer perceived as a steering factor of the development of arbitration within a transnational legal order. Rather, more and more regional regimes utilising arbitration (such as EU law) may have an impact on the fragmentation of transnational arbitration practice and private relationships generated by means of arbitration. European Regulatory Private Law, in both its internal and external dimensions, may serve as one example of such private dealings.

[106] *Novenergia II-Energy& Environment (SCA) (Petitioner) v The Kingdom of Spain (Respondent) Civil Action No 1, 18 cv 1148*, www.globalarbitrationreview.com/digital_assets/5fe65c30-3bfe-4d79-b3d3-34c8f32c6558/Memorandum-D.D.C.-18-cv-01148-dckt-000018_001-filed-2018-10-16.pdf; see also (in Swedish) www.italaw.com/sites/default/files/case-documents/italaw9746.pdf.

A. The Impact of Hans Micklitz's Scholarship on the Discussion at Hand

The argument in question has been largely inspired by the scholarship of Hans Micklitz. In particular, it builds off the hypothesis formulated by Hans Micklitz that European private law has recently transformed from a traditional model based on freedom of contract, party autonomy, and tort into a 'regulatory' model based on economic efficiency in EU regulated markets.[107] The new generation of the European private law, namely the European Regulatory Private Law is moving away from the 'social' dimension of traditional private law to the core of the European Economic Constitution, creating new challenges to individual contractors.[108] This results in the economisation of private law in the EU internal market, laying the foundations for the novel understanding of contractual rights and freedoms, as well as for new modes of contract enforcement in and outside the EU.[109]

In addition, other scholarly works by Hans are crucial for the present discussion. These especially concern his scholarship on the topic of access justice[110] and the transformations of the enforcement of private law scholarship more generally.[111]

A brief explanation of the distinction between the internal and external dimensions of European Private Regulatory Law is in order. The former concerns the scope of European private law within the EU, hence affecting Member States and the EU internal market. The latter refers to the reach of European private law outside the EU marketplace, hence potentially shaping economic transactions outside the EU internal market. Both concepts will be discussed in the context of the arbitration practice in and outside the EU in the sections below.

B. Internal and External Dimensions of European Regulatory Private Law and Arbitration

Arbitration is discussed here broadly. It concerns different out-of-court dispute resolution mechanisms including mediation, arbitration, ombudsperson, conciliation, and the like. This broad approach is in line with a broad understanding

[107] H-W Micklitz, 'The Internal vs the External Dimension of European Private Law – A Conceptual Design and a Research Agenda' *EUI Working Paper* Law 2015/35 ERC-ERPL-13 1, 1; H-W Micklitz, 'The Visible Hand of European Regulatory Private Law' [2008] EUI LAW; 2008/14 1; H-W Micklitz and D Patterson, 'From the Nation State to the Market: The Evolution of EU Private Law as Regulation of the Economy beyond the Boundaries of the Union?' in B Van Vooren et al, *The EU's Role in Global Governance: The Legal Dimension* (Oxford, Oxford University Press, 2013).

[108] Micklitz, 'The Internal vs the External Dimension of European Private Law' (above n 107) 1.

[109] See generally Micklitz, 'The Visible Hand of European Regulatory Private Law' (above n 107).

[110] H-W Micklitz, *The Politics of Justice in European Private Law. Social Justice, Access Justice, Societal Justice* (Cambridge, Cambridge University Press, 2008).

[111] H-W Micklitz and A Wechsler (eds), *The Transformation of Enforcement. European Economic Law in a Global Perspective* (Oxford, Hart, 2006).

of arbitration under EU law that stems mostly from the Directive on Consumer Alternative Dispute Resolution (ADR), the Regulation on Online Dispute Resolution (ODR), and the sector-specific directives that regulate different EU markets. Additionally, arbitration has a dual meaning here. It concerns both arbitration as a form of dispute resolution (procedural understanding) and arbitration practice (substantive understanding). The procedural dimension limits the discussion to the procedures through which arbitration applies to various fields of EU law. In turn, the substantive dimension concerns the ways in which arbitration practitioners have been shaping EU law in accordance with the dispute resolution patterns rooted in their day-to-day practices.

Historically, arbitration was rarely used in the context of EU law. This was so because arbitration was perceived as an instrument via which large businesses could avoid public justice systems and solve their disputes in private and in secrecy. This trend, sometimes called *vanishing trials*, began in the US but it quickly spread around the world, and is most recently visible in Europe.[112] As long as arbitration and ADR were used only for business disputes, the trend was not controversial. The situation changed when businesses started to apply arbitration in disputes with consumers. From this moment onwards, arbitration and ADR has been criticised for lacking the procedural safeguards that could protect weaker parties from potential abuses. Notably, this criticism did not stop arbitration from infiltrating new fields of law, including EU law. Furthermore, public officials and bodies, including the European Commission have begun to encourage arbitration in the resolution of disputes traditionally reserved for public courts. One reason for this is that arbitration is perceived as being cheaper and faster than courts that are often overburdened, and hence ineffective in terms of time and costs. Consequently, arbitration developed a new, public function, next to its traditional commercial function.[113]

The increasing use of arbitration in EU law is seen at both the EU and Member State levels. Regarding EU law developments, regulatory disputes within the EU regulated markets such as energy and telecommunications have been subject to arbitration and other ADR mechanisms.[114] There have also been reforms of consumer arbitration accompanying a number of ADR and ODR means, often based on their traditional commercial models.[115] Furthermore, national practices

[112] TJ Stipanowich, 'ADR and the "Vanishing Trial": The Growth and Impact of "Alternative Dispute Resolution"' (2004) 1 *Journal of Empirical Legal Studies* 843.

[113] BA Warwas, *The Liability of Arbitral Institutions: Legitimacy Challenges and Functional Responses* (Springer, 2016) ch 2.

[114] B Warwas, 'ADR in B2B Disputes in the EU Telecommunications Sector: Where Does the EU Stand and What Does the EU Stand For?' *EUI WP EUI LAW 2014/12*, 2014.

[115] As a result of the implementation of the following instruments: Directive 2008/52/EC of the European Parliament and of the Council of 21 May 2008 on Certain Aspects of Mediation in Civil and Commercial Matters, OJ L136; Directive 2013/11/EU of the European Parliament and of the Council of 21 May 2013 on Alternative Dispute Resolution for Consumer Disputes and Amending Regulation (EC) No 2006/2004 and Directive 2009/22/EC (Directive on Consumer ADR), OJ L165; Regulation (EU) No 524/2013 of the European Parliament and of the Council of 21 May 2013 on Online Dispute Resolution for Consumer Disputes and Amending Regulation (EC) No 2006/2004 and Directive 2009/22/EC (Regulation on Consumer ODR), OJ L165.

of arbitration within the EU have revealed the increased outsourcing of disputes of eminent social and public relevance to arbitration (for example, tax disputes in Portugal,[116] company disputes in Italy,[117] and arbitration within public administration in Spain[118]).

These developments promote the private enforcement of contracts by means of arbitration and ADR. They also suggest an increasing trust by European officials in private arbitration regimes and the role of arbitration practitioners in improving private enforcement in the EU. Together, these developments constitute the incremental privatisation of civil justice systems within the EU.

What is the impact of the privatisation of justice in the EU on the European private law and its regulatory aspect? What message does the EU send to contractors within and outside the EU when encouraging arbitration? The answer to this question is twofold.

First, from the perspective of the internal aspect of European Regulatory Private Law, I argue that the European Commission further supports the economisation of European law when outsourcing EU law disputes arising within the EU internal market to arbitration. Why is this so? Because the European Commission allows private arbitration actors to incorporate arbitration practices into European private law. Those practices mostly concern informal behavioural aspects of decision-making and problem solving by private arbitrators that are largely based on the patterns established by those actors in commercial arbitrations. Such practices may be indeed more effective than traditional public enforcement. At the same time, however, there are risks that with little public oversight of private arbitration by EU or Member States' officials and given the rather vague EU procedural framework on ADR stemming from the Consumer ADR Directive, the rights and freedoms of contractors will not be given full consideration vis-à-vis economic efficiency of the EU internal market. Hence, arbitration may serve as a tool to increase market efficiency to the detriment of individual contractors.

Second, from the perspective of the external dimension of European Regulatory Private Law, I argue that the EU, and especially the European Commission, uses arbitration to promote EU law, and in particularly EU private law outside the EU. This is especially so in transactions in which EU law applies outside EU borders. We see this, for example, in consumer law and its application in e-commerce transactions involving a foreign (non-EU) party. The implications of arbitration on further development of European Private Regulation Law follow in the sections below.

[116] Decree-Law no 10/2011 2011.

[117] The Italian Legislative Decree No 5 of 17 January 2003.

[118] Spanish Act 11/2011, of May 20, Reforming Act 60/2003, of December 23, on Arbitration, and Regulating Institutional Arbitration within the Public Administration.

C. Four Observations on the External Dimension of European Regulatory Private Law by Hans Micklitz: An Analysis

This section analyses the application of arbitration to European Regulatory Private Law and its implications from the perspective of the four observations on the external dimension of European regulatory private law formulated by Hans Micklitz. Those observations concern the shift in European private law:

(i) from legal rules to legal practice,
(ii) from formal law making to European governance,
(iii) from substantive law to procedural law, and
(iv) from private law to trade law.

The analysis below deals with the question on the role of arbitration in augmenting those changes in all four fields noted above. The discussion will concern both the internal and external dimension of European private law.

i. From Legal Rules to Legal Practice: Private and Public Functions of Arbitration and the Nature and Scope of the European Regulatory Private Law

Hans Micklitz argues that European regulatory private law, especially in its external dimension, encompasses less rules than traditional private law.[119] As such, the analysis of this law requires the examination of legal practices instead of legal rules to see how those scarce and multi-layered rules are applied in real life.

To understand the interplay between arbitration and European regulatory private law, it is necessary to distinguish between the traditional, commercial function of arbitration and its emerging public function, specifically in the EU law context. In fact, the distinction between private and public function of arbitration serves as a starting point for the analysis of the recent EU policies to promote arbitration and ADR in different types of disputes in the EU. What are the grounds of the legitimacy of those policies? They clearly relate to *economic efficiency* as defined by the traditional, commercial arbitration model applied in the EU. This model assumes that arbitration is expeditious and cost-effective. Is it the only reason why the European Commission decided to promote arbitration? We can already see that in order to examine the role of arbitration in the development of the European Regulatory Private Law we need to start with the examination of the legitimacy of the policies promoting arbitration in the EU. Such an examination will not concern rules per se. Rather, it will focus on the motivation of the EU officials in setting up new ADR framework in the EU and applying it both internally (within the EU) and externally (possibly also outside the EU).

[119] Micklitz, 'The Internal vs the External Dimension of European Private Law' (above n 107) 6–9.

The second step would be to look at the arbitration practices with the aim of investigating what patterns are applied by arbitration actors when interpreting and enforcing EU law. Although it is the EU and national regulations that include selected provisions on arbitration, the effectiveness of the emerging use of arbitration in EU law is largely dependent on the *application* of those rules in practice by businesses, arbitrators, and arbitral institutions. I claim here that arbitration contributes to the generation of European regulatory private law in its internal and external variant. Moreover, I argue that that such law is based on the new paradigm, where dispute resolution mechanisms inherently based on party autonomy, are applied in contracts to eventually limit such autonomy for the sake of economic efficiency. These arguments need to be proven based on the data on those practices. Such research could reveal other patterns. For example, Hans Micklitz notices that the EU rules on consumer ADR are designed in a way to ensure that they are not applied outside the EU.[120] He further wonders, however, whether this is in fact how those rules work in practice.[121] The research into the arbitration practices should address those questions in order to determine the practical role of arbitration in generating both the internal and external dimension of European regulatory private law.

ii. Experimentalist Governance versus Formal Law: New Modes of Governance and European Arbitration

Referring to the ground-breaking article by Charles Sabel and Jonathan Zeitlin on experimentalist governance, Hans Micklitz makes an argument that European Regulatory Private Law, especially in its external dimension is suitable for various forms of experimentation.[122] Indeed, similar observations can be made with regard to arbitration.

The application of arbitration to European Regulatory Private Law already suggests various forms of collaboration between private and public actors such as arbitrators and legislators, courts, and policy-makers at both EU and national level. This concerns rule-making in the field of arbitration but also their enforcement. Learning through differences, experimentation, and innovation may seem especially suitable in the field of EU arbitration and it can produce effective frameworks to enhance the development of European Regulatory Private Law.

iii. Substance versus Procedure: From Globalisation to Regionalisation and Back?

Hans Micklitz claims that there is no consistency regarding the rules on European Regulatory Private Law, especially in its external aspect.[123] It is clear that arbitration

[120] ibid, 9.
[121] ibid.
[122] ibid, 9–13.
[123] ibid, 14.

and ADR are procedural mechanisms. The question emerges of whether, and if so, how, different types of arbitration and ADR inform the substance of European regulatory private law. Here, two main issues need to be addressed: (1) from the perspective of *substance*, what are the new types of arbitration in the EU and how do they affect private law making in different sectors? (2) from the perspective of *procedure*, what are the legislative attempts to harmonise the arbitration procedure at the EU level and the Member States' level and how does it influence European Regulatory Private law?

The first question can be explained by means of consumer arbitration and ADR and their impact on consumer contract law. Although we tend to assume that consumer arbitration in the EU is based on a restrictive EU model of dispute resolution, in fact it is largely inspired by the American model that still favours businesses rather than consumers. The deficiencies of the current system of consumer arbitration in the EU were pointed out in the report on the 'Legal Instruments and Practice of Arbitration in the EU and Switzerland', prepared for the European Parliament.[124] They involved, inter alia, a flexible approach in Member States to the enforceability of arbitration clauses in contracts with consumers. This flexibility, that does not make consumer arbitration clauses inherently unenforceable in all Member States, creates the risk that less honest businesses will manipulate consumers to rely on arbitration even in cases in which businesses know that such clauses may not be enforced. This is largely the function of the 'Americanisation' of the European arbitration. It is hypothesised that there has been a shift from *globalisation* to *regionalisation* of arbitration understood here in the European context. This brings us to the procedural perspective.

Arbitration laws of Member States have been recently subject to increasing scrutiny by EU officials. The European Parliament has been gradually more and more interested in arbitration. Possible changes may be made to the general regulation of arbitration (currently rather vague) and in various sectorial arbitrations. This suggests a new paradigm in the European arbitration that may have far-reaching implications for the development of European Regulatory Private Law, as well as for the global arbitration practice. This regionalisation of arbitration implies that globalisation is no longer a steering factor in the international arbitration scene. Rather, more local, regional practices have begun utilising arbitration in specific types of disputes that often fall beyond commercial disputes traditionally resolved by means of arbitration. Once sanctioned through legislative changes, the new forms of arbitration may generate new dynamics for the contractual relationships inside and outside the EU. This would bring the discussion back to the global level of arbitration practice where different types of private laws are generated, depending on the regional regulations and/or local practice of arbitration.

Quite surprisingly, the idea of harmonising laws on both domestic and international arbitration (containing mostly procedural norms) at the EU level has met

[124] T Cole and others, 'The Legal Instruments and Practice of Arbitration in the EU, A Study for the Directorate General for Internal Policies Policy Department C: Citizens' Rights and Constitutional Affairs' (European Union, 2014) 204–14.

with a positive reaction by the European arbitration community.[125] The results of the large-scale survey of arbitration practitioners developed in the course of the aforementioned study on the *Law and Practice of Arbitration* for the European Parliament support this statement.[126] For example, when asked to evaluate the desirability of the EU taking action to harmonise national arbitration laws across the Member States, 29.46% of respondents survey-wide answered 'desirable', 10.24% of respondents answered 'very desirable', with only 14.52% of respondents answering 'very undesirable', 25.59% of respondents remaining 'neutral' and 20.19% of respondents answering 'undesirable'. Comparable results were generated with regard to the question on the desirability of the EU taking action to harmonise laws applicable to international arbitration. 32.23% of respondents answered 'desirable' and 15.49% of respondents answered 'very desirable'. The answers to the survey were provided by 871 arbitration practitioners from Europe. As such, these results may be treated as being representative of the recent trends in European arbitration practice mostly because of the large number of prominent practitioners taking part in the survey. This desire to have EU officials regulating arbitration practices within and outside the EU will also need to be subject to further research. Here, it will also be relevant to investigate the ongoing changes in the relationship between the CJEU, the European Commission, and arbitral tribunals, in all types of arbitration proceedings emerging in the EU context.

Harmonising arbitration laws would also be relevant for ensuring consistency between arbitration practices across Europe. It would allow better public understanding of the process. Currently, in almost each Member State, different arbitration practices exist. This becomes even more diverse if we start analysing them by different sector. The current status quo not only distorts the understanding of arbitration in the EU. It also hinders the impact of arbitration on European Regulatory Private Law, in a consistent manner.

iv. Private Law versus Trade Law: Arbitration and Trade Law

Finally, Hans Micklitz analyses the role of standards in the relationship between European Regulatory Private Law and trade law.[127] What is the relationship between arbitration, trade law, and European Regulatory Private Law?

It can be argued that arbitration has been applied to EU law widely by the European Commission. This concerns both the application of arbitration to various disputes emerging within the internal market and the recent promotion of

[125] This argument was already developed and presented in BA Warwas, 'The State of Research on Arbitration and EU Law: Quo Vadis European Arbitration?' (2016) *EUI Working Paper LAW* 2016/23 1, 59–60.

[126] Data of the Survey on the Law and Practice of Arbitration in the European Union, available on the website of the Transnational Dispute Management Journal at www.transnational-dispute management.com.

[127] Micklitz, 'The Internal vs the External Dimension of European Private Law' (above n 107) 16–17.

arbitration, in its reformed version called the Investment Court System in EU trade and investment agreements. Through the latter, the EU is trying to actively participate in the dispute settlement in international economic law, also entering into competition with WTO dispute settlement system.[128] Hence, arbitration is used here by the EU to advance consistent standards of dispute resolution in international economic law by means of which the external aspect of European Regulatory Private Law may be affected. The exact implications of this argument on the development of European Regulatory Private Law (if any) would need to be tested in future research.

The above discussion was aimed at depicting the possible role of arbitration in the development of European Regulatory Private Law. Following Hans Micklitz's distinction of four main variables of the external dimension of European Regulatory Private Law, my main argument was that the active promotion of arbitration in EU law by the European Commission turns arbitration into a tool to advance the development of European Regulatory Private Law, in its internal and external dimension. This is especially so because arbitration: (1) encompasses the important role of practitioners in shaping the substance of European Regulatory Private Law; (2) is an informal mechanism that allows new modes of governance and experimentation between private and public actors; (3) has a strong procedural element that could increase the consistency of European arbitration and hence also European Regulatory Private Law; and finally (4) has an increasing role in harmonising dispute settlement in international economic law. Future research should focus on the understanding of the substance of European Regulatory Private Law, and the role of arbitration in shaping it.

IV. Conclusions

In this chapter, we tried to present the new functions of arbitration (be it investor-state arbitration, commercial arbitration, or other types of arbitration) under EU law together with their potential legal and economic implications within and outside the EU. It remains to be seen what the exact implications of the *Achmea* judgment are. This is especially so in view of the eagerly awaited CJEU opinion regarding the compatibility of the Investment Court System under CETA with EU law. It was also signalled that arbitration has a potential role in shaping the content and the enforcement of private dealings within and outside the EU. This is so as it contributes to the development of a new generation of European private law, called European Regulatory Private Law by Hans Micklitz. All those developments need to be further tracked and examined to study the increasing role of private arbitration actors in EU law.

[128] This argument was first developed by B Warwas in 'EU Rules and Values, Transnational Legal Ordering, and International Arbitration' in H-W Micklitz and M Cantero Gamito (eds), *Standards, Contracts, Codes* (Edward Edgar, forthcoming).

15

The Energy Community in its Second Decade: Where Does it Stand and Where is it Heading?

ROZETA KAROVA*

I. Introduction

Back in 2009, I wrote the first academic review of the Energy Community, formally established in 2006 with the entry into force of the Energy Community Treaty, as a Working Paper of the European University Institute (EUI).[1] In that paper, as a first year PhD student under the supervision of Professor Micklitz (his first generation of doctoral students at the EUI), I looked into the rationale behind the establishment of the Energy Community and took note of the implementation of the EU electricity *acquis* in the South East Europe (SEE) countries. That was a basis for what later became a PhD thesis, defended at the Law Department of the EUI and resulted in a monograph published by Kluwer, titled *Liberalization of Electricity Markets and Public Service Obligations in the Energy Community*.[2] Besides Professor Micklitz, who found this topic interesting, and me – a student from the region who was curious to explore the reasons for establishment and to follow the development of the Energy Community – not many people were showing particular interest in the development of yet another regional initiative for the Western Balkans in such an important sector of the economy: energy.

Ten years after that first working paper on the topic, the Energy Community became a success story, the central piece in the EU external energy policy

* The author is a Senior Energy Lawyer at the Energy Community Secretariat in Vienna, which she joined in 2011. The views presented in this paper are personal views of the author and do not reflect the position of the Energy Community Secretariat.

[1] R Karova, 'Energy Community for South East Europe: Rationale behind and Implementation to date', RSCAS Working Paper No 12, 2009.

[2] R Karova, *Liberalization of Electricity Markets and Public Service Obligations in the Energy Community* (Kluwer Law International, 2012).

and a reference point for regional cooperation in energy. Therefore, I decided to contribute to this *liber amicorum* in honour of my dear supervisor, Professor Micklitz, by looking back at its developments and provide my views on what the Energy Community is in its second decade of existence.

I will start from the question I had in 2009 and look into whether the potential for EU membership was and still is the only motivator for the Contracting Parties for participating to the Energy Community. I will also discuss what are the limits, if any, of the Energy Community's expansion both geographically and in substance. Second, I will present briefly the developments of the Energy Community law through the years and will try to assess whether the EU energy law plays a role of a common denominator for sharing EU values, principles and rules beyond the EU's borders. Finally, I will try to present where the Energy Community stands now, what kind of role it plays and could play in the Energy Union, what its importance was for other regional initiatives for the Western Balkans and what kind of relationship, if any, it could have with other neighbouring regional initiatives in energy.

II. Why an Energy Community and What Kind of Energy Community?

The Energy Community Treaty concluded in 2005 between the EU and the SEE countries[3] is an international legally binding agreement between the EU and its neighbours for exporting sectoral *acquis*. The process had been initiated several years before the Treaty was signed through the so-called Athens Process, which resulted in signing two memoranda: one on electricity in 2002, and another one on gas in 2003.[4] The initial objective of the Treaty was the establishment of a regional energy market for SEE countries, which would later be integrated into the EU internal energy market even before the EU accession of the Contracting Parties.

The objective pursued by the Treaty is the creation of a single energy market, including the coordination of mutual assistance in the case of serious disturbance of the energy networks or external disruptions, which includes the formation of a common external energy trade policy.[5] The Treaty is based on EU rules and principles, adapting them to a certain extent to the specificities of its Parties, or rather to the institutional set-up of the Energy Community. Such EU principles are to be implemented fully by the Contracting Parties, following the European model

[3] The countries of the SEE were: the Republic of Albania, the Republic of Bulgaria, Bosnia and Herzegovina, the Republic of Croatia, the Republic of Macedonia, the Republic of Montenegro, Romania and the Republic of Serbia, as adhering parties, and, Kosovo through the United Nations Interim Administration Mission in Kosovo (UNMIK), pursuant to the United Nations Security Council 1244. Since 1 January 2007 Romania and Bulgaria have been full members of the EU.

[4] See more in n 2 above.

[5] Art 2 Energy Community Treaty.

of liberalisation of energy markets. Therefore, the Treaty creates the basis for the establishment of a common legal and regulatory framework for the functioning of the energy markets that would allow trading energy across the borders from Lisbon to Tbilisi in an open, transparent and competitive manner. Since its establishment, however, the Energy Community has changed substantially, and those changes will be addressed in the subsequent paragraphs.

A. From Pre-accession Tool to Reference Point for Cooperation in the Field of Energy

The Energy Community had initially been established as covering the EU and the territories of the SEE countries that are part of the Stabilization and Association Process (SAP) and that have a clear perspective for EU membership, aiming to consolidate the region after the conflicts of the 1990s. Namely, with the Athens Process, the countries in SEE were trying to stabilise their political and security situation at both a national and at a regional level by re-building friendly relations with their neighbours. It was a smart choice of the EU, to follow its own history when the main instrument for integration after the Second World War was signing two treaties specifically related to the energy sector.[6] At the same time, knowing that the Yugoslavian energy sector was quite advanced in terms of infrastructure development, good interconnections and almost no congestion, well planned generation capacities, as well as very advanced balancing markets (something on which the EU is still working today), it would have been a pity to leave the once interconnected energy sectors compartmentalised and striving for national self-sufficiency after the conflicts of the 1990s. This regional arrangement was also in line with the broader regional strategy of the EU for the SEE and the many regional initiatives undertaken towards the region in other fields.[7]

At that time, the Energy Community was seen as a waiting room for the Balkan countries in the framework of their pre-accession talks with the EU. It was not surprising that the EU launched (yet another) regional initiative. However, doing that through a legally binding Treaty to which the EU itself (and not its Member States) was a party, establishing a robust institutional framework, including provisions on enforcement of that legal framework, was telling already at that time about its importance and the potential role this community would play.

[6] Treaty of Paris establishing the European Coal and Steel Community, Paris, signed on 18 April 1951, entered into force 25 July 1952 and expired 50 years later in 2002; Euroatom Treaty creating the European Atomic Energy Community, Rome, signed on 25 March 1957, entered into force on 1 January 1958 and was concluded for an unlimited period.

[7] See R Karova, 'The Energy Community: Regional Ownership of an Integration Initiative in South East Europe' in B Cerovic and M Uvalic (eds), *Western Balkans' Accession to the European Union. Political and Economic Challenges* (Faculty of Economics of the University of Belgrade Publishing Centre, 2010) 313–42.

The Energy Community was initially established for a duration of ten years, thereby giving hope to the Contracting Parties that this might be the period in which they could become the EU Member States, or at least giving the politicians arguments for signing up to the difficult reforms of the energy sectors in a regionally-coordinated way and based on foreign (EU) rules. The hope had increased with seeing a few examples of the transition from Contracting Parties to Participants by Bulgaria and Romania in 2007 and later on Croatia in 2013, when those countries joined the EU. Macedonia had already received candidate status by the time that the Treaty entered into force, so even though it was too optimistic, the ten-year life span of the Energy Community did not seem like science fiction.

However, the Energy Community was later enlarged to countries that are part of the European Neighbourhood Policy (ENP), countries with no clear membership perspective. As from 1 May 2010 Moldova became a member, followed by Ukraine, which joined the Energy Community as from 1 February 2011, and as from 1 July 2017 Georgia is the newest Contracting Party. As the EU institutions note, there is nothing to prevent the further enlargement of the Energy Community. The EU Commission stated that:

> [w]idening the Energy Community could be considered for countries that have concluded or envisage to negotiate a Free Trade Agreement with the EU and demonstrate both willingness and ability to implement relevant EU legislation.

The European Parliament called '... for further expansion of the Energy Community via the ENP in line with the objectives of the Energy Community on the basis of mutual interest'.[8] The Council of the European Union stated that

> the Energy Community should be promoted as a framework for energy relationships with countries in the Western Balkans, Eastern Europe and other neighbouring countries willing and able to implement the relevant EU acquis.[9]

This expansion of the geographical scope of the Energy Community is reflected in the change of motivation and the rationale for the participation of the Contracting Parties to the process. Namely, in the early years when only countries with potential EU membership were Contracting Parties to the Treaty, the perspective of accession to the EU and not the European financial funds only, were the key driving force for undertaking difficult reforms in their energy sectors. The lack of membership perspective was considered to be insufficient in moving the reform process.[10] By involving the ENP participants in the Energy Community as Observers and then as Parties, shows that the needs of these countries (due to political

[8] European Parliament, Resolution on the European Neighbourhood Policy: towards a strengthening of the partnership – position of the European Parliament on the 2012 reports, 2013/2621(RSP), 23 October 2013, para 27.

[9] Council of the European Union, Follow-up to the European Council of 22.05.2013: Review of Developments on the External Dimension of the EU Energy Policy, 17756/13, 12.12.2013, p 8.

[10] See some of the first papers analysing this issue, above n 2; R Karova, 'Rationale behind the establishment of the Energy Community' (2010) *Law Department EUI Working Paper* 14.

and economic reasons) to secure better access to the EU's internal market and seeking to deepen their relations with the EU – or just to be part of a real European institution – appear to be a strong motivator despite the lack of 'membership carrot'.

At its tenth anniversary in 2016, the Energy Community had a different geographic scope than the original one, as its Contracting Parties consisted of six SAA members and two ENP members. On the one hand, obtaining ENP countries as Contracting Parties changed the motivation factor for participation to the Energy Community and moved it away from the membership dream. On the other hand, even the initial Contracting Parties faced stagnation in the enlargement process, for reasons ranging from the EU's internal problems (such as the financial crisis in 2009 or Brexit at present date) to the existence of unresolved political issues in the region that the EU Member States refused to import. At the same time, reforms of the energy markets and even regional integration in the original Contracting Parties from the SEE were not completed, so even the initial objectives of the Energy Community had not been achieved. It thus became clear that the duration of the Energy Community was to be extended. In 2011, well ahead of the expiry of the Treaty, the European Commission proposed an extension of the Treaty beyond 2016[11] and the Ministerial Council in 2013, acting unanimously, decided to extend its duration for another ten years.[12]

B. Evolution of the Energy Community Law and New Areas of Work

The substantive scope of the Energy Community Treaty, its objectives and the means for achieving those are limited to 'Network Energy', a concept that has been defined in Article 2(2) of the Treaty including 'electricity and gas sectors …'. Even though this concept indicated the Treaty's 'intention of strictly sectoral integration',[13] it has proved flexible and has been enlarged over the years. For example, the concept of Network Energy, and thus the scope of the Treaty, were enlarged in 2008 to include also the oil sector.[14] This means that provisions such as the principle of non-discrimination, competition and state aid rules, and free movement rules are also applicable to the oil sectors of the Parties to the Treaty.

Moreover, besides enlarging the scope of Network Energy covered by the Treaty, the scope of legislation and even areas of work covered by the Treaty has regularly undergone extensions. Article 25 of the Treaty, the so-called 'evolution clause',

[11] European Commission (2011) *Communication on Security of Energy Supply and International Cooperation 'The EU Energy Policy: Engaging with Partners Beyond Our Borders'* COM(2011) 539, Brussels, 7 September.

[12] Ministerial Council (2013) D/2013/03/MC-EnC, 24 October.

[13] J Navickaite, 'The Export of Acquis Communautaire in the EU External Relations: The Energy Community Treaty' (2013) *Leidykla 'Edukologija'* 41.

[14] Ministerial Council Decision No 2008/3/MC of 11 December 2008.

enables the Energy Community to take measures to implement amendments to the *acquis* in line with the development of EU law. Despite the fact that this provision does not impose an obligation[15] on the Energy Community to adopt the changes to the EU *acquis*, the development of the Energy Community legal order shows the great level of ambition by the Energy Community institutions responding positively to the Commission's proposals[16] for the adoption of new legislation. To this extent, the content of the *acquis* being an Energy Community law, contained in Title II of the Treaty has been regularly changed by simple majority of its members.

On the one hand, those changes relate to upgrading the adopted legal acts after their amendment or repeal within the EU. Such examples include replacing the second energy liberalisation package[17] which was an obligation for the Contracting Parties at the time of signing the Energy Community Treaty with the Third Energy Package[18] in 2011;[19] or upgrading the obligation to provide a plan for implementing the 2001 RES Directive[20] with an obligation to transpose and implement Directive 2009/28/EC.[21] On the other hand, they also include changes that include pieces of the *acquis* in areas that had barely been mentioned within the Energy Community Treaty. Namely, Article 35 of the Treaty stipulated that the 'Energy Community may adopt Measures to foster development in the areas of renewable energy sources and energy efficiency', based on several Ministerial Council decisions, Directive 2006/32/EC on energy end-use efficiency and energy services, Directive 2010/31/EU on energy performance of buildings and Directive 2010/30/EU on the indication by labelling became part of the Energy Community body of law. Now the Energy Efficiency Directive 2012/27/EU[22] is also binding on the Energy Community Contracting Parties.

[15] Art 25 Energy Community Treaty reads: 'The Energy Community may take Measures to implement amendments to the acquis communautaire described in this Title, in line with the evolution of European Community law'.

[16] Art 79 Energy Community Treaty.

[17] Art 11 Energy Community Treaty.

[18] Third energy liberalisation package encompasses: Directive 2009/72/EC of the European Parliament and of the Council of 13 July 2009 concerning common rules for the internal market in electricity, Directive 2009/73/EC of the European Parliament and of the Council of 13 July 2009 concerning common rules for the internal market in natural gas, Regulation (EC) No 714/2009 of the European Parliament and of the Council of 13 July 2009 on conditions for access to the network for cross-border exchanges in electricity, and Regulation (EC) No 715/2009 of the European Parliament and of the Council of 13 July 2009 on conditions for access to the natural gas transmission networks. These legal acts entered into force on 3 March 2011.

[19] Decision No 2011/02/MC-EnC, 06.10.2011 following a Ministerial Council, Recommendation No 2010/02/MC-EnC of 24 September 2010.

[20] Directive 2001/77/EC of the European Parliament and of the Council of 27 September 2001 on the promotion of electricity produced from renewable energy sources in the internal electricity market, OJ L283, 27 October 2001, 33–40.

[21] Ministerial Council Decision D/2012/04/MC-EnC, 18 October 2012.

[22] Directive 2012/27/EU of 25 October 2012 on energy efficiency, amending Directives 2009/125/EC and 2010/30/EU and repealing Directives 2004/8/EC and 2006/32/EC.

It is, however, most remarkable how from the very few legal acts in the area of the environment, limited to improving the situation in relation to network energy as stipulated in Article 2 of the Treaty,[23] this body of law is substantially enlarging. The area is slowly shifting to integrating climate issues in the context of the Energy Community,[24] thereby trying to keep up with the EU's willingness to lead in the decarbonisation of the energy sectors.

All in all, while in 2006 Title II of the Treaty referred to only 11 acts that had to be transposed and implemented by the Contracting Parties; the legal framework in 2018 amounts to 61 Decisions and 38 Procedural Acts adopted by the Ministerial Council and the Permanent High Level Group.

C. Fixed Institutional Set-up and Emerging Additional Bodies

The Energy Community Treaty established an institutional framework analogous to the EU.[25] The Treaty formalises the institutions already established by the 2002 Athens Memorandum, and such a strong institutional framework is one of the reasons for the success of the Energy Community. Those include political institutions, such as the Ministerial Council – its decision maker in charge with taking strategic decisions and giving directions to the Treaty or formally adopting or endorsing secondary legislation. In addition to adopting new *acquis*, it is also a decision-making body for dispute settlement. Another institution is the Permanent High Level Group (PHLG), composed of representatives of the ministries for energy of the Contracting Parties and the European Commission. There are also independent institutions, such as the Energy Community Secretariat, which has its seat in Vienna and is the central coordinating body of the Energy Community,[26] as well as the Energy Community Board of Regulators, which has an advisory role for regulatory matters. Finally, several fora have also been established (for electricity and gas set up by the Treaty, but also for oil based on a Ministerial Council decision) as platforms for the inclusion of civil society. Unlike the ECRB[27] and PHLG,[28] which could take decisions if so empowered by the Ministerial Council,

[23] The Environmental Impact Assessment Directive 85/337/EEC, Directive 1999/80/EC for the reduction of sulphur content of fuels and the Large Combustion Plants Directive 2001/80/EC. In addition, in 2013, the Ministerial Council agreed that in the case of new plants the Contracting Parties have to implement the provisions of the Industrial Emissions Directive as from 1 January 2018.

[24] Recommendation 2018/1/MC-EnC on preparing for the development of integrated national energy and climate plans by the Contracting Parties of the Energy Community of 3 January 2018, Policy Guidelines 03/2018-ECS on the development of National Energy and Climate Plans under Recommendation 2018/01/MC-EnC.

[25] European Commission, DG TREN: *Discussion and Consultation Note*, 3–4.06.2004.

[26] According to Art 70, the Director and the staff are not allowed to 'seek or receive instructions from any Party to the EnCT and shall act impartially and promote the interests of the Energy Community'.

[27] Art 58.c) Energy Community Treaty.

[28] Art 53.d) Energy Community Treaty.

the decision-making power of the Secretariat has been explicitly excluded by Article 67.d) of the Treaty.

Unlike the possibilities to enlarge the geographic and the substantive scope of the Treaty, the institutional setting is fixed. New institutions cannot be established without re-ratification of the Treaty. However, the substantive developments of the Energy Community and the new areas of work have been reflected in establishing a large number of bodies, in addition to task forces, committees and coordination groups.[29] One of the most prominent is the Advisory Committee, providing legal opinions in dispute settlement cases that has been established by the Dispute Settlement Rules adopted by the Ministerial Council in 2008 and amended in 2015.[30] It has five members, who are required to possess the qualifications required for appointment to the highest judicial offices in the respective Party, thus, to a certain extent, making up for the lack of a judicial decision-maker for enforcement. Another body is the Parliamentary Plenum established by the Ministerial Council in 2015, which by bringing together members of the parliaments of the Contracting Parties and the European Parliament, is involving the national legislative bodies in the Energy Community process and adds to the democratisation of the community.

III. EU Energy Law and its Role as Unifying Factor between Different Countries and Legal Jurisdictions

A common energy market[31] had to be established, even though there was no clear competence of the EU to take measures on energy matters. This has changed with the Lisbon Treaty,[32] which introduced Article 194 dealing specifically with energy[33] and providing a legal basis for the European Parliament and the Council, acting in accordance with the ordinary legislative procedure, to establish the measures necessary for achieving those objectives. In the early 1990s, the first more ambitious steps towards the liberalisation of the European energy market were taken by adopting sector-specific secondary legislation. This involved fixing of a specific

[29] www.energy-community.org/aboutus/whoweare.html.

[30] Ministerial Council, Procedural Act on the Rules of Procedure for Dispute Settlement under the Treaty, No 2008/01/MC-EnC, 27 June 2008.

[31] As defined in Art 8(a) of the Single European Act [1987] OJ L169/1: 'an area without internal frontiers in which the free movement of goods, persons, services and capital is ensured'.

[32] Consolidated versions of the Treaty on European Union and the Treaty on the Functioning of the European Union, Official Gazette of the European Union 2008/C115/01, 9 May 2008.

[33] Art 194 TFEU outlines that the energy policy of the EU is aiming to: (a) ensure the functioning of the energy market; (b) ensure security of energy supply in the Union; (c) promote energy efficiency and energy saving and the development of new and renewable forms of energy and (d) promote the interconnection of energy networks.

timetable for liberalisation in 1996 with the adoption of the first liberalisation package concerning both electricity and gas markets. The objective since this first generation of liberalisation directives was to open up energy markets through the gradual introduction of competition in generation and supply, thereby increasing the efficiency of the energy sector and the competitiveness of the European economy as a whole. Since then, three packages of liberalisation directives and regulations have been adopted, and in 2018, a political agreement was reached on the Clean Energy Package, including new legislation on electricity market design, the adoption of all acts is to be completed in early 2019. In addition to the liberalisation legislation, the EU *acquis* contains legislation on energy efficiency, renewables, and a large body on environmental and climate issues. With the Governance Regulation,[34] as part of the Clean Energy Package, integrated national energy and climate planning is being introduced for the first time.

Being a Community based on the rule of law, and being founded by a legally binding instrument, the Energy Community objectives stipulated in Article 2 of the Treaty are to be achieved by ensuring that the Contracting Parties adopt and implement the relevant *acquis communitaire* in areas such as energy, environment, competition and renewables.

As explained in the previous section, the Energy Community Treaty contains an evolution clause as an instrument to keep up with the developments of EU law. Despite the discretion of the Energy Community that *may* take Measures to implement amendments to the *acquis*,[35] I have already argued that such wording has been irrelevant in practice.[36] Namely, from the application of the second energy liberalisation package, the rules governing the electricity and gas sectors in the Contracting Parties have been upgraded to the third energy package within a couple of years after they entered into force in the EU. By adopting Policy Guidelines at its meeting in Skopje in 2018,[37] the Ministerial Council expressed the political commitment to follow up and adopt relevant pieces of the Clean Energy Package within the Energy Community already in 2019. This plan, if successful, will be the most ambitious so far in terms of timing, which corresponds with the political support of the Contracting Parties to the decarbonisation objective of the EU energy policy.

[34] Regulation (EU) 2018/1999 of the European Parliament and of the Council of 11 December 2018 on the Governance of the Energy Union and Climate Action, amending Regulations (EC) No 663/2009 and (EC) No 715/2009 of the European Parliament and of the Council, Directives 94/22/EC, 98/70/EC, 2009/31/EC, 2009/73/EC, 2010/31/EU, 2012/27/EU and 2013/30/EU of the European Parliament and of the Council, Council Directives 2009/119/EC and (EU) 2015/652 and repealing Regulation (EU) No 525/2013 of the European Parliament and of the Council, OJ L328, 21 December 2018, p 1–77.

[35] Art 25 EnCT.

[36] R Karova, 'The Dispute Settlement System of the Energy Community: Testing its Effectiveness' in D Buschle and K Talus (eds), *The Energy Community: A New Energy Governance System* (Intersentia, 2015).

[37] See above n 24.

Besides the flexibility of whether new pieces of legislation shall be adopted as Energy Community law or not, the Treaty also grants discretion to the Energy Community to adopt EU legislation when adopting it as Energy Community Law, both when following the *acquis* from Title II of the Treaty[38] and when adopting measures for its implementation.[39] This flexibility relates to both 'the institutional framework of the Treaty and the specific situation of each of the Contracting Parties'. However, beyond technical adaptations and adjustments to the institutional structure of the Energy Community, we have argued that 'flexibility to adapt has been used only very occasionally'[40] despite the fact that the EU rules have been drafted for countries that are, on the one hand, quite different and much more developed than the Contracting Parties, and which, on the other hand, take only their interests into account, and do not take into consideration the needs of the latter when adopting EU rules.

Moreover, the export of EU rules to the Contracting Parties through Title II of the Treaty has been 'designed as a strictly one-way street',[41] which is applicable only to the Contracting Parties thus creating obligations only for them – to transpose and implement the rules in question without covering the interface between the Contracting Parties and EU Member States. The Energy Community has also prepared to follow up with the timely adoption of technical rules based on the third liberalisation package, the so-called Network Codes and, for that reason, its institutions adopted procedural rules giving this power to the PHLG to adopt the Network Codes upon the Commission's proposal.[42] However, the adoption of Network Codes in the Energy Community has only started in 2018, and due to the legal and regulatory gap related to the lack of reciprocal obligations between the Contracting Parties and the EU Member States, the market-related Network Codes could not yet be adopted with simple adaptations under Article 24 of the Treaty and without amendments to the Treaty.

The Treaty contains provisions governing dispute settlement procedure in Articles 90–93 and in the Dispute Settlement Rules (DSR) adopted by the Ministerial Council in the form of a Procedural Act. The full procedure has been modelled upon the EU infringement procedure. Disputes between different countries[43] or

[38] Art 5 Energy Community Treaty.

[39] Art 24 Energy Community Treaty.

[40] D Buschle and R Karova, 'The EU's sectoral communities with neighbours: the case of the Energy Community' in S Gstöhl and D Phinnemore, *The European Union, its Neighbours, and the Proliferation of 'Privileged Partnerships'* (Routledge, forthcoming).

[41] ibid.

[42] Procedural Act No 01/2012 PHLG-EnC of the Permanent High Level Group of the Energy Community of 21 June 2012 laying down the rules governing the adoption of Guidelines and Network Codes in the Energy Community and Procedural Act No 02/2012 of the Energy Community Regulatory Board 2012/02 ECRB-EnC: Decision of 23 October 2012 of the Energy Community Regulatory Board on the Procedure for Issuing an Opinion of the Energy Community Regulatory Board on the Adoption of Network Codes adopted and/or amended under Regulation 714/2009 or Regulation 715/2009.

[43] See for instance Art 27 of the Energy Charter Treaty.

annulment procedures and preliminary rulings are not included in the scope of the DSR. The procedure does not cover disputes between private parties either.[44] Not having judicial enforcement, and the lack of financial penalties, have been seen as the main deficiencies of the Energy Community. This has also been an argument used by the EU Member States as a response to the quest for ensuring reciprocity in terms of mutual obligations.

In order to prevent this legal and regulatory gap from widening and affecting negatively the main objective of the Treaty – pan-European integration of energy markets – negotiations on amending the Treaty are ongoing. Those cover both the attempt to ensure mutual obligations also on the interface Contracting Parties – EU Member States, but also to strengthen enforcement of Energy Community law in the Contracting Parties.

Once the European rules become Energy Community law, Article 94 of the Treaty, which imposes an obligation on the Energy Community institutions to 'interpret any term or other concept used in the Treaty that is derived from EU Law in conformity with the case law of the ECJ and General Court',[45] tries to compensate for the lack of judicial interpretation and the lack of preliminary reference procedures.[46] This provision allows the Ministerial Council to give guidance in interpreting the Treaty itself, or to delegate that task to the PHLG. The same article, however, provides for a safeguard that 'such guidance shall not prejudge any interpretation of the acquis communautaire by the ECJ or General Court at a later stage'.

The EFTA Court held that even though '… the depth of integration of the EEA Agreement is less far-reaching than under the EC Treaty, its scope and objective goes beyond what is usual for an agreement under public international law'.[47]

Later on, the CJEU Opinion on the European Common Aviation Area (ECAA) confirmed that even very limited sectoral agreements could have the same nature and aim as the EEA.[48] In this line, I have already argued that the Energy Community Treaty is also an agreement *sui generis* and that the Energy Community establishes a new legal order confined to the energy sector.[49] Explicit recognition of the EU fundamental principles in the Treaty would allow the Contracting Parties that have an aspiration to EU membership to become familiar with these constitutional fundamentals and would strengthen the enforcement of Energy Community law.[50] The ongoing negotiations on a reform of the Energy Community

[44] Art 4 DSR.

[45] Art 94 EnCT.

[46] For a comparison with the EEA, the European Common Aviation Area (ECAA) and the Transport Community see nn 50 and 26 above.

[47] Case E-9/97, *Erla María Sveinbjörnsdóttir v Iceland* [1998] EFTA Court Report 95, para 59.

[48] ECJ Opinion 1/00, 18 April 2002.

[49] R Karova, 'The Application of the EU Constitutional Principles in the Energy Community; Reaping the Full Benefits of the Regional Integration' (2015) 3 *European Networks Law and Regulation Quarterly* 2.

[50] ibid, 11.

Treaty address direct applicability or granting the EU Regulations quasi-direct effect once adopted in the Energy Community, by explicitly recognising such effect in the Treaty.

The Energy Community serves the purpose of exporting EU rules and making them applicable to countries well beyond the EU's borders. This aims to ensure that same rules apply to the whole Energy Community (the whole EU and the Contracting Parties) and has obviously brought changes in the functioning of the energy markets in the latter. The reforms, in particular in the electricity and gas markets, have advanced. Back in 2009,[51] different obstacles to trade in energy based on lack of transposition of the second liberalisation package ranged from the necessity for tariff reforms, diverging market models, diverging eligibility thresholds in different Contracting Parties as well as obstacles to cross-border trade. And even in 2018, the implementation of the electricity *acquis* in most advanced cases is not above 70–80%, and the average implementation score in all areas under the Treaty is at around 43%.[52] This shows that the Energy Community has not fulfilled its mission, not even the short-term one of finalising the national energy sector reforms before heading to regional integration, and gradual inclusion in the internal energy market in the long term. However, in its Annual Implementation Report of 2018, the Secretariat has noted that the Contracting Parties have made progress in their first energy transition, that is 'a transition from foreclosed, post-socialist energy sectors in each Contracting Party to open and regionally integrated energy markets'. It has also reported that what appears to be an additional challenge with unfinished first energy transition, is actually the Energy Community's second energy transition – the energy transition currently transforming Europe and the rest of the world, ie the paradigm shift from liberalisation to decarbonisation.

Nevertheless, being part of the Energy Community, the Contracting Parties are members of the European family. They are under an obligation to reform their energy sectors, and to apply European rules to them. Since Energy Community law is not only confined to electricity and gas sectoral *acquis*, being part of the Energy Community means that also larger sets of rules and principles are obligatory for these countries. This includes energy efficiency, renewables, but also competition and state aid, principles of non-discrimination and transparency, legal certainty for investors and other market-based rules. Having that in mind, with all the gradual changes of the EU energy law, its ongoing integration with environmental/climate law, and despite the limited adaptations of the EU rules forming part of Energy Community law, it could be considered that the moving target of EU law acts as a common denominator for functioning of the pan-European energy markets. Such a common denominator is the instrument used for ensuring that the trading of energy takes place on an effective, competitive and transparent market allowing for legal certainty for investors and market participants.

[51] Karova (above n 1).

[52] Energy Community Secretariat, Annual Implementation Report, September 2018, p 7.

Besides the *acquis* exported through Title II of the Treaty, competition and state aid rules are also applicable to the energy sectors in the Contracting Parties in order to prevent trade in energy between the Contracting Parties from being affected.[53] No central enforcement authority exists in the Energy Community, and implementation depends on the effectiveness and efficiency of the national competition and state aid authorities, assisted by the Secretariat through the cooperation established by Article 2 of the Dispute Settlement Rules. Strengthening the effectiveness of competition and state aid enforcement is also subject to amendment within the ongoing negotiations for amending the Treaty.

Finally, Title III of the Treaty and Title IV have a different scope of application. They do not concern export of EU ready-made sectoral rules, but instead aim at regional integration between the Contracting Parties and the neighbouring EU Member States (Title III)[54] and between the Contracting Parties and the whole EU (Title IV).[55] Thus Title III, in addition to the Contracting Parties, applies also to the EU Member States that are surrounding the Contracting Parties, and Title IV is addressed to the whole Energy Community, ie the entire EU in addition to the Contracting Parties, and measure to be taken under this Title would apply to the whole territory of the Energy Community. However, it has already been noted that the Energy Community institutions are reluctant to adopt measures that would 'create genuine rules independent of its EU law origins' binding on the EU as well through its participation to the Energy Community.[56] The importance of this Title will be addressed in the following section.

IV. The Energy Community as a Success Story?

The Energy Community has proved useful and important, and not only for the SEE countries for which it was initially established. It has developed itself as an important central piece of the puzzle called the EU external energy policy. The EU institutions consider it a 'success story',[57] have recognised its importance in

[53] Art 18(2) Energy Community Treaty: 'Any practices contrary to this Article shall be assessed on the basis of criteria arising from the application of the rules of Articles 81, 82 and 87 of the Treaty establishing the European Community'.

[54] Title III contains obligations related to establishing mechanisms for operation of network energy markets, such as security of supply measures, provision of energy to citizens, harmonisation concerning the market designs and mutual recognition of licences as well as establishing mechanisms for crisis situations – safeguard measures.

[55] Title IV of the Treaty covers the free movement of network energy – electricity, gas and oil – and allows for further measures to be taken with a view to creating a single energy market. In addition, this Title IV establishes an external energy trade policy and importantly provides for a mechanism of mutual assistance between the Parties in the event of energy disruption.

[56] J Kopač and D Buschle, 'The Energy Community' in C Jones, *The Role of Gas in the EU's Energy Union* (Clays & Casteels, 2017) 203.

[57] Report from the Commission to the European Parliament and the Council under Article 7 of Decision 2006/500/EC, 10.3.2011, COM(2011) 105 final.

the EU's relations with its neighbouring countries by referring to the Energy Community as a 'reference point for the majority of the EU's neighbours'[58] and an institution with a 'strategic role' in relations with Ukraine.[59] In addition to its importance for internal integration and establishing regional and pan-European markets through export of EU rules and forming 'the basis for establishing a fully integrated regional energy market',[60] the Energy Community is one of 'the most successful policy frameworks of the European external energy policy'.[61]

It is in exactly this context that the Energy Community's existence for more than a decade is interesting when analysed in comparison to the other regional initiatives that the EU continues to establish for the Western Balkans, but also for its place and role within the Energy Union. In addition, since the Energy Community's scope – both geographic and substantive – is open to enlargement and expansion, its limits are not set in stone and confined with the signature of the Treaty. The Energy Community's functioning cannot be looked at in isolation without keeping an eye on developments in the neighbourhood (the East and the South).

A. Energy Community and the Energy Union

Upon an initial proposal made by the Polish Prime Minister and afterwards President of the European Council, Donald Tusk, in April 2014, calling upon the European countries to establish an energy union, the EU Commission's President has appointed a vice-president with a portfolio devoted to the realisation of an Energy Union. In February 2015, by publishing a Communication,[62] the EU Commission launched its Energy Union based on the three long-established objectives of EU energy policy: security of supply; sustainability; and competitiveness. With a view to achieving those objectives, the Energy Union focuses on several dimensions: energy security, solidarity and trust; the internal energy market; energy efficiency as a contribution to the moderation of energy demand;

[58] Communication from the Commission to the European Parliament, the Council, the European Economic and Social Committee and the Committee of the Regions on security of energy supply and international cooperation – The EU Energy Policy: Engaging with Partners beyond Our Borders, 7.9.2011, COM(2011) 539 final.

[59] European Parliament resolution of 13 March 2014 on the invasion of Ukraine by Russia (2014/2627(RSP)).

[60] European Parliament, resolution of 23 October 2013 on the European Neighbourhood Policy: towards a strengthening of the partnership. Position of the European Parliament on the 2012 reports (2013/2621(RSP)).

[61] Report on the review of developments on the external dimension of the EU energy policy by the Council of the European Union, 12 December 2013.

[62] Communication From The Commission To The European Parliament, The Council, The European Economic And Social Committee, The Committee Of The Regions And The European Investment Bank, A Framework Strategy for a Resilient Energy Union with a Forward-Looking Climate Change Policy, Brussels, 25.02.2015, COM 2015 (80) final.

decarbonisation of the economy; and research, innovation and competitiveness. Different actions have been taken and annual reports on the status of fulfilling those objectives are regularly published.[63]

The creation and the fulfilling of the Energy Union has become a major issue on the EU's political agenda. The legal framework has continued to develop as well, and a whole new energy package with more than 1,000 pages, so-called Clean Energy Package,[64] is to be adopted in early 2019. The Clean Energy Package redesigns European energy policy by a new governance system based on long-term strategies and integrated national energy and climate plans. The new legislation envisages a new electricity market design and ensures the EU's vision for energy efficiency and renewables by setting the 2030 binding targets. The EU already noted its progress made on the way to transition to a low-carbon, secure and competitive EU economy, and the Commission, on 28 November 2018, has presented its strategic long-term vision for a prosperous, modern, competitive and climate neutral economy by 2050.[65]

However, where the Energy Union was expected to make a difference is the area of external energy policy and the EU's external relations not only with the immediate neighbours but also beyond. An Energy Union bringing benefits for all its citizens, especially in the area of security of supply, could not make sense if confined within the EU's borders. It could only be considered important if it included the existing instruments of external energy policy, such as the Energy Community together with its Contracting Parties, some of which (for example Ukraine) are important for gas supply and transit of natural gas for the whole continent, as one of its central pieces.[66]

In this relation, it is important to note that the Energy Community already contains the means for allowing the coordination of external relations with its neighbours. Title IV of the Treaty, which is binding for all Contracting Parties and the whole EU, contains provisions some of which could not form part of even EU secondary legislation. In addition to Article 41, which relates to free movement of Network Energy across the whole Energy Community, this title contains a solidarity clause in Article 45 of the Treaty giving a right to each Party to the Treaty (the EU or a Contracting Party for example Ukraine) to request a meeting of the Ministerial Council, and giving power to the latter to take the necessary

[63] See www.ec.europa.eu/commission/priorities/energy-union-and-climate_en, last accessed 27 March 2019.

[64] Seewww.ec.europa.eu/energy/en/topics/energy-strategy-and-energy-union/clean-energy-all-europeans, last accessed 27 March 2019.

[65] Communication From The Commission To The European Parliament, The European Council, The Council, The European Economic And Social Committee, The Committee Of The Regions And The European Investment Bank, A Clean Planet for all: A European strategic long-term vision for a prosperous, modern, competitive and climate neutral economy, Brussels, 28 November 2018, COM(2018) 773 final.

[66] J Kopač and D Buschle, 'Crisis and structure: From Ukraine to a European energy union' (2014) Opinion at Europolitics.

measures in response to a disruption. Article 43 allows for a common external energy policy at the borders of the Energy Community, ie towards neighbours such as the Russian Federation or Azerbaijan, as the Energy Community is empowered to take measures necessary for the regulation of imports and exports of Network Energy to and from third countries with a view to ensuring equivalent access. It is not an overstatement that binding rules and obligations for the whole EU and the Contracting Parties is of utmost importance and should be used by the EU in the framework of its Energy Union. However, so far there has been a reluctance to use Title IV of the Energy Community Treaty, mostly coming from the difficulties of the EU as a Party to the Treaty in obtaining a common voice of its Member States that would empower the Commission to speak with one voice in the institutions of the Energy Community. Even though other titles of the Treaty allow for simple majority voting, unanimity is required for using Title IV, because a measure adopted under this title would be binding and would impose obligations on the whole EU. The full potential of the existing Energy Community Treaty has not been yet explored. In the Energy Union Communication of February 2015, the Commission envisaged that it will propose to strengthen the Energy Community, ensuring effective implementation of the EU's energy, environment and competition *acquis*, energy market reforms and incentivising investments in the energy sector. The goal would be closer integration of the EU and Energy Community energy markets.[67]

This statement follows the initiation of a reform of the Energy Community. The actual discussions on Treaty amendments were initiated in 2016, following the so-called Buzek report on Energy Community reform of the High Level Reflection Group from 2014 established by the Ministerial Council.[68] This group prepared a report assessing 'the adequacy of the institutional set up and working methods of the Energy Community in achieving the objectives of the Treaty'. In doing so, it has taken into account 'the organisation's evolution over the past years, including its extended membership, and to make proposals for improvements to the Ministerial Council in 2014'. The Report and the Energy Community Ministerial Council conclusions called for amendments to the Energy Community Treaty in order to

> … ensure that the organization can fully fulfil its objectives and live up to the requirements of a Single Energy Market based on the effective implementation of the acquis communautaire in the Contracting Parties on equal terms with EU Member States as well as on fair and equal conditions for access to markets and infrastructure.

The amendments to the Treaty have not yet been adopted, and the outcome will be important for strengthening the Energy Community within the framework of the Energy Union as well.

[67] See above n 64, 7.

[68] Ministerial Council, Procedural Act, PA/2013/04/MC-EnC: On setting up a High Level Reflection Group on the functioning of the Treaty, 24.10.2013.

B. The Regional Initiatives for the Western Balkans

In addition to the Energy Community, and following its example, the EU has established two other sectoral communities with those SEE countries which are at the same time Contracting Parties to the Energy Community. Those two other sectoral communities have been also established by way of legally binding international agreements. The European Common Aviation Area (ECAA) Treaty is signed between the European Community and its Member States with the SEE countries as well as Norway and Iceland. The Treaty establishing the Transport Community (TCT) was signed between the EU and the SEE countries and is more similar to the Energy Community Treaty. While the Energy Community Treaty was signed in October 2005 and entered into force in less than a year (in July 2006), the other two treaties took longer between signing and entering into force. The ECAA Treaty, even though signed in 2006, entered into force only on 1 December 2017, whereas the Transport Community Treaty, which followed the establishment of the South East Europe Transport Observatory (SEETO) in 2004 by the Memorandum of Understanding (MoU) on the Development of the South East Core Regional Transport, the TCT was published in Official Journal on 27 October 2017.

The main aim of these two sectoral communities is to deepen European integration of the Western Balkans in the field of transport, by allowing for progressive access to the transport market of the EU in exchange for the application of EU norms and regional market integration. The progressive and gradual integration is spelt out much more clearly than in the Energy Community Treaty. The regional component also seems not that important, and the implementation of the EU rules by the non-EU countries is assessed country-by-country on a case-by-case basis. Unlike in the Energy Community, where the Secretariat as an independent institution is assessing compliance by the Contracting Parties with the EU rules, in the other two communities, the European Commission is granted such power. As mentioned above, in the Energy Community, the legal and regulatory gap in the interface between Contracting Parties and EU Member States is not addressed in the original treaty. The Transport Community, on the other hand, contains a switch-on reciprocity clause, which addresses this issue.[69]

Other differences from the Energy Community Treaty relate to some of the horizontal substantive provisions. Namely, the ECAA contains a provision on the right of establishment in addition to the free movement of goods, in line with its objective for establishing an ECAA air carrier. In addition, the application of

[69] Art 3(3) of the Transport Community Treaty reads: 'where applicable provisions of the acts referred to in paragraph 1 give rise to obligations on the part of the EU Member States, those obligations shall apply to the EU Member States, following a decision adopted under the rules applicable within the EU based on an assessment by the European Commission with regard to the full implementation by the South East European Parties of the EU acts referred to in Annex I'.

competition and State aid rules is also different. While in the Energy Community Treaty there is a clear obligation for the application of those rules to the energy sectors, in the other two communities non-EU countries have to 'progressively adjust the state monopolies of commercial character', and to 'recognise the importance of the approximation of the existing State aid and competition rules'.

Other differences between the three communities relate to the institutional set-up and the enforcement of the obligations under the treaties. All of them have established their own supranational institutions, but the institutions defined in the Transport Community Treaty follow more closely those of the Energy Community, whereas the ECAA only establishes a Joint Committee.[70] None of the three communities has established a judicial body,[71] but both the ECAA and the Transport Community Treaty provide for preliminary references of national courts of non-EU countries to the CJ EU and stipulate the exclusive competence of the latter over questions concerning the legality of decisions of the EU institutions. The two new treaties also differ from the Energy Community because they do not provide for enforcement of the Treaty provisions through infringement proceedings of the kind developed in Article 258 TFEU. They envisage dispute settlement between parties, which 'may draw up a proposal for solution'. If a solution is not found, the parties to the dispute may bring the case before the Joint Committee in the ECAA or before the Regional Steering Committee in the Transport Community Treaty. If, after four months, a decision to resolve the dispute has not been taken, the parties to the dispute may refer the case to the CJEU.

Bearing in mind this short observation, and without assessing in detail the three sectoral communities, it could be concluded that the EU used the Energy Community's good example as an instrument for not only export of EU rules to its neighbours limited to different sectors, but also as an instrument for regional integration. Compliance with the EU rules is made a pre-condition for further integration, but also for benefiting from the EU funds.[72] What is not clear, at the moment, is whether this is the end of such initiatives, or whether the enlargement to the Western Balkans is slowly being replaced by sectoral agreements and legally binding instruments producing more and more obligations for the Contracting Parties and lacking more and more the main *carrot* – EU membership. This becomes more striking bearing in mind that the geographic scope of both the ECAA and the Transport Community is limited to the SEE countries, all of which have the potential membership perspective.

[70] For a short review of the differences, see n 45 above.

[71] For a comparison between Energy Community and the EEA Agreement, see R Karova, 'Enforcement record of the Energy Community' (2015) 5(3) *European Energy Journal* 61.

[72] See a reference to the Connectivity Agenda for the Western Balkans in the Transport Community Treaty, Art 28.

C. A Glimpse into the Energy Community's Neighbourhood

Most of the Eastern Partnership countries are now fully-fledged members of the Energy Community, meaning that they have all the rights but also all the obligations from the Energy Community Treaty. The other remaining three countries that are not Contracting Parties of the Energy Community are also in a certain manner involved in the process. Armenia is an Observer, Belarus has applied to become an Observer, and Azerbaijan is cooperating through the regional component of the EU4Energy project. Furthermore, through projects such as the Trans Adriatic Pipeline, for example, there is also a potential for the increase in the energy trading relationships with the Energy Community countries. Therefore, initiatives such as the Eurasian Economic Union (EEU), to which some of those countries participate, are also important.

On 29 May 2014, the Presidents of Belarus, Kazakhstan and the Russian Federation signed the Treaty on the Eurasian Economic Union, while Armenia and the Kyrgyz Republic became members in 2015.[73] The members agreed

> … to develop long-term mutually beneficial cooperation in the energy sector, conduct coordinated energy policies and gradually create common energy markets with a view to ensuring energy security.[74]

The aim of the EEU Treaty is to

> … effectively utilise the potential of the fuel and energy complex of the Member States, as well as to provide national economies with the main types of energy resources (electricity, gas, oil and petroleum products) [so it aims through] cooperation and coordination of energy policy [to gradually establish a] common energy markets.

Some of the principles on which such common markets would be based, correspond to the European principles.[75]

[73] A Decision approving the establishment of a common electricity market No 261, 4 December 2012.

[74] Art 79 of the Treaty on the establishment of the Eurasian Economic Union; Art 81 provides a legal basis for establishing common electricity market.

[75] Art 104 of the EAEUT establishes the procedure and terms of approval of concepts and programmes, as well as international agreements on the establishment of common energy markets. The principles relate to: (1) ensuring market pricing for energy resources; (2) ensuring the development of competition in the common markets of energy resources; (3) no technical, administrative and other barriers to trade in energy resources, equipment, technology and related services; (4) ensuring the development of a transport infrastructure for the common markets of energy resources; (5) ensuring non-discriminatory conditions for economic entities of the Member States in the common markets of energy resources; (6) creation of favourable conditions for attracting investments in the energy sector of the Member States; (7) harmonisation of national rules and regulations for the functioning of the process and business infrastructure of the common markets of energy resources.

The EEU Treaty governs the legal, institutional,[76] organisational and technical issues related to the creation of common energy (electricity, gas and oil) markets. Particularly, Section XX of the Treaty on Energy Industry defines the principles of cooperation, compilation of indicative (projected) balance of gas, oil and petroleum products, establishment of a common electricity market and common gas, oil and petroleum product markets and access to services of natural monopolies for the transportation of energy resources.[77] The common electricity market of the EEU is to be finalised by mid-2019, while the concepts for oil and gas are to be implemented in stages by 2024 and 2025 respectively.

For establishing a common electricity market, for example, the parties agreed to ensure the harmonisation of national legislation and gradually transform their national markets in order to create a common electricity market, providing non-discriminatory access of economic entities to the services of natural monopolies, in compliance with the national legislation of the Parties.[78] The EEU Concept on electricity sector introduced several new elements. Namely, in addition to the existing non-regulated bilateral contracts, a trading platform for centralised trading for both fixed-term contracts and on a day ahead basis (DAM) is envisaged. Common rules are to be developed for capacity allocation at interconnectors, based on the principles of priority for supply of domestic customers, as well as rules for non-discriminatory access to national transmission grids. The Concept also includes the requirement that tariffs for EEU-wide long-distance transmission shall not exceed those at the national level.

Even though such requirements resemble some of the elements from the *acquis*, the EEU common electricity market is also based on certain principles that are different from the European and Energy Community rules. Namely, the fact that priority shall be granted for satisfying demand at the national level before trading cross-border between EEU members is in contrast with the EU principles. That is, however, understandable bearing in mind that despite the common electricity market of the EEU being modelled on the EU's electricity market for continental Europe (bilateral market as well as DAM), the trade of electricity at the EEU common market will only concern the excess electricity. An electricity exchange would be a new element for cross-border electricity trading in the EEU, in addition to bilateral trading that is in place already. While in the EU, the end-customers were at the centre of the liberalisation and electricity sector reforms,

[76] Art 8 of the EAEUT. The following institutions have been established: The Supreme Council is the EAEU's supreme authority composed of Heads of State; The Intergovernmental Council consists of the Heads of Government; The Eurasian Economic Commission is a permanent supranational regulatory body of the EAEU. The Council (Deputy Heads of Government) of the Commission and the Board of the Commission support the operation and development of the EAEU; and the Court of the Eurasian Economic Union is the court of justice of the Eurasian Economic Union, which ensures the uniform application of the EAEU Treaty and other Union treaties by the EAEU member states and bodies.

[77] Section XX of the EAEUT.

[78] Agreement on Establishment of Common Electricity Market of the CIS 2007.

and the eligibility of each customer was to be ensured, only a wholesale regional DAM is envisaged in the EEU. No retail market opening and no retail market competition is planned (for the moment). While the abundance of transmission capacities within the EEU in principle allows for unrestricted trade (namely the capacity of the cross-border transmission lines would permit trading of about 30 GWh annually), just 6.5 GWh were actually traded in 2014.[79]

Belarus, for example, is a member of the EEU and a country that has applied to become an Observer to the Energy Community, looking towards increased trade of electricity with the Energy Community Parties (including EU Member States). In April 2018, the Secretariat observed that having a harmonised market model and introducing gradually compatible rules for governing the electricity sector would also complement the country's obligations undertaken within the Eurasian Economic Union, under which Belarus has committed to establishing a wholesale electricity market by mid-2019.[80] Armenia, which is an Energy Community Observer, has also been part of the EEU since 2015. The Secretariat noted that this country 'has thus chosen a policy orientation, which does not completely comply with the acquis communautaire'. However, it also concluded that besides the benefit of having enhanced trading of electricity with Georgia, harmonising the electricity market model and introducing gradually compatible rules for governing the Armenian electricity sector would also complement the obligations undertaken by Armenia within the Eurasian Economic Union.[81] Therefore, participation in the EEU does not prevent or contradict approximation (or even harmonisation) of these countries' rules with the EU rules governing energy markets, as the latter go beyond what is required under the EEU, but would go in line with the obligations undertaken under the EEU.

It is also interesting to note that the EEU is not an EU initiative, but the Russian Federation – the main exporter of natural gas for the EU – has initiated its establishment. Unlike the EU's and Energy Community's objective of integration of fragmented national markets, and sharing common principles and values, the EEU seems to rely on economic interests. Nevertheless, the EU's interest in promoting liberalisation and increased trade goes along with the interest in having neighbouring energy markets that follow similar principles and standards. In general, establishing a wholesale electricity market, following principles similar to the EU's electricity market for continental Europe, and a wholesale market following the European electricity market design in the Energy Community's neighbourhood, could bring benefits and increased trade potentials. Here once again, as argued in other papers, the Energy Community could play a role, by sharing experience – at a

[79] M Pastukhova and K Westphal, 'A common Energy market in the Eurasian Economic Union: Implications for the European Union and Energy Relations with Russia' (2016) 9 SWP Comments.

[80] Energy Community Secretariat, *Energy Governance in Belarus Policy Recommendations*, April 2018.

[81] Energy Community Secretariat, *Energy Governance in Armenia Policy Recommendations*, July 2017, p 11.

technical and expert level, by establishing contacts through its institutions with those of the EEU.[82] There can be no harm in offering assistance to countries and institutions that aim at following the European energy (at least electricity) market model, even if limited to wholesale markets, and that aim at regional integration of such liberalised energy markets.

Similarly, exporting the Energy Community experience to the Mediterranean would also be an interesting undertaking. Several years ago, the Council noted that the Ministerial meeting of the Union for the Mediterranean from December 2013 discussed '… a potential energy community of Union for the Mediterranean members'. For the EU, promotion of regulatory convergence is important, and the EU would support

> fostering regional integration and facilitating energy investment and trade, inter alia in the context of new fossil fuel discoveries in the area and the potential for renewable energies and energy efficiency ….

The Council has also called for the Union to 'continue to promote the EU energy acquis in third countries, when and where appropriate'.[83] Instead of creating a new Mediterranean energy community, and in particular provided that the Energy Community is reformed to allow for flexible and diverse membership, it could become attractive for countries from the Mediterranean, Turkey and others that do not have the strong incentive for joining an Energy Community that requires basically copy-paste of EU *acquis*. Turkey was one of the countries drafting the Energy Community Treaty and participating up to the last moment of negotiations as a potential Contracting Party. Turkey is even today cooperating with the Energy Community Parties, it is a member of the Regional Capacity Allocation Office for the allocating of cross-border capacities established in Montenegro, has also fully synchronised its electricity system with that of the EU, and its electricity TSO is a member of ENTSO-E (an institution for cooperation of electricity TSOs in wider Europe). These countries could easily become members of the Energy Community, if the institutions offer more flexibility, a differentiated membership, allowing for cherry-picking in terms of obligations, but – in such a case – also in terms of fewer rights.

V. Conclusions

The Energy Community Treaty was concluded for a period of ten years from the date of entry into force, and was initially designed as an institution preparing the Western Balkans countries for EU membership. It offered close regional integration and the chance to become part of the internal energy markets even before

[82] Above n 79, 6.
[83] Above n 61, 4, 8.

the countries became EU Member States. It also required reform of their energy sectors, and adoption of the EU *acquis* adapted to the institutional framework of the Treaty. With the extension for ten more years, it became clear that there is a need to amend the Treaty because, in the first years of its existence, the Energy Community showed flexibility and changed substantially not only its geographic scope by becoming a reference point for regional cooperation in energy instead of pre-accession tool, but its substantive scope – the body of law legally binding upon its members – grew substantially as well.

With the High Level Reflection Group report, several proposals for reforming the Energy Community have been put forward. Negotiations for amending the Treaty have been initiated and are expected to be completed by the end of 2019. Though it has become clear that there will be no substantial overhaul of the Energy Community, and many of the issues proposed by the Buzek Report are no longer on the table, the amendments are expected to bring several improvements both in terms of reciprocity between Contracting Parties and the EU, but also in terms of more efficient and effective enforcement of obligations under the Treaty.

As this chapter has shown, the Energy Community brought many benefits not only for the Contracting Parties but also for the EU itself. Having Ukraine and Georgia as its members, obliged to apply the EU rules in their energy sectors (albeit with certain exemptions as the Georgian Accession Protocol shows), is of utmost importance for the EU and its Member States. The place of the Energy Community, as its central element for the European external energy policy through its Energy Union, should not be neglected. Instead, its potential – including that of Title IV of the original Treaty – remains intact and available. The political support from the EU institutions is also there for years:

> Member States are satisfied with the progress achieved in the Energy Community in recent years and have underlined that it should continue to expand and should continue to focus on the practical implementation of the EU energy acquis and should broaden and deepen its scope on a case by case basis.[84]

The Energy Community has also served as inspiration, and following its success, the EU has proposed the creation of two more regional communities with the Western Balkans – the Transport Community and the ECAA – the potential of which is still to be explored. Being based on legally binding treaties as well, even though having different scope of rules and members, the strong institutional set-up and the reciprocity clause present (at least) in the Transport Community, as well as the competence granted to the CJEU, provide for potential for development and making a difference in the years to come. It remains to be seen whether those communities will develop as the Energy Community did, whether they would remain indeed steps for reforms and integration as pre-accession tools or whether such sectoral communities will appear in other sectors, and will slowly show

[84] Above n 61, 8.

that the EU aims to use those instead of accepting (all) the Western Balkans as EU members. Even though the current Commission has tried to revive the membership story, and to give some hope to the Western Balkans by setting some scenarios for accession, with the unresolved political issues in the region, it has become more and more clear that Montenegro is the only country that has a chance to join in the next five years.

At the same time, since the Energy Community has already established itself on the global energy scene, it should continue to be promoted as a framework for energy relationships with the EU neighbours. Moreover, even though full members could and should be only countries that can and are willing to apply the EU rules in full, it should be open for cooperation and accession to members with larger exemptions and with further Treaty changes, by the creation of a differentiated membership. At the same time, since the borders of energy trade, and even more energy flow, are not and could not be limited to the borders of the EU or the Energy Community, the Energy Union through the Energy Community should at least keep an eye on, and where appropriate establish relations with, other similar or different neighbouring communities. This should be a cooperation going beyond bilateral relations with countries such as Belarus, Armenia, Turkey or Switzerland. It could also aim at relating at different levels with associations such as the existing platforms for regional cooperation with European (Union for the Mediterranean) or without European (Eurasian Economic Union) influence. There can be only benefits in having similar if not (fully) harmonised rules, based on market principles, transparency and non-discrimination, governing the energy sectors beyond Energy Community's borders. The economic interests – if strong enough – might help to mitigate some political concerns, and such influence is expected to increase in the years of the second transition on which the EU and the Energy Community are embarking. The decarbonisation, the objective of having a climate-neutral economy, in which the energy sectors play an essential role, requires friends and even competitors who think alike and take over similar responsibilities. The EU could hardly aim at promoting its leadership in decarbonisation and climate neutrality without making use of the Energy Community, through which it could share the good experience already made.

PART III

The CJEU between the Individual Citizen and the Member States

16

Contestation and Accommodation: Constitutional and Private Law Pluralism(s) in the EU

BOŠKO TRIPKOVIĆ* AND JAN ZGLINSKI**

I. Introduction

This chapter aims to demonstrate that there are certain structural and theoretically significant similarities between constitutional and private law pluralism in EU law. While EU legal scholarship has been animated by the idea of constitutional pluralism for years, relatively little has been said about private law pluralism.[1] We think this is a mistake. The central claim of this chapter is that – if constitutional pluralism is understood in a wider sense – the difference between constitutional and private law pluralism is one of form and not of substance. Once this is done, the pluralist vocabulary perhaps loses some of its distinctiveness and allure as a conceptualisation that explains the specificities of European constitutional (dis)settlement; however, as we shall argue, what is gained is a more comprehensive analytic framework that is able to account for the multiplicity of interactions between European and Member State legal, political, and evaluative structures, and which is capable of integrating public and private law pluralisms into one coherent narrative.

This, of course, raises the question of what constitutional pluralism is, and what it means to understand it properly. One way of approaching this question would be to start from the leading accounts of constitutional pluralism and show how private law pluralism shares certain paradigmatic features with these conceptions. And this is, partly, what we shall do. But our account of constitutional pluralism, and pluralism more generally, is both wider and narrower than the existing conceptions. It is wider because we argue that the literature on constitutional pluralism

* Lecturer in Law, Birmingham Law School.
** Erich Brost Lecturer, Oxford Law Faculty and St Hilda's College.

[1] One notable exception is L Niglia (ed), *Pluralism and European Private Law* (Oxford, Hart, 2013). More recently, see also V Mak, 'Pluralism in European Private Law' (2018) 20 *Cambridge Yearbook of European Legal Studies* 202.

has often advanced a merely juridical conception of pluralism while neglecting its political aspects, and that it has predominantly focused on conflicts while not paying enough attention to cooperative processes that are present in both constitutional and private law. It is narrower because we, unlike many constitutional pluralists,[2] remain agnostic in this chapter as to whether a pluralist European legal space (public and private) is normatively more attractive than a theoretically (if not practically) possible unified legal framework.

We also aim to transcend the vocabulary of pluralism: we prefer, instead, to talk about the processes of *contestation* and *accommodation*. In our understanding, these processes are paradigmatic of the multitude of interactions in the European legal space, which are not necessarily constitutional or juridical in character. On the one hand, EU and Member States' institutions routinely contest each other's legally consequential propositions on the basis of the fundamental values of their polities: in the first part of the chapter, we aim to show that the competing claims of supreme constitutional authority by the Court of Justice of the EU (CJEU) and national courts are but one form in which this contestation occurs. On the other, there is a silent process of quotidian accommodation of these claims and disagreements that occurs behind the scenes of the grandiose legal and political conflicts. In the second part of the chapter, we aim to demonstrate that, despite the usual criticism of judicial institutions as being at the forefront of contestation, they – and in particular the CJEU – are responsible for much of this accommodation.

II. Contestation

A. Constitutional Contestation

The theory of constitutional pluralism has been developed to explain, and sometimes justify, the existence of multiple constitutional sites claiming ultimate legal-constitutional authority. Setting aside many important nuances, the state of the European constitutional situation (or predicament) can be explained by comparing the examples of such competing claims. As previously mentioned, we shall focus on the descriptive merits of constitutional pluralism.

The CJEU has, in *Internationale Handelsgesellschaft*, paradigmatically put forward its view of the constitutional order of Europe as follows:

> the law stemming from the Treaty, an independent source of law, cannot because of its very nature be overridden by rules of national law, however framed, without

[2] See M Poiares Maduro, 'Contrapunctual Law: Europe's Constitutional Pluralism in Action' in N Walker (ed), *Sovereignty in Transition* (Oxford, Hart, 2003) 502; N Krisch, *Beyond Constitutionalism – The Pluralist Structure of Postnational Law* (Oxford, Oxford University Press, 2010); K Jaklic, *Constitutional Pluralism in the EU* (Oxford, Oxford University Press, 2014).

> being deprived of its character as Community Law and without the legal basis of the community itself being called in question. Therefore, the validity of a Community measure or its effect within a Member State cannot be affected by allegations that it runs counter to either fundamental rights as formulated by the constitution of that state or the principles of a national constitutional structure.[3]

From the perspective of the CJEU, there can be nothing in domestic constitutional structures that would legally undermine the supremacy of EU law. This proposition has been met with a competing claim of ultimate legal authority by domestic constitutional courts. The German Constitutional Court's *Lisbon* judgment is a typical articulation of this attitude:

> The *ultra vires* review as well as the identity review may result in … Union law being declared inapplicable in Germany. … *ultra vires* review as well as the finding of a violation of constitutional identity is incumbent on the Federal Constitutional Court alone.[4]

The German Constitutional Court here denies the supremacy of EU law and retains its competence to ultimately decide on its compatibility with the domestic constitution. This is, in short, the crux of European constitutional conflict, or contestation, that pertains to (at least) two issues: first, depending on one's jurisprudential taste, the grounds that make the propositions of law true or the ultimate rule of recognition that determines the validity of legal acts in Europe;[5] and second, the authority that is competent to decide on this matter in the last instance.[6]

The theoretical innovation of constitutional pluralism lies primarily in the idea that there is no hierarchy between these competing claims and constitutional orders. As succinctly put by Neil Walker, '[t]he relationship between the orders … is now horizontal rather than vertical – heterarchical rather than hierarchical'.[7] The descriptive claim of constitutional pluralism is that there is no explanation or conceptualisation of such a constitutional situation that holds true from all these different constitutional perspectives and which would subsume them to a common constitutional standard or authority.[8] This claim rests on the assumption that there is a theoretical need to consider this issue from such a meta-perspective, in other words, it is not satisfactory to deny the existence of conflict by taking either the perspective of the CJEU or national constitutional courts as solely relevant.

[3] Case 11/70, *Internationale Handelsgesellschaft mbH v Einfuhr- und Vorratsstelle für Getreide und Futtermittel*, ECLI:EU:C:1970:114, para 3. This judgment consolidates and develops further the claims regarding the autonomy and supremacy of EU law made in Case 26/62, *Van Gend & Loos*, ECLI:EU:C:1963:1 and Case 6/64, *Costa/ENEL*, ECLI:EU:C:1964:66.

[4] BVerfGE 123, 267 – *Lisbon judgment*, para 241.

[5] N MacCormick, *Questioning Sovereignty – Law, State and Nation in the European Commonwealth* (Oxford, Oxford University Press, 1999).

[6] M Kumm, 'Who is the Final Arbiter of Constitutionality in Europe?: Three Conceptions of the Relationship Between the German Federal Constitutional Court and the European Court of Justice' (1999) 36 *Common Market Law Review* 351.

[7] N Walker, 'The Idea of Constitutional Pluralism' (2002) 65 *Modern Law Review* 317, 337.

[8] N Walker, 'Constitutional Pluralism Revisited' (2016) 22 *European Law Journal* 333, 333–34.

The weight, importance, and persistence of constitutional contestation in Europe is of such magnitude that we have good theoretical reasons to consider it a part of the same structure that stands in need of an integrated explanation, and that such explanation can neither arbitrarily opt for either of these conflicting perspectives, nor assume that the current situation is a transitional phase to a new constitutional settlement under a unified and uncontested authority or principle.[9] Put differently, constitutional pluralism claims certain comprehensiveness and situatedness for its explanation of European constitutional conflict: on the one hand, it is impossible to ignore the gravity of contestation and we need a theoretical understanding of the situation that would include all the implicated perspectives, and on the other, it is not credible to ignore the depth and endurance of this situation in the hope of a more familiar form of settlement that might come.

In light of these claims to comprehensiveness and situatedness, we find the predominantly juridical focus of constitutional pluralists peculiar. Granted, such legal contestation is real and has important doctrinal and theoretical consequences. And, at least in the domain of constitutional law, this phenomenon did arise in the context of the adjudicative processes and the judicial constitutionalisation of the European public space.[10] But we wish to suggest that there are weighty theoretical reasons – pertaining to the very same virtues of comprehensiveness and situatedness – to understand the European constitutional structure in the wider context of the political, social, and cultural contestation of which the judicial conflict forms only a part.[11] In our view, what is known as constitutional pluralism is not only a legal conundrum but a manifestation of the deeper political and social reality of European integration.

The claims of ultimate constitutional authority do not come from courts only. There are other constitutional forces that raise parallel claims, and their contestations have proven to be even more challenging. Let us use two well-known examples to illustrate this point. First, the rejections of the Constitutional Treaty (CT) in the referenda in France and the Netherlands in 2005 can be explained as fundamental contestations of further constitutionalisation of the European political and legal space. While the reasons for the rejections were complex, they signalled that the electorates in these two founding Member States still considered their own national constitutional frameworks to be the primary locus of constituent power formation, in much the same way as some of the highest domestic courts had considered their national constitutional documents to be expressions of such power and, thus, supreme.[12] As one of the consequences of these rejections,

[9] ibid, 337–47.

[10] See JHH Weiler, 'The Tranformation of Europe' (1991) 100 *Yale Law Journal* 2403.

[11] M Goldoni and MA Wilkinson, 'The Material Constitution' (2018) 81 *Modern Law Review* 567.

[12] See, for example, apart from already mentioned *Lisbon judgment* (above n 4) of the German Constitutional Court, similar claims made by the Italian Constitutional Court in *Frontini v Ministero delle Finanze* (1974) 2 *Common Market Law Review* 372, at 384 (couched in the language of sovereignty), and the French Conseil d'Etat in *Sarran and Levacher*, 30 October 1998 (couched more explicitly in the language of constituent power).

the provision on the supremacy of EU law in Article I(6) of the CT has been replaced by Declaration 17 concerning primacy in the Lisbon Treaty. In contrast to the CT, which was supposed to establish the principle of supremacy directly, as an independent constitutional principle, the declaration explicitly underlined the existing case law of the CJEU as the main parameter of supremacy. It is, of course, clear that such clarification need not – and, as the case law post-2009 shows, did not – have immediate legal consequences on the way supremacy operates in EU law, but it is also possible that the consequences of establishing supremacy in the CT would have changed the legal landscape in this regard by providing a clearer and stronger legal basis for the supremacy claims of the CJEU. What the example does show is that other, non-judicial forces participate and significantly affect the conversation about some of the constitutional issues that are among the principal questions of the judicial dialogue in the constitutional pluralist narrative.

Second, one of the motivating ideas behind the decision of the UK to leave the EU has been a sense of 'taking back control' of constitutional fundamentals in this Member State. While we do not suggest that the process of Brexit is unidimensional and can be traced back to a single motive,[13] the notion of taking back control certainly indicated that the electorate wished to retain the ability to decide on essential political questions against the perceived threat of interference from the EU level. The CJEU, as seen by leading Brexiters, was at the forefront of this threat.[14] This sentiment has been reflected in the UK government position throughout the negotiations on the withdrawal from the EU. The opening statement of the government's position paper on 'Enforcement and Dispute Resolution', to name but one example, stated: '[i]n leaving the European Union, we will bring about an end to the direct jurisdiction of the Court of Justice of the European Union (CJEU)'.[15] Again, as was the case with the rejection of the CT, we see different constitutional actors challenging the supremacy of EU law and the claim of ultimate authority of the CJEU.

To sum up, the theory of constitutional pluralism, although important and revealing in its descriptive version, ultimately neglects the non-judicial forms of constitutional contestation in Europe. Moreover, such contestation pertains to the

[13] See more in MJ Goodwin and O Heath, 'The 2016 Referendum, Brexit and the Left Behind: An Aggregate-level Analysis of the Result' (2016) 87 *The Political Quarterly* 323 and HD Clarke et al, 'Why Britain Voted for Brexit: An Individual-Level Analysis of the 2016 Referendum Vote' (2017) 70 *Parliamentary Affairs* 439.

[14] The Leave camp would frequently call the CJEU 'rogue'; see eg the 'framework for taking back control and establishing a new UK-EU deal after 23 June', available at www.voteleavetakecontrol.org/a_framework_for_ taking_back_control_and_establishing_a_new_uk_eu_deal_after_23_june.html, last accessed 27 March 2019. In his column in the *Telegraph*, Boris Johnson wrote, just before the Brexit referendum, that 'the UK will 'extricate itself' from 'the vast and growing corpus of law enacted [sic!] by a European Court of Justice from which there can be no appeal'.

[15] HM Government, 'Enforcement and Dispute Resolution: A Future Partnership Paper', available at assets.publishing.service.gov.uk/government/uploads/system/uploads/attachment_data/file/639609/Enforcement_and_dispute_resolution.pdf.

question that has been the focus of constitutional pluralist attention: competing claims of ultimate constitutional authority. If understood more broadly, European juridical-constitutional pluralism is only one form in which such contestation occurs, and is perhaps the tip of the iceberg of a more fundamental constitutional conflict that took the most radical shape in the Brexit referendum and the processes that have ensued.

B. Private Law Contestation

If we accept that these developments in the domain of constitutional law are part and parcel of the same pluralist dynamics, then it is possible to understand some of the developments in European private law through the pluralist lens. In that sense, it is first important to dispel the myth that EU law has had a much more significant impact on constitutional law than on private law in the Member States. As forcefully argued by H-W Micklitz, at least since the mid-1980s, a new regime of European regulatory private law has been steadily emerging, and the EU has been using law 'to open up and shape markets'.[16] The new private law as developed by the EU does not fit into the traditional conception of domestic private (contract and tort) law which is based on private autonomy and freedom of contract, and the grand codification projects of the nineteenth century. Instead, it is a form of economic law based on the logic of completing the internal market.[17] Its nature is regulatory and policy-oriented, while at the same time, almost of necessity, affecting the traditional rights-and-entitlements based private law in the Member States. Because of the lack of competences of the EU in the domain of private law, this new economic law was developed primarily through harmonisation and Article 114 TFEU.[18] The CJEU has also played a role in scrutinising national legislation that interfered with the processes of deregulation and removing barriers to trade based on the four freedoms (goods, persons, services, and capital).[19] The key notion that permeates all harmonisation attempts in the domain of private law is the policy goal of preventing market failure, which, in turn, often affects the domestic private law which might be

[16] H-W Micklitz, 'Monistic Ideology versus Pluralistic Reality: Towards a Normative Design for European Private Law' in Niglia (above n 1) 32. See also H-W Micklitz, 'European Private Law' in D Patterson and A Södersten (eds), *A Companion to European Union Law and International Law* (Chichester, Wiley-Blackwell, 2016).

[17] Micklitz, 'Monistic Ideology versus Pluralistic Reality' (above n 16) 40.

[18] As helpfully identified by Micklitz, the regulation and enforcement strategies of the EU take the form of development of sectoral rules and principles (horizontal and vertical), and the development of the 'general principles of civil law' by the CJEU; ibid, 45. On general principles of EU civil law, see N Reich, *General Principles of EU Civil Law* (Cambridge, Intersentia, 2013).

[19] H Collins, *The European Civil Code: The Way Forward* (Cambridge, Cambridge University Press, 2008) chs 1–3.

based on a different set of values, such as fairness or social justice.[20] It has thus been suggested that European private law has undergone a process of 'creeping' codification[21] and that – if it is understood in this wider sense, as economic-regulatory law – the EU's interference in the private law of the Member States has been of similar scope and magnitude as its interference in national constitutional law. And so has been the contestation of these processes in the Member States.

The case in point are the multifaceted and much debated attempts to develop a common European Civil Code. After longstanding lobbying from academics, politicians, and businesses, the EU Commission decided to launch an initiative for a unified European contract law in the early 2000s.[22] This initiative was intended to pave, in the long run, the way for a European Civil Code. The timing seemed consequential. Europe was preparing to adopt the CT, its first big 'c' constitution, which was meant to capture and symbolise the important evolution the European project had undergone since the Treaties of Paris and Rome. The adoption of a common contract law seemed a natural, even indispensable, element of this process, instrumental to establishing a meaningful political and social community in Europe based on shared conceptions of fairness and justice.[23] What followed was over a decade of intense political and scholarly debate.[24] Arguments were exchanged as to whether a common contract law was necessary or not, but also as to what such a contract law should look like. Yet, just as the CT never received approval, so the project of a common contract law was, after almost a decade-and-a-half, eventually abandoned.

The events and debates that took place during the (thus far) last phase of the private-law unification project are instructive. In 2011, the Commission proposed a Regulation on a Common European Sales Law (CESL). The draft Regulation aimed to create a sales law system that would exist simultaneously with the Member States' contract law, and would be optional in terms of its applicability to a specific contractual relationship.[25] The Parliament further proposed a limitation of the scope of the proposal to distant business-to-consumer contracts. Notwithstanding its narrow(er) scope, parliaments of seven Member States objected to CESL, it has

[20] ibid, 115–17.

[21] KP Berger, 'The Principles of European Contract Law and the Concept of the "Creeping Codification" of Law' (2001) 9 *European Review of Private Law* 21.

[22] Communication from the Commission to the Council and the European Parliament on European Contract Law, COM(2001) 398 final.

[23] This point is well captured in 'Social Justice in European Contract Law: A Manifesto' (2004) 10 *European Law Journal* 653 at 656: 'A common system of European contract law signifies an aspiration towards a shared European identity. It marks a commitment to an ever-closer union of peoples, of cultures, and of values'.

[24] From the academic side, two groups were the driving forces in this process: the so-called *Acquis* Group and the Study Group.

[25] Proposal for a Regulation on a Common European Sales Law COM/2011/0635 final.

never attained support in the Council, and the Commission has effectively, if not formally, withdrawn the proposal.[26]

The key objection to the proposal by the Member States was the lack of competence, as it would have been adopted under Article 114 TFEU without actually harmonising the law: it was meant to be optional and exist in parallel with national rules. While this formal argument has been at the surface of the criticisms voiced against the initiative, there are much deeper reasons that motivated it.[27] The first question was whether CESL was necessary to address the issue of different private law regimes potentially hindering cross-border trade. In the view of the Member States, the solution to this problem could be found in the domain of domestic private law structures coupled with international private law mechanisms devised at the EU level. This, of course, neglects the structures of European regulatory private law which have already taken up a significant legal space which is beyond the control of domestic institutions.[28] The argument is thus to be understood as a political plea for the preservation of national understanding of private law, which is supposed to be based on a different set of guiding principles and policy considerations. It concerns the justification of a new private legal order that would subvert the existing understandings of private law to the dynamics which put the internal market in the driving seat. As is the case in constitutional law contestation, the objections to CESL are in fact attempts to protect the core of values that underpin the Member States' private law and that are constitutive of the identities of their societies.

Part of the reason for this is, of course, historical. The codification of private law was, in countries such as France, Germany, and Italy, an enterprise of immense legal and political importance.[29] Although we have come to use the notion 'crowning glory', ascribed to the grand codifications back then, with a pinch of irony, the sentiment continues to exist in a weaker form. European states cherish their private law.[30] This has to with its content. Private law contains a great number of delicate value judgements. It captures, more than other segments of the legal order, the *Weltanschauung* of a polity. Private law rules determine when a person begins to exist, whom we can marry, under which circumstances we can fire or evict someone, and what happens with our belongings after we die. In doing so,

[26] EU Commission, Work Programme for 2015: A New Start, COM (2014) 910 final. Parts of the contract law harmonisation endeavour may, however, survive. A slimmed down version is pursued in the area of digital services; see Communication from the Commission to the European Parliament, to the Council, the European Economic and Social Committee and the Committee of Regions, 'A Digital Single Market Strategy for Europe', COM(2015) 192 final.

[27] As reported by Micklitz, the some of these reasons were couched in the languages of subsidiarity and proportionality: Micklitz, 'Monistic Ideology versus Pluralistic Reality' (above n 16) 43–44.

[28] ibid, 44.

[29] The same goes for the more recent civil codes adopted by several post-communist states.

[30] For a (critical) analysis of the French perspective on this point, see R Michaels, 'Code vs Code: Nationalist and Internationalist Images of the Code Civil in the French Resistance to a European Codification' (2012) 8 *European Review of Contract Law* 277.

it encapsulates a wide range of socio-cultural beliefs. In this non-mystical sense, authors like Savigny were therefore certainly right to emphasise the link between the spirit of a polity and its private law, and the differences among nations that are likely to arise from this. Thus, the European Civil Code was seen as an important element of building a community of value in the EU, and – at the same time – it was perceived as a significant threat to the values of national communities. While the pluralism debate primarily focused on the notion of constitutional identity that denotes the core evaluative commitments of domestic political communities,[31] we believe that there is a parallel notion of community's private law identity that causes similar contestations.

The judicial and political contestation of the supremacy of EU law that occurred in the constitutional law domain has its counterpart in European private law. On the one hand, the attempts to adopt the CT and the European Civil Code are in many ways analogous. Both have started as ambitious political projects of unification but have neglected the underlying social reality of domestically developed values that constitute and are constituted by the laws of the Member States. On the other, the resistance to supremacy in constitutional law and harmonisation in private law are, on this understanding, part of the same process regardless of the different institutional form they may take. If we look at the issue of pluralism through this wider lens, we are able to see that the process of contestation is not the exclusive domain of courts or constitutional law.

III. Accommodation

The second point we want to make is that, underneath these loud battles, there have been quiet acts of cooperation between the European and national legal orders. While in the first part we argued that contestation is not exclusively a juridical phenomenon, in this part we wish to turn our attention to courts and different forms of judicial accommodation. In particular, we will examine the case law of the CJEU, which, as far as the usual pluralist narrative goes, has been at the forefront of the processes of contestation. We aim to demonstrate that – despite the uncompromising position announced in rulings such as *Internationale Handelsgesellschaft* – the CJEU has, in reality, shown itself to be willing to accommodate certain practices and values adopted at the Member State level. We will illustrate this phenomenon with the aid of examples from the case law: for the constitutional realm, our evidence will comprise judgments on the four freedoms, EU citizenship and fundamental rights; for the private law realm, it will focus on jurisprudence from two core areas of European private law – consumer and anti-discrimination law (as applied to horizontal relationships).

[31] For the notion of constitutional identity, see B Tripkovic, *The Metaethics of Constitutional Adjudication* (Oxford, Oxford University Press, 2017) chs 2 and 6.

A. Constitutional Accommodation: Free Movement Law, EU Citizenship, and Fundamental Rights

As already explained, EU law has had a considerable impact on the constitutional orders of the Member States, affecting provisions relating to both constitutional process[32] and substance.[33] But this dynamic has, on occasion, also played out in the opposite direction, with national constitutional rules putting pressure on those of the EU. In these scenarios, the CJEU has usually been perceived as a deaf interlocutor, putting European constitutional concerns over national ones.[34] Recent years, however, have brought to light a number of cases that reveal a different approach on the part of the Court, one which is more respectful of domestic constitutional choices.

The *Omega* judgment is one example.[35] The city of Bonn prohibited the operation of a laser tag facility as local authorities took the view that the commercial exploitation of games involving 'playing at killing' violated human dignity, a fundamental right enshrined in Article 1(1) of the German Basic Law. The applicant, who had signed a franchise contract with a British company, alleged a breach of the freedom to provide services. Given that there was a clear restriction on Article 56 TFEU, the dispute all boiled down to the question whether the German authorities could invoke human dignity as a public policy ground to justify the ban. Legally, this was a true 'clash of the titans': a 'fundamental freedom'[36] of EU law collided with a foundational value of a national constitution.

The CJEU resolved this problem in an accommodating way. Drawing inspiration from the 'constitutional traditions common to the Member States' – a not all that obvious claim in light of the principle's peculiar status (justiciable right) and understanding in the *Grundgesetz* (influenced by the experience of national socialism) – it recognised human dignity as a general principle of *European* law,[37] only to announce that German authorities were at liberty to rely on their *local* conception of it. As free movement law allowed for different national systems and levels of protection, it was not necessary for a domestic measure 'to correspond to a conception shared by all Member States as regards the precise way in which the fundamental right or legitimate interest in question is to be protected'.[38] Thus, while Europeanising human dignity, the Court handed down the power to define

[32] Eg by demanding that lower courts declare inapplicable legislation breaching European law, even in systems of centralised constitutional review; see Case 106/77, *Simmenthal*, ECLI:EU:C:1978:49.

[33] Eg by shielding EU action from the need to comply with national fundamental rights; see *Internationale Handelsgesellschaft* (above n 3).

[34] See, most recently, Case C-399/11, *Melloni*, ECLI:EU:C:2013:107 (which is discussed in Section IV) and Case C-441/14, *Dansk Industri ('Ajos')*, ECLI:EU:C:2016:278.

[35] Case C-36/02, *Omega*, ECLI:EU:C:2004:614.

[36] Case C-112/00, *Schmidberger*, ECLI:EU:C:2003:333, para 59.

[37] *Omega*, above n 35, paras 33–34.

[38] ibid, para 37.

its contours to national authorities.[39] Ultimately, the prohibition was held to be justified.

A similar approach was pursued, in the context of EU citizenship, in *Sayn-Wittgenstein*, a case on the prohibition of using nobility titles in Austria.[40] The applicant, an Austrian luxury real estate agent, was adopted by a German 'prince' and, in line with German law, changed her name to 'princess von Sayn-Wittgenstein'. Although Germany, just like Austria, had abolished nobility upon becoming a republic in the wake of World War I, it adopted a laxer approach in relation to designations of nobility, which could be carried as part of a person's surname. The Austrian authorities first registered the new (German) name in the register of civil status but, some years later, corrected the entry to say 'Sayn-Wittgenstein' only.

The CJEU held that the discrepancy between the applicant's German and Austrian surnames was likely to cause a serious inconvenience for her. Therefore, the Austrian rules constituted an interference with the free movement of EU citizens (Art. 21(1) TFEU).[41] Submitting that the abolition of nobility had constitutional status nationally and served to implement the principle of equality, the Austrian government argued the legislation was justified on grounds of public policy. In this regard, the Court stressed that:

> [I]t must be accepted that, in the context of Austrian constitutional history, the Law on the abolition of the nobility, as an element of national identity, may be taken into consideration when a balance is struck between legitimate interests and the right of free movement of persons recognised under European Union law.[42]

Although derogation clauses had, in principle, to be interpreted narrowly, the circumstances justifying recourse to the concept of public policy could 'vary from one Member State to another and from one era to another': in the view of the CJEU, this warranted a 'margin of discretion' for the national authorities, especially when the national and constitutional identity was at stake.[43] Member States were free to choose between a republican form of government and a monarchy, between accepting and abolishing nobility, even if this, in cases like the applicant's, meant restricting EU constitutional rules.

The *Taricco* saga is another example of constitutional accommodation.[44] The litigation dealt with limitation periods in Italian criminal law and the principle of legality from Article 49(1) CFEU. Pursuant to Article 325(2) TFEU, Member States have the duty to take effective measures to counter fraud affecting the

[39] This deferential form of judicial review has become a frequent occurrence in the case-law on free movement rights; see J Zglinski, 'The Rise of Deference: The Margin of Appreciation and Decentralized Judicial Review in EU Free Movement Law' (2018) 55 *Common Market Law Review* 1341.

[40] Case C-208/09, *Sayn-Wittgenstein*, ECLI:EU:C:2010:806.

[41] ibid, paras 66–67.

[42] ibid, para 83.

[43] ibid, paras 87 and 92.

[44] Case C-105/14, *Taricco*, ECLI:EU:C:2015:555; Case C-42/17, *MAS ('Taricco II')*, ECLI:EU:C:2017:936.

financial interests of the Union. However, due to its short limitation periods, Italian criminal law often made it practically impossible to prosecute offences relating to VAT (which contributes to the EU's budget). When this state of affairs was brought to the attention of the CJEU in *Taricco I*, the Court ruled that domestic rules which prevented 'the imposition of effective and dissuasive penalties in a significant number of cases of serious fraud affecting the financial interests of the European Union' were incompatible with EU law.[45] For Italy, this constituted a serious problem: unlike many other supreme and constitutional courts (including the European Court of Human Rights), the *Corte Costituzionale* views limitation periods as a substantive element of the principle of legality. Consequently, if a limitation period is prolonged after the offence was committed, the defendant can claim a violation of the principle of *nulla poena sine lege*.

After *Taricco I* was rendered, 'all hell broke loose in Italy'.[46] Numerous courts found, based on the CJEU's ruling, that the domestic rules on limitation periods were inapplicable to cases concerning VAT fraud; countless criminal investigations were re-opened. This triggered proceedings before the Italian Constitutional Court, which decided to refer the matter to the CJEU once again. The Constitutional Court's order has been described as resorting to a 'carrot and stick' approach:[47] on the one hand, the *Corte* tried to persuade the CJEU to allow Italy to retain the substantive reading of the principle of legality in EU cases; on the other, it made clear that it would – should the CJEU decide otherwise – resort to its *controlimiti* doctrine[48] and refuse to apply EU law as an element of national constitutional identity was at stake.

In the *Taricco II* judgment, the CJEU repeated the principle from *Åkerberg Fransson* and *Melloni* whereby:

> national authorities and courts remain free to apply national standards of protection of fundamental rights, provided that the level of protection provided for by the Charter, as interpreted by the Court, and the primacy, unity and effectiveness of EU law are not thereby compromised.[49]

Yet, in contrast to *Taricco I*, the Court of Justice found that Italy could hold onto its domestic standard of protection, even though it was higher than that laid down in Article 49(1) CFEU. The national limitation periods were incompatible with Article 325(2) TFEU, but this was a problem that had to be resolved by the Italian legislature, ie for future cases. In the meantime, Italian courts were allowed to apply a substantive reading of the principle of legality, despite its adverse effects on EU law and the Union's financial interests.

[45] *Taricco* (above n 44).

[46] D Sarmiento, 'To Bow at the Rhythm of an Italian Tune', available at despiteourdifferencesblog.wordpress.com/2017/12/05/to-bow-at-the-rhythm-of-an-italian-tune/, accessed 27 March 2019.

[47] D Paris, 'Carrot and Stick. The Italian Constitutional Court's Preliminary Reference in the Case Taricco' (2017) 37 *Questions of International Law* 5.

[48] *Frontini* (above n 12).

[49] *Taricco II* (above n 44) para 47; Cases C-617/10, *Åkerberg Fransson*, ECLI:EU:C:2013:105, para 29, and *Melloni* (above n 34) para 60.

There are many things to be said about the *Taricco* saga. In terms of process, it was a forceful illustration of how cooperation between European and national courts can work if both sides are willing to listen.[50] In terms of substance, the CJEU let a Member State apply its own – more protective – fundamental rights standard in cases concerning EU law. Whether we see this as an exception to the supremacy of EU law (and the longstanding rule that national constitutional concerns cannot be invoked as grounds for deviating from European law[51]) or just as a recognition that Member States retain the competence to apply higher standards of fundamental rights protection in areas that have not or not fully been harmonised (such as criminal procedure),[52] *Taricco II* showed that the CJEU will sometimes accommodate national constitutional concerns, even when the concession is significant from the perspective of EU constitutional law.

B. Private Law Accommodation I: Consumer Law

Consumer law is the heartland of European private law: it was the consumer protection instruments adopted in the 1980s that truly gave birth to EU private law as a discrete domain.[53] One of the (slightly later) pieces of legislation is Directive 93/13/EEC on unfair terms.[54] It lays down requirements for standard terms in business-to-consumer transactions. The Directive's centrepiece is Article 3(1), which prohibits 'unfair' terms – defined to be clauses that, contrary to good faith, cause a significant imbalance in the parties' rights and obligations to the detriment of the consumer. It is complemented by an annex, which provides an indicative, ie non-binding, and non-exhaustive list of potentially problematic terms.

Disputes on Directive 93/13/EEC often revolve, at a level of substantive law, around the same question: is a particular clause unfair?[55] When the Directive

[50] See Sarmiento (above n 46).

[51] See Section II.A and the passage cited from *Internationale Handelsgesellschaft* (above n 3).

[52] C Rauchegger, 'National Constitutional Rights and the Primacy of EU law: M.A.S. (Case Note)' (2018) 55 *Common Market Law Review* 1521.

[53] Council Directive 85/374/EEC of 25 July 1985 on the approximation of the laws, regulations and administrative provisions of the Member States concerning liability for defective products [1985] OJ L210/29 (Product Liability Directive); Council Directive 85/577/EEC of 20 December 1985 to protect the consumer in respect of contracts negotiated away from business premises [1985] OJ L372/31 (Doorstep Selling Directive); Council Directive 87/102/EEC of 22 December 1986 for the approximation of the laws, regulations and administrative provisions of the Member States concerning consumer credit [1986] OJ L42/48 (Consumer Credit Directive); and, a little later, Council Directive 90/314/EEC of 13 June 1990 on package travel, package holidays and package tours [1990] OJ L158/59 (Package Holidays Directive).

[54] Council Directive 93/13/EEC of 5 April 1993 on unfair terms in consumer contracts [1993] OJ L95/29.

[55] There is another, numerically important strand of the case law which turns on procedural issues, notably on whether national judges can review the unfairness of a contractual term *ex officio*: see Cases C-240/98 to C-244/98, *Océano Grupo*, ECLI:EU:C:2000:346; Case C-473/00, *Cofidis*, ECLI:EU:C:2002:705; Case C-168/05, *Mostaza Claro*, ECLI:EU:C:2006:675; Case C-243/08, *Pannon*, ECLI:EU:C:2009:350; Case C-40/08, *Asturcom Telecomunicaciones*, ECLI:EU:C:2009:615; Case C-137/08, *VB Pénzügyi Lízing*, ECLI:EU:C:2010:659.

was adopted, serious clashes with national private laws on this issue seemed inevitable. Several Member States had control mechanisms for standard terms already in place, some of them for decades. Also, there was a divide between systems relying on 'good faith' (eg German law) and on the 'significant imbalance' between the contractual parties (eg English law) as a doctrinal yardstick.[56] As unfairness turned into a concept of EU law, it was expected that the CJEU would determine which of the clauses brought before it were (in)valid.

Yet, the Court, in *Freiburger Kommunalbauten*, one of the first preliminary references on the Directive, made a consequential choice.[57] First, it stated that, when assessing unfairness, the context of a standard term, notably the surrounding national law, needed to be given consideration. Second, it announced that it was for the national courts to decide whether a contractual term was unfair; the CJEU would limit itself to only 'interpreting [the] general criteria' used in the Directive. The Court's approach is, in a later judgment, usefully summarised as follows:

> As to the question whether a particular term in a contract is, or is not, unfair, Article 4 of Directive 93/13 provides that the answer should be reached taking into account the nature of the goods or services for which the contract was concluded and by referring, at the time of conclusion of the contract, to all the circumstances attending the conclusion of the contract. It should be pointed out in that respect that the consequences of the term under the law applicable to the contract must also be taken into account. *This requires that consideration be given to the national law.*
>
> It follows that, in the context of its jurisdiction under Article 267 TFEU to interpret European Union law, the Court may interpret general criteria used by the European Union legislature in order to define the concept of unfair terms. However, it should not rule on the application of these general criteria to a particular term, which must be considered in the light of the particular circumstances of the case in question, and so *it is for the national court to decide whether a contractual term* [...] *is to be regarded as unfair* in the light of all the circumstances attending the conclusion of the contract.[58]

The approach set out in *Freiburger Kommunalbauten* has been the basis for most of the CJEU's jurisprudence on the Unfair Terms Directive, and it remains (despite some subsequent, more activist rulings[59]) good law. Its effects are two-fold. Institutionally, it puts national courts in the driving seat when it comes to determining unfairness. National judges end up deciding – to an important extent, autonomously – whether certain contractual clauses are legal. Substantively, it makes national law a crucial factor in the examination of the unfairness of a term.

[56] H-W Micklitz and N Reich, 'The Court and Sleeping Beauty: The Revival of the Unfair Contract Terms Directive (UCTD)' (2014) 51 *Common Market Law Review* 771, 773.

[57] It should be mentioned that *Freiburger Kommunalbauten* departed from the more centralised review approach the CJEU had opted for in its first preliminary reference on the Unfair Terms Directive in *Océano Grupo* (above n 55).

[58] Case C-76/10, *Pohotovosť*, ECLI:EU:C:2010:685, paras 59–60.

[59] See, for instance, the case law on exclusive territorial jurisdiction clauses: *Océano Grupo*, *Pannon* and *VB Pénzügyi Lízing* (all above n 55).

In the balancing assessment that is required for identifying breaches of 'good faith' and the existence of a 'significant imbalance' between the contractual parties (see Article 3(1)), domestic private law becomes an important element in the calculus. Unfairness, thus, turns into what one could call a *semi-autonomous concept*: although laid down in EU legislation in general terms, it is concretised by national courts and infused with values and practices from national private law.

The *Pohotovosť* case illustrates this.[60] The disabled defendant, who lived on an invalidity pension of €370 per month, borrowed €664 from Pohotovosť, a Slovak credit company. When she became unable to pay the monthly instalments (in part due to the exorbitant annual percentage rate of over 95%), Pohotovosť filed an action before a local arbitration court. On the basis of the award that was delivered, the company applied for an enforcement order to recover a sum of €3,467. The final sum was, partly, so high because the annual penalty rate had been set at 91.25% in the credit agreement. One of the questions that arose in *Photovosť* was whether this was excessive.[61]

In its judgment, the Court of Justice began by explaining that Directive 93/13/EEC established a general prohibition of unfair contract terms and that point (1)(e) of the (indicative) annex even explicitly classified penalty clauses requiring consumers to pay a 'disproportionality high sum' as potentially invalid. Yet, when it came to the actual proportionality of the rate, the Court reiterated the principles from *Freiburger Kommunalbauten*: this issue was for the national court to decide and required a consideration of national private law.[62] That Slovakian rules prohibited penalties exceeding 9% mattered in this respect. And so did the referring court's initial assessment which found the rate set by Photovosť to be excessive.

Aziz is a further example.[63] The case turned on the validity of certain contractual terms used in a mortgage loan agreement, a politically sensitive topic in the aftermath of the 2008 financial crisis. Among the clauses challenged by the applicant was a default interest clause whereby the consumer, in the case of default, was automatically obliged to pay an annual default interest of 18.75%, without the need for any notice. Again, the unfairness potentially resulted from point (1)(e) of the Directive's annex and, again, the CJEU deferred to the referring court, which was instructed to assess:

> first, the rules of national law which would apply to the relationship between the parties, in the event of no agreement having been reached in the contract in question or in other consumer contracts of that type and, second, the rate of default interest laid down, compared with the statutory interest rate, in order to determine whether it is appropriate

[60] ibid.

[61] The other question of substantive law was whether the fact that the (extremely high) annual percentage rate had not been mentioned in the credit agreement constituted a violation of Art 1(2) of the Unfair Terms Directive.

[62] *Photovost* (above n 55) paras 59–60.

[63] Case C-415/11, *Aziz*, ECLI:EU:C:2013:164.

> for securing the attainment of the objectives pursued by it in the Member State concerned and does not go beyond what is necessary to achieve them.[64]

The validity of the clause, thus, depended on what was common under national law as well as on its proportionality, which was to be determined with reference to the statutory interest rate by the referring judge. In her opinion in *Aziz*, Advocate General Kokott explained that it was 'not the spirit and purpose of Directive 93/13 to level out differences between national legal cultures'.[65] Member States could decide how much was too much regarding default interest.[66]

The foregoing is not mean to suggest that the Unfair Terms Directive has remained ineffective or that is has, in substance, been fully 'nationalised'. The CJEU has been an active interlocutor in the conversation on standard terms[67] and, on occasion, has pushed Member States towards adopting higher levels of consumer protection. Especially in *Aziz* (and the avalanche of case law that followed the Court's ruling), the Directive functioned as an important 'legal irritant'[68] – one might even say disruptor – for Spanish private law. Yet, the Court of Justice, by adopting the approach from *Freiburger Kommunalbauten*, has interacted with national courts and legal orders in a manner which is respectful of national traditions and contexts.

C. Private Law Accommodation II: Anti-Discrimination Law

Although the EU has been active in the area of equality and anti-discrimination law from fairly early on,[69] there has been a proliferation of European anti-discrimination legislation since the 2000s as a result of the introduction of a Union competence in this domain in the Treaty of Amsterdam (Article 19 TFEU).[70]

[64] ibid, para 74.

[65] Case C-415/11, *Aziz*, Opinion of AG Kokott, ECLI:EU:C:2012:700, para 86.

[66] The CJEU's review of the other two terms challenged in *Aziz* followed the same basic approach; see *Aziz* (above n 63) para 73 ff.

[67] See Micklitz and Reich (above n 56); O Gerstenberg, 'Constitutional Reasoning in Private Law: The Role of the CJEU in Adjudicating Unfair Terms in Consumer Contracts' (2015) 21 *European Law Journal* 599.

[68] An idea going back to G Teubner, 'Legal Irritants: Good Faith in British Law or How Unifying Law Ends Up in New Divergencies' (1998) *Modern Law Review* 1.

[69] Council Directive 75/117/EEC of 10 February 1975 on the approximation of the laws of the Member States relating to the application of the principle of equal pay for men and women [1975] OJ L45/19 and Council Directive 76/207/EEC of 9 February 1976 on the implementation of the principle of equal treatment for men and women as regards access to employment, vocational training and promotion, and working conditions [1976] OJ L39/40.

[70] Council Directive 2000/43/EC of 29 June 2000 implementing the principle of equal treatment between persons irrespective of racial or ethnic origin [2000] OJ L180/22; Council Directive 2004/113/EC of 13 December 2004 implementing the principle of equal treatment between men and women in the access to and supply of goods and services [2004] OJ L373/37; Directive 2006/54/EC of the European Parliament and of the Council of 5 July 2006 on the implementation of the principle of equal opportunities and equal treatment of men and women in matters of employment and occupation (recast) [2006] OJ L204/23.

Among the various EU measures adopted, Directive 2000/78/EC establishing a general framework for equal treatment in employment and occupation (the so-called 'Equality Framework Directive') has shown to be a particularly significant instrument.[71] Binding both employers in the public and private sector, it prohibits discrimination on grounds of religion or belief, disability, age and sexual orientation. The application of the Directive has triggered sensitive conflicts with national laws and practices.[72] Let us take a look at the way the CJEU has recently resolved one such conflict.

In *Egenberger*, the Court of Justice was asked to rule on the case of a German journalist who, although non-religious, applied for a fixed-term employment with the Protestant Church.[73] The post-holder was meant to work on a report on the elimination of racial discrimination; being of Protestant denomination was listed as an essential prerequisite. When Ms Egenberger did not get the job – a Protestant candidate was chosen instead – she claimed that she had been discriminated on religious grounds. The crux of the dispute was whether the Church could demand that its employees, even for jobs without a strictly religious focus, needed to be Protestant. German law had, for decades, embraced an extremely deferential approach towards churches and church-run organisations. Pursuant to a constitutional rule dating back to the Weimar Constitution, religious organisations had the right to arrange and administer their affairs autonomously (the so-called 'privilege of self-determination' or 'church privilege').[74] As a consequence, courts limited their control of church activities, including those in the employment sector, to a (very lenient) review of 'plausibility'.[75]

The applicant contested this practice based on Directive 2000/78/EC and the principle of non-discrimination on grounds of religion.[76] Although prohibiting discriminatory behaviour, the Directive contains several derogation clauses by means of which differences in treatment can exceptionally be justified. One of them is Article 4(2), whereby Member States may, in relation to employment in churches and other religious organisations, allow unequal treatment where,

[71] Council Directive 2000/78/EC of 27 November 2000 establishing a general framework for equal treatment in employment and occupation [2000] OJ L303/16.

[72] Among the more memorable ones are: Case C-144/04, *Mangold*, ECLI:EU:C:2005:709; Case C-555/07, *Kücükdeveci*, ECLI:EU:C:2010:21; Case C-341/08, *Petersen*, ECLI:EU:C:2010:4; *Dansk Industri ('Ajos')* (above n 34) (all on age); Case C-147/08, *Römer*, ECLI:EU:C:2011:286 (sexual orientation); Case C-157/15, *Achbita*, ECLI:EU:C:2017:203; Case C-188/15, *Bougnaoui*, ECLI:EU:C:2017:204 (religion).

[73] Case C-414/16, *Egenberger*, ECLI:EU:C:2018:257.

[74] Art 137 of the Weimar Constitution, which continues to be applicable via Art 140 Basic Law.

[75] See BVerfGE 70, 138 – *Duty of Loyalty*; BVerfGE 57, 220 – *Bethel*. The German Federal Labour Court, who referred the case to the CJEU, had already on previous occasions expressed its dissatisfaction with the low level of protection employees of churches enjoyed as a result of the Constitutional Court's case law.

[76] For a thorough critique of the CJEU's use of the general (ie constitutional) principle of non-discrimination in *Egenberger*, see S Enchelmaier, 'The Magical Mystery of Words: "Direct Effect" and All That' (2019) *Yearbook of European Law* (forthcoming).

due to the nature or context of the activity, a person's religion constitutes a 'genuine, legitimate and justified occupational requirement, having regard to the organisation's ethos'. The central question of *Egenberger* was: how far did the scope of this derogation clause reach? Was the occupational requirement at stake – to be of Protestant denomination – 'genuine, legitimate and justified' in light of the employer's ethos?

The Court of Justice gave a nuanced answer. On the one hand, it found that the plausibility control applied in Germany was insufficient.[77] Article 4(2) was, as the Court emphasised, not only concerned with the autonomy of churches but equally aimed at protecting workers from being discriminated against on grounds of religion. Therefore, even the activities of religious organisations had to be subjected be 'effective judicial review'. This notably included an examination of whether imposing the occupational requirement was truly necessary (only if a 'probable and substantial' risk of causing harm to the Church's ethos or autonomy existed) and proportionate.[78] On the other hand, the CJEU deferred the latter assessment almost entirely to the national judiciary, providing marginal guidance only.[79] It held that it was for the referring court to decide on the justification and proportionality of the occupational requirement, the crucial problem of the dispute.

Although *Egenberger* is a bold judgment, it also demonstrates a cautious approach of the CJEU. While pushing the German courts – against a well-established constitutional tradition – towards a more thorough supervision of churches, the ruling gives them, on matters of substance, a great deal of discretion. It means that the national judiciary will, to a large extent, decide what is and what is not proportionate when it comes to employment in religious organisations. Proportionality analysis is an inherently complex and uncertain exercise, especially in disputes between private parties.[80] It requires, as the Court explains, the balancing of the competing rights and interests of both sides:[81] in cases of the *Egenberger* variety, this will notably be the principle of non-discrimination (Article 21(1) CFEU) and the right to an effective remedy (Article 47 CFEU) against freedom of religion (Article 10 CFEU) and possibly even – think, for instance, of church-funded hospitals[82] – the freedom to conduct business (Article 16 CFEU). The deference granted to national courts in this respect gives them the possibility to tailor their judgment to local values and convictions. One can imagine that

[77] *Egenberger* (above n 73) paras 42–59.

[78] ibid, paras 67–68.

[79] Compare this approach with judgments such as *Mangold*, *Kücükdeveci* (both above n 72) or, more recently, Case C-312/17, *Bedi*, ECLI:EU:C:2018:734, where the CJEU engaged in a full-blown review of the proportionality of the challenged Member State act.

[80] Although the Protestant and Catholic Church are bodies of public law (*Körperschaft des öffentlichen Rechts*), private-law instruments such as the *Kündigungsschutzgesetz* (Employment Protection Act) and the *Allgemeines Gleichbehandlungsgesetz* (General Law on Equal Treatment) apply to them.

[81] *Egenberger* (above n 73) para 80.

[82] See Case C-68/17, *IR v JQ*, ECLI:EU:C:2018:696 on the dismissal of a doctor from a hospital funded by the Catholic Church for divorcing and re-marrying.

a German, French and Polish court will reach very different conclusions when it comes to drawing a line between proportionate and disproportionate occupational requirements in the religious context. In fact, even within Germany, it is likely that a small-town judge in Bavaria will not share the view of their colleague in the city of Hamburg. (The referring judges from the Federal Labour Court eventually ruled in Ms Egenberger's favour.[83])

The daily legal reality of constitutional and private law in the EU is much more accommodating than is sometimes suggested. This, of course, does not mean that real conflicts no longer occur. Frictions do arise in the European legal space, some of them serious. In *Landtová*, the Czech Constitutional Court declared a CJEU judgment on retirement pensions to be ultra vires.[84] In *Gauweiler*, the *Bundesverfassungsgericht* threatened to disapply European law if the Luxembourg Court did not follow its interpretation on the limits of the OMT-program.[85] Most recently, the Danish Supreme Court ruled in *Ajos* that Denmark's Act of Accession did not cover judge-made principles;[86] as a consequence, the Court of Justice's jurisprudence on non-discrimination on grounds of age has ceased to apply under Danish law. But it is not only Member State courts that continue to nurture contestation. Sometimes, it is the CJEU that lacks the sympathetic ear for national constitutional concerns. *Melloni* is a case in point.[87] In what was its first preliminary reference ever, the Spanish Constitutional Court – evidently in the 'mood for dialogue'[88] – asked the CJEU whether the Charter allowed national judges to refuse the execution of an European Arrest Warrant if a domestic conception of the right to fair trial (*in casu*, concerning in absentia convictions) stipulated a higher level of protection than that of the EU. The CJEU not only said no, reminding the Spanish judges that 'rules of national law, even of a constitutional order, cannot be allowed to undermine the effectiveness of EU law'[89] – but it also failed to engage in any

[83] German Federal Labour Court, judgment of 25 October 2018 – 8 AZR 501/14 (*Egenberger*).

[84] Czech Constitutional Court, Case Pl ÚS 5/12 *Landtová*, judgment of 31 January 2012. The judgment was a reaction to the CJEU's decision in Case C-399/09, *Landtová*, ECLI:EU:C:2011:415.

[85] Case C-62/14, *Gauweiler*, ECLI:EU:C:2015:400. The German court, thereby, forced the CJEU into what some authors have called a game of 'chicken'; see M Kumm, 'Rebel Without a Good Cause: Karlsruhe's Misguided Attempt to Draw the CJEU into a Game of "Chicken" and What the CJEU Might do About It' (2014) 15 *German Law Journal* 203 and F Mayer, 'Rebels Without a Cause? A Critical Analysis of the German Constitutional Court's OMT Reference' (2014) 15 *German Law Journal* 111.

[86] Danish Supreme Court, Case no 15/2014 *Dansk Industri (DI) Acting for Ajos A/S v The Estate Left by A*, judgment of 6 December 2016. For an analysis, see M Madsen et al, 'Competing Supremacies and Clashing Institutional Rationalities: the Danish Supreme Court's Decision in the Ajos Case and the National Limits of Judicial Cooperation' (2017) 23 *European Law Review* 140; U Neergaard and KE Sørensen, 'Activist Infighting among Courts and Breakdown of Mutual Trust? The Danish Supreme Court, the CJEU, and the Ajos Case' (2017) 36 *Yearbook of European Law* 275.

[87] *Melloni* (above n 34).

[88] Cf G Martinico, 'Preliminary Reference and Constitutional Courts. Are You in the Mood for Dialogue?' in F Fontanelli et al (eds), *Shaping Rule of Law Through Dialogue* (Groningen, Europa Law Publishing, 2009) 221.

[89] ibid, para 59.

meaningful discussion about the referring court's (well-reasoned) position.[90] Contestation, thus, is and will continue to be an important element of European pluralism. However, as we explained, it may be time we focused our attention on accommodation as well.

IV. Conclusion

The story of European pluralism typically begins with the claim of supreme constitutional authority made by the CJEU, followed by the challenges to this claim put forward by certain courts in the Member States. We argued that this is not the complete picture, and aimed to unsettle this narrative in two primary ways. In the first part of this chapter, we argued that such judicial contestation is but one example of a wider process of contestation that has included other constitutional forces and actors, and has equally taken place in the realm of private law. In the second part of the chapter, we argued that contestation has, in both constitutional and private law, been accompanied by the phenomenon of accommodation, to which courts – and the CJEU in particular – have contributed significantly.

In this sense, the chapter aspired to set the record straight when it comes to the role of courts in European legal pluralism(s). On the one hand, they have played a significant part in the process of contestation, but they have not been the only actors that engaged in such contestation, perhaps not even the main actors. On the other hand, courts have not, as the usual story goes, merely encouraged contestation, but have also been an important vehicle for accommodation.

[90] See A Torres Pérez, '*Melloni* in Three Acts: From Dialogue to Monologue' (2014) 10 *European Constitutional Law Review* 308; D Sarmiento, 'An Instruction Manual to Stop a Judicial Rebellion (before it is too late, of course)', *Verfassungsblog*, available at verfassungsblog.de/an-instruction-manual-to-stop-a-judicial-rebellion-before-it-is-too-late-of-course/, accessed 27 March 2019.

17

The Psychology of Judicial Co-operation: The Preliminary Reference Procedure as a Therapeutic Relationship

BARND VAN LEEUWEN*

I. Context: The Psychology of Doing a PhD

The starting point of this chapter is to characterise the preliminary reference procedure in EU law as a 'therapeutic relationship', and to analyse the procedure from a psychoanalytical perspective. However, before the analysis is conducted, it should first be emphasised that the relationship between PhD supervisor and PhD researcher has many dimensions of a therapeutic relationship. In this relationship, I could not have wished for a better therapist than Hans Micklitz. Hans was always available, always willing to listen and to discuss, and always able to find a way forward. We often disagreed on the substance, and this 'conflict and resistance'[1] added an interesting dimension to our sessions. However, I am convinced that we both enjoyed the process. I am very grateful to Hans for his guidance, his commitment and his support.

The foundations of this chapter were written in October 2014 – a few months before I submitted the final version of my PhD thesis at the European University Institute in Florence. I had reached that stage of the PhD where you just want to get it over and done with, and I was battling with Hans over commas, footnotes and the relevance of the Unfair Contract Terms Directive to my argument. It was against this background that I turned to an entirely different subject to take my mind off the technicalities of European standardisation of services. For someone who for a

* Assistant Professor in EU Law, Durham University.

[1] 'Conflict and resistance' was one of the pillars of the European Regulatory Private Law project. See H-W Micklitz, 'The Visible Hand of European Private Law – The Transformation of European Private Law from Autonomy to Functionalism in Competition and Regulation' (2009) 28 *Yearbook of European Law* 3. See also H-W Micklitz and Y Svetiev (eds), 'A Self-Sufficient European Private Law: A Viable Concept?' *EUI Working Papers LAW* 2012/31.

long time had wanted to become a medical doctor[2] – and who 'compensated' for this by focusing heavily on the medical sector in his PhD – it did not come as a surprise that I started to read Freud.[3] I had always been interested in psychiatry, but primarily from a medical perspective. Freud opened up a new perspective, which I then enthusiastically started to link to EU law. This became an exercise in exploring 'the psychology of EU law'. As such, it was – and is – highly experimental, and this chapter and the ideas in it should not be taken too seriously. However, I feel sufficiently confident to 'go public' with it because, in linking some insights from psychoanalysis to the interaction between national courts and the Court of Justice of the European Union (CJEU) in the preliminary reference procedure, I touched upon many areas that have always been of interest to Hans: the importance of national legal culture;[4] the importance of knowing and understanding the full facts and background of a case;[5] and the preliminary reference procedure in EU law.[6] Therefore, this chapter should be well-suited to a book in Hans' honour.

II. Introduction: Linking Psychoanalysis and the Preliminary Reference Procedure

This paper will apply psychoanalytical concepts to the interaction between national courts and the CJEU in the preliminary reference procedure in EU law. Therefore, as a starting point, it is necessary to justify why such a psychoanalytical perspective should be adopted, and what its benefits are to law and to lawyers. There can be no doubt that there is a substantial amount of psychology in judicial decision-making. Courts consist of judges – human beings who individually or collectively engage in legal decision-making. This process takes place in the context of national, European and international developments which are likely to affect them in one way or another. These developments are not just limited to legal developments – social, economic and cultural factors have a similar impact.[7] Law is a product of society and court judgments are no different in that respect. Furthermore, there is a significant amount of psychology behind the interaction between courts – often

[2] In fact, during my time as a visiting researcher at the University of Cambridge in early 2014, I came very close to applying to study Medicine at the University of Groningen in the Netherlands (where I would eventually teach EU law from 2015 to 2017).

[3] S Freud, *Inleiding tot de Psychoanalyse* (Amsterdam, Wereldbibliotheek, 2013).

[4] See, for example, R van Gestel and H-W Micklitz, 'Why Methods Matter in European Legal Scholarship' (2014) 20 *European Law Journal* 292.

[5] See H-W Micklitz, *The Politics of Judicial Co-operation* (Cambridge, Cambridge University Press, 2005).

[6] ibid.

[7] See G Helleringer and KP Purnhagen, *Towards a European Legal Culture* (Oxford, Hart, 2014) and T Wilhelmsson et al (eds), *Private Law and the Many Cultures of Europe* (The Hague, Kluwer Law International, 2008).

described as a judicial dialogue[8] – such as in the preliminary reference procedure. The psychological dynamics have an important impact on *why* preliminary references are made and on *how* the CJEU deals with them. As a result, an analysis of these dynamics will have an explanatory role and will also give national courts and the CJEU more insight into the motivation behind their decisions in the context of the preliminary reference procedure. Ultimately, this insight will help national courts and the CJEU to decide how to act in concrete cases.

A second important justification for adopting a psychological perspective is that the relationship between the CJEU and national courts in the preliminary reference procedure has many characteristics of a 'therapy'. Through Article 267 TFEU, national courts and the CJEU are engaged in a long-standing relationship with the aim to assist national courts with questions about how they should deal with the requirements that EU law imposes on them. For these reasons, psychoanalysis might have something to contribute to a better understanding of the interaction between the CJEU and national courts in the preliminary reference.

In order to be able to analyse the interaction between the two courts, it is necessary to take a broader and historical perspective on the case law. Therefore, by way of illustration, I will analyse a number of preliminary references to the CJEU from a psychoanalytical perspective. Through this analysis, some of the dynamics between the CJEU and national courts will become clearer. This exercise should help us to better understand why national courts and the CJEU act in the way they do in the preliminary reference procedure. Furthermore, it may result in an increased degree of reflection and awareness on the part of both the CJEU and national courts about their role and impact in the preliminary reference procedure. As such, this chapter also aims to have a therapeutic effect itself.

First, a brief introduction to psychoanalysis will be given. Psychoanalysis was developed by the Austrian neurologist Sigmund Freud in the late nineteenth century.[9] Since then, it has continually been adapted to accommodate and reflect changes both in science and in society. It can best be described as a combination of a theory and methodology of treatment to identify unconscious mental processes which in one way or another have a negative impact on the psychological wellbeing of human beings. The patients are not usually aware of these processes, and psychoanalysis aims to make them conscious of how these mental processes are affecting them. This process occurs through a long series of analyses in which the psychoanalyst and the patient together attempt to deconstruct the various stages of development of the patient in order to better understand how they have affected – and how they are still affecting today – the patient. As a consequence of its historical approach, psychoanalysis is very much focused on the patient's

[8] See, for example, J van Dorp and P Phoa, 'How to Continue a Meaningful Judicial Dialogue about EU Law? From the Conditions in the CILFIT Judgment to the Creation of a New European Legal Culture' (2018) 34 *Utrecht Journal of International and European Law* 73.

[9] For a recent biography, see J Whitebook, *Freud: An Intellectual Biography* (Cambridge, Cambridge University Press, 2017).

interaction with family members – in particular with their parents. It does not offer a direct cure – it is not like medication – but it is intended that through the process of deconstructing the unconscious the mental processes become less of an obstacle to the patient. As such, psychoanalysis is a highly individualistic – and inevitably somewhat abstract – treatment. It is also quite elitist, in that relies on frequent sessions between analyst and patient for a long period of time. One must have both the time and means to be able to embark on such a project.

Any attempt to link psychoanalysis to the preliminary reference procedure in EU law could easily be dismissed as a challenging and somewhat artificial exercise. There are good reasons to be critical. Psychoanalysis is above all about individual human beings and about their personal development. As such, in law, it could be used to explain and to analyse criminal behaviour. It is more difficult to see how it could be applied to the interaction between judges in the preliminary reference procedure. As a result, some scepticism is entirely justified. Nevertheless, for all the reasons outlined above, I argue that it has something to add to a better understanding of the interaction between national courts and the CJEU in the preliminary reference procedure.

My argument will proceed in four steps:

(i) judges possess a legal 'mind', which is shaped by their national culture, national law and national legal training, in which EU law has to be accommodated;[10]
(ii) the preliminary reference procedure establishes a therapeutic relationship between national courts and the CJEU. The CJEU assists national judges with questions about how they should accommodate the demands imposed by EU law;
(iii) in this therapeutic relationship, psychoanalytical dynamics can be identified;
(iv) an analysis of these dynamics gives a better insight in the relationship and interaction between national courts and the CJEU in the preliminary reference procedure.

Each of these steps will now be discussed in turn.

III. Analysing the 'Psyche' of National Judges in EU Law

Before it is possible to analyse the therapeutic interaction between national courts and the CJEU in the preliminary reference procedure, the 'psyche' of national judges has to be analysed. After all, it is in this mind where the mental processes occur that can be analysed through psychoanalysis. Freud himself went through a number of stages of development in attempting to provide a 'map' of the mind.

[10] See J Smits, 'Legal Culture as Mental Software, or: How to Overcome National Legal Culture' in Wilhelmsson et al (above n 7) 133–43. See also Helleringer and Purnhagen (above n 7).

He started with what is usually called the 'topographical model'.[11] It consists of three stages: the unconscious, the preconscious and the conscious. In the unconscious mind, processes take place automatically – here, we find our deepest instincts, which are beyond introspection. This does not mean that they do not have an impact on our behaviour. They can come to light, by way of example, in dreams or in slips of the tongue – hence the term 'Freudian slips'. Our unconscious mind consists of a reservoir in which we have stored – and sometimes repressed – prior experiences, automatisms and memories. It should be contrasted with the conscious, where we are very much aware of the mental processes taking place. An important function of psychoanalysis is to bring processes which are taking place in the unconscious into the conscious. Such a process of deconstruction allows the patient to deal with the processes better through a process of realisation. In between the unconscious and the conscious we find the preconscious mind. Here, we find thought processes which are not sufficiently repressed to be incapable of becoming part of the conscious mind. It is possible for them to progress from the unconscious into the conscious. Therefore, the preconscious could be considered as a 'bridge' from the unconscious to the conscious.

Later on in his life, Freud developed a second model of the mind, which is commonly referred to as to the 'structural model'.[12] It is this model that will be used in this chapter. In fact, it does not represent a departure from the topographical model, but it can be seen as an additional model which interacts with the topographical model. For the structural model, Freud distinguished between the Id, the Ego and the Superego. The Id represents the human's most instinctive drives, such as desire, lust or aggression. It is already present from birth. As a consequence, much of it can be seen as genetic. The Superego is about the internal acceptance – the internalisation – of external influences which the human being considers should be complied with. Cultural rules or usages are often referred to. Much of this external influence comes from the parents, who through their education and upbringing attempt to convey on their child a particular system of what is wrong and what is right. As a result, the Superego can then be seen as an external conscience which has to be internalised. The Ego brings the two together and has to attempt to moderate between the instinctive drives of the Id and the internalised external pressure of the Superego. The Ego is the organised part of the mind, which constantly has to balance between the demands of the Id and Superego. As such, there is always an inevitable amount of pressure on the Ego, which is in a constant limbo to decide on the most rational course of action. It cannot come as a surprise that some minds are better able to cope with this pressure than others.

If this structural system of the mind is applied to the role of national judges in EU law, we could map the mind of national judges as follows. The Id stands

[11] S Freud, *The Interpretation of Dreams* (Ware, Wordsworth Editions, 1997).
[12] S Freud, *The Ego and the Id* (New York, WW Norton and Co, 1962).

for national law, national culture and legal training. In a manner which can sometimes be more and sometimes less conscious, national judges will instinctively respond to particular problems by reference to national law. This applies to the substance of their response as well as to their methodology. It necessarily means that the instinctive responses of judges are based on their particular national background.[13] Although there is a lot to say about it, the popular statement that every common lawyer is born as a common lawyer has at least a sense of truth in it.[14] The Superego represents EU law as an external influence and legal culture which imposes demands on the Id. Unlike the Id, it is not genetic – it does not come with birth. It is through the development of the law, including through the judgments of the CJEU, that national judges learn what demands are imposed upon them by EU law. It is then up to the Ego of national judges to deal with how best to balance the requirements imposed by the Superego with the more instinctive responses provided by the Id. In the Ego, national judges are forced to reach a response which is both acceptable to the Superego – EU law – and the Id – national law and legal culture. As has been explained above, this inevitably involves some tension. Moreover, some national judges will be more inclined to fall back on instinctive responses than others, and will be more likely to rely on the Id. Other national judges will take a more moderate approach and will be more willing or able to accommodate the external pressure imposed by the Superego.

I will illustrate this 'mapping' of the mind of national courts with two examples. First, a parallel can be drawn with the distinction between monism and dualism in international law. From a very simplistic point of view, monism believes that national and international law are part of the same unit – of the same 'all in one' legal system.[15] As a consequence, international law *is* national law. Dualism is based on the understanding that national law and international law are separate systems and that one has to accommodate the other. International law needs to find its way into national law through specific application. EU law has always had a difficult position in this discussion – some argue that EU law is genuinely supranational and on that basis directly applicable in national law, while others maintain the position that EU law is just a different kind of international law. For the purposes of this chapter, I only use the distinction to make the point that national courts in a system which is based on a monistic approach towards international law, such as the Netherlands, will have fewer problems with the accommodation of the Superego – EU law – in the Ego.

[13] See, again, Helleringer and Purnhagen (above n 7) and Wilhelmsson et al (above n 7).

[14] Hans definitely believes in this statement. I remember very well how he continued to refer to me as a Dutch lawyer, even though I studied Law in the UK and have never studied any Dutch law. See also P Legrand, 'The Impossibility of Legal Transplants' (1997) 4 *Maastricht Journal of European and Comparative Law* 111.

[15] See R Higgins, *Problems and Process: International Law and How We Use It* (Oxford, Clarendon Press, 1994).

They have a less difficult balancing exercise to perform. This is because the very presence of the Superego itself has already been genetically internalised in the Id. Although this does not mean that these national judges might have fewer questions about the exact scope or substance of the requirements imposed by EU law, they will at least be more instinctively inclined to accommodate EU law. Such an approach can be distinguished from judges in a system with a dualistic approach, such as the UK. They are much more likely to have to engage in a balancing exercise to find the appropriate balance between the Id – where parliamentary sovereignty,[16] for example, can be found – and the requirements imposed by the Superego of EU law.

A more practical example can be provided by looking at the *ex officio* application of EU law by national courts. We can take *Aziz* as an example.[17] In that case, Mr Aziz had concluded a mortgage agreement with a Spanish bank. The agreement contained excessive interest rates. He challenged these rates in the Spanish courts under the Unfair Contract Terms Directive (UCTD). However, the rules of Spanish civil procedure provided that he would only be able to do so *after* the forfeiture of his house. This would effectively deprive him of the protection of the UCTD. The Spanish court was uncertain about what to do. Would it have to rely on its own national civil procedure or would it have to do apply the provisions of the Directive? The CJEU gave a clear answer: the principle of effectiveness required that in this case Spanish civil procedure be set aside.[18] The judgment of the CJEU showed to the national court that it was unconsciously relying too much on the Id, and that the balance with the Superego had to be struck differently. It enabled Spanish courts to get rid of some of the unconscious demands imposed by national civil procedure by bringing them into the Ego and by contrasting them more directly with the Superego. To any EU lawyer the result of this case did not come as a surprise at all. In fact, most of the cases about the *ex officio* application of EU law go in the same direction. However, Spanish national courts apparently needed the preliminary reference procedure to feel more secure in departing from their instinctive responses based on national law.[19] Therefore, in this case, the preliminary reference procedure had a therapeutic effect on Spanish law. In the next section, I will explain how the relationship between national courts and the CJEU in the preliminary reference procedure can be construed as a therapeutic relationship.

[16] A Dicey, *The Law of the Constitution* (Oxford, Oxford University Press, 2013).

[17] Case C-415/11, *Mohamed Aziz v Caixa d'Estalvis de Catalunya*, ECLI:EU:C:2013:164. This case was chosen deliberately, because Hans was very intrigued by it. See H-W Micklitz, 'Unfair Contract Terms – Public Interest Litigation before European Courts' in V Colaert and E Terryn (eds), *Landmark Cases of EU Consumer Law: In Honour of Jules Stuyck* (Cambridge, Intersentia, 2013) 633.

[18] *Mohamed Aziz v Caixa d'Estalvis de Catalunya*, ibid, para 64.

[19] For more background, see P Gutierrez de Cabiedes and M Cantero Gamito, 'Country Report Spain' in H-W Micklitz and I Domurath, *Consumer Debt and Social Exclusion in Europe* (Abingdon, Routledge, 2015) 67.

IV. The Preliminary Reference Procedure as a Therapeutic Relationship

In the section above I have illustrated how the mind of national judges can be construed. In dealing with cases that raise issues of EU law, national judges can come up against problems when they are unable to balance the requirements imposed by the Superego with those of the Id. In such situations, they can make a reference to the CJEU in Luxembourg. Such preliminary references are never solely or exclusively about the interpretation of EU law. Both in the context of the case and also more generally, the preliminary reference procedure constitutes a mechanism through which national judges are helped to strike the right balance between national law and EU law. More importantly, through the preliminary reference procedure, the effect of certain instinctive responses of national judges – deeply hidden in their Id – can be made conscious. As a result, national courts might be better able to deal with the question of how to reconcile national law and EU law. On that basis, the CJEU would take the role of therapist. It should immediately be noted that the CJEU as a court has its own legal mind, which could probably be described as the inverse of national courts. For the CJEU, EU law is at the core of its Id, while national law is the Superego. It is too simple to deny that the CJEU is only concerned with the interpretation of EU law – the result of that interpretation inevitably involves a balancing act with national law. Any judgment of the CJEU in the preliminary reference procedure also involves a balancing exercise between national law and EU law. However, this exercise starts from a different perspective than national courts. This could lead one to conclude that the CJEU is not the ideal therapist for national courts. How could the CJEU help to uncover problems with the Id of national courts if its own Id is so instinctively directed towards EU law, and its most instinctive response would be that national law is irrelevant to the outcome of the therapy? The different starting point of the CJEU should not be a problem as long as the CJEU itself provides for sufficient scope to balance its own Id and Superego. This places the CJEU in a position of responsibility. It would even be possible to describe the relationship between national courts and CJEU as a therapeutic relationship in which the therapy goes in both directions – a mutually therapeutic relationship. On some occasions national courts would take the position of therapist, while in other situations the CJEU would remain the therapist. However, for the sake of clarity, in this paper I will assume that the CJEU maintains its role as therapist.

A patient seeks the help of a therapist or analyst if they feel that they are ill and cannot find a way out themselves. What does illness mean in the context of the preliminary reference? Article 267 TFEU provides that the CJEU is capable of giving rulings on the interpretation of the Treaties and on the validity and interpretation of acts of the institutions. The CJEU itself has given further guidance on the interpretation of Article 267 TFEU in *CILFIT*,[20] in which it held that national

[20] Case C-283/81, *CILIFT and Another v Ministry of Health*, ECLI:EU:C:1982:335.

courts of last instance were required to make a preliminary reference if the answer to a question of EU law was necessary to resolve the case and if it was not *acte clair* (ie the answer was so obvious that no help would be required) or *acte éclairé* (ie the CJEU had already dealt with the question before). *CILFIT* would seem to place a number of formal entrance requirements at the door of the CJEU as therapist. However, the reality is that these formal requirements are not strictly adhered to by the CJEU.[21] More frequently, national courts use the *CILFIT* doctrine as a way to refuse to engage in a therapeutic relationship with the CJEU, by refusing to accept that there are problems in balancing the Id with the Superego. This will be discussed in more detail below.

The preliminary reference procedure has created a long-term relationship between national courts and the CJEU. In principle, it is of unlimited duration. National courts know that they can rely on the CJEU to help them out if they are in need of clarification of what EU law requires from them. In this long-term relationship, one preliminary reference constitutes just a moment in time of that therapeutic relationship. However, it is important to realise that a preliminary reference is symptomatic of certain problems a national court has in balancing national law and EU law. There are psychological dynamics even behind the formulation of the question(s) of a preliminary reference. A preliminary reference has to be considered in the context of both national and EU law to understand those dynamics. The therapeutic relationship between national courts and the CJEU results in therapeutic dynamics, which are not dissimilar from the dynamics between Freud and his patients. As a consequence, some of the principles which Freud could identify in his patients through psychoanalysis can also be identified in the case law of the CJEU – or more generally, in its relationship with national courts. In the next sections, I will use three psychoanalytical concepts to analyse the interaction between national courts and the CJEU in different areas of EU law. For each concept, I will start with a description of how the concept is interpreted by psychoanalysts. I will then explain how it can be used to interpret what happened in the preliminary references.

V. Therapeutic Alliance: X and Van Dijk and Ferreira da Silva

Psychoanalytic therapy relies on a series of sessions between the psychoanalyst and patient. There has to be a certain frequency to these sessions – often, patient and therapists will meet at least three times a week for a number of years. For the therapy to be effective, it is crucial that the therapist and the patient develop a good

[21] See A Kornezov, 'The New Format of the *Acte Clair* Doctrine and its Consequences' (2016) 53 *Common Market Law Review* 1317.

working relationship. Trust is the foundation of this relationship. Similarly, it is important that the patient is genuinely committed to working with the therapist to explore the cause(s) of their problems, and to work together to try and find a workable solution. In psychoanalytical theory, the concept that is used to describe this commitment is 'therapeutic alliance' – or 'working alliance'.[22] In other words, the therapist and patient must have developed a good working relationship with a sufficient amount of trust for their sessions to be successful. The trust works in both ways: the patient has to trust the therapist, and the therapist has to have trust in the commitment of the patient. As such, there is a close link between therapeutic alliance and the concepts of transference and countertransference, which will be discussed below.

Article 267 TFEU makes it clear that lower national courts enjoy discretion in deciding whether to make a preliminary reference to the CJEU. Therefore, it can be presumed that the decision to make a preliminary reference – and to seek help from the therapist – is a choice which is freely made by national courts (often supported by the parties in the case). This is positive from the perspective of therapeutic alliance. However, national courts of last instance are under an obligation to make a preliminary reference – it is a 'compulsory referral' to their therapist. This obligation is complicated from a psychoanalytical point of view, because national courts of last instance are known to be difficult patients. Their position in the national judicial hierarchy – ie their superiority – gives them a certain sense of independence. Furthermore, national judges working in courts of last instance might be so experienced that they refuse to consider themselves as patients. As a result, they might be less inclined to make a preliminary reference. To deal with this tension, the CJEU developed two exceptions to the obligation of national courts of last instance to make a preliminary reference in *CILFIT*. The two exceptions were already introduced above. The *acte éclairé* principle means that national courts of last instance do not have to refer a case if the issue has already been solved in a previous judgment of the CJEU. The *acte clair* principle means that no reference has to be made if the court of last instance has no reasonable doubt about how the issue of EU law should be resolved.[23] To a significant extent, the *CILFIT* criteria have been developed for practical reasons, since they reduce the workload of the CJEU. At the same time, *CILFIT* is also about a sharing of responsibility between the CJEU and national courts of last instance. Moreover, it indicates that the CJEU is prepared to trust national courts of last instance to make the important assessment of whether the CJEU should get involved in the case.

Until recently, there were relatively few cases in which the CJEU was asked to provide guidance on how the *CILFIT* criteria should be interpreted by national courts. This resulted in a broad margin of appreciation for national courts in

[22] See D Freebury, 'The therapeutic alliance: a psychoanalytic perspective' (1989) 34 *Canadian Journal of Psychiatry* 772.

[23] *CILFIT* (above n 20) para 16.

deciding how the criteria should be applied. It also created the potential for abuse by national courts of last instance. Two recent judgments of the CJEU have provided further guidance on how the criteria should be interpreted. In *X and Van Dijk*, the Dutch Supreme Court had to rule on an issue of EU tax law.[24] The Supreme Court, which has a Chamber specialised in taxation, was of the opinion that the matter was *acte clair* and that no reference to the CJEU was necessary. However, it discovered that a lower national court – the Court of Appeal of Den Bosch – had just made a preliminary reference on precisely this issue. Interestingly, the Supreme Court then decided to make a preliminary reference on whether the fact that a lower national court had already made a preliminary reference on the same question prevented the Supreme Court from ruling that it was *acte clair*. The CJEU was sympathetic to the Dutch Supreme Court. It held that the fact that a preliminary reference had already been made by a lower national court did not prevent the Supreme Court from finding that it was *acte clair*. The CJEU emphasised that it was the 'sole responsibility' of national courts of last instance to decide whether an issue was *acte clair*.[25] If a lower national court had already made a reference on this issue, this was a factor which should be taken into account in that assessment. However, it did not prevent the Supreme Court from giving judgment. Similarly, the Supreme Court did not have to wait for the answer of the CJEU in the preliminary reference of the lower national court.

In *Ferreira da Silva*, the Portuguese Supreme Court's interpretation of the concept of 'transfer of a business' in an EU company law directive was challenged before the Portuguese courts.[26] The Portuguese Supreme Court had consistently refused to make a preliminary reference on this issue. However, after a judgment of the CJEU, it became clear that the Supreme Court had in fact misinterpreted the relevant directive. Mr Ferreira da Silva then brought a *Köbler* claim for state liability against the Portuguese state. The CJEU held that although the determination of whether an issue was *acte clair* was indeed the sole responsibility of the national court of last instance, in this case, there were a number of factors which made it impossible for the Portuguese Supreme Court to rule that this issue was *acte clair*.[27] The CJEU pointed to significant differences in the judgments of national courts, and also emphasised that courts in other Member States had reached different conclusions on this issue. Various preliminary references had been made to the CJEU. As a result, the Portuguese Supreme Court could not reasonably have come to the conclusion that the matter was *acte clair* and had committed a breach of the *CILFIT* doctrine. Ultimately, however, the CJEU held that the breach was not sufficiently serious to establish state liability.

[24] Case C-72/14 and C-197/14, *X v Inspecteur van Rijksbelastingdienst and Van Dijk v Staatssecretaris van Financiën*, ECLI:EU:C:2015:564.

[25] ibid, paras 57–58.

[26] Case C-160/14, *João Filipe Ferreira da Silva v Estado português*, ECLI:EU:2015:565.

[27] ibid, para 43.

On a first reading, the two judgments of the CJEU do not appear to be consistent. Although the CJEU emphasises the 'sole responsibility' of national courts of last instance in both cases, it rejected the assessment of the Portuguese Supreme Court. As a result, it is difficult to maintain that the assessment is solely made by the national court. It remains unclear to what extent the test for *acte clair* is an objective or subjective test. From a legal point of view, the distinction made by the CJEU in these two cases is unconvincing.[28] A possible justification could be that, in *X and Van Dijk*, the divergences were only 'vertically' within the same Member States, while in *Ferreira da Silva* there were also divergent interpretations 'horizontally' in different Member States. In any event, the outcome of the two cases can more easily be explained from a therapeutic perspective. If we look at the relationship between the Dutch Supreme Court and the CJEU, it is clear that the Dutch Supreme Court has historically been very willing to engage with the CJEU – as shown by the fact that a reference was made in *X v Van Dijk* itself. The number of preliminary references made by the Dutch Supreme Court is consistently high. As such, the therapeutic alliance between the Dutch Supreme Court and the CJEU is strong.[29] This relationship justifies the willingness of the CJEU to give more freedom to the Dutch Supreme Court to decide how to apply the *CILFIT* criteria. After all, it has sufficient trust that the outcome will be compatible with EU law – if there were doubts about this, the Dutch Supreme Court would refer. This is different from the Portuguese Supreme Court, which had made hardly any preliminary references to the CJEU before *Ferreira da Silva*. Therefore, the strict decision of the CJEU was justified from a therapeutic perspective. It had to be stricter to enforce and to improve the therapeutic alliance between the Portuguese Supreme Court and CJEU. This more hierarchical perspective on their relationship was necessary to encourage the Portuguese Supreme Court to engage more regularly with the CJEU.

VI. Transference and Countertransference: *Keck*

Through his contact with patients Freud discovered that they often displayed emotions towards him – their therapist – which could be traced back to experiences in their childhood. These emotions would be re-experienced again by patients and would be 'transferred' to the therapist.[30] As a result, it was possible that patients would fall in love with their therapist. Alternatively, patients could express very strong sentiments of unexplained anger towards the therapist.

[28] Others are more positive. See Kornezov (above n 21).

[29] See CWA Timmermans, 'De Hoge Raad en het Hof van Justitie van de EU als partners in de prejudiciële procedure' (2015) 4 *Tijdschrift voor Civiele Rechtspleging* 114.

[30] S Freud, 'The Dynamics of Transference' in *The Standard Edition of the Complete Psychological Works of Sigmund Freud, Volume XII (1911–1913)* (London, Hogarth Press, 1963).

A distinction should be made between positive transference – like a patient falling in love – and negative transference – a patient being aggressive or angry with the therapist. While Freud at first interpreted transference as a negative side-effect of psychoanalytical treatment, he later came to understand the phenomenon as an essential step in the treatment process. If the transference is interpreted correctly by the therapist, it can provide crucial information about processes which have taken place in the unconscious of the patient. It can then explain some of their current symptoms or problems. However, for transference to have a positive effect on the treatment, it is crucial that the therapist recognises it and responds appropriately to it. There is always a risk that the therapist acts on the transference – for example, by falling in love with the patient or by getting angry with the patient. Such responses – called countertransference – are to be avoided as they might put at risk the therapeutic process and relationship with the patient. All of this can be avoided by adequate interpretation of the initial transference of the patient, which requires the therapist to take a step back and to use the transference to make progress with the treatment.

In EU law, *Keck* represents one of the main examples of transference of national courts to the CJEU, which led to a process of countertransference by the CJEU.[31] As a result, the initial transference of the French court was not adequately acted upon, with years of uncertainty about the scope of application of the provision on the free movement of goods – now found in Article 34 TFEU – as a result. The facts of *Keck* are well-known. The case concerned French legislation which prohibited resale of goods at a loss. A number of supermarkets had engaged in this practice and prosecutions had been brought against their managers. In an attempt to avoid a conviction, the managers argued that the French legislation contravened the free movement provisions, because it made it more difficult to sell goods in comparison with Member States where no such prohibition existed. It is interesting and important to take the questions of the preliminary reference as a starting point. The French court referred to all potentially relevant provisions of EU law in its preliminary questions – including the free movement of goods, services and capital.[32] Moreover, it included the competition law provisions and the right to non-discrimination in (what is now) Article 18 TFEU. As such, it gave a clear message to the CJEU: 'This is too much for us, we have no idea which provisions are applicable and which are not, so you deal with it'. The implicit message of the French court, which was visually reflected in the enormous number of provisions of EU law to which it referred, was that EU law *itself* was getting too much and was being extended beyond its proper scope of application. As such, the way in which the question was put represented an instinctive response from the national court – it was felt that the Superego was imposing too much on the Id with the result

[31] Case C-267/91, *Criminal Proceedings against Bernard Keck and Daniel Mithouard*, ECLI:EU:C:1993:905.

[32] ibid, para 4.

that the Ego could no longer deal with it. It was a distinctively defensive reaction from the French court. This did not come as a complete surprise – there had been indications that national courts were unhappy with the potentially broad application of the free movement of goods after *Dassonville*.[33] The Sunday Trading cases in the UK had revealed this tension,[34] and Advocate General Tesauro had asked some fundamental questions about the aim of Article 34 TFEU in *Hünermund*.[35] However, there was more to it – although this interpretation could lead one to conclude that the irritation of the French court was directed against the CJEU, there was a deeper sentiment underneath. It is no surprise that the preliminary reference came from France. At the national level, there has always been a dominant view in France that the EU represents the market and stands for liberalisation of trade. France has always had a strong position of the state in the market – *Keck* could then be considered as the personification of the threat to that national tradition.[36] On that basis, it would not only represent the dissatisfaction of national courts with a broad interpretation of the scope of application of Article 34 TFEU by the CJEU, but an even deeper anxiety for the intrusion of the market – through the EU – in the national society and economy.

The response of the CJEU is equally well-known. It held that there was a certain category of measures – which it labelled as 'certain selling arrangements' – which did not come within the scope of the free movement of goods if they complied with two conditions.[37] The concept of 'selling arrangements' was a newly invented concept, which was not really defined in the judgment.[38] Furthermore, the CJEU found it necessary to expressly state that it was derogating from its previous case law, without in any way making it clear which cases were no longer good law. Despite the fact that the CJEU clearly recognised the underlying conflict represented by *Keck*, it still failed to provide a response which could be seen as responsible from a therapeutic point of view. The creation of the curious category of 'certain selling arrangements' – in combination with the unclear announcement that some of its previous case law had been overruled – constituted clear countertransference by the CJEU. It is important to understand that, through this judgment, the CJEU not only accepted that the French court had real and genuine fears about the intrusion

[33] Case C-8/74, *Procureur du Roi v Benoît and Gustave Dassonville*, ECLI:EU:1974:82.

[34] See Micklitz (above n 5). See also C Barnard, 'Sunday Trading: A Drama in Five Acts' (1994) 57 *Modern Law Review* 449.

[35] Opinion of AG Tesauro in Case C-292/92, *Ruth Hünermund and Others v Landesapothekerkammer Badem-Württemberg*, ECLI:EU:C:1993:863.

[36] This became particularly clear in the lead-up to the adoption of the Services Directive: E Grossman and E Woll, 'The French Debate over the Bolkestein Directive' (2011) *Comparative European Politics* 344. For more background, see J Flower, 'Negotiating European Legislation: The Services Directive' (2007) 9 *Cambridge Yearbook of European Legal Studies* 217.

[37] *Keck* (above n 31) para 16.

[38] S Weatherill, 'After Keck: Some Thoughts on How to Clarify the Clarification' (1996) 33 *Common Market Law Review* 887.

of EU law in the national economy, but also that these fears were justified. In acting upon these fears in the way that it did, the CJEU reaffirmed that there is constant pressure of EU law which imposes a threat to national law. If the preliminary reference represented a picture of EU law as an emperor looking to confiscate the land of the Member States, the judgment in *Keck* represented his hasty withdrawal from the battlefield. The problem with this is that the CJEU overacted in finding that cases like *Keck* fell outside the scope of free movement law. In so doing, it internalised the perception of EU law as unjustifiably encroaching on the regulatory autonomy of Member States.

The result was that the outcome of *Keck* has been the complete opposite of what the CJEU was trying to achieve – rather than to provide peace of mind to national courts, it reaffirmed their fears. This effect was increased by the uncertainty about the scope – or reach – of the judgment and about the question of which previous judgments had been overruled.[39] As a response to the transference of national courts it was too instinctive. What the CJEU should have done was to accept that the fear of the national court was genuine, but that it could adequately be dealt with *within* the scope of EU law. After all, there was a broad consensus that EU law should not come to the rescue of the supermarket managers in this case. This would have been a more responsible reaction from a therapeutic perspective. Taking the case outside the scope of EU law did not help the national court with how to balance the requirements of the Id and Superego – it was based on the fiction that they could be kept separate. Developments after *Keck* have shown that this interpretation of *Keck* might be correct. In subsequent cases, the scope of the category of certain selling arrangements has been limited and most cases about selling arrangements have been brought within the scope of EU law. The practical relevance of *Keck* has been minimised.[40] I would interpret these cases as an attempt by the CJEU to limit the effects of the original countertransference.

VII. Projective Identification: *Grogan*

Projection is a concept most of us will have heard about and will have experienced ourselves. It means that we project onto others something that we feel ourselves. As such, it serves as a kind of defence mechanism. For example, children who bully

[39] L Gormley, 'Reasoning Renounced? The Remarkable Judgment in *Keck and Mithouard*' (1994) 3 *European Business Law Review* 63.

[40] L Gormley, 'Inconsistencies and misconceptions in the free movement of goods' (2015) 40 *European Law Review* 925; I Lianos, 'In Memoriam Keck: the reformation of the EU law on the free movement of goods' (2015) 40 *European Law Review* 225; E Spaventa, 'Leaving Keck behind? The free movement of goods after the rulings in Commission v Italy and Mickelsson and Roos' (2009) 33 *European Law Review* 914; M Jesse, 'What About Sunday Trading …? The Rise of Market Access as an Independent Assessment Criterion under Article 34 TFEU' (2012) 3 *European Journal of Risk Regulation* 437.

other children could be seen as projecting on these children feelings of uncertainty which they are in fact experiencing themselves. Projection was developed into the more sophisticated concept of projective identification by Melanie Klein.[41] The patient splits their mind into a good and bad – the bad is subsequently projected onto someone else. The projection of the bad thoughts takes place unconsciously by the patient to protect them against potential harm. The patient will subsequently expect and look for the projected thoughts in the other person. As such, there is a very close link to transference. There is also a possible risk of countertransference by the therapist – which is here called counter-projection – in response to the projective identification.

In 1991, the CJEU delivered a controversial judgment in *Grogan*.[42] The national context is important and should be set out in detail. Ireland had a Catholic majority which, in accordance with the position of the Catholic Church, was strongly against abortion and in favour of the protection of foetuses. When the first anti-religious sentiments began to threaten the Catholic morals in Irish society, a lobby was started with the aim to provide constitutional protection to the right to life. After a referendum in 1983, Ireland became the first and only Member State of the EU in which the right to life of foetuses was expressly constitutionally protected. In a judgment in 1988, the Irish Supreme Court decided on the basis of this provision that family planning clinics in Ireland were not allowed to provide information to patients about the location and identity of abortion clinics in the UK.[43] The case had been brought by the Society for the Protection of Unborn Children (SPUC), a self-declared anti-abortion police whose main aim was to enforce the constitutional right to life of foetuses. This was not the end of the matter, and student societies became the next target of SPUC. These student associations habitually included in their student guides the addresses of abortion clinics in the UK. SPUC applied to the High Court to get an injunction to prevent student associations from putting this information in their student guides. At first instance, the High Court judge refused the injunction and expressed her intention to refer a number of questions to the CJEU. This decision was appealed to the Supreme Court before the preliminary reference had been made. The Supreme Court did not want to interfere with the High Court judge's decision to refer questions to the CJEU, but it did grant an injunction.[44]

The case obviously has to be read against the context of increasing criticism of the provision in the Irish Constitution and the lack of action on the part of the political apparatus. A constitutional amendment was unlikely to happen. Furthermore, it should be noted that the High Court judge in this case, Ms Justice Carroll, was

[41] M Klein, 'Notes on Some Schizoid Mechanisms' (1946) 27 *International Journal of Psychoanalysis* 99.

[42] Case C-159/90, *Society for the Protection of Unborn Children Ltd v Stephen Grogan and Others*, ECLI:EU:C:1991:378.

[43] *Attorney General (Society for the Protection of Unborn Children Ltd) v Open Door Counselling Ltd* [1988] IR 593.

[44] *Society for the Protection of Unborn Children Ltd v Grogan (No 1)* [1989] IR 753.

the first ever female High Court judge in Ireland. After her death in 2003, she was described as a 'superb role model for women'.[45] From that perspective, it does not come as a complete surprise that she referred the case to Luxembourg in an attempt to provoke movement in the deadlock of the Irish political situation. It was based on a more liberal view of morality. In referring the case to Luxembourg, the judge attempted to separate the 'bad' part of Irish law, or the Irish Constitution, and project it on the CJEU. The unconscious intention behind the reference was that the CJEU would also recognise the fear, that it would experience the same fear for conservative anti-abortion sentiments and that it would act on it. Because of the lack of national support, evidenced by the strong criticism by the Irish Supreme Court of her decision to refer questions to the CJEU, the preliminary reference constituted a defence mechanism to project the problems on the CJEU. There was an implicit hope in the reference that the CJEU would be able to at least provoke some movement in the situation.

With this in mind, the response of the CJEU was disappointing. Although it held that abortion constituted a service for the purposes of the right to free movement of services, it found that the case did not come within the scope of Article 56 TFEU. This was because the economic link between the student associations and the abortion clinics in the UK was too tenuous – they were not being paid by the clinics to advertise and they had no economic interest in the activity of the clinics.[46] From the perspective of EU law, the reasoning of the CJEU has been strongly criticised as providing an easy way out to avoid having to scrutinise the Irish Constitution under the free movement provisions. This was no doubt true and, from the perspective of legal reasoning, the criticism was entirely justified.[47] However, from a therapeutic point of view, the reaction of the CJEU was both convincing and appropriate. As I have explained above, the attempt to get the CJEU involved in what was essentially national politics in a field in which the EU had no competence constituted a defence mechanism by the Irish national court. By declining to bring the case within the scope of Article 56 TFEU, the CJEU emphasised the responsibility of the Irish courts – and of Irish society more broadly – to deal with these inherently cultural issues. Any attempt by the CJEU to intervene could have been seen as a counter-projection by the CJEU and as an implicit confirmation that it shared the same fears as the Irish court. It would have provoked much more of an outrage in Irish law and society – the Irish Supreme Court had already warned against this – which would have been counterproductive. Its complete refusal to get involved provided a clear signal to

[45] See www.rte.ie/news/2006/0115/71836-carrollm/, accessed 28 March 2019.

[46] *Grogran* (above n 43) paras 24–27.

[47] For a more detailed analysis, see S O'Leary, 'The Court of Justice as a Reluctant Constitutional Adjudicator: An Examination of the Abortion Information Case' (1992) 17 *European Law Review* 138; G de Búrca, 'Fundamental Rights and the Reach of Community Law' (1993) 13 *Oxford Journal of Legal Studies* 283; D Curtin, 'Case C-159/90, The Society for the Protection of Unborn Children Ltd v Grogan, Judgment of 4 October 1991' (1992) 29 *Common Market Law Review* 585.

Ireland that it had to deal with this issue itself. And so it did – in subsequent cases, the interpretation of the provision of the Irish Constitution became more flexible, which probably provided a more balanced response to a society with mixed views on this issue. Therefore, the intervention of the CJEU – or rather its lack of direct intervention – had an impact on the situation in Ireland. Finally, in 2013, legislation which provided a new interpretation of the Irish Constitution was introduced. This legislation allowed abortion in certain specific circumstances.[48] In 2018, after a strongly contested and debated referendum, the Irish Constitution was amended to remove the ban on abortion.[49]

VIII. Conclusion: Lessons for the Preliminary Reference Procedure from Psychoanalysis

If it is accepted that the relationship between national courts and the CJEU in the preliminary reference procedure can be defined as a therapeutic relationship in which psychoanalytical dynamics can be identified, the CJEU should consider using some techniques from psychoanalysis in the context of the preliminary reference procedure. In this conclusion, I will propose three techniques which could be used by the CJEU and national courts to improve their therapeutic relationship.

First, the CJEU should develop 'patient files' to be able to analyse patterns in the preliminary references which it receives from national courts. These patient files should contain information on the number of preliminary references made by national courts, the topics on which references are made, and the type of questions that have been asked (eg interpretation or validity). Ideally, these files would be made for different levels of national courts for each Member States. Courts of last instance would probably deserve their own file. As a result, the CJEU would have to create different files for the lower courts of each Member State, the appeal courts of each Member State and the courts of last instance of each Member State. In practice, the CJEU is likely to have all this information available – it may already have something like 'patient files'. The question is how the information is used. From a therapeutic perspective, the CJEU would have to place every preliminary reference in its context, and would have to identify how it related to previous references made by the same national court (or the same level of national court). Such an exercise would help to have a better understanding of the context of – and possibly the motivation behind – this particular preliminary reference. This would then help the CJEU to decide how to react to the preliminary reference.

[48] Protection of Life During Pregnancy Act 2013.

[49] Thirty-sixth Amendment of the Constitution Bill 2018 and Health (Regulation of Termination of Pregnancy) Bill 2018.

Second, national courts should be encouraged to describe their 'family history' while making a preliminary reference. This means that they should put the preliminary reference in the broader context of their relationship to other courts in the same Member State. How have their brothers and sisters dealt with the same issue (ie national courts of the same level)? How have their parents dealt with similar issues (national appeal courts), and what about their grandparents (national courts of last instance)? And to what extent has this affected the relationship between these courts? Some national courts may already do something like this when they submit a preliminary reference. However, it is again the *aim* of the exercise which is important. National courts should be encouraged to describe and analyse their relationship with their 'family members', and they should explain how the making of a preliminary reference can be linked to their relationship with their family members. This will help the CJEU to understand why a reference on a particular topic is made by a particular national court, and how this preliminary reference is linked to other cases at the national level. This will help to CJEU to better understand the aim and context of the preliminary reference.

Third, and finally, national courts should be encouraged to interact with the CJEU *during* the preliminary reference procedure. The CJEU should encourage more 'free association' on the part of national courts – the interaction should not stop after the preliminary reference has been sent to Luxembourg. This would mean that there would be more regular communication between the CJEU and the referring court, and that any questions or issues that might arise in the procedure could be clarified by the national court. This would probably require more fundamental changes to the current procedure of the CJEU. It could also lead to delays in the procedure. However, more effective communication between the CJEU and national courts is important. It could, for example, make it less likely that the CJEU would find it necessary to re-phrase questions. Similarly, the national courts could be asked to provide more information about particular provisions of national law. The result would be that the chances are higher that national courts are actually satisfied with the outcome of the preliminary reference – at least from a procedural point of view.

18

Law and Politics after Wightman: Taking Stock of Neo-Formalism in the EU

MARIJA BARTL* AND KEIVA CARR**

I. Introduction

Hans Micklitz is, on many accounts, a Renaissance scholar: versed in scholarship across geographies, times and disciplines, with academic productivity that few can match. Despite his many pursuits, Hans has always been the most generous and committed supervisor. He has motivated his students to read broadly, think deeply and be ambitious in their scholarship. His thoughtful supervision has moved many of us beyond our intellectual boundaries: we remain deeply grateful to Hans for his guidance during the most vulnerable, and the most beautiful, period of our lives.

When we started thinking about this contribution, we asked what brings Hans, Keiva and Marija together? Two things sprang to mind. First, our commonly held commitment to the EU project. While unquestionably critical observers of the EU, we all remain deeply concerned with its fate, intellectually and emotionally. It is for this reason that the CJEU's decision in *Wightman and Others*,[1] the most recent pronouncement on Brexit, issued mere weeks prior to the submission of this contribution, could not but form the object of our attention herein. Second, we also keenly remembered a piece of scholarship that Hans encouraged us to read and re-read – Duncan Kennedy's 'Three Globalisations of Legal Thought'[2] – a piece that has ultimately found its way into the scholarship of all of us.

* Associate Professor, Faculty of Law, University of Amsterdam.

** Legal Counsel, European Investment Bank. All opinion contained herein are strictly personal to the authors.

[1] Case C-621/18, *Andy Wightman and Others v Secretary of State for Exiting the European Union*, ECLI:EU:C:2018:999.

[2] D Kennedy, 'Three Globalizations of Law and Legal Thought: 1850–2000' in DM Trubek and A Santos (eds), *The New Law and Economic Development: A Critical Appraisal* (Cambridge, Cambridge University Press, 2006).

In this contribution then we, somewhat playfully, ask if there is anything we can learn from reading *Whitman and Others*[3] through the prism of Kennedy's 'Three Globalisations of Legal Thought'. In order to undertake this analysis, we will first, in Part II, set out the fundamental characteristics of Classical Legal Thought, The Social and Neo-Formalism. We then discuss the judgment *Wightman and Others*,[4] before proceeding to analyse the judgment in light of Kennedy's 'Three Globalisations' in Part IV. The main issue that we aim to shed light on is the relation between law and politics in the EU after *Wightman*. We will explore different legal consciousnesses that seem to co-exist in this judgment, each of which re-establishes the relationship between law and politics in the EU.

II. The Three Globalisations of Legal Thought

Following Kennedy, our employment of 'globalisation of legal thought' conjures a historical legal consciousness, which includes a set of legal and political arguments and tools rendering that consciousness the intellectual background of legal argumentation – the langue of legal discourse.

A. Classical Legal Thought

During the heyday of Classical Legal Thought (CLT) – from approximately 1850 until 1914[5] – contractual thinking presented the blueprint within which relations between individuals on the one hand as well as between countries on the other could be framed. CLT was characterised by a clear distinction between the public and the private, by individualism, and, interpretive formalism.

Contract law and will-theory stood in the centre of this legal consciousness. In CLT, the contract and private law rules were a set of rational derivations from first order principles: the individual and his will[6] were to be protected by governments as the rights of legal persons.[7] One may express the gist of this thinking as follows: I have private/sovereign rights and I owe no obligations toward others, save the harm principle. Individuals internally, and 'civilised' nations externally, could pursue their interests with minimal external interference, subject eventually to agreements accorded in line with their own preferred terms and conditions in disregard to potential power differentials.[8]

[3] *Wightman* (above n 1).
[4] Kennedy (above n 2).
[5] Kennedy (above n 2) 25.
[6] For a critique see RE Barnett, 'A Consent Theory of Contract' (1986) 86 *Columbia Law Review* 269.
[7] Kennedy (above n 2) 26; D Kennedy, 'From the Will Theory to the Principle of Private Autonomy: Lon Fuller's Consideration and Form' (2000) 100 *Columbia Law Review* 94.
[8] Indeed, it was for the above reasons that the imperialism of the contract was a construct that held significant theoretical and practical weight during the first globalisation. In essence, everything was

B. The Social

The dissatisfaction that arose in revolt of CLT began to ferment in the late 1800s and provided a forum which allowed for the embrace of a new legal consciousness, spreading from the 'Western' hemisphere across the world. Beginning in the early 1900s therefore, and lasting until the end of World War II, a reconstruction process was set in motion based on fundamental shifts from individualism to the interdependence and group rights, from formal equality to social justice and from private law as its core to social legislation. The second globalisation embedded a collective element, protecting individuals as constitutive elements of particular groups of society. The Social, in these terms, constituted an outright attack on the individualist nature of CLT.

We understand, therefore, the second globalisation of legal thought as the development of a legal consciousness that bestrode the will of individuals,[9] and to some extent sovereign nations, paving the way for arguments pertaining to interdependence and cooperation.[10] Internally, in regulatory terms, the law of the free market was slowly replaced by a new regulatory regime where market freedoms were balanced against radiating social concerns that aimed at protecting groups in society, eg workers, women, the disabled. In the international domain, the cooperation remained however hierarchical and exploitative – the League of Nations and Mandate system was succeeded by the United Nations, Bretton Woods, and a (failed) attempt to create a World Trade Organisation. Colonialism and economic exploitation in international proved much slower to wane.[11]

C. Neo-Formalism

Neo-Formalism grew from increased importance weighted on human and democratic rights, the rule of law, across the world. This third globalisation, what Kennedy refers to as the contemporary period, is more concerned with recognising and managing difference. In Kennedy's own words:

> Between 1945 and 2000, one trend was to think about legal technique, in the aftermath of the critiques of CLT and the social, as the pragmatic balancing of conflicting considerations in administering the system created by the social jurists. At the same time,

considered in a contractual light and therefore reduced to elements of a transaction – the will of the actors was key. According to The Will Theory, commitments made between parties to a contract were enforceable before courts because the parties freely chose to be bound by the contractual agreement.

[9] Take, for example, the development of labour law around which a legal *langue* aiming to reign-in the freedom of contract ideology and the regulation of private relations based solely on the will of the parties was developed. In this regard, we note that although freedom of contract remained intact, the Social paved the way for the imposition of obligations on, for example, employers, obligations essentially based on the recognition of social responsibilities and the development of the idea of social protection.

[10] Kennedy (above n 2).

[11] A Anghie, *Imperialism, Sovereignty and the Making of International Law*, vol 37 (Cambridge, Cambridge University Press, 2007).

> there was a seemingly contrary trend to envisage law as the guarantor of human and property rights and of intergovernmental order through the gradual extension of the rule of law, understood as judicial supremacy.[12]

The langue of Neo-Formalism saw a shift from individual rights and property rights that characterised the first globalisation, and from group rights and social rights that marked the globalisation of the social consciousness, to an increased focus on human rights in terms of policy analysis, policy-making and, more importantly for our scope here, adjudication.

To sum up, during the CLT the langue was based on a formalistic consensus of wills, the rights of individuals/states and a disregard for power disparities or vulnerability. During the second globalisation, the Social, more room was made for collective considerations and instrumental approaches to law, for social justice and protection. Towards the end of the Social, we see the emergence of an identity-based notion of rights, marking the beginning of the neo-formalist legal consciousness. During the spread of Neo-Formalism, the Social project is reintegrated into the legal discourse at the level of arguments about constitutional rights and balancing policy and identity. In this legal consciousness, political disputes are portrayed as legal disputes about the scope of one's rights, taking social justice into account as part of identity rights.

III. Wightman and Others

On 10 December 2018, the CJEU, in the context of a preliminary reference referred by the Court of Session, Inner House, First Division (Scotland, United Kingdom), handed down its seminal judgment in what has become known as 'the Brexit case'.[13] One short and concise question was referred for interpretation by the Court:

> Where, in accordance with Article 50 [TFEU], a Member State has notified the European Council of its intention to withdraw from the European Union, does EU law permit that notice to be revoked unilaterally by the notifying Member State; and, if so, subject to what conditions and with what effect relative to the Member State remaining within the European Union?

This is a short and concise question, with potentially explosive effects, given the possibility that any answer in the affirmative would pave the way to a third option for the UK, that is, to remain in the EU.

[12] Kennedy (above n 2) 22.
[13] *Wightman* (above n 1).

A. Opinion of Advocate General Campos Sánchez-Bordona

After having rejected the pleas concerning the admissibility of the question referred to the Court,[14] the Advocate General embarked on a three-step analysis.[15] First, he looked at the rules of public international law on the withdrawal of states from international treaties emphasising that the rules applicable under the Vienna Convention on the Law of Treaties can provide interpretative guidance for the case at hand since the principal question is not expressly dealt with in Article 50 TEU.[16] Second, the Advocate General proceeded to carry out a literal and contextual interpretation of Article 50. Through this interpretation, he emphasised the unilateral nature of a state's decision to withdraw from the EU, linking that to an expression of that state's sovereignty, conditional only upon a state's constitutional requirements.[17] In view of this construction, he opined that any revocation of an exit decision must also be considered as a manifestation of the sovereignty of the departing state[18] any that any decision to the contrary risks to deny common sense entailing a forced exit or even an indirect expulsion from the EU.[19] Indeed, in the view of the Advocate General, the notification decision of the UK can only indicate an intention to withdraw, consequently opening up a two-year period of negotiations during which the departing state remains a Member State of the Union, maintaining all rights that are implied with that membership until the withdrawal becomes effective.[20] In this regard, and in view of actual and current membership in the EU, the Advocate General references the principle of respect for the constitutional identity of the Member States, which, he submits, supports taking into account a change in the sovereign will of the departing state.[21] On this aspect, he links the objective of achieving an ever closer Union in submitting that a Member State should not be obstructed from continued EU membership[22] since any such obstruction would negate the rights acquired by EU citizens.[23] Bearing in mind the above arguments in favour of unilateral revocation, the Advocate

[14] The UK government had argued that the question referred was inadmissible, first due to its hypothetical and theoretical nature, and second because the Court has no competency to provide advisory opinions on constitutional matters.

[15] We will not analyse the third step, as it concerns the question of an agreed revocation, relevant only to the extent that the Court were to reject the possibility of unilateral revocation. However, the judgment of the Court rejected the possibility of a multilateral revocation on the basis it would transform a unilateral sovereign right into a conditional right subject to an approval procedure: *Wightman* (above n 1) para 72.

[16] AG's Opinion in Case C-621/18, *Andy Wightman and Others v Secretary of State for Exiting the European Union*, ECLI:EU:C:2018:978, para 82.

[17] ibid, paras 91–93.

[18] ibid, para 94.

[19] ibid, paras 110–12.

[20] ibid, paras 95–102 and 114–15.

[21] ibid, paras 130–32.

[22] ibid, para 133.

[23] ibid, paras 135–36.

General outlines the conditions under which unilateral revocation would be valid, noting that revocation should be carried out via a formal act of the departing state addressed to the European Council and should be adopted in accordance with national constitutional requirements. He notes the potential for abuse, recalling that it is limited by the principles of good faith and sincere cooperation.[24]

B. Judgment of the Court

The judgment of the Court was delivered on 10 December 2018. In setting out the provisions considered relevant to its judgment, that is, relevant provisions of the Vienna Convention, the relevant EU law including Articles 1 and 2 of the TEU and the text of the withdrawal clause of Article 50 and the relevant provisions of UK law, the Court delineated the legal framework within which its analysis was confined. It then proceeded with an analysis of the admissibility of the preliminary reference, confirming the existence of a dispute between the parties and the relevance of the question referred which required an interpretation of a provision of EU law. The Court concluded by finding the reference to be admissible.

The judgment proceeded to examine the substance of the dispute before noting that despite Article 50's silence on revocation of withdrawal from the Union, that same Article 50, in paragraph 2, refers explicitly to the notification of the 'intention' to withdraw. The Court notes that such an 'intention' can neither be definitive nor irrevocable[25] and is supported by the fact that Article 50(1) provides for unilateral withdrawal dependent solely on the sovereign choice of the Member State concerned.[26] In delineating the purpose of Article 50, the Court notes its two objectives: first, to enshrine the sovereign right of a Member State to withdraw from the EU; and second, to ensure that such a withdrawal takes places in an orderly fashion.[27] Endorsing the opinion of the Advocate General, the Court noted that the first objective of Article 50 supports the conclusion of a unilateral right to revoke notification until such time as a withdrawal agreement has not entered into force or for as long as the two-year negotiation period and any possible extension has not expired.[28] In doing so, the Court recognised the sovereignty of a state in deciding to retain its status as a Member State.[29] In referencing the principle of an ever closer union among the peoples of Europe, and the values of liberty and democracy[30] the Court noted that since a state cannot be forced to accede,

[24] ibid, paras 148 and 156.
[25] *Wightman* (above n 1) para 49.
[26] ibid, para 50.
[27] ibid, para 56.
[28] ibid, para 57.
[29] ibid, paras 59 and 60.
[30] ibid, paras 61–63.

against its will, to the Union[31] neither can it be forced to withdraw unwillingly. Any interpretation of the notification of an intention to withdraw from the Union which would translate to an inevitable withdrawal would amount to an exit inconsistent with the aims and values of the EU and the purpose of creating an ever closer union.[32] Furthermore, in the opinion of the Court, any such interpretation would produce negative consequences with regard to the rights of all Union citizens, effectively undermining the status of citizenship of the Union which is intended to be the fundamental status for all nationals. The final decision of the Court, therefore, found that.[33]

> Article 50 TEU must be interpreted as meaning that, where a Member State has notified the European Council, in accordance with that article, of its intention to withdraw from the European Union, that article allows that Member State – for as long as a withdrawal agreement concluded between that Member State and the European Union has not entered into force or, if no such agreement has been concluded, for as long as the two-year period laid down in Article 50(3) TEU, possibly extended in accordance with that paragraph, has not expired – to revoke that notification unilaterally, in an unequivocal and unconditional manner, by a notice addressed to the European Council in writing, after the Member State concerned has taken the revocation decision in accordance with its constitutional requirements. The purpose of that revocation is to confirm the EU membership of the Member State concerned under terms that are unchanged as regards its status as a Member State, and that revocation brings the withdrawal procedure to an end.

IV. *Wightman* through the Lens of the Three Globalisations (and Beyond)

What, if any, of the various elements of the legal langues pertaining to the Three Globalisations can be identified in the Court's judgment? And what can we learn from *Wightman* and the way it was decided about the status of the EU project?

To recall, the first globalisation of Classical Legal Thought was centred on legal formalism: the idea that law provided facilitative rules, formal equality and procedural fairness. In other words, the rules of the game applied to all in the same way – even if the outcomes were manifestly unjust. We portray this legal consciousness as 'law without politics'. The second globalisation, The Social, on the other hand, was typified by an understanding of 'law as the extension of politics'. Law in this period was overlain with an increased awareness of social obligations and the idea of social protection. When we come to the third globalisation, Neo-Formalism, we witness a change in legal grammar in an attempt to integrate 'politics in/through law', via rights discourse and the emergence of identity rights.

[31] Consolidated Version of the Treaty on European Union [2008] OJ C115/13 (TFEU), Art 49.
[32] *Wightman* (above n 1) paras 63 and 65–67.
[33] ibid, para 64.

Upon a first reading, *Wightman* reverts to the langue of the CLT. The importance the Court gives to will, and the sovereignty of the Member State in question is remarkable. The Court specifically notes that:[34]

> In those circumstances, given that a State cannot be forced to accede to the European Union against its will, neither can it be forced to withdraw from the European Union against its will. However, if the notification of the intention to withdraw were to lead inevitably to the withdrawal of the Member State concerned from the European Union at the end of the period laid down in Article 50(3) TEU, that Member State could be forced to leave the European Union despite its wish – as expressed through its democratic process in accordance with its constitutional requirements – to reverse its decision to withdraw and, accordingly, to remain a Member of the European Union.

This is a clear expression of a Member State's freedom and autonomy – states are free to join the Union, and they are free to leave. Therefore, Article 50 should be interpreted in such a way that any intention to leave the Union can be revoked in a unilateral fashion.

Yet there is another level of argument at play. Immediately before pronouncing its opinion on the notification of intention to withdraw, the Court states that:[35]

> As regards the context of Article 50 TEU, reference must be made to the 13th recital in the preamble to the TEU, the first recital in the preamble to the TFEU and Article 1 TEU, which indicate that those treaties have as **their purpose the creation of an ever closer union among the peoples of Europe**, and to the second recital in the preamble to the TFEU, from which it follows that the European Union **aims to eliminate the barriers which divide Europe.** It is also appropriate to underline the importance of **the values of liberty and democracy**, referred to in the second and fourth recitals of the preamble to the TEU, which are among the common values referred to in Article 2 of that Treaty and in the preamble to the Charter of Fundamental Rights of the European Union, and which thus form part of the very foundations of the European Union legal order [...] It must also be noted that, since **citizenship** of the Union is intended to be the **fundamental status of nationals of the Member States** [...] any withdrawal of a Member State from the European Union is liable to have a **considerable impact on the rights of all Union citizens**, including, inter alia, their right to free movement, as regards both nationals of the Member State concerned and nationals of other Member States (emphasis added).

These three paragraphs of the judgment seem to catapult the discussion into the political field. By saying that Article 50, a provision that at first sight seems to be of a purely procedural nature, should be interpreted in light of the overall aim of the Union as expressed in the Treaties, values of liberty and democracy, the Charter of Fundamental Rights and the impact any withdrawal from the Union would have on EU citizens, the Court openly politicises the interpretation of Article 50 and links it to these European values. By interpreting the will of the Member State

[34] ibid, paras 64–65.
[35] ibid, paras 61–62 and 64.

in line with European values, the Court recognises the links between national law and politics on the one hand and European law and politics on the other and incorporates, in its reasoning, national politics in advancing the European society-building project. In fact, in advancing the latter within the confines of considerations pertaining to the will of the state, the Court inadvertently encourages/burdens the Member State to consider the European society-building project in making any eventual decision to revoke, or not, its intention to exit the Union. In our view, this tends to go beyond the gist of Neo-Formalist thinking in the EU which has dominated EU law, and, more specifically, the CJEU's jurisprudence in recent decades.

In order to demonstrate, let us recall what we consider to be two of the main markers of the EU's globalisation – both neo-formal in nature. First, since the publication of the 1985 White Paper on the Completion of the Internal Market, we have seen an important re-constitution of the relation between law and politics in the EU. As noted by Micklitz, the While Paper constituted 'the starting point for the ongoing transformation of the European Community into a new supranational polity',[36] where, in a uniquely neo-formalist move, the EU's common and later internal market was presented as a technical project. The portrayal of the internal market as a technical exercise may have eased the political acceptance of regulations and directives; however, it also limited the politicisation of the EU internal market, downplaying the re-distributive and political nature of its regulation.

Second, EU citizenship has played a significant role in the neo-formal turn of the European project. In this regard, we note a marked shift from market and consumer citizens, that is, those citizens that were afforded specific rights (and duties) by virtue of their participation in the internal market project, to, eventually, what we recognise as the development of standalone citizens that derive rights (and duties) by virtue of that very status, a status that has been significantly built upon by the broad interpretation given to it by the CJEU. What we note is that, with regard to the former, rights and duties conferred by way of being a market player constructed a sort of dependency relationship between the Union as the addressor and the nationals of the Member States as the addressees. In more recent times though, and as can be deciphered from the judgment, the latter has developed into a status that weakens the market dependency element and rather sees a concept develop which produces its own legal effects.

In *Wightman*, and despite the opposition of the European Commission and the Council, and in an even more unequivocal fashion than the Advocate General, the Court moves to judge on the one hand with a clear CLT consciousness but, with reference to essential elements of the European project, thereby rather recalling the legal-political consciousness of the Social. Indeed, by setting the scene for a

[36] H-W Micklitz, 'The Visible Hand of European Regulatory Private Law – The Transformation of European Private Law from Autonomy to Functionalism in Competition and Regulation' in P Eeckhout and T Tridimas (eds), *The Yearbook of European Law 2009*, Volume 28 (Clarendon Press, Oxford 2009) 9.

possible unilateral revocation that unshackles national politics from supranational constraints (ie the agreement of the European Council) the Court gives large space to national politics, more voice to the British citizens and also ensures that the least number of constraints are placed on making sure that EU citizens remain so.

The Court takes this recognition even further when, in another conspicuously anti-neo-formalist move, the CJEU refuses to place additional legal safeguards against the abuse of the right to unilateral revocation, such as those for instance suggested by the Advocate General. While the revocation of the 'intention to withdraw' has to be a genuine expression of EU citizens' wish to remain in the EU, the quality of consent is not framed in legal terms of good faith and sincere cooperation, but rather left on the backdrop of political trust in the EU-British citizens and their constitutional procedures.

V. Conclusion

The *Wightman and Others* judgment may be a special case in the EU jurisprudence. In view of the pending Brexit, we can safely say that the EU may be at its lowest point for what concerns its pursuit of 'the ever closer union'. Yet, it is perhaps at this moment that EU law is at its best.

First, in rejecting the stance of the Commission and the Council on the form any revocation must take, the Court casts away any assumed position of strength the latter may have vis-à-vis the UK. Second, the Court, by embedding the discussion about UK sovereignty in the language of EU values and EU citizenship, manages to assert the extensiveness of the UK's sovereign rights within the context of the extensiveness of the political and democratic rights of EU-British citizens. Finally, the Court also makes clear that this status cannot be taken from the EU-British citizens by their fellow EU citizens, or the countries which represent them. On this reading, we suggest that the Court is, therefore, going beyond strict Neo-Formalism in upholding the will of the Member State but moving that classical consciousness beyond the economic union and any reduction to a give-take relationship. In the Union of the *Wightman and Others*, the politics and democratic rights of all citizens seem to have found their rightful place. Another contribution would be merited to explain why the Court has treated national politics in a very different manner in the economic crisis case law.[37]

[37] H Schepel, 'The Bank, the Bond, and the Bail-out: On the Legal Construction of Market Discipline in the Eurozone' (2017) 44(1) *Journal of Law and Society* 79.

19

Transforming the European 'Legal Field' by Strategic Litigation: A Research Agenda

BETÜL KAS*

I. Introduction

The EU constitutes a *transnational* legal order beyond the nation-state.[1] As an epitome of transnational law, it does not fit into the traditional dichotomy of national and international law.[2] The Court of Justice of the European Union (CJEU) characterised EC law as an independent legal order, which is distinct from both national and international law.[3] The EU legal order and the national legal systems occupy the same territorial and social space, which can be conceptualised as a 'hybrid legal space'.[4] Despite the tendency of the EU legal order towards denationalisation and transnational (re-)construction, it has retained its interaction with the domestic legal systems of the Member States. The EU legal order remains both normatively and institutionally intertwined with the national legal systems. Rules created by the EU must be implemented within the legal systems of the Member States. The effectiveness of EU law depends on the domestic adaptation

* Researcher at the Centre for the Study of European Contract Law of the University of Amsterdam. With this chapter, I would like to thank Hans Micklitz for his constant support and encouragement and for the inspiration that I draw from his work. I gratefully acknowledge funding by the NWO-subsidised research project 'Judges in Utopia', which is led by Chantal Mak.

[1] H-W Micklitz, 'A European Advantage in Legal Scholarship?' in R van Gestel et al (eds), *Rethinking Legal Scholarship. A Transatlantic Dialogue* (Cambridge, Cambridge University Press, 2017) 262 ff.

[2] K Tuori, 'Transnational law. On legal hybrids and perspectivism' in M Maduro et al (eds), *Transnational Law. Rethinking European Law and Legal Thinking* (Cambridge, Cambridge University Press, 2014) 17.

[3] The landmark rulings were Case 26/62, *Van Gend en Loos* [1963] ECR 1 and Case 6/64, *Costa v Enel* [1964] ECR 585.

[4] K Tuori, 'On Legal Hybrids' in Y Svetiev and H-W Micklitz (eds), 'Self-Sufficient European Private Law: A Viable Concept?' *EUI-ERC Working Papers 2012*, 72; see also PS Berman, 'Global Legal Pluralism' (2007) 80 *Southern California Law Review* 1155 ('hybrid legal spaces, where a single act or actor is potentially regulated by multiple legal or quasi-legal regimes').

to EU rules. The 'legal field'[5] – a social order comprising actors, positions and institutions – was recognised by sociologists and historians to have played a crucial role in the genesis of the European legal order.[6] Beyond that, it is suggested that the 'legal field' safeguards the effectuation of EU law in the national context.[7] The characteristics displayed by the EU's hybrid legal space provide a fruitful breeding ground for strategic actions by legal entrepreneurs, which gradually produce systemic change of the normative and institutional structure of the legal field in which the actors operate.[8] In other words, changes in the legal field are both products of the hybrid legal space and catalysts for its further growth.[9]

The aim of this chapter is to explore the transformation of the 'legal field' by drawing on the socio-legal reconstruction of the *Janecek* case.[10] The *Janecek* case concerns the private enforcement of EU environmental law before the national courts in the situation where the national authorities failed to comply with their planning obligations for clean urban air. The case reached the CJEU by request for a preliminary ruling by the Federal Administrative Court of Germany. A legal action based on rights derived from one of the EU's policy fields, which is initiated before a national court and reaches the CJEU via the preliminary reference procedure under Article 267 TFEU constitutes a fruitful starting point to investigate how the 'legal field' operates in and is shaped by the hybrid legal space. Following the trajectory of a case – ie an investigation of 'where from' EU law cases emerge and 'where to' they have a structuring effect – acknowledges that the EU legal order remains intertwined with the national legal systems. Taking the 'law in action' perspective of the legal realist reveals that no clear boundaries can be drawn between rights derived from the EU legal order and their enforcement by national institutions, remedies and procedures – substance and procedure mutually influence each other. The findings resulting from such a methodological

[5] The notion of the 'legal field' originates from P Bourdieu, 'The Force of Law: Toward a Sociology of the Juridical Field' (1987) 38 *Hastings Law Review* 805.

[6] A Vauchez, 'The Force of a Weak Field: Law and Lawyers in the Governance of the European Union' (2007) 2 *International Political Sociology* 28; A Vauchez, *Brokering Europe. Euro-lawyers and the Making of a Transnational Polity* (Cambridge, Cambridge University Press, 2015).

[7] T Pavone, 'From Marx to Market: Lawyers, European Law, and the Contentious Transformations of the Port of Genoa' (2018) *Law and Society Review* 1.

[8] Similarly, RD Kelemen, 'Eurolegalism and the European Legal Field' in A Vauchez and B de Witte (eds), *Lawyering Europe. European Law as a Transnational Social Field* (Oxford, Hart, 2013) 243; see also RD Kelemen, *Eurolegalism. The Transformation of Law and Regulation in the European Union* (Harvard University Press, 2011).

[9] Related to this, we might ask whether hybridity as a dynamic process (better termed in that sense as 'hybridisation') has to be thought of as a linear process or a loop. For Hans Micklitz's thoughts on this regarding the public/private divide, see H-W Micklitz, 'Rethinking the public/private divide' in Maduro et al (above n 2) 271. According to K Tuori, 'legal hybrids are – or at least should be – merely temporary creatures, awaiting their extinction through novel ways of legal conceptualising and mapping of our legal universe', see Tuori (above n 4) 67.

[10] Case C-237/07, *Janecek* [2008] ECR I-06221. I would like to gratefully acknowledge that the empirical material – semi-structured interviews with the actors involved in the litigation – was collected and analysed together with the sociologist Thomas Roethe.

approach might be transferable to all fields of EU law, ie they might concern the European legal order as a whole.[11] The chapter does not provide yet for a complete analysis of the transformation of the 'legal field'. Its preliminary findings result from the empirical material collected during my doctoral research, but draw novel insights.[12]

II. The Nature of the EU's *Hybrid* Legal Space

The 'hybrid legal space' which is occupied concurrently by the EU legal order and the national legal systems displays particular characteristics, which will be briefly explored in this section.[13] It will be shown that its nature is characterised by: (i) the EU's instrumentalisation of law to achieve the (political) objectives of integration; (ii) the horizontal fragmentation of the EU legal order into different policy fields; and (iii) the vertical fragmentation between EU policy-making and domestic implementation and enforcement.

A. 'Integration through Law' without Politics

Over 20 years ago, Weiler, Seccombe and Cappelletti published their seminal work on integration through law in the EU.[14] It has subsequently become a classic observation in European studies that law constitutes both the object and agent of integration – in both cases, law is constructed in instrumental terms.[15] The former's focus is on the legal process of bringing diverse national legal systems together in order to establish a new legal order. The latter's focus is on the process of framing through law the economic, social, and political spheres such as to achieve the goals of integration. Hence, the rule of law is supposed to replace force in

[11] This method – the socio-legal reconstruction of cases – has been employed by Hans Micklitz himself in his seminal monograph, *The Politics of Judicial Co-operation in the EU. Sunday Trading, Equal Treatment and Good Faith* (Cambridge, Cambridge University Press, 2009) set out at 40; similarly, the interdisciplinary analysis of the rulings of the CJEU in the light of 'thick' descriptions and contextual histories engaging with the actors involved behind the scenes of each case has been pursued in F Nicola and B Davies (eds), *EU Law Stories. Contextual and Critical Histories of European Jurisprudence* (Cambridge, Cambridge University Press, 2017).

[12] B Kas, '"Hybrid" collective remedies in the EU social legal order' (EUI, PhD thesis, 2017).

[13] The chapter refers deliberately to the EU legal order and not to the EU legal system; for the difference, see J Dickson, 'Towards a Theory of European Union Legal Systems' and K Culver and M Giudice, 'Not a System but an Order: An Inter-Institutional View of European Union Law' in J Dickson and P Eleftheriadis (eds), *The Philosophical Foundations of European Union Law* (Oxford, Oxford University Press, 2013) 25 and 54 respectively.

[14] M Cappelletti et al (eds), *Integration Through Law* (De Gruyter, 1986).

[15] R Dehousse and J Weiler, 'The Legal Dimension' in W Wallace (ed), *The Dynamics of European Integration* (Pinter, 1990) 234.

European politics.[16] On a foundational level, the instrumentalisation of law is meant to promote European identity and society building.[17] According to the understanding of the 'integration through law' project, law 'performs a role in ordering social life, translating the highly visible political acts into more mundane daily applications and, through this implementation, it determines the implications of the political decisions'.[18] They write further: 'integration aims at fundamental restructuring of society and societal attitudes, and these changes are reflected and promoted by the law'.[19] Thus, as summarised by Azoulai, '[l]aw affects social attitudes by creating norms and conferring rights and obligations on member states and private parties, but also by translating political and social actions into legal forms conveying the values of integratio'.[20]

The realisation of 'integration through law' therefore demands national actors to bring EU law into practice by invoking rights granted by EU law and by construing arguments on its basis.[21] The effectuation of EU law in local practice is secured by the EU's conferral of individual rights. Accordingly, it is crucial that rights derived from the EU legal order prove effective in local practice. The less effective EU rights are, the less likely identification by national actors with EU rights will be and hence integration will be weakened. The more attractive EU rights are across existing national communities, and the more effective they are in practice, the more likely it will be that rights will be able to cause a shift in loyalty from the Member States to the Union and to bind the communities in view of a 'collective identity' together.

B. Horizontal Fragmentation

The horizontal fragmentation of EU law has been most prominently expressed in the notion of the 'Many Constitutions of Europe'.[22] The EU legal order is structured along different policy fields, which reflect the policy-oriented competences that the Member States were ready to transfer to the EU. In line with the EU's logic of 'integration through law', law has been employed as the driving force for the process of integration along those diverse policy goals, which each developed

[16] L Azoulai, '"Integration through law" and us' (2016) *International Journal of Constitutional Law* 449, 451.

[17] Micklitz (above n 1) 267; see also C Mak, 'Europe-building through private law. Lessons from constitutional theory' (2012) 8 *European Review of Contract Law* 326; G Comandé, 'The Fifth European Union Freedom: Aggregating Citizenship … around Private Law' in H-W Micklitz (ed), *Constitutionalisation of European Private Law* (Oxford, Oxford University Press, 2014) 61; K Carr, 'Regulating the Periphery – Shaking the Core, European Identity Building through the Lenses of Private Law' *EUI-ERC Working Paper 2015*.

[18] Cappelletti et al (above n 14) 4.

[19] Cappelletti et al (above n 14) 42, 43.

[20] Azoulai (above n 16) 449, 451.

[21] C Sieburgh, 'A Method to Substantively Guide the Involvement of EU Law in Private Law Matters' (2013) 21 *European Review of Private Law* 1165.

[22] K Tuori and S Sankari (eds), *The Many Constitutions of Europe* (Ashgate Publishing, 2010).

within its own economic, social, and political context. Accordingly, the European legal order possesses multiple dimensions, which are functionally delimited. The EU legal order is not characterised by a formal and hierarchical order between its various sources, but is based on substantive order produced through policy-based coherence according to the EU's competences. Tuori grounds this characteristic of the EU legal order in the principle of conferral, which requires that Union legislative competences be grounded in express Treaty authorisations, whereas use of these competences is governed by the principles of subsidiarity and proportionality. Compared to the territorially delimited national legal order, the European legal order is therefore not comprehensive.[23] Each EU policy field defines not only its own scope of application *ratione materiae* but also *ratione personae*. That means that there is no uniform legal subject in EU law, but each policy field defines its own identity-based right holder.[24]

The substantive fragmentation of the EU legal order raises complex questions: we might ask how many substantively delimited legal orders there are or should be in the EU and whether there are equally developed. This issue is particularly pertinent when it comes to the European social legal order.[25] Economic integration spilled over to the 'Social':[26] with the adoption of the Single European Act (1986) the EU got entangled in an increasing number of policy fields and the originally conceived two-fold structure – whereby the EU level was committed to market building, while the Member States were to engage in social matters – was eroded.[27] It is debatable to what extent the EU social legal order is separate from and equally developed as the EU economic legal order. We might ask whether there are legal principles that permeate all of the substantively delimited legal orders.[28] On a smaller scale, the question could be posed whether there are legal concepts which could be transferred between diverse policy fields.

The EU's substantively structured legal orders are characterised by hybridity, ie they do not adhere to the formal mapping and basic systematisation of the law as conceived from a nation-state perspective.[29] Most prominently, EU law

[23] K Tuori, *European Constitutionalism* (Cambridge, Cambridge University Press, 2015) 21 ff.

[24] H-W Micklitz, 'The Legal Subject, Social Class and Identity-based Rights' in L Azoulai et al (eds), *Constructing the Person in EU Law: Rights, Roles, Identities* (Oxford, Hart, 2016) 285, 304 ff.

[25] Hans Micklitz asked whether the social legal order and citizens' rights order could be regarded as distinct legal orders separate from the economic legal order, see H-W Micklitz, 'The ECJ Between the Individual Citizen and the Member States – A Plea for a Judge-Made European Law on Remedies' in B de Witte and H-W Micklitz (eds), *The European Court of Justice and the Autonomy of the Member States* (Cambridge, Cambridge University Press, 2012) 355, 356–60.

[26] The meaning of the 'Social' has been elaborated by D Kennedy, 'Three Globalizations of Law and Legal Thought: 1850–2000' in D Trubek and A Santos (eds), *The New Law and Economic Development: A Critical Appraisal* (Cambridge, Cambridge University Press, 2006) 19.

[27] H-W Micklitz (ed), *The Many Concepts of Social Justice in European Private Law* (Cheltenham, Edward Elgar, 2011) 4.

[28] See for example T Tridimas, *The General Principles of EU Law* (Oxford, Oxford University Press, 2006) and N Reich, *General Principles of EU Civil Law* (Intersentia, 2014).

[29] Tuori (above n 4) 73.

does not observe the divide between private and public law prevalent in the national legal systems. Without an explicit competence in the area of private law, and leaving traditional concepts of private law largely aside, EU law had taken a considerable impact on the relationships between private parties with the goal of strengthening the internal market. This was the starting point of the ERC-funded research project entitled 'The Visible Hand of European Regulatory Private Law (ERPL) – The Transformation from Autonomy to Functionalism in Competition and Regulation' hosted by the European University Institute under the scientific guidance of H-W Micklitz, which explored the EU's contribution to the building of a private law beyond the boundaries of national private law.[30] The project's claim is that European private law is fundamentally different from national private law. National private law, as developed in the context of nation-state building in the nineteenth and twentieth centuries, is traditionally informed by notions of private autonomy and freedom of contract. European private law is regulatory law that sets out mandatory and default rules. This finding reflects the nature of the EU as a market state, which employs (private) law as a tool to construct and complete the internal market.[31]

C. Vertical Fragmentation

The European legal order(s) is (are) separated from – as well as interrelated with – the national legal systems.[32] The substantive and institutional level of 'self-sufficiency' from the domestic legal systems differs among the various European legal orders.[33] European integration strives for autonomy but depends largely on implementation by the Member States and lacks effective supranational enforcement and coercive powers. The EU draws legitimacy from a new political community – an 'ever closer relationship between the peoples of Europe' (Article 1 TEU) – but lacks the instruments to acquire a popular basis of legitimation.[34] The EU's identity rights-based approach pursued in a diverse range of policy areas and propelled by the case law of the CJEU is hoped to compensate – at least to some extent – for those shortcomings. In light of the limited administrative capacity of the EU to ensure the implementation of its own policies, the enforcement of Member States' compliance with EU law relies to a large extent on private

[30] H-W Micklitz, 'The Visible Hand of European Regulatory Private Law – The Transformation of European Private Law from Autonomy to Functionalism in Competition and Regulation' (2009) *Yearbook of European Law* 3.

[31] H-W Micklitz and D Patterson, 'From the Nation State to the Market: The Evolution of EU Private Law as Regulation of the Economy Beyond the Boundaries of the Union?' in B van Vooren et al (eds), *The EU's Role in Global Governance: The Legal Dimension* (Oxford, Oxford University Press, 2013) 59.

[32] Micklitz (above n 25) 355, 356.

[33] H-W Micklitz, 'Self-Sufficient European Private Law: A Viable Concept?' in Svetiev and Micklitz (above n 4).

[34] Azoulai (above n 16) 449, 452.

parties invoking EU law before national courts. Private parties and national courts become thereby not only part of the EU's institutional structure, framing policies in the language of individual rights has been promoted as a promise to enhance the EU's legitimacy.[35] It follows that the nature of the EU's transnational legal order guided by the logics of 'integration through law' can be linked with the judicialisation of politics, ie the greater role of courts in addressing public policy questions and political controversies.[36]

Although the judicial enforcement of rights originating from the EU legal order is of fundamental importance within the EU's architecture, the EU legal order is formally built on a distinction between rights and remedies and procedures.[37] Accordingly, it is for the Member States to provide the appropriate remedies and procedures for the enforcement of rights defined by the EU legal order. The so-called principle of procedural autonomy of the Member States is restricted by the principles of equivalence and effectiveness,[38] and the fundamental right to an effective remedy set out in Article 47 of the EU Charter of Fundamental Rights.[39] Domestic procedural autonomy in the enforcement of EU law remains a controversial subject. It seems to have lost its relevance as the EU is exerting an increasing influence on the national enforcement structures by borrowing its competence from the respective subject-related substantive area at stake. The growing European influence – whether resulting from subject-related secondary Union law, the case law of the CJEU or the role of the European Commission in a network of national authorities – raises the need for a new conceptualisation of the interplay between the European and the national level in enforcement matters.[40]

III. The *Janecek* Case

By the example of the *Janecek* case,[41] this section will demonstrate how the characteristics of the EU's hybrid legal space provide a breeding ground for strategic actions by legal entrepreneurs, which in turn have a transformative effect on the 'legal field' as a whole. A legal action based on rights derived from one of the

[35] RD Kelemen, 'Eurolegalism and Democracy' (2012) *Journal of Common Market Studies* 55, 58.

[36] R Hirschl, 'The Judicialization of Politics' in K Whittington and G Calderia (eds), *The Oxford Handbook of Law and Politics* (Oxford, Oxford University Press, 2008) 119.

[37] W van Gerven, 'Of Rights, Remedies and Procedures' (2000) *Common Market Law Review* 501.

[38] The classic statement of the procedural autonomy of the Member States can be found in Case 33/76, *Rewe*, ECLI:EU:C:1976:188, para 5 and Case 45/76, *Comet*, ECLI:EU:C:1976:191, para 13.

[39] A van Duin, 'Metamorphosis? The Role of Article 47 of the EU Charter of Fundamental Rights in Cases Concerning National Remedies and Procedures under Directive 93/13/EEC' (2017) *Journal of European Consumer and Market Law* 190.

[40] B Kas, 'Reshaping the boundaries of the enforcement of European social regulation: Unitas in Diversitate – the construction of a hybrid relationship' in Svetiev and Micklitz (above n 4) 119.

[41] This section constitutes a summary of the relevant findings of the socio-legal reconstruction of the *Janecek* case as comprehensively set out in ch 2 (pp 25–126) of my doctoral thesis, see Kas (above n 12).

EU's policy fields, which is initiated before a national court and reaches the CJEU by the preliminary reference procedure under Article 267 TFEU brings the characteristics of the EU's hybrid legal space together in a nutshell. This section will proceed in the following way: the *Janecek* case will be first embedded within its broader regulatory framework by contextualising the nature of the EU's hybrid legal space within the EU's air quality policy. Its implications for the 'legal field' will be unfolded by reconstructing the trajectory of the *Janecek* case. For that purpose, the preliminary reference to the CJEU will be traced, to show 'where from' it emerged, and 'where to' the CJEU judgment had a structuring effect.

A. The *Janecek* Case within its Regulatory Framework

The *Janecek* litigation and the court actions that followed deal with the regulation of urban air quality and the reduction of pollution to levels which minimise harmful effects on human health. The EU's air quality policy bears the characteristics of the EU's hybrid legal space. The ramifications of this will be contextualised by setting out: (i) the development of the EU's policy of regulating air quality; and (ii) the paradigmatic change its implementation had for Germany's regulatory approach.

i. The EU's Air Quality Policy

Environmental protection policies were first developed at the national level. From around the 1970s, the environment was established as a political category in Western European societies. The grassroots movements of the mid-1970s evolved during the late 1980s into new political parties which have altered the party-political spectrum in most Western European countries.[42] The original Treaty of Rome did not contain any provisions on environmental protection. While the EU became involved in environmental matters during the 1970s, due to the lack of a legal basis, the EU's environmental policy developed predominantly by the adoption of non-binding medium-term programmes for action. Legislative measures were piecemeal and motivated by the concern to establish a level playing field among the Member States. With the adoption of the Single European Act in 1986, the environment was recognised for the first time as a new Community policy in the Treaty and an increasing amount of environmental legislation was adopted, which linked environmental policies to the internal market legal basis. By gradually assuming a leading role in environmental matters, the EU has decoupled the policy field from its national welfare origin and re-established a policy

[42] P Knoepfel, 'Environmental Policy' in ME Hawkesworth and M Kogan (eds), *Encyclopedia of Government and Politics* (Routledge, 2004) 698 ff.

steered by the completion of the internal market.[43] The ensuing development of the EU's environmental policy reveals that it constitutes a field which is still torn between its foundation in the internal market and its autonomous justification in the protection of the environment.[44]

In line with this development, the first EU measures on air pollution were originally limited to regulating the sources of pollution, in particular from the 1970s, by setting product standards in terms of emission limit values for motor vehicles and fuels and, from the mid-1980s, by targeting emissions from industrial plants and mandating the adoption of the best available control technology to curb emissions.[45] From the early 1980s, the EU started to address air pollution by setting Community-wide standards for harmful pollutants in ambient air. The Commission's proposals, based on the recommendations of the WHO, were motivated by the protection of public health in urban areas. However, since the proposed mandatory limit values – substantiated by scientific knowledge on the harmful effects of the respective pollutants – were considered too strict by most Member States in the light of the economic and financial consequences that would result from their implementation, they were considerably watered down during the political decision-making process.[46]

Although the proper implementation of the directives adopting limit values for specific pollutants in ambient air proved problematic in practice, in the 1990s, the EU revived its approach. In view of the introduction of the principle of subsidiarity by the Maastricht Treaty, an approach based on air quality limit values for ambient air was the preferred way forward, as it left freedom to the Member States to choose the actual measures in order to achieve compliance with the limit values. The EU progressed towards a more holistic and integrated approach with the adoption of the Air Quality Framework Directive 96/62/EC.[47] The Directive harmonised the assessment, monitoring and management procedures for air quality to be adhered to by the national authorities designated by their respective Member State. The attainment of political agreement on the limit values was facilitated by the long-term applicability of the regime – compliance with the limit values was to be achieved in time periods of between 10 to 15 years. In the interim, under the oversight of the Commission, the Member States were required to prepare plans

[43] N de Sadeleer, *EU Environmental Law and the Internal Market* (Oxford, Oxford University Press, 2014) 8–11.

[44] C Hey, 'EU Environmental Policies: A short history of the policy strategies' in S Scheuer (ed), *EU Environmental Policy Handbook: A Critical Analysis of EU Environmental Legislation* (International Books, 2005) 17.

[45] E Louka, *Conflicting Integration: The Environmental Law of the European Union* (Intersentia, 2004) 132, 133.

[46] JD Liefferink, 'Environmental Policy on the Way to Brussels: The Issue of Acidicification between the Netherlands and the European Community' (PhD thesis, Landbouw Universiteit Wageningen, 1995) 92.

[47] Council Directive 96/62/EC of 27 September 1996 on ambient air quality assessment and management, OJ L296, 21 November 1996, p 55.

and programmes, setting out the measures to be gradually implemented in order to achieve compliance with the limit values within the specified time-frame. Once the transition period lapsed, the directive obliged the national authorities, where there is a risk of the limit values being exceeded, to draw up action plans indicating the measures to be taken in the short term, in order to reduce that risk and to limit the duration of such an occurrence. In addition, the directive introduced information rights for the public, which were intended to generate 'pressure from below' to ensure the proper implementation of the limit values.[48]

In the context of the Commission's 'Better Regulation' initiative of June 2002, the EU's air quality regime was streamlined, clarified and simplified by the adoption of Air Quality Directive 2008/50/EC.[49] Also in the new directive one of the key elements was the obligation of the national authorities to adopt air quality plans containing adequate measures to achieve compliance with the limit values in the shortest time possible. Moreover, acknowledging that even if the Member States have taken all reasonable measures, compliance with the limit values might not be possible, the directive introduced some flexibility in the implementation of the limit values by allowing, under specific conditions to be approved by the Commission, prolongation of the attainment dates for certain limit values such as for PM_{10} (ie compliance by June 2011) and NO_2 (ie compliance by January 2015).[50]

While air quality has been improving, the latest air quality report of the European Environmental Agency reports that concentrations of PM and NO_2 continue to exceed the EU limit values across Europe. Local road transport is seen as the major source of PM and NO_2 in Europe's urban areas. In view of the fragmentation of competences between the European and national level as well as between the governance levels within the Member States, the effective regulation of air pollution requires a coordinated approach.[51] For instance, taking the example of Germany, while the local authorities at the level of the *Länder* could impose measures related to traffic such as vehicle access restrictions or speed limits for urban areas and the federal government could adopt for example tax incentives for clean vehicles, the competence for the adoption of admission requirements for vehicles is vested in the EU. The *Janecek* litigation reveals how such a situation easily turns into a ping-pong situation where the local authorities shift responsibility to the EU for its failure to synchronise its regulation of vehicle admissions (the so-called Euro norms) with its air quality limit values (in particular for NO_2), while the EU claims that the grounds for exceeding limit values lie in the failure of the

[48] A Héritier et al, *Ringing the Changes in Europe: Regulatory Competition and the Transformation of the State: Britain, France, Germany* (W de Gruyter, 1996) 161, 162.

[49] Directive 2008/50/EC of the European Parliament and of the Council of 21 May 2008 on ambient air quality and cleaner air for Europe, OJ L152, 11 June 2008, p 1.

[50] Proposal for a Directive of the European Parliament and of the Council on ambient air quality and cleaner air for Europe COM(2005) 447 final, p 8.

[51] European Environmental Agency, Air Quality in Europe – 2018 report, EEA Report No 12/2018.

Member States to take sufficient measures within their competence to reduce pollution.[52] The *Dieselgate* scandal added a further dimension to the widespread failure of achieving compliance with the limit values in Europe's urban areas by raising questions about the proper enforcement of the Euro norms.[53]

ii. A Paradigmatic Change in Germany's Regulatory Approach

Germany's approach to regulating the sources of pollution can be traced back to the mid-nineteenth century, when the Prussian state empowered local authorities to restrict heavily polluting industrial facilities through the establishment of a permit system. The focus on the sources of pollution remained Germany's approach to regulating air quality, as illustrated by the Federal Emission Control Act of 1962[54] and the Ordinance on Large Combustion Plants of 1984.[55] Both rely on the precautionary and polluter-pays principles. The former requires that harmful environmental impacts are to be prevented, and that environmentally friendly variants are to be given preference at the construction and production stages. The polluter-pays principle implies a focus on the emission source, since measures are in principle to be taken vis-à-vis the polluter.[56]

Germany had assumed an active role in shaping the EU's approach to addressing pollution from stationary sources in the light of the best available control technology in the mid-1980s.[57] Conversely, the implementation of the EU's approach of managing air quality in light of binding limit values for pollutants resulted in a paradigmatic change of Germany's regulatory approach. The adoption of this new approach has not been unproblematic, as illustrated by two actions lodged by the European Commission against Germany before the CJEU for the failure to correctly transpose Directives 80/779/EEC and 82/884/EEC on limit values for sulphur dioxide, suspended particulates and lead in the air.[58]

[52] Interview with three representatives of the legal and scientific departments of the Bavarian State Ministry the Environment and Consumer Protection (the defendant in the *Janecek* case), 9 October 2012.

[53] See for instance N Hooftman et al, 'A review of the European passenger car regulations – real driving emissions vs local air quality' (2018) *Renewable and Sustainable Energy Reviews* 1.

[54] Gesetz zum Schutz vor schädlichen Umwelteinwirkungen durch Luftverunreinigungen, Geräusche, Erschütterungen und ähnliche Vorgänge (Bundes-Immissionsschutzgesetz).

[55] Dreizehnte Verordnung zur Durchführung des Bundes-Immissionsschutzgesetzes (Verordnung über Großfeuerungs-, Gasturbinen- und Verbrennungsmotoranlagen – 13. BImSchV); MA Schreurs, *Environmental Politics in Japan, Germany, and the United States* (Cambridge, Cambridge University Press, 2002) 48–53; see also H Pehle, 'Germany: Domestic Obstacles to an International Forerunner' in M Skou Andersen and D Liefferink (eds), *European Environmental Policy: The Pioneers* (Manchester University Press, 1997) 163.

[56] Héritier et al (above n 48) 40–41.

[57] Directives 84/360/EEC on the combating of air pollution from industrial plants and 88/609/EEC on the limitation of emissions of certain pollutants into the air from large combustion plants reflected this new approach and constituted the EU's first significant reaction to the problem of acid rain and the damage it caused to forests; see K Hanf, 'Air Pollution Policy in the European Union' in R Baker (ed), *Environmental Law and Policy in the European Union and the United States* (Praeger, 1997) 137–44.

[58] OJ L229, 30 August 1980, p 30; OJ L378, 31 December 1982, p 15.

Germany considered that its source-approach to pollution offered sufficient protection and that the concrete results which it has achieved amply satisfied the EU's air quality limit values. The CJEU criticised that Germany's implementation limited protection to the immediate neighbourhood of defined plants, while the directives had a wider scope of application, which concerns the entire territory of the Member States. The nuisances created by the pollutants at stake may originate elsewhere than in the plant subject to a requirement of authorisation, for example in a high density of road traffic or private heating systems. Therefore, the CJEU found that the general nature of the directives cannot be satisfied by a transposition confined to certain sources of pollution.[59] Moreover, the Court pointed out that Germany failed to set up a legal framework, which ensures that individuals are in a position to know with certainty the full extent of their rights, in order to rely on them, where appropriate, before the national courts.[60]

B. 'Where from' the *Janecek* Case Emerged

The decoupling of environmental policy from the Member States and the re-establishment of a legal-policy field at EU level denoted a paradigmatic change to Germany's regulatory approach to air pollution. While the source-approach was limited to the regulation of specified industrial installations, guaranteeing clean air in urban areas requires addressing additional industrial sectors, in particular the automobile industry, and most significantly, a change of social behaviour on a large scale in terms of society's mobility habits. The trajectory of the *Janecek* case illustrates how the underlying political stakes have been translated into legal argumentation, which in turn triggered a re-conceptualisation of legal protection in German administrative procedural law.[61] The role of the 'legal field' in this process will be unfolded by reconstructing from where the case emerged. To that effect, the following text sets out: (i) how the case was strategically constructed; (ii) the position that the German courts took; and (iii) the judgment that the CJEU rendered.

i. The Strategic Construction of the Case

According to the official legal documents, the reference for a preliminary ruling to the CJEU in the *Janecek* case arose out of the course of proceedings between

[59] Case C-361/88, *Commission v Germany*, ECLI:EU:C:1991:224, para 19; Case C-59/89, *Commission v Germany*, ECLI:EU:C:1991:225, para 22.

[60] Case C-361/88, *Commission v Germany*, ECLI:EU:C:1991:224, para 20; Case C-59/89, *Commission v Germany*, ECLI:EU:C:1991:225, para 23.

[61] G Kirchhof, 'Der rechtliche Schutz vor Feinstaub – subjektive öffentliche Rechte zu Lasten Vierter? Der Wechsel vom Emissions- zum Immissionsprinzip im Luftqualitätsrecht und die Folgen für das subjektive öffentliche Recht und die Verhältnismäßigkeitsprüfung' (2010) *Archiv des öffentlichen Rechts* 135.

Mr Janecek and the Bavarian authorities. Mr Janecek applied for an order requiring the authorities to draw up an air quality action plan for the territory of the city of Munich comprising the district where he lived. He demanded that the plan should include the short-term measures to be taken to ensure compliance with the limit value for PM_{10} in ambient air. The interviews with Mr Janecek and his lawyer (hereafter referred to as 'the lawyer') revealed that Mr Janecek acted as a stalking horse for a cause of much broader ramifications.[62] The case was strategically fabricated upon the initiative of the lawyer, who co-operated closely with an environmental NGO involved in the campaign 'No diesels without a filter' ('*Kein Diesel ohne Filter*').[63] The aim of this grouping of environmental organisations was to pressure the automobile industry to sell exclusively diesel-powered vehicles with pre-installed ecological filters. They were active by lobbying industry and politics aside from disseminating information in society about the health risks associated with long-term exposure to traffic-related air pollution.[64]

Based on the anticipation that the limit values for PM_{10}, which were due to become legally binding on the Member States as of 2005,[65] and the prediction that most German cities would not be able to achieve compliance, the lawyer developed the idea of initiating legal actions against the German state authorities, which would be forced to restrict traffic for diesel vehicles in the cities in order to ensure compliance with the limit values. That would indirectly force the automobile industry to adopt the environmentally-friendly filter technology. The lawyer entered into negotiations with various NGOs and reached agreement with one of them to provide the organisational and financial support for the legal actions. The interview with the lawyer revealed his awareness of pursuing legal-political work. He explained his ambition of creating cases whereby the methods and means theoretically discussed in legal literature are put into legal practice and to thereby structurally influence legal change.[66]

Filing legal actions before the German administrative courts in order to enforce the EU's regulatory framework for air quality requires observance of the domestic administrative procedural rules. The restrictive national doctrine of subjective-public rights, whose origin can be traced back to the nineteenth century, rendered it impossible to initiate legal actions in the name of the NGO itself. Judicial review had been confined to the protection of individual rights to

[62] Interview with the lawyer of Mr Janecek, 8 October 2012; interview with Mr Janecek, 9 October 2012.

[63] For the website, see www.duh.de/kein-diesel-ohne-filter/.

[64] See for instance 'Abschätzung positiver gesundheitlicher Auswirkungen durch den Einsatz von Partikelfiltern bei Dieselfahrzeugen in Deutschland', conducted by Dr Erich Wichmann (Direktor des Instituts für Epidemiologie der GSF, Neuherberg) for the Umweltbundesamtes Berlin, 7 June 2003, available at www.umweltbundesamt.de/sites/default/files/medien/publikation/long/2352.pdf.

[65] Council Directive 1999/30/EC of 22 April 1999 relating to limit values for sulphur dioxide, nitrogen dioxide and oxides of nitrogen, particulate matter and lead in ambient air, OJ L163, 29 June 1999, 41; Directive 1999/30/EC has been repealed by Directive 2008/50/EC.

[66] Interview with the lawyer of Mr Janecek, 8 October 2012.

ensure that courts do not interfere in the state's political decision-making on a case-by-case basis. Legal protection under German administrative law is therefore confined to norms, which not only serve to protect the general public interest but are intended to protect individual interests as well (referred to as the 'protective norm theory' (*Schnutznormtheorie*)). The protective norm theory shapes the rules of legal standing before the administrative courts and the different types of actions available. Accordingly, private parties are prevented from initiating legal actions in the collective or public interests. An objective control of administrative acts is excluded, aside from actions against the lack of administrative action.[67] From the mid-1950s, the case law of the Federal Administrative Court loosened the requirements by admitting neighbourhood actions in the context of industrial emissions. Private parties were granted standing if they were 'neighbours' of the beneficiary of an administrative action, and if they could invoke a norm that intends to protect their interests. Those actions have a tripartite structure: private parties may challenge an administrative licence, building or operation permit granted to another private party by a public authority, if they are able to establish an individual relationship between themselves and the dangers allegedly emanating from the respective facility.[68]

In view of the restrictive domestic rules and in order to spread the risk, four test-cases on behalf of individuals living in close proximity to air quality measuring stations in different German cities were initiated. Since the pollution, which was largely caused by local motor vehicle traffic, posed a significant threat to human health and the limit values for air quality were designed to protect human health, the lawyer argued that all persons who are permanently or repeatedly exposed to the pollutants are individually and directly affected. The proximity of the individuals' residences to the air quality measuring stations facilitated the claim that the limit values have been exceeded at their homes. While the legal actions were formally initiated by the individuals, their role remained passive, ie nothing beyond the power of attorney was required.[69]

The search of individuals willing to support the legal action created some difficulties, as did securing their long-term commitment to lengthy court proceedings, as illustrated by a prematurely terminated case in which the individual decided to move home three weeks before the oral proceedings began.[70] The legal action of Mr Janecek eventually reached the CJEU. Mr Janecek served as litigant for

[67] O Bühler, *Die subjektiven öffentlichen Rechte und ihr Schutz in der deutschen Verwaltungsrechtsprechung* (Berlin, Kohlhammer, 1914); M Greve, 'The Non-Reformation of Administrative Law: Standing to Sue and Public Interest Litigation in West German Environmental Law' (1989) *Cornell International Law Journal* 197; BW Wegener, 'Subjective public right – Historical Roots versus European and Democratic Challenge' in H Pünder and C Waldhoff (eds), *Debates in German Public Law* (Oxford, Hart, 2014) 219.

[68] BVerwG, 24.10.1967 – I C 64.65. See also UG Berger, *Grundfragen umweltrechtlicher Nachbarklagen: zum verwaltungsrechtlichen Drittschutz im Bauplanungsrecht, Immissionsschutzrecht und Kernenergierecht* (Heymann, 1982); Kirchhof, (above n 61).

[69] Interview with the lawyer of Mr Janecek, 8 October 2012.

[70] ibid.

4–5 years before he could move home to a low traffic road with his family. He pursued concurrently a political career in the green political party.[71] The lawyer anticipated from the very beginning either reaching one of the highest national courts or the CJEU in order to clarify the legal situation once and for all, and to facilitate subsequent actions in other cities. In order to reach that goal, in addition to finding a resilient individual willing to see through the various court instances, the strategic approach extended towards the choice of resistant defendants.[72]

In order to effectively further the interests of the campaign, it was not sufficient if traffic were only to be restricted in the specific street or area where the individual plaintiffs lived. Therefore, the legal actions required the authorities to set up action plans covering the whole urban territory and to include the measures that would immediately result in compliance with the limit values. This claim was based on the domestic implementation of Article 7(3) of the Air Quality Framework Directive 96/62/EC, which obliged national authorities to draw up action plans indicating the measures to be taken in the short term, where there is a risk of the air quality limit values being exceeded.[73] To support that claim, the lawyer relied on the judgments of the CJEU in Cases C-361/88, *Commission v Germany* and C-58/89, *Commission v Germany*, where it was held that whenever the exceeding of the limit value could endanger the health of the persons concerned, they must be in a position to rely on mandatory rules in order to be able to assert their rights.

ii. The Position of the German Courts

The German courts took diverging views as to whether Mr Janecek was entitled to request an action plan setting out the short-term measures to be taken to ensure compliance with the limit value for PM_{10}. The Administrative Court of Munich held that the domestic implementation of Article 7(3) of the Air Quality Framework Directive 96/62/EC did not substantiate a subjective right.[74] Even though the Bavarian Higher Administrative Court recognised Mr Janecek's subjective right to the preparation of an action plan, it denied that an action plan would have to ensure compliance with the limit values.[75] In both courts' reasoning, it was prevalent that the authorities enjoyed discretion as to the choice of measures to be included in the action plan and that the principle of proportionality requires that only those measures are taken within the framework of an action plan that carefully examine and adequately balance the interests of affected third parties, including the economic interests traders and road users. The Federal Administrative Court argued that a third party affected by pollution had no right to have an action plan drawn up. According to the court, action plans are to be drawn up by

[71] Interview with Mr Janecek, 9 October 2012.
[72] Interview with the lawyer of Mr Janecek, 8 October 2012.
[73] Section 47(2) of the Federal Emission Control Act (*Bundes-Immissionsschutzgesetz*).
[74] VG München, 26.07.2005 – M 1 K 05.1114.
[75] VGH Bayern, 18.05.2006 – 22 BV 05.2462.

the authority in the public interest and not to protect the subjective rights of third parties. The action plan as such would not directly result either in an improvement in ambient air quality or compliance with the limit values. The court even considered it counterproductive to accord this provision protective effect because that would lead to several claims of third parties, which would interfere with and delay the setting up of the action plan and disturb the goal of achieving a balance of interests. However, since it was not unequivocally resolved by EU law whether the right to require an action plan could be based on Article 7(3) of the Air Quality Framework Directive 96/62, the court decided to request a preliminary reference from the CJEU. In that regard, the court stressed that it is for the Member States to lay down detailed procedural rules to ensure that the rights granted to citizens under Community law are protected, provided the requirements of equivalence and effectiveness are adhered to. Since private parties can request the enforcement of specific measures independent of an action plan if the limit values are exceeded (such as, for instance, requesting the restriction of traffic in a particular street), domestic law would comply with the Community requirements.[76]

iii. The Judgment of the CJEU

In its judgment, the CJEU held that

> natural or legal persons directly concerned by a risk that the limit value or alert threshold may be exceeded must be in a position to require the competent authorities to draw up an action plan where such a risk exists, if necessary by bringing an action before the competent courts.[77]

The rather terse judgment of the CJEU, which was delivered without written opinion by the Advocate General, established a new remedy, namely a representative action, which was novel to both German and European law.[78] In view of the extensive and forcefully argued opposition by the Federal Administrative Court as to granting third parties the right to an action plan, whose view was supported by the governments of Austria and the Netherlands in their written observations submitted to the CJEU,[79] the questions at stake must not have posed particular

[76] BVerwG, Vorlagebeschluss vom 29.3.2007 - 7 C 9/06.

[77] *Janecek* (above n 2) para 39.

[78] L Krämer, *Focus on European Environmental Law* (Sweet & Maxwell, 1997) 97, 98: ('Normally, however, provisions, which provide for an obligation for administrative bodies to act are not of direct effect: they regularly lack the fifth condition, i.e. giving a "right", a favourable position to individuals. Therefore, where an administrative body is obliged, under a Community directive, to draw up a clean-up programme for waste, air or soil, or a monitoring programme for waste, this kind of obligation is not essentially improving the individual's position vis-à-vis the administrative body. […] Most of these provisions are unconditional and sufficiently precise, yet they generally concern normal administrative activity which does not reflect on the protected position of individuals').

[79] As summarised by the CJEU in *Janecek* (above n 2) paras 25–30.

difficulties for the CJEU. Indeed, the judgment was firmly based on earlier case law on the direct effect of directives. The CJEU did not frame the question as one relating to remedies covered by the procedural autonomy of the Member States.[80] Regarding the content of the action plans, the CJEU held that 'the Member States are not obliged to take measures to ensure that those limit values and/or alert threshold are never exceeded'.[81] Instead,

> it is for the Member States to take measures capable of reducing to a minimum the risk of the limit values and/or alert thresholds being exceeded and the duration of such an occurrence, taking into account all the material circumstances and opposing interests.[82]

The Member States enjoy discretion as to

> the adequacy of the measures which must be included in the action plan with the aim of reducing the risk of the limit values and/or alert thresholds being exceeded and the duration of such an occurrence, taking into account the balance which must be maintained between that objective and the various opposing public and private interests.[83]

C. 'Where to' the *Janecek* case had a structuring effect

From the claimant's perspective, the Court of Justice's ruling was considered to be a success. Although the CJEU did not confirm that the action plan had to achieve strict compliance with the limit values, the European citizen was given a 'right to clean air'.[84] After the CJEU's judgment, Mr Janecek and the Bavarian authorities withdrew their appeals against the judgment of the Higher Administrative Court, which thus became final. The Bavarian authorities were ordered to draw up an action plan that ensured compliance with the air quality limit values to the extent that was possible and proportionate. This resulted in the introduction of the low-emission zone in Munich and the prohibition of trucks from driving through the city centre.[85] The *Janecek* case resulted in a remarkable amount of follow-up actions, which aim not only to extend the scope of the newly-established remedy, but also to reach beyond the German legal system.

[80] *Janecek* (above n 2) para 40. However, in the *ClientEarth* case, by transferring the *Janecek* doctrine by analogy to Directive 2008/50, the CJEU framed the same issue in the light of the Member State's obligation to ensure judicial protection of an individual's rights under EU law and to provide remedies sufficient to ensure effective legal protection in the fields covered by EU law as provided for in Art 19(1) TEU, see Case C-404/13, *ClientEarth*, ECLI:EU:C:2014:2382, paras 52–56.

[81] *Janecek* (above n 2) para 44.

[82] *Janecek* (above n 2) para 45.

[83] *Janecek* (above n 2) paras 43–47.

[84] L Krämer, 'The Commission's Omission to Use Article 267 TFEU as a Tool to Enforce EU Environmental Law' (2016) *Journal for European Environmental and Planning Law* 255, 262.

[85] However, the road on which Mr Janecek lived was not made part of the low-emission zone.

i. Follow-up Actions in Germany

Until today, the German environmental NGO standing behind the *Janecek* litigation has initiated legal actions against more than 25 German cities for their failure to comply with the European air quality limit values for various pollutants.[86] In the light of the judgment of the CJEU in *Lesoochranárske zoskupenie*,[87] the lawyer was able to establish legal standing for the NGO in its own name before the German courts.[88] Beyond the setting up of an action plan, the NGO went on to request the courts to order the state authorities to change their action plans in order to ensure compliance with the limit values as soon as possible. Those actions have again reached the German Federal Administrative Court, which confirmed the collective legal standing of environmental NGOs in light of the CJEU judgment and the Aarhus Compliance Committee's case law on Article 9(3) of the Aarhus Convention.[89] Regarding the content of the action plan, the Federal Administrative Court held that the requirement to end the exceeding of the ambient air quality limit values as quickly as possible requires an evaluation of the measures that are suitable and proportionate to reduce emissions, particularly in the interests of promptly meeting the ambient air quality goals. This may lead to a restriction of the discretion for planning if only the selection of a specific measure could achieve compliance with the limit values.[90]

The degree to which the national courts enter into a substantive evaluation of the action plan determines whether the newly-established remedy remains of a mere procedural nature or gives rise to a substantive right to a clean environment. Initially, the remedy's effectiveness to achieve actual compliance with the ambient air limit values for pollutants was cast into doubt by the resistance of national courts to enter into a substantive evaluation of the measures set out in the air quality plans. That would be a matter for the administration with a view to a balancing of the various interests at stake. In light of the persistent failure to set up adequate air quality action plans, and the increasing pressure stemming from the legal actions for clean air, the position of the German courts has started to change in recent years. The Administrative Court of Düsseldorf stated that, in order to comply with the limit values as soon as possible, driving bans for certain diesel vehicles are legally possible and not excluded.[91] The Administrative Court of Stuttgart went a step further and ordered the state of Baden-Württemberg to consider a year-round ban on the use of diesel vehicles.[92] The Federal Administrative Court decided in February 2018 that diesel traffic prohibitions – while

[86] Deutsche Umwelthife, Klagen für saubere Luft, Hintergrundpapier, Stand: 22.10.2018, available at www.duh.de/fileadmin/user_upload/download/Projektinformation/Verkehr/Feinstaub/2018-10-22_Right-to-Clean-Air_Hintergrundpapier_D.pdf.

[87] Case C-240/09, *Lesoochranárske zoskupenie*, ECLI:EU:C:2011:125.

[88] Interview with the lawyer of Mr Janecek (applicant), 8 October 2012.

[89] BVerwG, 5.09.2013 – 7 C 21.12, paras 47–50.

[90] BVerwG, 5.09.2013 – 7 C 21.12, paras 61–63.

[91] VG Düsseödorf, 19.09.2016 – 3 K 7695/15.

[92] VG Stuttgart, 26.7.2017 – 13 K 5412/15.

respecting the principle of proportionality – are already possible today. While the court admitted that the currently applicable regulations of the Federal Emission Control Act do not permit such traffic prohibitions, they are, however, admissible taking into account EU law.[93]

ii. Actions across Europe

Since the cause for exceeding limit values of pollutants in the ambient air of Europe's cities lies mainly in urban road traffic, it is considered to be a local problem. Moreover, looking at the origin of the *Janecek* litigation, one might conclude that its implications are limited to the German legal context. However, the *Janecek* litigation resulted in a remarkable transnational effect in terms of the establishment of a cross-border co-operation of various NGOs, which share their legal experiences and strategies on the enforcement of the EU air quality legislation. The grouping received funding of €1,686,635 by an 'EU Life Project' from the European Commission.[94] The project, entitled 'Clean Air' (which ran from 1 September 2012 until 30 November 2015), aimed 'to give NGOs the competence through capacity building to use justice as an instrument for supporting the implementation of the Air Quality Directive'. The aim was to 'force administrations to really use effective instruments for the reduction of emissions'.[95] In order to achieve that goal, the project organised 11 legal workshops to inform NGOs and specialised lawyers about the EU air quality legislation and the possibilities of taking legal action to promote better implementation. Legal strategies that were successful were presented, and their applicability in diverse legal contexts discussed. The legal workshops resulted in *The Clean Air Handbook*, which includes an Annex of useful test cases for the enforcement of the European air quality legislation.[96] The initiative received further funding of €521,834 for the period from 1 August 2016 until 30 November 2019 under the 'LIFE Legal Actions – Legal Actions on Clean Air' Programme.[97] Both projects have been coordinated by the NGO standing behind the *Janecek* case. The websites of the projects provide an overview of the legal situations in various Member States and the legal actions that have been initiated so far. Some of the legal actions were successful in reaching the highest national courts, and further preliminary references to the CJEU have been submitted.[98]

[93] BVerwG, 27.2.2018 – 7 C 30.17; BVerwG, 27.2.2018 – 7 C 26.16.

[94] The EU LIFE Programme is the EU's financial instrument supporting environmental, nature conservation and climate action projects throughout the EU. See on this ec.europa.eu/environment/life/.

[95] For details on the project, see ec.europa.eu/environment/life/project/Projects/index.cfm?fuseaction=search.dspPage&n_proj_id=4265; see also www.cleanair-europe.org/en/home/.

[96] A Andrews, *The Clean Air Handbook – a practical guide to EU air quality law*, Version 2.0 – November 2015, available at www.clientearth.org/reports/20140515-clientearth-air-pollution-clean-air-handbook.pdf.

[97] For details on the project, see ec.europa.eu/environment/life/project/Projects/index.cfm?fuseaction=search.dspPage&n_proj_id=5820.

[98] See legal.cleanair-europe.org/legal/eu/; www.right-to-clean-air.eu/en/lawsuits-and-decisions/germany/.

IV. An Outlook

This chapter reconstructed the *Janecek* case as an entry point into the deep entanglement between law, society, and politics in the EU context. It revealed how the fragmentary nature of the EU's 'hybrid legal space' provides a breeding ground for strategic actions by legal entrepreneurs, which turn political disputes into legal argumentation. The judgment of the CJEU in *Janecek* did not close down the political battles that existed before, but redirected them towards legal disputes about the interpretation over the judgment's meaning and scope. The newly-established remedy changed the institutional role of the actors involved. On the surface, the individual within the preliminary reference procedure turned into a representative for the collective interests of all EU citizens suffering from air pollution. However, the distress suffered by Mr Janecek because of polluted air hardly played a role in the case. The follow-up developments demonstrated the institutionalisation of the monitoring function of collective entities. Their professionalism, funding and legal expertise are key factors for the effective enforcement of the EU air quality legislation. National courts have taken the role of political decision-makers by rendering judgments that have an impact beyond the conflict between the parties of the case. The role of the national authorities is at this point largely reduced to the execution of the judgments rendered. This development can be termed as a transformation of the 'legal field', which requires to be re-connected in future research to the broader political and legal dynamics of EU polity-building.

20

Defectiveness and Causation in Vaccine Liability Cases

The Jurisprudence of the Supreme Court of the United States and the Court of Justice of the European Union

MARCO RIZZI* AND LÉCIA VICENTE**†

I. Introduction

A vaccine is a substance that derives from or is similar to a particular infectious agent that causes a disease. Once introduced in the human body, the immune system recognises that substance and triggers the immune system's response, protecting the individual who received the vaccine against that particular agent. Vaccination is a crucial method of prevention, eradication and control of infectious diseases and a pillar of public health protection, saving more lives than any other medical treatment. However, despite being 'one of the greatest achievements of public health in the 20th century', vaccines have become, in time,

> ... victims of their own success. They had been so effective in preventing infectious diseases that the public became much less alarmed at the threat of those diseases, and much more concerned with the risk of injury from the vaccines themselves.

So begins the majority opinion, delivered by Justice Scalia, in *Bruesewitz v Wyeth*, decided by the Supreme Court of the United States (SCOTUS) in 2011.[1] Recent societal developments such as the rise and increasing pervasiveness of 'vaccine

* Senior Lecturer, University of Western Australia, Law School.

** Assistant Professor of Law, Louisiana State University Paul M Hebert Law Center.

† We would like to thank Christopher Minus, JD student at the University of Western Australia Law School for his research assistance, and Martin Gelter, Fordham University School of Law, for his comments. All mistakes remain our own.

[1] *Bruesewitz v Wyeth LLC* 562 US 223, 131 S Ct 1068, 179 L Ed 2d 1 (2011).

hesitancy' (if not overt hostility) in Europe and the United States (US) constitute a problematic issue for policymakers,[2] and are promoting a range of policy and legislative responses.[3] In this context, the recent jurisprudence of the Court of Justice of the European Union (CJEU) and the SCOTUS warrant reflection. The EU and the US are the two largest vaccine markets globally,[4] with a considerable overlap in the manufacturers.[5] The European Medicines Agency (EMA) and the United States Food and Drug Administration (FDA) have developed significant cooperative mechanisms to facilitate marketing authorisation procedures. While a detailed contextual analysis would fall beyond the scope of this chapter, it is worth keeping this background in mind when reading this contribution.

The reflection we undertake is two-pronged. We analyse the policy arguments put forth in crucial decisions by the European and American highest courts to sanction vaccine-related injuries. In parallel, we investigate the place and role of scientific evidence in the legal framework disciplining liability of vaccine manufacturers. In doing so, we will identify convergence and discrepancies with respect to policy, regulatory and legal approaches in Europe and the US. Admittedly, this analysis is limited to EU and US federal laws, regulations, and case law. We acknowledge that internal divergences exist (between states in the US and Member States in the EU), and these will be referred to when appropriate, but the focus is on the overarching approach that the two principal markets adopt in the face of alleged vaccine-related injuries.

Policy-wise, the recent jurisprudence of the CJEU has been leaning towards a plaintiff-oriented interpretation of the applicable legal framework,[6] the contours of which are defined by the European Product Liability Directive.[7] Critically, in

[2] For example HJ Larson, 'The State of Vaccine Confidence' (2018) 392 *The Lancet* 10161, 2244; HJ Larson et al, 'The State of Vaccine Confidence 2016: Global Insights Through a 67-Country Survey' (2016) 12 *EBio Medicine* 295.

[3] For a discussion of the mandatory vaccination schemes adopted in the US, Europe, and Australia, see K Attwell et al, 'Recent Vaccine Mandates in the United States, Europe and Australia: A Comparative Study' (2018) 36(48) *Vaccine* 7377.

[4] The World Health Organization (WHO) estimates that high-income countries constitute 82% of global vaccine sales regarding value. See www.who.int/immunization/programmes_systems/procurement/market/global_demand/en/, accessed on 28 March 2019.

[5] WHO estimates that 80% of global vaccine sales come from five large multinational corporations: ibid.

[6] CJEU, Case C-621/15, *W & Others v Sanofi Pasteur MSD SNC & Others*, ECLI:EU:C:2017:484. The case has sparked significant debate, see M Rizzi, 'A Dangerous Method: Correlations and Proof of Causation in Vaccine-Related Injuries' (2018) 9 *Journal of European Tort Law* 3; E Brosset, 'Distinguishing between Law and Science in Terms of Causation and the Hepatitis B Vaccine: *W v Sanofi Pasteur*' (2018) 55(6) *Common Market Law Review* 1899; T Verheyen, 'Full Harmonization, Consumer Protection and Products Liability: A Fresh Reading of the Case Law of the ECJ' (2018) 26(1) *European Review of Private Law* 119; E Ruiz Cairó, 'The Lack of Medical Research Does not Prevent an Injured Person from Proving the Defect of a Product and the Causal Link between the Defect and the Damage' (2017) 8(4) *European Journal of Risk Regulation* 798.

[7] Council Directive 85/374/EEC of 25 July 1985 on the approximation of the laws, regulations and administrative provisions of Member States concerning the liability for defective products, OJ L210, 7 August 1985, pp 29–33.

its most recent case *W & Others v Sanofi Pasteur*, the CJEU held that in product liability litigation involving vaccines, national courts might consider circumstantial evidence or indirect proof to make inferential conclusions regarding the defectiveness of the vaccine and its causal link to the lamented harm. On the contrary, in the US, the SCOTUS in *Bruesewitz v Wyeth* has maintained that it is not up to courts or juries to make judgments about vaccine design that would encroach upon scientific territories such as epidemiology. That type of judgement is instead a prerogative of the FDA and the National Vaccine Injury Compensation Program (NVICP). It is important to note that, in the US, generally speaking, courts are quite deferential to administrative agencies and unlikely to strike down agency decisions even in interpreting the law. The rationale is that agencies usually have expertise that courts do not have.[8] Furthermore, in *Bruesewitz v Wyeth*, the court held that not only is the design of the vaccine not subject to challenge in a tort action, but also that evidence of causation for other types of defect is to undergo a rigorous 'vetting' process to ascertain its scientific soundness.

Essentially the CJEU, taking up from the jurisprudence of French courts on this matter, has adopted a form of *dialectical* reasoning to define the nature and scope of the causal link under the Directive. The SCOTUS, on the other hand, stands firmly by a *deductive* reasoning, while following a purely textual or plain meaning approach to the black letter law of relevant provisions.[9]

There are two fundamental questions for us to consider. The first is whether the SCOTUS's jurisprudence is excessively rigid in an ambit characterised by rapid scientific developments and discoveries that should warrant more open-textured readings of legislative texts. The second question is whether the CJEU has conceded too wide a margin of manoeuvre for national courts when it opened the door to a system of presumptions for vaccine liability and, by the same token, whether it has endorsed a 'dangerous method'[10] for determining defectiveness and causation, which has the potential to elevate illogical reasoning to the status of legal proof. The point of interest is identifying which option achieves a better balance between public health concerns and individual rights, or whether a balancing act between the two approaches would be desirable.[11]

[8] 'A court must defer under Chevron to an agency's interpretation of a statutory ambiguity that concerns scope of agency's statutory authority, that is, its jurisdiction; no matter how it is framed, question a court faces when confronted with an agency's interpretation of a statute it administers is always, simply, whether agency has stayed within bounds of its statutory authority': *City of Arlington, Tex v FCC* 569 US 290, 133 S Ct 1863, 185 L Ed 2d 941 (2013).

[9] In particular 42 USC § 300aa–22(b)(1): '[n]o vaccine manufacturer shall be liable in a civil action for damages arising from a vaccine-related injury or death associated with the administration of a vaccine after October 1, 1988, if the injury or death resulted from side effects that were unavoidable even though the vaccine was properly prepared and was accompanied by proper directions and warnings'.

[10] As suggested by Rizzi (above n 6).

[11] A recent article suggests that the approach adopted by the CJEU in *Sanofi* achieves that balance, but it arguably does so without sufficiently discussing the full range of the judgment's potential consequences. See MS Holland, 'Liability for Vaccine Injury: The United States, the European Union, and the Developing World' (2018) 67 *Emory Law Journal* 415.

We organise the chapter as follows. We first discuss the legal framework governing the liability of vaccine manufacturers in the US and the EU. Then, we analyse the issues of defectiveness and causation in vaccine-related injuries as elaborated by the SCOTUS and the CJEU. We undertake the work of comparison through a *comparative matrix*. A comparative matrix is a two-entry table that lists key ancillary queries, the purpose of which is to help us address the overarching issue identified above. The matrix will provide essential material for the concluding *comparative synthesis*.

II. The Legal Framework

A. The United States Vaccines Act: Rationale and Implications

The National Childhood Vaccine Injury Act (NCVIA or Act) of 1986 (42 USC §§ 300aa-1 to 300aa-34) created two programs: a National Vaccine Program and a National Vaccine Injury Compensation Program. The National Vaccine Program concerns the establishment of optimal measures and lines of research to prevent human infectious diseases through immunisation and adverse reactions to vaccines. The National Vaccine Compensation Program sets forth the terms under which a judgment may award compensation for a vaccine-related injury or death. By creating these two programs, the main focus of the Act was to stabilise the vaccine market as well as promote an expedited system of compensation in order to overcome the inefficiencies and costs that both injured consumers and vaccine manufacturers had to bear.[12] Needless to say, those inefficiencies and costs have caused high levels of litigation in an area where the law is grey.

Here, we focus on the National Vaccine Injury Compensation Program (Compensation Program). It is a 'no-fault' compensation system by which vaccine manufacturers are not subject to general tort liability. According to § 300aa-22(b)(1) of the Act, no vaccine administrator or manufacturer may be made a party to a civil action (other than the civil actions that a defendant can specifically bring against the vaccine manufacturer pursuant to the compensation program) for damages resulting from a vaccine-related injury or death associated with the administration of a vaccine, after 1 October 1988.

The petitioner shall initiate the proceeding for compensation with the United States Court of Federal Claims. The clerk of the court shall immediately forward the petition to the chief special master, who will assign the filed petition

[12] 'Congress enacted the NCVIA to stabilize the vaccine market and expedite compensation to injured parties after complaints mounted regarding the inefficiencies and costs borne by both injured consumers and vaccine manufacturers under the previous civil tort compensation regime'. See *Sebelius v Cloer* 569 US 369, 133 S Ct 1886, 185 L Ed 2d 1003 (2013).

to a special master. A person who has allegedly sustained damages as a result of a vaccine-related injury or death associated with the administration of a vaccine cannot bring a civil action in an amount greater than $1000,00 or an unspecified amount against a vaccine administrator or manufacturer in a state or federal court. No such court may award damages in an amount greater than $1000,00 in a civil action for damages for such a vaccine-related injury or death unless the petitioner meets the following criteria. The petitioner must have filed for compensation under the Compensation Program beforehand. Additionally, the United States Court of Federal Claims must have issued a judgment on that petition, and the petitioner has elected to file a civil action after the court's final judgment. Alternatively, the petitioner must have elected to withdraw the petition they filed under the Compensation Program.

The preponderance of the evidence the petitioner provides with the petition determines the eligibility for compensation under the Compensation Program for a vaccine-related injury or death. The petition shall contain, except where provided in the Act, an affidavit, and supporting documentation, demonstrating that the person who suffered the injury or who died received a vaccine listed in the Vaccine Injury Table. If the petitioner did not receive such a vaccine, they must demonstrate that they contracted, directly or indirectly, the listed disease from another person who received the vaccine outlined in the Table. If the petitioner received the vaccine outlined in the Table, they must demonstrate the case has a relevant connection to the US. The petitioner demonstrates there is that relevant connection if they received the vaccine in the US, they were a citizen of the US deployed abroad when they received the vaccine, the person whom the petitioner contracted the disease from was a citizen of the US or a dependent of such a citizen.

The petitioner must demonstrate they sustained, or had significantly aggravated, any illness, disability, injury, or condition set forth in the Table in association with a vaccine listed in the Table, or that death resulted from the administration of such vaccine, and the first symptom or manifestation of the onset or of the significant aggravation of any such illness, disability, injury, or condition or death occurred within the time frame after vaccine administration set forth in the Table. If the Table does not outline the sustained or significantly aggravated illness, disability, injury, or condition, or their symptoms did not occur within the period set forth in the Table, the petitioner must demonstrate that a vaccine listed in the Table caused that illness, disability, injury, or condition.

The petitioner must demonstrate that they suffered the residual effects or complications of such illness, disability, injury, or condition for more than six months after the administration of the vaccine, or death resulted from the administration of the vaccine, or suffered such illness, disability, injury, or condition from the vaccine which resulted in inpatient hospitalisation and surgical intervention. The petitioner must demonstrate that they have not previously collected an award or settlement of a civil action for damages for such vaccine-related injury or death.

The petition should contain relevant documents such as maternal prenatal and delivery records, newborn hospital records, vaccination records associated with the vaccine allegedly causing the injury, pre- and post-injury physician or clinic records, all post-injury inpatient and outpatient records and, if applicable, a death certificate, or autopsy results. The petition may also include other relevant records relating to the person who suffered the injury or who died from the administration of the vaccine.

In addition to the content of the petition, a person is eligible to be compensated if they demonstrate by a preponderance of the evidence that the vaccine-related injuries or death are not due to factors unrelated to the administration of the vaccine as described in the petition. The Act specifies that the term 'factors unrelated to the administration of the vaccine' does not include any idiopathic, unexplained, unknown, hypothetical, or undocumentable cause, factor, injury, illness, or condition or any other factors such as infection, toxins, trauma or metabolic disturbances that, although not having a known connection to the vaccine involved, are shown to have been the agents or agents principally responsible for causing the petitioner's injuries or death.

In sum, if the petitioner shows by a preponderance of the evidence that the person who suffered the vaccine-related injury or who died: (i) received a vaccine listed in the Table or contracted the disease from someone who received such listed vaccine; (ii) that the vaccine-related injuries set forth in the Table are associated with the administration of a vaccine set forth in the Table; (iii) that the first symptoms occurred within the timeframe of the table; and (iv) that injury or death is not due to factors unrelated to the administration of the vaccine, the court will award the petitioners compensation for a vaccine-related injury or death. If the injuries and the timeframe within which they occur are off-Table, the petitioner must demonstrate, again by a preponderance of the evidence, that a vaccine listed in the Table caused those injuries.

B. The European Product Liability Directive: 'one size fits all'(?)

Unlike the US, the EU does not dictate special provisions for vaccine-related injuries compensation. Indeed, these fall within the scope of general legislation, which in turn situates them within the scope of application of the European Product Liability Directive (the Directive).

The Directive was approved more than three decades ago, in 1985. Its principal aim was levelling an uneven playfield, as divergent approaches to the tortious liability of producers for damages caused by defective products could negatively affect competition and free movement of goods among the Member States.[13] To remedy this unsatisfactory state of affairs, and after long and complex negotiations, the Council adopted the Directive to impose a strict liability regime on producers. A producer is broadly understood as anyone taking part in the

[13] See Preamble of the European Product Liability Directive.

manufacture of a finished product, including the producer of raw materials or a component or part, as well as anyone presenting themselves as producers by putting their names or trademarks or other distinguishing features of a product. The regime extends to the supplier of the product if the product is imported from outside the EU or generally when the producer cannot be traced (Article 3). The regime applies to all moveables, broadly defined and including moveable goods incorporated in immovable ones (Article 2). Despite the Preamble of the Directive mentioning consumer protection as a goal, the primary aim of the Directive was, at least originally, that of providing maximum harmonisation to the field across the internal market.[14]

For over half of its life, the Directive has remained a virtually dormant piece of legislation.[15] A series of reports by the Commission has repeatedly signalled that the European version of product liability, unlike its American counterpart, has faced significant structural obstacles in its quest to become a primary means of compensation for victims of defective products.[16] Academic literature has abundantly discussed the reasons for these difficulties.[17] Among others, it is worth mentioning the fact that the Directive does not detract from the rights an injured party may have under national contractual and non-contractual liability rules or pre-existing individual liability systems (as per Article 13). This deference of the Directive to the national systems of liability has *de facto* worked as an incentive for claimants (and their legal representatives) to file claims under existing national regimes.[18] Nonetheless, the Directive in time has progressively increased its impact, becoming a useful tool for claimants to reach out-of-court settlements as well as to litigate cases in national courts.[19] The latest report by the Commission in particular shows that this 'revival' of the Product Liability Directive is particularly significant in the raw materials market (21% of the claims) and pharmaceutical products (including vaccines, accounting for 16% of the claims).[20]

Relatively few cases reach the CJEU to seek the interpretation of the Directive's provisions, but, unsurprisingly, the overwhelming majority (67%) of cases referred for preliminary rulings stem from domestic litigation involving pharmaceutical products or medical devices. The 'one size fits all' nature of the Directive, designed to

[14] ibid. See also the recent commentary by Verheyen (above n 6).

[15] M Reimann, 'Product Liability in a Global Context: The Hollow Victory of the European Model' (2003) 11 *European Review of Private Law* 2.

[16] European Commission, COM (1995) 617 final; European Commission, COM (2000) 893 final; European Commission, COM(2006) 496 final; European Commission, COM(2011) 547 final; and European Commission, COM(2018) 246 final.

[17] See for example D Wuyts, 'The Product Liability Directive – More than two Decades of Defective Products in Europe' (2014) 5 *Journal of European Tort Law* 1.

[18] ibid, 2 ff.

[19] M Rizzi, 'Non-Measurable Negotiations – The EU between Transnational Pharmaceutical Regulation and Private Law' in M Cremona and H-W Micklitz (eds), *Private Law in the External Relations of the EU* (Oxford, Oxford University Press, 2016).

[20] European Commission, COM(2018) 246 final, p 4; the topic has also gained renewed prominence in academic debate, see for example P Machinkowski (ed), *European Product Liability – An Analysis of the State of the Art in the Era of New Technologies* (Intersentia, 2016).

apply transversally from the simplest to the most sophisticated of moveable goods, has raised several complex legal questions in situations characterised by structural uncertainty. As the Commission itself has explicitly conceded, the very language of the Directive and its focus on product defectiveness may be ill-suited to accommodate rapid technological advances that raise difficult challenges as regards methods of allocation of legal responsibility. Admittedly, the concerns are specifically raised in the context of the 'Fourth Industrial Revolution', with a focus on the emergence of artificial intelligence, machine learning algorithms and the Internet of Things.[21] However, there is an explicit acknowledgement that the notions of *defectiveness* and *causal link* as laid out in the Directive constitute significant (potentially fatal) obstacles to compensation for claimants injured by scientifically complex products such as pharmaceuticals, vaccines or medical devices.[22]

Whether this acknowledgement represents a concrete step towards reform of the regime of product liability in the EU (perhaps with the introduction of special regimes for specific categories of products) remains to be seen.[23] What is apparent, however, is that, in recent years, when referred a question on the matter, the CJEU has consistently issued markedly claimant-friendly readings of the Directive's provisions. This approach of the CJEU is arguably contributing to shifting the focus of European product liability from full harmonisation for internal market purposes, repositioning it more squarely within the realm of consumer protection – which, as argued in legal scholarship, may very be its more natural function.[24]

It is essential to take stock of this background when approaching the issue of liability of vaccine manufacturers. So far, relatively few vaccine cases have been litigated under EU product liability rules. Indeed, several Member States have special regimes in place to provide remedies for damages caused by vaccines. These include, for example, specific compensation funds, social security systems, and general regimes of civil liability.[25] The recent jurisprudence of the CJEU is shaping European product liability in a way that may induce increasing reliance on this old piece of legislation in cases involving scientifically complex products, including vaccines. It is, therefore, appropriate to discuss in more detail how the case law is transforming the two critical components (or most significant obstacles to compensation as per the Commission's observations) of this liability regime: defectiveness and causal link, which, together with the damage suffered, are what the injured party must prove to trigger the strict liability of the manufacturer (Article 4).

[21] European Commission, COM(2018) 246 final, p 8 ff.

[22] ibid, p 2 ff.

[23] Verheyen (above n 6) 133 suggests the argument.

[24] H-W Micklitz, 'Liability for Defective Products and Services' in N Reich et al (eds), *European Consumer Law* (Intersentia, 2014); see also S Whittaker, 'Introduction to Fault in Product Liability' in S Whittaker (ed), *The Development of Product Liability* (Cambridge, Cambridge University Press, 2010).

[25] See for example E Rajneri et al, 'Remedies for Damage Caused by Vaccines: A Comparative Study of Four European Legal Systems' (2018) 27 *European Review of Private Law* 1.

III. Defectiveness and Causation

A. Defectiveness

i. The Tripartite Nature of American Product Liability

Vaccines are unavoidably dangerous products. The reporting of adverse side effects such as high fevers, seizures or paralysis by parents who have vaccinated their children is not unusual. Litigation has often ensued as the next step to obtain remedies for situations that are not clear but are extremely painful for those involved, particularly the children.

In the US, the overarching goal of the NCVIA was to stabilise the vaccine market and the prices of vaccines as well as provide secure, quick, and fair compensation to children with a vaccine injury or whose death resulted from the administration of a vaccine. However, the compensation process is seemingly slower, more adversarial, costly, and off point than what the legislature initially intended.[26] For example, the Act provides tight schedules to submit documentation; it maintains that attorneys' fees are not to be paid in full, and it establishes that payments for compensation depend on whether the petitioner has made their elections according to the Act. Besides, considering the lack of definitive scientific evidence as to the side effects of vaccines, the decision of the special master to consider whether the presumptions outlined in the Table cover a particular injury may require a second judgment.

Petitioners may elect to file a civil action for damages arising from a vaccine-related injury or death for which they previously filed a petition under the Compensation Program. State law shall apply to such civil action. Nevertheless, petitioners must bring the civil action within the period prescribed by limitations of actions under state law applicable to such civil action. Once claimants have brought their lawsuits in a state or federal court subject to the tort law system of the state where the court sits, there are a few challenges they will face. Proving a vaccine injury, illness, disability, condition or death outside of the Table is reportedly hard. It is difficult to prove that a vaccine is defective, in which case the vaccine manufacturer would be strictly liable, that is, liable without fault. Depending on the circumstances, it may be extraordinarily burdensome or even impossible to prove causation, if and when the presumptions outlined in the Table do not cover such injuries, illness, disability, condition, or death and those injuries, illness, disability, condition, or death have manifested themselves outside of the timeframe maintained in the Table.

In practical terms, what happens if a petitioner rejects the judgment of the United States Court of Federal Claims and elects to seek tort relief from the vaccine manufacturer? The Act provides in § 300aa-22(b)(1) that:

> No vaccine manufacturer shall be liable in a civil action for damages arising from a vaccine-related injury or death associated with the administration of a vaccine after

[26] Holland (above n 11), p 433, 'The NVICP has not lived up to the expectations Congress set out for it – to be fair, consistent, non-adversarial, and speedy'.

> October 1, 1988, if the injury or death resulted from side effects that were unavoidable even though the vaccine was properly prepared and was accompanied by proper directions and warnings'.

Neither the Act nor the FDA yields detailed criteria for determining a defective vaccine. The next step is to determine the meaning of 'unavoidable' (are the side effects unavoidable even if there are no defects in the vaccine or are the side effects unavoidable regardless of whether or not the vaccine was defective?). Once that meaning is clear, it is important to consider whether the Act pre-empts or not states' tort law. If the Act does not pre-empt states' tort law, should states' tort law apply *prima facie*? If the Act pre-empts states' tort law, it is crucial to figure to what extent states' tort law can still promote legal innovation in an area of the law that is unsettled. The active action of the manufacturer should define the term 'unavoidable', that is, the manufacturer must have taken all preventive measures for a side-effect to be considered unavoidable. The use of the grammatical method of interpretation entails that the term unavoidable, referring to vaccines' side-effects, cannot be read alone due to the conjunction 'even though' used in the legal provision above. In that provision, the degree to which the vaccine manufacturer complied with the rules of adequate manufacturing and warning qualify the unavoidability of the vaccine side effects. The 'even though clause' of the statutory provision does not qualify the term 'unavoidable' concerning compliance with rules of adequate design.

The Restatement Second, Torts § 402A provides that[27]

> (1) One who sells any product in a defective condition unreasonably dangerous to the user or consumer or to his property is subject to liability for physical harm thereby caused to the ultimate user or consumer, or to his property, if: (a) the seller is engaged in the business of selling such a product; and (b) it is expected to and does reach the user or consumer without substantial change in the condition in which it is sold; and
>
> (2) The rule stated above applies although: (a) the seller has exercised all possible care in the preparation and sale of his product, and (b) the user or consumer has not bought the product from or entered into any contractual relation with the seller.

Product liability may be established on the grounds of defective manufacture, defective warning, and defective design.[28] Defective manufacture reveals a flaw in the production and marketing of the product; defective instructions or warning consists of inadequate instructions or warnings or a total failure to warn about the foreseeable risks of harm posed by the product; the existence of a reasonable alternative design reveals the existence of a defective design. Typically, claimants seeking damages for vaccine-related injuries or death under states' tort law, would have to show that the administered vaccine was defectively manufactured, labelled,

[27] See Restatement (Second) of Torts § 402A (1965). Many jurisdictions continue to follow the Restatement Second, Torts § 402A, even though the Restatement Third, Torts: Products Liability has superseded it.

[28] See Restatement (Third) of Torts: Prod Liab § 2 (1998).

or designed. However, by not referring to defective-design in the provision quoted above, it seems that the Act wanted to exclude vaccine manufacturers' liability for defective design. In other words, the Act seems to exclude design defects from the bulk of considerations that would trigger the manufacturer's responsibility in a typical action of product liability.

In *Bruesewitz v Wyeth*, the SCOTUS provided that:

> The 'even though' clause clarifies the word that precedes it. It delineates the preventive measures that a vaccine manufacturer *must* have taken for a side-effect to be considered 'unavoidable' under the statute. Provided that there was proper manufacture and warning, any remaining side effects, including those resulting from design defects, are deemed to have been unavoidable. State-law design-defect claims are therefore pre-empted.[29]

The jurisprudence of the SCOTUS interprets the Act in a way that limits the vaccine-manufacturers liability for design defects because according to the Court's reading of the Act the design of the vaccine itself 'is not open to question'. The Court takes this literal approach to the Act (without no or very little resort to external aids of interpretation like legislative history, statutory purpose, administrative agencies or expert medical opinions) because it refuses to make a complex epidemiological judgment about vaccine design which, it maintains, should be left to the FDA and the National Vaccine Program to do. Again, neither the FDA nor the National Vaccine Program establishes clear criteria to determine the defectiveness of a vaccine.

By generally excluding vaccine manufacturers from the tort law system of the states, the Act triggers a special regime of product liability for vaccines that pre-empts the states' tort law.[30] Put differently, in vaccine liability cases, states' tort law is not applied *prima facie*. The SCOTUS has interpreted the Act as pre-empting 'all design-defect claims against vaccine manufacturers brought by plaintiffs who seek compensation for injury or death caused by vaccine side effects'.[31]

Vaccine manufacturers are bound to the duty to improve their products in light of the most recent advances in science and technology. The fact that plaintiffs cannot enforce this obligation through a state tort law action for defective design because the Act pre-empts all design-defect claims for vaccine-related injuries or deaths, strips states' tort law of its ability to affect original and more equitable solutions for circumstances where the regulatory framework cannot be straightforwardly applied. Furthermore, the word 'unavoidable' requires that the manufacturer has taken all preventive measures for a side-effect to be considered unavoidable. That includes preventing design defects.[32]

[29] See *Bruesewitz v Wyeth* (above n 1).

[30] See *Schafer v American Cyanamid Co* CA1 (Mass), 20 F 3d 1 (1994).

[31] See *Bruesewitz v Wyeth* (above n 1).

[32] See *Mutual Pharmaceutical Co, Inc v Bartlett* 133 S Ct 2466 (2013) where the court points out that 'Under New Hampshire law, one who sells any product in defective condition unreasonably dangerous to the user or consumer or to his property is subject to liability for physical harm caused by product, even though he has exercised all possible care in preparation and sale of product'.

Indeed, design defects are the most speculative and difficult type of product liability claim to litigate.[33] Still, the active conduct of the vaccine manufacturer when it comes to being updated and finding safer alternative medical products is and should be subject to judgment. The approach to it should be normative, even if the lack of criteria to define a defective vaccine wearies any objective understanding. The realisation that the FDA and the National Vaccine Program do not set forth criteria to determine the defectiveness of vaccines leaves a vacuum that is unlikely to be filled entirely by the presumptions of the Table or by the procedural requirements of the Act.[34]

ii. EU Product Liability: A Unified Notion of 'Defectiveness'

The first observation to be made here is that the cornerstone of EU product liability is a unified notion of defectiveness, a characteristic that sets this regime apart from its American counterpart where manufacturing, warning, and design defects are neatly distinct categories. The Directive defines a product as defective when it lacks the safety 'which a person is entitled to expect, taking all circumstances into account' (Article 6). This broad definition, which the Directive effectively phrases as a restatement of the so-called *consumer-expectation test*, has opened a significant debate in legal scholarship as to its precise contours and implications.[35]

The test of defectiveness has been said to be both *objective* and *normative*.[36] The objectivity lies in the fact that it is the expectations of the public at large that are to be considered, not the individual preferences of the injured party. This objective dimension is reminiscent of the variously described concepts of reasonableness that permeate the civil liability systems of every Member State. While this implies that the specific idiosyncrasies or sensitivities of an individual plaintiff cannot be taken into account, when a product is clearly targeted at a specific group of people (for instance, patients with a particular condition), the manufacturer is expected to offer a level of safety that meets the expectations of that group. Indeed, while, the standard of liability remains the expectation of the public at large, the public can reasonably expect a level of safety adequate to the target group.[37]

On the other hand, the test is also said to be normative insofar as it will only take into account legitimate expectations of the public – and therefore not their

[33] See *Bruesewitz v Wyeth* (above n 1).

[34] See, however, KF Cloney, 'AIDS Vaccine Manufacturers v Tort Regime: The Need for Alternatives' (1992) 49 *Washington & Lee Law Review* 559, 583–584 ('The application of traditional tort theory to manufacturers greatly hinders the development and marketing of vaccines because of the difficulty in complying with the variety of state standards, the unpredictability of the protections within the tort system, the large damage awards, and the incompatibility of strict product liability with governmental regulation').

[35] Two recent and comprehensive contributions are D Fairgrieve et al, 'Product Liability Directive' in Machinkowski (above n 20); and Micklitz (above n 24).

[36] D Wuyts, 'The Product Liability Directive – More than two Decades of Defective Products in Europe' (2014) 5 *Journal of European Tort Law* 1, 8 ff.

[37] ibid; see also A Grubb and G Howells (eds), *The Law of Product Liability* (Butterworths, 2007) ch 4.

actual expectations, which may very well be superior.[38] The level of safety that one is entitled to expect depends on the circumstances of the case, and it is ultimately for the adjudicating court to make a decision. Anglo-Saxon jurists would refer to this limb of the test as its 'policy' component. The Preamble of the Directive gives a clear indication in this sense when it attributes particular prominence to the idea of ensuring a 'fair apportionment of risks' between manufacturers and injured parties. An argument can be made that for specific categories of products presenting standard features, the normative component of the safety test should be complemented by recourse to *risk-utility* factors, which are critical to the American model of product liability.[39] Studies have shown that, in applying the Directive to emerging cases, national courts in various Member States have at times given weight to these risk-utility factors, not as alternative tests of liability, but as tools to moderate the potentially distorting effects of a *pure* consumer-expectation test.[40]

In its latest case on the matter, *Boston Scientific*,[41] the CJEU has taken the opportunity to provide strong normative guidance to national courts in cases involving technologically complex health products. The facts of the case are well known: the quality control service of the manufacturer, Boston Scientific, detected an increased risk of failure in a series of implantable medical devices. The question for the court was whether this increased risk was sufficient to establish defectiveness for plaintiffs who had decided to have the devices removed and were seeking compensation. The decision of the CJEU is of extreme interest as it lays down a simple but astute blueprint for decision-making in cases involving complex products. In essence, a 'potential defect' exists and does meet the Directive's requirement when the product under scrutiny is part of the same group or same production series as others that show 'abnormal potential for damage'. In *Boston Scientific*, the issue that effectively decided the case was the fact that the very task of the products in question was preventing damage, specifically heart failure (the case involved implantable pacemakers and defibrillators). Therefore, any issue with the products preventing them from fulfilling that task was, in and of itself, to be considered a defect.[42]

The decision in *Boston Scientific* has triggered extensive debate in legal scholarship and attracted different reactions.[43] One aspect that is not entirely clear, for example, is the scope of application of the 'potential defect' category, and in particular, whether it is to be extended to any product falling within the scope of the Directive, or only to implantable medical devices, or somewhere in the middle. While a definitive answer will only come from the case law, it seems reasonable

[38] D Fairgrieve (ed), *Product Liability in Comparative Perspective* (Cambridge, Cambridge University Press, 2005).

[39] See D Owen, *Products Liability Law* (West Academic, 2015).

[40] D Fairgrieve et al, 'The Product Liability Directive: Time to get Soft?' (2013) 4 *Journal of European Tort Law* 1, 8.

[41] CJEU Joined Cases C-503/13 and 504/13, *Boston Scientific Medizintechnik GmbH v AOK Sachsen-Anhalt – Die Gesundheitskasse, Betriebskrankenkasse RWE*, ECLI:EU:C:2015:148.

[42] P Machnikowski, 'Product Defect and Damage' (2016) 7(2) *Journal of European Tort Law* 233.

[43] See for example L Bergkamp, 'Is there a Defect in the European Court's Defect Test? Musings about Acceptable Risk' (2015) 6(2) *European Journal of Risk Regulation* 309; and B Van Leeuwen and P Verbruggen, 'Resuscitating EU Product Liability Law?' (2015) 23 *European Review of Private Law* 899.

to suggest that, while generalised application may be unwarranted, it would be appropriate to apply this reasoning to products presenting an elevated degree of technological complexity, such as medical devices, pharmaceuticals, and vaccines (to limit the discussion to the field of health products).

Normatively, the decision in *Boston Scientific* represents an important restatement of the prevalence of consumer-expectation to the detriment of risk-utility factors. While this aspect has attracted criticisms,[44] *Boston Scientific* constitutes a commendable attempt to reconcile law and science in the allocation of responsibility while taking into account the high levels of vulnerability and reliance that patients must necessarily place on manufacturers. Interestingly, this notion of 'potential defect' shows substantial commonality with the category of 'general causation' elaborated in American toxic tort litigation – whereby the plaintiff must first show that the allegedly defective product is capable *in general* of causing the lamented harm in order to prove a causal link.

B. Causation

i. The American Case Law: Scientific Rigour or Blanket Protection?

A party to a lawsuit for vaccine-related injuries or death under the NCVIA must demonstrate by a preponderance of the evidence that: (i) they received a vaccine listed in the Table; (ii) the Table listed the injuries sustained; (iii) that the first symptoms occurred timely as specified on the Table; (iv) and that unrelated factors to the administration of the vaccine did not play a role in causing the injuries or death. If the petitioner is successful in showing these elements, the court will grant them a presumption of causation.[45] The presumptions outlined in the Table do not preclude litigation for vaccine-related injuries, whether the Table outlines such injuries or not. If the Table outlines the injuries, the petitioner may elect to file a tort law civil action if they are not pleased with the decision of the court. If the petitioner received a vaccine listed in the Table but suffered injuries not listed in the Table ('off-Table' injuries), they will not benefit from a presumption of causation. Instead, the petitioner must prove by a preponderance of the evidence that the injuries derived from the administration of the listed vaccine. In other words, the petitioner must prove causation in fact.[46]

[44] Bergkamp (above n 42) takes a very negative view. See also A Galasso and H Luo, 'How does Product Liability Risk Affect Innovation? Evidence from Medical Implants' (2018) *Harvard Business School*, Working Paper 19-002.

[45] 'In a table claim, under Vaccine Act, a claimant who shows that he received a vaccination listed in the Vaccine Injury Table, and suffered an injury listed in the table within a prescribed period, is afforded a presumption of causation.' See *Andreu ex rel Andreu v Sec'y of Dep't of Health & Human Servs* 569 F3d 1367 (Fed Cir 2009).

[46] Holland (above n 11).

In *Althen v Sec'y of Health & Human Servs*, the United States Court of Appeals provided that to prove causation in fact, the claimant must 'show a medical theory causally connecting the vaccination and the injury'. Such medical theory is persuasive if it is proven by 'a logical sequence of cause and effect showing that the vaccination was the reason for the injury'. The logical sequence is supported by 'reputable medical or scientific explanation', ie 'evidence in the form of scientific studies or expert medical testimony.[47] Additionally, the claimant must show there is a proximate temporal relationship between vaccination and injury'.[48] Once the plaintiff has proven causation in fact under *Althen*, they are entitled to recover, unless the defendant proofs by a preponderance of the evidence that the injuries were due to factors unrelated to the administration of the vaccine.[49]

Meeting the causality standard outlined in *Althen* is difficult, mainly because vaccines are inherently dangerous products. There has not been a consensus as to the proper standard for determining the admissibility of novel scientific evidence or expert witness testimony in American courts. *Frye v United States* established the 'general acceptance' standard by which expert opinion based on a scientific technique must be 'generally accepted' as reliable in the relevant scientific community in order to be admissible in a trial court.[50] The SCOTUS revoked this longstanding standard in *Daubert v Merrell Dow Pharmaceuticals Inc*, in light of the enactment of the Federal Rules of Evidence.[51] In that case, the SCOTUS held that in order to determine whether the expert is proposing to testify to scientific knowledge that will assist the trier of fact to understand or determine the facts, the judge must assess whether the reasoning or methodology underlying the testimony is scientifically valid and whether the trier of fact can adequately apply that reasoning or methodology to the facts at issue. As provided by the Court, 'The focus of the inquiry should rest solely on principles and methodology, not on the conclusions that they generate'. To this end, the judge ought to elaborate a checklist or a test where they inquire if the theory or technique has been tested, if it has been subject to peer review and publication, if the potential rate of error is known, and if the scientific community generally accepts the theory (in the words of the Court, this standard can yet have a bearing).[52]

[47] R Goldberg, 'Epidemiological Uncertainty, Causation, and Drug Product Liability' (2014) 59 *McGill Law Journal* 777 (discussing the differences in how the legal and scientific community define causation). See also L M Finley, 'Guarding the Gate to the Courthouse: How Trial Judges are Using their Evidentiary Screening Role to Remake Tort Causation Rules' (1999) 49 *DePaul Law Review* 335.

[48] *Althen v Sec'y of Health & Human Servs* 418 F3d 1274, 1278 (Fed Cir 2005). See also *Dillon v Secretary of Health and Human Services* (citing *Althen v Sec'y of Health & Human Servs*).

[49] V Walker et al, 'Annotating Patterns of Reasoning about Medical Theories of Causation, Association for Computational Linguistics', available at www.aclweb.org/anthology/W14-2101, accessed 28 March 2019 (examining the evidence used in several cases after *Althen v Sec'y of Health & Human Servs* to prove causation).

[50] *Frye v United States* 293 F 1013 (DC Cir 1923).

[51] *Daubert v Merrell Dow Pharm, Inc* 509 US 579, 113 S Ct 2786, 125 L Ed 2d 469 (1993).

[52] ibid. See also H Weiner et al, 'Medical Causation and Expert Testimony: Allergists at this Intersection of Medicine and Law' (2012) 12(6) *Curr Allergy Astma Report* 590.

According to the jurisprudence of the SCOTUS, courts function as gatekeepers of the scientific validity of expert evidence. This role is not unproblematic. First, it is questionable that all courts own the adequate skills to validate a specific scientific method. Second, court decisions are not subject to falsification and continuous revision. Consequently, the trier of fact may be called to judge the facts based on inconclusive or incomplete evidence. Third, the appreciation of the ultimate legal question depends on the knowledge that courts typically do not have. Courts interpret common law and statutory law. Fourth, even if the court has that type of knowledge, the line between judging the relevance and reliability of a scientific method and judging the results or facts is thin. The jury is expected to judge those results, not the judge. However, despite the difficulties, courts have been applying the *Daubert* test in a way that has revealed increased expertise in screening and validating expert opinions and scientific methods.[53]

To recover damages in strict liability for pharmaceutical product liability, a plaintiff must prove both general and specific causation. General causation establishes that a product is capable of causing injuries of the type the plaintiff sustained. Specific causation establishes that a product has caused the specific injuries the plaintiff suffered.[54] The *Daubert* test may not be easy for a plaintiff for that implies the plaintiff provide evidence that establishes not only general but also specific causation.[55] The stakes of scientific knowledge required to prove causation are very high, particularly in areas where science is yet to provide clear answers. The judicial evaluation of scientific evidence may end meritorious claims of plaintiffs against defendants whose liability rests uncheck.[56] This fact, together with the pre-emption of all design defect claims against vaccine manufacturers under states tort law, has often turned into blanket protection for vaccine manufacturers.

ii. The European Take: Autonomy of Legal Evidence or a Jump in the Dark?

As already discussed, unlike the US, the EU does not have a particular compensatory scheme to cover vaccine-related injury (although some Member States do). Injured parties must rely on the Directive. In order to trigger the liability of a manufacturer, Article 4 requires the injured party to prove the existence of a defect in the product, a damage, and a causal link between the defect and the damage. While both defect and damage are explicitly defined in the Directive (Article 6 and Article 9 respectively), the text is silent as regards the causal link, which remains

[53] *In re Bextra & Celebrex Mktg Sales Practices & Prod Liab Litig* 524 F Supp 2d 1166 (ND Cal 2007).

[54] *Sterling v Velsicol Chem Corp* 855 F2d 1188 (6th Cir 1988) and *Thompson v Underwood* 407 F2d 994 (6th Cir 1969); *Maryland Cas Co v Young* 211 Tenn 1, 362 SW 2d 241 (1962).

[55] *Meade v Parsley* No 2:09-CV-00388, 2010 WL 4909435 (SDW Va Nov 24, 2010).

[56] WM Ertmer, 'Just What the Doctor Ordered: The Admissibility of Differential Diagnosis in Pharmaceutical Product Liability' (2003) 56 *Vanderbilt Law Review* 1227, 1230.

regulated by national laws in observance of the principles of equivalence and effectiveness. In light of this observation, one can argue that, while the requirement of defectiveness forms the cornerstone of the liability system established by the Directive, causation plays an 'ancillary' role. Indeed, the Directive requires injured parties to prove that a defect in the product has caused the damage, not that the product in itself has done so. Furthermore, one should construe the choice not to regulate the causal link in the text of the Directive in a way that does not impair the effectiveness of a liability regime that came to be with the explicit goal of harmonising product liability rules throughout the single market. Indeed, different regimes of causation can significantly undermine that goal,[57] and even if we accept the argument that the principal aim of the Directive is really consumer protection, its harmonising purpose cannot be ignored.

The CJEU has recently had the opportunity to clarify the nature of the causal link mentioned in Article 4 of the Directive in its decision in *Sanofi*.[58] The case involved the claim brought by the family of a deceased French man who died of multiple sclerosis, which he allegedly contracted as a result of three injections of a hepatitis B vaccine manufactured by Sanofi Pasteur. The CJEU explicitly accepted that proof of causation in the face of alleged vaccine-related injury could rest upon 'serious, specific and consistent presumptions'. While such presumptions cannot translate into a shift of the burden of proof (which must remain with the plaintiff to avoid compromising the effectiveness of the Directive's regime), the decision allows the use of circumstantial evidence and inferential proof (a method based on the French notion of *présomption*).[59] We can make a number of observations about this judgment.[60]

First, the decision does not seem to take sufficiently into account the nuanced relationship between the requirements of defectiveness and that of causation. The two are distinct, albeit related. As discussed above, the cornerstone of the Directive is that a manufacturer incurs liability when *a defect* in their product causes damage, not merely when *the product as such* does so. In *Sanofi*, the CJEU refrains from discussing the relationship between proof of defectiveness and proof of causation. It instead seems to base its decision on the Advocate General's Opinion, which found it unproblematic for proof of causation and proof of defectiveness to rest on the same set of facts. The Advocate General's reasoning went even further and suggested that inferring defectiveness from proof of causation would be equally acceptable.[61] While the Court does not explicitly include this

[57] The argument is put forward in Rizzi (above n 6) 298 ff.

[58] *W & Others v Sanofi Pasteur MSD SNC & Others* (above n 6).

[59] Opinion of AG Bobek delivered on 7 March 2017, Case C-621/15, *W & Others v Sanofi Pasteur MSD SNC, Caisse primaire d'assurance maladie des Hauts-de-Seine & Carpimko*, ECLI:EU:C:2017:176, paras 30–34.

[60] For a detailed analysis of the case see Rizzi (above n 6); see also the literature referenced above (above n 6).

[61] Opinion of AG Bobek (above n 58) para 78.

observation in its judgment, it is worth noting that there seems to be a logical flaw in such reasoning. Indeed, if the causal link can be inferred from purely circumstantial evidence (as accepted by the Court), there is a concrete risk of rendering the separate and essential requirement of defectiveness void of any material significance – to the point where causation alone could determine whether or not a claim deserves compensation, thereby impairing the basic mechanism set by the Directive.

A second problem is the type of relationship between legal and scientific proof that this decision appears to put forward. It permits giving legal relevance to a series of circumstances that scientific literature considers dubious at best.[62] Take for example one of the circumstances considered relevant in *Sanofi*: the proximity in time between the injections and the onset of the disease. Attributing causal relevance to this fact *presupposes* the notion it tries to prove: that the vaccine *can* cause the injury in the first place. If we were to use the American categories, *Sanofi* potentially allows plaintiffs to establish specific causation on the basis of circumstantial evidence, while *presupposing* general causation. This type of tautological reasoning is not only unhelpful but potentially dangerous in the context of vaccines, where individual and public health concerns are intimately intertwined. While the decision in *Sanofi* has attracted some positive reactions,[63] it arguably leaves the door open to non-rigorous adjudications in a field where the relationship between law and science demands a constant and careful balancing exercise.

Sanofi must be set apart from *Boston Scientific* (although the CJEU refers to it in *Sanofi*), not only because *Boston Scientific* focuses on defectiveness and *Sanofi* on causation, but because of the quality of the respective reasonings. As discussed above, the court in *Boston Scientific* elaborated the notion of 'potential defect' to accommodate vulnerable plaintiffs for whom identifying an actual defect in a specific product may be impossible. However, it did so on the basis of a recognised (no matter if improbable) abnormal risk of harm. This approach appears to be a more considerate way to vindicate the autonomy of legal reasoning in situations of scientific uncertainty, without running the risk of unwarrantedly disregarding the need for credible evidence.

IV. Conclusion

This brief overview of liability regimes for vaccine related injuries in the US and Europe offers a vivid contemporary example of the classic Horatian ideal of

[62] The relevant scientific literature is discussed in Rizzi (above n 6) 301; and J Borghetti, 'Causation in Hepatitis B Vaccination Litigation in France: Breaking Through Scientific Uncertainty?' (2016) 91 *Chicago-Kent Law Review* 543.

[63] See Brosset (above n 6); Ruiz Cairó (above n 6).

aurea mediocritas.[64] Indeed, in the search for a balanced compromise between ensuring individual rights to compensation and protecting public health, neither the approach of the CJEU nor that of the SCOTUS is entirely satisfying. A more desirable solution arguably lies somewhere in the middle. Additionally, the work of comparison spells out jurisprudential differences in both legal systems. These differences have to do, in part, with the specificities of the legal and institutional frameworks in place for vaccine-related injuries. Differences can also be traced to how differently the civil and the common law traditions impact legal structures on both sides of the Atlantic.[65]

In the EU, the jurisprudence of the CJEU is more normative, and shows less deference to regulatory agencies when it comes to determining liability for defective products such as vaccines or other medical devices. This approach fosters a more active or, in a way, a more investigative role of the judge. By contrast, the jurisprudence of the SCOTUS is less normative, more deferential, and more analytical. Courts play the role of gatekeepers. On the one hand, this gatekeeping role enhances the position of the trier of fact as regards the evaluation of the circumstances of the case; but, on the other hand, it restricts their margin of manoeuvre, which is based on the stringent method validated by the SCOTUS. The comparative matrix below provides a succinct overview of the main points raised throughout the chapter. The comparative synthesis ensues:

Comparative Matrix		
Ancillary Research Questions	**CJEU**	**SCOTUS**
What elements of the causal link does a plaintiff need to establish?	The Directive does not define the elements of the causal link. It leaves the definition of those elements to national legal orders following the principles of effectiveness and equivalency.	The plaintiff must establish causation in fact, for which they must establish 'but for' causation and proximate cause. The but for test determines that the defendant's product is the cause of the event, which would not have occurred 'but for' the defendant's conduct. Proximate causation establishes that a defendant's product is a substantial factor in causing the plaintiff's injury.

(continued)

[64] Horace, *The Odes: New Translations by Contemporary Poets* (Princeton University Press, 2002). On the philosophy of the 'Golden Mean' see, the classic *Aristotle, The Nicomachean Ethics* (Penguin Books, 2004).

[65] See L Vicente, 'The Hohfeldian Concept of Share in Limited Liability Companies: A View from the Common and Civil Law Traditions' (2018) 33 *Tulane European & Civil Law Forum* 41 (scrutinising different methods of reasoning in the civil and common law traditions).

(Continued)

Comparative Matrix		
Ancillary Research Questions	**CJEU**	**SCOTUS**
Is the creation of a system of presumptions to prove the existence of a causal link acceptable?	Yes. Presumptions can be sufficient to demonstrate the existence of a causal link provided they are 'serious, specific and consistent'.	No. The NCVIA creates a system of presumptions listed on the Vaccine Injury Table. In a tort law civil action, no presumptions are allowed.
If a system of presumptions is acceptable, does it soften or shift the burden of proving causation for the plaintiff?	No. The burden remains on the plaintiff as the principle of effectiveness does not allow a shift of the burden of proof. This burden of proof shifting may be possible at the national level where the Members States follow liability regimes not based on the Directive.	No. The system of presumptions on the Table does not require the petitioner prove causation if the petitioner meets the requirements to file a petition for compensation under the NCVIA. In tort cases, no shift of the burden of proof is allowed.
Can causation be determined on the circumstantial evidence of the case?	Yes. The term *presumption* in the *Sanofi* case is interpreted to have the meaning of the French *présomption*, which indicates circumstantial evidence. Causation can be determined on such evidence provided it is 'serious, specific and consistent'.	No. The plaintiff must prove causation in fact, and that includes proving both general and specific causation. Proving causation requires passing the *Daubert* test, which demands more than circumstantial evidence.
Can the same set of facts constitute proof of causation and defectiveness?	Yes. *Sanofi* establishes that it is unproblematic to rely on the same sets of facts to establish both defectiveness and causal link.	No. The standards or criteria that the plaintiff must meet, and consequently the facts the plaintiff must prove in order to prove defectiveness and causation are different.

(continued)

(Continued)

Comparative Matrix		
Ancillary Research Questions	**CJEU**	**SCOTUS**
Does liability for vaccine-related injuries dispense the plaintiff from proof of causation?	No. Considering that the Directive is a 'one size fits all' solution for all movable goods, liability for vaccine-related injuries does not dispense plaintiffs from proving causation. National compensatory schemes not based on the Directive dispense plaintiffs from proving causation.	No. Product liability for vaccine-related injuries does not dispense the plaintiff from proving causation. To recover damages in strict liability, a plaintiff must prove both general and specific causation.
Is the concept of defectiveness central to the system of product liability?	Yes. A unitary notion of defectiveness forms the sole standard of liability under the Directive.	Yes. The concept of defectiveness is central to the determination of product liability. The US adopts a tripartite notion of defectiveness.
Is the concept of causation ancillary to that of defectiveness?	Yes. Arguably so, insofar as defectiveness is the cornerstone of the Directive while causation is left to national courts to determine from national rules.	No. The concept of causation is not ancillary to the concept of defectiveness. It is independently defined and cumulative to defectiveness.
Do courts distinguish between general and specific causation?	No. However, the notion of 'potential defect' elaborated in *Boston Scientific* introduces a similar distinction albeit within the test of defectiveness.	Yes. US courts distinguish between general and specific causation both in federal and state jurisdictions.
Is proof of general causation sufficient to establish a causal link between defect and damage?	No. However based on *Boston Scientific* it may be sufficient to prove a potential defect to establish defectiveness of a specific product.	No. To recover damages in strict liability, a plaintiff must prove both general and specific causation separately.

The European approach seems preferable to guarantee accessibility of remedial action to injured parties (when they cannot already benefit from alternative compensatory schemes) as it does not set an impossible evidential burden of proof in situations of scientific uncertainty. In a form of *de facto* observance of the precautionary principle, the jurisprudence of *Boston Scientific* and *Sanofi Pasteur* purposively interprets the Directive's text, the 'one size fits all' nature of which fails to adequately account for the difficulties set by litigation involving technologically advanced products such as vaccines – thereby undermining its effectiveness.

The American literal approach is arguably too restrictive, as it excessively curtails the scope of manufacturers' liability by denying design-defect claims in cases involving injuries that are not contemplated by the NVICP. However, as regards proof of causation, the conceptual division between general and specific causation developed by the American toxic tort case law and referred to by the SCOTUS in *Bruesewitz v Wyeth* is a helpful attempt to reconcile scientific evidence and legal causation – although, to fulfil its potential, it would require a less rigid interpretation of the 'gatekeeping' function.

Indeed, the CJEU's approach in *Sanofi* seems to go one step too far in allowing inferential proof of causation. It goes to the point that the inference (that the damage *caused* the vaccine in a given case) rests upon the very notion it purports to demonstrate (that the vaccine *can* cause the damage and is defective as it fails the Directive's safety test). In this sense, the CJEU has shown greater acumen in *Boston Scientific*, a decision that offers positive guidance to national courts in the complex task of integrating science and law, and it is within the perimeter of that reasoning that European product liability shows better potential to balance injured party compensation and public health protection.

21

The Usage of Solidarity in the Jurisdiction of the CJEU

ANNETT WUNDER*

'Solidarity is booming';[1] it has become a notion that is used frequently in the literature[2] as well as in the decisions of the Court of Justice of the European Union (CJEU).[3] It appears on its own, but sometimes it is linked with other terms like European solidarity,[4] national solidarity,[5] financial solidarity,[6] and furthermore, sometimes it is used as a synonym for equality[7] or identity.[8] The aim of this chapter is to explore the usage of solidarity in the jurisdiction of the CJEU. Therefore it is important to have a better understanding of what the term solidarity generally means. This knowledge may help us to better understand its usage in case law. In the first section of the chapter the meaning of solidarity is defined. In the second section I will look at the usage of that term in the case law of the CJEU. In the third section the findings are summarised.

* Social Court Frankfurt am Main, currently Research Associate at the German Federal Constitutional Court.

[1] E Denninger, 'Constitutional Law and Solidarity' in K Bayertz (ed), *Solidarity* (Kluwer Academic, 1999) 223.

[2] For instance: F de Witte, *Justice in the EU – The Emergence of Transnational Solidarity* (Oxford, Oxford University Press, 2015); M Klamert, 'Solidarität als Rechtsprinzip der europäischen Union' in M Knodt and A Tews (Hrsg), *Solidarität in der EU* (Baden Baden, Nomos, 2014) 19ff.

[3] Case C-67/96, *Albany* [1999] ECR I-5751; Cases C-115/97, C-116/97 and C-117/97, *Brentjens' Handelsonderneming BV* [1999] ECR I-6025; Case C-219/97, *Maatschappij Drijvende Bokken BV* [1999] ECR I-5751; Opinion of AG Jacobs in Cases C-180/98 to C-184/98, *Pavel Pavlov and Others* [2000] I-6451; Case C-157/99, *Smits/Peerbooms* [2001] ECR I-5473; Case C-385/99, *Müller-Fauré/van Riet* [2003] ECR I-4509.

[4] C Newdick, 'Citizenship, Free Movement and Health Care: Cementing Individual Rights by Corroding Social Solidarity' (2006) *Common Market Law Review* 1645, 1666.

[5] C Barnard, 'EU Citizenship and the Principle of Solidarity' in M Dougan and E Spaventa (eds), *Social Welfare and EU Law* (Oxford, Hart, 2005) 159 ff.

[6] Case C-209/01, *Bidar* [2005] ECR I-2119, para 56; Opinion of AG Maduro in Case C-281/06, *Jundt*, para 19; Opinion of AG Jacobs, in Case C-147/03, *Commission v Austria* [2005] ECR I-5969, para 53; Opinion of AG Geelhoed in Case C-209/01, *Bidar* [2005] ECR I-2119, paras 24, 31.

[7] Y Borgmann-Prebil, 'The Rule of Reason in European Citizenship' (2008) *European Law Journal* 328, 339.

[8] Discussed by M Ferrera, *The Boundaries of Welfare – European Integration and the New Spatial Politics of Social Protection* (Oxford, Oxford University Press, 2005) 1.

I. Solidarity – What Does it Mean? How is it Used?

A. Solidarity: A Linguistic Approach

The word solidarity (*solidaridad, solidarietà, Solidarität*) derives from the French *solidarité*. *Solidarité* goes back to the Latin word *solidum*,[9] which means dense, firm or solid.[10] Until the eighteenth century, solidarity was only used as a legal term in Europe.[11] As a legal concept, solidarity can be traced back, in Roman law, to the concept of obligation in solidum, which meant 'the unlimited liability of each individual member within a family or other community to pay common debts'.[12]

If we look to the *Oxford English Dictionary*'s definition of solidarity, it becomes immediately clear that the term has more than one meaning. Solidarity is one of those terms that is difficult to define, as its meaning is largely dependent on the context in which it is used.[13] The *Oxford English Dictionary* gives three different meanings, one of which is even further subdivided. According to the Oxford definition, the term means:

(1) the fact or quality, on the part of communities etc, of being perfectly united or at one in some respects, especially in interests, sympathies or aspirations or action of trade unions members,[14] construction of mankind,[15] construction between or with others;[16]
(2) community or perfect coincidence of (or between) interests;[17]
(3) in civil law a form of obligation involving joint or several responsibilities or rights.[18]

These definitions are similar to the understanding of *Solidarität* in German,[19] *Solidarité* in French,[20] *Solidarietà* in Italian and *Solidaridad* in Spanish.[21] What the understandings have in common is the sharing or pooling of interests to form a community on the one hand; and on the other the linkage (of that community) to rights, duties and obligations. Therefore, solidarity is linked to identification and integration with a group, and thereby associated with shared identity.[22]

[9] Espansa-Calpe, *Enciclopedia Universal ilustrada europeo americana* (Madrid 1966) Vol LMII, 141.
[10] Casell's, *Latin-English – English-Latin*, 560.
[11] Historic overview given by A Wildt, 'Solidarity: its history and contemporary definition' in Bayertz (above n 1) 209ff.
[12] K Bayertz, 'Four Uses of Solidarity' in Bayertz (above n 1) 3.
[13] G Khusshf, 'Solidarity as a Moral and Political Concept: Beyond the Liberal/Communitarian Impasse' in Bayertz (above n 1) 57, 64.
[14] *Oxford English Dictionary*, Vol 10, 972 Nr 1a.
[15] ibid, 972 Nr 1b.
[16] ibid, 972 Nr 1c.
[17] ibid, 972 Nr 2.
[18] ibid, 972 Nr 3.
[19] Wahrig, *Deutsches Wörterbuch* (Gütersloh 1978) 2419 Nr 1–2.
[20] Librairie Larousse, *Grand Laousse encyclopédique* (Paris 1964) Vol 9.
[21] *Enciclopedia Universal ilustrada europeo americana*, Vol LMVII, 141.
[22] C Barnard, 'Solidarity and New Governance in Social Policy' in G de Búrca and J Scott (eds), *Law and New Governance in the EU and the US* (Oxford, Hart, 2006) 153, 154.

B. Solidarity – Its Different Uses

Since the eighteenth century, the idea of solidarity has become an important political idea in both philosophy and the social sciences.[23] Bayertz distinguishes four different uses of solidarity. One use Bayertz distinguishes is between solidarity and liberation. In this pairing solidarity describes the formation of an interest group in order to express shared interests through social or political actions.[24]

Another use of solidarity is linked to morality, where references to solidarity are used to tie human beings to a moral community.[25] As a moral concept, solidarity means the commitment or the willingness [*Bereitschaft*][26] to act in accordance with the outcome of collective decision-making.[27] A number of scholars connects solidarity with justice and law [*Recht und Gerechtigkeit*].[28] As one example, Hartmann perceives solidarity as the strictly universal value that contains more than a joint responsibility to the whole.[29] According to Habermas, solidarity is related to equal treatment[30] in that such a right necessarily includes a commitment to active participation in the group or community. As such:

> Justice and Solidarity are two sides of the same coin, because practical discourse is a procedure which on one hand, allows every individual to make his or her 'yes' and 'no' felt, and thereby satisfies an individualistic understanding of equal rights. But, on the other hand, in moral discourse the social bond which requires all participants in argumentation to remain aware of their belonging to an unlimited community of communication remains intact. Only with the securing of the existence of the communication community, which demands of everyone in the ideal assumption of roles an unselfish, empathetic activity, can those relations of reciprocal recognition be reproduced, without which even the identity of each individual would be disintegrated.[31]

The third use concerns solidarity and society. Here solidarity is perceived as a decisive factor for community cohesion; it is considered as the 'inner cement holding society together'.[32] In this context, Durkheim's theory of the 'transformation of solidarity' plays an important and influential role. It deals with a division of labour, which creates the possibility for a transformation of solidarity among autonomous

[23] Bayertz (above n 12) 3; Wildt (above n 11) 209 ff.

[24] Bayertz (above n 12) 3, 16.

[25] ibid, 3, 5 ff.

[26] A Wildt in J Ritter and K Gründer (eds), *Historisches Wörterbuch der Philosophie, Band 9, Solidarität* (Schwabe Verlage Darmstadt, 1995) 1004.

[27] E Mason in E Craig (ed), *Routledge Encyclopedia of Philosophy* (1998) Vol 9, 23 ff.

[28] See for instance N Hartmann's chapter on law and solidarity in N Hartmann, *Ethik* (1926, translated and reprinted in 2002): N Hartmann, *Moral Values* (New Brunswick, 2003) Vol 2, 234 ff; R Houtepen and R ter Meulen, 'New Types of Solidarity in the European Welfare State' (2000) 8 *Health Care Analysis* 329, 336.

[29] Hartmann (2003) (above n 28) 235 ff.

[30] J Habermas, 'Justice and Solidarity: On the Discussion Concerning Stage 6' in E Wren (ed), *The Moral Domain* (Cambridge, MIT Press, 1990) 226, 244.

[31] J Habermas, *Autonomy and Solidarity* (London, Verso, 1986) 251 ff.

[32] Bayertz (above n 12) 3, 9 ff.

individuals, rather than its decline.[33] For Durkheim, solidarity was the main characteristic of the individualised society. He claimed that solidarity towards others is based on a sense of shared interests. However, as society has modernised, so has the division of labour: our understanding of solidarity must shift[34] from a solidarity that is mechanical, to one that is organic.[35]

Fourth, Bayertz points towards the relationship between solidarity and the welfare state. Solidarity and the redistribution of financial resources or public goods to individuals in need are closely correlated. Solidarity is formalised, in that it is seen as a decisive factor in determining levels of contribution to the scheme, as well as necessary distributions of benefits. Therefore, solidarity serves to legitimise the existence of the welfare state.[36]

The last two uses can also be distinguished by the terms formal or informal solidarity, or 'cold' and 'warm' solidarity. By informal or warm solidarity, the type of solidarity being referred to is that shown towards people with whom a personal relationship is established, whereas formal or cold solidarity refers to forms of solidarity among people who do not share personal relationships.[37] Formal solidarity is based on formal intermediaries, such as insurances or taxes, and regulated procedures of entitlement.[38]

Solidarity is either descriptively or normatively used. When used descriptively, solidarity refers to actually existing bonds and types of such bonds occurring between individuals, groups, or communities. When used in the normative sense, 'it is used as a postulate and the most frequently positively valued model of relations (bonds) between social entities'.[39]

Solidarity as a descriptive tool refers to the commitment to a group or to other members of a group and is therefore strongly related to a collective identity.[40] When used as normative idea, solidarity is related to the commitment to the well-being of others, and the recognition of special rights and obligations owed towards each other due to the ties established among the group members.[41] In this usage, solidarity is often linked with fraternity.[42] The literature points in many cases to the potential contribution solidarity can make to the social stability and coherence of a society.[43] Hence solidarity is regarded as instrumentally valuable.[44] This may

[33] ibid, 3, 13.
[34] H Entzinger, 'Open borders and the welfare state' in A Pécoud and P de Guchteniere (eds), *Migration Without Borders* (New York, Berghahn Books, 2007) 119, 121.
[35] ibid, 119, 121.
[36] Bayertz (above n 12) 3, 21.
[37] Entzinger (above n 34) 119, 121 ff.
[38] ibid, 119, 122.
[39] D Dobrzański, 'The Concept of Solidarity and its Properties' in T Buksiński and D Dobrzański (eds), *Eastern Europe and the Challenges of Globalization* (Washington, 2005) 135.
[40] U Preuss, 'National, Supranational and International Solidarity' in Bayertz (above n 1) 281, 285.
[41] U Steinvorth, The Concept and Possibilities of Solidarity, in Bayertz (above n 1) 30, 31.
[42] In detail: K Metz, 'Solidarity and History: Institutions and Social Concepts of solidarity in 19th Century in West Europe' in Bayertz (above n 1) 191, 192ff.
[43] E Durkheim, *The Division of Labour in Society* (New York, Free Press, 1964).
[44] Craig (above n 27) Vol 9, 23.

explain the appealing character of the notion. Solidarity is mainly perceived as a positive value. At the same time, there are those who claim its incompatibility with personal autonomy, in so far as it requires individuals to act in accordance with collective decision-making.[45] Entzinger emphasises that there is also an inherently exclusive aspect of solidarity in that it always implies including some people and excluding others.[46]

The term solidarity seems to have three different dimensions: first, it can be used as a tool to describe a group or society; second, it is a normative or moral idea; and third, solidarity can have an appealing character in encouraging an ethic of individual or public involvement. However, these three separate dimensions demonstrate solidarity's intrinsic ambiguity.

C. Solidarity as a Legal Concept

Solidarity is not only a philosophical and social science concept but a legal one as well. Solidarity as a legal concept dates back to Roman law.[47] Nowadays the fields of private as well as public law refer to solidarity as a legal concept.

In private law, solidarity is often related to legal terms such as good faith, fairness, the obligation to inform, or the obligation to advise or cooperate with the contracting partner. Solidarity or 'contract solidarity' [*Vertragssolidarität*[48]] is understood as a prerequisite for a relation between contracting parties. Contract solidarity puts limits on the freedom of contract in that solidarity rules represent limitations, regulations or mandatory rules, which apply in order to protect the weaker party.[49] As Lurger points out, the principle of solidarity is not only restricted to the protection of weaker parties or to standards of good faith; it also includes duties of cooperation and loyalty and further applies to general default rules such as the rules on breach of contract.[50]

When used in the field of public law, solidarity is often related to the welfare state and to welfare benefits, in respect to the contribution or redistribution of welfare benefits and other public goods to those in need. Solidarity in the context of the welfare state can play a role on three different levels: first, regarding the universal coverage or nature of a welfare scheme, where no one can opt out, and no one is excluded; second, when the funding of a scheme is related to an individual's income and not to the individual' risk; or third, when benefits are provided on equal terms according to medical need, without any consideration of the contribution to

[45] R Wolff, *In Defence of Anarchism* (California University Press, 1970).

[46] Entzinger (above n 34) 119, 121.

[47] J Ottmann, 'The Concept of Solidarity in National and European Law: The Welfare state and the European Social Model' (2008) *ICL Journal* 36, 38.

[48] B Lurger, *Vertragliche Solidarität* (Baden Baden, 1997).

[49] M Hesselink and G de Vries, *Principles of European Contract Law* (Kluwer, 2001) 54.

[50] B Lurger, 'Prinzipien eines europäischen Vertragsrechts: liberal, marktfunktional, solidarisch oder …?' (1998) *Electronic Journal of Comparative Law* 5.

the scheme. Although the use of solidarity varies in each of these mentioned levels, the underpinning idea is that the stronger members of a community contribute institutionally for the weaker ones.

In public law, solidarity is institutionalised as the relevant public goods are in the main provided by public institutions, according to proceduralised standards (institutionalised solidarity[51]). Therefore the modern type of solidarity is characterised by a rational 'taxable […] use of the bond of feeling'.[52] Tax law and social security law are tools to define solidarity. That is why – if solidarity is institutionalised – morality and solidarity can, to a certain extent, be separated.[53] However, institutions can only partly overcome a lack of non-institutionalised solidarity, because the institutions themselves are dependent on the agreement of people to act in a solidarity-enhancing manner,[54] in that they are dependent on the willingness of individuals to contribute.

What we can take from this short overview is that the notion of solidarity can describe more than one legal concept. In private law, solidarity refers to a general principle of contract aiming to ensure a degree of social justice by fostering the co-operating of the contracting parties, and avoiding antagonism,[55] whereas in public law solidarity stands as a synonym for the proceduralised contribution to public welfare schemes and the distribution of welfare benefits. As Bucher rightly claims:

> Solidarität ist denn auch nicht ein Begriff im logischen Sinne, sondern etwas anderes und viel mehr: ein Vorstellungskomplex, dessen Gehalt sich in einer zweitausendjährigen, sowohl in römischen wie germanischen Ursprüngen wurzelnden Rechtsentwicklung sich herausgebildet hat, ein Gehalt, der nicht mit einer Realdefinition abschließend erfasst werden kann […].[56]

D. Solidarity in European Primary Law

In European primary law solidarity is rarely mentioned. Solidarity was mentioned in the preamble of the ECSC Treaty of 1951:

> Recognising that Europe can be built only through real practical achievements which will first of all create real solidarity, and through the establishment of common bases for economic development.[57]

[51] J Rodger, 'Social Solidarity, Welfare and Post-Emotionalism' (2003) *Journal of Social Policy* 403 ff.

[52] Denninger (above n 1) 223, 230f.

[53] For that reason institutionalised solidarity inherits the danger that solidarity becomes meaning free: Denninger (above n 1) 223, 230 ff.

[54] M Baurmann, 'Solidarity as a Social and as a Constitutional Norm' in Bayertz (above n 1) 243, 251.

[55] Lurger (above n 48) 128, 137; T Wilhelmsson, *Social Contract Law and European Integration* (Dartmouth, 1994) 26 ff.

[56] E Bucher, 'Traditionale und analytische Betrachtungsweise im Privatrecht' in *Rechtstheorie, Zeitschrift für Logik, Methodenlehre, Kybernetik und Soziologie des Rechts*, Bd 1 (1970) 23, 39.

[57] European Communities, *European Union: selected Instruments taken from the Treaties*, Book I, Vol II, p 17.

A reference to solidarity was also made in the preamble of the Founding Treaty of the European Economic Community (EEC) in 1957:

> Intending to confirm the solidarity which binds Europe and the overseas countries and desiring to ensure the development of the prosperity, in accordance with the principle of the charter of the United Nation.[58]

The Maastricht Treaty, by which the European Community was established in 1993, referred to solidarity once in Article 2 TEC, where the promotion of solidarity among Member States is named as a task of the Community.[59] The Amsterdam Treaty[60] of 1999, amending the Maastricht Treaty, did not change this provision, whereas in the current version of the Treaty establishing the European Community, consolidated in the Treaty of Nice,[61] solidarity appears only twice, once in the preamble and once in Article 2 TEC, which refers to solidarity among the Member States. In the preamble, solidarity appears in the context of external relations as it refers to the intention of the treaty to confirm the solidarity which binds Europe and other countries overseas.[62]

In the Treaty of the European Union solidarity is mentioned four times.[63] Reference to solidarity are made in order either to describe an objective of the EU (as is the case in the preamble) or as a standard of behaviour for the Member States towards each other (as in Articles 11 and 23 TEU).

We can find more frequent references to solidarity in the Lisbon Treaty. Solidarity is mentioned 15 times within the Treaty.[64] In the preamble the desire is expressed 'to deepen the solidarity between their peoples while respecting their history, their culture and their traditions'. That solidarity is perceived as a general value is demonstrated by its usage in Articles 2 and 3 of the Lisbon Treaty. Article 2 refers to solidarity as a fundamental value of the EU, whereas in Article 3 solidarity is even mentioned twice. Here, named duties of the EU include the fostering of solidarity among generations and the use of solidarity[65] to encourage mutual respect among peoples.[66] Solidarity is mentioned in the preamble of the Charter of Fundamental Rights as a principle upon which the Union is based – while the Charter is not included in the Lisbon Treaty, it may become a binding source of primary law. Within the Charter solidarity is the headline of chapter IV, which contains social rights related to employment.

Noticeable also is the appearance of solidarity in the context of external relations. It appears in this content in Article 3(5) of the Lisbon Treaty and also in Articles 21(1) and 24(2), (3).

[58] European Communities, *European Union: selected Instruments taken from the Treaties*, Book I, Vol I, 103.
[59] OJ C340 of 10 November 1997.
[60] ibid.
[61] OJ C325 of 24 December 2002.
[62] OJ C325, C329/39 of 24 December 2002.
[63] Preamble, Art 11 para 2 TEU, Art 11 para 3 TEC and Art 23 para 1 TEU.
[64] Preamble, Art 2, 3.
[65] Art 3(3 II).
[66] Art 3(3 III).

However, in most of the cases solidarity refers to solidarity between Member States. It either refers to a political process conducted in a manner conducive to solidarity[67] or it is related, as in Articles 122 and 194 of the treaty, to the distribution of resources among the Member States. The ties between the Member States and the EU are specially emphasised in the solidarity clause in Article 222 of the Lisbon Treaty.

To conclude, we can see that solidarity is a notion known in primary European law, however the term refers more to a supranational solidarity, than to solidarity among individuals, because it is considered either in terms of solidarity between Member States and the EU, or in regard to the EU's external relations. It furthermore appears (as in Articles 2 and 3 of the Lisbon Treaty, or in the Charter of Fundamental Rights) in relation to social policy. However, it is often used there in an overly general manner. For instance, in Article 2, and in the preamble of the Charter of Fundamental Rights, solidarity is declared as a common value of the Member States, without specifying the term any further. In Article 3, it imposes a duty on the EU to promote solidarity between generations. In the Charter of Fundamental Rights, it is used as a chapter's title but does not provide a specific meaning: as it is not mentioned in the following provisions, it seems instead to be used as a more general synonym for 'the social'. That is why solidarity – while broadly used in primary law – remains an abstract concept.

II. Solidarity – How is it Used in Case Law?

A. Competition Law and Solidarity

By categorising the given case law, we can distinguish four different categories in which solidarity is used: (1) solidarity as a tool to describe the relationship between industrial partners;[68] (2) solidarity as a tool to describe structures and relationships among social partners and social bargaining;[69] solidarity as a negative element for defining economic activity related to the definition of undertakings in Article 101 TFEU;[70] and (4) solidarity as a positive element of defining services of general interests in the context of Article 106(2) TFEU.[71]

[67] Art 24(3), Art 31, Art 67(2), Art 80.

[68] Cases C-204/00 P, C-205/00 P, C-211/00 P, C-213/00 P, C-217/00 P and C-219/00 P, *Aalborg Portland A/S & Others* [2004] ECR I-123, para 331; Case T-279/02, *Degussa AG* [2006] ECR II-897, para 417; Case T-25/95, *Cimentries CBR (Cement)* [2000] ECR II-491, paras 1265, 2677, 3190.

[69] *Brentjens' Handelsonderneming BV* (above n 3); *Maatschappij Drijvende Bokken BV* (above n 3); Case C-222/98, *van der Wounde* [2000] ECR I-7111; *Pavel Pavlov and Others* (above n 3) paras 68, 70.

[70] Case C-159/91, *Poucet and Pistre* [1993] ECR I-637; *van der Wounde* (above n 69) para 2; *Pavel Pavlov and Others* (above n 3) para 2.

[71] *Albany* (above n 3); *Brentjens' Handelsonderneming BV* (above n 3); *Maatschappij Drijvende Bokken BV* (above n 3); Opinion of AG Jacobs in *Pavel Pavlov and Others* (above n 3).

The first notable point is that the notion of 'solidarity' is used quite often. The Court has referred to the term more often since the early 1990s. However, despite referring to solidarity, the Court has never actually defined the meaning of the term. Examining the four above mentioned groups, we see that the way the term is used varies.

The notion is introduced by the CJEU either as an additional element in defining the term economic activity used in Article 101(1) TFEU or to determine whether a provided service comes within the scope of Article 106(2) TFEU. Solidarity is used as an additional element to broaden the definition of either economic activity or services of general interest. It has to be noted that, in the context of Article 101(1) TFEU, solidarity is one element which is used to define economic activity[72] – if the economic character of a welfare scheme is denied then EU competition law is not applicable at all.[73] However, in the case of a welfare scheme exercising an economic activity, Article 106(2) TFEU is of importance, as if the scheme is considered to be providing a service of general interest,[74] and if the measure which is being exercised is proportionate, EU competition law is not applicable.[75]

By referring to solidarity, the Court has found a tool that can be used to exclude national welfare schemes from the application of EU competition law. Here the notion serves the purpose of delimiting the application of EU competition law to national welfare schemes.[76] As a result, it can be argued that the notion of solidarity is used to protect national welfare schemes in order to ensure their proper functioning.[77]

B. The Four Freedoms and Solidarity

In most of the cases in this area, it is not the Court, but the Advocates General, who refer to solidarity.[78] They search for an analogy between the four freedoms

[72] *Poucet and Pistre* (above n 70); Case C-136/12, *Consiglio di Stato Rom*, para 44 ff; Case C-437/09, *AG2R Prévoyance* [2011] ECR I-973, para 46 ff.

[73] W Frenz, *Sozialversicherungsträger unter Kartellrecht – Zur Europarechtskonformität von § 69 Abs. 2 SGB V* (ZESAR, 2013) 107, 108.

[74] S Wernicke, *Die gewandelte Bedeutung des Art. 106 AEUV: Aus den Apokryphen zum Kanon der Wirtschaftsverfassung* (EuZW, 2015) 281, 284.

[75] *Brentjens' Handelsonderneming BV* (above n 3); Case C-350/07, *Kattner Stahlbau GmbH* [2009] I-01503, para 42; W Sauter, 'Services of General Economic Interest and Universal Service in the EU' (2008) 2 *European Law Review* 167.

[76] J Cruz, 'Beyond Competition: Services of General Interest and European Community Law' in G de Búrca, *EU Law and the Welfare State* (Oxford, Oxford University Press, 2005) 169, 185; N Kaeding, *Europäisches Wettbewerbsrecht und gemeinsame europäische Werte in der Gesundheitsversorgung* (ZESAR, 2016) 259, 261.

[77] Barnard (above n 5); Barnard (above n 22) 153, 169 ff; N Boeger, 'Solidarity and EC Competition Law' (2007) *European Law Review* 319 ff.

[78] Opinion of AG Bot in Case C-179/14, *Celex-Nr* 62014 CC0179, para 204; Opinion of AG Stix-Hackl in C-76/05, *Schwarz* [2007] ECR I-6849, para 39.

and competition law.[79] However, although the Court does not refer to the term many times, it cannot be argued that it is unaware of the impact that the application of the four freedoms can have on national welfare schemes.[80] Instead of using solidarity as an element of definition or as an argument to exclude national welfare schemes from the application of EU law, the Court has taken a different approach when referring to solidarity, where the application of the four freedoms can be limited when the national scheme is endangered either through written or unwritten reasons of justification.[81] The Court has developed unwritten reasons of justification such as, for instance, the 'financial stability of a system'.[82] The development of unwritten reasons of justification displays a similar function to the introduction of an additional definitional element.

Regarding the four freedoms, it can be argued that a Europe-wide solidarity is fostered by the CJEU in the sense that markets are opened to ensure pan-European economic activity by either nationals requesting services abroad or foreign services providers or migrant EU citizens demanding services within the host Member State. By ensuring the functioning of the internal market, Europe-wide welfare is fostered and thereby a European form of solidarity is promoted as well. However, national solidarity will be protected where the member state can prove that the application of the four freedoms could endanger the stability of the national welfare scheme.[83] Yet, national solidarity will be prioritised over a Europe-wide form of solidarity only as far as the Member State can prove that its welfare scheme is in danger. The way the Court approaches the issue of the impact of the application of the four freedoms on national welfare systems shows that the Court is convinced of the idea that the improvement of Europe-wide economic activity is to the advantage of all, as it will lead to a fostering of welfare across the EU as a whole.[84]

[79] Opinion of AG van Gerven in C-145/88, *Torfaen* [1989] ECR I-3851, para 22; K Mortelmans, 'Towards a convergence of the application of the rules on free movement and competition?' (2001) *Common Market Law Review* 613.

[80] Barnard (above n 5).

[81] *Smits/Peerbooms* (above n 3) para 72; *Müller-Fauré/van Riet* (above n 3) para 73; Kaeding (above n 76) 259, 261.

[82] Case C-372/04, *Watts* [2006] ECR I-4325, para 103. Over the years the Court has further developed the unwritten reasons of justification. According to Snell the Court has recognised 20 different unwritten reasons of justification: J Snell, *Goods and Services in EC Law* (Oxford, Oxford University Press, 2002) 192.

[83] Case C-113/13, *Azienda sanitaria locale n 5 'Spezzino' and Others v San Lorenzo Soc coop sociale and Croce Verde Cogemacooperativa sociale Onlus*, ECLI:EU:C:2014:2440, para [33]; Y Borgmann-Prebil, 'The Rule of Reason in European Citizenship' (2008) *European Law Review* 323, 349.

[84] This point of view is expressed by AG Maduro in C-499/06, *Nerkowska*, para 23. McGowan discusses in detail how liberalisation can enhance a market society: McGowan, 'State Monopoly Liberalization and the Consumer' in D Geradin (ed), *The Liberalization of State Monopolies in the European Union and Beyond* (Kluwer, 1999) 207, 210 ff; critical: R Caranta, 'After *Spezzino*: A Major Loophole Allowing Direct Awards in the Social Sector' (2016) *EPPPL* 14, 17. He points out that 'the "good of the community" – or solidarity for what matters – is too generic a standard to provide, alone and without qualification, a justification to limitations imposed on the Treaty fundamental freedoms'.

C. EU Citizenship and Solidarity

The Court relies on solidarity as a tool for inclusion into the host society of migrant EU citizens, as well as to avoid social exclusion by extending the national solidarity pact to nationals living in other Member States. In the case of migrant EU citizenship, the granting of rights is based on the argument that the longer someone is lawfully resident in the host Member State, the thicker the solidarity ties to the host society become, and the more equal treatment can be obtained.[85] Contrary to that, in cases in which the export of benefits to nationals residing in other Member States were at stake, the extent of residency, as an expression of bondage to national solidarity, was not applied by the Court.[86] Instead, the CJEU has argued that, due to national citizenship, the bond to national solidarity could be presumed.[87]

Solidarity is applied differently in case law that does not concern entitlement to welfare benefits. In these cases, solidarity is used materially rather than formally. Solidarity has a linking function, in the sense that identity and solidarity are linked to each other as an expression of belonging to the Europeanised community as an active EU citizen.

When the CJEU extends social benefits to migrant EU citizens, a Europe-wide form of solidarity is promoted. This also holds true in the case of political rights, such as voting for the European Parliament and issues related to naming, as, in those cases, the decisions have been taken against the backdrop of a European sense of belonging, able to develop a European sense of identity and to form a European bond of solidarity.

Aspects of national solidarity are of importance when it comes to the export of social benefits abroad. The CJEU's judgments are based on the premise that nationals of one Member State share a certain degree of solidarity towards each other due to national bonds.[88] However, although the jurisprudence aims to strengthen the ties of national solidarity, the CJEU's decisions at the same time Europeanise national citizenship, since exclusion from the national solidarity pact is avoided in the case of those making use of the rights granted by the Treaty. Nevertheless, by drawing on the length of lawful residency as an indicator of linkage to the solidarity pact, the Court does pay attention to the impacts of its rulings on national schemes.[89] Because of this awareness, only incremental entitlement has been granted.[90]

[85] C Barnard, 'Social Policy revisited in the Light of the Constitutional Debate' in C Barnard (ed), *The Fundamentals of EU Law Revisited* (Oxford, Oxford University Press, 2007) 127 ff.

[86] *Nerkowska* (above n 84) para 21 ff.

[87] ibid, para 43.

[88] *Nerkowska* (above n 84) para 21ff.

[89] Case C-333/13, *Dano*, ECLI:EU:C:2014:2358; EuGH v 15.9.2015, Case C-67/14, *Alimanovic*, ECLI:EU:C:2015:597; Case C-299/14, *Garcia-Nieto*, ECLI:EU:C:2015:366; U Becker, *Migration und soziale Rechte* (ZESAR, 2017) 101, 104; J Greiser and D Ŝuŝnjar, *Der Anspruch auf Teilhabe an Sozialleistungen im Europäischen Wirtschaftsraum und in der Schweiz* (ZESAR, 2015) 60, 67.

[90] Further discussed in Becker (above n 89) 101, 104. Critical: A Wallrabenstein, *Die Gleichheit der Freiheit* (ZESAR, 2016) 349, 353ff; D Frings and C Janda, 'Die Sozialbürgerschaft und das Ende der

III. Conclusion

In competition law, solidarity is put forward by the CJEU as a means of strengthening national solidarity, whereas regarding the market freedoms and EU citizenship, the use of solidarity is oriented more towards the EU itself. In the latter case, the notion can foster national solidarity[91] and a Europe-wide solidarity,[92] as the CJEU recognises the need to protect national solidarity bonds.[93] Rights granted through market freedoms and EU citizenship can be limited if national schemes could be endangered by the application of EU law, but since the burden of proof for the Member States is higher than in competition law, it is a rather difficult condition for the Member States to fulfil.[94]

Before we turn to possible explanations for the different approaches, it must be emphasised that the appearance of the word 'solidarity' in case law is not coherent as such. Solidarity takes different meanings within the case law and serves different functions too. As the notion is not coherently used, it is difficult to understand the notion as such, and to extract general features. Even though the Court uses the same technical vocabulary, the aims, purposes and results of referring to it are diverse.

Studying the case law, it becomes clear that there is a linguistic ambiguity to the Court's notion of solidarity; it can mean anything and nothing. In some cases, solidarity can be 'translated' as identity, as socially belonging to a group or community, as a mutual commitment, as well as a synonym for obligation or distribution. Sometimes it is an argument, sometimes part of a definition, sometimes a premise or a moral/ethnical value, and sometime a vision or an aim. Solidarity is not applied as a coherent normative model.

Interestingly, the notion starts to appear in European law exactly when its relevance seems to be diminishing at the national level, in the sense that the national liberalisation process has led to a weakening of solidarity elements at the national level. At the same time, solidarity's importance at the European level may be just beginning to appear.

A. Explanatory Model or Out of the Blue? Is There an Explanatory Model by Which These Different Approaches Can be Explained?

The variations in usage of solidarity might be influenced by the aspect of 'territorialisation versus de-territorialisation' of welfare, to which I would like to

europäischen Solidarität' in C Janda and S Beichel-Benedetti (eds), *Hohenheimer Horizonte. Festschrift für Klaus Barwig* (Baden-Baden, 2018) 153.

[91] Barnard (above n 5); Barnard (above n 22) 153, 169 ff.

[92] Opinion of AG Maduro in *Nerkowska* (above n 84) para 23.

[93] *Dano* (above n 89); *EuGH* (above n 89); *Alimanovic* (above n 89); *Garcia-Nieto* (above n 89).

[94] Frings and Janda (above n 90).

draw attention. Welfare has, for decades, been perceived as a task to be fulfilled by the nation-state, and so the provision of welfare has been closely linked to territory.[95] The territorialisation principle means that welfare is provided within the territory of the nation state,[96] whereas de-territorialisation refers to the fact that the territorial state no longer monopolises welfare provision. This is due to the opening of national welfare schemes by allowing exportation of welfare benefits outside the nation state's territory on the one hand and through the inclusion of foreigners into the system on the other.[97]

Examining the case law, we can see that the jurisprudence differs in its approach to the principle of territorialisation. In competition law the Court does not touch upon it, while the jurisprudence on market freedoms and the provisions on EU citizenship have enacted a process of de-territorialisation. One explanation for this might be that in these areas, the general functioning of the system is at stake and not solely the application of the law in an individual case. Another reason could be that competition law deals less with the granting and export of social rights than with participation in the market, as it deals, in the field of social welfare, with the mode or method of providing welfare. On the other hand, the case law regarding the market freedoms and EU citizenship mainly concerns the granting of rights through the opening-up of national welfare schemes, either to include migrant EU citizens or to allow the exportability of welfare benefits abroad. Therefore, regarding EU citizenship and the four freedoms (but not competition) the jurisprudence has played an important role in limiting the territorial principle by ensuring a gradual de-territorialisation process. Interestingly, solidarity becomes a legal buttress both in competition law and for free movement, as it justifies either the territorial principle or acts in favour of 'de-territorialisation'. The same notion (solidarity) is used to argue in favour of keeping a national system closed as well as for its opening-up, so solidarity is used to determine the extent of integration.

Connected to the aspects of de-territorialisation and territorialisation is the implications the jurisprudence has for (consumer) rights, in which solidarity plays an important role. We have to bear in mind that the application of competition law has its primary effects on competitors, and that it has an effect on the citizen as a consumer in a secondary sense, whereas the application of the four freedoms as well as EU citizenship concerns primarily the status and rights of the individual consumer or citizen. Strengthening of a European form of solidarity is here equated with fostering internal market participation. In the area of free movement, European integration can come with limited negative effects, since the fostering of a European solidarity in this context does not, contrary to the general application of competition law, involve a restructuring of the national scheme as such. The latter provisions generally only apply to cross-border cases, with the Court

[95] D Sindbjerg-Martinsen, 'The De-Territorialization of Welfare?' in de Búrca (above n 76) 89, 98 ff.
[96] Ferrera (above n 8) 126.
[97] A Hemerrijck, 'EU social policy beyond national welfare regime' in M Burgess and H Vollaard (eds), *State Territoriality and European Integration* (Routledge, 2006) 197, 222.

recognising the right of the Member States to restrict the granted right when the functioning of their national schemes is hampered.

As an addition to the common definition of economic activity, solidarity can become a tool to limit competition law, or as a way to consider and balance divergent interests, such as the need to ensure competition as well as the proper functioning of social schemes. Solidarity is utilised for a general weighing of the respective public and private interests, whereas towards the market freedoms and EU citizenship the purpose is to ensure the access of individuals, leading to a more individual weighing process to take place. When pondering the different interests in the context of EU citizenship, solidarity serves the purpose of substantiating a sense of belonging to a community, whereas in the area of the market freedoms solidarity is primarily perceived as a European solidarity in the sense that the opening of national markets to foreign providers enables the latter to participate. By strengthening economic activity and involvement solidarity is fostered[98] and it is assumed that the overall social welfare will also benefit.[99]

We have to bear in mind that solidarity is perceived as an important value that makes us feel good. It is a notion that touches upon our emotions. The common perception that solidarity is valuable for all of us, and necessary to some extent to ensure social order, is an explanation of why references to solidarity continue to be made. It is appealing to argue with reference to solidarity in spite of the difficulties in determining what the notion means.[100] The ambiguity of the term makes its usage rather attractive, as it can mean both anything and nothing. However, arguing with reference to a value that everyone agrees on, but which everyone also understands in a different way, can make a decision more plausible at first glance, diminishing its critics. That may be why solidarity is a valuable tool for approaching matters such as the balancing of social and economic rights.[101] Having the different modes of usage of solidarity in the case law in mind, I have the impression that the Court uses solidarity more when it wants to depart from a principle set out in European law and much less if the case law is an example of continuity in the jurisprudence. Looking at competition law as well as the jurisprudence involving EU citizenship, we can see the following: in competition law, the term economic activity was defined by settled case law, but this case law did not seem to be appropriate when applied to social security schemes. The Court has modified its jurisprudence by introduction solidarity as an additional element to, for instance, its definition of economic activity. This element, which cannot be directly linked to the wording of the Treaty, limits the scope of competition law when compared to the former case law. A similar approach is taken regarding the interpretation of

[98] In this sense AG Maduro could be understood: see Opinion of AG Maduro in Case C-438/05, *Viking*, para 68.

[99] Opinion of AG Sharpston in Case C-34/09, *Zambrano*, para 154.

[100] A Alharbi, 'Towards a performative theory of solidarity discourse' (2018) 5(1) *Cogent Arts & Humanities*.

[101] Klamert (above n 2) 31.

the provisions on EU citizenship, for example, when introducing the incremental approach to entitlement for welfare benefits or when establishing criteria regarding naming, or participation in the elections of the European Parliament.

It is the ambiguity of the term 'solidarity' that makes its use so attractive. Solidarity embodies a welcomed value, which is seen as linked to the social nature of the EU. There is a powerful symbolism inherent in the language of the Court when it speaks of solidarity.[102] Although its meaning can seldom be deduced from the wording of the Treaty, and a definition cannot be easily extracted from the case law of a Court which uses it in various manners, it can be argued that solidarity refers to a European solidarity in a normative sense. Concerning the four freedoms, the underpinning idea is an economic solidarity embedded in the internal market,[103] whereas when solidarity refers to national solidarity, it serves as a description that displays a national rather than a European value.

There is no solid European legal concept behind solidarity, since the notion is not applied coherently in the jurisprudence.[104] The use of the term 'solidarity' by the CJEU is more than symbolism, since it can serve as a buttress for different national and European ideas and values; however, the Court uses not only one but many legal conceptions of solidarity.

[102] S O'Leary, 'Solidarity and Citizenship Rights in the Charter of Fundamental Rights of the European Union' in de Búrca (above n 76) 39, 77.

[103] See Opinion of AG Maduro in *Viking* (above n 98) para 68.

[104] Klamert (above n 2) 31.

INDEX

www.ingramcontent.com/pod-product-compliance
Ingram Content Group UK Ltd.
Pitfield, Milton Keynes, MK11 3LW, UK
UKHW020229290926
15470UKWH00002B/441

9 781509 932580